COMPLETE
HOME GUIDE TO
MEDICAL
ILLNESSES

Dr. Warwick Carter
MB. BS, FRACGP

HINKLER
BOOKS

**2100
DISEASES
DESCRIBED
AND
EXPLAINED**

This book is intended as a reference volume only, not as a manual for self treatment. If you suspect that you have a medical problem, please seek competent medical care. The information here is designed to help you make informed choices about your health. It is not intended as a substitute for any treatment prescribed by your doctor.

Published by
Hinkler Books Pty Ltd
17-23 Redwood Drive
Dingley Victoria 3172 Australia
www.hinklerbooks.com.au

ISBN: 1 86515 231 5

Printed and bound in Australia

To
Jane, Deb & Jacqui

Complete
Home Guide To
Medical Illnesses

Dr. Warwick Carter

From Abetalipoproteinaemia to Zygomycosis,
from Warts to Menétrière's Disease,
from Dandruff to Ingrown Toenails,
from Cancer to the Common Cold,
from Orf to von Recklinghausen's Disease of Multiple
Neurofibromatosis,
from Kidney Stone to Disseminated Superficial Actinic
Porokeratosis,
from Capgras Syndrome to Bat Ears.
Over 2100 diseases
described and explained
in a common format.

Preface

Every day we hear of diseases — from friends, relatives, in the media or books, or from doctors. Often the names are meaningless medical jargon, at other times they result in feelings of dread or hopelessness. Some are thought to be simple, but are actually more complex, while the reverse is true of others.

The more individuals know about diseases, their cause, symptoms, investigation, treatment, complications and likely outcome, the better they can cope with them, or understand what others have to deal with.

This book covers them all — over 2100 disease names covered in over 1200 entries. Everything is explained, from one end of the alphabet (Abetalipoproteinaemia) to the other (Zygomycosis), from the very simple (Warts) to the exotic (Menétrière's Disease), from the top of the body (Dandruff) to the bottom (Ingrown Toenails), from the serious (Lung Cancer) to the mild (Common Cold), from the shortest name (Orf) to the longest (von Recklinghausen's Disease of Multiple Neurofibromatosis), from simple names (Kidney Stones) to almost unpronounceable tongue twisters (Disseminated Superficial Actinic Porokeratosis), from the bizarre (Capgras Syndrome) to the cosmetic (Bat Ears).

The amusing (Itchy Upper Arm Syndrome) and the distressing (Infertility), the self explanatory (Cat Scratch Disease) and the inexplicable (Charcot-Marie-Tooth Disease), may appear within a few pages of each other. Psychiatric diseases (Clérambault Syndrome) appear next to developmental abnormalities (Cleft Lip and Palate). Unexpected names (Christmas Disease), unavoidable conditions (Baldness), extremely rare diseases (Mokola Virus Infection), tragic diseases (Huntington's Chorea), sad diseases (Diogenes Syndrome), historic diseases (Kuru), addictions (Narcotic Addiction), sexual problems (Vaginismus), injuries (Colles' Fracture), headline grabbers (Flesh Eating Disease), the self inflicted (Alcoholism), abbreviations (Flu) and poisoning (Lead Poisoning) are all discussed.

Both common names (Ear Wax) and the medical terminology (Cerumen) for every disease are used, and are extensively cross referenced.

Have I missed any diseases? Certainly. Will you discover them? Probably not, because it is unlikely that any lay person will come across a disease that is not discussed.

Remember this is a book about diseases (diagnoses), not symptoms (the things that you feel). There is a very blurred line between these two (eg. is constipation a symptom or a disease? — probably both), and I have tried to err on the side of caution in listing these as diseases, but something like a sore throat is definitely a symptom and not a disease, as it is necessary to determine which one of a number of diseases (eg. Pharyngitis, Tonsillitis, Uvulitis) is responsible for a sore throat.

Whether you are using this book to look up specific problems, or just perusing it to discover gems that interest you, I trust and hope that you will find it both interesting and informative.

Warwick Carter
Brisbane, June 2000

Format

Disease Name
(Alternate Names)

DESCRIPTION: A description of the disease in simple terms

CAUSE: The cause of the disease (eg. name of responsible bacteria, behaviour or genetics)

SYMPTOMS: The symptoms (sensations) that a patient with the disease may experience

INVESTIGATIONS: The investigations necessary to prove the presence of the disease

TREATMENT: The most common forms of treatment available

COMPLICATIONS: Any complications of the disease or its treatment

PROGNOSIS: The likely outcome of the disease

See also Other Relevant Disease(s)

Alternate Disease Name
See Disease Name

NB: For the definitions of technical terms used in the text see the glossary on the following pages.

Not all sections listed above are relevant for all diseases.

Glossary

Abdomen	The belly. Part of the body between the lower ribs and pelvis that contains the intestine and other organs.
Acute	Sudden, recent onset, severe.
Allergen	Substance (pollen, food etc.) that starts an allergy reaction within the body.
Antibodies	Protein particles used by the body to attack invading infections, allergens or foreign material.
Arthroscopy	Insertion of a thin tube into a joint to enable the interior of the joint to be examined or operated upon.
Benign	Not cancerous.
Biopsy	Taking a small sample of (usually abnormal) tissue by using a large bore needle, or cutting with a scalpel.
Bone scan	See radionucleotide scan below.
Chromosome	Microscopic thread like structure in every cell, each of which carries many thousands of genes. Humans have 46 chromosomes arranged in 23 pairs.
Chronic	Persistent, long lasting.
Colonoscopy	Examination of the large intestine (colon) with a two metre long flexible tube that magnifies and illuminates the gut, and is passed into the colon through the anus.
Congenital	Something (eg. a deformity) that exists from the moment of birth.
CT or CAT Scan	Computerised (axial) tomography. X-rays that are enhanced by computers to allow cross sectional views of the body, and show soft tissue as well as bone.
Echocardiogram	A type of ultrasound that shows the structure and function (blood flow) of the heart.
Electrocardiograph (ECG)	Measurement of the electrical activity of the heart through wires that are attached to the arms, legs and chest.
Electroencephalography (EEG)	Measurement of the electrical activity of the brain through wires that are attached to the scalp.
Electromyography (EMG)	Measurement of the electrical activity of muscles through wires that are attached to needles into, or skin over, the muscle(s) under investigation.
Endoscopy	Passing a flexible or rigid tube into any body cavity (eg. bowel) to enable the interior of the cavity to be examined.
Familial	Condition that may occur regularly in a family, and pass from one generation to the next.

Gastroscopy	Examination of the oesophagus (gullet), stomach and first part of the small intestine (duodenum) through a long flexible tube that magnifies and illuminates the gut, and is passed in through the mouth.
Gene	A molecule of DNA (deoxyribo nucleic acid) occurring on a chromosome in a cell that determines one of the characteristics of a person. There are several million genes in every human, and every cell carries identical genes.
Intravenous	Injection given directly into a vein.
Laparoscopy	Examination of and operation on the interior of the abdomen through a rigid or flexible tube that magnifies and illuminates the interior of the abdomen, and is passed in through a one centimetre incision in the skin. Usually, several endoscopy tubes are introduced simultaneously.
Malignant	Cancerous.
MRI scan	Magnetic resonance imaging exposes the body to an extremely powerful magnetic field that when switched on and off, produces electromagnetic signals within tissue that can be collected and interpreted. The signal varies with the water content of the tissue, and can therefore show soft tissues better than bone.
PET scan	Positron emission tomography measures the chemical activity of the brain and how it is working by producing an image that differentiates those areas where a lot of chemical activity is taking place from those where there is little. A radioactive substance is injected, and more is absorbed by the most chemically active areas of the brain, which then emit radiation (positrons) that can be detected and computer enhanced to form an image.
Radionucleotide scan	A radioactive substance that is taken up by a specific organ is injected into the body, and the nuclear energy it gives off when it reaches bone or other tissue is picked up by a gamma camera (picks up radiation instead of light) to give a picture of how the tissue is functioning.
Ultrasound	High-frequency sound waves introduced into the body through a probe on the skin surface bounce off tissues of different density in different ways, and the reflected sound waves can be converted into a picture of the organ under investigation.

A

Abetalipoproteinaemia
(Bassen-Kornzweig Syndrome)

DESCRIPTION: Rare abnormality of body fat metabolism (chemistry).

CAUSE: Congenital birth defect that prevents absorption of fat and vitamin E from food and prevents production of necessary body fats in the liver.

SYMPTOMS: Child with foul smelling fatty diarrhoea, low body weight, retarded growth, poor coordination, abnormal sensations and pigmented retina at back of the eye.

INVESTIGATIONS: Abnormal red blood cells, and very low levels of fats (cholesterol and triglycerides) in the blood.

TREATMENT: Fat restricted diet, special dietary supplements and vitamin E.

COMPLICATIONS: Permanent brain damage.

PROGNOSIS: Poor.

See also Vitamin E Deficiency

Abortion, Spontaneous
See Miscarriage

Abscess

DESCRIPTION: A collection of pus in a tissue cavity. There are two main types of abscesses — those under the skin, and those that occur in internal body organs (called an **empyema** on the surface of the lungs or brain).

CAUSE: The destruction of normal tissue by bacterial, or rarely fungal, infection. If significant tissue destruction occurs, the destroyed cells accumulate as pus, and an abscess forms. May be a complication of a skin infection (cellulitis — see separate entry), follow surgery, appendicitis or similar internal infection, or be due to a penetrating injury.

SYMPTOMS: Skin abscess — appear as a red, painful swelling that is initially hard to touch, but as the pus formation increases, becomes soft and obviously fluid-filled. Eventually a head forms that bursts and allows the pus to escape. Internal abscess — can occur in almost any organ, and often not found until they are a large size. Cause a fever and a general feeling of being unwell. The organs most commonly affected include the brain, liver, breast, lung, tonsils (causing quinsy — see separate entry) and teeth.

INVESTIGATIONS: Skin abscesses are obvious. Internal ones may be suspected by the result of blood tests, but ultrasound scans or laparoscopy may be needed to confirm the diagnosis.

TREATMENT: Skin abscess — in the early stages antibiotics are given by mouth or injection, and hot compresses applied to the area. Once pus is present, the abscess is drained, scraped out, and the drain hole kept open by a small piece of cloth (a wick) to allow further pus to escape quickly.

Internal abscess — antibiotics used to stop the spread of the infection but will not cure the abscess and the pus must be removed by an open operation under a general or local anaesthetic.

COMPLICATIONS: Particularly nasty abscesses may develop around the anus and require quite major surgery to drain the pus.

PROGNOSIS: Most abscesses will slowly reduce in size and heal. If left untreated, a patient may become severely ill, with new abscesses forming in surrounding tissues.

See also Cellulitis; Lung Abscess; Quinsy

Acanthosis Nigicans

DESCRIPTION: Skin condition of the neck, groin, palms and armpits that appears in four forms — true benign, benign, malignant and pseudo.

CAUSE: True benign — inherited trait, that often runs in families, starts in childhood, is more common in girls and worsens with puberty.

Benign — often associated with hormonal abnormalities in Cushing syndrome, pituitary gland disorders or polycystic ovaries and develops in late childhood or early adult life. Mildest form.

Malignant — reaction to cancer in other parts of the body (eg. stomach, breast, lung) and starts in late life. Most severe form.

Pseudo — occurs in obese women who have a dark complexion.

SYMPTOMS: All forms cause thick, ridged skin covered in multiple dark brown or black small polyps, giving the skin a velvety appearance.

INVESTIGATIONS: Diagnosed by skin biopsy.

TREATMENT: True benign — no specific treatment.

Benign — treatment of the underlying hormonal imbalance.

Malignant — treatment of the underlying cancer.

Pseudo — weight loss.

PROGNOSIS: True benign — Often settles in early adult life.

Other forms — only improve with successful treatment of cause.

Accelerated Conduction Syndrome
See Wolff-Parkinson-White Syndrome

Achalasia
(Oesophageal Achalasia)

DESCRIPTION: Loss of muscle contractions in the lower two thirds of the gullet (oesophagus).

CAUSE: Degeneration of the nerves supplying the muscles of the oesophagus that starts between 25 and 60 years of age.

SYMPTOMS: Gradually worsening difficulty in swallowing that initially affects solids more than liquids, fullness and discomfort behind the breast bone (sternum), regurgitation of unswallowed food (particularly at night), weight loss and cough.

INVESTIGATIONS: Barium swallow X-ray diagnostic. Endoscopy (passing a flexible tube down the oesophagus) can further evaluate the severity of the disease and allow pressure measurements to be made in the oesophagus.

TREATMENT: Dilation of the narrowed section of the oesophagus using a balloon, medications (eg. nifedipine) that relax the lower oesophagus, and surgery.

COMPLICATIONS: Inhalation of regurgitated food can cause cough, lung damage and infections. Increased risk of cancer in the oesophagus.

PROGNOSIS: Most cases well managed by appropriate treatment.

Achilles Tendon Rupture
See Ligament or Tendon Rupture

Acne
(Pimples)

DESCRIPTION: Skin infection that can vary from the occasional spot to a severe disease that may cause both skin and psychological scarring. Normally occurs in teenagers, but may develop later in life, particularly in women. Usually more severe in teenage males, but starts earlier in females. Affects Caucasians (whites) more than Negroes or Chinese races. **Acne vulgaris** is a severe form that almost invariably results in scarring of the face, back and chest. **Acne conglobata** affects mainly the buttocks and chest and causes skin abscesses and severe inflammation.

CAUSE: A blockage in the outflow of oil from a few of the millions of tiny oil glands in the skin caused by dirt, flakes of dead skin, or a thickening and excess production of oil. Once the opening of the oil duct becomes blocked the gland becomes dilated with thick oil, inflamed and eventually infected. Hormonal changes at puberty are the major aggravating factor, as they cause changes to the thickness of the oil. Pregnancy, menopause and the oral contraceptive pill may all influence pimples in this way. Acne may be worsened by stress (either psychological or physical), illness (eg. a common cold), skin pressure (eg. spectacles on the bridge of the nose or tight collars), increases in skin humidity (eg. a fringe of hair or nylon clothing), and the excessive use of cosmetics (further block the oil duct openings). The severity also depends on hereditary factors. There is no evidence that diet, chocolate, vitamins or herbs have any effect on acne.

SYMPTOMS: A white or black headed skin eruption, with a surrounding red area of infection. The face, upper chest, upper back and neck are most commonly affected.

INVESTIGATIONS: None normally necessary.

TREATMENT: The skin should be kept clean with a mild soap and face cloth, and simple oil drying, antiseptic and cleansing creams or lotions used. Further treatment involves combinations of antibiotics (eg. tetracyclines) that may be taken in the short term for acute flare ups or in the long term to prevent acne, skin lotions or creams containing antibiotics and/or steroids, and changing a woman's hormonal balance by putting her on the oral contraceptive pill or using other hormones. In rare cases it is necessary to see a skin specialist for isotretinoin (which can cause birth deformities if used during pregnancy), steroid injections (eg. triamcinolone) into the skin around particularly bad eruptions, and abrading away the skin around scars. The treatment of adults with maturity onset acne is more difficult than juvenile acne.

COMPLICATIONS: May cause both skin and psychological scarring. Picking acne spots can cause serious secondary bacterial infections that can spread deep into the skin (cellulitis).

PROGNOSIS: Cannot be cured, but the majority of cases can be reasonably controlled. Eventually settles with age.

Acne Conglobata
See Acne

Acne Rosacea
See Rosacea

Acne Vulgaris
See Acne

Acoustic Neuroma
(Acoustic Neurinoma)

DESCRIPTION: A usually benign (non-cancerous) tumour of the insulating sheath which covers the acoustic nerve (nerve which conducts the sense of hearing to the brain) which often develops at the point where the nerve passes through a small hole in skull to enter the brain.

CAUSE: Not known.

SYMPTOMS: A ringing noise, followed by deafness in the affected ear are the early symptoms. As it increases in size other symptoms may include pain, dizziness and, because of pressure on other nearby nerves that supply the eye, a lack of tears in the eye and double vision. Headache does not occur until the tumour is very large.

INVESTIGATIONS: A CT scan can usually show the tumour accurately.

TREATMENT: Surgical removal of the tumour in a very intricate operation.

COMPLICATIONS: Removing larger tumours may result in unavoidable permanent deafness and possibly other nerve damage.

PROGNOSIS: The smaller the tumour at the time of surgery, the better the final result. Tumours less than 2 cm. in diameter can normally be removed without any problem.

Acquired Immune Deficiency Syndrome
See AIDS

4

Acrocephalopolysyndactyly
See Carpenter Syndrome

Acrocephalosyndactyly of Apert
(Apert Syndrome)

DESCRIPTION: Very rare disorder of hand and head development.

CAUSE: Familial. Premature fusion of the bones that make up the skull and abnormal development of the fingers.

SYMPTOMS: Head rises to a point, eyes protrude, the cheeks are sunken and two or more fingers are fused together.

INVESTIGATIONS: None diagnostic.

TREATMENT: Surgery to separate fingers and open up the suture lines between the skull bones.

COMPLICATIONS: Mental retardation.

PROGNOSIS: No cure.

See also Carpenter Syndrome

Acromegaly

DESCRIPTION: Excess growth in specific parts of the body due to a growth hormone imbalance.

CAUSE: Excess production of growth hormone in the pituitary gland, which sits underneath the brain. Growth hormone is required for the normal growth of a child, but if it is produced inappropriately later in life, acromegaly results. The most common reason for this is a tumour in the pituitary gland, but occasionally tumours elsewhere can secrete the hormone.

SYMPTOMS: Excessive growth of the hands, feet, jaw, face, tongue and internal organs. Patients also suffer headaches, sweating, weakness, and loss of vision. A woman's menstrual periods will stop.

INVESTIGATIONS: Blood tests can be used to prove the diagnosis, and X-rays and CT scans of the skull can detect the tumour.

TREATMENT: Specialised microsurgery through the nose, and up into the base of the brain, to remove the tumour. Occasionally irradiation of the tumour may be performed. Usually hormone supplements must be taken long term to replace those normally produced by the destroyed pituitary gland.

COMPLICATIONS: Diabetes insipidus (see separate entry) is a common complication of the disease and its treatment.

PROGNOSIS: Treatment is very successful, particularly in younger adults.

Acrophobia
See Phobia

Actinomycosis

DESCRIPTION: An uncommon bacterial infection of the skin, particularly the face.

CAUSE: The bacteria *Actinomycoses* normally live in the mouth and assist with food digestion, but if they enter into damaged tissue in other parts of the body they cause an infection in which the bacteria are difficult to identify.

SYMPTOMS: Hard, inflamed lumps in the skin that develop into abscesses and discharge pus. Other areas that may be infected include tooth sockets after an extraction, and the gut. Other symptoms include a fever, and constant severe pain in any infected area.

INVESTIGATIONS: Swabs taken from discharging pus in an attempt to identify the responsible bacteria.

TREATMENT: The infection is resistant to simple treatments, and a 6-week or longer course of penicillin and other antibiotics, initially by injection, is necessary. Abscesses are surgically drained and affected tissue may need to be excised (cut out).

COMPLICATIONS: Abscesses may persist for many months.

PROGNOSIS: Cure difficult, but usually possible. Permanent scarring may be left behind.

Acute Brain Syndrome
(Acute Confusional Syndrome)

DESCRIPTION: Abrupt onset of confusion in an elderly person.

CAUSE: Common in suddenly hospitalised or relocated elderly patients due to disorientation.

SYMPTOMS: Elderly person who is psychotic, and has clouding of consciousness, impaired thought processes, poor short-term memory, strange illusions, misinterpretations, anxiety, irrational fears, loss of interest in life, restlessness and apathy. Some patients experience hallucinations that involve the sensations of vision, touch, hearing and smell.

INVESTIGATIONS: Diagnosed by psychiatric assessment.

TREATMENT: Careful nursing, psychotherapy and medications (eg. haloperidol).

COMPLICATIONS: Sedatives may aggravate confusion.

PROGNOSIS: Often persist, but may settle spontaneously with time.

See also Alzheimer's Disease; Psychosis

Acute Bronchitis
See Bronchitis, Acute

Acute Confusional Syndrome
See Acute Brain Syndrome

Acute Febrile Neutrophilic Dermatosis
See Sweet Syndrome

Acute Hepatic Porphyria

DESCRIPTION: One of a number of different types of porphyria, which is an uncommon liver disease.

CAUSE: An inherited disease that passes from one generation to the next but causes symptoms in only 10% of those affected.

SYMPTOMS: Symptoms develop at the time of puberty with vague abdominal pains, nausea, vomiting and abnormal sensations. As the disease progresses, the abdominal pains may become severe, but nothing abnormal can be found in the abdomen. In advanced cases, nerve pain, paralysis, personality changes and fits may occur. The urine turns a dark purple colour, then brown, if left standing. Some patients may have the otherwise quiescent disease triggered by severe infections, starvation, some drugs or steroids.

INVESTIGATIONS: Diagnosed by special blood tests.

TREATMENT: Treatment involves careful genetic counselling of families and avoiding factors (eg. crash diets, emotional stress, alcohol, certain drugs) that may precipitate an attack. Controlled by the use of a complex drug regime.

COMPLICATIONS: Liver damage, which may progress to liver failure or liver cancer (hepatoma), and nerve damage which may cause varying forms of paralysis.

PROGNOSIS: May be controlled, but not cured. Death may occur due to the paralysis of the muscles of breathing.

See also **Porphyria Cutanea Tarda**

Acute Leukaemia
See Leukaemia, Acute Lymphatic; Leukaemia, Acute Myeloid

Acute Kidney Failure
See Kidney Failure, Acute

Acute Pyelonephritis
See Pyelonephritis, Acute

Acute Renal Failure
See Kidney Failure, Acute

Adams-Stokes Syndrome
See Stokes-Adams Syndrome

ADD
See Attention Deficit Hyperactivity Disorder

Addiction
See Alcoholism; Amphetamine Abuse; Cocaine Addiction; Marijuana Abuse; Narcotic Addiction

Addisonian Crisis
See Addison's Disease

Addison's Disease
(Adrenocortical Insufficiency; Chronic Hypoadrenocorticism)

DESCRIPTION: Rare underactivity of the outer layer (cortex) of the adrenal glands which sit on top of each kidney, and produce hormones (chemical messengers) such as cortisone that control the levels of vital elements in the body and regulate the breakdown of food.

CAUSE: In most cases, the reason for adrenal gland failure is unknown, but tuberculosis is a possible cause.

SYMPTOMS: Weakness, lack of appetite, diarrhoea and vomiting, skin pigmentation, mental instability, low blood pressure, loss of body hair and absence of sweating.

INVESTIGATIONS: Diagnosed by special blood tests that measure the body's response to stimulation of the adrenal gland.

TREATMENT: A combination of medications (eg. steroids such as cortisone) to replace the missing hormones. Dosages vary greatly from one patient to another. Frequent small meals high in carbohydrate and protein are eaten, and infections must be treated rapidly. Patients must carry an emergency supply of injectable cortisone with them at all times.

COMPLICATIONS: Diabetes, thyroid disease, anaemia, and eventual death. Sudden onset of disease is known as an **Addisonian crisis**, which may be rapidly fatal.

PROGNOSIS: Treatment can give most patients a long and useful life, but they cannot react to stress (both physical and mental) adequately, and additional treatment must be given in these situations. The ultimate outcome depends greatly on the patient's ability to strictly follow all treatment regimes.

See also Congenital Adrenal Hyperplasia; Schmidt Syndrome; Waterhouse-Friderichsen Syndrome

Adenitis
(Infected Glands; Lymphadenitis; Lymph Node Inflammation)

DESCRIPTION: An infection or inflammation of one or more lymph nodes, usually in the neck, armpit or groin.

CAUSE: Lymph nodes are collections of white cells designed to remove and destroy invading bacteria and viruses. Sometimes the infection overwhelms the lymph node, or cancer spreads from another part of the body, causing it to become painful and enlarged.

SYMPTOMS: Red, sore and swollen lymph nodes, and the patient develops a fever and feels ill.

INVESTIGATIONS: Blood tests may be performed to identify serious infections, or in cases where cancer is suspected.

TREATMENT: If the infection is bacterial, the treatment is antibiotics. Viral infections, such as mumps and glandular fever, will need to run their course, with rest and pain-killers the only treatment. Cancerous lymph nodes need to be surgically removed.

COMPLICATIONS: An untreated infection may cause an abscess (see separate entry).

All lymph nodes that cause discomfort must be examined by a doctor as the adenitis may be due to a cancer.

PROGNOSIS: Most bacterial infections settle well with antibiotics. Cancer prognosis varies depending on the type.

See also Abscess; Cancer; Mesenteric Adenitis; Sialitis

Adenocarcinoma of the Lung
See Lung Cancer

ADHD
See Attention Deficit Hyperactivity Disorder

Adhesions

DESCRIPTION: A relatively uncommon but potentially serious and disabling complication of any surgery within the abdomen.

CAUSE: During an operation, minor damage to tissue in the abdominal cavity occurs. If two areas of damaged tissue come into contact they may heal together and form an adhesion, which is a tough fibrous band that can later stretch across the abdominal cavity between the two surgically damaged points. More common if there is an infection in the abdomen (eg. burst appendix), but sometimes occur after relatively minor surgery. More common in short, fat females, but the reason for this is unknown.

SYMPTOMS: Most produce no symptoms, but if a loop of bowel is trapped it can become obstructed. More commonly, adhesions cause a persistent colic in the gut as the intestine winds tightly around the fibrous bands, or the adhesion may tear and bleed, leading to more pain.

INVESTIGATIONS: No totally diagnostic tests available, but sometimes abnormalities are seen on an ultrasound scan of the abdomen.

TREATMENT: More surgery to cut away the adhesions, during which extreme care must be taken to prevent any bleeding into the abdomen and any unnecessary injury to the bowel.

COMPLICATIONS: Bowel obstruction may lead to gangrene, perforation and peritonitis.

PROGNOSIS: A few months or years after treatment the adhesions may re-form, and the symptoms start again. Very difficult problem to deal with, and often no permanent solution.

See also Asherman Syndrome

Adhesive Capsulitis
See Frozen Shoulder

Adie's Pupil
See Holmes-Adie Syndrome

Adrenal Gland Insufficiency
See Addison's Disease

Adrenal Hyperplasia, Congenital
See Congenital Adrenal Hyperplasia

Adrenocortical Hyperfunction
See Cushing Syndrome

Adrenocortical Insufficiency
See Addison's Disease

Adrenogenital Syndrome
See Congenital Adrenal Hyperplasia

Adult Respiratory Distress Syndrome
See Respiratory Distress Syndrome, Adult

Affective Disorder
See Depression

Afferent Loop Syndrome
DESCRIPTION: Complication of major surgery to the stomach.
CAUSE: Only occurs after operations to the stomach known as Bilroth II gastrectomy and gastrojejunostomy that are performed for severe peptic ulcers or cancer and leave a redundant loop of bowel. Operation results in failure of the bowel to move food along and distension of the bowel.
SYMPTOMS: Belly pain after eating relieved by vomiting, poor food absorption and fatty faeces.
INVESTIGATIONS: Barium meal X-ray abnormal, and fat level in faeces high.
TREATMENT: Tetracycline or lincomycin antibiotics, and further surgery to bowel.
COMPLICATIONS: Pernicious anaemia because of failure of vitamin B12 absorption.
PROGNOSIS: Difficult to treat.

African Trypanosomiasis
See Sleeping Sickness

Agammaglobulinaemia
(X-linked Agammaglobulinaemia)
DESCRIPTION: Inherited inability of the bone marrow and thymus gland to produce gammaglobulin, which is essential for establishing and maintaining the immune system. Only occurs in boys.
CAUSE: Familial (passed from one generation to the next) condition that is passed on by women, but only affects males.

SYMPTOMS: Recurrent severe infections that start in infancy.

INVESTIGATIONS: Blood tests and bone marrow biopsy.

TREATMENT: Antibiotics to control infections, immunoglobulin injections on a regular basis, bone marrow transplant.

COMPLICATIONS: Increased incidence of cancers.

PROGNOSIS: Poor unless successful bone marrow transplant possible.

See also Immunodeficiency

Agoraphobia
See Phobia

Agranulocytosis
(Malignant Leucopenia)

DESCRIPTION: Lack of white blood cells which are normally produced in the bone marrow, and inability of the body to defend itself from infection.

CAUSE: Often no apparent cause, but may be due to a rare adverse reaction to some drugs (eg. suphonamides, thiouracil), heavy metal poisoning or a complication of leukaemia and aplastic anaemia (see separate entries).

SYMPTOMS: Severe, uncontrollable bacterial and viral infections.

INVESTIGATIONS: Diagnosed by examining blood and a bone marrow sample under a microscope.

TREATMENT: Blood transfusion, potent antibiotics by injection.

PROGNOSIS: Often fatal.

AIDS
(Acquired Immune Deficiency Syndrome;
Human Immunodeficiency Virus [HIV] Infection)

DESCRIPTION: An infection caused by a retrovirus known as the human immuno-deficiency virus (HIV) which destroys the body's defence mechanisms and allows severe infections and cancers to develop. It is spread by the transfer of blood and semen from one person to another. First identified in 1983, it was initially only a disease of homosexuals and drug addicts, but although these remain the most affected groups in developed countries, it is promiscuous heterosexual contact that is the most common method of transmission in poorer countries. Those who are infected with the human immunodeficiency virus are said to be HIV positive. The disease has been classified into several categories. A patient can progress to a more severe category but cannot revert to a less severe one.

CAUSE: AIDS is a relatively hard disease to catch. It can NOT be caught from any casual contact, or from spa baths, kissing, mosquitoes, tears, towels or clothing. Only by homosexual or heterosexual intercourse with a carrier of the disease, by using contaminated needles, or blood from a carrier, can the disease be caught. If someone does come into sexual or blood contact with an AIDS carrier, it is possible for the virus to cross into their body. The body's defence mechanisms may then fight off the virus and leave the person with no illness whatsoever, or the AIDS virus may spread throughout the body to cause an HIV infection. In 1996 there were 22 million people in the world with an HIV infection, 14 million of them in Africa. There are 6.5 million deaths every year from AIDS. The incidence varies from 2 in every 100,000 people in China, to 115 in Australia, 2100 in Thailand and 20,000 in Uganda (the world's highest rate).

SYMPTOMS: Once the HIV virus enters the body it may lie dormant for months or years. During this time there may be no or minimal symptoms, but it may be possible to pass the infection on to another sex partner, and babies may become infected in the uterus of an infected mother.

HIV category 1 — a glandular fever-like disease that lasts a few days to weeks with inflamed lymph nodes, fever, rash and tiredness.

HIV category 2 — no symptoms.

HIV category 3 — persistent generalised enlargement of lymph nodes.

HIV category 4 (AIDS) — varied symptoms and signs depending on the areas of the body affected. May include fever, weight loss, diarrhoea, nerve and brain disorders, severe infections, lymph node cancer, sarcomas, and other cancers.

INVESTIGATIONS: Blood tests are positive at all stages of HIV infection, but there may be a lag period of up to three months or more from when the disease is caught until it can be detected. Tests are available to allow blood banks to screen for AIDS.

TREATMENT: There is no cure or vaccine available at present. Prevention is the only practical way to deal with AIDS. Condoms give good, but not total, protection from sexually catching the virus, and drug addicts may be educated not to share needles. Once diagnosed as HIV positive patients should not give up hope, because they may remain in the second stage for many years. Prolonging this stage can be achieved by the regular long term use of potent antiviral and immunosupportive medications, stopping smoking, exercising regularly, eating a well-balanced diet, resting adequately and avoiding illegal drugs.

COMPLICATIONS: In stage 4 patients are very susceptible to any type of infection or cancer from the common cold to pneumonia, septicaemia and multiple rare cancers (eg. Kaposi's sarcoma) because the body's immune system is destroyed by the virus.

PROGNOSIS: May remain at the category 2 level for many years, possibly even decades. Up to half of those who are HIV positive do not develop category 4 disease for more than ten years. On the other hand, no-one with category 4 HIV (AIDS) has lived more than a few months, and sufferers develop severe infections and cancers that eventually kill them.

See also Kaposi's Sarcoma

Air Sickness
See Motion Sickness

Alagille Syndrome
DESCRIPTION: Developmental abnormality of the lung, liver and brain.
CAUSE: Congenital condition localised to chromosome 20.
SYMPTOMS: Narrowing of the pulmonary arteries in the lungs, poorly developed bile drainage system in the liver, liver damage and jaundice (yellow skin), deep set eyes, prominent forehead and mental retardation.
INVESTIGATIONS: Chromosomal analysis used to make diagnosis.
TREATMENT: Surgical correction of artery and bile duct abnormalities.
COMPLICATIONS: Worsening heart, lung and liver disease.
PROGNOSIS: Poor.

Albinism
(Albino)
DESCRIPTION: Uncommon disorder of skin pigmentation.
CAUSE: Inherited. Melanocytes (skin pigment cells) fail to develop.
SYMPTOMS: Skin lacks pigment cells and is very pale pink in colour, regardless of racial ancestry. The iris (coloured part of the eye) also lacks pigment and appears pink because of the blood vessels in it.
INVESTIGATIONS: None necessary.
TREATMENT: None available.
COMPLICATIONS: Very susceptible to sunburn, skin disorders and eye damage.
PROGNOSIS: No cure, but normal life expectancy.

Albino
See Albinism

Albright Syndrome
(McCune-Albright Syndrome)
DESCRIPTION: Abnormal formation of bone and body chemistry abnormalities.
CAUSE: Congenital. Usually occurs in young females.
SYMPTOMS: Early puberty and abnormal bone formation in fibrous tissue. Some patients have an overactive thyroid gland and acromegaly (see separate entry).
INVESTIGATIONS: Abnormal bone deposits show on X-ray. Specific blood and urine tests are also abnormal.
TREATMENT: Surgical correction of bony deformities and steroids.
PROGNOSIS: Variable results from treatment.

Alcoholism
DESCRIPTION: A long standing addiction to alcohol that affects as many as 3% of the population.
CAUSE: The excessive use of alcohol on a regular basis to relieve tension or anxiety.

13

Alcoholism

There is also a genetic tendency, so that if one of your parents or siblings is an alcoholic, your risk of developing alcoholism is increased.

SYMPTOMS: An alcoholic is someone who has three or more of the following symptoms or signs:
— drinks alone;
— tries to hide drinking habits from others;
— continues to drink despite convincing evidence that it is damaging their health;
— disrupts work or social life because of alcohol;
— craves alcohol when none is available;
— appears to tolerate the effects of alcohol well;
— blacks out for no apparent reason;
— binges on alcohol;
— averages six standard alcoholic drinks a day;
— has abnormal liver function blood tests.

INVESTIGATIONS: Blood tests on liver function and alcohol levels may confirm diagnosis. An ultrasound scan of the liver may show damage (cirrhosis).

TREATMENT: Counselling, professional treatment programs in hospital, supportive groups (eg. Alcoholics Anonymous), medications to ease withdrawal and prevent relapses (eg. disulfram, naltrexone).

COMPLICATIONS: Social complications include disruption to family life, verbal and physical abuse of children and wife/husband, poor performance at work, repeated loss of jobs or failure to gain promotion, loss of friends and chastisement from relatives, the physical risks of drink-driving and being injured in falls or industrial accidents, the increased risk of eventual suicide. Medical complications include liver cirrhosis (hardening of the liver — see separate entry); nutritional deficiencies (eg. beriberi — see separate entry); brain damage can cause depression, memory loss, irrational behaviour and a form of insanity known as the Wernicke-Korsakoff psychosis (see separate entry); damage to the nerves supplying the rest of the body can result in peripheral neuropathy (see separate entry); degeneration of the cerebellum (the part of the brain that is at the back of the head) can cause permanent incoordination, difficulties in walking and performing simple tasks.

Withdrawal from alcohol may cause delirium tremens (see separate entry).

PROGNOSIS: The medical effects of alcoholism can be serious to the point where they can significantly alter the quality of life and shorten the life of the alcoholic.

See also Amnestic Syndrome; Beriberi; Cirrhosis; Delirium Tremens; Fetal Alcohol Syndrome; Pancreatitis; Peripheral Neuropathy; Wernicke-Korsakoff Psychosis

Aldosteronism
See Conn Syndrome

Allergic Conjunctivitis
(Atopic Conjunctivitis)

DESCRIPTION: An allergic reaction involving the surface of the eye.

CAUSE: If a pollen, dust or other substance to which a person is allergic lands on the eye, an allergic reaction will occur. Allergic conjunctivitis is often associated with hay fever and often only occurs at certain times of the year.

SYMPTOMS: Redness, itching, blurred vision and watering of the eye. In severe cases the white of the eye may swell dramatically and balloon out between the eyelids. There may be a clear, stringy discharge from the eyes, as well as excessive tears, and if the lower eyelid is turned down it appears to be covered with a large number of tiny red bumps.

INVESTIGATIONS: Blood and skin tests can be undertaken to identify the responsible substance in some patients.

TREATMENT: Prevented by the regular use of sodium cromoglycate drops throughout the allergy time of year. Attacks can be treated by antihistamine tablets and eye drops such as levocabastine. Simple eye drops available over the counter from chemists and containing artery-constricting medications can be used in milder cases.

COMPLICATIONS: Rarely, ulceration of the eye surface may occur.

PROGNOSIS: Appropriate treatment usually settles the symptoms rapidly.

See also Allergy; Conjunctivitis; Hay Fever

Allergic Eczema

DESCRIPTION: A skin rash caused by an allergic reaction.

CAUSE: Many substances (allergens) have the ability to cause an allergic reaction in an individual. In most cases, the first exposure of a patient to a substance causes no reaction, but this sensitises the patient, and subsequent exposure can then cause an allergic reaction. Drugs, chemicals, metals, elements, plants, preservatives, rubber, cement, etc., may all be responsible. The reaction is worse if the patient is hot and sweaty, if the substance is caught in clothing, or is present at a point of skin flexion (eg. in the groin, under breasts, armpit). The condition is relatively uncommon in the young, and very common in the elderly. The sites of the rash correspond to the points where the allergen has touched the skin, and this may give a clue to its cause.

SYMPTOMS: Red, scaling, itchy rash.

INVESTIGATIONS: Once a substance is suspected, it can be confirmed by 'patch testing', where a patch of the substance is applied to the skin, and the reaction noted.

TREATMENT: If possible, the allergen should be avoided. Otherwise, the rash is controlled by steroid creams on weeping areas, and steroid ointments on dry and scaling areas. In severe cases, steroids may need to be given by tablet or injection.

COMPLICATIONS: Unavoidable exposure to an allergen can cause a persistent rash that is difficult to treat.

PROGNOSIS: Most patients respond well to treatment for a particular attack, but the rash may recur on subsequent exposure to the allergen.

See also Allergy; Atopic Eczema; Dermatitis; Eczema

Allergic Rhinitis
See Hay Fever

Allergy

DESCRIPTION: An excessive reaction to a substance which in most people causes no reaction.

CAUSE: Significant allergies occur in 10% of the population. An allergy may be triggered by almost any substance including foods, pollens, dusts, plants, animals, feathers, furs, mould, drugs, natural or artificial chemicals, insect bites and gases. Some individuals are far more susceptible to a wide range of substances than others and the tendency to develop allergies may be inherited. Allergy reactions may be very localised (eg. at the site of an insect bite, or in just one eye), may occur suddenly or gradually, may last for a few minutes or a few months, may involve internal organs (eg. lungs), or be limited to the body surface (eg. skin or nose lining). When a person is exposed to a substance to which they are allergic, the body reacts by releasing excessive amounts of histamine from mast cells that are found in the lining of every body cavity and in the skin. Histamine is required at times to fight invading substances, but when released in excess, it causes tissue inflammation and an allergic reaction.

SYMPTOMS: May cause a wide range of symptoms including itchy skin and eyes, diarrhoea, redness and swelling of tissues, a runny nose and skin lumps, depending on the area of the body affected.

INVESTIGATIONS: Screening blood tests can determine if a patient is suffering from an allergy. An allergy to specific substance can be detected by skin or blood tests. In the skin test, a minute amount of the suspected substance is scratched into a very small area of skin and the reaction of that skin area is then checked for a reaction a day or so later. In blood tests, specific antibodies to invading allergic substances are sought and identified.

TREATMENT: Depends on where the allergy occurs, its severity, and its duration. Antihistamine drugs are the main treatment and may be given by tablet, mixture, injection, nose spray or cream, but some types may cause drowsiness. A severe attack may require steroid tablets or injections, adrenaline injections, or in very severe cases, emergency resuscitation (see anaphylaxis). There are a number of medications (eg. sodium cromoglycate, steroid sprays, nedocromil sodium) that can be used on a regular basis to prevent allergic reactions. If the substance that causes an allergy can be identified, further episodes may be prevented by desensitisation which involves giving extremely small doses of the allergy-causing substance to the patient by injection, and then slowly increasing the dose over many weeks or months until the patient can completely tolerate the substance.

COMPLICATIONS: Severe allergic reactions may kill a patient by causing the throat to swell shut, acting on the heart to cause irregular beats, or inducing a critical lung spasm. A small number of highly allergic patients must carry an emergency supply of injectable adrenaline with them at all times.

PROGNOSIS: Most allergies can be successfully treated and prevented. Some allergies can be cured by desensitisation.

See also Allergic Conjunctivitis; Anaphylaxis; Angioneurotic Oedema; Hay Fever; Hives; Prurigo; Serum Sickness

Alopecia Areata

DESCRIPTION: Common cause of patchy hair loss.

CAUSE: Family history in about 20% of patients, fungal infections and drugs used to treat cancer may be responsible, but in most cases no specific cause can be found. Stress and anxiety are not usually a cause. Different to baldness in that it can occur at any age, in either sex, in any race, and more common under 25 years of age.

SYMPTOMS: A sudden loss of hair in a well-defined patch on the scalp or other areas of body hair (eg. pubic area, beard, eyebrows). Starts suddenly, and a bare patch 2 cm or more across may be present before it is noticed. The hairless area may slowly extend for several weeks before stabilising. Several spots may occur simultaneously, and may merge together as they enlarge. If the entire body is affected, the disease is called **alopecia totalis**, which is not a different disease, just a severe case of alopecia areata.

INVESTIGATIONS: None usually necessary, but skin biopsy sometimes performed.

TREATMENT: Strong steroid creams, injections of steroids into the affected area, and irritant lotions.

COMPLICATIONS: Sunburn to exposed scalp skin.

PROGNOSIS: In 90% of patients, regrowth of hair eventually recurs, although the new hair may be totally white and it may take many months or years. The further the bare patch is from the top of the scalp, the slower and less likely the regrowth of hair. It is rare to recover from total hair loss.

See also Baldness; Loose Anagen Syndrome; Telogen Effluvium

Alopecia Totalis
See Alopecia Areata

Alport Syndrome

DESCRIPTION: Rare developmental problem of the kidneys that occurs only in boys.

CAUSE: Familial (passes from one generation to the next in families) but both parents must be carriers for it to occur.

SYMPTOMS: Deafness, progressive glomerulonephritis (see separate entry), and blood in the urine. Some patients have recurrent middle ear infections, and eye cataracts.

INVESTIGATIONS: Blood found in urine and kidney function blood tests abnormal.

TREATMENT: None available.
COMPLICATIONS: Disease recurs in transplanted kidneys.
PROGNOSIS: No cure. Kidney failure inevitable.
See also Glomerulonephritis

Altitude Sickness
(Mountain Sickness)

DESCRIPTION: Lung damage caused by lack of oxygen at high altitudes.
CAUSE: Ascending rapidly to heights over 3000m. A slow ascent is less likely to cause problems than a rapid one. Impossible to predict who will be affected, how rapidly or at what altitude.
SYMPTOMS: Starts with headache, shortness of breath, and excessive tiredness, followed by inability to sleep, nausea, vomiting, diarrhoea, abdominal pains and a fever. Fluid fills the lungs, patients start coughing up blood, the heart races, and they may eventually drown as blood fills the lungs.
INVESTIGATIONS: None normally necessary.
TREATMENT: A rapid descent to a lower altitude is the only effective treatment for severe cases, although mild cases may recover with rest at high altitude. Fluid removing drugs (diuretics) may be used in an emergency to remove fluid from the lungs. Acetazolamide and dexamethasone may be given during the climb for prevention. Oxygen in cylinders is used by very high altitude climbers.
COMPLICATIONS: Permanent lung and other organ damage may result from a severe attack.
PROGNOSIS: May be life-threatening unless a lower altitude can be reached.

Alveolitis
See Idiopathic Pulmonary Fibrosis

Alzheimer's Disease
(Second Childhood; Senile Dementia)

DESCRIPTION: The most common form of dementia in the elderly, but may start as early as the mid-fifties.
CAUSE: A faster than normal loss of nerve cells in the brain, the exact cause of which is unknown, but studies suggest specific genes may predispose a person to the disease, and there is a familial tendency (runs in families from one generation to the next).
SYMPTOMS: Initially causes loss of recent memory, loss of initiative, reduced physical activity, confusion and loss of orientation (confused about place and time). Progresses to loss of speech, difficulty in swallowing which causes drooling, stiff muscles, incontinence of both faeces and urine, a bedridden state and eventually the patient is totally unaware of themselves or anything that is happening around them.
INVESTIGATIONS: Reduced brain volume and wasting may show on a CT scan. The

diagnosis is primarily a clinical one made by a doctor after excluding all other forms of dementia by blood tests, X-rays, electroencephalogram (EEG) and sometimes taking a sample of the spinal fluid. The progress of the disease can be followed by tests of skill, general knowledge, simple maths, etc.

TREATMENT: Medication is useful for restlessness and insomnia, and a number of medications are now being used experimentally to slow the progression of the disease. In women, hormone replacement therapy after menopause reduces the incidence of Alzheimer's disease, and slows its progress. Visits by the family general practitioner, physiotherapists, occupational therapists, home nursing care and health visitors are the main forms of management. Many claims have been made for various herbal remedies, but none have proved to be beneficial.

COMPLICATIONS: Some patients may not deteriorate for some time, then drop to a lower level of activity quite suddenly. Admission to a nursing home or hospital is eventually necessary.

PROGNOSIS: No cure, and treatments are aimed at keeping the patient content. From diagnosis to eventually death takes seven years on average.

See also Dementia; Organic Brain Syndrome; Pick's Disease

Amaurosis
See Leber Congenital Amaurosis

Amblyopia

DESCRIPTION: A decrease in vision in one or both eyes.

CAUSE: Numerous causes including squint, cataracts, severe short sight (myopia) or a lack of good nutrition, particularly vitamin B (often occurs in alcoholics and is aggravated by tobacco smoking). All causes result in degeneration of the light sensitive area (retina) at the back of the eye.

SYMPTOMS: Dimness and blurring of vision and reduced colour differentiation.

INVESTIGATIONS: Specific tests on visual function, and examination of the retina with an ophthalmoscope (magnifying light).

TREATMENT: Correct the cause by spectacles, covering the better eye to stimulate the poorer one, eye muscle surgery or vitamin B supplements, good diet and not smoking.

COMPLICATIONS: Permanent damage to optic nerve and blindness.

PROGNOSIS: Steadily progressive to virtual blindness in affected eye(s) unless adequately treated.

See also Strachan Syndrome and other diseases listed under Vision Problems

American Trypanosomiasis
See Chagas' Disease

Amnestic Syndrome
DESCRIPTION: Complication of alcoholism involving the brain.
CAUSE: Lack of thiamine (vitamin B3) caused by alcoholism.
SYMPTOMS: Sudden onset of short term memory disturbances, and permanent loss of memory of period when affected.
INVESTIGATIONS: Blood tests show low levels of thiamine, liver damage and presence of alcohol.
TREATMENT: Treat alcoholism.
COMPLICATIONS: Other complications of alcoholism.
PROGNOSIS: Poor, as alcoholism is well advanced by this stage.
See also Alcoholism

Amoebiasis
(Amoebic Dysentery)
DESCRIPTION: Infestation of the gut with single-celled animals (amoebae). Relatively common in many third-world countries.
CAUSE: Swallowed amoebae usually infest the gut and liver, and very rarely the brain and lung. Amoebae are passed out with the faeces, and if this contaminates food or water, they can be picked up by others. Some people have very mild infections and act as carriers, steadily infecting more and more people.
SYMPTOMS: Abdominal pain, diarrhoea, mucus and blood in the faeces, fever, and in severe cases the bowel may rupture, leading to peritonitis and death.
INVESTIGATIONS: Diagnosed by finding the amoebae in the faeces when examined under a microscope, or by special blood tests that detect antibody changes caused by amoebae.
TREATMENT: Controlled by strict attention to personal hygiene, cooking food and boiling water. Treated with one or more of a number of drugs to kill the amoebae, but they have significant side effects and may need to be used for several weeks. An abscess needs to be drained surgically.
COMPLICATIONS: If the amoebae enter the liver from the gut, an abscess (see separate entry) can form in the liver and cause severe pain.
PROGNOSIS: If left untreated, severely affected patients will die, but modern treatment methods lead to the total recovery of the majority.

Amoebic Dysentery
See Amoebiasis

Amphetamine Abuse
('Speed')
DESCRIPTION: Synthetic addictive chemical that is available illicitly as tablets ('speed'), or as a faster acting powder that is smoked ('ice').
CAUSE: Amphetamines are stimulants, that in some situations are used medically (eg. methylphenidate is used for the treatment of attention deficit disorder).

Possibly one in every 100 people is dependent upon illicit drugs, and a far higher percentage have experimented with them at one time or another.

SYMPTOMS: When used inappropriately cause increased activity, euphoria and a feeling of increased mental and physical ability. Tolerance develops quickly, and with time, higher and higher doses must be used to cause the same effect.

INVESTIGATIONS: Blood and urine tests can detect the presence of amphetamines.

TREATMENT: The treatment options available are:
— gradual withdrawal while receiving counselling and medical support
— immediate drug withdrawal ('cold turkey') while hospitalised
— half-way houses that remove the patient from the environment in which drug taking is encouraged
— individual or group psychotherapy.

COMPLICATIONS: Adverse effects include a rapid heart rate, sweating, dry eyes, increased blood pressure that may cause heart problems, confusion and disorientation. Long term use may cause delusions, paranoia, hallucinations, and serious psychiatric disturbances. Withdrawal results in severe depression and drowsiness.

PROGNOSIS: Reasonably good. Not as addictive as heroin, but more than marijuana.

See also other problems listed under Addiction

Amsterdam Dwarf
See de Lange Syndrome

Amyloidosis

DESCRIPTION: A rare disease in which millions of microscopic fibres made of a dense amyloid protein infiltrate and replace the normal tissue of different parts of the body. The kidneys, lungs, heart and intestine are commonly involved.

CAUSE: The disease may be triggered by another disease, such as tuberculosis, rheumatoid arthritis, cancer or drug abuse, but in many cases no apparent cause can be found.

SYMPTOMS: Extremely variable symptoms, depending on which organs are involved.

INVESTIGATIONS: Microscopic examination of a sample taken from an involved organ reveals a dense jelly formed by the protein fibres, rather than normal tissue.

TREATMENT: No treatment available.

COMPLICATIONS: Pneumonia, kidney infections, heart failure.

PROGNOSIS: Death within three years of diagnosis on average.

Amyotrophic Lateral Sclerosis
(Lou Gehrig Disease)

DESCRIPTION: Rare form of motor neurone disease (see separate entry) that affects the nerves that supply the muscles of the body. Sometimes known as Lou Gehrig disease after a 1930s American baseballer who developed the condition.

CAUSE: Absolute cause unknown, but may run in families, and results in a steadily progressive degeneration of the motor nerves in the body.

SYMPTOMS: Muscle weakness that usually starts in the hands or feet, muscle cramps and twitches, difficulty in swallowing and talking, drooling of saliva, inability to cough effectively, reduced tongue movement, and progressive weakness up the arms and legs. Eventually the muscles used for breathing are involved.

INVESTIGATIONS: Electrical tests of the motor nerves to determine how well they are functioning, and a nerve biopsy.

TREATMENT: No cure available, and treatment is aimed at relieving muscle spasm, assisting feeding, preventing infections, aiding breathing and making the patient as comfortable as possible. Physiotherapy on a very regular basis is essential.

COMPLICATIONS: Lung infections such as pneumonia develop, and often lead to death.

PROGNOSIS: Steadily progressive to death within three to five years.

See also Kugelberg-Welander Syndrome; Motor Neurone Disease; Werdnig-Hoffman Syndrome

Anaemia

DESCRIPTION: A low level of haemoglobin in the blood.

CAUSE: Haemoglobin is a complex compound that is found in red blood cells, gives these cells their colour, and is used to transport oxygen in the blood from the lungs to the organs. A major component of the haemoglobin molecule is iron. There are many different types of anaemia which vary widely in their cause and severity.

SYMPTOMS: Tiredness and weakness due to insufficient oxygen reaching the organs. Other symptoms may include pins and needles in the arms and legs, palpitations, abnormally curved finger nails, dizziness and shortness of breath. Skin and eye colour are poor guides to the severity of anaemia.

INVESTIGATIONS: The level of haemoglobin in blood can be tested by a pathology laboratory. Further blood tests determine the type of anaemia present.

TREATMENT: Depends on type and cause, but a blood transfusion may be necessary in severe cases.

PROGNOSIS: Depends on cause and type of anaemia.

See also Aplastic Anaemia; Haemolytic Anaemia; Iron Deficiency Anaemia; Pernicious Anaemia; Sickle Cell Anaemia; Spherocytosis

Anaerobic Infections

DESCRIPTION: Infection anywhere in the body by bacteria that do not require oxygen (anaerobes).

CAUSE: Bacteria such as *Prevotella* in the lungs and throat, *Bacteroides* and *Clostridia* in the bowel and belly, and numerous types in the female genital tract and brain.

SYMPTOMS: Depends on organ infected. Often multiple organs involved, pus produced is foul smelling, and numerous small abscesses form in infected organs.

INVESTIGATIONS: Culture of pus, fluid or tissue from infected organ identifies responsible bacteria.

TREATMENT: Appropriate antibiotics. Surgical drainage of abscesses.

COMPLICATIONS: Permanent damage to infected organs.

PROGNOSIS: Depends on organ and bacteria, but usually good response to appropriate antibiotics.

Anal Atresia

DESCRIPTION: Failure of the anus to develop at birth.

CAUSE: Congenital.

SYMPTOMS: Infant does not pass faeces, fails to feed and becomes bloated. Vomiting may occur at a late stage.

INVESTIGATIONS: Diagnosed by examining the anus.

TREATMENT: Quite major surgery to initially form a colostomy (opening the gut onto the belly skin) to drain the bowel of collected wastes, create a new anus, then join up the gut again.

PROGNOSIS: Reasonable results from surgery, but some children end up with a permanent colostomy.

Anal Fissure
(Fissure in Ano)

DESCRIPTION: A split in the anus.

CAUSE: Develops when the anus has overstretched and torn during an episode of constipation.

SYMPTOMS: Intermittent pain and bleeding similar to that of a pile.

INVESTIGATIONS: Cause of constipation may need to be determined.

TREATMENT: Keeping the motions soft and using a medicated ointment.

COMPLICATIONS: Scarring and narrowing of the anus.

PROGNOSIS: Good if constipation controlled.

See also Piles; Proctitis

Anal Fistula
(Fistula in Ano)

DESCRIPTION: A serious problem caused by a serious infection around the anus.

CAUSE: An abscess, bacterial infection or cancer damages the tissue between the rectum and skin, allowing a false tube (fistula) to form between the rectum inside the anus, and the skin beside the anus.

SYMPTOMS: Liquid faeces leaks through the fistula onto the skin which becomes inflamed and painful.

INVESTIGATIONS: Special dye may be injected into the drainage point of the fistula and then X-rayed to see where it runs to.

TREATMENT: Quite difficult surgery is necessary to close the fistula.

COMPLICATIONS: Rarely a fistula may develop between the last part of the rectum and the vagina or bladder.

PROGNOSIS: Progress after surgery may be difficult, but most patients recover completely.

Anal Inflammation

See Anal Fissure; Anal Fistula; Proctalgia Fugax; Proctitis; Pruritus Ani; Rectal Prolapse

Anal Itch

See Pruritus Ani

Anaphylactic Shock

See Anaphylaxis

Anaphylactoid Purpura

See Henoch-Schoenlein Syndrome

Anaphylaxis
(Anaphylactic Shock)

DESCRIPTION: Immediate, severe, life-threatening reaction to an allergy-causing substance.

CAUSE: Insect stings (eg. bees, hornets, wasps, ants) and injected drugs are the most likely causes. It is rare for inhaled, touched or eaten substances to cause this reaction.

SYMPTOMS: Patient rapidly becomes sweaty, develops widespread pins and needles, may develop a generalised flush or red rash, or swelling in one or more parts of the body (possibly including the tongue, throat and eyelids), starts wheezing, becomes blue around the lips, may become incontinent of urine, loses consciousness, convulses and stops breathing. Swelling of the tongue and throat may cause death by suffocation if air is unable to pass into the lungs.

INVESTIGATIONS: No time for tests during attack. Blood and skin tests to identify responsible substance can be very carefully performed at a later time.

TREATMENT: First aid — patient placed on their back with the neck extended to give the best possible airway, and mouth-to-mouth resuscitation and external cardiac massage may be necessary.

Medical treatment — emergency medical assistance necessary, as an injection of a drug such as adrenaline, hydrocortisone, aminophylline and an antihistamine (this is the preferred order) can reverse the reaction and save the patient's life. Patients who are aware that they may have an anaphylactic reaction often carry an adrenaline injection with them at all times to be used in an emergency.

PROGNOSIS: Patients respond well to appropriate treatment, but death may occur within minutes if medical help is not immediately available.

See also Allergy

Anaplastic Carcinoma of the Thyroid Gland
See Thyroid Cancer

Ancylostomiasis
See Hookworm

Andersen Syndrome
See Glycogen Storage Diseases

Anencephaly
DESCRIPTION: Failure of the brain to develop.
CAUSE: Congenital abnormality.
SYMPTOMS: Infant with no forehead and minimal skull development behind face.
INVESTIGATIONS: Diagnosis usually obvious.
TREATMENT: None available.
PROGNOSIS: Incompatible with life, and infant dies within hours of birth.

Aneurysm
DESCRIPTION: Ballooning out of one part of an artery (or the heart), at a point where the artery becomes weakened. May be a slight bump on the side of an artery, a quite large bubble, or a long sausage-shaped extension along an artery. Any artery may be affected, but the most serious ones involve the aorta (the main artery down the back of the chest and abdomen — **aortic aneurysm**) and arteries in the brain (**cerebral aneurysm**). Different types are categorised by their shape. The most common are **saccular** or **berry aneurysms** which are direct balloonings on the side of an artery. The most sinister are the **dissecting aneurysms**, where only part of the artery wall is damaged (often by cholesterol plaques — arteriosclerosis) and the blood penetrates in between the layers of the artery wall, slowly splitting them apart, and extending along the artery.
CAUSE: Weakness in arteries may be caused by plaques of cholesterol, high blood pressure, injury to the artery or a congenital (present since birth) weakness in the wall of an artery. The heart wall may be damaged by a heart attack, and the weakened area can bulge out as an aneurysm. There is a slight hereditary tendency.
SYMPTOMS: Usually no symptoms, unless the aneurysm is very large or presses on a nerve, but the aneurysm may burst, leading to a massive loss of blood or damage to surrounding organs (eg. brain), or they may extend to the point where they put pressure on other arteries, and cut off the blood supply to vital organs (eg. kidney).
INVESTIGATIONS: Diagnosed on X-ray after special dye has been injected into the artery. Very large aneurysms may be seen on a plain X-ray. CT scans and magnetic resonance imaging (MRI) may also detect an aneurysm.
TREATMENT: The rupture of an aneurysm on a major artery can lead to death within seconds, or a slow leak may allow surgeons enough time to undertake a major operation to repair or replace the leaking artery. If an aneurysm is found

incidentally, it may be operated upon to prevent it bursting, or left alone and regularly checked for any increase in size. In the brain, a small aneurysm may be clipped with a tiny U-shaped piece of silver to prevent it from leaking. It is vital to control blood pressure and avoid aggravating factors such as smoking and strenuous exercise.

PROGNOSIS: Extremely variable, depending on the site and severity of any rupture, but there is a significant overall mortality rate.

See also Tolosa-Hunt Syndrome

Angelman Syndrome
(Happy Puppet Syndrome)

DESCRIPTION: Rare cause of intellectual impairment.

CAUSE: Congenital due to damage on chromosome 15. One case occurs in every 25,000 children.

SYMPTOMS: Severe mental retardation, inability to talk, abnormal walk, intractable seizures, inappropriate laughter, small head, abnormal facial structure.

INVESTIGATIONS: Diagnosed by chromosome analysis.

TREATMENT: None available.

PROGNOSIS: Shorter than normal lifespan.

Angina
(Angina Pectoris; Ischaemic Heart Disease)

DESCRIPTION: Pain caused by an inadequate blood supply (ischaemia) to part of the heart muscle.

CAUSE: Due to a narrowing of one or more of the three small arteries that supply blood to the heart muscle. This narrowing may be due to hardening of the arteries, or a spasm of the artery caused by another disease, smoking, excitement, heavy meals or stress. Angina may lead to a heart attack, or a heart attack may cause angina, but they are two different problems. In a heart attack, part of the heart muscle dies.

SYMPTOMS: A pressure-like, squeezing pain or tightness in the chest, usually central, that starts suddenly, often during exercise, and settles with rest, but may occur at almost any time and may extend into the left arm, neck, upper abdomen and back. It is uncommon during sleep.

INVESTIGATIONS: Diagnosis may be difficult as the pain has usually subsided when the patient sees a doctor, and all blood tests and electrocardiographs (ECG) may be normal. Sometimes a stress ECG must be performed under strict medical supervision to recreate the pain and observe the abnormal ECG pattern. Coronary angiography is a type of X-ray that can detect narrowed arteries around the heart. A more sophisticated test involves injecting radio-isotopes into the bloodstream, and measuring their uptake by the heart muscle.

TREATMENT: Prevention involves tablets or skin patches (eg. nitrates, beta-blockers or calcium channel blockers) that are used regularly to keep the arteries as widely dilated as possible. Smokers must stop smoking.

Treatment of an acute attack involves immediately resting, and spraying glyceryl trinitrate under the tongue, or placing a tablet containing nitroglycerine, nifedipine or a similar drug under the tongue to dilate the heart arteries and relieve the attack. If a narrowed artery can be found it can be bypassed by a coronary artery bypass graft (CABG) operation. Balloon angiography is a technique that involves passing a tiny deflated balloon through the arteries in the leg or arm, into the heart, and then into the small narrowed arteries around the heart, then inflating it to enlarge the narrowed artery. Sometimes a stent (tube shaped metal grid) is left behind to ensure that the artery does not close down again.

COMPLICATIONS: About 5% of all patients with angina will have a heart attack each year, and half of these will die from that heart attack. Heart failure can gradually affect those remaining, reducing their mobility and eventually leading to premature death. High blood pressure, diabetes and an irregular heart beat are unfavourable findings and will also lead to an early death.

PROGNOSIS: Most people with angina can have their symptoms prevented and relieved by medication. Many patients with narrowed arteries can be successfully treated by surgery.

See also Heart Attack; Intermediate Coronary Syndrome

Angina, Vincent's

See Gingivostomatitis; Necrotising Ulcerative Gingivostomatitis

Angioedema

See Familial Angioedema; Hives

Angioma

See Haemangioma

Angioneurotic Oedema

DESCRIPTION: Abnormal swelling (oedema) of tissue around the body openings in the face.

CAUSE: Allergic reaction, usually to a pollen, dust, chemical or other substance that has blown into the eye or nose, food that has touched the lips, or from rubbing the face with a contaminated finger.

SYMPTOMS: A sudden, severe swelling of tissues around the eye, nose or mouth. May be slightly itchy, but not usually painful or tender.

INVESTIGATIONS: None necessary.

TREATMENT: Antihistamine tablets or injections. Severe cases may need steroids.

COMPLICATIONS: Rarely swelling may be very severe and affect breathing.

PROGNOSIS: Good response to treatment.

See also Allergy; Anaphylaxis

Angiosarcoma

DESCRIPTION: Form of cancer involving arteries and veins, that often occurs in the liver or on the skin of the face and scalp.

CAUSE: Unknown.

SYMPTOMS: Red-purple tumour on the skin or in internal organs. General symptoms vary with location.

INVESTIGATIONS: Internal tumours difficult to detect. Angiograms (blood vessels X-rayed after injecting a dye) or CT and MRI scans may be used.

TREATMENT: Extensive surgical resection of tumour and surrounding tissue.

COMPLICATIONS: May extend very deeply into tissue of face.

PROGNOSIS: Variable depending on stage of tumour development, but often poor.

See also Cancer; Stewart-Treves Syndrome

Angiostrongyliasis
(Eosinophilic Meningoencephalitis)

DESCRIPTION: Infestation of the brain and surrounding membranes (meninges) by the nematode worm *Angiostrongylus cantonensis*. Occurs on Pacific islands, in west Africa, south Asia and in the Caribbean.

CAUSE: Worms normally occur in the gut of rats. Eggs pass out with rat faeces, are eaten by snails, prawns or fish, and then pass to humans if these foods are eaten when poorly cooked. May directly enter humans if food contaminated by rat faeces (eg. salads) are eaten. The swallowed eggs hatch into larvae which migrate through the bloodstream to the brain and meninges. Incubation period one to three weeks.

SYMPTOMS: Severe headache, fever, neck stiffness, nausea, vomiting and abnormal nerve sensations.

INVESTIGATIONS: Blood tests show non-specific changes. CT and MRI scans may show presence of worms in brain.

TREATMENT: No specific treatment available.

COMPLICATIONS: May spread into the eye and cause blindness.

PROGNOSIS: Symptoms persist for several months until the worm dies, and then most patients recover completely. Rarely there may be permanent brain damage and death.

See also other conditions listed under Nematode Infestation

Aniridia

DESCRIPTION: Rare eye developmental abnormality with two subtypes, **Miller syndrome** (associated with Wilms tumour and subnormal mentality), and **Gillespie syndrome** (associated with mental retardation and poor coordination).

CAUSE: Inherited genetic defect.

SYMPTOMS: The iris (coloured part of the eye) is missing and vision is poor. Both eyes usually affected.

INVESTIGATIONS: Defect is obvious on simple eye inspection.

TREATMENT: None available except for complications.
COMPLICATIONS: Glaucoma (see separate entry) is very common. Clouding of the cornea (outer surface of the eye) and lens (cataract) may occur.
PROGNOSIS: No cure, and very poor vision usually occurs.
See also other conditions listed under Eye Diseases

Anisakiasis

DESCRIPTION: Infestation of the stomach by the nematode worm *Anisakid*.
CAUSE: Normally infests the gut of whales, seals and dolphins. Eggs are passed out in the faeces of these animals, swallowed by small shellfish, which in turn are eaten by squid, mackerel, herring, salmon, tuna and other fish. Enter the human stomach by eating raw fish.
SYMPTOMS: Nausea, vomiting, and severe upper abdominal pain occurs within hours of eating infested fish. Diarrhoea occurs later. Pain spreads to lower abdomen, becomes intermittent, and may last for years (chronic stage).
INVESTIGATIONS: No specific diagnostic test. Diagnosis difficult and often delayed until part of the bowel is removed surgically or gastroscopy detects a worm.
TREATMENT: Surgical excision of worms from the stomach and intestine.
COMPLICATIONS: Severe allergy reactions may occur in the acute stage. Bowel obstruction in the chronic stage.
PROGNOSIS: Cure difficult. Symptoms usually prolonged. Rarely life threatening.
See also other conditions listed under Nematode Infestation

Ankle Sprain
See Sprain

Ankylosing Spondylitis

DESCRIPTION: A long-term inflammation of the small joints between the vertebrae in the back. More common in men, usually starts in the late twenties or early thirties, but progresses very slowly.
CAUSE: Unknown.
SYMPTOMS: Starts gradually with a constant backache that may radiate down the legs. Stiffness of the back becomes steadily worse, and eventually the patient may be bent almost double by a solidly fused backbone in old age.
INVESTIGATIONS: Diagnosis by X-rays of the back, and specific blood tests.
TREATMENT: Anti-inflammatory drugs such as indomethacin, naproxen, aspirin and (in resistant cases) phenylbutazone. Regular physiotherapy can help relieve the pain and stiffness even in advanced cases.
COMPLICATIONS: May be associated with a number of apparently unrelated conditions, including arthritis of other joints, heart valve disease, weakening of the aorta and inflammation of the eyes.
PROGNOSIS: May settle spontaneously for a few months or years, before progressing further. No cure available, but treatment can give most patients a full life of normal length.

Anorexia Nervosa

DESCRIPTION: Eating disorder that usually occurs in young white women in Western society. Almost unknown in American Negroes and British Indians, and totally unknown in third-world countries. About one in every 200 women between 13 and 30 in developed countries may be affected.

CAUSE: May start with a psychological shock (eg. rejection by a boy friend, fear of a new situation, stress at school, bad sexual experience) and is due to an inappropriate body image which makes the patient feel grossly overweight, or have an abnormal fear of becoming overweight, when they may be normal or underweight.

SYMPTOMS: An extreme dislike of food accompanied by excessive exercising, a cessation of menstrual periods, diffuse hair loss, intolerance of cold, slow pulse, irregular heart beat and complex hormonal disorders. Patients may practice deceit to fool their family and doctors by appearing to eat normal meals but later vomit the food, use purgatives to clean out their bowel, or hide food during the meal. May become seriously undernourished and emaciated, to the point of death, if adequate treatment is not available.

INVESTIGATIONS: No specific blood or other test that can confirm the diagnosis, but tests may be undertaken to ensure that there is no other cause for the weight loss or lack of appetite.

TREATMENT: Very difficult, prolonged and requires the attention of expert psychiatrists and physicians. Initial hospital admission is almost mandatory, and any relapses should also be treated by hospitalisation. Punishment for not eating must be avoided, but friendly encouragement and persuasion by family and friends is beneficial in both improving the patient's self- esteem and food intake. Medications (eg. tricyclic antidepressants) are not successful without accompanying psychiatric help, which is required for many years.

COMPLICATIONS: Patients are more susceptible to infection. In advanced stages the heart, kidney and liver may fail.

PROGNOSIS: Relapses are common, and suicide frequently attempted. Long term outcome can vary from complete recovery to death within a year or two. Statistically, 30% suffer some long term adverse health effects, and as many as 25% eventually die from the disease.

See also Bulimia Nervosa

Anorgasmia
(Orgasm Failure)

DESCRIPTION: Failure of a woman to have an orgasm during sexual intercourse.

CAUSE: Different women require different degrees and types of stimulation to have an orgasm, which is a reflex, in the same way as a tap on the knee causes a reflex. Some women can only orgasm by stimulation of the clitoris, others require prolonged intercourse, while others may orgasm frequently and easily with merely breast stimulation or thinking about sex. A woman may find that one particular sex position causes orgasm more easily than other positions.

SYMPTOMS: A woman may be sexually responsive, enjoy sex and have the physical signs of erotic arousal, but she may still fail to have an orgasm.

INVESTIGATIONS: None diagnostic.

TREATMENT: Treatment is difficult. The woman should be taught relaxation techniques which are accompanied by masturbation by hand or mechanical devices in order to bring herself to orgasm. Once she has experienced orgasm in this manner, she can move to the next stage of treatment with a male partner. This may involve the man using his hand to stimulate her to orgasm, or by using different sex positions (eg. man behind woman) during which the woman can stimulate her own clitoris. The supervision of a sex therapist (psychiatrist or psychologist) in this process is invaluable.

PROGNOSIS: Treatment often successful if woman and her partner are well motivated.

See also other diseases listed under **Sex Problems**

Anterior Chest Wall Syndrome
See Tietze Syndrome

Anterior Compartment Syndrome

DESCRIPTION: Leg pain in athletes.

CAUSE: Increased pressure in the rigid compartment between the bones in the lower leg (tibia and fibula) and the fibrous tissue surrounding the muscles. Caused by exercise stress (eg. long distance running).

SYMPTOMS: Pain in the front and outside fleshy part of the lower leg that is worse with exercise.

INVESTIGATIONS: None diagnostic.

TREATMENT: Rest, anti-inflammatory medications, physiotherapy, and rarely surgical relief of the pressure.

COMPLICATIONS: In severe cases there may be difficulty in pulling up the foot due to nerve compression.

PROGNOSIS: Settles slowly with treatment.

Anterior Impingement Syndrome
(Footballer's Ankle)

DESCRIPTION: Persistent painful inflammation of tissues around the ankle.

CAUSE: Repeated forced upward flexion of the ankle, as in kicking.

SYMPTOMS: Chronic ankle pain that is worse with running or descending stairs, ankle stiffness, pain on upward flexion of the ankle.

INVESTIGATIONS: X-ray of the ankle shows bony growths on the upper surface of the talus bone at the top of the foot just in front of the ankle, and on the lower end of the tibia (shin bone).

TREATMENT: Rest, anti-inflammatory medications, and surgical removal of the bony overgrowths.

COMPLICATIONS: Without rest, pain steadily worsens until walking becomes impossible.
PROGNOSIS: Good if treatment plan followed correctly.
See also Impingement Syndromes

Anthrax

DESCRIPTION: A skin infection common of farmers, meat workers, veterinarians and others who come into close contact with animals.
CAUSE: The bacterium *Bacillus anthracis* which is found in cattle, horses, sheep, goats and pigs. Caught by bacteria entering the body through scratches and grazes, or rarely by inhalation into the lungs.
SYMPTOMS: A sore appears at the site of entry, then nearby lymph nodes become inflamed, a fever develops, followed by nausea, vomiting, headaches and collapse.
INVESTIGATIONS: Diagnosis confirmed by microscopic examination of smears from the skin sores, or from sputum samples. Specific blood tests may also detect the disease.
TREATMENT: Antibiotics (eg. penicillin or tetracycline) by injection.
COMPLICATIONS: If the infection enters the lung, a severe form of pneumonia results. May also spread into the bloodstream.
PROGNOSIS: Treatment clears skin form of the disease effectively in most cases. Anthrax pneumonia is very serious, and a significant proportion of these patients die.

Antiphospholipid Syndrome

DESCRIPTION: Uncommon blood clotting condition that is more common in young women.
CAUSE: Congenital (present since birth) lack of blood chemicals that prevent blood from clotting while circulating in the arteries and veins.
SYMPTOMS: Repeated blood clots (thrombosis — see separate entry) in arteries and veins, that may cause serious complications and organ damage, depending on their position.
INVESTIGATIONS: Diagnosed by specific blood tests.
TREATMENT: Anticoagulants taken constantly to prevent blood from clotting.
COMPLICATIONS: Women patients tend to have repeated miscarriages.
PROGNOSIS: No cure, but good control.

Anxiety Neurosis
See Neurosis

Aortic Aneurysm
See Aneurysm

Aortic Arch Syndrome
See Takayasu's Arteritis

Aortic Regurgitation
See Aortic Valve Incompetence

Aortic Stenosis
See Aortic Valve Stenosis; Coarctation of the Aorta

Aortic Unfolding

DESCRIPTION: The aorta is the main artery of the body and is about 2cm. across. It starts from the top of the heart, bends (or folds) over, and then runs down the back of the chest and belly along the inside of the backbone. It looks like an upside down 'J'.

CAUSE: With ageing the bend in the aorta as it curls around from the top of the heart to run down the back of the chest becomes a less sharp bend. The aorta does not fold over on itself as much as it did before, and so in medical jargon, the aorta is said to be 'unfolded'.

SYMPTOMS: Normally none.

INVESTIGATIONS: Unfolding revealed by an X-ray of the chest.

TREATMENT: None necessary.

COMPLICATIONS: The aorta may be unfolded and dilated by an aneurysm (see separate entry).

PROGNOSIS: A sign of advancing age, and nothing more.

Aortic Valve Incompetence
(Aortic Regurgitation)

DESCRIPTION: A leak of the aortic valve in the heart which sits between the left ventricle and the aorta, and normally stops blood that has been pumped out to the body from running back into the heart.

CAUSE: Rheumatic fever, endocarditis, high blood pressure, syphilis or a birth defect.

SYMPTOMS: If only a slight leak is present, there will be no symptoms, but if the leak worsens, the patient will become short of breath, develop chest pain, and become very tired.

INVESTIGATIONS: Diagnosed by echocardiography (ultrasound) or passing a catheter through an artery and into the heart.

TREATMENT: Medications to reduce blood pressure may give relief, but if possible, surgical correction should be undertaken once symptoms are present.

COMPLICATIONS: May be significant leakage before symptoms occur, and then the patient may deteriorate rapidly with heart failure.

PROGNOSIS: Depends on severity. Good if mild or surgical replacement of valve possible.

See also other diseases listed under Heart Valve Disease

Aortic Valve Stenosis

DESCRIPTION: Narrowing of the aortic valve in the heart which sits between the left ventricle and the aorta, and normally stops blood that has been pumped out to the body from running back into the heart. An aortic stenosis prevents the blood from being easily pumped from the heart into the aorta.

CAUSE: May be congenital (present at birth) or develop because of rheumatic fever (see separate entry) or hardening of the valve from high blood pressure and/or high cholesterol levels.

SYMPTOMS: Often absent in mild cases, but when more serious, chest pain (that may progress to angina), fainting with exercise and an irregular heartbeat occur.

INVESTIGATIONS: Diagnosed by hearing a typical murmur produced by the blood rushing through the narrowed valve, echocardiography (ultrasound) or passing a catheter through an artery and into the heart.

TREATMENT: Once symptoms occur, surgery to correct the narrowing should be performed.

COMPLICATIONS: Heart failure or attack due to the excessive load placed on the heart muscle.

PROGNOSIS: Good results if surgery possible. Half those with symptoms will die within three years without surgery.

See also other diseases listed under Heart Valve Disease

Apert Syndrome
See Acrocephalosyndactyly of Apert

Aphthous Ulcers
See Mouth Ulcers

Aplastic Anaemia

DESCRIPTION: A very rare, but extremely serious form of anaemia.

CAUSE: Caused by a failure of the bone marrow and spleen to produce new red blood cells. As old red blood cells die, they are not replaced, leading to a rapidly progressive and severe anaemia. Reasons for the failure of the blood cell production include poisons, toxins, insecticides, nuclear irradiation, severe viral infections and some drugs. In more than half the cases, no cause can be found.

SYMPTOMS: In addition to the normal symptoms of anaemia of weakness, tiredness and pallor, these patients have a fever, bleeding into the skin, a rapid heart rate, and increased susceptibility to infection.

INVESTIGATIONS: Diagnosed by examining a blood film under a microscope.

TREATMENT: Repeated blood transfusion can keep the patient alive in the short term only. Any cause must be eliminated if it can be found. Steroid drugs may control the condition, but the only effective long term cure is a bone marrow transplant. The donor must be closely related to the patient, but cannot be one of the parents. Brothers and sisters are usually the best donors.

The procedure involves taking a small amount of bone marrow from the pelvic bone or breast bone of the donor, and injecting it into the bone marrow of the patient.

COMPLICATIONS: Rejection is a far greater problem with a bone marrow transplant than with other forms of transplant. Heart, lung and other organ failure may occur suddenly.

PROGNOSIS: Unfortunately, up to half the patients will eventually die from the condition.

See also Anaemia

Apophysitis of the Tibial Tuberosity
See Osgood-Schlatter's Disease

Apotemnophilia
DESCRIPTION: Very rare psychiatric disturbance.

CAUSE: May be a sexual fetish, or an abnormal discomfort with body shape and structure.

SYMPTOMS: Patient wishes to have a body part, usually an arm or leg, amputated.

INVESTIGATIONS: None diagnostic.

TREATMENT: Detailed psychiatric assessment and psychotherapy. Some patients actually have surgery to remove a limb.

COMPLICATIONS: Often very difficult to convince surgeons to amputate a healthy limb, and patients seek unregistered surgeons to perform the procedure in unhygienic conditions, risking infection and death.

PROGNOSIS: Very difficult to treat, but surgery does cure some carefully selected patients.

Appendicitis
DESCRIPTION: Infection of the appendix, which is a narrow dead end tube about 12cm. long that attaches to the caecum (first part of the large intestine). An almost unknown condition in poorer countries for dietary reasons, and the lack of fibre in Western diets is often blamed, although its incidence is steadily falling due to better dietary education. In other mammals, particularly those that eat grass, the appendix is an important structure which aids in the digestion of cellulose, but in man it serves no useful purpose.

CAUSE: If the narrow tube of the appendix becomes blocked by faeces, food, mucus or some foreign body, bacteria start breeding in the closed-off area behind the blockage.

SYMPTOMS: Pain around the navel that soon moves to the lower right side of the abdomen just above the pelvic bone and steadily worsens. Often associated with loss of appetite, slight diarrhoea and a mild fever.

INVESTIGATIONS: No specific diagnostic test, but blood and urine tests are done to exclude other causes of pain. The removed appendix will be sent to a pathologist to confirm the diagnosis.

TREATMENT: The only effective treatment is surgical removal of the appendix in a simple operation (appendectomy) which takes about 20 minutes. The usual hospital stay is only two days, and patients return to work in seven to ten days. The operation is sometimes done through laparoscopes (1cm. diameter tubes). The surgeon looks through one and operates through two others, leaving only three tiny scars scattered across the belly. This speeds recovery so that sometimes only a single night is required in hospital.

COMPLICATIONS: If untreated, the appendix becomes steadily more infected, full of pus, and eventually bursts to cause peritonitis (see separate entry).

PROGNOSIS: Very good results from treatment.

See also Peritonitis

Arachnoiditis

DESCRIPTION: A form of meningitis involving the middle of the three membranes (meninges) that surround and support the brain and spinal cord. The nerves leaving the brain or spinal cord may become compressed and their function affected.

CAUSE: Infection, inflammation or scarring of the arachnoid membrane. May be a rare complication of spinal surgery, injection of drugs into the spine or a myelogram (X-ray of the spinal cord after injection of a dye).

SYMPTOMS: Severe pain in nerves affected by the inflammation, usually affecting both sides of the body. Sometimes there is paralysis of muscles supplied by these nerves.

INVESTIGATIONS: Reflexes involving affected nerves are absent.

TREATMENT: Delicate surgery may be attempted to release trapped nerves. Various medications used to reduce nerve inflammation and pain.

PROGNOSIS: Treatment often unsatisfactory and symptoms persist long term.

See also Meningitis

Arachnophobia
See Phobia

Arcus Senilis

DESCRIPTION: Common eye pigmentation disorder.

CAUSE: Deposition of fats around the edge of the iris (coloured part of the eye) in the elderly and those with abnormally high blood fat levels.

SYMPTOMS: White ring around the iris of both eyes. Vision is unaffected.

INVESTIGATIONS: Blood fat levels should be checked, but no diagnostic tests necessary.

TREATMENT: None necessary.

COMPLICATIONS: None.

PROGNOSIS: No cure, but mild cosmetic problem only.

Arnold-Chiari Malformation
See Syringomyelia

Arrhythmia
Any irregular rhythm of the heart.
See Atrial Extrasystoles; Atrial Fibrillation; Long QT Syndrome; Lown-Ganong-Levine Syndrome; Paroxysmal Atrial Tachycardia; Paroxysmal Ventricular Tachycardia; Sick Sinus Syndrome; Ventricular Extrasystoles; Ventricular Fibrillation; Wolff-Parkinson-White Syndrome

Arsenic Poisoning
DESCRIPTION: Swallowing arsenic compounds.

CAUSE: May be encountered in smelting (eg. gold, lead, zinc and nickel), wood preservatives, pesticides, herbicides and some folk remedies. Lethal dose is about 150mg.

SYMPTOMS: Diarrhoea, bleeding from the bowel, nausea, vomiting, low blood pressure, belly pains, delirium, fitting, coma and death.

INVESTIGATIONS: Detected in specific blood tests.

TREATMENT: Induce vomiting if recently swallowed, and go to hospital, where the stomach will be pumped out and activated charcoal given. Copious fluids are given by a drip into a vein to flush out the poison, and medications are given to neutralise it.

PROGNOSIS: Depends on age and weight of patient, and dose of arsenic.

Arterial Gas Embolism
See Bends

Arteriosclerosis
(Atherosclerosis; Hardening of the Arteries)
DESCRIPTION: Degeneration of the arteries in the body, making them hard and inelastic. Usually associated with atherosclerosis, the excessive deposition of hard fatty plaques and nodules within the artery and its wall.

CAUSE: Usually occurs in the elderly, and those who have a high blood level of cholesterol. May also be caused and aggravated by high blood pressure. Hard fatty deposits form at points of turbulence within a major artery (eg. the junction of two arteries, or a bend in the artery) to narrow the artery and gradually restrict the flow of blood to the tissues beyond.

SYMPTOMS: Depends which arteries are affected. An affected artery is less able to cope with pressure changes and more likely to rupture, causing a leak of blood, sometimes into vital structures such as the brain. Patients cannot cope with sudden changes in position (eg. getting out of bed) without becoming dizzy or light-headed. If the leg arteries are involved, the leg muscles become painful, particularly when climbing slopes or stairs (claudication). If heart arteries are involved, angina occurs. If arteries to the brain are involved, the patient may develop a multitude of bizarre symptoms, become light headed, dizzy, confused, or black out as the brain does not receive sufficient blood to operate correctly.

INVESTIGATIONS: Diagnosed by doppler flow (ultrasound) studies on the movement of blood through arteries, and by angiograms (artery X-rays) in which an X-ray visible dye is injected to outline an artery. Cholesterol levels can be checked by a fasting blood test.

TREATMENT: Better prevented than treated, by keeping cholesterol levels and blood pressure within normal limits. Narrowed arteries can be opened slightly with medications that relax the muscles in the artery walls, or that ease the passage of blood cells through the narrowing. There are three types of surgery possible:

— bypass grafts use tubes of synthetic material, or arteries or veins from elsewhere in the body, to bypass the blocked area.

— endarterectomy involves opening the blocked artery and cleaning out the fatty deposits.

— balloon angioplasty is used to dilate blocked arteries by passing a fine tube, with a deflated balloon at the end, along an artery and into the narrowed segment where the balloon is inflated, forcing open the blockage. Sometimes a stent (tube shaped metal grid) is left behind to keep the artery open.

COMPLICATIONS: An embolism occurs when a piece of the hard fat within the artery, breaks away, and travels with the blood along the arteries to a point which is too narrow for it to pass. This causes no problem in most parts of the body, but if the blockage is in the heart or brain, a heart attack or stroke will occur.

PROGNOSIS: Medication can help many cases. Surgery can be extremely successful in curing the condition.

See also Angina; Claudication; Hypercholesterolaemia; Transient Ischaemic Attacks

Arteriovenous Fistula

DESCRIPTION: Abnormal connection (fistula) between an artery and a vein.

CAUSE: May be congenital (developmental abnormality), or due to an injury or cancer. Sometimes surgically created in the forearm for insertion of a shunt used for kidney dialysis.

SYMPTOMS: Depends on site and severity. An abnormal pulsating lump may be seen or felt. May reduce the blood supply to vital organs, and affect their function.

INVESTIGATIONS: Diagnosed by arteriography (X-ray of blood vessels) in which a dye is injected into an artery and its movement through the fistula into the vein recorded.

TREATMENT: Surgical closure or destruction of the fistula.

COMPLICATIONS: Blood clots can form in the turbulent blood flow in a fistula, and travel through the veins to the heart and lungs to cause a pulmonary embolus (see separate entry).

PROGNOSIS: Surgical results are usually very good.

See also Fistula

Arteritis
See Temporal Arteritis; Takayasu's Arteritis

Artery, Hardened
See Arteriosclerosis

Arthritis
See Ankylosing Spondylitis; Gout; Osteoarthritis; Pigmented Villonodular Synovitis; Polymyalgia Rheumatica; Pseudogout; Psoriasis; Reiter Syndrome; Rheumatic Fever; Rheumatoid Arthritis; Ross River Fever; Scleroderma; Septic Arthritis; Sjögren Syndrome; Still's Disease; Synovitis; Systemic Lupus Erythematosus etc.

Asbestosis
DESCRIPTION: A lung disease caused by the inhalation of fine asbestos particles over a prolonged period of time.

CAUSE: Asbestos particles are long, thin filaments, that easily become trapped in the small air tubes (bronchioles) of the lung. The lower part of the lungs is most commonly affected, and it occurs almost exclusively in asbestos factory workers, processors and miners who inhale free-floating particles of asbestos in their workplace. Swallowing small amounts of asbestos or touching asbestos in any form is harmless. Smoking will aggravate the condition.

SYMPTOMS: Sufferers develop shortness of breath, cough, and in advanced cases, blue lips and swollen finger tips. As the disease progresses the patient may have no exercise tolerance and suffer symptoms similar to severe asthma or emphysema.

INVESTIGATIONS: Easily diagnosed on chest X-ray.

TREATMENT: None available other than removing the person from exposure to further asbestos dust and performing regular chest X-rays to detect mesothelioma as early as possible.

COMPLICATIONS: Mesothelioma (see separate entry), a rapidly progressive form of lung cancer.

PROGNOSIS: 7% of those with asbestosis develop mesothelioma. Others suffer from varying degrees of lung impairment.

See also Emphysema; Lung Cancer; Mesothelioma

Ascariasis
DESCRIPTION: The roundworm (*Ascaris lumbricoides*, one of a group of worms known as nematodes) infests the human gut.

Ascariasis

CAUSE: Adult roundworms that are between 20 and 40cm long live in the small intestine. After fertilisation, the females release a large number of microscopic eggs that pass out in the faeces and can survive for many years in the soil. In areas where human faeces is used as a fertiliser, it is easy for them to be swallowed again on food; or if sewerage contaminates the water supply, they may be swallowed in a drink. Once swallowed, the eggs hatch into larvae that burrow through the gut wall into the bloodstream and move through the heart into the lungs. There they penetrate into the small air tubes (bronchioles) of the lung, wiggle their way up through larger airways to the back of the throat from where they are swallowed again to enter the small intestine and grow into mature adults that may live for up to a year. Infections with roundworms are very widespread in Indonesia, south-east Asia and other less developed countries.

SYMPTOMS: At all stages the larvae and worms can cause symptoms including a cough, shortness of breath, fever, wheezing, chest pain, abdominal pains and discomfort, nausea and gut obstruction.

INVESTIGATIONS: The diagnosis is confirmed by finding eggs in the faeces.

TREATMENT: A number of drugs are available to treat the disease, but they often have side effects.

COMPLICATIONS: If severe infestations are left uncontrolled, the worms may move into the gall bladder and pancreas, rupture the bowel, and cause other severe complications that may result in death.

PROGNOSIS: If patients are given the correct treatment at a relatively early stage of the disease, full recovery is normal.

See also other conditions listed under Nematode Infestation

Ascites

DESCRIPTION: Accumulation of fluid in the abdomen.

CAUSE: Many causes including widespread infection (eg. tuberculosis), heart failure, cirrhosis of the liver, kidney failure, various cancers (eg. ovary, liver, lymph tissue), inflammation of any organ in the abdomen (eg. pancreatitis), and malnutrition (causes the typical distended stomach of children suffering from lack of protein in their diet).

SYMPTOMS: If there is a lot of fluid, the abdomen will become swollen and distended.

INVESTIGATIONS: Fluid can be taken from the abdomen by a needle for analysis, ultrasound and CT scans, and blood tests used in an attempt to identify the cause.

TREATMENT: Cause must be treated.

PROGNOSIS: Depends on cause.

Asorbic Acid Deficiency and Excess
See Scurvy; Vitamin C Excess

Aseptic Meningitis
See Meningitis

Asherman Syndrome
DESCRIPTION: Complication of pregnancy from retaining the placenta (afterbirth).

CAUSE: If part of the placenta is retained after childbirth it must be removed, or the woman may continue to bleed, become infected or infertile. The operation is carried out using a small sharp edged spoon with a long handle (curette) to scoop out the remaining placental tissue. If it is carried out too vigorously, the lining of the uterus may be damaged and adhere to the opposite wall, obliterating the cavity inside the uterus where a baby would normally grow during pregnancy. This also prevents the lining of the uterus from developing in the future.

SYMPTOMS: Menstrual periods stop, and the woman is infertile.

INVESTIGATIONS: Hysteroscopy (looking into the uterus through a thin tube).

TREATMENT: No effective treatment available.

PROGNOSIS: The woman is unable to fall pregnant again, but is otherwise unaffected.

See also Adhesions

Asperger Syndrome
DESCRIPTION: Personality disorder that is much more common in males.

CAUSE: Unknown.

SYMPTOMS: Unable to feel emotion or empathy, acts inappropriately in social contacts, may be violent, have poor communication skills, and may be poorly coordinated. Other characteristics that sometimes occur include poor posture, poor imagination and the inability to memorise organised data.

INVESTIGATIONS: No specific tests, and diagnosis made after extensive psychiatric assessment.

TREATMENT: Long term psychotherapy by a psychiatrist.

COMPLICATIONS: Often become involved with criminal acts of violence and end up in jail.

PROGNOSIS: Poor.

Aspergillosis
DESCRIPTION: A fungal infection of a wide range of tissues in the body including the ears, lungs, sinuses and skin (particularly burns) that is normally a minor irritation, but in patients who have poor immunity (eg: AIDS or taking chemotherapy for cancer), it may become critically serious if internal organs are infected.

CAUSE: The fungus *Aspergillus* which passes easily from one person to another.

SYMPTOMS: Often a very minor problem, and may cause no symptoms. If the lungs are infected, causes asthma like symptoms with a wheeze and cough.

INVESTIGATIONS: Diagnosis confirmed by examining sputum or other secretions that are infected, and by a specific antibody test on the blood.

TREATMENT: Depends on severity. If internal organs involved, high doses of potent antifungal drugs such as Amphoterecin B are used.

PROGNOSIS: Normally no problems, but half of the immunocompromised patients with lung aspergillosis will die, even in the best centres.

See also other diseases listed under **Fungal Infections.**

Asthma
(Wheezy Bronchitis)

DESCRIPTION: A temporary narrowing of, and excess production of phlegm in, the small airways (bronchioles) through which air flows into and out of the lungs. The narrowing is caused by a spasm in the tiny muscles which surround the bronchioles. One in ten Australians suffers from some degree of asthma.

CAUSE: The absolute cause is unknown, but certain triggers (eg. colds and other viral infections, temperature changes, allergies, exercise, smoke, dust and other irritants) may start an attack in susceptible individuals. The tendency to develop asthma runs in families along with hay fever and some forms of eczema to give a 15 times greater chance of developing the condition.

SYMPTOMS: Attacks may build up slowly over many weeks and the individual may be barely aware of the deterioration in lung function, or a severe attack may start within a minute or two of exposure to a trigger. The narrowing of the airways causes shortness of breath and wheezing, coughing, particularly in children, and tightness and discomfort in the chest. Asthmatics have more trouble breathing out than breathing in.

INVESTIGATIONS: Diagnosed by respiratory function tests which involve blowing into a number of different machines which either draw a graph or give an electronic reading. The patient's response to medication is also checked on these machines. Once diagnosed it is important to identify any trigger substances if possible by trial and error, or with blood and skin tests.

TREATMENT: Prevention — all but the mildest asthmatics should be using steroid or anti-allergy inhalations to prevent attacks. Severe asthmatics may need to use prednisone tablets to both prevent and treat their attacks. Those who react to specific substances may benefit from allergen desensitisation.

Treatment — best method is by aerosol sprays which take the medication directly into the lungs where they act to dilate the airways and liquefy the thick mucus. Many of these can have their effectiveness and ease of use improved, particularly in children, if a spacing device or machine nebuliser is used. Mixtures and tablets are also available, but they work more slowly and have greater side effects. Very severe attacks may require oxygen by mask and injections of adrenaline, theophylline or steroids.

COMPLICATIONS: Prednisone and other steroids may have significant side effects if used for a long time. People can die rapidly from a sudden, severe asthma attack.

PROGNOSIS: Asthma cannot be cured, but doctors can control the disease very effectively in the vast majority of patients.
See also Allergy; Hyper-Reactive Airways Disease

Astigmatism

DESCRIPTION: Uneven vision clarity.
CAUSE: The curvature of the cornea (front surface of the eye) is uneven causing light rays to focus unevenly on the retina (light sensitive cells at back of the eye).
SYMPTOMS: Vision is blurred in some areas of the visual field, and clear in others.
INVESTIGATIONS: Specific tests on vision using varying lenses.
TREATMENT: Specifically designed spectacles are now being replaced by laser radial keratotomy, a procedure in which the corneal curvature is corrected.
PROGNOSIS: Good vision obtained with either spectacles or laser treatment.
See also Keratoconus and other diseases listed under Vision Problems

Astrocytoma

DESCRIPTION: Slow growing, low grade malignant or benign tumour arising in the connective cells of the brain.
CAUSE: Unknown.
SYMPTOMS: Often very mild and confusing in the early stages, and as a result it may be quite large before it is detected. Common symptoms include visual disturbances, abnormal gland function, paralysis of facial muscles, incoordination and difficulty in walking.
INVESTIGATIONS: Visualised by CT and MRI scans. Biopsy required for final diagnosis.
TREATMENT: Surgery to remove growth, and the parts that cannot be removed are treated by drugs. Because of their size when diagnosed, they sometimes cannot be completely removed.
COMPLICATIONS: Rarely may become aggressively malignant and progress rapidly.
PROGNOSIS: Often cured if complete surgical excision possible. The outcome is often better in children.
See also Glioma and other tumours listed under Brain Cancer

Ataxia

See Ataxia Telangiectasia; Friedrich's Ataxia; Marinesco-Sjögren Syndrome; Xeroderma Pigmentosa

Ataxia Telangiectasia

DESCRIPTION: Developmental abnormality of the lower back part of the brain (cerebellum) and skin in a child under ten.
CAUSE: Familial (inherited) genetic disorder linked to chromosome 11. Both parents must be carriers for condition to occur.
SYMPTOMS: Dilated blood vessels under and in the skin (telangiectasia), abnormal

side to side eye movements (nystagmus), poor coordination (ataxia) and abnormal reflexes. Other symptoms may include difficulty in talking, abnormal sensations, muscle twitching and jerking.

INVESTIGATIONS: Chromosome analysis abnormal.

TREATMENT: Medications to try and control symptoms.

COMPLICATIONS: Significantly increased risk of many types of cancer, particularly lymphomas, leukaemia and breast cancer in both patients and those who carry the gene but are not otherwise affected.

PROGNOSIS: No cure.

See also Friedrich's Ataxia

Atherosclerosis
See Arteriosclerosis

Athlete's Foot
(Tinea Pedis)

DESCRIPTION: A fungal infection of the toes.

CAUSE: The responsible fungi can be found everywhere in the environment in the form of hardy microscopic spores that may survive for decades before being picked up and starting an infection. Between the toes they cause a type of tinea commonly known as athlete's foot because athletes sweat and wear close fitting shoes that lead to the ideal warm, damp environment favoured by fungi.

SYMPTOMS: Sore, red, cracks in the skin under and between the toes.

INVESTIGATIONS: Normally none necessary, but swabs may be taken to identify the responsible fungus.

TREATMENT: Antifungal creams, lotions and powders. In resistant cases, antifungal tablets may be taken.

COMPLICATIONS: A secondary bacterial infection of the damaged skin.

PROGNOSIS: Responds well to treatment, but often recurs, particularly if treatment ceased too soon.

See also Fungal Infections

Atopic Conjunctivitis
See Allergic Conjunctivitis

Atopic Dermatitis
See Atopic Eczema

Atopic Eczema
(Atopic Dermatitis)

DESCRIPTION: An abnormal reaction of skin to an irritating substance.

CAUSE: Atopy is the tendency to develop a sudden, excessive sensitivity to a substance. It is similar to allergy, but not the same, as no previous exposure to the substance is required. The rash may be triggered by changes in climate or diet, stress or fibres in clothing, and tends to occur in areas where the skin folds in upon itself (eg. groin, arm pits, inside elbows, eyelids). It is more common in winter and urban areas, has a peak incidence between 6 and 12 months of age, and there is an hereditary tendency. Up to a third of the population are atopic, but only 5% of children will develop this skin condition.

SYMPTOMS: Extremely itchy rash, but any blisters that form are rapidly destroyed by scratching which changes the normal appearance of the eczema, so that it appears as red, scaly, grazed skin that may be weeping because of a secondary bacterial infection. With repeated irritation, the skin may become hard, thickened, and pebbly.

INVESTIGATIONS: In most cases, the responsible substance cannot be identified. Skin and blood tests can be performed to tell if a person has an atopic tendency.

TREATMENT: Soothing moisturising creams, steroid creams to reduce inflammation and itch, and soap substitutes to prevent drying the skin. In severe cases, steroid and antihistamine tablets are necessary.

COMPLICATIONS: A secondary infection of the rash may occur, resulting in enlarged and tender lymph nodes in the neck, groin and armpit.

PROGNOSIS: No cure, but effective control can be obtained in the most cases. The majority of children grow out of the condition.

See also Allergic Eczema; Dermatitis; Eczema

Atrial Extrasystoles

DESCRIPTION: Abnormal heart beat.

CAUSE: An abnormal nerve impulse from part of the left atrium (smaller chamber on the left side of the heart) fires off before the normal heart pacemaker.

SYMPTOMS: Momentary irregularity in the heart beat that may occur very infrequently, or every three or four beats.

INVESTIGATIONS: Diagnosed by electrocardiograph (ECG).

TREATMENT: Often none necessary, but if frequent, medications can be given to regulate heart rhythm.

COMPLICATIONS: May progress to atrial flutter (see atrial fibrillation entry).

PROGNOSIS: Good response to treatment.

See also other conditions listed under Arrhythmia

Atrial Fibrillation

DESCRIPTION: The heart has two small chambers (atria) which receive blood from the lungs and body through large veins, and two large chambers (ventricles) which pump blood out through arteries to the lungs and body. Atrial fibrillation occurs if the atria beat in a rapid uncoordinated manner, and as a result the ventricles (main pumping chambers of the heart) will receive only an intermittent blood supply from the atria, and will beat in a very irregular rhythm. If the atria beat rapidly, but not fast enough to cause irregular contractions by the ventricles, the condition is **atrial flutter.**

Atrial Fibrillation

CAUSE: May occur in normal people at times of stress, but more commonly as a reaction to heart damage such as a heart attack or infection. Other causes include an overactive thyroid gland, heart valve damage, severe high blood pressure, lung damage that restricts blood flow (eg. emphysema), or because of imbalances in body chemistry.

SYMPTOMS: Very irregular pulse, tiredness due to low blood pressure, palpitations and sometimes chest pains, shortness of breath and fainting.

INVESTIGATIONS: Diagnosed by an electrocardiograph (ECG).

TREATMENT: Numerous medications available to control heart rhythm. If uncontrolled, an anticoagulant (eg. warfarin) should be used to prevent an embolism.

COMPLICATIONS: An embolism (blood clot) that may cause a stroke or death if it travels through arteries to the brain. Increased risk of heart failure and heart attack.

PROGNOSIS: Most cases can be controlled by medication, but if persistent there is a small mortality rate due to complications.

Atrial Flutter
See Atrial Fibrillation

Atrial Septal Defect

DESCRIPTION: Hole between the two atria (smaller upper chambers) in the heart that creates an abnormal blood flow within the heart.

CAUSE: Congenital birth defect.

SYMPTOMS: Very variable depending on size of hole. Often no symptoms in an infant, but as they grow may include blue tinged skin (cyanosis) from poor circulation of blood through lungs, thickened finger tips (clubbing) because of poor oxygen supply, slow growth rate, increased incidence of lung infections, tiredness and weakness.

INVESTIGATIONS: Characteristic murmur heard. Electrocardiogram (ECG), echo-cardiogram (ultrasound of heart), and cardiac catheterisation (passing a pressure measuring tube through an artery or vein into the heart) demonstrate heart abnormalities.

TREATMENT: Open heart surgery to close defect if symptoms occur.

COMPLICATIONS: May cause atrial fibrillation, cor pulmonale (high blood pressure in lungs — see separate entry), heart failure and be associated with mitral valve stenosis.

PROGNOSIS: Very small holes may close spontaneously. Good results from surgery.

See also Ellis-van Creveld Syndrome; Ventricular Septal Defect and other conditions listed under Heart Diseases

Atrophic Vaginitis
(Post-Menopausal Vaginitis; Senile Vaginitis)

DESCRIPTION: A lack of vaginal moisture and lubrication. The vagina is kept moist by the production of a mucus from glands in and around it, that become more active during sexual stimulation.

CAUSE: After the menopause, the female hormone oestrogen is no longer produced by the ovaries. This hormone stimulates the vaginal glands to produce mucus, but without oestrogen, they do not function.

SYMPTOMS: Older women complain of a dry, sore, itchy vagina.

INVESTIGATIONS: Blood tests can measure oestrogen level.

TREATMENT: Simple moisturising creams can be applied when the vagina is irritated, but give only temporary relief. Best solution is to replace the missing oestrogen long term by using a vaginal cream once or twice a week, oestrogen tablets daily, skin patches once or twice a week, or implants every few months. Dosages must be slowly adjusted to suit each individual woman.

COMPLICATIONS: Ulceration and bacterial infection of the vagina. Increased risk of prolapse (see separate entry).

PROGNOSIS: Good results from treatment.

See also Menopause; Vaginal Prolapse

Attention Deficit Disorder
See Attention Deficit Hyperactivity Disorder

Attention Deficit Hyperactivity Disorder
(ADHD)

DESCRIPTION: Attention deficit hyperactivity disorder (ADHD) is a very complex behaviour problem. A subtype is **attention deficit disorder (ADD)** in which there is no excess activity.

CAUSE: Patients are most commonly males who inherit the disorder from their fathers side of the family, and it affects between 3 to 8% of primary school students. Boys show more aggressive and impulsive symptoms, while girls seem to have a lack of attention due to daydreaming.

SYMPTOMS: These children are often fidgeting, unable to remain seated for long, unable to play quietly, easily distracted, unable to sustain attention, always impatient, have difficulty in following instructions, often move from one incomplete task to the next, talk excessively, often interrupt or intrude, do not seem to listen, have poor short term memory, often lose items and engage in physically dangerous activities. Most are average or above average in intelligence, but due to their genuine inability to pay attention and control their impulsiveness often do not take in all of the information in school. 30% have a reading disorder and 10-15% have other academic disabilities.

INVESTIGATIONS: No specific diagnostic tests. Final diagnosis usually made by a child psychiatrist.

TREATMENT: Psychostimulant medication (eg. methylphenidate), behaviour modification with the assistance of a psychologist, social skills training, family counselling and occupational therapy. Many professionals have conflicting ideas about the best form of treatment, and it is a process of trial and error to find the best treatment for an individual. Diet modification is commonly thought to be useful, but there is no evidence to support this.

COMPLICATIONS: May lead to criminal activity in the teens and early adult life.

PROGNOSIS: Every individual will respond differently to treatment, but most grow out of the problem in the mid-teens.

See also Episodic Dyscontrol Syndrome; Hyperkinetic Syndrome

Auriculotemporal Syndrome
See Frey Syndrome

Autism

DESCRIPTION: A social developmental disorder.

CAUSE: May be an abnormality in the development of the brain due to damage during growth as a foetus, at birth, or in the first years of life. Absolute cause is not known.

SYMPTOMS: Child fails to develop normal social skills, language skills and communication skills. Often excessively preoccupied with a particular type of behaviour and very resistant to change or education. Repetitive habits are common. Occasionally have exceptional talents in a particular area (eg. maths or music — the idiot savant syndrome — see separate entry).

INVESTIGATIONS: No diagnostic tests, but CT brain scans sometimes show non-specific abnormalities. Electroencephalograms (EEG) are usually normal, except in those who develop epilepsy.

TREATMENT: No effective treatment.

COMPLICATIONS: Epilepsy occurs in up to 30% of cases.

PROGNOSIS: Remain mentally retarded and require care throughout their life. Life expectancy is close to normal.

See also Idiot Savant Syndrome

Autoimmune Diseases

DESCRIPTION: A group of diverse conditions that cause the body to inappropriately reject some of its own tissue.

CAUSE: Unknown, but often follow stress or viral infections.

SYMPTOMS: Depend on specific tissue rejected and type of disease.

INVESTIGATIONS: Blood tests and tissue biopsy.

TREATMENT: Depends on tissue involved, but steroids commonly used.

See also specific autoimmune diseases (eg: Nephrotic Syndrome; Polymyalgia Rheumatica; Rheumatoid arthritis; Scleroderma; Sjögren Syndrome; Systemic Lupus erythematosus; Temporal Arteritis etc.)

Autonomic Neuropathy

DESCRIPTION: Damage to nerves (neuropathy) of the autonomic nervous system, which perform most of the subconscious automatic tasks required by the body, including telling the sweat glands when to operate.

CAUSE: Usually a complication of diabetes which results in the blocking of tiny arteries. If the very small arteries supplying nerves become blocked, that nerve does not receive the oxygen and nutrition it needs, and dies. May also occur with alcoholism, amyloidosis, Parkinson's disease, and other rarer syndromes.

SYMPTOMS: Patient cannot sweat in some areas of the skin, blood pressure drops to cause fainting, impotence, incontinence of urine, and bowels do not contract in the correct rhythm resulting in severe constipation.

INVESTIGATIONS: No specific tests for neuropathy. Cause must be investigated.

TREATMENT: No specific treatment for autonomic neuropathy. The specific cause must be carefully controlled.

PROGNOSIS: Depends on degree of nerve damage. Some recovery may be possible if cause corrected.

See also Diabetes Mellitus

Avascular Necrosis of the Femoral Head
(Hip Avascular Necrosis)

DESCRIPTION: Death of the bone at the top end (head) of the femur (thigh bone) which forms the hip joint.

CAUSE: Failure of the blood supply to the head of the femur. Absolute cause unknown in most cases, but may follow an injury or fracture to the femur, or inflammation (vasculitis) of an artery. Common problem in deep sea divers.

SYMPTOMS: Severe hip pain that spreads down to the knee, and is made worse by movement or standing. Gradually the movement of the hip becomes more and more restricted, and the thigh muscles become thinner (wasted) on the affected side.

INVESTIGATIONS: Diagnosed by characteristic changes on an X-ray.

TREATMENT: Prolonged bed rest in early stages. Surgery to replace the head of the femur in advanced cases.

PROGNOSIS: Reasonable results from surgery.

Azorean Disease
See Machado-Joseph Syndrome

B

Baby Colic
See Infantile Colic

Baby Measles
See Roseola Infantum

Bacillary Dysentery
See Shigellosis

Back Diseases
See Ileolumbar Syndrome; Intervertebral Disc Prolapse; Kyphoscoliosis; Kyphosis; Lordosis; Lumbago; Piriformis Syndrome; Posterior Facet Syndrome; Scheuermann's Disease; Sciatica; Scoliosis; Spinal Stenosis; Spondylitis; Spondylosis; Spondylolisthesis etc.

Bacteraemia
DESCRIPTION: Very common low grade bacterial infection of blood. More severe infections are termed septicaemia (see separate entry).
CAUSE: May be associated with other serious illnesses such as leukaemia, cancer and AIDS. Most spread from urinary, intestinal, lung or gall bladder infections. Many are very low grade and persistent. Almost any type of bacteria may be responsible.
SYMPTOMS: Fever, chills and rapid breathing. Some patients have a normal, or even low, temperature.
INVESTIGATIONS: Abnormal white blood cell levels. Responsible bacteria can be cultured from the blood and identified.
TREATMENT: Treat underlying disease if possible, and appropriate antibiotics.
COMPLICATIONS: Infection may spread to other organs, or worsen into septicaemia.
PROGNOSIS: Most recover well with treatment, but more serious in those with significant underlying disease.
See also Septicaemia

Bacterial Conjunctivitis
See Conjunctivitis

Bacterial Endocarditis
See Endocarditis

Bacterial Meningitis
See Meningitis

Bacterial Vaginitis
See Vaginitis, Bacterial

Baker's Cyst
DESCRIPTION: Relatively common cause of knee pain and swelling.

CAUSE: Joints contain a lubricating (synovial) fluid within a synovial membrane that totally encloses the joint. A cyst can form at the back of the knee when part of the synovial membrane pushes out between two muscles to form an outpocketing. Commonly occur in athletes who stress their legs (eg. long distance runners).

SYMPTOMS: A lump behind the knee that causes no discomfort, or it may become inflamed and tender, or most seriously, it may rupture to cause sudden severe pain.

INVESTIGATIONS: Presence can be proven by an ultrasound scan.

TREATMENT: Surgical excision before rupture. With a ruptured cyst the patient is rested, the leg is kept elevated, and steroids are injected into the knee to protect the joint lining from the loss of fluid and seal the leak.

PROGNOSIS: Good.

Balanitis
DESCRIPTION: Inflammation or infection of the head of the penis (the area normally covered by the foreskin in uncircumcised men) or the tip of the clitoris in women.

CAUSE: Bacteria (common), fungi (eg. thrush — also common), and micro-organisms such as amoebae and Trichomonas (uncommon). Irritants such as chemicals, urine (in incontinent men) and dermatitis may also be responsible.

SYMPTOMS: Head of the penis or clitoris becomes tender, painful and there may be weeping sores present.

INVESTIGATIONS: Swab taken to identify responsible organism.

TREATMENT: Antibiotic or antifungal creams and/or tablets. Irritants must be removed, or the penis protected by a barrier cream or condom. Dermatitis may be difficult to treat and require a variety of creams and ointments.

COMPLICATIONS: In recurrent cases, circumcision may be required.

PROGNOSIS: Depends on cause, but generally good response to treatment.

See also Chancroid; Phimosis

Baldness
(Male Pattern Baldness)
DESCRIPTION: Loss of scalp hair in men.

CAUSE: A very strong sex linked hereditary tendency. Very rare in women, but passes through the female line to men in later generations. Very uncommon in Negroes and Chinese races, but more common in Caucasian men whose ancestors came from northwest Europe (Celts).

SYMPTOMS: Almost always gradual hair loss, starting at the front of the scalp on either side, or in a circular area on top. Usually accompanied by excess hair on the body due to higher levels of testosterone. The connection between baldness and sexual potency is unproven.

INVESTIGATIONS: None usually necessary.

TREATMENT: Minoxidil tablets or scalp lotion slow or stop hair loss, hair transplants, scalp flap rotation or a wig.

PROGNOSIS: Usually progresses steadily but slowly throughout adult life. Treatments moderately successful.

See also Alopecia Areata; Telogen Effluvium

Bard-Pic Syndrome

DESCRIPTION: Complication of advanced cancer of the pancreas.

CAUSE: The enlarging pancreas puts pressure on the bile duct which runs nearby, preventing bile from leaving the liver and entering the small bowel.

SYMPTOMS: Progressive jaundice (yellow skin), loss of appetite and weight loss.

INVESTIGATIONS: Blood tests show increasing levels of bilirubin, and CT or ultrasound scans show cancer of pancreas.

TREATMENT: Surgery to relieve pressure on bile duct.

PROGNOSIS: Almost invariably fatal.

See also Pancreatic Cancer

Barlow Syndrome

DESCRIPTION: Heart valve abnormality.

CAUSE: May be genetic. Mitral valve between the small (atrium) and large chambers (ventricle) on the left side of the heart slips out of place (prolapses).

SYMPTOMS: Sometimes no symptoms, but may cause an irregular heart rhythm, fainting and transient ischaemic attacks (see separate entry).

INVESTIGATIONS: Diagnosed by hearing characteristic abnormal heart sound and echocardiography (form of ultrasound scan).

TREATMENT: No treatment necessary if no symptoms. Beta-blocker tablets for mild symptoms. Surgical repair of valve if severe. Antibiotic cover to prevent endocarditis.

COMPLICATIONS: Endocarditis (internal heart infection) may occur with any dental procedure or other infection. Antibiotics are taken to prevent this.

PROGNOSIS: Good.

See also Mitral Valve Incompetence

Barmah Forest Virus

DESCRIPTION: Viral blood infection that is more common in males than females and in the elderly, and is limited to the eastern states of mainland Australia.

CAUSE: Arbovirus infection spread from one person to another by mosquito bites. Carriers, who have no symptoms, can donate the virus to a mosquito that bites them.

SYMPTOMS: Arthritis that moves from joint to joint, muscle aches and pains, fevers that come and go, headaches and sometimes a rash.

INVESTIGATIONS: Diagnosis confirmed by a specific blood test.

TREATMENT: Medication (eg. pain killers, anti-inflammatories) to relieve symptoms.

COMPLICATIONS: None significant.

PROGNOSIS: No specific cure, but settles with time and rest. Recurrences possible.

See also Ross River Fever

Barrett Syndrome
(Barrett Oesophagitis)

DESCRIPTION: Narrowing at the lower end of the oesophagus (gullet) from stomach acid reflux.

CAUSE: Reflux oesophagitis (see separate entry) causes inflammation and ulceration of the lower part of the oesophagus. If left untreated for years, repeated irritation causes scarring and narrowing.

SYMPTOMS: Difficult and painful swallowing as well as the symptoms of reflux oesophagitis.

INVESTIGATIONS: Barium meal X-ray or gastroscopy.

TREATMENT: Medication to control the acid reflux and dilation of the stricture by passing gradually larger dilators down the throat while the patient is anaesthetised. Occasionally more radical surgery is required.

COMPLICATIONS: If left untreated affected area may become cancerous.

PROGNOSIS: Good if patient complies with treatment. Poor if cancer develops.

See also Hiatus Hernia; Reflux Oesophagitis

Bartholin's Cyst

DESCRIPTION: Infection of the Bartholin's glands, which are mucus-secreting glands that open through small ducts onto the inside lips of a woman's vulva. They produce mucus to keep the female genitals moist, and secrete extra fluid to act as a lubricant during sexual intercourse.

CAUSE: Gland duct becomes blocked by thick mucus, it swells up into a cyst, and becomes bacterially infected.

SYMPTOMS: Tender, painful lump in the vulva that makes sex very painful, and even sitting uncomfortable. Occasionally, the duct may block intermittently, causing the cyst to swell and then subside.

INVESTIGATIONS: None normally necessary, but sometimes a swab is taken to identify the responsible bacteria.

TREATMENT: Antibiotics by mouth to settle the infection, and surgery to drain away the pus and open up the cyst.

COMPLICATIONS: An abscess may form in the adjacent tissues.

PROGNOSIS: Good results from treatment. Persistent without treatment.

See also Vaginitis, Bacterial

Bartter Syndrome

DESCRIPTION: Rare kidney condition that is far more common in females than males.

CAUSE: Inherited. Caused by failure of kidney to conserve adequate potassium in the blood. Inherited disorder giving the body chemistry effects of Conn syndrome (see separate entry) without high blood pressure.

SYMPTOMS: Child or young adult with short stature, frequent passing of large quantities of urine day and night (often causing bed wetting) and muscle weakness. Some patients develop muscle spasms and cramps, a craving for salt, and in advanced stages vomiting and constipation occur.

INVESTIGATIONS: Numerous blood and urine tests are abnormal.

TREATMENT: Indomethacin to reduce kidney inflammation, medication (eg. spironolactone) to reduce potassium loss, and potassium supplements.

PROGNOSIS: No cure.

See also Conn Syndrome

Basal Cell Carcinoma
(BCC; Rodent Ulcer)

DESCRIPTION: A cancer of the deeper (basal) layers of the skin.

CAUSE: Caused by prolonged exposure to sunlight, most commonly on the face and back. Generally not as serious as the more superficial squamous cell carcinomas (SCC), but occur at an earlier age than SCCs but rarely before 25 years.

SYMPTOMS: Appear as shiny, rounded lumps that often change in size and colour, or they may present as an ulcer that fails to heal. The ulcer often has a pearly, rounded edge.

INVESTIGATIONS: Whenever a BCC is suspected, it should be removed surgically. The specimen is then sent to a pathologist for examination to ensure that the diagnosis is correct, and that all the tumour has been removed.

TREATMENT: Surgical excision, irradiation or diathermy.

COMPLICATIONS: BCCs do NOT spread to other parts of the body.

PROGNOSIS: If correctly treated, they can be completely healed, but if left until large, significant plastic surgery may be necessary. Untreated, the cancer will slowly invade deeper tissues, and after many years may cause death.

See also Gorlin-Goltz Syndrome

Basal Cell Carcinoma Naevus Syndrome
See Gorlin-Goltz Syndrome

Bassen-Kornzweig Syndrome
See Wolff-Parkinson-White Syndrome

Bat Ears

DESCRIPTION: Minor ear deformity.

CAUSE: Inherited.

SYMPTOMS: Prominent protruding ears.

TREATMENT: An operation can be performed to pin back the bat ears by taking a wedge of skin and tissue from behind the ear, and then the tissue is sewn down again. Normally not performed until child is a teenager. Recovery takes only a couple of weeks.

COMPLICATIONS: Bruising and infection are uncommon complications of surgery.

PROGNOSIS: Excellent results from surgery.

Bazin's Disease

See Erythema Induratum

BCC

See Basal Cell Carcinoma

Beal Syndrome
(Contractural Arachnodactyly)

DESCRIPTION: Uncommon disorder of cartilage and limbs.

CAUSE: Inherited.

SYMPTOMS: Long slim arms and legs, long fingers and toes, multiple joint contractures (particularly knees), calf muscle wasting and abnormal crumpled ears. Some patients have worsening curvature of the spine (kyphoscoliosis), mitral heart valve disease, holes in the heart and a poorly developed aorta.

INVESTIGATIONS: None diagnostic.

TREATMENT: Surgery to correct heart defects.

PROGNOSIS: No cure. Joint contractures improve spontaneously.

See also Marfan Syndrome

Becker's Muscular Dystrophy

DESCRIPTION: Form of muscle wasting.

CAUSE: Inherited condition.

SYMPTOMS: Onset in late childhood or the early teens of progressive and permanent weakening and wasting of muscles around the shoulders and hips.

INVESTIGATIONS: Diagnosed by electrical studies of muscle action, and muscle biopsy.

TREATMENT: No effective treatment, but physiotherapy is beneficial.

PROGNOSIS: No cure, but patients often have a normal life span.

See also other diseases listed under Muscular Dystrophy

Becker's Naevus

See Naevus

Beckwith-Wiedemann Syndrome

DESCRIPTION: Rare developmental abnormality of the abdominal wall.

CAUSE: May be familial (run in families).

SYMPTOMS: Infant whose intestine lies outside the abdominal cavity, but under the skin. Other symptoms may include an enlarged tongue, generally larger intestines than usual, and low blood sugar levels from poor food absorption.

INVESTIGATIONS: X-rays and CT scans will be used to check for other abnormalities and determine method of treatment.

TREATMENT: Infant is fed through a drip into a vein, and the intestine is surgically replaced in the abdomen after the baby has grown for a few months.

COMPLICATIONS: Damage or infection to the exposed intestine or the overlying skin.

PROGNOSIS: Long term results from surgery are good.

Bed Sore
(Pressure Ulcer)

DESCRIPTION: Ulcer formation in skin on which the body rests. Most commonly affected areas are the heels, buttocks, back of the head and over the lower part of the backbone.

CAUSE: If blood supply to the skin is significantly reduced, the affected skin dies. When pressure is applied to the skin for many hours without relief, the area will break down into an ulcer. Elderly, infirm, paralysed or unconscious patients who spend long periods in bed, or sitting, may not have the ability to move themselves or the sensation necessary to prompt movement, so that a particular area of skin may carry a great deal of the body's weight for a prolonged period of time.

SYMPTOMS: A deep punched out ulcer that may penetrate to muscle or bone.

TREATMENT: Prevention involves moving patient regularly so that no area bears pressure for a prolonged period of time. Sheep skins, ripple mattresses, water beds and other devices are placed under affected patients to spread their weight as much as possible. Cured by avoidance of any further pressure to the area, antibiotic dressings, special absorbent bandages or dressings, and, in resistant cases, surgical treatment to cover the area with a skin graft.

COMPLICATIONS: Sores may become infected very easily. Once affected, the same area is very susceptible to future damage, and extra precautions must be taken to avoid their recurrence.

PROGNOSIS: Often difficult to heal, but persistence is usually effective.

See also Ulcer, Skin

Bed Wetting
(Enuresis)

DESCRIPTION: Embarrassing problem that affects up to one in ten five-year-olds and one in 200 adults.

CAUSE: Urine is retained in the bladder by the contraction of a ring-shaped bundle of muscle (sphincter) that surrounds the bladder opening. To pass urine the sphincter relaxes, and muscles in the wall of the bladder and around the abdominal cavity, contract to squirt the urine out in a steady stream. Bed-wetters tend to sleep very deeply, and during the deepest phases of this sleep, when all the main muscles of the body are totally relaxed, the sphincter also relaxes. Because there is no associated contraction of the muscles in the bladder wall or elsewhere, the urine just dribbles out slowly, not in a hard stream.

SYMPTOMS: Unwanted passing of urine while asleep.

INVESTIGATIONS: Exclude any cause by urine tests and kidney ultrasound or X-rays.

TREATMENT: Several steps in treatment regime, but do not start before five years of age:

— restrict fluids for three hours before bedtime, take child to the toilet during the night, and establish a reward system for dry nights.

— bed-wetting alarm that consists of a moisture-sensitive pad that is placed under the patient, a battery and an alarm. When it becomes wet from the first small dribble of urine, it sounds the alarm, the patient is woken, and can empty the bladder before returning to sleep. After a few weeks use, most people learn to waken before the alarm.

— amitriptyline (Tryptanol) every night to alter the type of sleep. Over a few weeks, the dosage is slowly lowered and hopefully, the bad sleep habits and bed-wetting do not return.

— desmopressin nasal spray at bed time acts on the pituitary gland in the brain, and this instructs the kidney to reduce the amount of urine produced during the night.

— psychotherapy in the most resistant cases.

COMPLICATIONS: Premature treatment can cause permanent sleep disturbances in a child. No serious long term consequences.

PROGNOSIS: In most cases, controlled by cooperation between doctor, patient and family.

See also Incontinence of Urine

Bee Sting
See Sting, Bee or Wasp

Behçet Syndrome

DESCRIPTION: Serious condition that results in widespread apparently unconnected symptoms.

CAUSE: Unknown.

SYMPTOMS: Recurrent severe mouth and genital ulcers, inflammation of the eye, arthritis and brain abnormalities such as convulsions, mental disturbances, partial paralysis and brain inflammation. Other symptoms may include rashes (eg. erythema nodosum — see separate entry), skin ulcers, inflamed veins and blindness.

INVESTIGATIONS: None specifically diagnostic, but numerous non-specific blood tests abnormal.

TREATMENT: Unsatisfactory. Steroids and immune suppressant medications are used.

PROGNOSIS: Usually follows a long course with spontaneous temporary remissions. Seriously disabling and sometimes fatal.

Bell's Palsy

DESCRIPTION: A form of neuropathy (nerve inflammation).

CAUSE: Facial muscles are controlled by a nerve which comes out of a hole in the skull just below and in front of the ear. From there, it spreads like a fan across the face to each of the tiny muscles that control facial expressions. Inflammation of the nerve at the point where it leaves the skull causes the facial muscles to stop working. The exact reason for this inflammation is unknown.

SYMPTOMS: Sudden paralysis of the facial muscles on one side only. The patient can no longer smile or close the eye properly. There may be some mild to moderate pain at the point where the nerve leaves the skull beside the ear, but this settles after a few days. There may also be a disturbance to taste sensation.

INVESTIGATIONS: None diagnostic.

TREATMENT: No treatment is necessary for most patients, but in the elderly, if the paralysis is total, or if there is severe pain, treatment with high doses of prednisone (a steroid) may be tried, provided it is started within five days of onset.

COMPLICATIONS: 10% of patients are significantly affected long term by facial paralysis. Rarely crocodile tears syndrome occurs (see separate entry).

PROGNOSIS: Two thirds of patients recover completely within a few weeks with no treatment, while most of the others obtain almost complete recovery.

See also Crocodile Tears Syndrome

Bends
(Arterial Gas Embolism; Caisson Disease)

DESCRIPTION: Development of nitrogen gas bubbles in the blood due to sudden ascent from a deep dive.

CAUSE: In breathing, oxygen and nitrogen are taken into the lungs, and pass across a fine membrane to be dissolved into the blood. If the air pressure is high, more gases will be dissolved into the blood. Divers must breathe air at a pressure equivalent to the depth of water in which they are diving. When divers surface, they must do so slowly, or the lower pressure in shallow water or ashore will allow the dissolved gases to come out of solution and form tiny bubbles in the blood. The same phenomenon can be seen when the top is removed from a bottle of carbonated soft drink and it starts to fizz.

SYMPTOMS: May occur immediately or up to 6 hours later and depend on the fitness, age, and weight of the diver, and the amount of physical exertion undertaken. Joint pain, weakness, shortness of breath, dizziness, visual disturbances, pins and needles sensation, rashes, inability to speak, headache and confusion are common. Pain may be excruciating and if left untreated may progress to coma and death. The 'bends' name derives from the posture adopted in an attempt to relieve the pain.

TREATMENT: If possible, dive again to the appropriate depth, and resurface slowly, while being supervised. If impractical, give aspirin and oxygen and transport patient to a decompression chamber. The patient is repressurised in the chamber, and then over several hours or days the pressure is slowly reduced back to normal again.

COMPLICATIONS: Permanent joint damage from gas bubbles in joint fluid.

PROGNOSIS: Extremely variable, as it depends on the depth of the dive, the length of the dive, the individual diver's characteristics, and the delay before recompression commences. Death is common without treatment.

Benign Familial Chronic Pemphigus
See Hailey-Hailey Disease

Benign Lymphoepithelial Condition
See Mikulicz Disease

Bernard-Soulier Syndrome

DESCRIPTION: Prolonged bleeding from any minor cut and worse than normal bruising.

CAUSE: Inherited defect of platelets (blood cells essential for clotting) which fail to stick together to form a clot.

SYMPTOMS: Excessive bleeding, particularly from mouth and nose. Bruises and red spots and patches under skin, particularly on feet.

INVESTIGATIONS: Blood tests on platelet function and bleeding time.

TREATMENT: Blood transfusions on a regular basis.

COMPLICATIONS: Aggravated by aspirin.

PROGNOSIS: Lifelong defect that may cause significant disability.

See also Glanzmann Syndrome

Beriberi
(Vitamin B$_1$ Deficiency)

DESCRIPTION: Nutritional deficiency of vitamin B$_1$.

CAUSE: Lack of thiamine (vitamin B$_1$) in the diet of those who are malnourished, have food idiosyncrasies, overcook their food, in alcoholics (who obtain nutrition from alcohol and neglect normal food) and in those who require abnormally large amounts of thiamine due to an overactive thyroid gland or prolonged fever.

SYMPTOMS: Early stages — multitude of vague complaints including tiredness, loss of appetite, twitching, and muscle cramps and pains.

Late stages — swollen joints, shooting pains, paralysis of feet and hands, and heart abnormalities.

INVESTIGATIONS: Diagnosed by specific blood tests.

TREATMENT: Thiamine supplements (initially by injection in severe cases) and a well-balanced diet.

COMPLICATIONS: Permanent organ damage possible in advanced cases.

PROGNOSIS: Rapid response to treatment with recovery in a few days. Eventually fatal without treatment.

See also Alcoholism

Berry Aneurysm
See Aneurysm

Beta Cell Tumour
See Insulinoma

Bezoar
See Trichobezoar

Bilharzia
See Schistosomiasis

Biliary Colic
See Gallstones

Binge-Purge Syndrome
See Bulimia Nervosa

Bipolar Affective Disorder
(Manic-Depressive)

DESCRIPTION: Severe swings in mood that start most commonly around 30 years of age and almost never after 60.

CAUSE: Unknown.

SYMPTOMS: Dramatic changes in mood from very depressed to manic (see separate entries) and vice versa. When depressed patient is sad, loses interest in pleasure, loses weight, wakes through night and cannot get back to sleep, becomes restless, fatigues easily, feels worthless, cannot concentrate and may think of death. In the manic stage which may follow days, or even hours after the depression, the patient has an inflated self esteem, decreased need for sleep, is very talkative, has sudden changes in thoughts, poor attention span, increased sexual activity including promiscuity, spends excessively and takes risks.

INVESTIGATIONS: No specific diagnostic tests. Diagnosis made after careful assessment by a doctor.

TREATMENT: Medications to control mood swings (eg. lithium, valproic acid, carbamazepine).

COMPLICATIONS: Risk of suicide in depressive phase, and of self injury from dangerous activities in manic phase.

PROGNOSIS: Generally good response to treatment.

See also Depression; Mania; Schizophrenia

Bipolar Personality

See Bipolar Affective Disorder; Depression; Mania

Bird Fancier's Lung

See Psittacosis

Bite

See Funnel Web Spider Bite; Red-Back Spider Bite; Sting, Bee or Wasp; Snake Bite; Tick Bite

Black Death

See Plague, Bubonic

Blackfan-Diamond Syndrome
(Erythrogenesis Imperfecta)

DESCRIPTION: Very rare disorder of infants in which red blood cells fail to develop.

CAUSE: Unknown.

SYMPTOMS: Progressively worsening anaemia and abnormal facial appearance.

INVESTIGATIONS: Blood tests abnormal.

TREATMENT: Blood transfusion and intermittent steroids. Bone marrow transplant.

PROGNOSIS: Poor unless successful bone marrow transplant possible.

Blackwater Fever

See Malaria

Bladder Infection

See Cystitis

Blastocystis

DESCRIPTION: An organism that is widespread in every part of the world, and normally lives in humans without causing any symptoms. Only in cases where there is a very heavy infestation, the patient is particularly sensitive to the organism, or the patient has a deficient immune system (eg. AIDS) do symptoms occur.

CAUSE: A microscopic animal (protozoan) that infests the intestine. Spreads from person to person by a wide range of intermediates that include everything from the house fly to the earth worm, as well as other animals and humans.

61

SYMPTOMS: Often no symptoms, but when they occur patients develop diarrhoea, belly pains, nausea and loss of appetite.

INVESTIGATIONS: Diagnosis can be made by examining a sample of faeces under a microscope.

TREATMENT: Often none necessary, but if required, the antibiotic metronidazole is used.

COMPLICATIONS: Rarely an infestation of the lungs may occur.

PROGNOSIS: Normally self limiting and settles in a few days. Treatment will clear the organism from the gut.

Blastomycosis

DESCRIPTION: A serious fungal infection of the lungs and skin.

CAUSE: The fungus *Blastomycoses dermatitidis* which is found in the soil in tropical areas, may be inhaled in dust. Person to person infection does not occur. Far more common in men than women.

SYMPTOMS: Severe pneumonia-like illness with fever, mucus producing cough, muscle pains, tiredness, weight loss and skin sores.

INVESTIGATIONS: Sputum samples and swabs from skin sores can be taken in an attempt to identify the responsible fungus. Chest X-rays are abnormal.

TREATMENT: Regular injections into a vein with potent antifungal drugs (eg. amphotericin B, ketaconazole) for several months.

COMPLICATIONS: May spread to brain, bone, joints, lymph nodes, prostate gland and cause skin ulcers that are slow to heal.

PROGNOSIS: Difficult to cure. Mortality rate 15%.

See also Fungal Infections

Blepharitis

DESCRIPTION: Common inflammatory condition of the eyelid edges.

CAUSE: Bacterial infection, allergy or a reaction to an environmental factor.

SYMPTOMS: Both eyelids become red, covered with scales, sore and itchy. In advanced cases the eyelashes may fall out, and ulcers form on the lid margins.

INVESTIGATIONS: None normally necessary, but sometimes swabs are taken to identify any responsible bacteria.

TREATMENT: Cleaning away the scales several times a day with moist cotton wool, and applying antibiotic ointment to the affected areas of the eyelids.

PROGNOSIS: Difficult to cure and often recurrent.

Blighted Ovum
See Miscarriage

Bloch-Sulzberger Syndrome
(Incontinentia Pigmenti)

DESCRIPTION: Rare skin disease of newborn infants. Affects females only as males die as a foetus and are passed as a miscarriage.

CAUSE: Congenital.
SYMPTOMS: Lines of grouped blisters on skin that become warty then subside to leave pigmented streaks. May also cause brain, dental and eye abnormalities.
INVESTIGATIONS: Abnormal blood tests.
TREATMENT: None available.
PROGNOSIS: Incurable.

Blocked Tear Duct
See Conjunctivitis

Blood Poisoning
See Septicaemia

Blood Pressure, High
See Cor Pulmonale; Hypertension

Blood Pressure, Low
See Hypotension; Postural Hypotension

Blood Transfusion Reaction
See Transfusion Reaction

Bloom Syndrome
DESCRIPTION: Extremely rare developmental problem that occurs in Jews.
CAUSE: Familial genetic abnormality.
SYMPTOMS: Small at birth, light sensitive skin, underdeveloped cheeks, leukaemia and other malignant diseases. Some have spider naevi (blood vessels) on the facial skin.
INVESTIGATIONS: Blood levels of immunoglobulins (body defence proteins) low.
TREATMENT: None available.
COMPLICATIONS: People who are carriers of the gene, but do not suffer from the syndrome, are prone to developing malignant disease.
PROGNOSIS: Death in adolescence common.

Blount's Disease
DESCRIPTION: Abnormal curvature of the main bone on the inner side of the lower leg (the tibia).
CAUSE: Upper inner part of the tibia grows too slowly because of a dietary iodine deficiency, which results in thyroid gland abnormalities.
SYMPTOMS: Outcurving of the tibias in both lower legs.
INVESTIGATIONS: Diagnosed by X-ray of the tibia and blood tests on the thyroid gland.
TREATMENT: Iodine supplements in the diet.
PROGNOSIS: Curvature of tibia may be permanent if not diagnosed until disease has been present for some years.

Blue Baby
See Fallot's Pentalogy; Fallot's Tetralogy; Fallot's Trilogy; Ventricular Septal Defect

Blue Diaper Syndrome
DESCRIPTION: Rare metabolic (body chemistry) defect.
CAUSE: Due to defect in absorption of a protein (tryptophan) from the gut. This is degraded by the body to other substances (indoles) which are passed out and react with napkin starch to produce a blue stain.
SYMPTOMS: Mental retardation, deposition of calcium in tissues and formation of calcium based kidney stones.
INVESTIGATIONS: High levels of calcium in blood.
TREATMENT: None available.
PROGNOSIS: No cure.

Blue Naevus
DESCRIPTION: A non-cancerous mole that may be found anywhere on the body, usually appears on older children and teenagers, but may develop at any age.
CAUSE: Overproduction of pigment in the deeper layers of the skin by melanocytes (skin cells that are responsible for pigment production).
SYMPTOMS: A dark blue coloured mole.
INVESTIGATIONS: None necessary.
TREATMENT: None necessary unless cosmetically unacceptable, when it can be surgically excised.
PROGNOSIS: Not serious, but remains life long unless removed.

Blue Rubber Bleb Naevus Syndrome
DESCRIPTION: Rare disorder of small blood vessels in skin and bowel.
CAUSE: Congenital overgrowth of capillaries.
SYMPTOMS: Multiple blue tinged rubbery growths (blebs or haemangiomas — see separate entry) in skin and small bowel that bleed easily.
INVESTIGATIONS: Blood found in faeces, and blood tests show anaemia and low levels of iron.
TREATMENT: Surgical removal of affected gut and skin blebs, iron supplements and blood transfusions.
COMPLICATIONS: Blebs may develop in liver, spleen and brain.
PROGNOSIS: Poor. No cure.
See also Haemangioma

Body Dismorphic Disorder
See Obsessive Compulsive Neurosis

Boerhaave Syndrome

DESCRIPTION: Spontaneous rupture of the oesophagus (gullet).

CAUSE: Often follows gluttony.

SYMPTOMS: Sudden severe chest pain and collapse.

INVESTIGATIONS: Gastroscopy reveals the rupture.

TREATMENT: Surgical repair of oesophagus.

COMPLICATIONS: Permanent stricture (narrowing) at site of repair.

PROGNOSIS: May be fatal.

Boil
(Furuncle)

DESCRIPTION: A small superficial abscess.

CAUSE: A hair follicle infected by bacteria. People who are very hairy will develop more boils. Commonly affected areas are the armpits, buttocks and groin.

SYMPTOMS: Acutely painful, red and tender lump. Gradually enlarges, causing more and more pain until it ruptures, discharging pus.

INVESTIGATIONS: Patients with diabetes or kidney failure are particularly susceptible to boils, and recurrent attacks should lead a doctor to exclude these diseases as a cause.

TREATMENT: Antibiotic tablets, applying antiseptic or antibiotic ointment to the boil, and when pus is obviously present, lancing the boil with a scalpel or needle. Repeated attacks may require long-term antibiotic treatment, antiseptic soaps and antiseptic lotions applied regularly.

COMPLICATIONS: Infection can spread to cause boils in other areas. In severe cases, the infection may enter the blood stream to cause septicaemia. Boils should never be squeezed, as the pus they contain may rupture internally, and spread through the blood stream to the brain and other vital organs. A **carbuncle** is several boils in a limited area that join together to form an interconnecting infected mass that will degenerate into an abscess.

PROGNOSIS: Most infections settle quickly with treatment.

See also Abscess; Folliculitis; Furunculosis, Ear; Septicaemia

Bone, Broken
See Fracture

Bone Cancer

DESCRIPTION: Cancer affecting any bone in the body. There are many different forms depending on which bone cell types are involved, including osteomas, fibrosarcoma, enchondroma (start in cartilage), chondrosarcoma, osteoclastoma (giant cell tumours), osteosarcoma and Ewing's tumours. The last two have separate entries in this book.

CAUSE: No known cause. The most common type is that which spreads from cancer in another tissue (metastatic cancer) such as the breast and prostate.

SYMPTOMS: Common symptoms are bone pain and swelling, although many types of bone cancer may show no symptoms until the disease is quite advanced. Painful or swollen joints, and limitation of joint movement are also possible.

INVESTIGATIONS: Diagnosis involves X-rays, CT scans, bone scans, bone biopsy and blood tests.

TREATMENT: Involves a combination of amputation, surgical removal, irradiation and drugs, depending on that exact type of cancer present.

COMPLICATIONS: Pathological fractures may occur at the site of the fracture because the bone is weakened at that point.

PROGNOSIS: The outcome is extremely variable, depending on the type of cancer, the stage at which it is diagnosed, the position in the body, the age of the patient and the response to treatment. Metastatic cancers usually have a far poorer outcome than cancers that actually start in the bone.

See also Ewing's Tumour; Metastatic Cancer; Osteosarcoma

Bone Infection
See Osteomyelitis

Bonnet Syndrome
See Charles Bonnet Syndrome

Bornholm Disease
(Pleurodynia)

DESCRIPTION: The pleura is the smooth membrane that surrounds the lungs. Bornholm disease is a viral infection that attacks the pleura at the point where the diaphragm attaches to the ribs at the back of the chest.

CAUSE: The *Coxsackie* virus. Bornholm disease is named after a Danish island.

SYMPTOMS: Patients experience sudden, severe, lower chest pain that is aggravated by chest movements such as a deep breath or cough. Other symptoms include a fever, headache, nausea, and sore throat. There is marked tenderness of the lower ribs.

INVESTIGATIONS: None necessary.

TREATMENT: No treatment is available. The patient is given rest and aspirin until the disease settles.

COMPLICATIONS: In rare cases it is possible for the virus to spread to the testes and brain.

PROGNOSIS: Settles spontaneously after two or three weeks.

See also Coxsackie Virus Infection

Botulism

DESCRIPTION: An extremely severe form of food poisoning.

CAUSE: Home-preserved fruits and vegetables, and very rarely commercially canned foods, are responsible for harbouring the bacterium *Clostridium botulinum* which is capable of producing an extremely potent poison (toxin) that attacks the nervous system.

SYMPTOMS: Twelve to 36 hours after eating inadequately preserved food, the patient develops double vision, difficulty in swallowing and talking, a dry mouth, nausea and vomiting. The muscles become weak, and breathing becomes steadily more difficult.

INVESTIGATIONS: Blood tests can detect toxin.

TREATMENT: Patient must be hospitalised immediately and put upon an artificial breathing machine (ventilator) to maintain lung function once the paralysis occurs. An antitoxin is also available for injection.

PROGNOSIS: Death occurs in about 70% of patients unless adequate medical treatment in a major hospital is readily available. In the best circumstances, up to 25% of patients will still die.

See also Food Poisoning

Bowel Cancer
See Colo-Rectal Cancer

Bowen's Disease
DESCRIPTION: A precancerous skin condition.

CAUSE: May be found anywhere on the body and are caused by exposure to sunlight or arsenic compounds.

SYMPTOMS: Appear as a sharply edged red patch covered with a fine scale.

INVESTIGATIONS: Biopsy or excision required to make diagnosis.

TREATMENT: Should be surgically removed or chemically destroyed.

COMPLICATIONS: Can progress to become a squamous cell carcinoma (SCC).

PROGNOSIS: Very good.

See also Squamous Cell Carcinoma of the Skin

Bow Legs
(Genu Varum)
DESCRIPTION: Normal in toddlers and a common condition of young children, diagnosed when a significant outward bending of the legs is observed when the child stands straight and the ankles are together.

CAUSE: A developmental and growth problem. In rare cases due to rickets, poorly healed fractures of the leg bones or other very uncommon diseases.

SYMPTOMS: Awkward way of walking and possible knee and ankle discomfort.

INVESTIGATIONS: Sometimes an X-ray of the knees may be taken.

TREATMENT: In virtually all cases the problem corrects itself without any treatment. In rare cases a wedge may be inserted into the outside edge of the shoes to turn the foot slightly inwards. Very rarely, if the problem continues into the early teenage years and causes difficulty in walking or abnormal appearance and posture, an operation may be necessary.

COMPLICATIONS: None significant.

PROGNOSIS: Very good.

See also Knock Knees

Brachioradialis Pruritus
See Itchy Upper Arm Syndrome

Brachmann-de Lange Syndrome
See de Lange Syndrome

Brain Aneurysm
See Aneurysm

Brain Cancer or Tumour
See Astrocytoma; Craniopharyngioma; Glioma; Medulloblastoma; Meningioma;
Pinealoma: Retinoblastoma

Brain Haemorrhage
See Subarachnoid Haemorrhage; Subdural Haematoma

Brain Syndrome, Organic
See Organic Brain Syndrome

Breakbone Fever
See Dengue Fever

Breast Cancer
(Mammary Carcinoma)

DESCRIPTION: Cancer that develops in the breast tissue of women or men. The most common form of cancer in women with one in every 700 women over 18 developing breast cancer every year.

CAUSE: The absolute cause is unknown but it is more common in women who have a close relative (mother, sister, daughter) with the disease, in women who have not had a pregnancy, have not breast fed, have had a first pregnancy after 35 years, in white women, those who have had uterine cancer, and in higher socioeconomic groups. On the other hand, women who start their periods late and those who have an early menopause have a lower incidence of breast cancer. About 2% of all breast cancers occur in men as they have a tiny amount of breast tissue present just under the nipple.

SYMPTOMS: A hard, fixed, tender lump in the breast. The nipple skin itself can become cancerous causing a thick, firm, rubbery feeling to the nipple (see Paget's disease of the nipple). There are many other causes of lumps in the breast — less than one in ten breast lumps examined by a doctor is cancerous.

INVESTIGATIONS: The most important method of detecting breast cancer is monthly self examination. The diagnosis is made by X-ray mammogram, needle biopsy and ultrasound scan of the breast. If despite negative tests the lump persists, it may be removed for examination by a small operation through a cosmetic incision that follows the line of the coloured area around the nipple, or the skin fold under the breast.

TREATMENT: A disfiguring radical mastectomy (removal of the breast and underlying muscles) is an operation of the past except in the most advanced cases of breast cancer. It has been replaced by simple mastectomy in which only the breast is removed, leaving a cosmetically acceptable scar and scope for later plastic reconstruction of the breast. Often the lymph nodes under the arm will be removed at the same time. In women with early cancer, equally good results can be obtained by removal of the lump alone. A course of radiotherapy and/or chemotherapy (drugs) may also be given.

COMPLICATIONS: The cancer may spread to nearby lymph nodes, the lungs and bones. Lymphoedema (hard swelling — see separate entry) of the adjacent arm as a result of lymph nodes being removed from armpit.

PROGNOSIS: Up to 2/3 of all patients with breast cancer can be cured. In early cases the cure rate rises to over 90%.

See also Paget's Disease of the Nipple; Stewart-Treves Syndrome

Breast Enlargement, Male
See Gynaecomastia

Breast Infection
See Mastitis

Briquet Syndrome
(Somatisation Disorder)

DESCRIPTION: Psychiatric disorder of perceived illness.
CAUSE: Form of hysteria. Family history common.
SYMPTOMS: Multiple, unexplained, recurrent symptoms with no physical basis.
INVESTIGATIONS: All normal.
TREATMENT: Psychiatric counselling.
PROGNOSIS: Usually intractable.
See also Conversion Disorder

Brittle Bone Disease
See Osteogenesis Imperfecta

Broken Bone
See Fracture

Bronchial Carcinoma
See Lung Cancer

Bronchiectasis

DESCRIPTION: Scarring and permanent over dilation of damaged air carrying tubes (bronchi) within the lungs.

CAUSE: Bronchi may be damaged from birth by cystic fibrosis or childhood immune deficiencies. May develop in adult life due to recurrent attacks of bronchitis, pneumonia or the inhalation of toxic gases, but smoking is by far the most common cause.

SYMPTOMS: Constant cough that brings up large amounts of foul phlegm. Patient may cough up blood, become anaemic and lose weight.

INVESTIGATIONS: X-ray of the chest reveals characteristic changes that confirm the diagnosis.

TREATMENT: Regular physiotherapy to clear the chest of sputum, and antibiotics when necessary to control infection. Other medications to open up the clogged airways (bronchodilators), liquefy sputum (mucolytics) and assist the coughing (expectorants) may be necessary. It is essential for smokers to stop. In severe cases where a limited part of the lung is badly affected, that section may be surgically removed.

COMPLICATIONS: Frequent attacks of pneumonia and other lung infections.

PROGNOSIS: Usually very slowly progressive, but aggressive treatment slows this progression.

See also Bronchitis; Emphysema; Pneumonia and other conditions listed under Smoking

Bronchiolitis
(Respiratory Syncitial Virus Infection)

DESCRIPTION: A lung infection of children under two years of age.

CAUSE: The respiratory syncitial virus (RSV). Tends to occur in epidemics.

SYMPTOMS: Infant with a cough and wheeze, shortness of breath and a runny nose. In severe cases, the child may be very weak, blue around the mouth and dehydrated.

INVESTIGATIONS: Doctors hear sounds in the chest that enable the diagnosis to be made. In the early stages, chest X-rays can be normal, but later a characteristic pattern shows in the lungs.

TREATMENT: Antibiotics cannot cure this viral condition but are sometimes given to prevent pneumonia. Bronchodilator medications may be used but often are of little help. Placing the child in a warm room with a humidifier, or in a steam tent may give relief. More severe cases will require hospitalisation, where oxygen may be administered into a steam tent to assist with breathing.

COMPLICATIONS: In rare cases permanent lung damage and even death may result.

PROGNOSIS: The vast majority of cases settle without complications in a few days to a week.

Bronchitis, Acute

DESCRIPTION: A very common infection of the major tubes (bronchi) that carry air within the lungs. Occurs in two very different forms, acute and chronic.

CAUSE: Commonly caused by viruses, frequently by bacteria, and rarely by fungi. Spreads easily from one person to another on the breath.

SYMPTOMS: Fever, chest aches and pains, headache, tiredness, and a productive cough with dark yellow or green mucus.

INVESTIGATIONS: Diagnosed by listening to the chest through a stethoscope. In early stages, X-rays may be normal, but later shows characteristic changes. Sputum may be cultured to identify any bacteria present, and the correct antibiotic to treat it.

TREATMENT: Viral infections settle with time, rest, inhalations, bronchodilators (open up the bronchi) and physiotherapy. If a bacteria is responsible, antibiotics can be prescribed.

COMPLICATIONS: Pneumonia, a bacterial infection of the smaller tubes and air pockets in the lung, may develop if treatment is delayed.

PROGNOSIS: Bacterial infections settle rapidly with antibiotics. Viral bronchitis settles in about ten days in most patients, but may persist for several weeks in the elderly or debilitated.

See also Bronchitis, Chronic; Pneumonia

Bronchitis, Chronic

DESCRIPTION: Long term inflammation of the larger airways (bronchi) in the lungs. A form of chronic obstructive airways disease.

CAUSE: Repeated attacks of acute bronchitis, long-standing allergies, or constant irritation of the bronchi by noxious gases, particularly those found in tobacco smoke (most common cause).

SYMPTOMS: Persistent moist cough, shortness of breath (particularly with exertion), constant tiredness, blue lips and swollen ('clubbed') finger tips.

INVESTIGATIONS: Thickened and scarred bronchi, and poor air entry to the lungs, show up quite markedly on a chest X-ray.

TREATMENT: Physiotherapy, bronchodilators (medications to improve air flow), and antibiotics to treat any infection.

COMPLICATIONS: May progress to emphysema, and is sometimes associated with lung cancer.

PROGNOSIS: A semi-permanent condition for which there is no effective cure, but effective treatment can keep the condition under control for many years.

See also Bronchitis, Acute; Emphysema; Lung Cancer; Pneumonia

Bronchitis, Wheezy
See Asthma

Bronchogenic Carcinoma
See Lung Cancer

Bronchopneumonia
See Pneumonia

Brown-Séquard Syndrome

DESCRIPTION: Uncommon spinal cord condition.

CAUSE: Injury, transverse myelitis (see separate entry), overgrowth of arteries (angioma), tumours or compression of the spinal cord.

SYMPTOMS: Muscle spasm and loss of position sense on one side of the body, loss of pain and temperature sense on the opposite side, with light touch sensation preserved and muscle strength lost on both sides.

INVESTIGATIONS: CT and MRI scans of spinal cord.

TREATMENT: Treat cause if possible.

PROGNOSIS: Often no cure.

See also Paraplegia

Brucellosis
(Undulant Fever)

DESCRIPTION: An infection of cattle, goats and pigs, which can spread to man, and most commonly infects meat workers, veterinarians and farmers. Causes pregnant cattle to miscarry, and can spread rapidly through a herd.

CAUSE: The bacteria *Brucella abortus*, *Brucella melitensis* or other species of *Brucella*, enter a human through a cut or graze in the skin, or is swallowed. Found in raw meat and unprocessed milk.

SYMPTOMS: Fever, tiredness and intermittent sweats occur initially. After several weeks further symptoms of headache, swollen painful joints, loss of appetite and abdominal pains (from a large spleen and/or liver) develop. The fever may come and go for many months in a low-grade chronic form of the disease (thus undulant fever).

INVESTIGATIONS: Specific blood tests are diagnostic.

TREATMENT: Antibiotics (eg. tetracycline) and rest until all symptoms have settled. Animals may be vaccinated to prevent them from catching the disease, but not humans.

COMPLICATIONS: Occasionally may involve the lung, brain and heart, causing specific problems in those areas. Long-term complications include arthritis, and bone weakness.

PROGNOSIS: Good response to treatment, but may recur over several years and require further courses of treatment.

See also Q Fever

Bruise
(Haematoma)

DESCRIPTION: Leakage of blood into tissue under the skin.

CAUSE: Occurs due to a surface (eg. body is struck by a blunt object) or internal (eg. fracture of a bone, severe sprain) injury that ruptures blood vessels. If an artery ruptures, a bruise will form very rapidly, but more slowly and with less swelling if a vein ruptures. Patients on medication (eg. warfarin, aspirin) which reduces the speed at which blood clots form will bruise far more easily. Nonsteroidal anti-inflammatory medications and other less commonly used drugs may also increase bleeding, and therefore bruising. Women bruise more than men, particularly around the menopause, because hormonal changes may make blood vessel walls weaker and allow them to rupture easily. A number of uncommon diseases (eg. haemophilia, scurvy, aplastic anaemia) also reduce the speed at which clots form.

SYMPTOMS: Tender swelling with a blue/black tinge to the overlying skin. Blood under pressure can track its way between layers of tissue so that bruising may occur not only at the site of the injury, but some distance away (eg. a kick to the calf may cause a spot bruise on the calf, but a day or two later bruising may appear around the ankle).

INVESTIGATIONS: None normally necessary unless a clotting defect is suspected.

TREATMENT: Initially the affected area should be cooled with ice wrapped inside a cloth, elevated and rested. Paracetamol or codeine should be used as a pain reliever, not aspirin which may increase the amount of bruising. Wrap a firm supportive bandage around the damaged area to give support, reduce movement, and prevent further bleeding.

COMPLICATIONS: Patients with excessive bruising should have a blood test to check that their clotting mechanism is working normally.

PROGNOSIS: With time and rest the swelling will reduce, the bruise will go from blue/black to purple, brown and finally yellow before disappearing. There may be some residual swelling and firmness at the bruise site due to the formation of fibrous scar tissue and the skin over the area may dry out and flake off.

Bruton Syndrome

DESCRIPTION: Deficiency of the immune system in which inadequate amounts of immunoglobulin (used to fight infection and cancer) are produced.

CAUSE: Congenital.

SYMPTOMS: Child develops severe infections, leukaemia and lymphomas.

INVESTIGATIONS: Marked blood test abnormalities.

TREATMENT: Human gamma globulin injections. Treat infections, leukaemia and lymphoma (see separate entries).

PROGNOSIS: Very poor.

See also diseases listed under Leukaemia and Lymphoma

Bruxism

DESCRIPTION: Grinding of teeth.

CAUSE: Commonly a sign of stress or tension, may be a nervous habit, or during sleep can occur with nightmares. Very common in patients with mental retardation.

Bruxism

SYMPTOMS: Jaw moves constantly to grind teeth together, often to the point where a grinding sound can be heard.

INVESTIGATIONS: None normally necessary.

TREATMENT: A mild muscle relaxing and anxiety reducing medication (eg. diazepam) is sometimes appropriate. A dentist should check the teeth regularly.

COMPLICATIONS: Prolonged bruxism may cause permanent damage to the teeth.

PROGNOSIS: Usually responds to medication, but may be persistent otherwise.

Bubonic Plague
See Plague, Bubonic

Buerger's Disease
(Smoker's Foot; Thromboangiitis Obliterans)

DESCRIPTION: Abnormal blood clot formation associated with inflammation and obliteration of arteries resulting in the progressive loss of fingers, toes, then arms and legs.

CAUSE: Occurs only in smokers, and nearly always in men. Toxins in tobacco smoke cause inflammation in sections of the small arteries in the hands and feet which causes a clot to form in the artery, and the tissue beyond the blockage becomes painful, white and eventually gangrenous. Starts in the fingers and toes, and slowly moves further up the arteries in the arms and legs.

SYMPTOMS: Initially pain in the foot when walking, which settles with rest. Red tender cords caused by clot filled (thrombosed) arteries may be felt under the skin, and a finger or toe may be white and have reduced sensation. The next stage is characterised by pain at rest, loss of pulses in the hands and feet and ulcers around the nails. Cold weather aggravates symptoms. Further progression results in gangrene.

INVESTIGATIONS: Ultrasound (doppler) tests on involved arteries shows reduced or absent blood flow.

TREATMENT: Try to stop patient from smoking, but they are far more addicted than the average smoker, and rarely succeed. Surgery to the nerves supplying the arteries to make them totally relax may be tried, but amputation of affected tissue is usually necessary. A limb may eventually be totally amputated, but often over several operations as each successive area becomes deprived of blood.

COMPLICATIONS: Blood clots may form in vital organs, permanently damaging them.

PROGNOSIS: Poor, and usually slowly progresses to death unless the patient can stop smoking.

Budd-Chiari Syndrome

DESCRIPTION: Rare syndrome affecting liver function.

CAUSE: Abnormal blood clot blocking the main vein leading from the liver, because of a liver tumour or blood clotting disease.

SYMPTOMS: The liver and spleen become dramatically enlarged, abdominal pain and fluid accumulates in the belly.

INVESTIGATIONS: Diagnosed by CT and ultrasound scans, liver biopsy and radionucleotide scans.

TREATMENT: Liver transplant only option.

COMPLICATIONS: There may be significant bleeding into the upper intestine.

PROGNOSIS: Usually fatal within two years of diagnosis unless a liver transplant can be performed.

See also other diseases listed under Liver Diseases

Bulimia Nervosa
(Binge-Purge Syndrome)

DESCRIPTION: A psychiatric disturbance of body perception almost invariably occurring in middle to upper class young females, that may be associated with anorexia nervosa (see separate entry). The main difference between these diseases is the way in which the patients see themselves — the bulimic has a fear of being fat, the anorexic has a desire to be thin.

CAUSE: No known specific cause, but patients tend to be high achievers, perfectionists, desperately eager to please others and have an anxious personality.

SYMPTOMS: Voracious and continuous consumption of huge quantities of food followed by purging, vomiting and the use of fluid tablets in order to maintain a normal weight. Secretive, and appear to eat normally in public, but binge eat and vomit in private.

INVESTIGATIONS: Blood tests may show changes in body chemistry due to repeated vomiting and purging.

TREATMENT: Close family support, psychotherapy and careful medical monitoring over a period of several years.

COMPLICATIONS: Menstrual irregularities, sore throat, bowel problems, dehydration, lethargy, and dental problems due to the repeated exposure of the teeth to stomach acid. Suicide can be a risk in severe cases.

PROGNOSIS: Most patients recover, and go on to lead normal lives.

See also Anorexia Nervosa

Bullous Impetigo
See Scalded Skin Syndrome

Bullous Pemphigoid
See Pemphigoid

Bunion
(Hallux Valgus)

DESCRIPTION: Foot deformity causing discomfort.

CAUSE: If the big toe is constantly pushed across towards the smaller toes by tight shoes, it may become semipermanently deformed in this direction. The end of the long bone in the foot behind the toe bones is then able to push against the skin. A protective, fluid-filled sac (a bursa) forms between the bone end and the skin and slowly enlarges to form a bunion.

SYMPTOMS: A lump at the base of the big toe that may become tender and painful. Usually start in childhood but may not cause significant discomfort until adult life.

INVESTIGATIONS: An X-ray of the foot is sometimes performed.

TREATMENT: A number of surgical procedures are available, but in elderly people it may be preferable for a protective pad to be worn inside soft or especially made shoes.

COMPLICATIONS: Uncommonly, a bunion may become infected.

PROGNOSIS: Treatment is usually effective in correcting discomfort, but the foot may continue to appear slightly abnormal.

Burn

DESCRIPTION: The severity of a burn depends on the area covered by the burn and the depth of the burn. They are categorised as first degree (superficial), second degree (partial thickness) and third degree (full thickness).

CAUSE: A burn may be caused by hot fluids (scald), flame (eg. clothing catching alight), dry heat (eg. touching a stove hot plate) or radiation (eg. sunburn).

SYMPTOMS: First degree — red or grey in colour, and are not blistered initially, but can be very painful.

Second degree — blistered initially, then moist and red or white after the blister bursts. Tissue under the burn becomes progressively more swollen for several days. Often not as painful as first degree burns, as the nerve endings have been partially destroyed.

Third degree — sometimes difficult to differentiate from second degree burns unless there is obvious tissue charring or exposed fat, muscle or bone. Appear tough and leathery, and may be almost any colour, but there is usually no pain as the sensory nerve endings have been totally destroyed.

INVESTIGATIONS: None normally necessary for minor burns, but patients hospitalised with serious burns will have regular blood tests to check for dehydration and body chemistry disorders.

TREATMENT: First aid — no matter how mild or serious, all burns should initially be treated by immersion in cool water, or covering the area with a wet cloth, for at least 30 minutes. Those with severe burns may need mouth-to-mouth resuscitation and external cardiac massage.

First degree — soothing antiseptic creams and moderate to strong pain-killers may be required for the first two or three days.

Second degree — antibiotic cream or other dressings.

Third degree — skin grafts are required for all but small areas.

Extensive second and third degree — life threatening because of the loss of body fluids through the burn area and the absorption of large amounts of toxic waste products into the blood that can cause kidney and liver failure. Once in a hospital burns unit patients can be kept alive on a ventilator and fluids can be replaced through drips into a vein. Antiseptic paints, creams, amniotic sac membrane (recovered from the placenta of mothers who have just delivered a baby) or pig skin may be used to protect wounds after the burnt tissue has been cleaned or cut away (surgical debridement). Pressure may be applied in various ways to reduce scarring. Skin taken from unburnt areas of the body is grafted to areas that have been totally destroyed in a late stage of treatment. Tissue cultures of the patient's own skin cells, or those of a donor, are used in severe cases to replace missing skin. Rehabilitation takes months or years, and may involve plastic surgery to correct contractures (tight scars) or improve appearance. Physiotherapists, occupational therapists, and even speech pathologists (for inhaled hot gas burns) will all play a part.

COMPLICATIONS: First degree — do not cause major problems and heal readily without scarring.

Second degree — scarring only results if the burn becomes infected or otherwise further damaged.

Third degree — scarring occurs. Burns may become infected and require antibiotics. Pneumonia, kidney and heart failure are common complications of severe burns.

PROGNOSIS: First degree — heal rapidly.

Second degree — take between two and four weeks to heal.

Third degree — varies widely depending on the extent, position and severity of the burn, and the availability of a hospital burns unit. Patients under 2 years and over 60 have a higher death rate. Burns to the face, hands, feet and groin are more difficult to treat, and have a poorer outcome. Any victim with more than 20% of the body surface burnt is considered to be critically injured, and it is rare for patients to survive a burn of more than 70% of the body surface.

Burning Vulva Syndrome
(Vulvodynia)

DESCRIPTION: Painful condition of vulva that is NOT due to an infection or skin disease.

CAUSE: Unknown.

SYMPTOMS: Exquisite tenderness of vulva.

INVESTIGATIONS: All investigations normal. Diagnosis made by excluding any other possible cause.

TREATMENT: Loose clothing, reduce washing and avoid soap, avoid irritation of area (including sexual activity) until healed.

PROGNOSIS: Usually settles with time, but often prolonged.

Bursitis

DESCRIPTION: Inflammation or infection of a bursa. Every moving joint in the body contains synovial fluid to lubricate it. This fluid is produced in small sacs (bursae) that surround the joint. The fluid passes from the bursae through tiny tubes into the joint space, from where it is slowly absorbed into the bone ends.

CAUSE: Caused by an injury to the area, an infection entering the joint or bursa, or by arthritis. The most common sites for bursitis are the point of the elbow, over the kneecap (housemaid's knee), and the buttocks.

SYMPTOMS: Swelling of a joint, or joint surrounds, that may or may not be painful. The skin over the bursa may become red.

INVESTIGATIONS: None normally necessary.

TREATMENT: In cases of simple inflammation, local heat, rest, splinting and pain-killers only required. Recurrent or persistent cases may have the synovial fluid in the bursa removed by a needle, and steroids injected back into the sac to prevent further accumulation of fluid.

COMPLICATIONS: If the bursa becomes infected, antibiotic therapy and surgical drainage of pus are necessary.

PROGNOSIS: Good, but recurrences possible.

See also Housemaid's Knee

Burst Ear Drum
See Tympanic Rupture

C

Caisson Disease
See Bends

Calcium, Excess
See Hypercalcaemia

Calcium Pyrophosphate Deposition Disease
See Chondrocalcinosis; Pseudogout

Calculus, Renal
See Kidney Stone

Californian Encephalitis
See la Crosse Encephalitis

Callosity
See Callus

Callus
(Callosity)
DESCRIPTION: Abnormal thickening of skin.

CAUSE: Recurrent injury to, or rubbing of, an area of skin.

SYMPTOMS: Local area of increased keratin (hard yellow skin) build up, usually over a bony prominence.

INVESTIGATIONS: None necessary.

TREATMENT: Remove pressure if possible (eg. correct footwear, protective pads). Careful peeling away of the layers of keratin with a scalpel or apply salicylic acid ointment.

COMPLICATIONS: May become painful, and rarely infected, if trimmed excessively.

PROGNOSIS: Usually persist long term, but controlled well by treatment.

Campylobacter Enteritis
DESCRIPTION: Intestinal infection that occurs worldwide in both developed and developing countries.

CAUSE: Bacterial infection of the intestine by *Campylobacter jejuni* which spreads from one person to another or from animals by water or food (particularly dairy products) that are contaminated by faeces. Incubation period of 2 to 6 days.

SYMPTOMS: Fever, cramping belly pains and watery diarrhoea.

INVESTIGATIONS: Culture of faeces can identify the responsible bacteria.

79

TREATMENT: A diet with minimal fat and plenty of fluids. If the infection is prolonged, antibiotics such as erythromycin may be used.

COMPLICATIONS: None serious.

PROGNOSIS: Usually settles without treatment in a few days, but rarely may persist for weeks.

See also Gastroenteritis; Shigellosis

Cancer
(Carcinoma; Malignancy; Neoplasm; Sarcoma)

DESCRIPTION: Cancer occurs when otherwise normal cells start rapidly multiplying into cells that are abnormal in shape, size and function. The abnormal cancer cells affect the cells around them, prevent them from functioning normally, and this enables the cancer to spread further.

CAUSE: The specific cause of cancer is unknown, but sun exposure, a low-fibre diet and smoking are well-known precipitating factors. It is not just one disease process, dozens of different types of cancer occur in various parts of the body, and each type causes different problems and responds differently to treatment. There are two main groups of cancer — **sarcomas** start in connective tissue (bone, cartilage, muscle and fibre) while **carcinomas** are originate in the epithelial cells (tissue comprising the external and internal linings of the body).

SYMPTOMS: The early symptoms of cancer are a lump or thickening anywhere in the body, sores that will not heal, unusual bleeding or discharge, change in bowel or bladder habits, persistent cough or hoarseness, change in a wart or mole, indigestion or difficulty in swallowing, and loss of weight for no apparent reason.

INVESTIGATIONS: Depends upon the organ involved and may include blood tests, urine tests, sputum tests, faeces tests, X-rays, endoscopy, radioactive scans, ultrasound scans, microscopic examinations, magnetic resonance imaging and biopsies.

TREATMENT: May involve surgery to remove the growth, drugs that are attracted to and destroy abnormal cells, irradiation of the tumour with high-powered X-rays, or combinations of these three methods.

COMPLICATIONS: Spread of the cancer to other areas of the body (metastatic cancer).

PROGNOSIS: Over half of all cancers can be cured, and that excludes the skin cancers that rarely cause death. The cure rate is far higher in those who present early to a doctor, because the less the cancer has spread, the easier it is to treat.

See also specific cancer types (eg. Angiosarcoma; Astrocytoma; Basal Cell Carcinoma; Bone Cancer; Bowen's Disease; Breast Cancer; Carcinoid Syndrome; Cervical Cancer; Choriocarcinoma of the Uterus; Colo-Rectal Cancer; Erythroplasia of Queyrat; Ewing's Tumour; Glioma; Hodgkin's Disease; Insulinoma; Kaposi's Sarcoma; Leukaemia; Liver Cancer; Lung Cancer; Medulloblastoma; Melanoma;

Meningioma; Mesothelioma; Metastatic Cancer; Mouth Cancer; Multiple Endocrine Neoplasia Type 2; Mycosis Fungoides; Non-Hodgkin's Lymphoma; Oesophageal Cancer; Osteosarcoma; Ovarian Cancer; Paget's Disease of the Nipple; Pancreatic Cancer; Parotid Tumour; Prostate Cancer; Retinoblastoma; Skin Cancer; Squamous Cell Carcinoma of the Skin; Stewart-Treves Syndrome; Stomach Cancer; Teratoma; Testicular Cancer; Thyroid Cancer; Trousseau Syndrome; Tumour Lysis Syndrome; Turcot Syndrome; Uterine Mole; Werner Syndrome; Wilms' Tumour etc.)

Cancer of the Cervix
See Cervical Cancer

Cancer of the Oesophagus
See Oesophageal Cancer

Cancer of the Ovary
See Ovarian Cancer

Candidiasis
See Thrush

Cannabis Abuse
See Marijuana Abuse

Capgras Syndrome
(L'Illusion de Sosies)

DESCRIPTION: Rare cause of psychosis.

CAUSE: Unknown, but may be a form of, and associated with, schizophrenia.

SYMPTOMS: Psychotic delusion that a near relative has been replaced by a double or impersonator. May be transient in the elderly.

INVESTIGATIONS: EEG (electroencephalogram) is often abnormal.

TREATMENT: No specific treatment available, but medications used for schizophrenia may be tried.

PROGNOSIS: No cure, and control often unsatisfactory.

Capillaritis
(Pigmented Purpura)

DESCRIPTION: A harmless skin condition caused by leaky capillaries under the skin that become inflamed. Blood passes through small gaps between the cells which make up the capillary walls and tiny red dots appear on the skin. These join together to form a flat red patch, which becomes brown and then slowly fades away over weeks to months.

CAUSE: Usually unknown. Occasionally arises as a reaction to a medication, a food additive or a viral infection, or may flare after exercise.

SYMPTOMS: There are several different types of capillaritis —

81

Capillaritis

Schamberg's disease (progressive pigmented purpura) — most common type. Crops of red-brown flat patches with tiny red spots on their borders appear on the lower legs and other parts of the body.

Gourgerot-Blum disease (pigmented purpuric lichenoid dermatosis) — less common. The patches are thickened and itchy, rather like eczema.

Majocchis purpura (purpura annularis telangiectodes) — dilated capillaries as well as brown patches and red spots. The patches gradually spread outwards.

Lichen aureus — a solitary brown-yellow patch that is very persistent and often overlies a varicose vein.

INVESTIGATIONS: None necessary.

TREATMENT: Discontinue medication for several months if possible to see if condition improves. Avoid food preservatives and artificial colouring agents. Steroid creams help itching but rarely clear the capillaritis. If the lower leg is affected, consider wearing compression elastic stockings.

COMPLICATIONS: None significant.

PROGNOSIS: No cure, but it can disappear within a few weeks, recur from time to time, or persist for years.

Capsulitis
See Frozen Shoulder

Carbuncle
See Boil

Carcinoid Syndrome

DESCRIPTION: A cancer that starts in argentaffin cells inside the small intestine, stomach or lung.

CAUSE: Argentaffin cells are responsible for producing a number of essential hormones (eg. serotonin) for the functioning of the gut and body in general. When these cells become cancerous, they produce excessive amounts of these hormones, which causes unusual symptoms.

SYMPTOMS: May develop very rapidly, and patients can become severely ill in a few days. Symptoms include hot flushes of the face, swelling of the head and neck, diarrhoea and stomach cramps, asthma and bleeding into the skin.

INVESTIGATIONS: Blood or urine tests can be carried out to identify the high levels of serotonin and other hormones.

TREATMENT: Prednisone (a steroid) is used in the emergency treatment of the disease, and other medications are given to control the other symptoms. Drugs such as interferon can sometimes be used to destroy the cancer cells.

COMPLICATIONS: The site of the cancer is often very difficult to find, as it is usually very small and slow growing. It also tends to spread at an early stage to other areas, so even if the original is removed, the syndrome may continue due to the production of hormones in high levels by newly formed and very small cancers in multiple sites.

PROGNOSIS: Because of its slow growth rate, it may take 10 or 15 years for the disease to progress from the stage of being a nuisance that requires constant medication, to being life-threatening.

Carcinoma
See Cancer

Carcinoma of the Cervix
See Cervical Cancer

Cardiac Failure
See Congestive Cardiac failure

Cardiac Myxoma
See Myxoma

Cardiomyopathy
(Hypertrophic Cardiomyopathy)

DESCRIPTION: Hypertrophic cardiomyopathy means enlarged heart muscle disease ('hypertrophic' means over developed, 'cardio' refers to the heart, 'myo' to muscle, and 'pathy' to disease). Diseases and weakness of the heart muscle are very common in older people due to the aging process.

CAUSE: Almost any disease from an infection to a heart attack can cause cardiomyopathy, and so the term may be used when the exact nature of the heart disease present is unknown. Drugs, tumours and high blood pressure may also be responsible.

SYMPTOMS: May be a trivial illness that is barely noticed by the patient, or may cause tiredness, weakness, shortness of breath and chest pains (angina).

INVESTIGATIONS: Diagnosed by chest X-ray demonstrating an enlarged heart, ECG and echocardiogram.

TREATMENT: Medications such as digoxin, captopril, disopyramide, sotalol and a number of others, may be prescribed to strengthen the heart muscle and make it contract more efficiently.

COMPLICATIONS: Can be a progressive disease that leads inevitably to death or the need for a heart transplant.

PROGNOSIS: Depends on the cause, but in most cases can be controlled reasonably.
See also Angina; Congestive Cardiac Failure

Carney's Complex
DESCRIPTION: Rare growths within heart.
CAUSE: Familial (runs in families) genetic defect.
SYMPTOMS: Soft benign growths of tissue (myxomas) within the atria (smaller chambers) of the heart and spotty pigmentation inside the mouth and nose.

Some patients have skin growths, and tumours in the adrenal glands that may cause Cushing syndrome (see separate entry).

INVESTIGATIONS: Echocardiography (ultrasound scan of heart) is abnormal.

TREATMENT: Surgical removal of myxomas.

COMPLICATIONS: Myxomas may interfere with heart function and recur after surgery.

PROGNOSIS: Reasonable, depending on location and size of myxomas.

Carotenaemia
See Hypervitaminosis A

Carotodynia Syndrome
DESCRIPTION: Blood vessel spasm and inflammation that affects one side of the face and neck.

CAUSE: Migraine-like reaction of carotid artery in neck.

SYMPTOMS: Discomfort to intense pain in and behind angle of the jaw that spreads across the face and temple, tender carotid artery in the neck, stiff neck muscles and swelling of the neck (oedema). Some patients develop a runny nose, Horner syndrome (see separate entry) and hoarseness.

INVESTIGATIONS: No diagnostic test, but blood tests and X-rays need to be done to exclude other possible causes of symptoms (eg. temporal arteritis, dental abscess, jaw joint arthritis).

TREATMENT: Medications such as pizotifen and propranolol can prevent attacks.

PROGNOSIS: Settles in a few hours to days. Most cases can be prevented.

See also Migraine

Carpal Tunnel Syndrome
DESCRIPTION: A form of repetitive strain injury to the wrist.

CAUSE: Caused by the excessive compression of the arteries, veins and nerves that supply the hand as they pass through the carpal tunnel in the wrist. This tunnel is shaped like a letter 'D' lying on its side and consists of an arch of small bones which is held in place by a band of fibrous tissue. If the ligaments become slack, the arch will flatten, and the nerves, arteries and tendons within the tunnel will become compressed. It is far more common in women and in those undertaking repetitive tasks or using vibrating tools and in pregnancy.

SYMPTOMS: Numbness, tingling, pain and weakness in the hand.

INVESTIGATIONS: X-rays of the wrist, and studies to measure the rate of nerve conduction in the area confirm the diagnosis.

TREATMENT: Splinting the wrist, fluid tablets to reduce swelling, nonsteroidal anti-inflammatory medications, and occasionally injections of steroids into the wrist. Most patients will eventually require minor surgery to release the pressure.

COMPLICATIONS: Permanent damage to the structures in the wrist and hand can occur if not treated.

PROGNOSIS: The operation normally gives a lifelong cure.

See also Cubital Tunnel Syndrome; de Quervain's Tenosynovitis; Guyton's Canal Syndrome; Tarsal Tunnel Syndrome

Carpenter Syndrome
(Acrocephalopolysyndactyly)
DESCRIPTION: Very rare developmental disorder.
CAUSE: Familial. Premature fusion of the bones that make up the skull and face, and abnormal development of the fingers and toes.
SYMPTOMS: Peculiar facial structure and appearance, skull deformity, reduced number of fingers that are fused together and abnormally placed on hand, two or more toes that are fused together, obesity, mental retardation and small genitals.
INVESTIGATIONS: None diagnostic.
TREATMENT: Plastic surgery for deformities.
PROGNOSIS: No cure.
See also Acrocephalosyndactyly of Apert

Car Sickness
See Motion Sickness

Cataract
DESCRIPTION: Damage to the lens in the eye resulting in reduced vision.
CAUSE: A cloudy lens in the eye, which may be present from birth, or may be caused by injury or infection to the eye, but the cause in older people is unknown. Most people over 70 years of age have some degree of cataract formation.
SYMPTOMS: Reduced, cloudy vision with poor colour discrimination.
INVESTIGATIONS: Diagnosed by examining the eye with an ophthalmoscope (magnifying light).
TREATMENT: Initially treated with powerful spectacles, but eye surgery to replace the damaged lens is the best solution. Only one eye (usually the worst one) will be operated upon initially. Once this has recovered, the second eye may be repaired. The procedure can be done under a general or local anaesthetic, and involves cutting open the top of the eye at the edge of the iris (the coloured part of the eye), removing the damaged lens by gentle suction, and inserting an artificial lens in its place.
COMPLICATIONS: Dislocation of the new lens, or infection of the eye are uncommon.
PROGNOSIS: More than 95% of patients achieve excellent results with surgery.
See also other diseases listed under Vision Problems

Cat Scratch Disease
DESCRIPTION: A curious condition caused by a scratch from a cat claw, often to the face.

CAUSE: The bacterium *Bartonella henselae* that may be present on cat paws. When a person is scratched by a cat, the bacteria enter the damaged tissue.

SYMPTOMS: A few days after being scratched, about one third of patients develop a scab-covered sore at the site of the scratch. Between one and three weeks later, a fever and headache occur, and are accompanied by enlarged lymph nodes in the groin and the side of the neck or armpit nearest the scratch. Occasionally the infected nodes develop into an abscess.

INVESTIGATIONS: No specific tests to confirm the diagnosis, and blood tests merely show that an infection is present, but not what has caused the infection.

TREATMENT: None available or necessary. Sometimes it is necessary to surgically drain an abscess.

COMPLICATIONS: Very rarely a form of encephalitis (brain inflammation — see separate entry) and skin rashes may occur.

PROGNOSIS: Usually settles spontaneously within a week or two.

Catatonic Syndrome

DESCRIPTION: Psychiatric or neurological (brain damage) disorder that affects muscle control.

CAUSE: Usually associated with schizophrenia, but may be due to brain tumours or inflammation, strokes, drugs, poisons and body chemistry disorders.

SYMPTOMS: Increased muscle tone at rest that disappears during movement, sudden impulsive movements and excitement.

INVESTIGATIONS: Multiple investigations (eg. blood tests, CT scan) carried out to determine cause.

TREATMENT: Hospitalisation, medications (eg. haloperidol, fluphenazine, thiothixene), psychotherapy, behavioural and social therapy.

PROGNOSIS: Depends on cause.

Cattarh
See Post-Nasal Drip

Causalgia
(Complex Regional Pain Syndrome Type Two)

DESCRIPTION: Abnormal reaction to a nerve injury resulting in excessive inappropriate stimulation of the nerve.

CAUSE: Injury to a nerve in a limb.

SYMPTOMS: Three phases occur.

Phase one — swelling and intermittent severe burning pain of the forearm and hand, or lower leg and foot, starting within three months of a nerve injury.

Phase two — thin, shiny, cool skin that sweats excessively replaces normal skin on the affected limb three to six months after the injury, and pain continues.

Phase three — after a further three to six months, the skin becomes very thin, scar tissue develops in the limb, and affected joints become contracted, painful and immobile.

INVESTIGATIONS: No specific diagnostic tests. Electromyography (EMG — measurement of electrical impulses in muscles) may be abnormal.

TREATMENT: Unsatisfactory. Physiotherapy, anti-inflammatory drugs and steroids have been tried.

COMPLICATIONS: Permanent disability involving the affected limb common.

PROGNOSIS: Poor. Symptoms often persist long term.

See also Reflex Sympathetic Dystrophy Syndrome

CCF
See Congestive Cardiac Failure

Celiac Disease
See Coeliac Disease

Cellulitis

DESCRIPTION: A bacterial infection of the tissue immediately under the skin.

CAUSE: May start from a bite or wound, but sometimes for no apparent reason.

SYMPTOMS: The area affected is hot, red, tender, swollen and painful. The infected area slowly spreads, and once the lymphatic system becomes involved, red streaks may run towards the nearest lymph nodes (adenitis — see separate entry), the patient will develop a fever and become quite ill.

INVESTIGATIONS: A swab may be taken from any sore to determine the type of bacteria responsible, and the appropriate antibiotic to treat it.

TREATMENT: Antibiotic tablets or injections (eg. penicillin).

COMPLICATIONS: An abscess may develop in the tissue if treatment is delayed. Rarely, the infection may spread to the blood to cause septicaemia (see separate entry).

PROGNOSIS: Most cases respond rapidly to antibiotics.

See also Abscess; Adenitis; Erysipelas; Septicaemia

Cerebral Aneurysm
See Aneurysm

Cerebral Infarct
See Stroke

Cerebral Palsy
(Spastic)

DESCRIPTION: Brain condition causing abnormal uncontrolled muscle spasms.

CAUSE: Usually due to abnormal development of the brain before birth, or rarely to brain damage around the time of birth because the baby is deprived of oxygen for several minutes.

SYMPTOMS: Varies dramatically from one patient to another depending on area of brain damaged. Some have slight difficulty in controlling one limb, others may be unable to talk clearly, yet others may be totally unable to care for themselves in any way. Mental functioning may be completely normal, or there may be significant mental retardation.

INVESTIGATIONS: Electroencephalograms (EEG) which measure brain waves, electromyelograms (EMG) which measure the electrical conduction in muscles, and CT scans of the brain and spine may be abnormal. Blood tests are usually normal.

TREATMENT: Most help comes from teams of nurses, physiotherapists, occupational therapists, social workers and volunteers. Medications may be used to treat skin, intestinal and arthritic complications. Operations to correct deformities and release spasm in limbs can complement medications which reduce the uncontrollable twitching that may occur. Paramedical staff can teach the patient how to control an unwilling body. Emotional and psychiatric support is often necessary.

COMPLICATIONS: Often associated with epilepsy due to brain damage. High incidence of arthritis, pressure ulcers, chest infections and peptic ulcers. May be resultant emotional and social problems.

PROGNOSIS: No cure. Some symptoms can be eased. Life expectancy less than average.

Cerebral Thrombosis
See Stroke

Cerebral Tumour
See Astrocytoma; Glioma; Medulloblastoma; Meningioma; Pinealoma

Cerebro-Hepato-Renal Syndrome
See Zellweger Syndrome

Cerebrovascular Accident
See Stroke

Cerumen
See Ear Wax

Cervical Cancer
(Cancer of the Cervix)

DESCRIPTION: Cancer of the cervix involves the part of the uterus (womb) which opens into the top of the vagina. It is one of the more common forms of female cancer.

CAUSE: More common in women who have multiple sexual partners, smokers, and much more common in women who have been infected with the human pappiloma virus which causes genital warts (see separate entry). Very rare in virgins.

SYMPTOMS: May be no symptoms for several years after the cancer is present, then abnormal vaginal bleeding, foul discharge, pain and/or bleeding on intercourse, and discomfort in the lower abdomen may occur.

INVESTIGATIONS: May be detected at an early stage by a Pap smear test. If a Pap smear result is suspicious the cervix will be more closely examined through a microscope that looks into the vagina (a colposcope). Biopsy of a suspicious area can confirm the diagnosis.

TREATMENT: Easily treated in early stages by burning away the cancerous area with diathermy or laser, or a cone-shaped area of tissue may be excised. These forms of treatment do not interfere with the woman's ability to fall pregnant, or function normally in her sexual responses. Only if the cancer is advanced is a hysterectomy required or radiation therapy used.

COMPLICATIONS: If left untreated it may spread to the lymph nodes in the pelvis, the uterus, ureters and other organs.

PROGNOSIS: 99% of early stage cancer is cured, 65% of cases with medium stage survive, but only 5% of those with spread outside the pelvis are alive after five years.

See also Genital Warts

Cervical Rib Syndrome
See Naffziger Syndrome

Cervix Cyst
See Nabothian Cyst

Cestode Infestation
See Tapeworms

CFS
See Chronic Fatigue Syndrome

Chagas' Disease
(American Trypanosomiasis)

DESCRIPTION: Infestation by a parasite that is widespread in tropical America from Texas to Bolivia. Goes through three stages — acute, latent and chronic.

CAUSE: The protozoan (single celled) parasite *Trypanosoma cruzi* which is transmitted from wild animals to humans by bug bites to the skin or bug faeces in the eye.

SYMPTOMS: Sore develops on skin at site of bite or in the eye, and in many patients, no other symptoms ever occur until after a latent stage lasting 10 to 30 years when a chronic stage with heart disease occurs causing irregular heart rhythm, congestive heart failure, and pulmonary thromboses (see separate entries). A minority of patients go through an acute illness which causes enlarged lymph nodes near the bite, fever, tiredness, headache, and enlarged liver and spleen.

INVESTIGATIONS: Diagnosed by specific blood tests, but may be undetectable in the latent stage.

TREATMENT: Generally unsatisfactory. Medications may be tried in the acute stage, but are of no use in the chronic stage.

COMPLICATIONS: Acute heart or brain infection may be rapidly fatal. Long term infection may cause severe heart disease.

PROGNOSIS: Fatal in 10% of acute illnesses. Death from heart disease occurs in chronic stage.

See also Sleeping Sickness

Chalazion

DESCRIPTION: Bacterial infection of an oil gland (Meibomian gland) deep within an eyelid.

CAUSE: Blockage of the duct draining the gland.

SYMPTOMS: Painful, red, tender swelling in an eyelid.

INVESTIGATIONS: None necessary.

TREATMENT: Antibiotic eye ointment, and sometimes either cutting open or cutting out the infected gland.

COMPLICATIONS: May be recurrent, and rarely infection can spread further into the eyelid.

PROGNOSIS: Good response to treatment.

See also Meibomian Cyst and other conditions listed under Eye Diseases

Chancroid

DESCRIPTION: Sexually transmitted infection that is rare in developed countries, and more common in the tropics and Asia.

CAUSE: The bacteria *Haemophilus ducreyi*.

SYMPTOMS: Three to five days after sexual contact with a carrier, a sore develops on the penis or vulva which rapidly breaks down to form a painful ulcer. Several sores and ulcers may be present at the same time. Lymph nodes in the groin then swell up into hard, painful lumps, that may degenerate into an abscess and discharge pus. The patient is feverish and feels ill. Some patients develop a mild form with minimal symptoms, but they can transmit the disease. This is particularly common in women, where the sores may be hidden internally in the vagina.

INVESTIGATIONS: Diagnosed by taking swabs from the sores and identifying the bacteria present in the pus, or skin tests that often remain positive for life.

TREATMENT: Antibiotics (eg. azithromycin, ciprofloxacin).

COMPLICATIONS: Balanitis (infection of penis head) and phimosis (contracture of foreskin).

PROGNOSIS: Very good with treatment.

See also Balanitis; Phimosis

'Change of Life'
See Menopause

Charcot-Marie-Tooth Disease

DESCRIPTION: Gradually progressive degeneration of nerves that supply the arms and legs.

CAUSE: Familial (runs in families) genetic abnormality.

SYMPTOMS: Patients initially have an abnormal gait (way of walking) and foot deformities in late childhood or early adult life. Gait gradually worsens over several years with weakness and loss of sensation in the legs, and later the arms. Paralysis of both arms and legs is the eventual result.

INVESTIGATIONS: Diagnosed by nerve biopsy.

TREATMENT: None available.

PROGNOSIS: No cure.

CHARGE Syndrome

DESCRIPTION: Serious developmental abnormality of the heart, intestine and eye. Name is an acronym for major clinical features.

CAUSE: Congenital.

SYMPTOMS: Coloboma (gap) in the iris (coloured part) and retina of the eye, Heart structure abnormalities, failure of the Anus to develop, Retarded growth and development, under developed Genitals, Ear abnormalities and deafness. Some patients also have failure of the oesophagus to develop, paralysis of some face muscles, kidney abnormalities, structural brain defects, cleft lip and palate, and defects in the glands that secrete hormones.

INVESTIGATIONS: Defects diagnosed by a combination of CT and ultrasound scans.

TREATMENT: A feeding tube is put into the stomach, anus and heart abnormalities are surgically corrected if possible, and plastic surgery for other deformities.

PROGNOSIS: Often die soon after birth, but if infant survives first year, prognosis is reasonable.

Charles Bonnet Syndrome

DESCRIPTION: Psychological disturbance associated with isolation.

CAUSE: Often found in widows deprived of any company or outside contact.

SYMPTOMS: Vivid, elaborate and recurrent hallucinations in elderly patients with poor vision and depression.

INVESTIGATIONS: None diagnostic.

TREATMENT: Psychological counselling and support, and psychiatric treatments.

COMPLICATIONS: Hallucinations of smell, taste and sounds.

PROGNOSIS: Variable, but most patients end up in an institution.

Chédiak-Higashi Syndrome

DESCRIPTION: Inherited failure of white blood cells to function or develop.

CAUSE: Familial (runs through families) condition.

SYMPTOMS: Recurrent skin infections, partial albinism (loss of skin pigment) and a lack of white blood cells. Some patients have a large liver and spleen, and severe respiratory infections.
INVESTIGATIONS: Blood tests show abnormal and low number of white cells.
TREATMENT: Antibiotics for bacterial infections, steroids, bone marrow transplants and vitamin C supplements.
COMPLICATIONS: Severe infections almost anywhere in body.
PROGNOSIS: Poor.

Cheyne-Stokes Respiration
DESCRIPTION: Serious abnormality of breathing.
CAUSE: Damage to the respiratory (breathing) centre in the brain from a stroke or tumour, meningitis, uraemia (kidney failure), drug (eg. narcotic, barbiturate) overdose or advanced heart disease (eg. congestive cardiac failure). Final stage of many long term fatal diseases.
SYMPTOMS: Breaths that gradually decrease in frequency until a temporary stop occurs. Breathing then restarts and the frequency builds to a maximum before the cycle repeats itself.
INVESTIGATIONS: Cause needs to be determined.
TREATMENT: Treat cause if possible.
PROGNOSIS: In most cases a sign of imminent death, but with some causes may be reversed.

Chiari-Frommel Syndrome
DESCRIPTION: Late complication of pregnancy and breast feeding.
CAUSE: Usually due to a tumour in the hormone controlling pituitary gland under the brain, but there are other rare causes.
SYMPTOMS: Failure of menstrual periods to restart after breastfeeding finished following confinement, and continued production of breast milk.
INVESTIGATIONS: Blood tests show abnormal hormone production by the pituitary gland, and a CT or MRI scan reveals the pituitary tumour.
TREATMENT: Surgery to remove pituitary tumour.
PROGNOSIS: Good results from surgery.

Chickenpox
(Varicella)
DESCRIPTION: A generalised infection with the virus Herpes zoster.
CAUSE: Infection occurs when the virus that can be found in the fluid-filled blisters that cover the body of patients, as well as in their breath and saliva, passes to another person. Patients are infectious for a day or two before the spots appear, and remain infectious for about eight days. The incubation period is 10 to 21 days.
SYMPTOMS: Early symptoms are similar to those of a cold, with a vague feeling of being unwell, headache, fever and sore throat. The rash usually starts on the

head or chest as red pimples, then spreads onto the legs and arms, and develops into blisters before drying up and scabbing over. New spots may develop for three to five days, and it may be two weeks or more before the last spot disappears.

INVESTIGATIONS: None usually necessary.

TREATMENT: Bed and home rest until the patient feels well, and medications to relieve the itch (eg. calamine lotion, antihistamines), fever and headache. There is now a vaccine available.

COMPLICATIONS: Complications are more common in adults, and include chest infections and a type of meningitis. It is unusual for the pock marks to scar unless a secondary bacterial infection occurs. Once you have had chickenpox, the virus never leaves your body but migrates to the nerves along your spinal cord where it remains for the rest of your life, and may be reactivated years later at times of stress to give the patient the painful rash of shingles.

PROGNOSIS: Complete recovery within ten days normal. Once you have had chickenpox, it is unlikely (but not impossible) that you will ever have it again.

See also Congenital Varicella Syndrome, Shingles

Chiclero's Ulcers
See Cutaneous Leischmaniasis

Chilblains

DESCRIPTION: Mild form of frostbite (see separate entry).

CAUSE: Exposure to extreme cold.

SYMPTOMS: Itchy, red skin spots develop on the fingers, toes and other exposed areas such as the nose. The spot may form a blister, and the itching is aggravated by warmth.

INVESTIGATIONS: None normally necessary.

TREATMENT: Gradual warming in a warm room. The fingers or toes should NOT be immersed in hot water or placed near a heater or fire, nor should the area be rubbed or massaged as this may cause further damage.

COMPLICATIONS: Damaged skin may become infected and require antibiotics. Recurrent chilblains can lead to a permanent scar forming at the site.

PROGNOSIS: If not exposed to further cold, the skin will heal in a day or two.

See also Frostbite; Hypothermia

Chinese Restaurant Syndrome

DESCRIPTION: Abnormal reaction to food preservatives.

CAUSE: Caused by overuse of sodium glutamate in food and aggravated by alcohol.

SYMPTOMS: Facial pressure, headache, nausea, chest pain and a burning sensation of head and chest.

INVESTIGATIONS: None necessary.

TREATMENT: Aspirin or paracetamol.

PROGNOSIS: Settles spontaneously after 12 to 48 hours.

Chlamydial Infections

DESCRIPTION: Infection by any one of a number of different types of *Chlamydiae* that can cause diseases in birds (particularly parrots), and koalas as well as humans.

CAUSE: *Chlamydiae* are a group of organisms that are not bacteria, but closely resemble bacteria. They act as parasites inside human cells, cause the destruction of the cell where they multiply, and then move on to infect more cells. Transmitted sexually or by close contact with other patients or infected animals.

SYMPTOMS: May cause pneumonia (psittacosis), eye infections (trachoma), and infections of the urethra (urine tube from bladder to outside — non-specific urethritis), vagina (pelvic inflammatory disease) and genitals (lympho-granuloma venereum).

INVESTIGATIONS: Difficult to diagnose, but swabs from affected area are sometimes positive. Blood tests can also be used to make the diagnosis with internal infections.

TREATMENT: Infections settle with appropriate antibiotics.

COMPLICATIONS: Depends on area infected.

PROGNOSIS: Generally good.

See also Lymphogranuloma Venereum; Non-Specific Urethritis; Psittacosis; Trachoma

Chlamydial Urethritis
See Non-Specific Urethritis

Chloasma
(Melasma)

DESCRIPTION: Pigmentation disorder of the skin that occurs almost invariably in women, and more commonly in those with a dark complexion.

CAUSE: Deposits of pigment often triggered by pregnancy or starting the oral contraceptive pill.

SYMPTOMS: Excessive skin pigmentation of the forehead, cheeks, upper lip, nose and nipples.

INVESTIGATIONS: None necessary.

TREATMENT: Unsatisfactory. Numerous blanching agents have been tried with minimal success.

COMPLICATIONS: None.

PROGNOSIS: Usually fades slowly over several years.

Choledocoduodenal Fistula
See Fistula

Cholecystitis

DESCRIPTION: Infected gall bladder. The gall bladder collects and stores bile produced by the liver, and contracts to squeeze it out onto food when necessary. Bile is used to break down and digest fats.

CAUSE: Almost always due to the presence of gallstones. Many different bacteria can be responsible for the infection.

SYMPTOMS: Pain in the upper right abdomen and behind the lower right ribs that often goes through to the back. Patients have a fever, indigestion, nausea and sometimes irregular bowel habits.

INVESTIGATIONS: Ultrasound scans can detect gallstones, and sometimes thickening of the wall of the gall bladder which is characteristic of infection. Blood tests are often normal, but sometimes show non-specific signs of infection or liver stress.

TREATMENT: Antibiotics to settle the gall bladder infection and surgery to remove the stones (cholecystectomy).

COMPLICATIONS: Rarely there may be spread of the infection to the liver and other surrounding tissues. Sometimes an abscess forms in or around the gall bladder.

PROGNOSIS: Good response to treatment.

See also Gallstones

Cholelithiasis
See Gallstones

Cholera

DESCRIPTION: Severe infection of the bowel that occurs in areas with poor hygiene.

CAUSE: The bacterium *Vibrio cholerae* that is swallowed with contaminated water or food. The bacteria multiply rapidly in the body to irritate the gut, cause diarrhoea, and then pass out in faeces, contaminate water supplies, and infect others.

SYMPTOMS: Very severe diarrhoea with blood in the faeces and rapid dehydration that may lead to death. A huge amount of fluid is lost from the body in a short time. The patient shivers, has a below normal temperature, shallow breathing, muscle cramps and becomes comatose.

INVESTIGATIONS: Sample of faeces cultured in a laboratory to identify the responsible bacteria.

TREATMENT: Replacing fluid loss by a drip into a vein (preferable) or an electrolyte mixture by mouth. An emergency mixture to rehydrate a patient can be made by mixing a level teaspoon of salt and eight level teaspoons of sugar or glucose into a litre of boiled water. This should be given freely to more than replace the fluid lost in the diarrhoea. A course of tetracycline antibiotic will kill the infecting bacteria in the gut. A vaccination against cholera is available but gives less than 60% protection.

COMPLICATIONS: Permanent damage to organs from dehydration.

PROGNOSIS: Untreated, the death rate varies from 35% to 80%, but with proper

care, 98% should survive. From the time of onset to death from dehydration can be a matter of a day or two in adults and only a few hours in children.
See also Gastroenteritis; Shigellosis; Typhoid Fever

Cholesteatoma

DESCRIPTION: A serious complication of middle ear infections or blockage of the eustachian tube (runs through the centre of the head from the middle ear to the back of the nose to equalise ear pressure).

CAUSE: A sac on the ear drum develops which is filled with chronically infected material that antibiotics cannot reach. The infected sac slowly enlarges and eats away surrounding bone, including the fine bones which transmit sound vibrations from the ear drum to the hearing mechanism in the inner ear.

SYMPTOMS: Minimal until the condition is well advanced when ear discomfort and deafness occur.

INVESTIGATIONS: Diagnosed by examining the ear with an otoscope (magnifying light).

TREATMENT: Surgical removal of the sac of infected material.

COMPLICATIONS: If left too long before treatment, permanent deafness may occur.

PROGNOSIS: Usually good results from surgery.

See also Otitis Media

Cholesterol, Excess
See Hypercholesterolaemia

Chondrocalcinosis
(Calcium Pyrophosphate Deposition Disease)

DESCRIPTION: Form of arthritis due to cartilage damage.

CAUSE: Deposition of calcium pyrophosphate in the cartilages lining major joints. Familial (passed from one generation to the next), or due to abnormalities in the body's metabolic processes (eg. diabetes mellitus, hypothyroidism, haemochromatosis).

SYMPTOMS: Affected joints become painful and swollen.

INVESTIGATIONS: X-rays show abnormal calcium deposits in joints.

TREATMENT: Anti-inflammatory medications.

PROGNOSIS: Usually recurrent attacks occur, but each attack can be reasonably controlled.

See also Pseudogout

Chondrodermatitis Nodularis Chronica Helicis

DESCRIPTION: Painful inflammatory condition affecting the ear of middle-aged and elderly men.

CAUSE: Pressure on the ear between the head and pillow at night. Occurs in people who usually sleep on one side, may be due to a minor injury (eg. tight headgear or telephone headset), or by exposure to cold. Reduction in the blood supply to the ear with aging prevents healing.

SYMPTOMS: A benign tender lump a few millimetres across in the cartilaginous part of the ear that is exquisitely tender. There is often a tiny central core which may discharge a small amount of scaly material.

INVESTIGATIONS: None normally necessary.

TREATMENT: Avoid sleeping on the affected ear, use a soft pillow with a hole in it if necessary, and wear a warm hat over the ears when outside in the cold and wind. May be treated with a cortisone injection, frozen with liquid nitrogen or surgically removed. If ulcerated, antibiotic ointment may be applied.

COMPLICATIONS: Ulcer formation on the ear.

PROGNOSIS: Annoying but not serious. 10% recurrence rate after surgery.

Chondromalacia Patellae

DESCRIPTION: Disease of the knee cap (patella) that occurs only in teenagers and young adults. The patella is designed to glide smoothly over the end of the femur (the thigh bone) as the knee is bent and straightened. The under-surface of the patella is covered with a very smooth layer of cartilage, but in chondromalacia, the cartilage becomes softened, pitted, uneven and damaged, and the knee cap grates across the femur instead of gliding.

CAUSE: Often difficult to determine, but it can be caused by recurrent dislocation of the knee cap, or by falling repeatedly on the knee.

SYMPTOMS: Pain deep in the knee which is worse on bending the knee or kneeling. When the knee is moved, a fine grating sensation may be felt.

INVESTIGATIONS: Arthroscopy (looking into the knee joint through a thin tube) may be necessary to confirm the diagnosis.

TREATMENT: Firm bandaging and rest, but sometimes splinting or a plaster cast may be required for a few weeks. If pain persists for months, surgery to modify or remove the knee cap may be necessary.

COMPLICATIONS: Rarely, permanent knee pain may occur and resist all treatment.

PROGNOSIS: Majority of cases settle with simple treatments.

See also Patello-Femoral Pain Syndrome

Chondrosarcoma
See Bone Cancer

Chorda Tympani Syndrome

DESCRIPTION: Uncommon nerve disorder.

CAUSE: Irritation of the chorda tympani nerve.

SYMPTOMS: Abnormal sweating under the chin after eating.

INVESTIGATIONS: Specific nerve conduction tests may be performed.

TREATMENT: Surgically cutting the chorda tympani.

PROGNOSIS: Annoying problem rather than serious. Good result from treatment.

Chorea
See Huntington's Chorea; Rheumatic Fever; Sydenham's Chorea

Choriocarcinoma of the Testicle
See Testicular Cancer

Choriocarcinoma of the Uterus
(Invasive Uterine Mole)
DESCRIPTION: A rare form of cancer involving the placenta during pregnancy.

CAUSE: 4% of women with uterine moles (see separate entry) develop cancer in the abnormal tissue. This may occur some time after apparently successful treatment of the mole.

SYMPTOMS: During pregnancy, an abnormal vaginal bleed or discharge occurs, and the womb feels much larger than expected.

INVESTIGATIONS: Ultrasound scan and abnormal blood tests occur, but diagnosis depends upon biopsy of the abnormal placental tissue.

TREATMENT: May sometimes be successfully treated with surgical removal of the uterus (hysterectomy) and cytotoxic drugs.

COMPLICATIONS: Can also very rarely occur with an apparently normal pregnancy and a live baby.

PROGNOSIS: Poor for mother, foetus invariably dies.

See also Uterine Mole

Christmas Disease
(Factor IX Deficit, Haemophilia B)
DESCRIPTION: A lack of one of the essential factors responsible for the clotting of blood.

CAUSE: An inherited lack of factor IX. The gene for the disease is carried by women on the X chromosome, but can only affect men (sex linked inheritance).

SYMPTOMS: Excessive bleeding from a cut, severe bruising from a minor injury, bleeding into joints to cause arthritis, internal bleeding into the gut and other organs.

INVESTIGATIONS: Specific blood tests can confirm the diagnosis.

TREATMENT: Injections of the missing coagulation factor to prevent excessive bleeding when it occurs. Insufficient is available to be given regularly to prevent bleeding. The factor is obtained from blood donations.

COMPLICATIONS: Arthritis, infertility, damage to other organs from bleeding, chronic weakness, shorter than normal lifespan.

PROGNOSIS: Statistically, half the children of a woman who carries the responsible gene will have the disease. No permanent cure available. Incidence 1:40,000.

See also Haemophilia A; von Willebrand's Disease

Chronic Bronchitis
See Bronchitis, Chronic

Chronic Fatigue Syndrome
(CFS; ME; Myalgic Encephalomyelitis; Post-Viral Syndrome; Royal Free Disease; Tapanui Flu)

DESCRIPTION: A persistent tiredness and easy fatigue that persists for many months for no obvious reason.

CAUSE: Possibly caused by a virus, but some patients find that certain foods aggravate the condition. It is possible it is actually several diseases that overlap with their symptoms, and due to a combination of infection, immune deficiencies, auto-immune type condition (where the body rejects its own tissue), chronic inflammation, stress and psychiatric disturbances. It is a matter of debate whether the distressing symptoms cause the psychological problems, or vice versa.

SYMPTOMS: The diagnosis can only be confirmed if in the following list both major criteria are met, plus six symptoms and two signs from the minor criteria

Major criteria

— New persistent or intermittent, debilitating fatigue severe enough to reduce or impair average daily activity below 50% of normal activity for a period of more than 6 months

— Exclusion of all other causes by thorough clinical evaluation, and blood tests

Minor criteria — Symptoms

— Generalised fatigue lasting more than 24 hours following levels of exertion that would have been easily tolerated previously

— Vague headache

— Unexplained general muscle weakness

— Muscle pains

— Arthritis that moves from joint to joint without any apparent damage to the joint

— One or more of the following problems (avoidance of bright lights, forgetfulness, irritability, confusion, poor concentration, depression, intermittent visual disturbances, difficulty thinking)

— Inability to sleep, or excessive sleepiness

— Rapid onset over hours or days of major criteria

Minor criteria — Signs

Documented by a physician on at least two occasions at least a month apart

— Mild fever greater than 38.6°C

— Sore throat with no pus present

— Tender enlarged lymph nodes in neck or arm pit

INVESTIGATIONS: No specific diagnostic tests, but numerous blood tests may show minor abnormalities. Tests are performed to exclude any other possible cause.

TREATMENT: No specific treatment available, but patients can benefit by having an understanding doctor who may use antidepressants, anti-inflammatory medication, steroids and other drugs that may be helpful.

PROGNOSIS: No cure, but with time, most cases slowly improve. Some patients are left with long term tiredness so severe that they are unable to return to work or undertake normal daily activities.

Chronic Hypoadrenocorticism
See Addison's Disease

Chronic Kidney Failure
See Kidney Failure, Chronic

Chronic Leukaemia
See Leukaemia, Chronic Lymphocytic; Leukaemia, Chronic Myeloid

Chronic Obstructive Airways (Pulmonary) Disease (COAD)
See Bronchitis, Chronic; Emphysema; Pneumoconiosis

Chronic Pyelonephritis
See Pyelonephritis, Chronic

Chronic Renal Failure
See Kidney Failure, Chronic

Churg-Strauss Syndrome
DESCRIPTION: Inflammatory condition of the lungs and other organs.
CAUSE: Unknown, but may be an autoimmune condition.
SYMPTOMS: Asthma, generalised inflammation of blood vessels in two or more organs other than the lungs, and high levels of eosinophils (cells characteristic of allergy reaction) in the blood. Some patients also have inflamed nerves in the arms and legs giving strange sensations and pain, heart disease, bleeding into the lung, normal lung tissue replaced by fibrous tissue, diarrhoea, a rash and glomerulonephritis (kidney inflammation — see separate entry).
INVESTIGATIONS: Blood levels of eosinophils high, other blood cell and enzyme abnormalities, and abnormal lung and other organ biopsy.
TREATMENT: Medications such as prednisone, cyclophosphamide and azathioprine.
COMPLICATIONS: Permanent organ damage.
PROGNOSIS: Guarded. Long term follow-up essential.

Ciguatera Poisoning
DESCRIPTION: Form of seafood poisoning.
CAUSE: Eating reef fish that contain the ciguatera toxin. The fish itself is not affected, and there are no tests for differentiating safe from toxic fish. Generally the larger the fish, the more likely it is to be toxic. The poison is produced at certain seasons by a microscopic animal (Dinoflagellida) that proliferates on tropical reefs. This is eaten by very small fish, who are then eaten by bigger fish, who are then eaten by still bigger fish. There may be a dozen steps along this chain, with the poison being steadily concentrated in the fish tissue at every step. Ciguatera is present in a low concentration in

most reef fish, but only when it exceeds a certain concentration does it cause problems in humans. There are far higher concentrations in the gut, liver, head and roe of reef fish, which should never be eaten or used to make fish soup, and it cannot be destroyed by cooking.

SYMPTOMS: Vary dramatically from one patient to another, depending on the amount of toxin eaten, the size of the victim, and the individual reaction. May include unusual skin sensations and tingling, diarrhoea, nausea, abnormal sensation, headaches and irregular heartbeats. Unusual tingling sensations may persist for years.

INVESTIGATIONS: No diagnostic tests.

TREATMENT: No treatment or antidote, but medication may be used to control symptoms.

COMPLICATIONS: Subsequent serious attacks may be triggered by eating tiny amounts of ciguatera that may be present in fish that others can eat without adverse effects.

PROGNOSIS: Patients with a mild reaction recover in a few days, but severe attacks may cause symptoms for a couple of months. Death is rare, but possible, usually occurs within 36 hours of the onset of the attack, and is caused by the effects of the toxin on the heart and blood vessels. Toxin is naturally eliminated from the body.

Circumscribed Neurodermatitis
See Lichen Simplex

Circumscribed Scleroderma
See Morphoea

Cirrhosis

DESCRIPTION: Slowly developing damage to the liver resulting in it becoming hard and enlarged as normal tissue is replaced by fibrous scar tissue.

CAUSE: Recurrent attacks of hepatitis A, one attack of hepatitis B, other liver infections, excess alcohol intake, gall stones, a number of rare diseases that affect the liver (eg. haemochromatosis, Wilson's disease, Gaucher's disease — see separate entries), toxins, poisons (eg. arsenic) and drugs (eg. methotrexate, isoniazid).

SYMPTOMS: Itchy skin without a rash, jaundice (yellow skin), diarrhoea, abdominal discomfort.

INVESTIGATIONS: The diagnosis is confirmed by blood tests, and ultrasound and/or CT scans of the liver.

TREATMENT: Other than a liver transplant, there is no cure for cirrhosis. Patients must stop all further alcohol intake to reduce further damage. Vitamin supplements and nutritious diets are recommended. Medication can be prescribed to ease some symptoms.

COMPLICATIONS: Liver failure and portal hypertension (see separate entry).

Cirrhosis

PROGNOSIS: The liver tends to become steadily more damaged until it ceases to function completely.

See also Alcoholism; Hepatitis A; Hepatitis B and other diseases listed under Liver Diseases

CJD
See Creutzfeldt-Jakob Disease

Claudication

DESCRIPTION: Term used to describe the pain experienced when blood supply to muscles is inadequate.

CAUSE: Blood supply to leg muscles is reduced below requirements. The arteries to one or both legs may be narrowed by cholesterol deposits (atherosclerosis) and an adequate amount of blood may not get through. Any activity will require extra supplies of oxygen and nutrition, which the narrowed arteries cannot supply.

SYMPTOMS: Aching pain in the leg with exercise, particularly climbing slopes or stairs, that eases with rest.

INVESTIGATIONS: Doppler ultrasound scan will show reduced blood flow in affected arteries.

TREATMENT: Medications to strengthen heart and open arteries. Surgery may be necessary to bypass the blockage.

COMPLICATIONS: Ulcers may form on skin and be difficult to heal.

PROGNOSIS: Reasonable results from treatment.

Claustrophobia
See Phobia

Cleft Lip and Palate
(Hare Lip)

DESCRIPTION: A congenital deformity of the upper lip and palate (roof of mouth).

CAUSE: From four to seven weeks after conception, every foetus has a double cleft lip; and from the fifth to twelfth weeks, every foetus has a double cleft palate. These clefts normally close before birth, but in one child in 800 it is incomplete.

SYMPTOMS: May vary from a barely noticeable notch just off centre in the upper lip, to a complete wide split of the upper lip and full length of the palate on both sides.

INVESTIGATIONS: Sometimes detected late in pregnancy by an ultrasound scan of the foetus. After birth, sophisticated X-rays and CT scans of the face and skull will be undertaken before any surgical repair to accurately determine the extent of the problem.

TREATMENT: The aims are to ensure that the child has good speech, to enhance facial appearance, and to produce the best possible jaw function and dental

102

bite. Surgical repair of the lip is normally performed between two and six months after birth. Infants with a double cleft lip must have special dental treatment to reshape their upper jaw prior to surgical repair of the lip. The palate repair is normally done at about one year of age. Modern surgery now makes it possible to correct the problem in older people who have a poorly repaired or unrepaired cleft palate.

COMPLICATIONS: The upper jaw does not grow as well as the lower jaw, so special dental and orthodontic care is necessary until the child has finished growing. They also need careful monitoring to ensure their hearing is adequate.

PROGNOSIS: Very good results from surgery.

See also Lip-Pit Syndrome

Clérambault Syndrome
(de Clérambault Syndrome; Erotomania)

DESCRIPTION: Fixed single minded psychiatric delusion (monomania).

CAUSE: Inadequate dependent personality, often after period of real dependency on a person (eg. doctor during pregnancy and labour).

SYMPTOMS: Fixed delusional conviction that another is in love with them despite minimal contact. Majority of patients are female and may persecute or stalk the victim, who is often a doctor.

INVESTIGATIONS: No diagnostic test. Diagnosed by psychiatric assessment.

TREATMENT: Psychoanalysis, and drugs such as phenothiazines and clomipramine.

COMPLICATIONS: Legal action may need to be taken to stop stalking. Object of affection is sometimes attacked and harmed if advances are rejected.

PROGNOSIS: Poor prognosis. Treatment extremely difficult and often unsuccessful. Certification occasionally necessary.

Climacteric
See Menopause

Clostridial Myositis
Gangrene, Gas

Club Foot
(Talipes Equinovarus)

DESCRIPTION: Defect in the development of the foot. More common in boys than girls, and one or both feet may be affected.

CAUSE: Congenital.

SYMPTOMS: The foot is turned in so that the sole of the foot faces the other foot, and if the infant was to walk, it would walk on the outside edge of the foot. Often associated with under development of the muscles that move the ankle joint.

INVESTIGATIONS: None necessary. Usually obvious at birth.

TREATMENT: Should begin soon after birth by splinting the foot into the correct position for many months in mild cases, and surgery to correct the deformity in more severe cases and those that do not respond to splinting.

COMPLICATIONS: If treatment is delayed, there may be permanent deformity of the foot, due to a distorted growth of the bones around the ankle.

PROGNOSIS: Good results from treatment.

Cluster Headache

DESCRIPTION: Severe, intermittent one-sided headaches that occur in clusters lasting from days to weeks.

CAUSE: Attacks may be triggered by alcohol, stress, exercise, certain foods and glare. More common in middle-aged men.

SYMPTOMS: Severe, one-sided pain around the eye that occurs daily for weeks and then subsides, only to flare again months later. May be quite disabling, and are often accompanied by a congested nostril on the same side as the headache, a watery red eye and weakness on the affected side of the face.

INVESTIGATIONS: No specific diagnostic tests available.

TREATMENT: Once present, these headaches are very difficult to control. Normally a matter of trial and error to determine the most effective regime in any individual. The inhalation of pure oxygen may settle an otherwise intractable attack in a few minutes. Prevention is far better than cure, and medications such as propranolol, ergotamine, lithium and amitriptyline can be used on a regular basis to prevent further attacks. In severe cases prednisone is prescribed.

COMPLICATIONS: None significant.

PROGNOSIS: Prevention is reasonably successful, but treatment is difficult.

See also Migraine; SUNCT Syndrome

CMV
See Cytomegalovirus Infection

Coagulation, Disseminated Intravascular
See Disseminated Intravascular Coagulation

COA(P)D
(Chronic Obstructive Airways [Pulmonary] Disease)
See Bronchitis, Chronic; Emphysema; Pneumoconiosis

Coarctation of the Aorta
(Aortic Stenosis)

DESCRIPTION: A narrowing of the aorta, which is the main artery running from the heart through the chest and down the back of the abdomen. Only a short segment is normally affected and the severity of symptoms depends on the degree of narrowing. Usually diagnosed at birth or shortly afterwards, although milder cases may not be detected until the child undergoes rapid growth in the early teenage years.

CAUSE: Congenital condition (present since birth) that is more common in boys than girls. Often associated with abnormalities of the aortic heart valve.

SYMPTOMS: Children develop headaches, leg pain with exercise and frequent nose bleeds. The blood pressure is high in the arms, but low in the legs.

INVESTIGATIONS: Usually discovered by hearing a characteristic murmur when listening to the chest caused by the blood rushing through the narrowed section of the aorta. Diagnosis can be confirmed by an ultrasound scan.

TREATMENT: Surgical correction of the narrowing with a synthetic patch to open up the aorta to its correct diameter.

COMPLICATIONS: Severe coarctation can restrict blood flow to the lower half of the body and cause heart failure as it strives to pump the blood past the obstruction.

PROGNOSIS: Results of surgery are very good, but without surgery, 75% of babies die in the first year of life.

See also Aortic Valve Stenosis

Cocaine Addiction
('Crack')

DESCRIPTION: Naturally derived addictive substance that is available as a white crystalline powder, and can be administered by sniffing it into the nostrils (most common), injection into a vein, or smoking. Usually diluted with sugars such as lactose and glucose to less than 50% purity. 'Crack' is a concentrated form of cocaine.

CAUSE: Cocaine is a stimulant that is used in medicine as a local anaesthetic and constrictor of blood vessels. It is manufactured from the leaves of the coca plant which is native to South America. Users tend to be depressed and have a poor self-image and ego. Possibly one in every 100 people is dependent upon illicit drugs in western society, and a far higher percentage have experimented with them at one time or another.

SYMPTOMS: Effect is only brief, and causes mood enhancement, increased energy and generalised stimulation of all senses. With continued use, the duration of the pleasant effects becomes shorter and shorter, requiring further doses every 15 to 30 minutes to maintain the desired effect.

INVESTIGATIONS: Blood and urine tests can detect the presence of cocaine.

TREATMENT: The treatment options available are:
— Gradual withdrawal while receiving counselling and medical support
— Immediate drug withdrawal ('cold turkey') while hospitalised
— Half-way houses that remove the patient from the environment in which drug taking is encouraged
— Individual or group psychotherapy.

COMPLICATIONS: Adverse effects of the drug include a high fever (which may cause brain damage and death), high blood pressure (which may cause strokes), reduction of the desire to breath (which may stop breathing completely and cause death), irregular heart beats (which may cause a heart attack), delusions, paranoia, hallucinations, insomnia and convulsions (which may lead to loss of consciousness and unintentional self-injury).

PROGNOSIS: Reasonably good. Not as addictive as heroin, but more than marijuana.

See also other problems listed under Addiction

Coeliac Disease
(Celiac Disease; Coeliac Sprue; Non-Tropical Sprue)

DESCRIPTION: A disease of the small intestine that usually starts in childhood, and persists into early adult life, often settling in middle age.

CAUSE: Congenital condition caused by a genetic error that prevents the small intestine from absorbing fats and, to a lesser extent, carbohydrates and protein, because the intestine becomes sensitised to gluten. Gluten is found in wheat, oats, barley and rye cereals, and may be used as a bulking agent in prepared foods such as sausages.

SYMPTOMS: Patients are unable to tolerate any form of gluten in their intestine. If it is eaten they develop large, foul-smelling, frothy, fatty motions. This causes weight loss, anaemia and generalised weakness due to lack of nutrition and a failure to absorb vitamins A, D, E and K (the fat soluble vitamins).

INVESTIGATIONS: Initially diagnosed by a series of blood and faeces tests, but the final diagnosis can only be confirmed by taking a biopsy (sample) of the lining of the small intestine.

TREATMENT: Responds to a diet free of gluten, high in calories and protein, and low in fat.

COMPLICATIONS: Rashes and weak bones, as well as a failure to grow and foul diarrhoea may occur if untreated.

PROGNOSIS: In most patients it is completely controlled by diet. Once they reach adult life, many patients find they can slowly introduce gluten containing products to their diet without ill effect.

See also Tropical Sprue

Coeliac Sprue
See Coeliac Disease

Coffin-Lowry Syndrome

DESCRIPTION: Developmental abnormality affecting multiple organs.

CAUSE: Sex linked inheritance affecting boys only, but females act as carriers.

SYMPTOMS: Prominent lips, coarse facial features, tapering fingers, reverse eye slant, mental retardation and excess curvature of the spine (kyphosis and scoliosis — see separate entries).

INVESTIGATIONS: No diagnostic tests.

TREATMENT: None available.

PROGNOSIS: No cure.

Coffin-Siris Syndrome
DESCRIPTION: Genetic developmental abnormality.
CAUSE: Familial (runs in families) but both parents must be carriers.
SYMPTOMS: Poorly developed toe nails, very hairy at birth but sparse hair in later life, mental retardation and coarse facial features.
INVESTIGATIONS: No diagnostic tests.
TREATMENT: None available.
PROGNOSIS: No cure, but reasonable life expectancy.

Cogan Microcystic Corneal Dystrophy
See Corneal Dystrophy

Cogan Syndrome
DESCRIPTION: Rare ear, eye and other organ inflammation with rapid onset in young adults.
CAUSE: Unknown.
SYMPTOMS: Eye surface inflammation, ringing in the ears (tinnitus), dizziness and deafness. Some patients develop a fever, enlarged tender lymph nodes, joint aches and pains, belly pain, enlarged spleen, black faeces from blood leaking into the bowel and heart abnormalities (eg. aortic valve disease).
INVESTIGATIONS: Non-specific blood tests showing inflammation are positive. No specific diagnostic test.
TREATMENT: Medications such as corticosteroids and cyclophosphamide.
PROGNOSIS: Variable self-limiting course.

Cold, Common
(Coryza)
DESCRIPTION: Very common viral infection of the upper respiratory tract.
CAUSE: One or more of several hundred different rhinoviruses. It is a distinct entity from influenza, which is caused by a different virus. Spreads from one person to another in droplets of moisture in the breath, in a cough or in a sneeze. Once inhaled, the virus settles in the nose or throat and starts multiplying rapidly. Crowds, confined spaces (eg. buses, aircraft) and air conditioners that recycle air are renown for spreading the virus. Most adults have a cold every year or two, usually in winter. Children, because they have not been exposed to these viruses before and so have no immunity to them, may have ten or more infections a year.
SYMPTOMS: Sore throat and nose, runny and/or blocked nose, sneezing, cough, phlegm in the back of the throat, headache, intermittent fever and tiredness.
INVESTIGATIONS: None necessary.
TREATMENT: No cure or prevention possible. The symptoms can be eased by aspirin or paracetamol for headache and fever, and medications for the cough, sore throat, runny nose and blocked sinuses. The more the patient rests, the faster the infection will go away. Many vitamin and herbal remedies are touted

as cures or preventatives, but when subjected to detailed trials, none can be proved to be successful.

COMPLICATIONS: A secondary bacterial infection may cause pharyngitis or sinusitis.

PROGNOSIS: Usually lasts for about a week, but some people have a briefer course, while in others the first cold may lower their defences so that they can catch another one, and then another, causing cold symptoms to last for many weeks.

See also Influenza; Laryngitis; Pharyngitis; Sinusitis

Cold Sore
(Herpes Simplex Type 1 Infection)

DESCRIPTION: A skin infection, usually around the nose or mouth, with the virus Herpes simplex type 1.

CAUSE: Initially, the infection is caught as a child, when it is a simple mouth infection. The virus then migrates to the nerve endings around the lips and nose, and remains inactive there for many years. It may later reactivate at times of stress or illness to cause cold sores. It is passed from one person to another by direct contact (eg. kissing). 60% of the population are infected and remain carriers throughout their lives. Sores are uncommon before five years of age, and the incidence decreases in old age. Recurrences tend to develop at the same spot.

SYMPTOMS: Characterised by redness and soreness of the affected area, followed a day or two later by an eruption of small blisters, which rapidly burst to leave a shallow, weeping, painful ulcer. In severe cases, there may be a mild fever, and the lymph nodes in the neck may become tender and enlarged.

INVESTIGATIONS: None normally necessary, but if required the diagnosis can be confirmed by taking special swabs from the sore.

TREATMENT: If treated by appropriate creams and lotions immediately the redness and discomfort is felt and before the blisters form, it may be possible to stop further progress. Once the cold sore is established, a cure is not normally possible, but drying, antiseptic and anaesthetic creams or lotions may be used. Patients who are severely affected on a regular basis may use expensive aciclovir or famciclovir tablets continuously to prevent infections.

COMPLICATIONS: An additional bacterial infection, is the only common complication.

PROGNOSIS: The sore heals and the pain eases in about a week. Some patients have only one attack of cold sores in their lives, while others develop one every month. Over many years, most patients find that their attacks become less frequent.

See also Genital Herpes; Whitlow

Colic
See Gallstones; Infantile Colic; Intestinal Colic; Kidney Stone

Colitis
See Irritable Bowel Syndrome; Pseudomembranous Colitis; Ulcerative Colitis

Colles' Fracture

DESCRIPTION: Common fracture of the forearm bones (ulna and radius) which are bent back and broken just above the wrist.

CAUSE: Landing on the outstretched hand during a fall.

SYMPTOMS: Pain, swelling, tenderness and a backwards deformity of the forearm bones just above the wrist.

INVESTIGATIONS: Diagnosed by an X-ray.

TREATMENT: The bones must be put back into place under an anaesthetic and held in position by plaster.

COMPLICATIONS: Persistent deformity if incorrectly aligned.

PROGNOSIS: Normally heal well after six weeks in plaster in an adult, three to four weeks in a child.

See also Fracture; Scaphoid Fracture; Smith's Fracture

Collet-Sicard Syndrome
See Sicard Syndrome

Colo-Rectal Cancer
(Large Bowel Cancer)

DESCRIPTION: Cancer of the large bowel, which forms the last two metres of the intestine.

CAUSE: Absolute cause is unknown, but a low fibre diet may be a factor and there is a family tendency. More common in men, and most develop in the last 10cm of the gut.

SYMPTOMS: Alteration in normal bowel habits, passing blood with the faeces, weight loss, colicky pains in the abdomen and constant tiredness. A large cancer can be felt as a hard lump in the abdomen.

INVESTIGATIONS: A colonoscopy and/or barium enema X-ray will confirm the diagnosis. Blood tests may show anaemia due to the constant slow leaking of blood from the cancer. People with a bad family history can have a faeces sample tested for blood. A positive test is an indication to investigate further.

TREATMENT: Major surgery to remove the cancer, the bowel for some distance above and below the cancer, and the surrounding lymph nodes. Regular examinations of the colon are required lifelong to detect any recurrence.

COMPLICATIONS: Gut obstruction or perforation which allows faeces to leak into the abdomen, and causes peritonitis (see separate entry). Up to 3% of patients may die during or immediately after surgery.

PROGNOSIS: If cancer has not spread away from the large intestine, two out of three patients will survive for five years. If the cancer has spread, the survival rate drops steadily, depending on the degree of spread.

See also Cancer

Colour Blind

DESCRIPTION: The normal form of colour blindness is between red and green, but other colour combinations may be added to these colours.

CAUSE: Inherited, and nearly always occurs in men.

SYMPTOMS: An inability to differentiate between colours, usually red and green. Rarely all colour vision is lost with the patient seeing only black and white.

INVESTIGATIONS: Ishihara test — cards covered in coloured dots, with numbers hidden amongst the dots.

TREATMENT: None available.

COMPLICATIONS: Those planning to work as an electrician or commercial pilot, or in some other areas where colour differentiation is vital, may not be allowed to undertake these careers.

PROGNOSIS: No cure. Usually merely a nuisance. Most patients live happily with the problem, and adapt so completely that they are not aware of its existence.

Coma
(Unconscious)

DESCRIPTION: A state of deep unconsciousness from which the patient cannot be aroused. The brain stops functioning normally and cannot be stimulated.

CAUSE: Very wide range of causes including head injury, bleeding in or around the brain (eg. stroke), brain tumour or infection (eg. meningitis, encephalitis), after an epileptic seizure, overdoses of drugs or alcohol, severe dehydration, very low blood pressure, heart attack or rhythm abnormality, uncontrolled diabetes, severe lung diseases (eg. pneumonia), poisons and numerous other diseases and conditions.

SYMPTOMS: Unrousable loss of consciousness. Depth of coma assessed by the Glasgow coma scale—

EYE OPENING (E)	POINT SCORE
● Spontaneous opening	4
● Open to verbal command	3
● Open to pain	2
● No response	1

MOTOR RESPONSES (M)

● Obeys verbal command	6
● Responds to painful stimuli by:—	
— localises pain	5
— withdraws from painful stimulus	4
— abnormal flexion	3
— extensor response	2
— no response	1

VERBAL RESPONSES (V)

● Oriented and converses	5
● Disoriented and converses	4
● Inappropriate words	3
● Incomprehensible sounds	2
● No response	1

COMA SCORE = E + M + V

3 = very deeply comatose 15 = completely conscious and alert

INVESTIGATIONS: A wide range of blood, urine, X-ray, CT and ultrasound scan, and cerebrospinal fluid (CSF — the fluid around the brain) tests will be performed in order to determine the cause.

TREATMENT: A coma is always serious and needs immediate medical treatment, but correct treatment will depend on identifying the cause.

PROGNOSIS: Depends on cause and very unpredictable. Some comas last for years while others may be quite brief.

See also Concussion; Post Traumatic Cerebral Syndrome; Subarachnoid Haemorrhage; Subdural Haematoma

Common Cold
See Cold, Common

Complex Regional Pain Syndrome Type One
See Reflex Sympathetic Dystrophy Syndrome

Complex Regional Pain Syndrome Type Two
See Causalgia

Concussion

DESCRIPTION: Bruising of part of the brain that can vary in severity from mere giddiness and a headache for an hour or two, to a complete loss of consciousness, sometimes lasting for weeks.

CAUSE: A moderate to severe blow on the head (generally at the back) or a severe shake of the body.

SYMPTOMS: Temporary, partial or complete loss of consciousness, 'seeing stars', shallow breathing, nausea and vomiting, paleness, coldness and clamminess of the skin, blurred or double vision, and possibly loss of memory.

INVESTIGATIONS: Skull X-ray and CT scan may be performed to exclude fracture or other complications, but do not specifically diagnose concussion.

TREATMENT: Lie the patient down, keep them warm and comfortable, apply cold compresses applied to the brow or the site of injury, and do not give anything to eat or drink for the first few hours after the injury. Paracetamol may be used for pain, but aspirin should be avoided. Keep the victim under observation for at least 24 hours for signs of more serious injury.

COMPLICATIONS: There may be slow bleeding into the brain, which can cause problems hours or days later. The symptoms are a worsening headache, continued vomiting, drowsiness, stupor, deliriousness or other mental changes, collapse, fits, blackouts, giddiness, clear or bloodstained fluid draining from the nose or ears. If any of these symptoms occur, get medical advice immediately.

PROGNOSIS: Recovery within a few hours or days normal.

See also Coma; Post Traumatic Cerebral Syndrome; Subarachnoid Haemorrhage; Subdural Haematoma

Condylomata Acuminata
See Genital Warts

Congenital Adrenal Hyperplasia
(Adrenogenital Syndrome)

DESCRIPTION: Condition affecting the adrenal glands which sit on top of each kidney, in which they are over stimulated to produce abnormal steroids in the body which affect sexual development.

CAUSE: Familial (runs in families), but both parents must be carriers for the condition to be present.

SYMPTOMS: In girls the clitoris becomes enlarged, high blood pressure occurs, and at puberty the breasts are very small, pubic hair pattern is masculine, hair may develop excessively on the body, and female characteristics are reduced. A rare form causes excessive development of male characteristics in boys.

INVESTIGATIONS: Diagnosed by specific blood and genetic tests.

TREATMENT: Surgical correction of abnormal genitalia, and medication to correct hormonal imbalances.

COMPLICATIONS: Infertility and confused gender assignment if treated late.

PROGNOSIS: Good results if treated very early. Relatively normal life expectancy.

See also Addison's Disease; Conn Syndrome

Congenital Dislocation of Hip
See Hip Dislocation

Congenital Poikiloderma
See Rothmund-Thomson Syndrome

Congenital Syphilis
See Syphilis

Congenital Varicella Syndrome

DESCRIPTION: Severe viral infection of a pregnant woman and her child.

CAUSE: Varicella zoster (chickenpox virus) infection of a foetus before birth, when the mother develops chickenpox between 13 and 20 weeks of pregnancy.

SYMPTOMS: Thick scars on skin, mental retardation from wasting of the brain, paralysis of varied muscles of the face and elsewhere, eye abnormalities, Horner's syndrome (see separate entry), wasting of limbs and spinal curvature.

INVESTIGATIONS: Diagnosed before birth by ultrasound, chorionic biopsy (taking a sample of the placenta) and amniocentesis (putting a needle into the fluid around the baby).

TREATMENT: Aciclovir is being used experimentally in pregnant women with chickenpox to prevent this complication. May be prevented in future by using a chickenpox vaccine. No treatment available for the child other than correction of deformities if possible.

COMPLICATIONS: Significant risk of death in the foetus.
PROGNOSIS: Damage to child is permanent.
See also Chickenpox, Shingles

Congestive Cardiac Failure
(CCF; Heart Failure; Ventricular Failure)

DESCRIPTION: A failure of the heart to pump blood effectively.

CAUSE: Many conditions including heart attacks, heart infection (see endocarditis; myocarditis; pericarditis), narrowing or leaking of heart valves, high blood pressure, narrowing of the aorta (aortic stenosis), irregular heart rhythm, alcoholic heart damage, severe anaemia and an overactive thyroid gland (hyperthyroidism) may cause cardiac failure. In many elderly patients, there can be a multitude of causes, or no specific cause at all for heart failure. In these cases, the condition is treated as a disease in itself.

SYMPTOMS: Patients complain of being short of breath when exercising or climbing stairs, or in more advanced cases they may be short of breath constantly or only when lying down at night. Other symptoms include a hard dry cough, passing excess urine at night, general tiredness and weakness, a rapid heart rate, weight loss, chest and abdominal discomfort and swelling of the feet, ankles and hands. Severely affected patients may be unable to speak a full sentence without taking a breath and a blue tinge develops on and around the lips.

INVESTIGATIONS: The diagnosis can often be made without resorting to any tests. The exact cause of the CCF may be found by blood tests, chest X-rays and electrocardiograms (ECG). Echocardiograms and cardiac catheterisation (passing a tube through a vein into the heart) are sometimes undertaken if surgical treatment is being contemplated.

TREATMENT: Correction of any specific cause for the heart failure if possible, lowering high blood pressure and controlling any irregular heart rhythm. Sometimes surgical correction of a heart valve deformity is possible. A diet low in salt, and avoiding strenuous exercise can often be beneficial. Medications to remove excess fluid from the body (diuretics) and to strengthen the action of the heart (eg. digoxin, ACE inhibitors) are in common use. More sophisticated drugs are available for use in difficult cases. Oxygen may be supplied to seriously ill patients.

COMPLICATIONS: Angina and a heart attack may occur.

PROGNOSIS: Unless an underlying correctable cause can be found, heart failure cannot be cured, only controlled. The condition usually slowly worsens with time. It may take many years before serious incapacitation or death occurs.

See also Anaemia; Aortic Stenosis; Cor Pulmonale; Endocarditis; Hypertension; Hyperthyroidism; Myocarditis; Pericarditis

Conjunctivitis

DESCRIPTION: Inflammation of the outer surface (cornea) of the eye, due to an allergy (see allergic conjunctivitis entry), or a viral or bacterial infection.

CAUSE: Bacterial — most common form of conjunctivitis. Due to bacteria infecting the thin film of tears that covers the eye. Very easily passed from one person to another (eg. a patient rubs their eyes with a hand, then shakes hands, and the second person then rubs their eyes). Babies suffering from a **blocked tear duct** may have recurrent infections. Tears are produced in the lacrimal gland beyond the outer edge of the eye, move across the eye surface and then through a tiny tube at the inner edge of the eye that leads to the nose. If the duct is too small in an infant, or is blocked by pus or phlegm, the circulation of tears is prevented and infection results.

Viral — any one or more of a number of viruses infecting the cornea. Not quite as easily transmitted as bacterial conjunctivitis.

SYMPTOMS: Bacterial — yellow or green pus forms in the eyes and may stick the eyelids together. The eyes are bloodshot and sore. Almost invariably involves both eyes.

Viral — slight pain or an itch, redness of the eye and often a clear sticky exudate.

INVESTIGATIONS: Rarely, resistant infections make it necessary to take a swab from the eye to determine the exact bacteria or virus responsible.

TREATMENT: Bacterial — antibiotic drops or ointment on a regular basis until the infection clears. A blocked tear duct may be probed and cleared if conjunctivitis persists in a baby for several months, but most grow out of the problem.

Viral — the most difficult form to treat as there is no cure for most viral infections, but Herpes virus infections can be cured by anti-viral drops. Soothing drops and ointment may be used, but time is the main treatment.

COMPLICATIONS: Bacterial — if allowed to persist, may cause scarring of the eye surface and a deterioration in sight.

Viral — none serious.

PROGNOSIS: Bacterial — rapidly cured by antibiotics.

Viral — may persist for several weeks until the body's own defences overcome the infection.

See also Allergic Conjunctivitis; Trachoma and other diseases listed under Eye Diseases

Conn Syndrome
(Aldosteronism; Hyperaldosteronism)

DESCRIPTION: A rare disease due to overactivity of the adrenal glands which sit on top of each kidney.

CAUSE: A tumour in one of the adrenal glands, or other even rarer diseases, causes excessive amounts of the hormone aldosterone to be produced by the gland. Aldosterone controls the amount of salt in the body. If the level of salt in the blood drops, more aldosterone is secreted by the adrenal gland, and it acts on the kidney to reduce the amount being lost in the urine. The tumour is not a cancer, but the increased aldosterone production causes excess salt to be retained in the body.

SYMPTOMS: Excess salt causes high blood pressure, increased urine production, muscle weakness, pins and needles sensations, headache and thirst.

INVESTIGATIONS: Diagnosis confirmed by blood tests, and a CT or MRI scan. Radioactive substances that concentrate in the abnormal adrenal gland may also be given to a patient in whom the disease is suspected, and the degree of concentration of the substance in each adrenal gland can then be measured.

TREATMENT: The tumour of the adrenal gland can be removed surgically. Medications may be required to control the symptoms and high blood pressure before the operation.

COMPLICATIONS: May be the cause of high blood pressure that does not respond to normal treatments.

PROGNOSIS: Most cases can be cured by surgery, while the others can be controlled by medication.

See also Bartter Syndrome; Congenital Adrenal Hyperplasia; Hypertension

Conradi-Hunermann Syndrome

DESCRIPTION: Developmental abnormality of the heart, skin and limbs.

CAUSE: Congenital.

SYMPTOMS: Defect between the two main chambers in the heart (ventricular septal defect), patent ductus arteriosus (see separate entries), unequal limb shortness and large skin pores.

INVESTIGATIONS: X-rays show abnormal bone mineralisation.

TREATMENT: Surgery for heart defects.

PROGNOSIS: No cure.

See also Ventricular Septal Defect

Conrad Syndrome

DESCRIPTION: Developmental abnormality.

CAUSE: Congenital.

SYMPTOMS: Cataracts in the eyes, limb contractures, deafness and mental retardation.

INVESTIGATIONS: Abnormal long bone ends (stippled epiphyses) seen on X-ray.

TREATMENT: Surgery for cataract and limb contractures.

PROGNOSIS: No cure. Reasonable life expectancy.

Constipation

DESCRIPTION: Variation from normal regular bowel habits to infrequent passing of a motion. Normal can vary from two or three times a day to two or three times a week, or even once a week in some individuals. Constipation increases with age and is far more common in the elderly than the young.

Constipation

CAUSE: Hard dry motions are usually due to inadequate fluid intake, eating too much junk food with too little fibre, or lack of exercise. May also be due to repeatedly ignoring signals to pass a motion and allowing the bowel to become distended, which reduces the urge to eliminate and the problem becomes self-perpetuating. Other causes vary from inactivity (invalids in bed for long periods), pregnancy and the side effects of many medications (eg. codeine), to diseases such as an underactive thyroid gland, gut tumours, psychiatric conditions and diabetes.

SYMPTOMS: Infrequent passing of hard faeces. To be medically significant, constipation must cause discomfort in the abdomen, pain around the anus, bleeding, tears (both pronunciations of the word are appropriate), piles or another problem.

INVESTIGATIONS: Extensive investigations (eg. colonoscopy, barium enema X-ray) may be necessary to determine cause in persistent cases.

TREATMENT: Treat cause if possible. Change the diet by avoiding white bread, pastries, biscuits, sweets and chocolates, and adding plenty of fluids and fibre containing foods such as cereals, vegetables and fruit. If necessary, fibre supplements may be used. Laxatives are the next step, but dependence can develop rapidly. They vary in effectiveness and strength, but the weakest ones (eg. paraffin, other oils, senna and cascara) should be tried first. As a last resort, enemas may be used to clear out the lower gut.

COMPLICATIONS: Long term unrelieved constipation may result in megacolon (see separate entry).

PROGNOSIS: Depends on cause, but can usually be well managed by appropriate treatment.

See also Megacolon

Constrictive Pericarditis
See Pericarditis

Contact Dermatitis
(Housewife's Dermatitis; Irritant Eczema)

DESCRIPTION: One of the most common forms of dermatitis.

CAUSE: Soaps, medicated creams, detergents, chemicals, solvents, cosmetics, perfume, jewellery, metals, rubber and plants are the most common substances causing contact dermatitis. Substances that a person has used or touched regularly for many years without any adverse effect may suddenly cause a reaction. This is particularly common with solvents, dyes, rubber, inks and cosmetics. More common on exposed parts of the body, but may occur on other areas if, for example, underclothes are washed in a detergent to which the patient reacts.

SYMPTOMS: The affected area of skin is red, itchy, swollen, burns and may blister. After a few days, it may become crusted and weep.

INVESTIGATIONS: A person's reaction to suspect agents may be undertaken, but these tests, in which a patch of skin is exposed to a substance to test its response, are often inconclusive.

TREATMENT: If the substance causing the dermatitis can be identified and avoided, the problem is solved. Gloves can be used to avoid detergents, soap substitutes used for washing, and changes in occupation to avoid solvents. If the irritating substance can be tracked down, it may be possible to desensitise the patient. The main treatment is a steroid cream, lotion or ointment. Placing a plastic dressing over the dermatitis and cream increases the effectiveness of the treatment. In severe cases, steroids may need to be given in tablet form, or even by injection.

COMPLICATIONS: The dermatitis may become secondarily infected by bacteria, when antibiotics are required.

PROGNOSIS: Provided the causative agent is not touched again, the dermatitis should settle with treatment, and not recur.

See also Dermatitis

Contractural Arachnodactyly
See Beal Syndrome

Conversion Disorder
(Hysteria)

DESCRIPTION: Psychiatric disorder related to stress.

CAUSE: Conversion of inner psychological conflicts into physical symptoms. May be a serious preceding emotional upset. Tends to occur more in the poorly educated and some cultures (eg. southern European, Middle East).

SYMPTOMS: Varying abnormalities of bodily function for no apparent or discoverable reason. Fitting and paralysis are a common effects.

INVESTIGATIONS: All tests normal, including electromyography (electrical testing of muscles) and EEG (electroencephalogram).

TREATMENT: Psychiatric counselling, behaviour modification, and family involvement in socialisation.

COMPLICATIONS: 'Doctor shopping' may result in dependence on sedatives and pain killers.

PROGNOSIS: Long term management difficult, and success depends on combination of psychiatrist, patient and family.

See also Briquet Syndrome; Hypochondriasis; Stress

Cori Syndrome
See Glycogen Storage Diseases

Corneal Dystrophy

DESCRIPTION: Degeneration of the cornea, the clear dome over the pupil and iris (coloured part of the eye), with formation of dots, cysts, cracks or other deformities in the normally clear membrane. Many different subtypes known

Corneal Dystrophy

(eg. Cogan microcystic dystrophy, Reis-Bücklers dystrophy, Meesmann dystrophy, Schnyder dystrophy).

CAUSE: Usually an inherited characteristic.

SYMPTOMS: Deterioration of vision due to damage to, and distortion of, the cornea.

INVESTIGATIONS: Eye examined with a magnifying light (ophthalmoscope) to see corneal damage.

TREATMENT: Surgical replacement of the cornea with a transplanted cornea, or laser destruction of abnormalities in the cornea.

COMPLICATIONS: Significant deterioration in vision may occur, and disease may recur in transplanted cornea.

PROGNOSIS: Good results from treatment. Progressive sight deterioration without treatment.

Corneal Ulcer
See Eye Ulcer

Cor Pulmonale
(Pulmonary Hypertension; Right Heart Failure)

DESCRIPTION: Enlargement of the right side of the heart, which pumps blood through the lungs, and increased blood pressure in the lungs.

CAUSE: Lungs damaged by emphysema (see separate entry), smoking, inhaled coal dust or asbestos, recurrent lung infections or a number of rarer lung diseases may be so abnormal that the blood has difficulty in passing through them. The right side of the heart must work harder to force the blood through the damaged lungs which causes a significant rise in the blood pressure in the right heart and lungs. This causes further damage to arteries and worsens the disease. The heart muscle thickens and enlarges, and because of the lung damage, inadequate oxygen enters the blood, which further compounds the problem.

SYMPTOMS: Patients have a cough that produces clear or blood-stained phlegm, a wheeze, shortness of breath with any exertion and general weakness. In advanced cases the ankles may be swollen, nausea and indigestion may occur, and the liver enlarges.

INVESTIGATIONS: Diagnosed by a chest X-ray and by an electrocardiogram (ECG). Other investigations include cardiac catheterisation (passing a tube through a vein into the heart to measure the blood pressure), echocardiography and angiography.

TREATMENT: Medication can be prescribed to strengthen the heart, open the lungs and cure any lung infection. Physiotherapy can help drain phlegm from the lungs, and oxygen may be used to relieve the shortness of breath.

COMPLICATIONS: Patients are susceptible to lung infections such as bronchitis and pneumonia.

PROGNOSIS: No cure is possible and patients steadily deteriorate over many years to eventually die from heart attacks, pneumonia or other complications of the disease.

See also Congestive Cardiac Failure; Emphysema

Coryza
See Cold, Common

Costen Syndrome

DESCRIPTION: Jaw joint abnormality.

CAUSE: Due to abnormal stress on jaw (temporomandibular) joint and muscles used in chewing.

SYMPTOMS: Ear pain and discomfort, headache in the temples, ringing in the ears (tinnitus), impaired hearing, and top and bottom teeth do not meet properly (malocclusion).

INVESTIGATIONS: X-rays of temporomandibular joint with mouth open and closed show abnormality.

TREATMENT: Dental or surgical correction of malocclusion.

PROGNOSIS: Reasonable results from treatment.

Costochondral Syndrome
See Tietze Syndrome

Cot Death
(SIDS; Sudden Infant Death Syndrome)

DESCRIPTION: Sudden unexpected death of an apparently normal healthy child in whom a subsequent detailed post-mortem examination reveals no cause for the death. Affects two out of every 1000 children between the ages of one month and one year.

CAUSE: Unknown, but there are many theories. It is not infectious or contagious, nor are they due to suffocation, choking or allergies. Occurs in both bottle and breast fed babies and there is no relationship between immunisation and cot death. No evidence that vitamins, dietary supplements or any medication can prevent the syndrome. If one baby in a family dies from cot death, there is some evidence that subsequent babies are at a higher risk. Babies who sleep face down are more susceptible, and it is strongly recommended that babies should never be placed on their stomachs to sleep. Another theory implicates high body temperatures due to over wrapping or dressing a baby, so that it cannot sweat effectively.

SYMPTOMS: A baby is put to bed and some hours later is found dead. There is no evidence of disturbed sleep and no cry is heard.

INVESTIGATIONS: Any tests performed before death are normal, and autopsy results are normal.

TREATMENT: Imperative that parents receive adequate and immediate counselling by trained professionals as they develop an acute sense of guilt, thinking that they are in some way responsible, and fear that someone will blame them for the death of their child due to neglect or mistreatment, but this is not so. Other children in the family will also be affected because they are often unable to understand or accept the tragedy. Some parents have found their

119

child on the verge of death, lying blue in the cot and not breathing, and rousing them has started breathing again. After such an event, these babies can be monitored by a sensing device that sounds an alarm if breathing stops for more than a few seconds. Only a very select group of infants require this type of care.

Cowden Disease
(Multiple Hamartoma Syndrome)

DESCRIPTION: Multiple non-cancerous lumps of overgrown blood vessels (hamartomas) in the stomach.

CAUSE: Inherited.

SYMPTOMS: Abdominal discomfort, vomiting blood, black motions and anaemia from bleeding hamartomas.

INVESTIGATIONS: Diagnosed by gastroscopy and biopsy.

TREATMENT: Destruction of hamartomas by coagulation (electrical burning or laser) through a gastroscope.

COMPLICATIONS: Continued severe bleeding may necessitate removal of part or all of the stomach.

PROGNOSIS: Reasonable.

See also Polyposis Coli

Coxsackie Virus Infection

DESCRIPTION: Virus infections which can cause varied symptoms in different individuals.

CAUSE: The *Coxsackie* virus. There are two main types of *Coxsackie* virus (A and B), but these are further broken down into more than 50 subtypes.

SYMPTOMS: Depends on where the infection occurs. May cause viral meningitis, cold like symptoms, fevers, ulceration of the mouth and throat (**herpangina**), inflammation of the pleura around the lungs (Bornholm disease), hand foot mouth disease (see separate entries), myositis (inflammation of muscles), and inflammation of the heart or the pericardium that surrounds the heart.

INVESTIGATIONS: None usually necessary.

TREATMENT: No cure other than time and rest, but symptoms may be eased by appropriate medication when necessary.

COMPLICATIONS: Rarely, if the heart is infected, it may be permanently damaged.

PROGNOSIS: Most patients recover uneventfully unless the heart is involved.

See also Bornholm Disease; Hand Foot Mouth Disease; Meningitis; Stomatitis

Crabs
(Pubic Pediculosis)

DESCRIPTION: Infestation of the pubic hair with a parasitic insect.

CAUSE: Caused by lice, *Phthirus pubis*, that live by sucking blood from the soft pubic skin. Caught by being in close bodily contact with someone who already has an infestation (eg. during sex), but as the lice can survive away from humans for a time, they can also be caught from borrowed clothing, towels or bedding.

SYMPTOMS: Often there are no symptoms and many people are unaware of its presence. In others the lice cause an itchy rash in the pubic area, which may be raw and bleeding from constant scratching. Secondary skin infections may develop in these sores, and this infection can cause further symptoms including a fever and enlarged glands in the groin.

INVESTIGATIONS: Lice may be seen by examining the pubic hair through a magnifying glass.

TREATMENT: A number of lotions are available to kill the crabs. The affected individual, and all sex partners, must be treated simultaneously to prevent reinfestations occurring. All clothing and bedding must be thoroughly washed in hot water. A repeat treatment after 24 hours and again after seven days is advisable in order to kill any lice that have hatched in the interim.

COMPLICATIONS: Antibiotics may be required to treat secondary infections.

PROGNOSIS: Correct treatment should result in a complete cure.

See also Head Lice

'Crack'
See Cocaine Addiction

Cradle Cap
See Seborrhoeic Eczema

Cramps, Leg and Muscular
See Leg Cramps

Craniopharyngioma

DESCRIPTION: Uncommon slowly growing brain tumour that occurs in the centre of the brain, puts pressure on the optic (vision) nerve, and is more common in children and young adults.

CAUSE: Unknown.

SYMPTOMS: Partial or total blindness in one or both eyes, headache, vomiting, personality and mental changes.

INVESTIGATIONS: Diagnosed by a CT or MRI scan.

TREATMENT: Irradiation and sometimes surgery.

COMPLICATIONS: Short stature, failure of puberty in children and other hormonal abnormalities due to pressure on the pituitary gland.

PROGNOSIS: Treatment is unsatisfactory.

Craniostenosis

DESCRIPTION: Congenital deformity of the head.

CAUSE: Skull fails to grow and expand due to premature fusion of the joints (sutures) between the bones that make up the skull.

SYMPTOMS: Brain damage, mental retardation, convulsions and a small deformed skull.

INVESTIGATIONS: Closed sutures seen on X-ray.
TREATMENT: Sometimes surgical splitting of sutures is attempted, but generally no treatment.
PROGNOSIS: Poor results from surgery. Life expectancy significantly shortened.

Creeping Eruption
See Cutaneous Larva Migrans

CREST Syndrome

DESCRIPTION: Name is an acronym for symptoms. Known as CRST syndrome if oesophagus is not involved.
CAUSE: Unknown.
SYMPTOMS: Calcinosis (the formation of hard calcium containing nodules under the skin), Raynaud's phenomenon (fingers and toes to become cold and blue — see separate entry), oesophageal (Esophageal — American spelling) inflammation causing difficulty in swallowing, Sclerodactyly (thickening and hardening of the skin on the fingers and toes) and Telangiectasia (multiple dilated blood vessels in the skin).
INVESTIGATIONS: Diagnosed by a biopsy of affected tissue.
TREATMENT: Medications to ease symptoms.
COMPLICATIONS: Scleroderma.
PROGNOSIS: No cure. Usually slowly progressive.
See also Scleroderma

Cretinism

DESCRIPTION: Hypothyroidism in a child, which occurs in one in every 4000 births.
CAUSE: The thyroid gland in the front of the neck is responsible for producing a substance called thyroxine which acts on every cell in the body to control the rate at which it works. In cretinism, the thyroid gland fails to function correctly from birth.
SYMPTOMS: Impaired brain development and mental retardation which may be severe.
INVESTIGATIONS: Diagnosed by specific blood tests that are routinely performed on all babies at birth.
TREATMENT: Thyroxine tablets or mixture.
COMPLICATIONS: Usually some degree of brain damage due to lack of thyroxine in the foetus before birth.
PROGNOSIS: Most cretins can function normally in society with their intelligence and functional capacity only slightly below average. No further deterioration once treatment started.
See also Hypothyroidism

Creutzfeldt-Jakob Disease
(CJD; Spongieform Encephalitis)

DESCRIPTION: Prion (virus like) infection of the brain.

CAUSE: Rare spontaneous cases have occurred where the source of infection is unknown, but in more recent times it has been spread by the use of growth hormone extracted from the pituitary gland of corpses, and given to children who have inadequate growth. Rarely, transmission has also occurred through some corneal and meninges organ transplants. In the United Kingdom during the late 1980s and early 1990s, cattle were fed a protein supplement that included the ground up carcasses of sheep. Some of these sheep suffered from a disease called **scrapie**, which was caused by the same prion as CJD. These cattle developed **mad cow disease**, and when slaughtered for consumption by humans, passed on the prion to cause CJD.

SYMPTOMS: May lay dormant for years after the prion enters the body, before attacking the brain. Progressive dementia, tremors, incoordination, drowsiness, emotional instability and speech difficulties.

INVESTIGATIONS: Diagnosis difficult.

TREATMENT: None available.

PROGNOSIS: Leads inevitably to death, often within a year of diagnosis.

See also Kuru

Cri du Chat Syndrome

DESCRIPTION: Brain development abnormality.

CAUSE: Congenital.

SYMPTOMS: Mental retardation, eyes set wide apart in face, small head, round face, low set ears, cat-like cry ('cri du chat') as newborn. Cat cry disappears with age.

INVESTIGATIONS: Chromosome studies show deletion of short arm of 5th chromosome.

TREATMENT: None available.

PROGNOSIS: No cure.

Crigler-Najjar Syndrome

DESCRIPTION: Severe jaundice (yellow skin) that occurs in newborn infants.

CAUSE: The congenital lack of an enzyme from the liver that results in liver failure.

SYMPTOMS: Jaundice only early symptom. May result in permanent brain damage and premature death.

INVESTIGATIONS: Blood tests show abnormal liver function and lack of enzyme.

TREATMENT: Phenobarbitone sometimes slows progression of the disease.

COMPLICATIONS: May be related to Gilbert and Tourette syndromes (see separate entries).

PROGNOSIS: Often poor.

Crocodile Tears Syndrome

DESCRIPTION: Complication of Bell's palsy (see separate entry).

CAUSE: Possibly due to regenerating nerves that normally control salivary glands being misdirected to the tear gland during recovery from Bell's palsy.

SYMPTOMS: Tears pour from affected eye when eating.

INVESTIGATIONS: No diagnostic tests.

TREATMENT: Surgically cutting the responsible abnormal nerve fibres.

PROGNOSIS: Good response to treatment.

See also Bell's Palsy

Crohn's Disease
(Regional Enteritis)

DESCRIPTION: A chronic inflammation and thickening of the wall of the intestine that usually occurs in the lower part of the small intestine (ileum), but may occur anywhere between the stomach and the anus. Usually affects young adults, and despite treatment, often continues for the rest of the patient's life. When the intestine of these patients is examined at operation, segments of bowel from a few centimetres to a metre or more in length are found to have a wall that is several times thicker and much firmer than normal. May vary from a minor irritation to being a very serious disease as patients have episodes of relatively good health for months or years, then become acutely ill again.

CAUSE: Unknown.

SYMPTOMS: Moderate to severe intermittent lower abdominal pain (colic), alternating diarrhoea and constipation (with the diarrhoea being more common), intermittent fever, loss of appetite, passing excess wind and weight loss.

INVESTIGATIONS: Diagnosis confirmed by a barium meal X-ray and follow through, or if the lower intestine (colon) is involved, a barium enema or colonoscopy.

TREATMENT: Surgically removing the worst affected segments of intestine, and controlling diarrhoea and pain with medication, followed by a high-calorie, high-vitamin, low-residue diet with calcium supplements. Vitamin injections are sometimes necessary if food absorption is very poor. Anaemia, dehydration and diarrhoea are signs of a poorly maintained diet. Antibiotics are given to treat bowel infections, and steroids to control flare-ups of the disease.

COMPLICATIONS: In severe cases the bowel may rupture into the bladder, vagina or through the skin around the anus, bowel obstruction may occur, as may bowel perforation and, in rare cases, death.

PROGNOSIS: No permanent cure. Even after extensive surgery, 60% of patients develop new affected segments of intestine. Although the mortality rate of these patients is slightly increased, most live relatively normal and long lives.

Cronkhite-Canada Syndrome

DESCRIPTION: Thickening of the lining of the stomach, small bowel and colon to form non-cancerous polyp-like lumps.

CAUSE: Unknown.

SYMPTOMS: Abdominal discomfort, irregular bowel habits, bleeding from bowel to give dark or black motions. Other symptoms include abnormal skin pigmentation (particularly of the palms and soles), poorly developed finger and toe nails, hair loss and diarrhoea.

INVESTIGATIONS: Diagnosed by gastroscopy or colonoscopy.

TREATMENT: None available.

PROGNOSIS: No cure.

See also Cronkhite Syndrome

Cronkhite Syndrome

DESCRIPTION: Same as Cronkhite-Canada syndrome (see above) but without the bowel polyps.

CAUSE: Unknown.

SYMPTOMS: Abnormal skin pigmentation (particularly of the palms and soles), poorly developed finger and toe nails, hair loss and sometimes diarrhoea.

INVESTIGATIONS: No specific diagnostic test.

TREATMENT: None available.

PROGNOSIS: No cure, but not serious.

See also Cronkhite-Canada Syndrome

'Crotch Rot'
See Tinea Cruris

Croup

DESCRIPTION: Minor respiratory infection of childhood.

CAUSE: Viral infection low down in the throat (pharynx).

SYMPTOMS: Seal-like barking cough, difficulty on breathing in, and excessive chest movement with breathing in a child under five years of age. Usually only a slight fever, and minimal throat pain.

INVESTIGATIONS: When the throat is examined using a mirror it is seen to be red and swollen.

TREATMENT: Nurse the child in a warm, moist, steamy environment (eg. use a vaporiser). Paracetamol for fever or discomfort, and lots of fluid to prevent dehydration. In more serious cases, a steam and oxygen tent may be used in hospital to assist breathing.

COMPLICATIONS: Very rarely, the child may develop severe swelling in the throat that totally obstructs breathing, which is a critical emergency.

PROGNOSIS: Vast majority of children recover spontaneously within a day or two.

Crouzon Syndrome

DESCRIPTION: Developmental abnormality of the face.

CAUSE: Familial.

SYMPTOMS: Abnormal growth and shape of face and skull, protruding eyes, squint and loss of vision in one or both eyes.
INVESTIGATIONS: Skull X-ray abnormal.
TREATMENT: Major facial surgery.
PROGNOSIS: No cure, but reasonable results from surgery, depending on severity of deformities.

CRST Syndrome
See CREST Syndrome

Cryptococcosis
DESCRIPTION: Fungal infection of the lungs.
CAUSE: Infection by the fungus *Cryptococcosis neoformans* which is caught by inhalation of the fungal spores into the lungs. Often carried by pigeons, and found in their droppings, which when dry can be inhaled as a dust.
SYMPTOMS: Often no symptoms. Those with severe infections may have chest pain and a cough. Those with reduced immunity (eg. AIDS) develop pneumonia like symptoms.
INVESTIGATIONS: Diagnosis is difficult. Chest X-ray shows abnormalities, but is not diagnostic. Sputum tests may be positive for the fungus, but are usually negative. Biopsy of lung often necessary to make diagnosis.
TREATMENT: Often none necessary, but in severe cases antifungal medications (eg. amphotericin B, flucytosine) are given.
COMPLICATIONS: May spread from lungs to brain to cause a serious form of encephalitis (see separate entry). Rarely may spread to skin and bones.
PROGNOSIS: Usually settles spontaneously in lungs. May be fatal in brain.
See also Fungal Infection

Cryptogenic Fibrosing Alveolitis
See Idiopathic Pulmonary Fibrosis

Cryptorchidism
See Testicle, Undescended

Cryptosporidiosis
DESCRIPTION: Common parasitic infestation of the gut of humans and animals. Usually only causes symptoms in patients with a damaged immune system (eg. AIDS) or other illnesses.
CAUSE: The parasite *Cryptosporidium* which spreads from animals to humans in water contaminated by faeces.
SYMPTOMS: Often minimal symptoms, but when they occur may include watery diarrhoea, belly discomfort and pains, and less commonly weight loss, nausea and a mild fever.

INVESTIGATIONS: Diagnosis made by examining a sample of faeces under a microscope.
TREATMENT: Low fat diet, medications to ease diarrhoea and plenty of fluid. No medication is effective against the parasite itself.
COMPLICATIONS: None significant.
PROGNOSIS: Very good.
See also Campylobacter Enteritis; Shigellosis

Cubital Tunnel Syndrome

DESCRIPTION: Damage to one of the nerves supplying the forearm and hand. Often both sides affected.
CAUSE: Due to the the ulnar nerve becoming trapped under muscles below the elbow, sometimes after an injury, but often for no apparent reason.
SYMPTOMS: Loss of sensation in the little (5th.) finger and half of the ring (4th.) finger, and wasting and weakness of some muscles to and in the hand.
INVESTIGATIONS: X-ray usually normal, but specific nerve conduction studies and electromyograms (EMG) of muscle function abnormal.
TREATMENT: Surgical release of trapped ulnar nerve.
PROGNOSIS: Good result from treatment.
See also Carpal Tunnel Syndrome

Cushing Syndrome
(Adrenocortical Hyperfunction; Hyperadrenocorticism)

DESCRIPTION: Syndrome resulting from excessive amounts of steroids in the blood.
CAUSE: The hypothalamus is the part of the brain that decides how much natural steroid is required. It sends nerve messages to the pituitary gland, which sits under the centre of the brain and it sends a chemical message to the adrenal glands that sit on top of each kidney. These produce the steroids required by the body. Tumours or overactivity (may be triggered by pregnancy or stress) in the hypothalamus, pituitary gland or adrenal gland can result in the overproduction of steroids. May also be due to taking excessive amounts of steroids (eg. prednisone) for medical reasons.
SYMPTOMS: Fat face, fatty deposits on the upper back (called a buffalo hump), obesity of the abdomen and chest with thin arms and legs, high blood pressure, impotence, cessation of menstrual periods, skin infections and pimples, headaches, backache, excess hair growth on the face and body, mood changes, excessive bruising, thinning of the bones (osteoporosis — which can cause bones to fracture easily), stretch marks on the breasts and abdomen, kidney stones, and generalised weakness.
INVESTIGATIONS: Complex blood tests can confirm the diagnosis, but finding the cause can be very difficult, and CT scans and magnetic resonance imaging (MRI) may be used to find very small tumours.
TREATMENT: If a tumour can be found in the adrenal or pituitary gland, it is surgically removed. Other treatments include irradiation of the pituitary gland,

or removal of both adrenal glands. Drug treatment is generally unsuccessful, but if both adrenal glands are removed it is necessary to supply steroids and other hormones by taking tablets or having injections regularly. If due to taking steroid medication, the dosage of this should be reduced if possible.

COMPLICATIONS: Strokes, heart attacks, broken bones, diabetes, increased susceptibility to infections (particularly of the skin and urine), and psychiatric diseases. Nelson syndrome (see separate entry) is a complication of treatment.

PROGNOSIS: Depends on its cause. Some tumours of the adrenal or pituitary glands are very aggressive and spread to other areas to continue the syndrome, and these patients have a poor life expectancy. In others, a lifelong cure may be obtained by removing a localised tumour. If caused by excessive steroid medication, the syndrome is cured by stopping the medication, but the patient may require the steroids for control of asthma, rheumatoid arthritis or other diseases, and they must tread a very narrow path between the side effects of the medication and the necessary treatment of a disease.

See also Nelson Syndrome; Pseudocushing Syndrome

Cutaneous Larva Migrans
(Creeping Eruption)

DESCRIPTION: Skin infestation by a larval nematode worm.

CAUSE: The burrowing of hookworm larvae through the skin. The larvae hatch from dog or cat faeces, mature in the soil and then penetrate human skin.

SYMPTOMS: Several centimetre long red, very itchy, twisting tracks in and under the skin. Large blisters may form later.

INVESTIGATIONS: None normally necessary, but skin biopsy sometimes diagnostic.

TREATMENT: Medication by mouth and ointment to kill the larvae, and other creams to ease the skin irritation.

COMPLICATIONS: Secondary bacterial infection of skin damaged by both the larvae and scratching.

PROGNOSIS: Larvae cannot mature in humans, die after several weeks, and the skin tracks slowly heal.

See also Visceral Larva Migrans

Cutaneous Leischmaniasis
(Chiclero's Ulcers; Oriental Sore; Uta)

DESCRIPTION: Ulcerating skin infection caused by a protozoan (single cell animal).

CAUSE: Infection by the protozoan *Leischmania tropica*, *Leischmania aethiopica*, *Leischmania mexicana*, or *Leischmania peruviana* depending upon the geographic location. Transmitted from one person to another by sandflies. Occurs throughout the tropics in Asia, Africa and particularly America.

SYMPTOMS: Depending upon responsible protozoan may cause a self healing ulcer (Oriental sore), persistent multiple mutilating sores and ulcers (Chiclero's ulcers), or widespread non-ulcerating plaques on the skin.

INVESTIGATIONS: Smears taken from ulcer edge show the protozoan under a microscope. Specific blood tests may be positive.

TREATMENT: Single ulcers treated with heat packs, cryotherapy (freezing), radiotherapy or specific ointments. Widespread disease is difficult to treat but numerous medications may be tried. Antibiotics are given for secondary infections.

COMPLICATIONS: Secondary bacterial infection of sores can allow rapid spread of protozoan and gross disfigurement.

PROGNOSIS: Depends on infecting organism and form of disease. Single ulcers often heal after a few months, but widespread disease may be steadily progressive without treatment.

See also Kala-Azar; Mucocutaneous Leischmaniasis

Cutis Hyperelastica
See Ehlers-Danlos Syndrome

Cutting Teeth
See Teething

CVA
See Stroke

Cyanide Poisoning

DESCRIPTION: Inhaling or swallowing compounds containing cyanide.

CAUSE: Cyanide is used in fumigation, photography, electroplating, rubber processing, metal cleaning and some other industries. It is found naturally in numerous seeds including cherry, plum, peach, pear and apricot. Lethal dose depends on form, but is about 250mg. of sodium cyanide.

SYMPTOMS: Headache, fainting, dizziness, anxiety, rapid heart rate, burning in the mouth and throat, shortness of breath, high blood pressure, nausea, vomiting, bitter almond breath, coma, convulsions and death.

INVESTIGATIONS: Detected by specific blood tests.

TREATMENT: Some medications may be effective as an antidote. Pure oxygen should be given by mask.

PROGNOSIS: Depends on age, weight and fitness of patient, and dose of cyanide.

Cyclothymic Disorder
See Depression

Cyst
See Baker's Cyst; Bartholin's Cyst; Hydatid Cyst; Lipoma; Meibomian Cyst; Nabothian Cyst; Ovarian Cyst; Polycystic Kidney; Polycystic Ovarian Syndrome; Sebaceous Cyst

Cystic Duct Syndrome

DESCRIPTION: Condition of the cystic duct (which drains the gall bladder) that mimics gallstones. The gall bladder is normal.

CAUSE: Inflammation or infection of the cystic duct causing obstruction of the duct by scar tissue or swelling.

SYMPTOMS: Pain in the upper right abdomen with eating due to gall bladder contraction, and pale fatty poorly digested faeces due to lack of bile.

INVESTIGATIONS: X-ray of gall bladder (cholangiogram) abnormal.

TREATMENT: Removal of the gall bladder and cystic duct (cholecystectomy).

PROGNOSIS: Good result from surgery.

See also Gallstones

Cystic Fibrosis
(Fibrocystic Disease)

DESCRIPTION: A congenital disease of all mucus glands in the body due to genetic damage that occurs in 1:2000 children.

CAUSE: No known cause, and there is nothing parents can do to prevent the occurrence of the disease.

SYMPTOMS: Extremely varied symptoms because it is a disease of mucus glands throughout the body, but particularly those in the lungs and gut. In the lungs, the mucus becomes thick and sticky, the lungs clog up, become infected, and the lung tissue is destroyed. In the gut, excess mucus is produced, food cannot be absorbed correctly, and diarrhoea occurs. Because the glands in the reproductive organs are involved, these patients are usually sterile, and so cannot pass the disease on to their children. Glands in the skin produce sweat that is far saltier than that of normal people.

INVESTIGATIONS: Diagnosed by measuring the amount of salt in sweat, chest X-rays, abnormal lung function tests, and faeces tests. The condition cannot be detected before birth, but screening of parents to see if they are potential carriers is sometimes successful.

TREATMENT: Physiotherapy several times every day to clear the lungs is critical. Antibiotics are used to treat lung infection, and medications to open up the airways (bronchodilators) and loosen the thick mucus (mucolytics) are prescribed. Regular vaccination against lung infections are essential. As a final solution, a heart and lung transplant may be performed.

COMPLICATIONS: Severe lung infections, lung damage and heart failure.

PROGNOSIS: No cure. Outcome depends on the patient's dedication to following a comprehensive treatment program. Many survive into their 30s with continued intensive therapy.

Cystinosis

DESCRIPTION: Very rare disorder that results in the deposition of crystals of cystine in the eyes, bone marrow, lymph nodes, white blood cells, kidneys and other organs. Two forms of the disease — infantile which is widespread, and adult which affects only the eyes.

CAUSE: Familial (runs in families).

SYMPTOMS: Infants are very small, feverish, vomit constantly, pass excess urine and become dehydrated.

Adults have eye pain, intolerance to bright light and headaches.

INVESTIGATIONS: Diagnosis is difficult and is confirmed by seeing crystals in white blood cells when blood sample is examined under a microscope.

TREATMENT: No effective treatment.

COMPLICATIONS: Kidney failure may be a late complication in adults.

PROGNOSIS: Death from kidney failure before the age of ten is usual with infant form. Some reduction in life expectancy with adult form.

Cystitis
(Bladder Infection)

DESCRIPTION: An infection of the urinary bladder that usually occurs in women, with less than 10% occurring in men because the longer length of their urethra (the tube leading from the bladder to the outside).

CAUSE: A bacterial infection that can enter the bladder by coming up the urethra from outside the body, or through the bloodstream to the kidneys and then the bladder. Entry from the outside is far more common, and often due to irritation of the urethra with sex. Slackness of the muscle ring that controls the release of urine from the bladder can also allow bacteria to enter the bladder. This damage may be caused by childbirth or prolapse of the womb, and may eventually cause incontinence with a cough or laugh.

SYMPTOMS: Burning pain on passing urine, pain in the pelvis, the desire to pass urine very frequently and blood may be seen in the urine.

INVESTIGATIONS: Urine culture to identify the responsible bacteria and correct antibiotic. Further investigations such as X-rays and ultrasound scans of the bladder and kidneys may be performed, to exclude more serious causes of recurrent cystitis.

TREATMENT: Appropriate antibiotic tablets for a week or two, and urinary alkalinisers (in the form of a powder that makes a fizzy drink). Drinking extra fluid will help wash the infection out of the bladder. Passing urine immediately after sex sometimes prevents infections.

COMPLICATIONS: May spread up the ureters to the kidneys to cause acute pyelonephritis.

PROGNOSIS: Usually easily and effectively treated.

See also Pyelonephritis, Acute

Cystitis, Interstitial
See Interstitial Cystitis

Cystocoele
See Vaginal Prolapse

Cytomegalovirus Infection
(CMV)

DESCRIPTION: Extremely common viral infection affecting between 10% and 25% of the entire population at any one time. Infection rate may be in excess of 80% in homosexual men. May be a serious illness in patients who have reduced immunity due to treatment with cytotoxic drugs for cancer, have suffered other serious illnesses, are anaemic, suffering from AIDS or other immune affecting diseases, or who are extremely run-down from stress or overwork.

CAUSE: Infection with the cytomegalovirus (CMV). Normally passes from one person to another in saliva or as droplets in the breath, but may also spread through blood transfusions or sexual contact.

SYMPTOMS: In all but a tiny percentage of infected people, there are absolutely no symptoms, and they appear and feel totally well. Adults with reduced immunity develop a fever, headaches, overwhelming tiredness, muscle and joint pains, enlarged lymph nodes and a tender liver.

INVESTIGATIONS: Detected by specific blood tests, and the virus may be found in sputum, saliva, urine and other body fluids.

TREATMENT: No specific treatment. Aspirin and/or paracetamol are used to control fever and pain, and prolonged rest is required for recovery.

COMPLICATIONS: In patients with severely reduced immunity, pneumonia and hepatitis may develop. If a pregnant woman with reduced immunity acquires a significant CMV infection, her baby may be affected in the womb and be born with liver damage (jaundice), enlarged liver and spleen, poor ability to clot blood, bruises, mental retardation, and one in six are deaf.

PROGNOSIS: Uneventful recovery expected in normal patients. In immune compromised patients, pneumonia and hepatitis may be fatal.

D

da Costa Syndrome
(Effort Syndrome)

DESCRIPTION: Heart function abnormality.

CAUSE: Psychiatric disorder with no underlying cause.

SYMPTOMS: Persistent palpitations triggered by anxiety, exercise or stress.

INVESTIGATIONS: ECG (electrocardiograph) abnormal, and blood pressure shows a high systolic and low diastolic reading (wide pulse pressure).

TREATMENT: Resistant to psychiatric care. Beta-blocker medications used.

PROGNOSIS: Symptoms usually controlled by medication, but cure is difficult.

Dandruff

DESCRIPTION: A very common form of scalp irritation.

CAUSE: Over a period of a few weeks, new cells are produced deep in the skin, slowly move out to the surface, thin out to form a hard scaly layer, and eventually slough off. Dandruff is an acceleration of this process in which the rate at which cells are produced on the scalp is increased. A fungal infection of the scalp may cause this increased rate of cell loss. Emotional stress, overworking, hot climates and a poor diet all aggravate dandruff.

SYMPTOMS: Excess cell production results in the formation of skin flakes on the scalp. The underlying skin may be inflamed and itchy.

INVESTIGATIONS: Severe cases of dandruff may need to be differentiated from other skin diseases such as psoriasis by a biopsy.

TREATMENT: Good scalp hygiene, and an anti-dandruff lotion or shampoo. Resistant cases may be helped by steroid scalp lotions and antifungal lotions or gels.

COMPLICATIONS: None significant.

PROGNOSIS: Most patients have recurrences, with bad and good periods, often for no apparent reason. Control is normally possible.

See also Seborrhoeic Eczema

Dandy Syndrome

DESCRIPTION: Very rare abnormality of the inner ear.

CAUSE: Damage to the vestibular apparatus (balance and position mechanism) in both inner ears.

SYMPTOMS: Total loss of balance, horizon bounces up and down as patient walks, and dizziness.

INVESTIGATIONS: CT or MRI scan of inner ear may be abnormal.

TREATMENT: None available. Dizziness may be eased by medication.

PROGNOSIS: No cure.

Dandy-Walker Syndrome

DESCRIPTION: Brain developmental abnormality.

CAUSE: Failure of the central portion of the cerebellum (lower back part of brain) to develop.

SYMPTOMS: Very large head, vomiting, irritability, poor head control, cleft palate, and abnormal side to side eye movements (nystagmus). Some patients have an abnormal way of walking (gait), headaches, multiple cysts in the kidneys, abnormal lumbar vertebrae, subnormal mentality and delayed muscle control.

INVESTIGATIONS: MRI and CT scans of the skull are abnormal.

TREATMENT: Brain surgery may prevent further deterioration of symptoms.

PROGNOSIS: No cure.

Darier's Disease

DESCRIPTION: Rare skin condition that usually starts between 8 and 15 years of age, and affects the face, back, scalp, groin and armpits.

CAUSE: Inherited disorder causing the production of abnormal keratin (hardening substance in skin). May flare with heat and sweating.

SYMPTOMS: Small, brown, firm lumps on the skin that slowly enlarge and become covered in greasy scales. May appear as small pits on the soles and palms.

INVESTIGATIONS: Diagnosed by skin biopsy.

TREATMENT: Salicylic acid and retinoic acid ointments.

COMPLICATIONS: Lumps in the skin may merge together to form a hard crusted plaque. Nails become brittle, ridged and discoloured in persistent cases. Secondary bacterial infections may occur. May be associated with subnormal mentality and reduced height in some patients.

PROGNOSIS: May settle spontaneously in early stages. Prolonged disease difficult to control.

Deaf

See Acoustic Neuroma; Alport Syndrome; Cholesteatoma; Congenital Syphilis; Ear Wax; Eustachian Tube Blockage; Jervell-Lange-Nielsen Syndrome; Johanson-Blizzard Syndrome; Leopard Syndrome; Maroteaux-Lamy Syndrome; Ménière's Disease; Morquio Syndrome; Osteogenesis Imperfecta; Otityis Media; Oto-Palatal-Digital Syndrome; Otosclerosis; Pendred Syndrome; Refsum Syndrome; Treacher-Collins Syndrome; Tympanic Rupture; Usher Syndrome; Vogt-Koyanagi-Harada Syndrome; Waardenburg-Klein Syndrome etc.

de Clérambault Syndrome

See Clérambault Syndrome

Deep Vein Thrombosis
(DVT)

DESCRIPTION: Blood clot (thrombosis) in one of the veins inside the calf or thigh muscles.

CAUSE: May occur after surgery, with heart failure, poor circulation, cancer, varicose veins, or as an uncommon side effect of oral contraceptives.

SYMPTOMS: Pain and tightness in the calf which is worse when walking.

INVESTIGATIONS: Diagnosed by ultrasound scan or special X-ray (venogram) of the leg. Blood tests can show that there is a blood clot somewhere in the body, but not its location.

TREATMENT: Anticoagulant drugs, elevation of the the legs, firm elastic stockings and strict bed rest. In complex or persistent cases surgery may be undertaken to remove the clot or prevent its spread to the lungs. As a form of prevention, patients having major operations may be given special stockings to wear during and after the operation, the foot of the bed may be elevated, and leg exercises encouraged. After a thrombosis, further clots may be prevented by low dose aspirin or medications such as warfarin.

COMPLICATIONS: If the clot in the veins becomes fragile, small pieces may break off and travel to the heart and then into the lungs where one of the small lung (pulmonary) arteries becomes blocked (pulmonary embolism). The lung beyond this blockage then dies which may have serious effects for the patient. Women who have had blood clots anywhere in the body should not use the contraceptive pill.

PROGNOSIS: With appropriate treatment, most patients recover in four to six weeks without complications.

See also Postphlebitic Syndrome; Pulmonary Embolism; Superficial Venous Thrombosis; Thrombosis

Defibrination Syndrome

DESCRIPTION: Life threatening abnormality of blood clotting.

CAUSE: Very severe infection or shock after an accident may cause inappropriate blood clotting within arteries and veins. This causes the level of fibrinogen in the blood to drop to a low level. Fibrinogen is essential for the clotting of blood, so patients with this critical problem, then start to bleed profusely. Rarely may follow childbirth.

SYMPTOMS: After suffering excessive internal clotting which may affect their brain, heart, lungs, limbs and other organs, patients start to bleed excessively internally (eg. into the gut and kidney), externally (eg. intractable nose bleeds) and into the skin (eg. massive bruises).

INVESTIGATIONS: Diagnosed by specific blood tests.

TREATMENT: Rapid transfusion of freshly donated compatible blood and other blood concentrates to stop bleeding, heparin given intravenously to stop abnormal clotting, and treating the underlying cause of the syndrome if possible.

COMPLICATIONS: Permanent organ damage common in survivors.

PROGNOSIS: Significant mortality rate.

See also Shock

Dehydration

DESCRIPTION: Occurs when there is inadequate water in the body, which is normally 80% water.

CAUSE: Severe diarrhoea and/or vomiting, water deprivation, burns, diabetes mellitus, diabetes insipidus, peritonitis and kidney disease.

SYMPTOMS: Thirst, dry mouth, slack skin, sunken eyes, weight loss, rapid heart rate, weakness and lethargy.

INVESTIGATIONS: Blood tests can accurately determine the degree of dehydration.

TREATMENT: Giving a solution of water and electrolytes (vital elements) by mouth if possible, or intravenously. In an emergency, a mixture containing a level teaspoon of salt and eight level teaspoons of sugar or glucose into a litre of boiled water may be given by mouth. Plain water should not be given as it will pass straight through the body.

COMPLICATIONS: Because of their lower body weight, children will dehydrate far more rapidly than adults.

PROGNOSIS: A decrease of 5% in water volume can cause significant disease, and a 10% loss may be fatal in children. Very good response to correct treatment.

Deja Vu

DESCRIPTION: Abnormal feeling of familiarity.

CAUSE: Occurs in normal people but is more commonly associated with some types of epilepsy or psychiatric disorders.

SYMPTOMS: Feeling of intense familiarity when confronted with someone, something, or a place that is actually totally unknown.

INVESTIGATIONS: EEG (electroencephalogram) to measure brain activity if symptoms are recurrent and distressing.

TREATMENT: Epilepsy medications in very low doses usually very effective.

PROGNOSIS: Very good.

See also Epilepsy

de Lange Syndrome
(Amsterdam Dwarf; Brachmann-de Lange Syndrome; Lange Syndrome)

DESCRIPTION: Developmental dwarfism.

CAUSE: Congenital.

SYMPTOMS: Small head, severe mental retardation, bushy eyebrows that meet in centre, low birth weight and failure to thrive, low hair line, and excess hair on the skin.

INVESTIGATIONS: None specific.

TREATMENT: None available.

COMPLICATIONS: Skeletal malformations.

PROGNOSIS: Rarely survive beyond 10 years.

Delirium Tremens
(DTs)

DESCRIPTION: Complication of alcoholism.

CAUSE: Occurs when an alcoholic is deprived of alcohol and may start within 24 to 72 hours.

SYMPTOMS: Mental confusion, tremor, hallucinations, excessive sensitivity to all sensations, body chemistry disturbances, sweating, occasionally seizures and rarely death.

INVESTIGATIONS: Body chemistry disorders detected by blood tests.

TREATMENT: Medications to reverse adverse effects of alcohol withdrawal, intravenous fluids and observation in hospital.

PROGNOSIS: Successfully managed in hospital, but may be dangerous in other situations.

See also Alcoholism

Dementia
('Second Childhood')

DESCRIPTION: A progressive deterioration of mental capacity in the elderly with a gradual onset and steady deterioration over many years.

CAUSE: No specific cause, but may be worsened by arteriosclerosis (hardening of the arteries), and alcohol or drug abuse.

SYMPTOMS: Deterioration in intellect, leading to confusion, irrational behaviour, inappropriate reactions, poor or jumbled speech patterns, hallucinations (both visual and auditory), and loss of short term memory. Some patients become uninhibited in their language and habits, and may act in a socially unacceptable manner. Symptoms are often worse at night.

INVESTIGATIONS: No diagnostic blood or other tests. In advanced stages, a CT scan of the brain will show abnormalities.

TREATMENT: The patient should be kept in a pleasant, safe, non-threatening environment with adequate medical, nursing, physiotherapy, occupational therapy and general support services. Medications may be given for irrational behaviour, hallucinations and violent tempers, but do not affect the disease process.

COMPLICATIONS: Death from pneumonia, caused by immobility.

PROGNOSIS: No cure. Patients progressively deteriorate until death.

See also Alzheimer's Disease; Organic Brain Syndrome; Pick's Disease

Demons-Meigs Syndrome
See Meigs Syndrome

Denervation Syndrome

DESCRIPTION: Complication of surgery to the stomach or oesophagus.

CAUSE: Damage to the vagus nerve that supplies the stomach.

SYMPTOMS: Gas bloat syndrome (see separate entry), diarrhoea, stomach dilatation, and failure of the stomach to empty at the normal rate.

INVESTIGATIONS: Gastroscopy abnormal.

TREATMENT: Diet, and surgery to open the valve (pylorus) that controls drainage from the stomach (pyloroplasty).

PROGNOSIS: Management difficult.

See also Gas Bloat Syndrome

Dengue Fever
(Breakbone Fever)

DESCRIPTION: Mosquito spread generalised viral infection that is very common in Indonesia, New Guinea, Vanuatu and Fiji, as well as tropical countries in other parts of the world.

CAUSE: Virus spread from person to person by the bite of the *Aedes* mosquito. Incubation period is usually three to seven days, but may stretch out to two weeks.

SYMPTOMS: Sudden onset of a high fever, chills, and a severe aching of the back, head and legs (thus breakbone fever). Over the next few days a sore throat, blotchy skin and depression develop. These symptoms then totally cease for a day or two, before the second phase of the disease commences. This is similar to the first phase, but generally milder, and is usually accompanied by a rash that starts on the hands and feet and spreads to cover the entire body with the exception of the face. In severe cases, skin bleeding, and bleeding into the gut with accompanying diarrhoea can occur.

INVESTIGATIONS: Diagnosis confirmed by specific blood tests.

TREATMENT: No cure. Aspirin and anti-inflammatories (eg. ibuprofen) are given for fevers and pains, and prolonged rest is required. A vaccine is not yet available.

COMPLICATIONS: Patients may become dehydrated because of diarrhoea, and require fluid replacement.

PROGNOSIS: Complete recovery occurs, but may take several months.

Depression
(Affective Disorder; Melancholia; Nervous Breakdown)

DESCRIPTION: A disease, not just a state of mind, that affects 30% of people at some time in their life. Patients are not able to pull themselves together and overcome the depression without medical aid, although a determination to improve the situation helps the outcome.

CAUSE: An imbalance of chemicals that normally occur in the brain to control mood. If too much of one chemical is produced, the patient becomes depressed — if too much of another, the patient becomes manic. May be associated with hormonal changes that occur during a woman's menstrual cycle or with menopause.

SYMPTOMS: There are two types of depression with different causes—

Endogenous depression — no obvious reason for the constant unhappiness, and patients slowly become sadder and sadder, more irritable, unable to sleep, lose appetite and weight, and feel there is no purpose in living. They may feel unnecessarily guilty, have a very poor opinion of themselves, feel life is hopeless and find it difficult to think or concentrate. After several months they usually improve, but sometimes it can take years. When they do start to improve, some patients with depression go too far the other way and become over-happy or manic. These patients are said to be **manic depressive**, have **bipolar personality** (generally severe swings of mood) or **cyclothymic disorder** (milder mood changes).

Reactive depression — the sadness that occurs after a death in the family, loss of a job, a marriage break-up or other disaster. Patients are depressed for a definite reason, and with time, will be often be able to cope with the situation, although some patients do require medical help.

INVESTIGATIONS: No diagnostic blood tests or brain scans, and diagnosis depends on the clinical acumen of the doctor.

TREATMENT: Numerous medications that control the production or activity of the depressing chemicals in the brain are available (eg. Prozac, Aropax, Zoloft, Sinequan, Prothiaden, Efexor, Serzone), but most antidepressant drugs work slowly over several weeks. Hospitalisation in order to use high doses of drugs or other treatments, and to protect the patient from the possibility of suicide, is sometimes necessary when the disease is first diagnosed. The other form of treatment used is shock therapy (electroconvulsive therapy — ECT), which is a safe and often very effective method of giving relief to patients with severe chronic depression.

COMPLICATIONS: Untreated depression may lead to attempted or actual suicide, which can be seen as a desperate plea for help.

PROGNOSIS: Medication and counselling by a general practitioner or psychiatrist will control the vast majority of cases.

See also Bipolar Affective Disorder; Mania; Postnatal Depression; Seasonal Affective Disorder

de Quervain's Tenosynovitis
(de Quervain's Tenovaginitis)

DESCRIPTION: Inflammatory condition of the wrist.

CAUSE: Caused by repetitive wrist action.

SYMPTOMS: The prominent bone (radial styloid) at the side of the wrist above the thumb becomes painful, tender and swollen, and there is pain with wrist movement.

INVESTIGATIONS: None necessary.

TREATMENT: Anti-inflammatory medications, rest (in a splint if necessary), and steroid injections around radial styloid.

PROGNOSIS: Good response to treatment.

See also Carpal Tunnel Syndrome

de Quervain's Tenovaginitis
See de Quervain's Tenosynovitis

de Quervain's Thyroiditis
(Sub-acute Thyroiditis)

DESCRIPTION: A relatively common form of thyroid gland inflammation.

CAUSE: Occurs most commonly in women between 25 and 45 and is thought to be the result of a viral infection.

SYMPTOMS: Painful swelling of the thyroid gland at the front of the neck, pain around the neck to the ears, difficulty in swallowing and symptoms of hyperthyroidism (see separate entry) such as rapid heart rate and excess sweating.

INVESTIGATIONS: Diagnosed by blood tests and biopsy of the thyroid gland.

TREATMENT: There is no specific cure available. Aspirin usually relieves the pain and swelling, and propranolol controls the thyrotoxicosis.

COMPLICATIONS: Heart damage from the excess production of thyroid hormone.

PROGNOSIS: Satisfactory control usually possible, and settles spontaneously with time.

See also Hyperthyroidism; Thyroiditis

Dermatitis

DESCRIPTION: Any inflammation of the skin. There are many different types of dermatitis.

CAUSE: Often very difficult to determine, for although the skin is the most visible of our organs, its diseases are very diverse and often difficult to diagnose.

SYMPTOMS: Almost any rash can be called dermatitis.

INVESTIGATIONS: Often none necessary as simple treatments work. If necessary, biopsy, skin and blood tests will be performed.

TREATMENT: In most cases simple steroid anti-inflammatory creams will control dermatitis.

COMPLICATIONS: May become persistent and widespread.

PROGNOSIS: Depends on type and cause.

See also Contact Dermatitis; Dermatitis Artefacta; Dermatitis Herpetiformis; Dermatitis Medicamentosa; Eczema; Exfoliative Dermatitis; Neurodermatitis; Photodermatitis; Psoriasis; Razor Rash; Xeroderma Pigmentosa and other conditions listed under Skin Diseases

Dermatitis Artefacta

DESCRIPTION: A rash that is deliberately self-inflicted to attract attention or obtain special treatment.

CAUSE: Patients may be disturbed psychiatrically, prisoners, deprived of affection or attention, senile or confused. They may use heat, sharp instruments, sandpaper, chemicals or their fingernails to create the rash. Women are five times more likely to have the condition than men.

SYMPTOMS: The rash can be extraordinarily varied in its form, and quite bizarre in its presentation. It usually does not respond to treatment, and occurs on unusual parts of the body.

INVESTIGATIONS: No tests prove any cause for the rash.

TREATMENT: Psychiatric counselling and medication, and dressings that cannot be easily removed by the patient. Plaster casts may occasionally be necessary to stop a patient constantly picking at an ulcer that will not heal.

COMPLICATIONS: The rash may become infected or gangrenous.

PROGNOSIS: If effective psychiatric care given, treatment is usually successful.

See also Dermatitis

Dermatitis, Atopic
See Atopic Eczema

Dermatitis Herpetiformis

DESCRIPTION: An uncommon blistering itch that occurs on the elbows, knees and backside.

CAUSE: Several different causes, including gluten which is found in many cereals.

SYMPTOMS: Small, intensely itchy, fluid-filled blisters on red, inflamed skin. Often appears scratched and bleeding because of the almost irresistible itching.

INVESTIGATIONS: Diagnosed by biopsy of a skin blister.

TREATMENT: Avoiding gluten containing cereals, or using very potent steroid creams or tablets.

COMPLICATIONS: Often persistent.

PROGNOSIS: Can be cured by avoiding any cause that can be discovered, otherwise control may be difficult.

See also Dermatitis

Dermatitis Medicamentosa
(Drug Eruption; Toxic Erythema)

DESCRIPTION: Inflammation of skin.

CAUSE: Abnormal reaction to a medication.

SYMPTOMS: Sudden onset of bright red, itchy rash. Some patients have a fever, tiredness, joint pains, headache and nausea.

INVESTIGATIONS: Diagnosis often difficult, and usually no specific test.

TREATMENT: Stop use of responsible medication, antihistamines for itch, and steroid creams or tablets.

COMPLICATIONS: Blood cell damage, severe allergy reactions (anaphylaxis), kidney and liver damage may occur.

PROGNOSIS: Usually settles with cessation of the responsible medication, but if complications occur, may be serious.

See also Allergy; Dermatitis; Erythema Multiforme

Dermatofibroma
(Histiocytoma)

DESCRIPTION: Common non-cancerous fibrous skin lumps that usually occur on the legs and arms.

CAUSE: Unknown, but may arise at the site of a minor injury such as an insect bite or thorn prick.

SYMPTOMS: Firm yellow-brown nodule in the skin, that if squeezed forms a dimple because the skin is tethered to the nodule.

INVESTIGATIONS: None necessary unless there is concern that it might be cancerous, when it is excised.

TREATMENT: None necessary unless cosmetically unacceptable, when it can be removed surgically, frozen (cryotherapy) with liquid nitrogen or injected with a steroid.

COMPLICATIONS: None significant.

PROGNOSIS: Usually persist for years unless surgically removed.

Dermatomyositis
(Polymyositis)

DESCRIPTION: A rare disease that combines a persistent rash with muscle weakness. When it occurs without the rash (which is present in only 40% of cases) it is called polymyositis.

CAUSE: Unknown. Commonly attacks those in late middle-age.

SYMPTOMS: A gradually progressive weakness and pain of the muscles in the neck, upper arms, shoulder, buttocks and thighs. Patients may also develop a dusky red rash on the cheeks and nose, shoulders and upper chest and back. The eyelids are often swollen and appear bruised. Unusual symptoms include redness and bleeding under the nails, cold hands, and a scaly rash over the knuckles.

INVESTIGATIONS: Diagnosed by blood tests, muscle biopsy and by measuring the muscle's electrical activity.

TREATMENT: Drugs such as steroids, methotrexate and azathioprine are commonly used.

COMPLICATIONS: Ten percent risk of developing cancer. Rare complications may involve the heart and lungs.

PROGNOSIS: No cure. Most patients can lead a relatively normal life, although a minority are disabled by muscle weakness.

See also diseases listed under Myositis

de Toni-Fanconi-Debré syndrome
See Fanconi Syndrome

Devic's Disease
(Devic Syndrome; Neuromyelitis Optica)

DESCRIPTION: Inflammatory condition of spinal cord and optic (eye) nerve that usually occurs in Asians.

CAUSE: Autoimmune condition often associated with a recent viral or bacterial infection.

SYMPTOMS: Eye pain and vision disturbances, neck or back pain, followed by altered sensations (eg. pins and needles, loss of sense of touch) and muscle weakness in the body below the area of back pain.

INVESTIGATIONS: Diagnosed by an MRI scan.

TREATMENT: Steroids may be tried, but are often ineffective.

PROGNOSIS: May be some recovery, but effects usually permanent.

See also Transverse Myelitis

Diabetes Insipidus

DESCRIPTION: Form of failure of the pituitary gland which lies in the centre of the brain. Diabetes insipidus has nothing to do with the common sugar diabetes (diabetes mellitus). Diabetes means frequent and excessive passing of urine, and it is this symptom that the victims of both diseases share.

CAUSE: An uncommon disease that may be triggered by a head injury, or develop slowly over many months because of a brain infection, tumour or stroke. It is caused by a failure of the pituitary gland to produce the hormone vasopressin that controls the rate at which the kidney produces urine. Without this hormone, the kidney constantly produces large amounts of dilute urine.

SYMPTOMS: Patients have a huge urine output, are constantly thirsty, lose weight, develop headaches and muscle pains, become easily dehydrated, and may have an irregular heart beat.

INVESTIGATIONS: Diagnosed by a series of ingenious blood and urine tests after exposing the patient to varying degrees of water intake.

TREATMENT: Controlled by regular injections of vasopressin which last from one to three days. Milder cases can be treated with a nasal spray containing a synthetic form of vasopressin, but this only lasts for a few hours.

COMPLICATIONS: A rare variation of diabetes insipidus occurs when the kidney fails to respond to vasopressin, even when it is being produced normally by the pituitary gland.

PROGNOSIS: Cannot be cured, but usually well controlled. Some cases do settle spontaneously, but most patients require life long treatment.

Diabetes Mellitus
(Sugar Diabetes)

DESCRIPTION: Excessive levels of glucose in the blood. Glucose is used as fuel by every cell in the body. When glucose is eaten, it is absorbed into the blood from the small intestine. Once it reaches a cell, it must cross the fine membrane that forms its outer skin. This is normally impermeable to all substances, but insulin has the ability to combine with glucose and transport it across the membrane from the blood into the interior of the cell. Insulin is made in the pancreas, which sits in the centre of the abdomen. There are two totally different types of diabetes — **juvenile diabetes (type 1 or insulin**

dependent diabetes mellitus — IDDM) and **maturity onset diabetes (type 2 or non-insulin dependent diabetes mellitus — NIDDM)**. Diabetes affects approximately 2% of the population, with 90% of diabetics suffering from the maturity onset form. The cause and treatment of the two types is quite different.

CAUSE: Juvenile diabetes — a lack of insulin production by the pancreas. Most people develop this type as a child or in early adult life.

Maturity onset diabetes — far more common in obese patients. There is adequate insulin production, but cells throughout the body fail to respond to the insulin.

SYMPTOMS: Juvenile diabetes — excessive tiredness, thirst, excess passing of urine, weight loss despite a large food intake, itchy rashes, recurrent vaginal thrush infections, pins and needles and blurred vision. Patients become steadily weaker because their muscles and other organs cannot work properly.

Maturity onset diabetes — similar symptoms, but less thirst and urinary frequency, and more visual problems, skin infections and sensory nerve problems than those with the juvenile form. Many patients are totally without symptoms when the diagnosis is discovered on a routine blood or urine test.

INVESTIGATIONS: — Blood and urine glucose levels are high in untreated or inadequately treated patients.

— A blood glucose tolerance test (GTT) is performed to determine the severity of both types of diabetes. After fasting for 12 hours, a blood sample is taken, then a sweet drink is then swallowed, and further blood samples are taken at regular intervals for two or three hours. The pattern of absorption and elimination of blood glucose will give the diagnosis.

— By measuring the amount of glucose in certain blood cells, the average blood glucose level over the past three months can also be determined.

— The level of insulin can also be measured in blood.

Juvenile diabetes — daily self-testing is necessary to ensure that disease control is adequate. Both blood and urine tests for glucose are available, but the blood tests are far superior.

Maturity onset diabetes — regular blood testing of glucose levels is also necessary, but normally on a weekly rather than daily basis. Urine tests are often inaccurate in the elderly, as their kidney function may be reduced to the point where glucose cannot enter the urine.

TREATMENT: Diet is essential in both forms because the amount of glucose eaten is not normally constant, and diabetics lack the means of adjusting the amount of glucose in their blood with insulin. The diet must restrict the number of kilojoules (calories) being eaten, and sugar in all its forms should be eaten only with great caution. Fat should not account for more than a third of the total calories, and cholesterol intake should be restricted. Protein should be obtained more from poultry and fish than red meats. Carbohydrates other than sugar can be consumed freely. Grains and cereals with a high fibre content should be the main part of the diet. Artificial sweeteners such as aspartame

(NutraSweet) can be used to flavour food and drinks. Fat cells can react abnormally to insulin very easily, and so overweight diabetics must lose weight. Exercise is encouraged on a regular daily basis. Patients should carry glucose sweets with them at all times to use if their blood sugar levels drop too low.

Juvenile diabetes — when first diagnosed, patients are often quite ill, and most are hospitalised for a few days to stabilise their condition. Insulin injections must be given regularly several times a day for the rest of their life. Initially derived from pigs and cattle, human insulin has now been produced by genetic engineering techniques. Insulin cannot be taken by mouth as it is destroyed by acid in the stomach, but can be injected into any part of the body covered by loose skin, although the same site should not be used repeatedly. The newer pen-style delivery systems enable diabetics to easily dial the required dose and inject as necessary with minimal inconvenience. There are many different types of insulin that vary in their speed of onset and duration of action.

Maturity onset diabetes — education of patients with this type of diabetes is very important, so that they understand what they can and cannot eat and drink. Older people who develop diabetes can often have the disease controlled by diet alone or a combination of tablets and diet. Tablets (eg. tolbutamide, chlorpropamide, glibenclamide, glipizide) make the cell membrane respond to insulin again. Weight loss is a vital part of treatment because if normal weight levels can be maintained, the disease may disappear.

COMPLICATIONS: Juvenile diabetes — an increased risk of both bacterial and fungal skin and vaginal infections, the premature development of cataracts in the eye, microscopic haemorrhages and exudates that destroy the retina at the back of the eye, damage to the kidneys that prevents them from filtering blood effectively, poor circulation to the extremities (hands and feet) that may cause chronic ulcers and even gangrene to the feet, the development of brown skin spots on the shins, and sensory nerve damage (**diabetic neuropathy**) that alters the patient's perception of vibration, pain and temperature. There are also complications associated with treatment such as a 'hypo' in which too much insulin is given, excess exercise undertaken or not enough food is eaten, and blood glucose levels drop (hypoglycaemia) to an unacceptably low level. The patient becomes light-headed, sweats, develops a rapid heart beat and tremor, becomes hungry, then nauseated before finally collapsing unconscious. Glucose drinks or sweets given before collapse can reverse the process, but after collapse, an injection of glucose is essential. In an emergency, a sugary syrup or honey introduced through the anus into the rectum may allow a diabetic to recover sufficiently to take further sugar by mouth. Rarer complications of treatment are adverse reactions to pork or beef insulin, and damage to the fat under the skin if the same injection site is used too frequently. Diabetic ketoacidosis (see separate entry) is the most severe complication.

Maturity onset diabetes — the elderly are very susceptible to all the complications listed above, particularly foot damage and eye damage. High blood pressure is more common than in the average person of their age.

PROGNOSIS: With the correct treatment and careful control, patients with both types of diabetes should live a near-normal life, with a near-normal life span.

See also Diabetic Ketoacidosis; Mauriac Syndrome

Diabetes Type One and Two
See Diabetes Mellitus

Diabetic Ketoacidosis

DESCRIPTION: Severe complication or initial presentation of diabetes mellitus.

CAUSE: A build-up of waste products and glucose in the bloodstream because of untreated or under-treated diabetes. Patients who are careless about their treatment, diet and self-testing may be affected. Almost invariably, it is the juvenile insulin dependent diabetics that develop this complication.

SYMPTOMS: Mental stupor, nausea, vomiting, shortness of breath and eventually coma.

INVESTIGATIONS: Blood sugar is very high and other blood and urine tests abnormal.

TREATMENT: Emergency injections of insulin, but urgent hospital treatment is necessary to control the situation adequately.

COMPLICATIONS: If left untreated, death will occur due to kidney, heart or brain damage.

PROGNOSIS: Good with prompt medical care, but permanent organ damage if treatment is delayed.

See also Diabetes Mellitus

Diabetic Neuropathy
See Diabetes Mellitus

Diarrhoea

DESCRIPTION: The frequent and excessive discharge of watery fluid from the bowel. Diarrhoea is really a symptom of disease rather than a disease itself.

CAUSE: Common causes include eating or drinking to excess, allergies to certain foods or medications, side effect of antibiotics (alter the balance of bacteria normally found in the gut), emotional stress or excitement, food poisoning and a viral infection (gastroenteritis). More serious causes include a vast range of diseases such as bacterial dysentery, thyroid disorders, diabetes, bowel tumours, diverticulitis, ulcerative colitis and poisons.

SYMPTOMS: Frequent loose bowel motions, often associated with abdominal pains, nausea and vomiting.

INVESTIGATIONS: Faeces may be examined to determine cause, along with blood tests and sometimes colonoscopy and X-rays.

TREATMENT: Determine and treat the cause if possible. Mild attacks dealt with by diet and fluids, more serious ones require medication to slow the flow, and severe attacks may need fluids to be replaced by an intravenous drip.

COMPLICATIONS: Dehydration is the main problem, and the risk is much greater in children under five years of age.

PROGNOSIS: Depends on cause, but bowels can usually be controlled by correct treatment.

See also specific causes of diarrhoea (eg. Addison's Disease; Amoebiasis, Appendicitis; Campylobacter Enteritis; Carcinoid Syndrome; Cholera; Ciguatera Poisoning; Cirrhosis; Coeliac Disease; Crohn's Disease; Cystic Fibrosis; Dengue Fever; Food Poisoning; Gastroenteritis; Giardiasis, Intestinal; Hookworm; Hyperthyroidism; Insecticide Poisoning; Iron Poisoning; Irritable Bowel Syndrome; Mesenteric Adenitis; Pellagra; Peritonitis; Pinworms; Pseudomembranous Colitis; Schistosomiasis; Shigellosis; Strongyloidiasis; Tapeworms; Toxic Shock Syndrome; Trichinosis; Trichuriasis; Tropical Sprue; Typhoid Fever; Ulcerative Colitis; Weil Syndrome etc.)

DIC
See Disseminated Intravascular Coagulation

Diencephalic Syndrome
DESCRIPTION: Reaction to a brain tumour.

CAUSE: Due to a tumour in the part of the brain known as the anterior hypothalamus.

SYMPTOMS: Significant weight loss, pale complexion, vomiting and abnormal side to side eye movements (nystagmus). Patients may also develop wasting of the nerves to the eyes (optic atrophy) and blindness, tremor, sweats, low blood sugar and frequent passing of urine.

INVESTIGATIONS: Diagnosed by a CT or MRI scan.

TREATMENT: Sometimes surgery possible, but often inoperable.

PROGNOSIS: Poor.

di George Syndrome
(Thymic Hypoplasia)
DESCRIPTION: Failure of the thymus gland (which lies behind the upper end of the breast bone), and parathyroid glands (which lie in the front of the neck) to develop properly.

CAUSE: Congenital.

SYMPTOMS: Muscle spasms in a newborn infant, recurrent severe infections, wide spread eyes.

INVESTIGATIONS: Abnormal blood tests and lymph node biopsy.

TREATMENT: Thymic tissue transplantation.

COMPLICATIONS: Unusual cancers possible.

PROGNOSIS: Death inevitable unless successful thymus transplant possible.

See also Immunodeficiency; Nezelof Syndrome

Diogenes Syndrome

DESCRIPTION: Social disorder that is more a symptom of underlying problem than a disease in itself.

CAUSE: Numerous psychiatric disturbances (eg. schizophrenia).

SYMPTOMS: Recluse who lives alone in filth and squalor, and usually male. They may be involved in drug abuse and mentally subnormal.

INVESTIGATIONS: Numerous blood and other tests performed to determine cause of mental disorder.

TREATMENT: Treat any underlying cause, then specifically treat psychoses and dementia.

PROGNOSIS: Depends on cause.

See also Dementia; Psychosis; Schizophrenia

Diphtheria

DESCRIPTION: Childhood respiratory infection that is now rare in developed countries.

CAUSE: Infection of the throat and trachea (the tube leading to the lungs) by the bacterium *Corynebacterium diphtheriae* which releases a toxin that is responsible for most of the symptoms and complications. Spreads from one person to another in the breath. Incubation period two to seven days.

SYMPTOMS: Sore swollen throat, fever, nasal discharge, hoarse voice, overwhelming tiredness, weakness and muscle aches. A thick, grey, sticky discharge forms a membrane across the throat that the patient constantly fights to clear.

INVESTIGATIONS: Diagnosis confirmed by throat swabs, and heart involvement by an electrocardiograph (ECG).

TREATMENT: Rapid, early treatment is critical and involves diphtheria antitoxin injection, antibiotics (kill the bacteria but do not remove the toxin), and medications to control or prevent complications. In severe cases a tracheotomy (cut into the front of the throat) is performed to allow air into the lungs. Totally prevented by vaccination in infancy.

COMPLICATIONS: May affect the heart, nose, skin and nerves. Survivors may be affected for life by damage to the heart or lungs.

PROGNOSIS: Death rate varies from 10% to 30%, and most deaths occur within the first day or two. Survivors improve in a few days, but must be kept at rest for at least three weeks to prevent complications, as it will take this time for all the toxin to be removed from the body.

See also Whooping Cough

Discoid Eczema
(Nummular Eczema)

DESCRIPTION: A persistent rash that is often confused with a fungal infection.

CAUSE: Unknown. Occurs mainly in young adults.

SYMPTOMS: The rash appears as discs of scaling, red, thickened skin on the back of the forearms and elbows, back of the hands, front of the legs and the tops of the feet. The affected areas can vary in size from a few millimetres to three centimetres or more.

INVESTIGATIONS: Diagnosis confirmed by biopsy.

TREATMENT: Steroid creams are effective, but antihistamine tablets are sometimes needed for the itch.

COMPLICATIONS: None significant.

PROGNOSIS: The rash heals rapidly with correct treatment, but unfortunately, there is a tendency for recurrences. Attacks usually cease after 6 to 12 months.

See also Eczema

Discoid Lupus Erythematosus

DESCRIPTION: Uncommon disfiguring inflammatory skin disease.

CAUSE: Autoimmune disease in which the body inappropriately rejects patches of skin for no known reason.

SYMPTOMS: Distinct red plaques on the face (particularly the cheeks), scalp and ears that worsen with sun exposure. Permanent facial hair loss and loss of pigmentation in dark skinned races may also occur.

INVESTIGATIONS: Diagnosis confirmed by a skin biopsy. Some specific blood tests may be abnormal.

TREATMENT: Protecting the affected skin from the sun, strong steroid creams, injections of steroids into the lesions and medications such as chloroquine, dapsone and retinoic acid. All these must be used with great care as they have significant side effects.

COMPLICATIONS: Cosmetic facial disfigurement.

PROGNOSIS: Often persistent, and only 60% of patients adequately controlled.

See also Systemic Lupus Erythematosus

Disc, Slipped

See Intervertebral Disc Prolapse

Dislocation

DESCRIPTION: A dislocation occurs when the surfaces of a joint are totally displaced, one from the other. If there is partial separation of the joint surfaces, it is a subluxation.

CAUSE: May be a birth defect (eg. congenital dislocation of the hips), due to a severe injury, or be a complication of severe arthritis in a joint. The following information applies only to dislocations caused by an injury.

SYMPTOMS: The joint will be painful, swollen and difficult or impossible to move and the shape of the joint will be distorted.

INVESTIGATIONS: Diagnosed by an X-ray.

TREATMENT: Treated by manipulating the bones of the joint back into their correct position as soon as possible while the patient is appropriately anaesthetised. Immediately after the injury, this can sometimes be done quite easily as the damaged muscles around the joint will not yet have gone into a spasm.

Severely damaged ligaments and cartilages around a joint may need to be surgically repaired. Movement of the joint through its full range soon after correction of the dislocation, without putting it under any stress, is the best way of bringing a joint back to full recovery.

COMPLICATIONS: Inevitably, cartilages and ligaments, and possibly muscles and tendons around a dislocated joint will be stretched, strained or torn by the dislocation. A dislocation can be associated with pinching a nerve or blood vessel, or the premature development of arthritis. Once dislocated, a joint may dislocate very easily in the future. A joint that dislocates repeatedly may require an operation to tighten the ligaments and muscles around it. A dislocation may also be associated with a fracture.

PROGNOSIS: Depends on joint and cause of dislocation, but generally very good recovery occurs.

See also Hip Dislocation; Monteggia Fracture; Shoulder Dislocation

Dissecting Aneurysm
See Aneurysm

Disseminated Intravascular Coagulation
(DIC)

DESCRIPTION: A rare and horrendous blood reaction to many different types of severe disease (eg. septicaemia, cancer).

CAUSE: Excessive blood clotting occurs within normal arteries and veins in one area, which uses up all the available blood clotting factors in the body, so that excessive bleeding occurs elsewhere.

SYMPTOMS: Blood supply to an organ (eg. kidney, liver, brain), finger or limb is cut off partially or completely to cause loss of function, gangrene or scarring. Followed by severe and damaging bleeding internally to other organs, externally into the skin and from most body openings.

INVESTIGATIONS: Diagnosed by specific blood tests.

TREATMENT: Transfusion of fresh blood to replace lost clotting factors. Amputation of affected fingers, toes, or limbs may be necessary.

COMPLICATIONS: Permanent organ (eg. stroke if brain affected) or limb damage.

PROGNOSIS: Sudden death in severe cases. Most survivors are damaged in some way.

Disseminated Lupus Erythematosus
See Systemic Lupus Erythematosus

Disseminated Sclerosis
See Multiple Sclerosis

Disseminated Superficial Actinic Porokeratosis
(DSAP)

DESCRIPTION: Unusual condition that increases the risk of sun damage to the skin in people of European descent. Affects sun exposed areas, appearing mainly on the cheeks, forearms and lower legs and occurs more frequently in women than men.

CAUSE: Inherited. Half the children of an affected parent will have the condition, but only if they have excessive sun exposure will it be a problem. New spots may be caused by ultraviolet light in sun lamps. The average age of onset is about 40, and severity increases steadily with age. Does not occur in childhood.

SYMPTOMS: Spots that begin as a 1-3 mm cone shaped lump, brownish red or brown in colour and usually around a hair follicle. It expands and a slightly raised dark brown ring develops and spreads out to a diameter of 10 mm or more. The skin within the ring is thin and mildly reddened or slightly brown. Sweating is absent in affected areas and sun exposure may cause itching. Becomes more prominent in the summer and may improve in winter.

INVESTIGATIONS: Diagnosed by skin biopsy.

TREATMENT: No satisfactory treatment, but cryotherapy (freezing) and creams containing 5 fluoro-uracil, tretinoin or alpha hydroxy acid may be tried. Important to reduce sun exposure by wearing long sleeves shirts and slacks and using sunscreens.

COMPLICATIONS: Centre of area may ulcerate and crust. Development of true skin cancer is very uncommon.

PROGNOSIS: No cure, but reasonable control.

Distal Muscular Dystrophy

DESCRIPTION: A rare progressive and permanent weakening and wasting of muscles.

CAUSE: Inherited condition.

SYMPTOMS: Onset in middle age and the elderly. Progresses very slowly, with weakness of the hands and feet initially, before slowly moving up the arms and legs.

INVESTIGATIONS: Diagnosed by electrical studies of muscle action, and muscle biopsy.

TREATMENT: No effective treatment, but physiotherapy is beneficial.

PROGNOSIS: No cure.

See also other diseases listed under Muscular Dystrophy

Diverticular Disease
See Diverticulitis

Diverticulitis

DESCRIPTION: Infection or inflammation occurring in diverticulae (outpocketings) that develop on the colon (large intestine). When no infection or inflammation is present, the condition is called **diverticular disease** of the colon. Very common in older people, but the incidence is slowly decreasing in developed countries as the amount of fibre in the diet is increasing.

CAUSE: If fibre is lacking in the diet, almost everything eaten is absorbed, and there is little to pass on in the faeces. If there is no bulk in the motions, there is a tendency towards constipation, and pressure builds up in the colon as the hard, dry food remnants are moved along towards the anus. The pressure increases in the last metre or so of the bowel to cause ballooning out of the bowel wall between the muscle bands that run along and around the gut. With time, these outpocketings become permanent and form small diverticulae in which faecal particles can be trapped to cause infection and inflammation.

SYMPTOMS: Intermittent cramping pains in the lower abdomen, alternating constipation and diarrhoea, excess flatus (wind), and noisy bowels.

INVESTIGATIONS: Diagnosed by barium enema X-ray or colonoscopy of the large bowel.

TREATMENT: Acute attacks treated with antibiotics and medications that reduce gut spasm. Sometimes treatment must be continued long term to prevent recurrences. Fibre supplements are added to the diet, and faecal softeners prevent constipation. In severe cases, surgery may be necessary to remove the affected sections of bowel, particularly if the bowel starts to bleed from chronic irritation or if an abscess forms. If fibre is added to the diet once the disease is present, it will not lead to a cure, but will prevent the formation of more diverticulae and therefore limit the severity of the disease.

COMPLICATIONS: An abscess may form in one of the diverticulae, and this may rupture causing peritonitis.

PROGNOSIS: Acute attacks normally settle quickly with treatment. Once diverticulae are present, they are permanent, and periodic infections occur.

Donovanosis
See Granuloma Inguinale

Double Pneumonia
See Pneumonia

Down Syndrome
(Mongolism; Trisomy 21)

DESCRIPTION: A genetic defect causing various body and organ malformations.

CAUSE: Congenital defect due to the presence of three copies of chromosome 21 instead of two (one from each parent). Occurs in one in every 600 births overall, but rises to a rate of one in every 100 for mothers over 40 years of age.

SYMPTOMS: Considerable variation between individuals. Common characteristics include poor muscle tone, joints that move further than normal, slanted eyes, a flattened facial appearance (accounting for the former name of 'mongolism'), small stature, some measure of intellectual disability, small nose, a short broad hand and finger prints that have a whorl with the loop on the thumb side of the finger tip and other abnormal features. Other characteristics may include a fissured protruding tongue, short neck, widely spaced first and second toes, dry skin, sparse hair, small genitals, small ears, poorly formed teeth, and a squint.

INVESTIGATIONS: Usually easily recognised and diagnosed at birth. Diagnosis before birth is possible from the fifteenth week of pregnancy by amniocentesis (taking a sample of fluid from around the foetus) or chorionic villus (placenta) biopsy.

TREATMENT: None specific, but plastic surgery may help some deformities.

COMPLICATIONS: More than average medical attention for ear, nose and throat infections is often necessary. More severe health problems include abnormal heart formation, abnormal formation of the intestines (especially the duodenum), a clouded lens in the eye, infertility and a higher than normal incidence of leukaemia.

PROGNOSIS: No cure, but provided there are no serious heart abnormalities, the life expectancy is close to normal. Good education and physiotherapy are effective in helping patients achieve a relatively normal life.

Dracunculiasis
(Guinea Worm Disease)

DESCRIPTION: Worm infestation that occurs only in humans. Found in west and central Africa, and uncommonly in south Asia and Arabia.

CAUSE: The nematode (round worm) *Dracunculus medinensis*. Caught by swallowing water contaminated by microscopic crustaceans (copepods — water fleas) that contain the worm larva. In the stomach these are released, burrow through the stomach wall into the bloodstream, and migrate to the fat under the skin where they mature. After mating the male worm dies, but the mature female worm, which may be 60 to 80 cm. long, moves to the skin surface where it forms a sore, and through this discharges eggs every time the skin comes into contact with water. The eggs are then swallowed by the copepods where the cycle starts again. The worms eventually die and emerge through the skin sore, or occassionally remain under the skin. The full cycle takes 9 to 14 months.

SYMPTOMS: Generalised itching, fever, shortness of breath and nausea can occur when larvae are in the blood. Redness, burning and itching at site of skin sores, usually on the foot or leg. After worm dies a red, tender ulcer forms.

INVESTIGATIONS: Smears from skin sores show eggs when examined under a microscope.

TREATMENT: Patient should rest with affected leg elevated. Worms can be individually removed by exposing one end and then slowly drawing them out a centimetre at a time over several days. Medications cannot kill worms, but may encourage them to be expelled through a sore.

COMPLICATIONS: Secondary bacterial infection of an ulcer can spread to the surrounding skin (cellulitis). Abscesses can form under the skin (particularly if a worm is broken during removal), in joints or rarely in other organs that are reached by worms.

PROGNOSIS: Ulcers heal after a month or two. Most patients recover eventually.

Dressler Syndrome

DESCRIPTION: Complication of heart attack.

CAUSE: Hypersensitivity reaction causing inflammation of the pericardium (fibrous sac that contains the heart — see pericarditis entry).

SYMPTOMS: Chest pain and fever. Some patients develop lung inflammation (pneumonitis) and shortness of breath.

INVESTIGATIONS: Blood tests and ECG (electrocardiograph) used to differentiate syndrome from new heart attack.

TREATMENT: Indomethacin or corticosteroids.

PROGNOSIS: Settles spontaneously, with or without treatment.

See also Heart Attack; Pericarditis

Drowning
(Immersion)

DESCRIPTION: Immersion in a swimming pool, dam, river or the ocean. Fresh water drowning is more serious than salt water due to greater lung damage.

CAUSE: Drowning occurs because the lungs partially fill with water and the larynx (windpipe) goes into spasm and blocks air from entering the lungs.

SYMPTOMS: Breathing stops, often after vomiting swallowed water. The heart will stop beating soon afterwards.

INVESTIGATIONS: In hospital, blood tests and chest X-rays may be done after the patient is stabilised to check for lung damage and the level of oxygen in blood.

TREATMENT: Cardiopulmonary resuscitation started as soon as possible (in the water if necessary) and continued for at least an hour. Transfer to a hospital as quickly as possible. Resuscitation continued in hospital until doctors determine it is no longer appropriate. Follow up nursing in an intensive care unit.

COMPLICATIONS: Permanent lung or brain damage possible if resuscitation started too late.

PROGNOSIS: Variable, but competent cardiopulmonary resuscitation can save an amazing number of lives.

Drug Addiction

See Alcoholism; Amphetamine Abuse; Cocaine Addiction; Marijuana Abuse;
Narcotic Addiction

Drug Eruption

See Dermatitis Medicamentosa

Drusen

DESCRIPTION: Degenerative condition of the retinal macular (central area of light sensitive cells at the back of the eye) in late middle age and the elderly.

CAUSE: Degenerative condition.

SYMPTOMS: Steadily worsening central vision. Edge (peripheral) vision is often normal.

INVESTIGATIONS: Diagnosed by examining the eye through a magnifying light (ophthalmoscope) and injecting a bright dye (fluorescein) into the artery supplying the eye.

TREATMENT: None available.

PROGNOSIS: Slowly progressive.

See also Macular Degeneration

Dry Eye Syndrome
(Xerophthalmia)

DESCRIPTION: Very common problem, the incidence increasing with age.

CAUSE: An effect of old age due to reduced tear production.

SYMPTOMS: Dry scratchy irritated eye.

INVESTIGATIONS: Small piece of blotting paper placed under lower eye lid remains dry (Schirmer tear test).

TREATMENT: Artificial tear drops or ointment, lubricating inserts under lower lids, and surgical blockage of tear duct at inner corner of eye to prevent tear drainage.

COMPLICATIONS: Eye ulcers and infections. Severe forms known as kerato-conjunctivitis sicca (see separate entry).

PROGNOSIS: No cure, but reasonable control with treatment.

See also Keratoconjunctivitis Sicca and other conditions listed under Eye Diseases

DSAP
See Disseminated Superficial Actinic Porokeratosis

DTs
See Delirium Tremens

Duane Syndrome

DESCRIPTION: Rare abnormality of nerve supply to eye muscles. Vision remains normal.

CAUSE: Congenital absence of 6th nerve which supplies some eye movement muscles.

SYMPTOMS: Inability to move eye horizontal resulting in a variable squint.

INVESTIGATIONS: None normally necessary.

TREATMENT: Surgery if squint severe.

PROGNOSIS: No cure, but severity of squint may be reduced by treatment.

See also other conditions listed under Eye Diseases

155

Dubin-Johnson Syndrome

DESCRIPTION: Developmental abnormality of the liver.

CAUSE: Congenital abnormality of liver cell function.

SYMPTOMS: Jaundice (yellow skin) in a newborn infant.

INVESTIGATIONS: Blood tests show high levels of bilirubin, liver biopsy abnormal and gall bladder cannot be seen on special X-rays (cholecystogram) as it does not contain any bile.

TREATMENT: None necessary.

PROGNOSIS: Settles slowly.

See also Rotor Syndrome

Dubowitz Syndrome

DESCRIPTION: Developmental abnormality.

CAUSE: Familial, but both parents must be carriers.

SYMPTOMS: Low birth weight baby with drooping eyelids (ptosis), small jaw, sparse hair, short stature, mild mental retardation and eczema.

INVESTIGATIONS: Chromosome studies abnormal.

TREATMENT: None available.

PROGNOSIS: No cure.

Duchenne Muscular Dystrophy

DESCRIPTION: A progressive and permanent weakening and wasting of muscles.

CAUSE: Sex linked inherited condition affecting only males. Females can be carriers, and statistically half the sons of a carrier are affected.

SYMPTOMS: Starts in infancy or early childhood, and progresses rapidly with worsening weakness of the pelvic, shoulder, arm and leg muscles resulting in inability to walk by 12 years of age. Eventually the muscles essential for breathing are affected.

INVESTIGATIONS: Diagnosed by specific blood tests, electrical studies of muscle action, and muscle biopsy.

TREATMENT: No effective treatment or cure is available, but physiotherapy is beneficial.

COMPLICATIONS: Curvature of the spine (kyphoscoliosis — see separate entry).

PROGNOSIS: Eventually leads to death in the twenties or thirties.

See also other diseases listed under Muscular Dystrophy

Ductus Arteriosus
See Patent Ductus Arteriosus

Dumping Syndrome
(Postgastrectomy Syndrome)

DESCRIPTION: Complication of gastrectomy operation in which part of the stomach is surgically removed for diseases such as cancer and incurable peptic ulcers.

CAUSE: Occurs in 10% of postgastrectomy patients because of sudden

156

overstretching of the small stomach by food and stimulation of the Vagus nerve, which supplies the stomach, intestine and heart.

SYMPTOMS: Sweating, rapid heart rate, pallor, belly discomfort and cramps, nausea and weakness. Some patients experience fainting, vomiting and diarrhoea. All symptoms occur within 20 minutes of eating.

INVESTIGATIONS: None diagnostic.

TREATMENT: Frequent small meals with low carbohydrate content. No fluids with meal. Sedatives and anticholinergics (stomach muscle relaxing medication).

COMPLICATIONS: Damage to the oesophagus (gullet) from repeated vomiting and reflux of stomach acid.

PROGNOSIS: No cure.

Duodenal Ulcer
See Ulcer, Peptic

Dupuytren's Contracture of the Hand

DESCRIPTION: A fibrous sheet (the palmar aponeurosis) stretches under the skin of the palm to give it a smooth appearance, strength and firmness, and to protect and control the movement of the muscle tendons that cross under it to the fingers. If damaged, the palmar aponeurosis may become scarred, contract and thicken into hard lumps that can be felt under the skin. As the damage progresses, the contraction of the fibrous sheet pulls on the tendons that run underneath it to prevent their free movement. Men are affected more than twice as often as women.

CAUSE: Unknown, but may be due to a poor blood supply to the hand (eg. diabetes), the use of vibrating tools (eg. jack hammers), injury to the hand from repeated blows (eg. catching cricket balls), and there is a tendency for the condition to occur in successive generations.

SYMPTOMS: One or more hard, fixed nodules under the skin of the palm that gradually extend lengthwise along the palm to cause discomfort and loss of finger mobility. Eventually the fingers cannot be fully extended, and contract into a claw-like appearance. The ring and little fingers are usually more severely affected than the others.

INVESTIGATIONS: None necessary.

TREATMENT: Relatively minor operation to carefully cut away the thickened part of the palmar aponeurosis and free the tendons.

COMPLICATIONS: Rarely a similar condition can occur in the sole of the foot (Ledderhose's disease — see separate entry).

PROGNOSIS: Without treatment there is complete loss of hand function as it contracts into a fist. Surgery very successful, but a slow recurrence after operation, which may require further surgery, is quite common.

See also Ledderhose's Disease

DVT
See Deep Vein Thrombosis

Dyscontrol Syndrome, Episodic
See Episodic Dyscontrol Syndrome

Dysentery
See Amoebiasis; Shigellosis

Dyshidrosis
See Pompholyx

Dyspepsia, Nervous
See Irritable Bowel Syndrome

Dysplastic Naevus Syndrome
DESCRIPTION: Potentially serious skin condition.
CAUSE: Unknown, but probably congenital.
SYMPTOMS: More than 40 moles on body greater than 10 mm in diameter with irregular pigmentation and a poorly defined irregular edge. Usually occur on the trunk.
INVESTIGATIONS: Diagnosed by biopsy and microscopic examination.
TREATMENT: Excision of some moles, and regular observation of all moles.
COMPLICATIONS: Often progress to malignant melanomas.
PROGNOSIS: No cure, but controlled by excising any that become suspicious.
See also Melanoma

Dystrophia Adiposgenitalis
See Fröhlich Syndrome

Dystrophia Myotonica
See Myotonic Dystrophy

E

Ear Drum Rupture
See Tympanic Rupture

Ear Infection
See Mastoiditis; Otitis Externa; Otitis Media

Ears, Protruding
See Bat Ears

Ear Wax
(Cerumen)

DESCRIPTION: Ear wax is secreted naturally in the outer ear canal by special glands, and slowly moves out to clear away dust and debris that enters the ear. It also acts to keep the skin lining the canal lubricated and to protect it from water and other irritants. The ear is designed to be self-cleaning, and attempts to clean it may pack the wax down hard on the eardrum or damage the ear canal.

CAUSE: Ear wax may cause problems if excess is produced, the wax is too thick, the ear canal is narrow, or the person works in a dusty and dirty environment. When wax builds up on the eardrum, it cannot transmit vibrations on to the inner ear. Water entering the ear during bathing or swimming may cause the wax to swell.

SYMPTOMS: Gradual loss of hearing, itching and sometimes pain.

INVESTIGATIONS: Seen by examining the ear with a magnifying light (otoscope).

TREATMENT: Removed by syringing, suction or fine forceps. In syringing, warm water is gently squirted into the ear to dislodge the wax, with large lumps being removed by forceps. The use of wax-softening drops may be necessary to facilitate the removal of particularly large or hard accumulations of wax. Those with recurrent problems should use wax-softening drops on a regular basis.

COMPLICATIONS: Infection may start in the skin of the outer ear canal under the wax causing worse pain.

PROGNOSIS: No serious problems expected.

Eastern Equine Encephalitis
See Equine Encephalitis

Eaton-Lambert Syndrome
(Myasthenic Syndrome)

DESCRIPTION: Rare syndrome that affects motor nerve function.

CAUSE: Autoimmune reaction (inappropriate rejection of the body's own nerve tissue) similar to myasthenia gravis.

Eaton-Lambert Syndrome

SYMPTOMS: Muscle weakness that affects varying groups of muscles.
TREATMENT: Immunosuppressive drugs.
COMPLICATIONS: Increased risk of lung cancer.
PROGNOSIS: Poorer than for myasthenia gravis.
See also Myasthenia Gravis

Ebola Virus

DESCRIPTION: An extremely contagious form of viral haemorrhagic fever (viral infection of the blood) that occurs in central and west Africa, and the Philippines.
CAUSE: The virus is spread by monkeys and from person to person in conditions of poor hygiene. Outbreaks have occurred in the Congo, Sudan, Ivory Coast and the Philippines. Epidemics are often hospital based. Good personal hygiene and using masks and gowns prevents the spread of infection.
SYMPTOMS: Muscle pains, headache, sore throat, joint pains, diarrhoea, vomiting, red eyes and abnormal bleeding.
INVESTIGATIONS: Blood tests show significant abnormalities.
TREATMENT: No cure or vaccine for prevention, and treatment is restricted to managing the symptoms and nursing care. Patients must be nursed in strict isolation.
COMPLICATIONS: Internal bleeding causes death.
PROGNOSIS: Fatal in about 80% of patients.
See also Lassa Fever; Marburg Virus

Ebstein Anomaly

DESCRIPTION: Abnormal development of tricuspid valve and some nerve pathways in heart.
CAUSE: Congenital.
SYMPTOMS: The tricuspid valve between the atrium and ventricle on the right side of the heart is under developed, slips down into the right ventricle, and leaks (regurgitates). This results in right heart failure (cor pulmonale), and some patients develop blue skin (cyanosis), paroxysmal atrial tachycardia or Wolff-Parkinson-White syndrome (see separate entries).
INVESTIGATIONS: Echocardiography (ultrasound scan of heart) is abnormal.
TREATMENT: Medication to control heart contraction (eg. propranolol), and surgery to replace tricuspid valve and cut abnormal nerve pathways in the heart.
COMPLICATIONS: Some patients have irreparable heart defects.
PROGNOSIS: Reasonable results from treatment.
See also Cor Pulmonale; Tricuspid Valve Regurgitation

EBV Infection
See Glandular Fever

Echinococcosis
See Hydatid Disease

Eclampsia

DESCRIPTION: A rare but very serious disease that occurs only in pregnancy. Very rare in developed countries because most women undertake regular antenatal visits. Pre-eclampsia is a condition that precedes eclampsia, and this is detected in about 10% of all pregnant women. The correct treatment of pre-eclampsia prevents eclampsia.

CAUSE: The exact cause is unknown but may be due to the production of abnormal quantities of hormones by the placenta. More common in first pregnancies, twins and diabetes, and normally develops in the last three months of pregnancy, but may not develop until labour commences.

SYMPTOMS: Not until pre-eclampsia is well established does the patient develop the symptoms of headache, nausea, vomiting, abdominal pain and disturbances of vision. Eclampsia causes convulsions, coma, strokes, heart attacks and death of the baby.

INVESTIGATIONS: Excess protein is found in the urine. Doctors diagnose pre-eclampsia by noting high blood pressure, swollen ankles and excessive weight gain (fluid retention).

TREATMENT: Pre-eclampsia is treated by strict bed rest, drugs to lower blood pressure and remove excess fluid, sedatives, and in severe cases, early delivery of the baby. Eclampsia is treated by the emergency delivery of the baby, usually by caesarean section.

COMPLICATIONS: Death of the mother is possible if pregnancy is not terminated quickly.

PROGNOSIS: Full recovery probable for mother if treated correctly. Baby is at high risk.

See also Pre-Eclampsia

E. coli Infection
See *Escherichia coli* Infection

Ectopic Pregnancy
(Tubal Pregnancy)

DESCRIPTION: A pregnancy that starts and continues to develop outside the uterus (womb). The most common site for an ectopic pregnancy is in a Fallopian tube, which leads from the ovary to the top corner of the uterus. A pregnancy in the tube will slowly dilate it until it eventually bursts. This will cause severe bleeding into the abdomen and is an urgent, life- threatening situation for the mother. Other possible sites include on or around the ovary, in the abdomen or pelvis, or in the narrow angle where the Fallopian tube enters the uterus. About one in every 200 pregnancies is ectopic.

CAUSE: Pelvic inflammatory disease, salpingitis, endometriosis and appendicitis

161

increase the risk of ectopic pregnancies, as they cause damage to the Fallopian tubes or surrounding tissue.

SYMPTOMS: Symptoms may be minimal in early stages, but most women have abnormal vaginal bleeding or pains low in the abdomen. When the ectopic pregnancy ruptures the Fallopian tube, sudden severe pain is felt and the woman collapses.

INVESTIGATIONS: Ultrasound scan may be performed to confirm the exact position of the ectopic pregnancy.

TREATMENT: Surgery to save the mother's life is essential when an ectopic pregnancy ruptures as the woman can bleed to death very rapidly. If the ectopic site is the Fallopian tube, it is usually removed during the operation.

COMPLICATIONS: Adhesions in the pelvis may cause ongoing gynaecological and bowel problems.

PROGNOSIS: If a Fallopian tube is removed, the woman can still fall pregnant from the tube and ovary on the other side. It is very rare for a foetus to survive.

Ectropion

DESCRIPTION: Out turning of the lower eyelid, which is a common problem in the elderly.

CAUSE: Slackness of tissue in eyelid with ageing or injury.

SYMPTOMS: Tears cannot be retained in the eye and trickle down the cheek.

INVESTIGATIONS: None necessary.

TREATMENT: Surgery to tighten up the lower lid.

COMPLICATIONS: Increased risk of eye surface infection or ulceration.

PROGNOSIS: Good results from surgery.

See also Dry Eye Syndrome

Eczema

DESCRIPTION: A large number of skin diseases that cause itching and burning of the skin.

CAUSE: The many different forms of eczema also have innumerable causes, both from within the body (eg. stress) and outside (eg. allergies, chemicals).

SYMPTOMS: The appearance of an eczema depends more on its position on the body, duration, severity and degree of scratching than the actual cause. Typically appears as red, swollen, itchy skin that is initially covered with small fluid-filled blisters that later break down to a scale or crust.

INVESTIGATIONS: Often none necessary, but a biopsy is usually diagnostic.

TREATMENT: Depends upon cause of eczema, but steroid creams and tablets are commonly used.

COMPLICATIONS: A secondary bacterial infection of the skin may occur.

PROGNOSIS: Depends on cause.

See also Allergic Eczema; Atopic Eczema; Contact Dermatitis; Dermatitis; Discoid Eczema; Lichen Simplex; Photosensitive Eczema; Seborrhoeic Eczema; Varicose Eczema and other conditions listed under Skin Diseases

Edwards Syndrome
(Trisomy 18)
DESCRIPTION: Rare developmental disorder.
CAUSE: Congenital.
SYMPTOMS: Small jaw, heart malformations, rounded soles (rocker-bottom feet).
INVESTIGATIONS: No diagnostic tests.
TREATMENT: None available.
PROGNOSIS: No cure.

Effort Syndrome
See da Costa Syndrome

Ehlers-Danlos Syndrome
(Cutis Hyperelastica; Elastic Skin Syndrome)
DESCRIPTION: Abnormality of skin development with eight clinically and genetically different variants.
CAUSE: Congenital.
SYMPTOMS: Over extendable joints, excessively elastic and fragile skin, scarring of skin and growths on knees and elbows.
INVESTIGATIONS: Diagnosed by skin biopsy.
TREATMENT: None available.
COMPLICATIONS: Premature arthritis.
PROGNOSIS: No cure. Normal life expectancy.

Eisenmenger Syndrome
DESCRIPTION: Failure of an artery near the heart that bypasses the lungs before birth, to close immediately after birth.
CAUSE: Developmental abnormality.
SYMPTOMS: Patent ductus arteriosus causes abnormal blood flow in the lungs and heart, and high blood pressure in the lungs (cor pulmonale — see separate entry).
INVESTIGATIONS: A machinery like murmur can be heard, ECG (electro-cardiograph), echocardiogram (ultrasound of heart), and cardiac catheterisation (passing a pressure measuring tube through an artery or vein into the heart) are all abnormal.
TREATMENT: Medication (indomethacin) is sometimes successful, but surgery is often needed to close the ductus arteriosus.
COMPLICATIONS: Permanent lung or heart damage.
PROGNOSIS: Good results from treatment. Fatal if untreated.
See also **Patent Ductus Arteriosus**

Ejaculation Problems
See Failure of Ejaculation; Impotence; Premature Ejaculation; Retrograde Ejaculation

Ejaculatory Failure
(Failure Of Ejaculation; Retarded Ejaculation)

DESCRIPTION: Male equivalent of a failed orgasm in the female.

CAUSE: Some men can ejaculate when masturbating, or with oral sex, but not with vaginal sex. May be a drug side effect, psychological, inhibited personality, subconscious or conscious anxiety, or fear of losing self-control.

SYMPTOMS: Inability to ejaculate during sexual intercourse.

INVESTIGATIONS: Any significant underlying disease should be excluded.

TREATMENT: Progressive desensitisation with the assistance of a cooperative sex partner, who initially masturbates patient to ejaculation, and over a series of weeks, learns to bring him almost to the point of ejaculation by hand stimulation before allowing vaginal sex. Another technique involves additional stimulation of the penis during intercourse by the woman massaging the penis with her fingers while the man thrusts in and out of the vagina. Distracting the man from consciously holding back the ejaculation by passionate kissing or other stimulation of the face or back during intercourse may also help.

COMPLICATIONS: Infertility.

PROGNOSIS: Reasonable results with commitment to treatment program.

See also other diseases listed under **Sex Problems**

Ekbom Syndrome
See Restless Legs Syndrome

Elastic Skin Syndrome
See Ehlers-Danlos Syndrome

Elbow Fracture/Dislocation
See Monteggia Fracture

Elephantiasis
See Filariasis

Elephant Man Deformity
See Proteus Syndrome

Ellis-van Creveld Syndrome

DESCRIPTION: Developmental abnormality of heart and limbs.

CAUSE: Familial, but both parents must be carriers.

SYMPTOMS: Extra fingers and toes, tongue tied to floor of mouth, small nails, short arms and legs, small chest and holes in the heart (atrial septal defect, ventricular septal defect — see separate entries).

INVESTIGATIONS: No diagnostic tests, but echocardiogram (ultrasound of heart), and cardiac catheterisation (passing a pressure measuring tube through an artery or vein into the heart) demonstrate heart abnormalities.

TREATMENT: Surgical repair of heart and cosmetic defects where possible.
COMPLICATIONS: Permanent heart damage.
PROGNOSIS: No cure, but reasonable results from surgery.

Embolism, Pulmonary
See Pulmonary Embolism

Embryoma
See Testicular Cancer

Emphysema

DESCRIPTION: A form of chronic obstructive airways disease caused by permanent destruction of the small air absorbing sacs (alveoli) in the lungs.
CAUSE: Caused by smoking, exposure to other noxious gases, or recurrent attacks of bronchitis or pneumonia. With these irritants the alveoli break down into larger cavities which are surrounded by scar tissue and have less surface area to absorb oxygen. About 3% of the population develop emphysema, and most are smokers.
SYMPTOMS: Constant shortness of breath and repetitive coughing, a barrel shaped chest and excessive sputum. Because of their constant exertion to breathe they become wasted and emaciated.
INVESTIGATIONS: Diagnosed by chest X-rays and by breathing into machines (eg. spirometers, peak flow meters) that analyse lung function. There may also be changes in blood tests and electrocardiograms (ECG).
TREATMENT: Involves physiotherapy to make the damaged lung work as effectively as possible, drugs by tablet or spray to open up the lungs to their maximum capacity, and antibiotics to treat infection. In severe cases, steroids by inhalation or tablet are given, and as a last resort oxygen is used. Smokers must stop their habit. Vaccination against influenza and pneumonia may prevent a fatal illness.
COMPLICATIONS: Recurrent attacks of bronchitis and pneumonia, right heart failure (cor pulmonale) and pneumothorax.
PROGNOSIS: No cure possible and slowly progressive. The complications eventually cause death.
See also Bronchitis, Chronic; Cor Pulmonale; Lung Cancer; Pneumonia; Pneumothorax

Emphysema, Subcutaneous
See Subcutaneous Emphysema

Empyema
See Abscess

Encephalitis

See Angiostrongyliasis; Creutzfeldt-Jakob Disease; Equine Encephalitis; Japanese Encephalitis; la Crosse Encephalitis; Murray Valley Encephalitis; Rabies; Reye Syndrome; St.Louis Encephalitis; West Nile Encephalitis

Encephalomyelopathy, Subacute Necrotising

See Leigh Disease

Enchondroma

See Bone Cancer

en Coup de Sabre

See Morphoea

Endocarditis

DESCRIPTION: A bacterial or fungal infection inside the heart, usually on the heart valves.

CAUSE: Normally develops slowly over many weeks or months in an already damaged heart, or may rarely cause sudden illness in a previously healthy person. The heart valves may be malformed from birth, damaged by disease (eg. rheumatic fever), distorted by cholesterol deposits, scarred by heart attacks or an artificial heart valve may have been inserted to replace a damaged valve.

SYMPTOMS: Many and varied, and some patients, particularly the elderly, may have almost no early symptoms. Most patients have a fever, and other complaints include night sweats, fatigue, tiredness, palpitations, rapid heart rate, loss of appetite, chills, joint pains, muscle pains, weight loss, swollen joints, paralysis, headache, chest pain, nose bleeds and other minor problems.

INVESTIGATIONS: Diagnosed by taking blood and culturing it in the laboratory in order to detect any bacteria. Other blood tests and an ECG (electro-cardiograph) may also be diagnostic.

TREATMENT: Urgent hospital treatment is essential. Large doses of antibiotics, often penicillin, are given by injection for several weeks. Other treatments include correction of anaemia and controlling the damage done to other organs. Major heart surgery is sometimes required, particularly if the infection is fungal. Prevention is better than cure, and patients who have had rheumatic fever or any other heart disease should have a preventative course of penicillin before and during an operation or dental procedure.

COMPLICATIONS: The infection causes clumps of bacteria to grow inside the heart, and pieces can break off and travel through the arteries to cause severe problems elsewhere in the body. In the brain they can block an artery and cause a stroke. In other organs they may cause blindness, kidney failure, joint damage and bowel problems. Almost any part of the body may be affected. Further complications such as heart attack and stroke can occur years after the disease appears to have been cured.

PROGNOSIS: 60% of patients with endocarditis recover completely, another 30% survive, but with significant restrictions on their lifestyle caused by damage to the heart or other organs, while in about 10% of cases death occurs. Untreated, death is inevitable. When a fungus is responsible (most commonly in intravenous drug abusers), the outcome is far worse.
See also Rheumatic Fever

Endogenous Depression
See Depression

Endometriosis
DESCRIPTION: The presence of cells that normally line the uterus (womb) in abnormal positions in the pelvis and abdomen. 2% of all women affected at some time.
CAUSE: The uterus is lined with endometrial cells that during the second half of a woman's monthly cycle may accept a fertilised egg and allow it to grow into a baby. If no pregnancy occurs, these cells degenerate, break away from the inside of the uterus, and are carried out of the body in a woman's period. From the top of the uterus, a Fallopian tube leads out to each of the two ovaries. In a small number of women, the endometrial cells go into and through these tubes to settle in abnormal positions around the ovary, on the outside of the uterus, or in the pelvic cavity, where they can start growing and spread further. These cells still respond to the woman's hormonal cycle every month, will bleed with every period, releasing blood in places where it can cause symptoms. They can irritate the bladder, or settle on the outside of the intestine.
SYMPTOMS: Depends on site of endometrial deposits, but pelvic pain, often worse at the time of a period, is usual. May also cause uterus and bowel cramps, diarrhoea and frequent passage of urine due to bladder irritation.
INVESTIGATIONS: Can only be diagnosed by examining a woman's pelvis by means of an open operation or laparoscopy.
TREATMENT: Various medications (eg. hormones, danocrine) taken as tablets, implants or nasal sprays for many months settle mild to moderate cases. Removal of endometrial deposits is normally possible by laparoscopy (passing a number of small tubes into the abdomen), but open operation may be necessary to remove large amounts of abnormal tissue. As a last resort, a hysterectomy may be performed.
COMPLICATIONS: Endometrial cells may block the Fallopian tubes to cause infertility.
PROGNOSIS: Most patients are cured with medication and/or surgery, but some will be left permanently infertile. Artificial means of fertilisation can help these women conceive, as their ovaries still function normally.
See also Infertility, Female

167

Enteric Fever
See Typhoid Fever

Enteritis
See Campylobacter Enteritis; Crohn's Disease; Gastroenteritis; Shigellosis

Enterobiasis
See Pinworms

Enterocolitis, Necrotising
See Necrotising Enterocolitis

Entropion
DESCRIPTION: Inturning of the eyelashes.

CAUSE: Eyelid injury or infection.

SYMPTOMS: Eyelashes rub irritatingly on the eye surface.

INVESTIGATIONS: None necessary.

TREATMENT: Plucking of eye lashes gives temporary relief, but problem often recurs when they regrow. Cured by surgery to permanently destroy a small number of damaged eye lashes, or change shape of eyelid.

COMPLICATIONS: Ulceration or infection of eye surface.

PROGNOSIS: Good results from treatment. Blindness possible if left untreated long term.

See also other conditions listed under Eye Diseases

Enuresis
See Bed Wetting

Eosinophilia-Myalgia Syndrome
DESCRIPTION: Food intolerance.

CAUSE: Triggered by ingestion of large amount of the protein L-tryptophan in a sensitised person.

SYMPTOMS: Severe muscle and joint pain, cough, shortness of breath, swelling of feet and ankles, thick skin, rashes and nerve pain.

INVESTIGATIONS: Large number of reactive white blood cells (eosinophils) seen in blood sample.

TREATMENT: No specific treatment. Avoid eating L-tryptophan.

PROGNOSIS: Most patients recover quickly, but one in a hundred die within a few hours.

Eosinophilic Meningoencephalitis
See Angiostrongyliasis

Epicondylitis
See Golfer's Elbow; Tennis Elbow

Epidemic Polyarthritis
See Ross River Fever

Epidermal Naevus
See Naevus

Epidermolysis Bullosa
DESCRIPTION: Rare skin disease of which there are several subtypes.

CAUSE: Familial (runs in families).

SYMPTOMS: Slightest injury to the skin causes large, firm blisters. In infants blisters develop on knees and hands as the child starts to crawl, but later may occur anywhere. In severe forms disease continues throughout life, the fingers may become bound together by scar tissue, the mouth and throat may be involved, and nails and teeth may be damaged. On healing, blisters leave behind a scar that causes significant disfigurement.

INVESTIGATIONS: Diagnosed by skin biopsy.

TREATMENT: Steroids are the only treatment available, but are not particularly effective. Avoiding injury to the skin is imperative.

COMPLICATIONS: Cancer may develop in the affected tissue.

PROGNOSIS: No cure. Subtypes vary in severity from an inconvenience to life-threatening.

Epididymo-Orchitis
(Testicular Infection)
DESCRIPTION: A bacterial or viral infection of the testicle and epididymis.

CAUSE: The sperm produced in a testicle passes into a dense network of fine tubes that forms a lump on the back of the testicle called the epididymis. These join up to form the sperm tube (vas deferens) that takes the sperm to the penis. Epididymo-orchitis is an infection of both the epididymis and testicle. Orchitis is an infection of the testicle alone, but the infection is almost invariably present in both places.

SYMPTOMS: Men with a bacterial epididymo-orchitis are acutely uncomfortable, have a painful swollen testicle, and a fever.

INVESTIGATIONS: Blood tests may show the presence of infection in the body.

TREATMENT: Appropriate antibiotics, aspirin or paracetamol for pain relief, ice may be applied to the scrotum, and a supportive bandage or jock-strap worn. If the infection is caused by a virus such as mumps, there is no effective treatment available.

COMPLICATIONS: Occasionally an abscess will form, which must be surgically drained. A painful testicle can also be caused by torsion of the testis (see separate entry), which is a surgical emergency requiring immediate treatment.

169

Any boy or man, particularly in the teenage years or early twenties, who develops a painful testicle, must see a doctor immediately — day or night.

PROGNOSIS: With the correct treatment, bacterial epididymo-orchitis resolves in a couple of days, and usually does not cause any problems with fertility or masculinity. In cases of viral infection there may be problems with fertility in later life.

See also Torsion of the Testis

Epiglottitis
(HiB Infection)

DESCRIPTION: Uncommon throat infection that is an acute medical emergency requiring urgent hospitalisation.

CAUSE: The epiglottis is a piece of cartilage that sticks up at the back of the tongue to stop food from entering the wind pipe (trachea) when we swallow. If it becomes infected by bacteria (most commonly *Haemophilus influenzae B*), it can swell up rapidly. Most common in children under five years of age.

SYMPTOMS: A very sore throat, fever and obvious illness.

INVESTIGATIONS: Diagnosis confirmed by a side-on X-ray of the neck that show the swollen epiglottis. Throat swabs are taken to identify the infecting bacteria. Sometimes blood tests are also performed.

TREATMENT: Antibiotics to cure the infection and paracetamol to reduce fever and pain. Some hospitals routinely anaesthetise children and put a tube through the mouth or nose and down the throat to prevent the airway from blocking. A vaccination against *Haemophilus influenzae B* (HiB) is now routinely given to all children at two, four, six and 18 months of age.

COMPLICATIONS: In young children, if the epiglottis swells excessively, or is disturbed by trying to eat solids or by the tongue depressing stick of a doctor examining the mouth, it can cover the wind pipe completely and rapidly cause death through suffocation. For this reason a doctor will give the throat only a cursory examination before arranging the immediate transfer of the child to hospital. If the airway is obstructed in hospital, an emergency tracheotomy (an operation to make a hole into the wind pipe through the front of the neck) is performed to allow the child to breathe. HiB may also cause a severe form of meningitis.

PROGNOSIS: The infection usually settles in a few days. Provided there has been no airway obstruction, the outcome is excellent.

See also Haemophilus Influenzae B Infection

Epilepsia Partialis Continua
See Myoclonus

Epilepsy

DESCRIPTION: A brain condition causing recurrent seizures (fits).

CAUSE: May be congenital or acquired later in life after a brain infection, tumour, injury or with brain degeneration in the elderly. Chemical imbalances in the body, kidney failure and removing alcohol from an alcoholic or heroin from an addict may also trigger the condition. Fits are caused by a short-circuit in the brain after very minor and localised damage. This then stimulates another part of the brain, and then another, causing a seizure. Triggers such as flickering lights, shimmering televisions, certain foods, emotional upsets, infections or stress can start fits in some patients.

SYMPTOMS: May vary from very mild absences in which people just seem to loose concentration for a few seconds or stumble (**petit mal epilepsy**), to uncontrolled bizarre movements of an arm or leg and abnormal sensations (**temporal lobe epilepsy** or **partial seizures**), to a **grand mal convulsion** which last for a minute or two and during which the patient becomes rigid, falls to the ground, stops breathing, muscles go into spasm, abnormal movements occur and the patient may urinate, pass faeces and become blue. Petit mal epilepsy is far more common in children and teenagers than adults. Patients normally remain conscious during partial seizures. After recovering from a grand mal fit, the patient has no memory of the event, is confused, drowsy, disoriented and may have a severe headache, nausea and muscle aches. Many patients with epilepsy develop warning auras before an attack which can be a particular type of headache, change in mood, tingling, light-headedness or twitching.

INVESTIGATIONS: An EEG (electroencephalogram) to measure the brain waves, blood tests to exclude other diseases and a CT scan of the brain to find any structural abnormality.

TREATMENT: Many different anti-epileptic drug combinations in tablet or mixture form are used to control epilepsy. Regular blood tests ensure that the dosage is adequate. Medication must be continued long term, but after several years without fits, a trial without medication may be undertaken. Epileptics must not put themselves in a position where they can injure themselves or others.

COMPLICATIONS: Status epilepticus is a condition where one grand mal attack follows another without the patient regaining consciousness between attacks.

PROGNOSIS: Most forms of epilepsy can be well controlled with appropriate medication.

See also Cerebral Palsy; Deja Vu; Landau-Kleffner Syndrome; Sturge-Weber Syndrome

Epiloia
See Tuberous Sclerosis

Episcleritis
DESCRIPTION: Common inflammation of the outer surface of the eye in young adults.

CAUSE: Unknown.

SYMPTOMS: Uncomfortable, tender redness of one section of the white of the eye.

INVESTIGATIONS: None necessary.
TREATMENT: None usually necessary, but persistent cases settle with steroid eye drops.
COMPLICATIONS: May become lumpy and thickened, and take longer to settle.
PROGNOSIS: Usually settles without treatment in one or two weeks.
See also Scleritis

Episodic Dyscontrol Syndrome

DESCRIPTION: Psychiatric disturbance not related to recognised mental disorders (eg. schizophrenia).
CAUSE: Unknown.
SYMPTOMS: Physical abuse of family, severe episodes of alcohol intoxication, impulsive sexual misconduct, irresponsible social behaviour.
INVESTIGATIONS: No specific diagnostic test, but tests (eg. EEG, CT scan) performed to exclude brain tumour.
TREATMENT: Avoid alcohol, medication (eg. phenytoin, thioridazine), and legal restraints.
COMPLICATIONS: Almost invariably end up in prison for violent crimes.
PROGNOSIS: Poor.
See also Attention Deficit Hyperactivity Disorder

Epispadias
See Hypospadias

Epistaxis
(Nose Bleed)

DESCRIPTION: Air is warmed and moistened as it enters the body by blood vessels lining the nostrils which are very close to the moist surface. The lining can dry out and crack, or it can be damaged easily.
CAUSE: Injury to the nose, blowing the nose too vigorously, drying with hot dry weather, local infections inflame the mucous lining of the nose, rheumatic fever, measles, polyps or tumours in the nose, high blood pressure, high altitude and most often for no apparent reason.
SYMPTOMS: Bleeding from the nostrils(s) and sometimes down the back of the throat.
INVESTIGATIONS: If repetitive, investigations to exclude specific causes performed.
TREATMENT: Sit (not lie) still and hold the nostrils firmly without letting go for ten minutes. Ice applied to the nose will also help. If bleeding continues after repeating above three times, medical attention is necessary to find and treat the cause of the bleeding (eg. cauterising the bleeding point with heat, removing a nasal polyp).
COMPLICATIONS: Very rarely repeated severe nose bleeds may cause anaemia.
PROGNOSIS: Depends on cause. Most settle quickly with treatment.

Epstein-Barr Virus Infection
See Glandular Fever

Equine Encephalitis
(Eastern Equine Encephalitis; Venezuelan Equine Encephalitis; Western Equine Encephalitis)
DESCRIPTION: Viral infection of the brain first identified in horses.

CAUSE: Virus spread from birds and horses to man by a mosquito. Various sub-types found in the United States, central America and northern South America. More common in warmer months. Incubation period five to ten days.

SYMPTOMS: Rapidly progressive with fever, belly pains, dizziness, sore throat, cough, headache, neck stiffness, nausea, vomiting, tiredness, disturbed mental functions, disorientation, coma and death.

INVESTIGATIONS: Tests on blood and the fluid around the brain are abnormal.

TREATMENT: No specific treatment available, and no vaccine available.

COMPLICATIONS: Causes permanent brain damage in many survivors.

PROGNOSIS: Acute attack lasts for one to three weeks, but complete recovery may take months. Mortality rate of up to 75% with eastern form, but only 10% in other forms. Worse in children and elderly.

See also Encephalitis

Erb-Duchenne Palsy
(Erb's Palsy)
DESCRIPTION: Rare complication of a difficult birth affecting arm function.

CAUSE: Pulling too hard on the head during a difficult delivery of a baby stretches and damages the nerves running from the neck across the top of the shoulder to the muscles in the upper arm. The muscles are not damaged, but without a nerve supply, they cannot function.

SYMPTOMS: Inability to move the upper arm away from the body, fully bend the elbow, or turn the hand so that the palm faces backwards when the arm is beside the body. The arm hangs limply by the side, and if treatment is unsuccessful, it appears withered and wasted as the child grows older.

INVESTIGATIONS: Nerve conduction studies sometimes performed.

TREATMENT: Splinting the shoulder in a position that allows the nerves to grow back and recover.

PROGNOSIS: More than nine out of ten cases recover with adequate treatment, usually within a month, but sometimes it takes six months.

See also Klumpke Palsy

Erb's Muscular Dystrophy
(Limb Girdle Dystrophy)
DESCRIPTION: A rare gradually progressive muscle-wasting disease.

CAUSE: May occur in the one family in successive generations, or appear for no apparent reason.

173

SYMPTOMS: Affects the muscles around the shoulder and pelvis, and progresses at a variable rate from its onset between ten and thirty years to cause severe disability in mid-life.

INVESTIGATIONS: Muscle biopsy diagnostic.

TREATMENT: No treatment available other than physiotherapy and occupational therapy.

PROGNOSIS: Severity varies significantly between patients, some being only moderately inconvenienced while others are severely disabled and unable to care for themselves.

See also Muscular Dystrophy

Erb's Palsy
See Erb-Duchenne Palsy

Erectile Failure
See Impotence

Erotomania
See Clérambault Syndrome

Erysipelas

DESCRIPTION: Infection of the skin, most commonly involving the cheek, but any area of the body may be affected.

CAUSE: Any one of a large number of bacteria, but usually *Streptococci*. May start at the site of a scratch, crack or bite, but often there is no apparent cause.

SYMPTOMS: Red, swollen, painful, hot skin. The patient may be feverish, shiver and feel very ill.

INVESTIGATIONS: Swabs sometimes taken to identify the responsible bacteria.

TREATMENT: Antibiotic (eg. penicillin, erythromycin).

COMPLICATIONS: Fluid-filled blisters may develop on the infected area.

PROGNOSIS: Was a very serious disease and often killed children before effective antibiotics were available. Recovery is rapid once antibiotics started, and heals without scarring.

See also Cellulitis

Erythema Induratum
(Bazin's Disease)

DESCRIPTION: Skin disease that usually affects the calves and back of the upper arms of young and middle aged adults.

CAUSE: Unknown, but has been associated with tuberculosis in the past.

SYMPTOMS: Painful, soft, purplish lumps (nodules) that gradually join together and ulcerate.

INVESTIGATIONS: Sometimes necessary to biopsy a lump to make diagnosis.

TREATMENT: None necessary in most cases. Steroids in persistent cases.
PROGNOSIS: Most heal without treatment in a few months, but leave a permanent scar.

Erythema Infectiosum
See Fifth Disease

Erythema Multiforme

DESCRIPTION: Acute inflammation (redness) of the skin and moist (mucus) membranes lining body cavities. Name can be loosely translated as 'red spots of many shapes'.
CAUSE: May be triggered by drugs, bacterial or viral infections, cold sores and other Herpes infections, or may appear for no apparent reason. 75% occur after a Herpes or cold sore infection, and half of the remainder are caused by drugs — particularly sulpha antibiotics. Attacks caused by cold sores and other infections tend to be mild, but those that occur as a result of drug sensitivity can be very severe.
SYMPTOMS: Sudden development of several types of rash simultaneously. The easiest rash to identify appears as multiple red, sore rings on the skin with a pale centre that vary in diameter from a few millimetres to 2 or 3cm. Other forms include red patches, swollen lumps, fluid-filled blisters, itchy red stripes, and painful hard dome-shaped bumps. The insides of the mouth and the vagina, and the eye surface, may be involved with ulcers developing in some cases. Rash may occur anywhere, but is more common on the front of the leg, over the shoulders, above and below the elbow on the outside of the arm, and on the soles and palms. Most patients have only a mild fever, but those severely affected may be acutely ill with a very high fever and generalised weakness.
INVESTIGATIONS: No blood or other tests can confirm the diagnosis.
TREATMENT: If a drug is suspected as the cause, it is immediately ceased. If an infection is thought responsible, this is treated appropriately. Discomfort minimised with pain-killers such as paracetamol and aspirin, and with creams, lotions and dressings to ease the skin irritation. Steroid tablets taken in severe cases.
COMPLICATIONS: Stevens-Johnson syndrome (see separate entry).
PROGNOSIS: No cure, but the vast majority of cases are mild and settle in two to four weeks. Severe cases may persist for up to six weeks, and in rare cases, with lung involvement (Stevens-Johnson syndrome) in the elderly or chronically ill, death may occur. Recurrent attacks are quite common.
See also Stevens-Johnson Syndrome

Erythema Nodosum

DESCRIPTION: An unusual skin inflammation.
CAUSE: The cause is unknown, but may be a reaction to certain bacterial infections,

medications (eg. penicillin) or more serious underlying diseases (eg. leukaemia, tuberculosis, syphilis, hepatitis B or ulcerative colitis).

SYMPTOMS: Very tender, painful red lumps that develop on the front of the leg, usually below the knees. Less commonly affected areas include the arms, face and chest. Patients also have a fever, joint pains and general tiredness.

INVESTIGATIONS: Diagnosis confirmed by skin lump biopsy. Other tests are done to find any underlying cause.

TREATMENT: If a cause can be found, this is treated (eg. infection) or removed (eg. medication). No specific treatment, but steroids and pain-killers may ease the symptoms.

COMPLICATIONS: Skin ulcers.

PROGNOSIS: Lasts about six weeks before slowly disappearing. No serious after-effects, but recurrences are common.

See also Loeffler Syndrome

Erythrasma

DESCRIPTION: Common superficial skin infection. Usually affects the groin, armpit and under the breasts.

CAUSE: Infection of the outermost layer of the skin by the bacteria *Corynebacterium minutissium.*

SYMPTOMS: Well defined, red-brown, scaling, slightly itchy patches that slowly enlarge and become wrinkled.

INVESTIGATIONS: Skin scrapings culture can identify the responsible bacteria.

TREATMENT: Antibiotic tablets (eg. tetracycline, erythromycin) and ointments (eg. fusidic acid).

PROGNOSIS: Responds well to treatment.

Erythroderma, Generalised
See Exfoliative Dermatitis

Erythrogenesis Imperfecta
See Blackfan-Diamond Syndrome

Erythroplasia of Queyrat

DESCRIPTION: Form of skin cancer on the penis.

CAUSE: Unknown, but much rarer in circumcised males.

SYMPTOMS: Raised, velvety, red patch on the head of the penis.

INVESTIGATIONS: Diagnosed by biopsy.

TREATMENT: Anti-cancer cream containing 5-fluorouracil.

COMPLICATIONS: May spread onto the foreskin and break down into an ulcer.

PROGNOSIS: Good results from treatment.

See also Squamous Cell Carcinoma of the Skin

Escherichia coli Infection
(*E. coli* Infection)
DESCRIPTION: A bacteria normally found in the gut where it usually causes no harm, but if it finds its way into other organs, or overgrows to excessive numbers in the gut, may cause a serious infection.

SYMPTOMS: Depends on site of infection (eg. cystitis, pyelonephritis, pneumonia, diarrhoea, septicaemia, cholecystitis — see separate entries).

INVESTIGATIONS: Swab or sample taken from infected area to determine bacteria responsible for infection and appropriate antibiotic.

TREATMENT: Antibiotics.

COMPLICATIONS: Some forms are resistant to common antibiotics, making control more difficult.

PROGNOSIS: Usually respond rapidly to correct treatment.

Esophageal Cancer
See Oesophageal Cancer

Esophagitis
See Reflux Oesophagitis

Esotropia
See Squint

Espundia
See Mucocutaneous Leischmaniasis

Essential Hypertension
See Hypertension

Essential Tremor
(Familial Tremor)
DESCRIPTION: Muscle tremor that usually commences in the twenties.

CAUSE: Inherited condition.

SYMPTOMS: Tremor of hands at rest that worsens with emotional upsets and slowly deteriorates with advancing age.

INVESTIGATIONS: Attempts are made to find a cause (eg. CT scan of brain), but all are negative.

TREATMENT: Numerous medications to reduce tremor are available.

PROGNOSIS: No cure, but reasonable control usually possible.

See also Parkinson's Disease

Eustachian Tube Blockage
DESCRIPTION: Blockage of the eustachian tube which runs from the middle ear to the back of the nose, and is used to equalise air pressure between the middle ear and the outside air with changes in altitude.

CAUSE: Any condition which causes the excess production of phlegm (eg. common cold, sinusitis, hay fever), particularly if there is a sudden change in altitude (eg. flying).

SYMPTOMS: Pressure discomfort in the ear that may become painful, deafness and a constant feeling that swallowing will ease the discomfort. Worsened by changes in altitude.

INVESTIGATIONS: Bulging ear drum can be seen using an otoscope (magnifying light). Sometimes specific pressure tests are carried out on the ear drum.

TREATMENT: Steam inhalations, medications (eg. pseudoephedrine, bromhexine), decongestant nasal sprays and valsalva manoeuvre (holding the nose, closing mouth and trying to breathe out to force air into the ears). In persistent cases a small slit may be put in the ear drum (myringotomy) to ease the pressure.

COMPLICATIONS: If altitude changes, ear drum may burst. Persistent blockage may lead to a middle ear infection (otitis media).

PROGNOSIS: Settles slowly without treatment, and slightly faster with treatment, but may persist for weeks.

See also Cholesteatoma; Glue Ear; Otitis Media; Tympanic Rupture

Ewing's Tumour

DESCRIPTION: A form of bone cancer that usually occurs in young adults but can develop in children.

CAUSE: Unknown.

SYMPTOMS: Almost any bone in the body may be affected, including the vertebrae of the back. There is pain, swelling and tenderness at the site of the tumour, and the patient develops a fever and becomes anaemic.

INVESTIGATIONS: Diagnosis made by X-ray and bone biopsy.

TREATMENT: Involves surgical removal if possible, plus irradiation and potent anti-cancer (cytotoxic) drugs.

COMPLICATIONS: Pathological fractures may occur in the weakened bone.

PROGNOSIS: With intensive treatment a 50% cure rate can be achieved.

See also Bone Cancer

Exfoliative Dermatitis
(Generalised Erythroderma)

DESCRIPTION: A form of dermatitis in which there is extensive peeling of skin.

CAUSE: Often associated with drugs or foods, such as gold injections (used for rheumatoid arthritis), sulphonamide antibiotics, some diabetes tablets and some anti-inflammatory medications. Exposure to heavy metals (eg. lead in battery factories) may also be responsible.

SYMPTOMS: Widespread scaling, peeling and redness of the skin.

INVESTIGATIONS: Patch testing of the skin may be undertaken to determine the cause.

TREATMENT: Removal of the substance that causes the rash, and steroid creams to ease the inflammation.

COMPLICATIONS: Rarely may become very severe and debilitating.
PROGNOSIS: Good, if the trigger substance can be found, but still may take many
  months to settle.
See also Dermatitis

Exposure
See Hypothermia

External Hordeolum
See Stye

Extrasystoles
See Atrial Extrasystoles; Ventricular Extrasystoles

Eye Cancer
See Retinoblastoma

Eye Diseases
See Allergic Conjunctivitis; Amblyopia; Aniridia; Arcus Senilis; Astigmatism;
Cataract; Chalazion; Colour Blind; Conjunctivitis; Corneal Dystrophy; Drusen; Dry
Eye Syndrome; Duane Syndrome; Ectropion; Entropion; Episcleritis; Eye Ulcer;
Floaters in Eye; Glaucoma; Holmes-Adie Syndrome; Keratoconjunctivitis Sicca;
Keratoconus; Leber Congenital Amaurosis; Long-Sighted; Macular Degeneration;
Meibomian Cyst; Posner-Schlossman Syndrome; Presbyopia; Retinal Detachment;
Retinitis Pigmentosa; Retinoblastoma; Scleritis; Short-Sighted; Stagardt Syndrome;
Stye; Tolosa-Hunt Syndrome; Trachoma; Usher Syndrome; Vogt-Koyanagi-Harada
Syndrome etc.

Eye Floaters
See Floaters in Eye

Eye Ulcer
(Corneal Ulcer)
DESCRIPTION: Ulceration of the cornea, the transparent outside covering on the
  front of the eye.
CAUSE: Injuries to the surface of the eye (eg. scratch), or infections. Herpes
  simplex, the virus that causes cold sores and genital herpes, is the most
  common cause of all eye ulcers. Fungal infections causing ulcers are commonly
  seen in farm workers, but may develop in others when steroid eye drops are
  being used. Bacterial conjunctivitis seldom causes ulcers unless treatment is
  neglected. Two rare causes are a deficiency in vitamin A (eg. in people on
  fad diets, or with inability to absorb vitamin A because of diseases of the bile
  duct) which results in a very dry eye, and prolonged exposure of the eye in
  unconscious patients who do not blink.

Eye Ulcer

SYMPTOMS: Pain and watering in the eye, redness of the whites of the eye, and the discharge of sticky pus if an infection is responsible.

INVESTIGATIONS: A swab may be taken from the eye to identify the organism responsible for an infection.

TREATMENT: Appropriate eye drops for bacterial and fungal eye infections. Serious Herpes virus infections can be treated with special anti-viral eye drops and ointment, and through a microscope, minor surgery to remove the active viral areas at the edge of the ulcer may be undertaken.

COMPLICATIONS: Permanent scarring of the cornea and reduced vision. If necessary, a scarred cornea can be surgically replaced by a corneal transplant.

PROGNOSIS: Depend upon the cause and response to treatment. Ulcers caused by an injury usually heal within a few days without treatment. Most viral infections settle without treatment after a few weeks of discomfort, but in some patients, particularly those who are otherwise in poor health or on potent drugs for other serious diseases, the infection can steadily worsen to cause severe eye ulceration. Bacterial and fungal infections respond rapidly to treatment. Good result from corneal transplantation.

See also Conjunctivitis

F

Factor VIII Deficit
See Haemophilia A

Factor IX Deficit
See Christmas Disease

Failure of Ejaculation
See Ejaculatory Failure

Faint
(Syncope)
DESCRIPTION: A sudden brief loss of consciousness.

CAUSES: Stress, anxiety, fright, over exertion, lack of sleep, lack of food, heat, dehydration, lack of ventilation, prolonged standing, hormonal fluctuations.

SYMPTOMS: Light headedness, dizziness, slight nausea, darkening of vision, and loss of consciousness resulting in a fall or collapse. Usually occurs when standing, but sometimes when sitting.

INVESTIGATIONS: None usually necessary. If repeat attacks occur, other diseases that may cause this condition (eg. low blood sugar, low blood pressure, irregular heart beat, infections, anaemia) must be excluded by blood tests and electrocardiographs.

TREATMENT: The patient usually recovers quickly once lying, but should only rise slowly and when completely well.

COMPLICATIONS: Injuries incurred during the fall.

PROGNOSIS: The cause is usually obvious, and provided it can be prevented, recurrences are unlikely.

See also Stokes-Adams Attacks; Vasovagal Syndrome

Fallot's Pentalogy
DESCRIPTION: A developmental abnormality of the heart present at birth resulting in five defects:
— hole between the upper chambers (atriums) of the heart
— hole between the lower chambers (ventricles) of the heart
— narrowing of the artery leading to the lungs (pulmonary artery)
— the opening of the heart into the aorta (main artery of the body) shifted from the left side of the heart to the right
— enlargement of the right side of the heart

CAUSE: Not known

SYMPTOMS: Blue baby, very short of breath, very weak, fails to thrive.

INVESTIGATIONS: Special X-rays of heart and chest, echocardiograms (ultrasound

181

pictures of heart function), electrocardiographs (ECG), measurement of oxygen concentration in blood, catheters inserted into heart through veins.

TREATMENT: Open heart surgery, often on several occasions.

PROGNOSIS: Most patients respond well to surgery, and can lead a normal life.

See also Fallot's Tetralogy; Fallot's Trilogy

Fallot's Tetralogy
(Tetralogy of Fallot)

DESCRIPTION: A developmental abnormality of the heart present at birth resulting in four defects:
— hole between the lower chambers (ventricles) of the heart
— narrowing of the artery leading to the lungs (pulmonary artery)
— the opening of the heart into the aorta (main artery of the body) shifted from the left side of the heart to the right
— enlargement of the right side of the heart

CAUSE: Not known.

SYMPTOMS: Blue baby, very short of breath, very weak, fails to thrive.

INVESTIGATIONS: Special X-rays of heart and chest, echocardiograms (ultrasound pictures of heart function), electrocardiographs (ECG), measurement of oxygen concentration in blood, catheters inserted into heart through veins.

TREATMENT: Open heart surgery, often on several occasions.

PROGNOSIS: Most patients respond well to surgery, and can lead a normal life.

See also Fallot's Pentalogy; Fallot's Trilogy; Ventricular Septal Defect

Fallot's Trilogy

DESCRIPTION: A developmental abnormality of the heart present at birth resulting in three defects:
— hole between the lower chambers (ventricles) of the heart
— narrowing of the artery leading to the lungs (pulmonary artery)
— enlargement of the right side of the heart

CAUSE: Not known.

SYMPTOMS: Blue baby, short of breath, weak, fails to thrive.

INVESTIGATIONS: Special X-rays of heart and chest, echocardiograms (ultrasound pictures of heart function), electrocardiographs (ECG), measurement of oxygen concentration in blood, catheters inserted into heart through veins.

TREATMENT: Open heart surgery.

PROGNOSIS: Most patients respond well to surgery, and can lead a normal life.

See also Fallot's Pentalogy; Fallot's Tetralogy

Familial Angioedema

DESCRIPTION: A rare, severe form of tissue reaction that runs in families.

CAUSE: Inherited.

SYMPTOMS: Sudden severe swelling of the tongue or throat.

INVESTIGATIONS: None diagnostic.

TREATMENT: Treated with a wide variety of rather unusual drugs including danazol (also used for infertility) and the sex hormone methyltestosterone.
COMPLICATIONS: Throat and tongue swellings may block the airway and be fatal.
PROGNOSIS: No cure, but most cases can be controlled.
See also Hives

Familial Mediterranean Fever

DESCRIPTION: Inherited condition that occurs only in people from the Middle East and eastern Mediterranean area.
CAUSE: Cause unknown, but slightly more common in males than females.
SYMPTOMS: Starting in the teens or twenties, the patient develops recurrent severe attacks of a high fever, arthritis, belly pains and pleurisy (inflammation of the membrane over the lungs). Skin rashes may also occur. All symptoms settle after 24 to 48 hours, but will recur after a period that can vary from days to months or even years.
INVESTIGATIONS: There is no specific blood or other test that can diagnose the condition, and so many patients are not diagnosed until they have had several attacks.
TREATMENT: Medication to relieve the pain and inflammation during attacks.
COMPLICATIONS: Amyloidosis (see separate entry) may develop.
PROGNOSIS: Good unless amyloidosis develops.
See also Amyloidosis

Familial Polyposis
See Polyposis Coli

Familial Tremor
See Essential Tremor

Fanconi Syndrome
(de Toni-Fanconi-Debré Syndrome)

DESCRIPTION: Rare defect of kidney function that may be congenital (present from birth) or follow diseases such as cystinosis, glycogen storage diseases, Wilson's disease and others.
CAUSE: Failure of the kidney to adequately deal with numerous chemicals and elements.
SYMPTOMS: Abnormalities in the blood levels of calcium, phosphate, potassium and sugar.
INVESTIGATIONS: Diagnosed by specific blood and urine tests.
TREATMENT: Supplements of missing calcium and potassium, increased water intake and specific dietary restrictions.
COMPLICATIONS: The bone disease osteomalacia (see separate entry) and kidney failure may develop. Eye and brain abnormalities may accompany the congenital form.
PROGNOSIS: Good if carefully managed.

Fascioscapulohumeral Muscular Dystrophy

DESCRIPTION: A progressive and permanent weakening and wasting of muscles.

CAUSE: Inherited condition that may commence at any age.

SYMPTOMS: Very slowly progressive permanent weakness of muscles that initially involves the face and shoulders. Later the hip and leg muscles are involved.

INVESTIGATIONS: Diagnosed by electrical studies of muscle action, and muscle biopsy.

TREATMENT: No effective treatment, but physiotherapy is beneficial.

PROGNOSIS: No cure but a normal life span is usual.

See also other diseases listed under Muscular Dystrophy

Fat Cyst
See Lipoma

Fatigue Fracture
See Stress Fracture

Favus
(Witkop)

DESCRIPTION: Fungal infection of the scalp.

CAUSE: The fungus *Trichophyton schoenleinii*.

SYMPTOMS: Redness of the scalp followed by matting of the hair and gradual formation of a thick off-white crust on the skin.

INVESTIGATIONS: Examination of the skin under a microscope shows characteristic changes.

TREATMENT: Griseofulvin or other antifungal tablets for several weeks.

COMPLICATIONS: Permanent skin damage and hair loss occurs with severe infections.

PROGNOSIS: Good if treated early.

Felty Syndrome

DESCRIPTION: Patients have a very large spleen and a low level of both red and white blood cells in the bloodstream.

CAUSE: The premature destruction of red and white blood cells by the spleen. Often associated with advanced rheumatoid arthritis.

SYMPTOMS: Significant discomfort in the abdomen because of the enlarged spleen, which may put pressure on veins that pass through it. This pressure can cause dilation of the veins that surround the upper part of the stomach. These dilated veins may be attacked by the acid in the stomach, put under stress by vomiting, and damaged by food entering the stomach, ulcerate and bleed. Other symptoms may include a fever, leg ulcers, darkly pigmented skin patches, and tiny blood blisters under the skin.

INVESTIGATIONS: Diagnosis confirmed by blood tests that estimate the type and age of cells in the blood stream.

TREATMENT: Surgical removal of the spleen.

COMPLICATIONS: Patients may become quite ill, very anaemic and vomit blood. If the bleeding continues, patients may die from loss of blood into the stomach.

PROGNOSIS: After removal of the spleen patients react more slowly to infections, and must ensure that they are treated early in the course of any bacterial or viral infection. Regular influenza and pneumococcal vaccinations are recommended.

Femoral Hernia

DESCRIPTION: A hernia due to a small piece of intestine being forced through a point of weakness in the groin, just underneath the skin, where the femoral artery passes through a small hole as it leaves the abdomen and passes to the front of the thigh. More common in women than men.

CAUSE: Pressure in the abdomen from heavy work, lifting or childbirth.

SYMPTOMS: A small lump under the skin of the groin, that may be intermittently painful.

INVESTIGATIONS: Clinical diagnosis. No tests normally required, but ultrasound scan may be necessary in fat patients.

TREATMENT: Surgical repair of the hernia. If constant pain occurs in the hernia, urgent surgery is necessary.

COMPLICATIONS: Very easy for the trapped intestine to become pinched, twisted, and gangrenous.

PROGNOSIS: Recurrence rate after surgery is about 5%.

See also Hernia

Fetal Alcohol Syndrome

DESCRIPTION: Damage to the fetus before birth resulting in numerous deformities.

CAUSE: Excessive alcohol consumption by the mother for a prolonged period during pregnancy.

SYMPTOMS: Baby small for dates at delivery, and has excessive body hair, small finger nails, underdevelopment of the central part of the face and mild mental retardation. Less common symptoms include a small head and small jaw.

INVESTIGATIONS: Clinical diagnosis on history from mother and observation.

TREATMENT: None available for baby. Mother should be advised as strongly as possible not to drink alcohol to excess during pregnancy.

COMPLICATIONS: Poor coordination, poor concentration and reduced muscle tone.

PROGNOSIS: Permanent damage may be done to baby. If recovery to normal developmental levels does not occur by one year of age, further improvement is unlikely.

See also Alcoholism

Fibrillation
See Atrial Fibrillation; Ventricular Fibrillation

Fibrocystic Disease
See Cystic Fibrosis

Fibroids of the Uterus
(Uterine Fibroids)

DESCRIPTION: The formation of one or more hard fibrous balls in the wall of the uterus (womb).

CAUSE: The uterus is made up of muscular, fibrous and glandular tissue. After childbirth, the uterus shrinks back to its usual size. The stress on the uterus during pregnancy may result in some minor injury to the fibrous tissue in its wall, and after the uterus shrinks, it may repair itself in an abnormal way.

SYMPTOMS: When the uterus contracts to force out the blood and wastes during a period, the fibroids distort the uterus causing painful cramps and sometimes heavy menstrual bleeding.

INVESTIGATIONS: Usually detected on pelvic examination, but the diagnosis may be confirmed by an ultrasound scan of the abdomen, laparoscopy or special X-rays of the uterus.

TREATMENT: A hysterectomy to remove the uterus, or if the woman wishes to have more children, the individual fibroids can be cut out of the uterus.

COMPLICATIONS: Rarely any serious complications.

PROGNOSIS: Cured by appropriate surgery.

Fibromyalgia Syndrome
See Fibrositis

Fibromyositis
See Fibrositis

Fibrosarcoma
See Bone Cancer

Fibrosing Alveolitis, Cryptogenic
See Idiopathic Pulmonary Fibrosis

Fibrositis
(Fibromyalgia Syndrome; Fibromyositis)

DESCRIPTION: Widespread inflammation of muscles that is more common in women, particularly in middle age.

CAUSE: Unknown. Aggravated by poor sleep. May be temporary, recur regularly, or in rare cases last for years.

SYMPTOMS: Mainly aching, tender and stiff muscles in varying parts of the body. Other symptoms include tiredness, insomnia, bladder irritability and passing urine frequently. Touching certain areas of muscle causes sudden, severe pain, while nearby areas are quite unaffected.

INVESTIGATIONS: No specific tests can confirm the diagnosis.

TREATMENT: Heat, massage, exercise, anti-inflammatory drugs, and medication to relax the patient and assist in sleeping. Some are helped by physiotherapy.

COMPLICATIONS: None.

PROGNOSIS: Persists intermittently for some months then usually subsides, regardless of what treatment is given. Treatments usually give relief while disease process continues its course.

Fibrous Dysplasia
See Albright Syndrome

Fifth Disease
(Erythema Infectiosum; *Parvovirus* Infection; Slapped Cheek Disease)

DESCRIPTION: Common childhood viral disease that last from two to five days, but occasionally may persist for weeks. Occurs in epidemics every few years. Virtually every child will eventually develop the infection before their teenage years.

CAUSE: Infection caused by the *Parvovirus*.

SYMPTOMS: Red flushed cheeks, paleness around the mouth and a red patchy rash on the arms and legs. Many children will have very mild symptoms that may be overlooked, or confused with german measles (see separate entry).

INVESTIGATIONS: None necessary.

TREATMENT: None necessary.

COMPLICATIONS: Rarely joints may become sore and inflamed.

PROGNOSIS: Complete recovery is normal.

See also German Measles.

Filariasis
(Elephantiasis)

DESCRIPTION: A disease of the lymphatic system (waste drainage ducts) that occurs in tropical Asia, Africa and America.

CAUSE: Caused by a microscopic worm (filarial nematode) that is transmitted from one person or animal to another by mosquitoes.

SYMPTOMS: Inflammation of the lymph nodes and fever. After repeated attacks, the lymph channels of the lymphatic system that carry waste products become blocked by the worm, wastes cannot escape from the legs, arms and scrotum, and they slowly enlarge to a huge size to give the characteristic appearance of elephantiasis.

INVESTIGATIONS: Diagnosed by seeing the infecting worm in a drop of blood under a microscope.

TREATMENT: Elevation of the affected limb, medication to kill the worm, and surgery to remove the swollen tissue. Residents of affected areas should avoid mosquito bites and take medication constantly to prevent the disease.

COMPLICATIONS: Amputation of a limb is sometimes necessary.

PROGNOSIS: Difficult to treat, effective use of damaged limbs may never return, and long term medication may be necessary.

Fissure in Ano
See Anal Fissure

Fistula

DESCRIPTION: The formation of a false passage (connection) between any two hollow organs within the body, or from a hollow organ to the skin. Fistulas can form between an artery and a vein (**arteriovenous fistula**), the bowel and bladder (**rectovescical fistula**), bowel and vagina (**rectovaginal fistula**), bowel and skin (**anal fistula**), gall bladder and bowel (**choledocoduodenal fistula**) etc. Sometimes fistulas are surgically produced to drain an otherwise blocked organ (eg. gall bladder to bowel).

CAUSE: An abscess, bacterial infection, stone, inflammation or cancer damages the tissue between the two organs, allowing a fistula to form between them.

SYMPTOMS: The contents of one organ (eg. intestine) can leak into the other (eg. bladder). Symptoms vary depending on what organs are involved.

INVESTIGATIONS: Special dyes may be injected into the fistula and then X-rayed to see where it runs to.

TREATMENT: Quite difficult surgery is necessary to close a fistula.

COMPLICATIONS: May cause serious damage or infection to one or both of the organs involved.

PROGNOSIS: Most patients recover completely after surgery.

See also Anal Fistula; Arteriovenous Fistula

Fistula in Ano
See Anal Fistula

Fit
See Epilepsy

Fitz-Hugh-Curtis Syndrome

DESCRIPTION: Infection and inflammation of tissue around the liver caused by the bacterium *Chlamydia trachomatis*.

CAUSE: Complication of a sexually transmitted infection of the Fallopian tubes (salpingitis — see separate entry) that lead from the ovaries to the uterus.

SYMPTOMS: Upper abdominal pain worse lying down and turning, vaginal discharge, vulval itch, pain on passing urine.

INVESTIGATIONS: Sample of fluid in abdominal cavity examined for presence of responsible bacteria.

TREATMENT: Tetracycline antibiotics for patient and partner(s).

COMPLICATIONS: Infertility from salpingitis.

PROGNOSIS: Usually cured by appropriate antibiotics.

See also Salpingitis

Fixed Drug Eruption

DESCRIPTION: Persistent skin rash.

CAUSE: Reaction to a drug (eg: blood pressure medications, thiazide diuretics — fluid tablets) that may have been taken for years without previous reaction.

SYMPTOMS: Widespread, itchy, red, patchy, raised rash.

INVESTIGATIONS: Biopsy of rash sometimes necessary.

TREATMENT: Stop taking suspected drug, then use steroid creams and antihistamine tablets. In severe cases steroid tablets may be necessary.

COMPLICATIONS: None serious.

PROGNOSIS: May persist for months or years after causative drug ceased, but most eventually subside.

Flash Burns to Eye

DESCRIPTION: Superficial burn to the surface of the eye (cornea).

CAUSE: Looking at a welding arc or ultraviolet light for a prolonged time.

SYMPTOMS: The eye is very painful, red and sometimes swollen. Pain may not develop until 6 to 12 hours after exposure.

INVESTIGATIONS: Examination of the surface of the eye with a magnifying device.

TREATMENT: Prescribed eye drops, pain-killing tablets, and covering the eye until it has recovered. The only effective first-aid measure is a cold, wet compress.

COMPLICATIONS: Severe or recurrent eye burns can cause scarring and blindness that can only be corrected by a corneal transplant.

PROGNOSIS: Most settle completely within 24 hours.

See also Keratitis

Flat Feet
(Pes Planus)

DESCRIPTION: Occurs when the arch on the inside of the foot is in continuous contact with the ground when the person is standing barefoot on a smooth hard surface. The foot may also be slightly twisted outwards. All infants are flat-footed, as the arch only develops after the age of two years.

CAUSE: In children a flat foot is an inherited or congenital disorder. In adults the causes may be obesity because the foot must carry excess weight, severe foot arthritis, and occupations that requires prolonged standing.

SYMPTOMS: Most patients have no symptoms or discomfort.

INVESTIGATIONS: Rarely, X-ray of the foot may be necessary.

TREATMENT: No treatment other than well fitting shoes is normally required. Wedging of the shoes to tilt the foot outwards, weight reduction, arch supports, foot exercises and physiotherapy are occasionally used.

COMPLICATIONS: An awkward gait, knock-knees and distorted shoes, but rarely any pain or discomfort.

PROGNOSIS: In later life, patients are more likely to develop arthritis in the foot and strain their feet more easily.

See also Pes Cavus

Flesh Eating Disease
See Necrotising Facsiitis

Floaters in Eye

DESCRIPTION: An intermittent or constant abnormality of vision.

CAUSE: A collection of cells or protein in the thick fluid that fills the eyeball, which casts a shadow on the light-sensitive retina at the back of the eye. The floater forms because of bleeding into the eye, a detached retina, infection, or no cause may be found. Diabetes, leukaemia, high blood pressure, and rarer conditions may cause bleeding into the eye.

SYMPTOMS: A spot in the field of vision. The spot may continue to move across the visual field after the moving eye comes to rest — thus the name floater.

INVESTIGATIONS: Because a serious condition may be responsible, all patients with floaters must be investigated to exclude any disease.

TREATMENT: Only treated if causing significant trouble. If necessary, a laser can destroy the floater while a doctor uses a microscope to look into the eye.

COMPLICATIONS: A detached retina can be repaired by a laser in the early stages, but if left, may cause permanent blindness.

PROGNOSIS: Most floaters dissipate with time.

Floppy Baby Syndrome

DESCRIPTION: Partial widespread muscular paralysis in an infant.

CAUSE: Babies fed honey contaminated with dust containing *Clostridium botulinum* are affected by the toxin produced by this bacteria.

SYMPTOMS: Infant is unable to use some of its muscles and becomes very floppy.

INVESTIGATIONS: Test on faeces for the infecting bacteria.

TREATMENT: No specific treatment available.

PROGNOSIS: Usually settles spontaneously with time. Rarely fatal.

See also Botulism

Floppy Eyelid Syndrome

DESCRIPTION: Persistent drooping of the upper eyelid.

CAUSE: Obesity and the deposition of excess fat in the eyelid structures.

SYMPTOMS: Inability to fully open or close eyelid, inflamed red eye, spontaneous turning out of upper eyelid during sleep.

INVESTIGATIONS: Cause of severe obesity needs to be determined.

TREATMENT: Weight loss, tape eyelid shut at night, surgery to remove fat from eyelid.

COMPLICATIONS: Ulceration of the eye surface.

PROGNOSIS: Poor, as most patients do not lose sufficient weight, and problem becomes chronic.

Flu
See Influenza

Focal Dermal Hypoplasia
See Goltz Syndrome

Focal Nodular Myositis
DESCRIPTION: A muscle affecting condition.
CAUSE: Unknown.
SYMPTOMS: Causes painful nodules that may come and go in varying muscles.
INVESTIGATIONS: Diagnosed by biopsy of nodules in muscles.
TREATMENT: None satisfactory.
PROGNOSIS: No cure, but may settle spontaneously.
See also other diseases listed under Myositis

Foetal Alcohol Syndrome
See Fetal Alcohol Syndrome

Follicular Ovarian Cyst
See Ovarian Cyst

Folliculitis
DESCRIPTION: A bacterial infection of hair follicles which occurs mainly on the neck, upper lip and in the groin. More common in men than women.
CAUSE: Numerous different bacteria may be responsible, but *Staphylococcus aureus* is the most common. Infection is more likely in diabetics, those with poor hygiene, and with oily skin.
SYMPTOMS: A sore, tender, and sometimes itchy pus-filled blister appears on the skin surrounded by red skin.
INVESTIGATIONS: A swab may be taken from a blister in resistant cases to identify the bacteria responsible for the infection and the correct antibiotic to treat it.
TREATMENT: Antibiotic ointments are applied to the sores. In severe cases antibiotic tablets are taken. Personal hygiene must be scrupulous. Long-term use of antibiotics and antiseptic soaps may be required.
COMPLICATIONS: A boil or abscess may form. The latter will need to be cut open and drained.
PROGNOSIS: The infection is often difficult to cure, and attacks may recur for several months or years.
See also Abscess; Boil

Fong Syndrome
(Nail-Patella Syndrome)
DESCRIPTION: Congenital abnormality of finger and toe nails, and the knee cap.
CAUSE: Genetic inheritance.
SYMPTOMS: Gross nail defects, small or absent knee caps, bony outgrowths of the pelvic bone, elbow joint abnormalities.

INVESTIGATIONS: Excess protein is found in the urine, X-rays show bony abnormalities.
TREATMENT: Plastic and orthopaedic surgery.
COMPLICATIONS: Kidney failure.
PROGNOSIS: Patients have persistent knee problems and premature arthritis.

Food Poisoning

DESCRIPTION: An illness involving the intestine caused by eating contaminated food.
CAUSE: Bacteria, or a toxin produced by bacteria, present in contaminated food. Many different types of bacteria may be responsible. Foods that are particularly likely to be responsible are dairy products, fish, chicken or other meat that has been inadequately refrigerated, fried foods, meat dishes that have been reheated, and stale bread.
SYMPTOMS: Vomiting, diarrhoea, nausea, fever and stomach cramps. Small amounts of blood may be vomited or passed in the motions. Most attacks develop suddenly within one to eight hours of eating the contaminated food, but may take up to 24 hours.
INVESTIGATIONS: No specific investigation can diagnose the cause in an individual, but a suspect food can be tested to see if it is contaminated. Strongly suspected when a number of people are affected simultaneously. May be confused with gastroenteritis.
TREATMENT: Usually no treatment is necessary other than a clear fluid diet. Antibiotics are rarely necessary.
COMPLICATIONS: In the very young and elderly, dehydration may be a problem, and intravenous drips in hospital may be required.
PROGNOSIS: Most attacks settle within six to twelve hours.
See also Botulism; Gastroenteritis

Footballer's Ankle
See Anterior Impingement Syndrome

Foot Ganglion
See Ganglion of a Tendon

Fox-Fordyce Disease
(Hidrosadenome; Lichen Axillaris)

DESCRIPTION: Rare skin disease that occurs in women between 15 and 50 years of age.
CAUSE: Unknown, but possibly due to a hormonal imbalance that causes blockage of the sweat glands in the affected areas.
SYMPTOMS: Extremely itchy groups of small, firm skin coloured lumps in the armpits, groin and on the nipples. Worsens during a menstrual period.
INVESTIGATIONS: None specific.
TREATMENT: Steroid creams, and taking the oral contraceptive pill to reduce hormone fluctuations.

COMPLICATIONS: Scratching may damage skin and allow a secondary bacterial infection.

PROGNOSIS: Persists long term, but may be cured by pregnancy.

Fracture
(Broken Bone)

DESCRIPTION: A break in any bone in the body. There are several different types of fracture—
- hair line fracture — tiny crack part way through a bone
- greenstick fracture — abnormal flexion in a child's soft bone wrinkling one surface only
- simple fracture — a single break across the whole width of a bone
- avulsion fracture — a small fragment of bone is pulled off at the point where a muscle, tendon or ligament attaches
- impacted fracture — the forcible shortening of a bone as one fragment of bone is pushed into another
- comminuted fracture — two, three or more breaks in the one bone
- depressed fracture — a piece of bone (often in the skull) is pushed in below the level of the surrounding bone
- compound fracture — the skin over the fracture is broken by a bone end
- pathological fracture — a break in a bone bone weakened by osteoporosis (see separate entry), cancer or other disease

CAUSE: Abnormal violence, pressure, force or twisting applied to a bone.

SYMPTOMS: Pain that is worse with use of the bone, swelling and tenderness at the site of the fracture, bruising over or below the fracture, loss of function of the limb or area.

INVESTIGATIONS: X-rays show most fractures, but sometimes a CT scan or bone scan is necessary.

TREATMENT: The bone fragments must be aligned as perfectly as possible after manipulation under an anaesthetic if necessary, and fixed in position with plaster, pins, plates, or screws. It is normally necessary to prevent movement in the joints at either end of the broken bone. The exact treatment will vary considerably from one bone to another, with some fractures requiring minimal fixation (eg. fracture of humerus — upper arm bone), while others require major surgery (eg. fracture of hip — see separate entry).

COMPLICATIONS: Movement at the fracture site may cause failure to heal, chronic pain may occur at fracture site, fractures requiring surgery and compound fractures are susceptible to infection, death of bone tissue can occur in small fragments.

PROGNOSIS: The majority of fractures can be successfully treated with an eventual return to full function of the bone.

See also entries under specific types of fracture (eg. Colles' Fracture; Hip Fracture; Humerus Fracture; March Fracture; Monteggia Fracture; Osteogenesis Imperfecta; Pott's Fracture; Scaphoid Fracture; Smith's Fracture; Stress Fracture)

Fragile X Syndrome

DESCRIPTION: Inherited cause of mental retardation in males.

CAUSE: Abnormal gene carried on the X chromosome. Men have only one X sex chromosome matched to a small Y sex chromosome, while women have two X sex chromosomes and the faulty gene's activity can be replaced by the one on the good X chromosome. Women carry the abnormal gene from one generation to the next.

SYMPTOMS: Mental retardation, excess activity, epilepsy and autism (see separate entry). Often large babies, with large ears, forehead and jaw.

INVESTIGATIONS: Diagnosed by examination of the genes in a cell sample taken from the blood after birth, or by a sample from the placenta taken before birth.

TREATMENT: No cure. Treatment involves the use of appropriate support services and medication to reduce the excitement and excess activity. Genetic counselling of families is essential.

COMPLICATIONS: Short sightedness, enlarged testes, cleft palate and slack joints.

PROGNOSIS: Life long disability.

France's Triad

DESCRIPTION: The simultaneous occurrence of asthma, aspirin sensitivity and allergic rhinitis (hay fever) in a patient.

CAUSE: Unknown.

SYMPTOMS: Symptoms of the three conditions above. Aspirin sensitivity may take many forms (see Allergy and Anaphylaxis entries).

TREATMENT: Individual diseases treated.

COMPLICATIONS: Nasal polyps.

PROGNOSIS: The same as that of the contributing diseases.

See also Allergy; Anaphylaxis; Asthma; Hay Fever

Freeman-Sheldon Syndrome
(Whistling Face Syndrome)

DESCRIPTION: An inherited condition that affects the hands, feet and face.

CAUSE: Genetic abnormality that can be present in several generations of a family.

SYMPTOMS: Club feet, deformed hands, pursed lips, difficulty in opening mouth, fixed facial grimace.

TREATMENT: May be helped by plastic and orthopaedic surgery.

PROGNOSIS: Lifelong disability.

Freiberg's Disease

DESCRIPTION: Inflammation of the toe end of the first or second metatarsal (long bones in foot).

CAUSE: Form of avascular necrosis (death of bone due to poor blood supply) due to stress fracture or other injury to the bones from repeated jumping, running etc.

SYMPTOMS: Pain, swelling and tenderness over the ball of the foot that is worse when walking.

INVESTIGATIONS: X-rays show bone deformity.

TREATMENT: Prolonged rest in early stages, or surgery in advanced cases.

COMPLICATIONS: Premature arthritis of other joints in the foot due to abnormal stresses from limping.

PROGNOSIS: Treatment only moderately successful and persistent pain may occur, although most settle as nerves in the affected bone are destroyed.

Frey Syndrome
(Auriculotemporal Syndrome)

DESCRIPTION: Abnormal function of a nerve on the side of the face.

CAUSE: A disturbance to a nerve on the affected side of the head after injury, infection or surgery.

SYMPTOMS: Flushing and sweating of the ear and temple on one side of the head with eating.

TREATMENT: Surgery to the involved nerve.

PROGNOSIS: Some success from surgery, but may persist long term.

Friedrich's Ataxia
(Spinocerebellar Degeneration)

DESCRIPTION: Inherited condition causing damage to the base of the brain and spinal cord which usually starts in childhood or early adult life.

CAUSE: Degeneration of nerves in the cerebellum (lower back part of the brain) and spinal cord.

SYMPTOMS: Abnormal way of walking, incoordination, clumsiness, weakness and abnormal sensation.

INVESTIGATIONS: Nerve conduction studies, CT and MRI scans.

TREATMENT: None available.

COMPLICATIONS: Heart inflammation and degeneration.

PROGNOSIS: Death in early adult life is normal.

Frigidity

DESCRIPTION: A woman who is unable to experience any pleasure or arousal from sexual stimulation.

CAUSE: Usually a psychological problem and not a physical one, which may be a result of a woman's strict upbringing, a loathing for sex that has been conditioned by an oppressive mother or violent father, an unfortunate early sexual experience, an unwanted pregnancy, a rape or other assault. Other causes include pain with intercourse, postnatal depression after birth, life stress (eg. moving house or changing jobs), and the hormone drop associated with menopause. Certain prescribed drugs and hormones may also be responsible.

SYMPTOMS: With sexual stimulation there is no lubrication of the vagina, enlargement of the nipples or clitoral tenseness.

Frigidity

INVESTIGATIONS: Sex hormone studies may be undertaken.

TREATMENT: Requires a very understanding partner and a very slow teaching process, usually with the help of a psychiatrist or psychologist. Stimulation of non-erotic parts of the body to relax the woman over a period of weeks, followed by stimulation of more erotically sensitive areas, slowly breaks down the barriers.

COMPLICATIONS: May be responsible for infertility.

PROGNOSIS: Most women respond to appropriate treatment after many sessions over several months.

See also other diseases listed under Sex Problems

Fröhlich Syndrome
(Dystrophia Adiposgenitalis)

DESCRIPTION: Rare syndrome that has its onset after puberty when there is a loss of sexual function and libido.

CAUSE: A lack of sex hormones, which in turn may be due to a tumour of the pituitary gland in the centre of the brain.

SYMPTOMS: Loss of sexual development and activity, the skin becomes thin and wrinkles prematurely, body hair is scanty, scalp hair becomes very fine, fat may deposit around the buttocks and genitals.

INVESTIGATIONS: All hormones are checked by blood tests, CT scan of pituitary gland.

TREATMENT: Sex hormone supplements. Surgery for any tumour.

COMPLICATIONS: Responsible tumour may be malignant.

PROGNOSIS: No cure, but long term control possible.

Frostbite

DESCRIPTION: The freezing of living tissue that occurs most commonly in the toes, but fingers, ears and nose may also be affected.

CAUSE: Exposure of flesh to very cold conditions.

SYMPTOMS: The severity of the frostbite depends on the depth to which the freezing has penetrated. Early symptoms are numbness, itching and a pricking sensation. As the freezing penetrates deeper, stiffness and shooting pains will occur, the skin is white or yellow, and the toe or finger becomes immobile.

TREATMENT: Slow and gradual thawing of frozen tissue in warm water. Rapid rewarming or overheating further damages the tissue. Never warm an area affected by frostbite by rubbing or massage. If two people are present, thawing each others toes by placing them in the other person's armpit is an ideal method. After thawing, the tissue should be kept protected and warm. No dressings should be applied, but the affected areas should be left exposed in a warm room. Antiseptics may be applied to blisters and antibiotics given for infection. Only after several days or weeks is amputation of affected fingers or toes considered, as recovery may occur from an apparently hopeless situation. Moist gangrene is an indication for immediate amputation.

COMPLICATIONS: Freezing of the skin itself is not particularly serious, but if the freezing penetrates to the bone, the tissue will die, and the finger or toe requires amputation. Late stages of frostbite are characterised by blistering, swelling, black colouration and gangrene.

PROGNOSIS: Depends on severity of freezing. Any area that has been frostbitten will be more susceptible to frostbite in future.

See also Chilblains; Hypothermia

Frozen Shoulder
(Adhesive Capsulitis)

DESCRIPTION: A shoulder that for no apparent reason becomes stiff and limited in its range of movement.

CAUSE: Unknown. Overuse of the joint may be an aggravating factor.

SYMPTOMS: Joint stiffness usually starts slowly and worsens gradually over a period of days or weeks. There may also be a constant ache in the joint.

INVESTIGATIONS: X-rays are taken to exclude other causes, but in a frozen shoulder the X-rays are normal.

TREATMENT: Rest in a sling, with periods of gentle movement several times a day under the supervision of a physiotherapist. Anti-inflammatory drugs and mild to moderate strength pain-killers are prescribed. In severe cases, steroid tablets are taken or injections given into the joint. If recovery is delayed, the shoulder may be moved around while the patient is anaesthetised to break down any adhesions that have formed.

COMPLICATIONS: Persistent limitation of movement and pain.

PROGNOSIS: Most cases last 6 to 12 months, then slowly recover regardless of any treatment.

Fuchs Heterochromic Cyclitis
See Fuchs Uveitis Syndrome

Fuchs Uveitis Syndrome
(Fuchs Heterochromic Cyclitis)

DESCRIPTION: Gradually worsening form of iritis (inflammation of the iris — coloured part of the eye). Usually affects young adults and only one eye.

CAUSE: Degeneration of the cells responsible for colour in the iris. May be congenital.

SYMPTOMS: The irises gradually become different colours and the vision is irregularly blurred.

INVESTIGATIONS: Diagnosed by eye examination.

TREATMENT: None available except for complications.

COMPLICATIONS: Cataracts and glaucoma (see separate entries) may occur.

PROGNOSIS: No cure.

See also Iritis

197

Fulminant Meningococcaemia
See Waterhouse-Friderichsen Syndrome

Functional Indigestion
See Irritable Bowel Syndrome

Fungal Infection
(Mycoses)

DESCRIPTION: Infection of the skin, mouth, gut or vagina (common), or an internal organ (rare) by a fungus, which is a type of microscopic plant.

CAUSE: Exposure of damaged tissue, or a patient with reduced immunity, to a fungus.

SYMPTOMS: Depends on the site of infection.

INVESTIGATIONS: Swab taken of infected site for culture and examination under a microscope.

TREATMENT: Antifungal creams, lotions, pessaries, tablets and injections.

COMPLICATIONS: Rarely may spread to the lungs, brain and other internal organs.

PROGNOSIS: Infections of skin, vagina, mouth and gut respond well to treatment. Infections of lungs, brain and other organs are very difficult to cure.

See also specific types of fungal infection (eg. Aspergillosis; Athlete's Foot; Blastomycosis; Cryptococcosis; Mycetoma; Onychogryphosis; Pityriasis Versicolor; Thrush; Tinea; Zygomycosis etc.)

Fungal Nail Infection
See Onychogryphosis

Fungal Skin Infection
See Athlete's Foot; Pityriasis Versicolor; Tinea

Funnel Web Spider Bite

DESCRIPTION: The eastern Australian funnel-web spider is a large black, furry spider about 2-3cm across. It lives in rock crevices, burrows, post holes, under houses or around dead tree roots.

SYMPTOMS: The bite is intensely painful, and the victim will usually be frightened and distressed. Further symptoms include tingling around the mouth, muscular spasm or weakness, excessive sweating, profuse salivation, nausea, abdominal pain, numbness, coughing up of secretions from the lungs, weeping eyes, cold shivers and breathing difficulty.

INVESTIGATIONS: None normally necessary, but swabs may be taken from the bite site for venom identification.

TREATMENT: Keep the victim calm and move them as little as possible, apply pressure immobilisation to the limb and get medical help as soon as possible. Check the victim's breathing and pulse regularly, and give mouth-to-mouth resuscitation if breathing stops, and cardiopulmonary resuscitation if the pulse stops. An effective antivenine injection is available.

COMPLICATIONS: Ulcer formation and scarring at site of bite.

PROGNOSIS: Death may occur, but is uncommon. Excellent results from antivenine.

Furuncle
See Boil; Furunculosis, Ear

Furunculosis, Ear

DESCRIPTION: A boil that involves a hair follicle in the outer canal of the ear.

CAUSE: Bacteria such as *Staphylococcus aureus* (the golden staph) invade the roots of the fine hairs in the ear canal, often after an injury to the ear canal from a cotton bud, hair pin or other foreign object.

SYMPTOMS: An excruciatingly painful swelling that may completely close the ear canal. If the infection is deeper, there may be less swelling and only a patch of redness on one side of the ear canal. The pain is aggravated by chewing and may spread to the lymph nodes on that side of the neck. Eventually it may burst and discharge pus.

INVESTIGATIONS: A swab is taken to culture the particular bacteria that is causing the infection, and to select the correct antibiotic. Furuncles are more common in diabetics and in cases of recurrent infection, tests should be done to exclude any other disease. X-rays are occasionally necessary to ensure that surrounding bone has not been damaged.

TREATMENT: A wick (thin ribbon of cloth or tiny material tube) soaked in an antibiotic and soothing ointment is gently placed in the ear canal and changed every day or two. A course of antibiotics by tablet or injection is also given. Scratching the ear canal with any object is forbidden. Heat can help relieve the pain.

COMPLICATIONS: Most furuncles burst spontaneously, but some deep-seated infections may form an abscess that must be lanced to drain the pus. Rarely, the infection can penetrate to bone and from there to the sinuses or brain.

PROGNOSIS: Most respond well to appropriate treatment.

See also Abscess; Boil; Otitis Externa

G

Galactokinase Deficiency
See Galactosaemia

Galactosaemia
(Galactokinase Deficiency)

DESCRIPTION: A disturbance of the way in which the sugar galactose in milk is metabolised (broken down).

CAUSE: A congenital lack of the liver enzyme galactokinase that is responsible for galactose metabolism.

SYMPTOMS: Vomiting, failure to thrive, liver disease, mental retardation and eye cataracts in an infant.

INVESTIGATIONS: Specific diagnostic tests on red blood cells.

TREATMENT: Strict dietary avoidance of all milk products.

COMPLICATIONS: Increased risk of infection.

PROGNOSIS: A strict diet will prevent all the symptoms except mental retardation.

Gallstones
(Biliary Colic; Cholelethiasis)

DESCRIPTION: The development of one or more stones in the gall bladder.

CAUSE: The liver produces bile which is stored in the gall bladder. Bile is required to help in the digestion of food, and when this is required in the gut, the gall bladder contracts to squeeze out the bile. If the bile becomes too concentrated it may precipitate out as a stone. Up to 10% of men over 60 years of age, and 20% of women over 60 have some gallstones.

SYMPTOMS: Larger stones block the bile duct, and when the gall bladder contracts with eating, the movement of the stone in the duct causes severe intermittent pain (colic) in the upper right side of the abdomen. The pain can also be felt in the back at the lower end of the shoulder blade. Indigestion, burping and passing wind rectally (farting), are common. If the stone becomes stuck, constant severe pain results, and an emergency operation is required to clear it.

INVESTIGATIONS: The presence of gallstones is confirmed by an ultrasound scan, or special X-rays (cholecystograms) taken after a dye which concentrates in the bile has been swallowed or injected. In difficult cases, X-rays of the gall bladder can be performed by passing a gastroscope into the small intestine and then injecting dye through the opening into the bile duct (endoscopic retrograde cholecystopancreatography — ERCP). Blood tests to check liver function are usually normal unless a gallstone is blocking the bile duct and preventing waste products leaving the liver.

TREATMENT: A low fat diet will reduce demands on the gall bladder for bile and reduce painful spasms. Most effective treatment is surgery to remove the gall bladder. The operation can be performed by open exposure of the gall bladder or by laparoscopic surgery. If stones are very low in the common bile duct they may be removed by an instrument that is passed through the mouth and stomach into the intestine (an endoscope). Patients who are too ill for an operation may use a drug that slowly dissolves some gallstones over many months. Lithotripsy is a treatment in which the stones are shattered by a high-frequency sound wave, but it is only suitable for a small number of cases.

COMPLICATIONS: Infection of the gall bladder (cholecystitis) when its drainage is blocked by a stone. The patient is feverish, nauseated and in constant pain. In extreme cases, an infected gall bladder will rupture and cause peritonitis.

PROGNOSIS: Surgery is completely successful in the vast majority of patients.

See also Cholecystitis; Mirizzi Syndrome

Gambling, Pathological

DESCRIPTION: A preoccupation with gambling for its own sake, that becomes more intense when under stress.

CAUSE: Pathological gambling is a psychiatric illness which normally starts in the teenage years, but intensifies in early adult life. It may be triggered by stress. Patient's children are more likely to develop the problem.

SYMPTOMS: Most are men who gamble alone, try to conceal their gambling and losses, gamble more when they lose, are unable to confine losses to a budget, borrow money to gamble, and may steal money to gamble. They experience an intolerable build up of tension when there is an opportunity to gamble, that can only be relieved by partaking in the bet.

TREATMENT: Group therapy run by psychiatrists, psychologists and groups such as Gamblers Anonymous are the most successful treatments. Only rarely are drugs prescribed to quieten a particularly manic phase.

COMPLICATIONS: Serious family, social and financial loss.

PROGNOSIS: Often, not until a crisis such as bankruptcy, gaol or separation from a wife results will the sufferer seek, or be forced to undertake, any form of treatment.

See also Obsessive Compulsive Disorder

Ganglion of a Tendon

DESCRIPTION: A benign thin-walled cyst filled with a thick, clear fluid that develops on a tendon of the wrist, hand or foot.

CAUSE: Tendons slide within fibrous sheaths which prevent the tendon from slipping out of position around a joint. The tendon is surrounded by a thin film of lubricating fluid within the sheath. A tiny puncture in the sheath allows some of the lubricating fluid around the tendon to escape and form a firm lump under the skin.

SYMPTOMS: A disfiguring hard lump develops on a tendon on the back of the hand, wrist or less commonly on the top of the foot.

INVESTIGATIONS: None normally needed.

TREATMENT: Either a minor operation in which the ganglion is cut away from the tendon, or a needle is inserted into the ganglion to withdraw the thick fluid within, and a small amount of a steroid solution is then injected.

COMPLICATIONS: Painful bleeding into the ganglion, painful pressure on a nerve, or infection.

PROGNOSIS: Many settle spontaneously, may recur after injection, usually permanently cured by surgery.

Gangrene, Gas
(Clostridial Myositis)

DESCRIPTION: Death of tissue caused by a gas producing bacteria.

CAUSE: The *Clostridium welchii* bacterium can infect a deep wound into which air cannot penetrate. These 'anaerobic' bacteria are widespread, but cannot survive if exposed to oxygen. They produce a chemical (toxin) that destroys damaged muscle and produces a foul-smelling gas.

SYMPTOMS: The wound becomes painful and swollen, and surrounding skin discolours. Pressure over the area produces a crackling sound as tiny gas bubbles in the damaged tissue burst. A smelly discharge issues from the wound. The patient becomes feverish, delirious and comatose.

INVESTIGATIONS: A swab taken from the wound shows the bacteria under a microscope. Gas bubbles in infected tissue can be seen on X-ray.

TREATMENT: Massive doses of penicillin by injection and gas gangrene antitoxin, but this is only beneficial if given very early in the infection. Surgery to cut away affected tissue is essential. High-pressure oxygen chambers normally used to treat divers with the bends may force oxygen into the tissues to destroy the bacteria.

COMPLICATIONS: Destruction of red blood cells, damage to the liver and kidney.

PROGNOSIS: Depends on the site of the wound, and the severity of the infection. There is a significant death rate.

Gardner Syndrome

DESCRIPTION: Inflammatory condition of the large bowel.

CAUSE: Inherited.

SYMPTOMS: Multiple polyps in their large bowel that may bleed, multiple skin cysts, bony growths on the jaw, other tumours of soft tissue throughout the body.

INVESTIGATIONS: Colonoscopy or barium enema X-ray.

TREATMENT: Regular colonoscopy to remove bleeding and cancerous growths. Sometimes necessary for part or all of the large gut to be removed.

COMPLICATIONS: Bowel cancer.

PROGNOSIS: Good, provided regular colonoscopies prevent cancer or detect it early.

See also Colo-Rectal Cancer; Polyposis Coli

Gas Bloat Syndrome

DESCRIPTION: Inability to burp or vomit.

CAUSE: Complication of surgery to the stomach.

SYMPTOMS: Significant discomfort when swallowed air builds up in the stomach.

INVESTIGATIONS: Barium meal X-ray and gastroscopy abnormal.

TREATMENT: Medications and diet to reduce gas build up. Further surgery to relieve obstruction.

PROGNOSIS: Surgery usually successful, but may persist despite treatment.

See also Denervation Syndrome

Gas Embolism
See Bends

Gas Gangrene
Gangrene, Gas

Gastric Carcinoma
See Stomach Cancer

Gastric Ulcer
See Ulcer, Peptic

Gastrinoma
See Zollinger-Ellison Syndrome

Gastritis

DESCRIPTION: Inflammation of the stomach.

CAUSE: Many factors including stress, gut infections, drugs (particularly aspirin and anti-arthritis drugs), alcohol excess, overindulgence in food, stomach cancer and allergies.

SYMPTOMS: Intermittent symptoms of nausea, vomiting, loss of appetite, a feeling of fullness, upper abdominal discomfort or pain, and possibly indigestion for a few hours or days, or constant discomfort for weeks or months.

INVESTIGATIONS: Gastroscopy reveals the inflamed red stomach lining.

TREATMENT: Depends upon the cause. Antacids or anti-ulcer drugs. Anti-anxiety drugs may be used when appropriate. Drug-induced gastritis will require the removal of the drugs, substituting other drugs, or if the medication is essential, adding anti-ulcer or antacid medications to control the continuing symptoms.

COMPLICATIONS: Peptic ulcers and stomach cancer.

PROGNOSIS: Dependent upon the cause, and varies from one patient to another.

See also Ulcer, Peptic

Gastro-Oesophageal Reflux
See Reflux Oesophagitis

203

Gastroenteritis
(Viral Enteritis)

DESCRIPTION: A viral infection of the gut.

CAUSE: The rotavirus is one of the most common viruses responsible, particularly in children. Often appears in epidemics, and usually in spring or early summer. Passes from one person to another through contamination of the hands and food.

SYMPTOMS: Uncomfortable feeling in the stomach, gurgling, cramping pains and then vomiting. A few hours later the vomiting starts to ease, and diarrhoea develops. Lasts from one to three days.

INVESTIGATIONS: Usually none necessary. Faeces tests if another cause is suspected and blood tests for dehydration.

TREATMENT: Specific diet to replace the fluid and vital salts that are rinsed out of the body by the vomiting and diarrhoea, and then careful reintroduction of foods. In adults, medications can be used to slow diarrhoea. Paracetamol can be used for belly pain.

COMPLICATIONS: Young children may become rapidly dehydrated and require urgent hospitalisation. Some children develop an intolerance to milk sugar (lactose) after the infection, and this may prevent them from returning to a normal diet for weeks or months.

PROGNOSIS: Almost everyone recovers in a few days.

See also Dehydration

Gaucher Disease

DESCRIPTION: Excess accumulation of fat in cells throughout the body.

CAUSE: Inherited condition more common in eastern Europeans and Jews. Due to the lack of a liver enzyme.

SYMPTOMS: Enlargement of the spleen, anaemia, damage to bones in the back and thigh, and bone pain.

INVESTIGATIONS: Diagnosed by specific blood tests and tissue biopsy.

TREATMENT: None available.

COMPLICATIONS: Fractures of softened bones. Poor liver function and lung involvement.

PROGNOSIS: Reasonable life expectancy unless lungs become damaged.

'Gay'
See Homosexuality

Gay Bowel Syndrome

DESCRIPTION: Inflammation of anus and rectum from anal intercourse.

CAUSE: Homosexuals who practise frequent anal sex can develop a chronic inflammation and infection of their lower bowel.

SYMPTOMS: Diarrhoea, a constant feeling of wanting to pass faeces when none is present, a mucus discharge from the anus.

INVESTIGATIONS: The responsible bacteria can be identified by a faeces test.
TREATMENT: Appropriate antibiotics to cure the bowel infection.
COMPLICATIONS: Ulcer formation and bleeding in the rectum.
PROGNOSIS: Good, but depends on personal habits.

Generalised Erythroderma
See Exfoliative Dermatitis

Genital Herpes
(Herpes Simplex Type 2 Infection)
DESCRIPTION: Contagious viral infection of the genitals.
CAUSE: The *Herpes simplex type 2* virus is caught by sexual contact with someone who already has the disease. It is possible, but unlikely, for the virus to be caught in hot spa baths and from a shared wet towel. If sores are present, there is a good chance of passing the disease on, but a patient is also infectious for several days before a new crop of sores develop. Condoms give limited protection against spreading the disease.
SYMPTOMS: Once a person is infected with the virus, it settles in the nerve endings around the vulva or penis, and remains there for the rest of that person's life. With stress, illness or reduced resistance, the virus starts reproducing and causes painful blisters and ulcers on the penis or scrotum (sac) in the male; and on the vulva (vaginal lips), and in the vagina and cervix (opening into the womb) of the female. The first attack may occur only a week, or up to some years, after the initial infection. An attack will last for two to four weeks and then subside. After weeks, months or years, a further attack may occur. Women are affected more severely and frequently than men.
INVESTIGATIONS: Diagnosed by taking a swab from the ulcer or a blood test.
TREATMENT: Antiviral tablets and ointments will control an attack, and can be taken for months or years to prevent further attacks.
COMPLICATIONS: If a baby catches the infection from the mother during delivery, it can cause severe brain damage in the child. For this reason, if a woman has a history of repeated herpes infections, she may be delivered by caesarean section. The incidence of gynaecological cancer is increased and in rare cases it can cause encephalitis (brain infection).
PROGNOSIS: Good control with modern medications.
See also Cold Sores; Sexually Transmitted Diseases

Genital Warts
(Condylomata Acuminata; Venereal Warts)
DESCRIPTION: The development of warts on the genitals because of a sexually transmitted viral infection.
CAUSE: The human papilloma virus (HPV) which is transmitted from one person to another only by sexual intercourse or other intimate contact, is responsible. It is not possible to catch it from toilet seats or spa baths. The incubation

period varies from one to six months. Condoms can give some protection against the infection.

SYMPTOMS: The growth of warts, sometimes of a large size, on the penis in men and in the genital area of women. Appear as flat, pale areas on the skin, or as the dark-coloured, irregularly-shaped lumps. Both men and women can be carriers without being aware they are infected. In women genital warts may develop internally where they are difficult to detect.

INVESTIGATIONS: Small warts seen if a special stain is applied.

TREATMENT: Antiviral cream applied three times a week for up to four months, acid paints or ointments, freezing with liquid nitrogen, or burning with electric diathermy or laser.

COMPLICATIONS: Anyone with genital warts should also have tests performed to check for the presence of other venereal disease. A significant proportion of women with this infection will develop cancer of the cervix which can only be detected at early stage by regular Pap smears.

PROGNOSIS: Treatment often prolonged, and warts tend to recur, but with careful watching and rapid treatment of any recurrence the infection will eventually settle.

See also Cervical Cancer and other conditions listed under Sexually Transmitted Diseases

Genu Valgum
See Knock Knees

Genu Varum
See Bow legs

Geographic Tongue

DESCRIPTION: Smooth red patches with greyish margin scattered over the tongue in a map-like pattern.

CAUSE: Excessive shedding of the cells on the surface of the tongue. May be due to an allergy or severe infection, but usually has no apparent cause.

SYMPTOMS: None, other than strange appearance of tongue.

INVESTIGATIONS: Sometimes tests to exclude a specific cause may be necessary.

TREATMENT: None necessary.

COMPLICATIONS: None.

PROGNOSIS: Usually settles after a few weeks.

German Measles
(Rubella)

DESCRIPTION: Contagious viral infection caused by a *Togavirus*.

CAUSE: The virus is widespread in the community, with epidemics occurring every few years. Spreads from one person to another with coughs and sneezes. Incubation period is two to three weeks. Can be caught only once in a lifetime, but may be so mild that it is completely overlooked.

SYMPTOMS: Occurs commonly in children, and produces a fine rash over the body that lasts only two or three days, is not itchy, and is not accompanied by the sore eyes and cold symptoms associated with common measles. There are often some enlarged lymph nodes at the back of the neck, and in severe cases there may be a fever, runny nose and joint pains.

INVESTIGATIONS: A blood test is sometimes done to confirm the disease or determine the immune status of a pregnant woman.

TREATMENT: Paracetamol for fever and discomfort is all that is necessary. Vaccination is simple and effective. All children are now given mumps, measles and rubella as a combined vaccine at one and five years of age.

COMPLICATIONS: Causes blindness, deafness, heart damage and other serious effects to the babies of pregnant mothers who catch the disease between the sixth and twelfth weeks of pregnancy.

PROGNOSIS: Excellent.

See also Measles; Roseola Infantum

Gerstmann Syndrome

DESCRIPTION: Loss of ability to remember previously known objects or learned skills.

CAUSE: Damage to the dominant side of the brain by a stroke, tumour or other injury.

SYMPTOMS: Inability to recognise objects or people, write, calculate simple maths or distinguish left from right.

INVESTIGATIONS: CT and MRI scans of the brain, blood tests to exclude other diseases.

TREATMENT: If possible, the cause of the brain damage is corrected.

PROGNOSIS: Poor.

Gerstmann-Straussler-Scheinker Syndrome

DESCRIPTION: Inherited form of degeneration in the lower parts of the brain.

CAUSE: Thought to be caused by a prion (infectious self replicating protein particle).

SYMPTOMS: Onset in mid-life with clumsiness, unsteadiness, poor coordination and abnormal way of walking.

INVESTIGATIONS: CT and MRI scans of brain.

TREATMENT: None available.

COMPLICATIONS: Tremor, loss of speech, deafness, blindness.

PROGNOSIS: Slowly progressive to death.

Gianotti Crosti Syndrome

DESCRIPTION: Skin rash that usually affects children between the ages of 6 months and 12 years. Often occurs in clusters, with multiple children who are in contact being affected, and usually follows an upper respiratory tract infection.

Gianotti Crosti Syndrome

CAUSE: Skin response to viral infection (eg. Hepatitis B, Epstein Barr virus, Coxsackie viruses, Echo viruses, respiratory syncitial virus).

SYMPTOMS: Over 3 or 4 days multiple slightly raised dull red spots develop on the thighs and buttocks, then spread to the arms and face. Later spots often look purple, especially on the legs, due to leakage of blood into them from capillaries. The patient may feel quite well or have a mild fever, there may be a mild itch, slightly enlarged lymph nodes in the armpits and groins, and an enlarged liver.

INVESTIGATIONS: Abnormal specific viral blood tests and liver function tests.

TREATMENT: No specific treatment, but a mild steroid cream may be used for the itch.

COMPLICATIONS: Underlying viral disease may cause complications.

PROGNOSIS: The rash fades in 2-8 weeks with mild scaling. Recurrence is unlikely but has been reported.

Giant Cell Arteritis
See Temporal Arteritis

Giant Cell Tumour
See Bone Cancer

Giardiasis, Intestinal

DESCRIPTION: A very common protozoan (microscopic single celled animal) infection of the intestine. Far more common in children than adults.

CAUSE: *Giardia lamblia* is the parasite responsible. It can enter the small intestine via the mouth and pass from one person to another by poor personal hygiene. Eggs are found in the faeces, and faecal contamination of water supplies is a common method of infection. From the time giardia eggs are swallowed, it may be one to three weeks before symptoms develop or the parasite can be found in the faeces.

SYMPTOMS: Most patients have no symptoms. In more severe cases, mild diarrhoea, foul-smelling stools, smelly flatus (farts), general tiredness, an uncomfortable feeling in the abdomen, nausea, vomiting, burping and cramping pains in the abdomen may occur.

INVESTIGATIONS: Diagnosed by examining a sample of faeces under a microscope and identifying the eggs or live giardia.

TREATMENT: Most cases clear spontaneously after many weeks or months. Essential to treat all members of the patient's family, and any other close contacts. A number of different single-dose treatments are available as tablets or mixtures. The only form of prevention is scrupulous personal hygiene.

COMPLICATIONS: Malnutrition, particularly amongst Aborigines and children in third-world countries, from the constant diarrhoea which prevents proper food absorption. People with the parasite but without symptoms can easily pass on the infection.

PROGNOSIS: The vast majority of cases settle rapidly with treatment.

Gilbert Syndrome

DESCRIPTION: An uncommon inherited cause of poor liver function.

CAUSE: Lack of a specific enzyme (glucuronyl transferase) that breaks down proteins in the liver.

SYMPTOMS: Usually none, but may cause a dark complexion (mild jaundice) from an excess level of bilirubin in the blood.

INVESTIGATIONS: Liver function blood tests are abnormal long term.

TREATMENT: No treatment is normally necessary, but in selected cases medication can be given to trigger the activity of the missing enzymes.

COMPLICATIONS: Patient more susceptible to other forms of liver damage (eg. from excess alcohol)

PROGNOSIS: No cure, but usually no adverse effects suffered by patient.

Giles de la Tourette Syndrome
See Tourette Syndrome

Gillespie Syndrome
See Aniridia

Gingivitis
See Gingivostomatitis

Gingivostomatitis
(Vincent's Angina)

DESCRIPTION: Inflammation of the gums (gingivitis) and mouth lining (stomatitis).

CAUSE: Due to bacterial infection, poor hygiene or malnutrition.

SYMPTOMS: Ulceration and pain of the gums, and inside of the mouth and lips.

INVESTIGATIONS: Swab from ulcer shows responsible bacteria. Blood tests show presence of infection.

TREATMENT: Appropriate antibiotic and anti-inflammatory mouth washes and gels.

COMPLICATIONS: May be associated with malignancy (eg. leukaemia).

PROGNOSIS: Good with appropriate treatment.

See also Necrotising Ulcerative Gingivostomatitis; Stomatitis

Gland Infection
See Adenitis; Glandular Fever

Glandular Fever
(Infectious Mononucleosis; Kissing Disease)

DESCRIPTION: Very common viral infection of the lymph nodes (glands) in the neck, armpit, groin and belly. Almost invariably occurs in teenagers or in the early twenties.

CAUSE: Due to the Epstein-Barr virus (EBV) which is passed from one person to another through the breath. The patient is infectious while s/he has the tender lymph nodes. Good personal hygiene is important to prevent further spread.

SYMPTOMS: Sore throat, raised temperature, large lymph nodes in the neck and other parts of the body, extreme tiredness, and generally feeling miserable. Usually lasts about four weeks, but in some patients it may persist for several months.

INVESTIGATIONS: A blood test can prove the diagnosis, but may not turn positive until ten days after the onset of the symptoms.

TREATMENT: No specific cure. Patient must rest as much as possible, take aspirin or paracetamol for the fever and aches, and use gargles for the sore throat.

COMPLICATIONS: Some antibiotics (eg. penicillin) can cause a widespread rash if taken while glandular fever is present. Other complications are very uncommon, but include secondary bacterial infections, infected spleen, or in even rarer cases the liver, heart and brain may be involved.

PROGNOSIS: Very good, but recurrences possible in the following year or two at times of stress or lowered resistance.

Glanzmann Syndrome

DESCRIPTION: Recurrent episodes of prolonged bleeding from lining of mouth, nose and vagina.

CAUSE: Inherited defect in structure of platelets (blood cells essential for clotting).

SYMPTOMS: Excessive bleeding and bruising, particularly involving moist membranes lining body cavities.

INVESTIGATIONS: Blood tests on bleeding time and platelet function.

TREATMENT: Platelet transfusions on a regular basis.

COMPLICATIONS: Anaemia from excessive bleeding, bleeding into vital organs and joints.

PROGNOSIS: Lifelong problem resulting in significant disability.

See also Bernard-Soulier syndrome

Glaucoma

DESCRIPTION: An increase in the pressure of the half-set jelly-like fluid inside the eyeball that damages the eye and affects the vision. Three types occur — chronic, acute and congenital.

Chronic glaucoma (open-angle glaucoma) — the most common type with a slow onset over years. It usually occurs in both eyes simultaneously and runs in families.

Acute glaucoma (angle-closure glaucoma) — the worst type, as it develops in a few hours or days, but usually involves only one eye. Permanent blindness can result.

Congenital glaucoma occurs in babies who are born with the condition.

CAUSE: The eye is filled with a thick clear fluid (aqueous humour) that is slowly secreted by special cells within the eye, while in another part of the eye the fluid is removed, allowing a slow but steady renewal. If there is a blockage to the drainage of the fluid from the eye while new fluid continues to be secreted, the pressure inside the eye increases, and damage occurs to the light-sensitive retina at the back of the eye. Other conditions may also cause glaucoma including eye tumours, infections and injury. In rare cases drugs (eg. steroids) may be responsible.

SYMPTOMS: Chronic — initially affects peripheral vision, which is how far you can see to the sides and up and down while looking straight ahead. One in every 75 people over 40 years have this type of glaucoma.

Acute — a rapid deterioration in vision, severe pain, rainbow-coloured halos around lights, nausea and vomiting. May start after a blow to the eye, or for no discernible reason.

Congenital — earliest sign is the continual overflow of tears from the eye, and the baby turns away from lights rather than towards them as a normal.

INVESTIGATIONS: Diagnosed in most cases by measuring the pressure of the fluid within the eye. This can be done by anaesthetising the eye surface with eye drops and then resting a pressure measuring instrument (tonometer) on the surface of the eye while the patient is lying down, or by using a machine that directs a puff of air onto the eye to measure the pressure. Glaucoma may also be detected by measuring deterioration in peripheral vision using a computerised device, charts or by following a white dot on a large black screen. More complex tests, including examining the eye through a microscope to determine the nature and seriousness of the glaucoma.

TREATMENT: Regular use of eye drops and/or tablets reduces the pressure in the eye. In serious cases, laser microsurgery to the tiny drainage canals in the front of the eye is necessary. Congenital glaucoma always requires surgical treatment.

COMPLICATIONS: Immediate treatment of acute glaucoma is essential if the sight of the eye is to be saved.

PROGNOSIS: Without treatment, glaucoma progresses inexorably to total blindness. If the disease is detected early, glaucoma in most patients can be successfully controlled but not cured.

See also Posner-Schlossman Syndrome and other diseases listed under Eye Diseases

Glaucomatocyclitic Crisis
See Posner-Schlossman Syndrome

Glioblastoma
See Glioma

Glioma
(Glioblastoma; Malignant Astrocytoma)
DESCRIPTION: Form of brain cancer arising from the cells that support and surround the nerve cells in the brain.

Glioma

CAUSE: Unknown, but higher incidence in some families and occupations (eg. petroleum processing).

SYMPTOMS: Variable symptoms may include personality changes, seizures, weakness in some areas and abnormal sensations.

INVESTIGATIONS: CT and MRI scans can usually identify the location of the tumour, but a biopsy is necessary to make a definitive diagnosis.

TREATMENT: Brain surgery and radiation therapy.

COMPLICATIONS: Bleeding into the tumour may suddenly worsen the symptoms.

PROGNOSIS: Very poor.

See also other tumours listed under Brain Cancer

Globus
(Globus Hystericus)

DESCRIPTION: Psychological stress causing a throat spasm.

CAUSE: An intermittent spasm of the muscles in the oesophagus (gullet) in very emotionally stressed people, particularly women.

SYMPTOMS: Sensation of a constant lump in the throat, that patients feel will interfere with swallowing, but usually does not.

INVESTIGATIONS: All investigations of the oesophagus and throat are normal.

TREATMENT: Usually settles with time and reassurance, but sometimes anti-anxiety medication is necessary.

PROGNOSIS: May persist for months, but eventually settles in most patients.

Glomerulonephritis
(Nephritis)

DESCRIPTION: A degenerative disease of the glomeruli and nephrons in the kidneys that occurs in two forms — acute and chronic. Glomeruli are microscopic cups in the kidney where the waste products are filtered out of the blood to form urine, while the nephron is the tiny tube that carries the urine away from the glomerular cup. Thus the term glomerulonephritis (inflammation of the glomeruli and nephrons).

CAUSE: Acute glomerulonephritis is often triggered by a bacterial infection but may start as a result of other diseases in the body or for no identifiable reason. It is more common in children than adults, in third-world countries and amongst Aborigines, but quite rare in affluent societies.

Some patients do not recover from acute glomerulonephritis, and they develop worsening kidney function which results in chronic glomerulonephritis.

SYMPTOMS: Acute — the patient feels tired, has no appetite, develops headaches, has a low-grade fever and tissues may become swollen.

Chronic — usually no symptoms until the kidneys start to fail and excessive levels of waste products build up in the bloodstream. Symptoms may then include a low urine output, loin (kidney) pain, swelling of the ankles and around the eyes, and cloudy urine.

INVESTIGATIONS: The diagnosis is confirmed by examining the urine under a microscope, when blood cells and cell fragments are seen. Blood tests can determine how effectively the kidneys are functioning. There may be an increase in blood pressure.

TREATMENT: Acute — antibiotics for any infection that is present, and keeping the patient at rest until the kidneys recover. In severe cases, a special low-protein, high-carbohydrate diet is required, and medication may be required to lower the blood pressure. In the rare cases that deteriorate further, an artificial kidney machine may be needed for a short time.

Chronic — there is no specific treatment other than continuation of the low-protein, high-carbohydrate diet. A large intake of fluids is also desirable.

COMPLICATIONS: Acute — about 5% of patients develop the nephrotic syndrome and permanent kidney damage. May progress to the chronic form.

Chronic — infection, injury or strenuous exercise may cause a sudden deterioration in kidney function.

PROGNOSIS: Acute — most patients recover completely in a month or so, but in severe cases it may take a year or more. Very rarely death may occur.

Chronic — most patients live relatively normal lives for 20 or 30 years before kidney failure occurs, at which point dialysis or a kidney transplant is necessary.

See also Alport Syndrome; Nephrotic Syndrome

Glomus Tumour

DESCRIPTION: Painful, but benign, skin discolouration.

CAUSE: Developmental defect of nerve tissue in the skin.

SYMPTOMS: One or more painful, pink to purplish lumps (nodules) on the skin of the hands or feet. Pain worse with heat or pressure.

INVESTIGATIONS: Examination of the removed nodule under a microscope diagnostic.

TREATMENT: Surgical removal.

COMPLICATIONS: May occur under the nails.

PROGNOSIS: Cured by removal, otherwise persist life long.

Glossopharyngeal Neuralgia

DESCRIPTION: Uncommon inflammation of the glossopharyngeal (ninth cranial) nerve which supplies the tongue and throat.

CAUSE: Unknown.

SYMPTOMS: Intense intermittent pain in the throat that radiates to the tongue and ear and may be triggered by swallowing. May be associated with fainting, slow pulse and low blood pressure.

INVESTIGATIONS: No specific diagnostic test.

TREATMENT: Medications (eg. carbamazepine) may be tried, but often cutting and destroying the nerve is the only solution.

COMPLICATIONS: Permanent numbness of one side of the throat and tongue after cutting nerve.

PROGNOSIS: Sometimes resolves spontaneously, but treatment often unsatisfactory.
See also Trigeminal Neuralgia

Glue Ear
(Middle Ear Effusion)

DESCRIPTION: The accumulation of mucus in the middle ear.

CAUSE: Develops when phlegm and mucus from the nose pass up the thin eustachian tube into the middle ear. It is difficult for these thick, sticky secretions to escape through the eustachian tube to the back of the nose, particularly if the adenoids which surround the opening of the tube into the nose are swollen.

SYMPTOMS: Feeling of blockage in the affected ear similar to that felt when ascending a mountain and being unable to 'pop' the ears clear. Also associated with reduced hearing.

INVESTIGATIONS: Examination of the ear by an otoscope (magnifier and light) shows an opaque and bulging ear drum. Special instruments can measure the pressure in the middle ear.

TREATMENT: The surgical insertion of a small tube (grommet) through the ear drum to relieve the pressure is often necessary. Recurrent cases may require the surgical removal of the adenoids.

COMPLICATIONS: May be responsible for middle ear infections (otitis media) and deafness.

PROGNOSIS: Very good after appropriate treatment, but may recur after grommets fall out.

See also Eustachian Tube Blockage; Otitis Media

Glycogen Storage Diseases

DESCRIPTION: A number of rare inherited or congenital conditions including McArdle syndrome, von Gierke syndrome, Cori syndrome, Hers syndrome, Pompe syndrome and Andersen syndrome.

CAUSE: The enzymes and other natural chemicals in the liver that are necessary to process carbohydrates in food into glycogen and make it available to the body as a form of energy fuel, are missing or inactive.

SYMPTOMS: The different diseases vary in their symptoms and effects depending upon which enzymes and chemicals are affected. Most patients have low blood sugar, large livers, short stature, subnormal mentality, and may bleed excessively and fail in their development to progress through puberty. Other forms causes muscle pain and weakness.

INVESTIGATIONS: The diagnosis can be confirmed by appropriate blood tests and a liver biopsy.

TREATMENT: Special diets and liver transplant sometimes assist.

PROGNOSIS: Varies from minimal effects throughout life to death in infancy, depending on which type of glycogen storage disease is present.

Gnathostomiasis

DESCRIPTION: Parasitic infection that occurs in southeast and east Asia.

CAUSE: Larvae of the nematode worm *Gnathostoma spinigerum*. Mature worms found in the gut of dogs and cats, from where larvae pass out in faeces to contaminate water where they are swallowed by water fleas. These are eaten by ducks, fish, frogs, eels etc. Eating uncooked fish or poorly cooked flesh, or applying poultices of frog flesh enables the parasite to enter humans. The larvae can complete their life cycle in humans by developing into worms in the gut, where they cause minimal symptoms, or the larvae may migrate abnormally into the brain, lungs, eye, skin, kidneys or other tissue.

SYMPTOMS: Depends on site of infestation. Pain, itch, lump and redness around affected area and a fever.

INVESTIGATIONS: No specific diagnostic test.

TREATMENT: Medications (eg. albendazole) to kill worms and larvae usually given, but results are unsatisfactory.

COMPLICATIONS: Eye invasion may cause blindness, while in the brain paralysis and severe pain may occur.

PROGNOSIS: Depends on site involved. In the skin, red itchy lumps come and go for years. In the brain, may be fatal.

Goitre
(Thyroid Gland Enlargement)

DESCRIPTION: An enlargement of the thyroid gland which lies over the throat just below the Adam's apple.

CAUSE: An enlarged thyroid gland indicates that it is malfunctioning either by producing too much (hyperthyroidism) or too little (hypothyroidism) of the hormone thyroxine. A goitre can also be due to the development of cysts or tumours in the gland, or a lack of iodine in the diet (iodine is essential for the production of thyroxine).

SYMPTOMS: A lump or swelling in the front of the neck that moves under your fingers when you swallow.

INVESTIGATIONS: Blood tests can determine the activity of the thyroid gland and the amount of thyroxine being produced. An ultrasound or radionucleotide scan will show any tumours or cysts.

TREATMENT: Depends on the cause — surgery for an overactive gland (see hyperthyroidism) or thyroid supplements for an underactive one (see hypothyroidism). In most developed countries a goitre due to a lack of iodine has been eliminated since the introduction of iodised table salt, bread and milk.

COMPLICATIONS: Depends on the cause.

PROGNOSIS: The enlargement usually settles with appropriate treatment.

See also Hyperthyroidism; Hypothyroidism; Painful Thyroiditis Syndrome; Pendred Syndrome

Golfer's Elbow
(Medial Epicondylitis)

DESCRIPTION: Inflammation of the tendon on the inside of the bony lump on the back of the elbow (olecranon).

CAUSE: Overstraining of the extensor tendon at the inner back of the elbow due to excessive bending and twisting movements of the arm. In golfers it is not normally one stroke that strains the tendon, but repeated episodes of overstretching caused by hitting the ground with the club during a stroke. This leads to tears of the minute fibres in the tendon, scar tissue forms which is then broken down again by further strains. May also occur in tradesmen who undertake repetitive tasks, housewives, musicians and many others who may put excessive strain on their elbows.

SYMPTOMS: Painful inflammation occurs, which can be constant or may only occur when the elbow is moved or stressed. The whole forearm can ache in some patients, especially when trying to grip or twist with the hand.

INVESTIGATIONS: None usually necessary.

TREATMENT: Prolonged rest is most important. Exercises to strengthen the elbow and anti-inflammatory drugs may also be used. Cortisone injections may be given in resistant cases. The strengthening exercises are done under the supervision of a physiotherapist and involve using your wrist to raise and lower a weight with the palm facing up. Some patients find pressure pads over the tendon, or elbow guards (elastic tubes around the elbow) help relieve the symptoms and prevent recurrences by adding extra support.

COMPLICATIONS: Not easy to treat and can easily become chronic.

PROGNOSIS: No matter what form of treatment is used, most cases seem to last for about 18 months and then settle spontaneously.

See also Tennis Elbow

Goltz Syndrome
(Focal Dermal Hypoplasia)

DESCRIPTION: Rare condition of abnormal skin development.

CAUSE: Due to partial or complete absence of normal skin in affected areas.

SYMPTOMS: Scar-like areas of very thin skin on scalp, thighs and sides of pelvis.

INVESTIGATIONS: Biopsy of affected area of skin examined under microscope to make definite diagnosis.

TREATMENT: No cure, but some areas may be improved by plastic surgery.

COMPLICATIONS: Lack of body and scalp hair, nail abnormalities.

PROGNOSIS: Permanent disfiguration unless small area can be corrected by plastic surgery.

Gonorrhoea
('Clap')

DESCRIPTION: A common sexually transmitted bacterial infection.

CAUSE: Caused by the bacterium *Neisseria gonorrhoeae* which can only be caught by having sex with a person who already has the disease. It has an incubation period of three to seven days after contact. Some degree of protection can be obtained by using a condom.

SYMPTOMS: The symptoms vary significantly between men and women.

Women — may be minimal symptoms with a mild attack. When symptoms do occur they include a foul discharge from the vagina, pain on passing urine, pain in the lower abdomen, passing urine frequently, tender lymph nodes in the groin, and fever.

Men — symptoms are usually obvious with a yellow milky discharge from the penis, pain on passing urine and, in advanced cases, inflamed lymph nodes in the groin.

With anal intercourse, a rectal infection with gonorrhoea can develop and cause an anal discharge, mild diarrhoea, rectal discomfort and pain on passing faeces. Oral sex can lead to the development of a gonococcal throat infection.

INVESTIGATIONS: Confirmed by examining a swab from the urethra, vagina or anus under a microscope and culturing the bacteria on a nutrient substance. There are no blood tests available for gonorrhoea. Other sexually transmitted diseases should also be tested for when gonorrhoea is diagnosed, as they may be contracted at the same time. For this reason, blood tests are often ordered when treating anyone with any form of venereal disease.

TREATMENT: Readily treated with a course of penicillin until recently, but many strains of gonorrhoea are now resistant to penicillin and more potent antibiotics are required. All sexual contacts of the infected person need to be notified as they may be carriers of the disease and unaware of the presence of the infection. After treatment, a follow-up swab is important to ensure that the infection has been adequately treated.

COMPLICATIONS: Women — the infection can involve the uterus and Fallopian tubes to cause salpingitis and pelvic inflammatory disease (see separate entries) which can result in infertility and persistent pelvic pain. Babies born to mothers with the infection can develop a gonococcal conjunctivitis (eye infection).

Men — if left untreated the prostate can become infected, which can cause scarring of the urine tube (urethra), permanent difficulty in passing urine and reduced fertility.

Both sexes — gonorrhoea may enter the bloodstream and cause septicaemia (see separate entry). An unusual complication is gonococcal arthritis, which causes pain in the knees, ankles and wrists. Other rarer complications include infections of the heart, brain and tendons.

PROGNOSIS: More than 95% of cases of gonorrhoea can be cured by the appropriate antibiotics.

See also Sexually Transmitted Diseases

Goodpasture Syndrome

DESCRIPTION: A rare failure of the body's immune system.
CAUSE: Unknown.
SYMPTOMS: Shortness of breath, coughing, recurrent nose bleeds, significant anaemia, kidney damage and iron deposition in vital organs throughout the body.
INVESTIGATIONS: Diagnosed by blood tests and a lung biopsy.
TREATMENT: Treatment is often unsatisfactory, and involves potent medications, artificial cleaning of the blood by dialysis, and kidney transplantation.
PROGNOSIS: Serious.

Gorlin-Goltz Syndrome
(Basal Cell Carcinoma Naevus Syndrome)

DESCRIPTION: Rare condition of children characterised by the development of multiple basal cell carcinoma (BCC) skin cancers and other abnormalities.
CAUSE: Inherited.
SYMPTOMS: Multiple BCCs, calcification of areas of the brain, abnormal vertebrae and ribs, multiple cysts in the jaw and pitting of the palm.
INVESTIGATIONS: X-rays of jaw, vertebrae and ribs.
TREATMENT: Excision of jaw cysts and basal cell carcinomas.
COMPLICATIONS: Other characteristics that may be present include a large head, skin cysts, depressed breast bone, lumps of fibrous tissue in the heart, cleft lip, and extra fingers and toes.
PROGNOSIS: Recurrence of skin cancers and jaw cysts after excision is common.
See also Basal Cell Carcinoma

Gourgerot-Blum Disease
See Capillaritis

Gout
(Hyperuricaemia)

DESCRIPTION: Exquisitely tender, red and painful joint.
CAUSE: Excess blood levels of uric acid, which is produced as a normal breakdown product of protein in the diet. Normally uric acid is removed by the kidneys, but if excess is produced or the kidneys fail to work efficiently, high levels build up in the body and precipitate as crystals in the lubricating fluid of a joint. Under a microscope the crystals look like double ended needles. An alcoholic binge or eating a lot of meat can start an attack in someone who is susceptible. There is a tendency for the disease to run in families. Nearly all victims are men and it usually starts between 30 and 50 years of age.
SYMPTOMS: A very red, swollen and excruciatingly painful joint. The most common joint to be involved is the ball of the foot, but almost any joint in the body may be involved. In severe attacks, a fever may develop, along with a rapid heart rate, loss of appetite and flaking of skin over the affected joint. Attacks

start very suddenly, often at night, and may occur every week or so, or only once in a lifetime.

INVESTIGATIONS: High levels of uric acid found on blood tests. A needle may be used to take a sample of fluid from within the joint for analysis in difficult cases.

TREATMENT: Management takes two forms — treatment of the acute attack, and prevention of any further attacks.

Acute attack — combination of nonsteroidal anti-inflammatory drugs (eg. indomethacin) and colchicine. Rest of the affected joint to control the pain and prevent further damage is important.

Prevention — taking tablets (eg. allopurinol, probenecid) daily for the rest of the patient's life to prevent further attacks, not consuming excess alcohol, keeping weight under control, drinking plenty of liquids to prevent dehydration, avoiding overexposure to cold, not exercising to extremes and avoiding foods that contain high levels of purine producing proteins which metabolise to uric acid (eg. prawns, shellfish, liver, sardines, meat concentrates and game birds).

COMPLICATIONS: Uric acid crystals can form lumps (tophi) under the skin around joints and in the ear lobes. More seriously, the crystals may damage the kidneys and form kidney stones. If the prevention tablets are missed an attack of gout can follow very quickly.

PROGNOSIS: Controlled and prevented easily, provided the patient understands the problem and cooperates with treatment.

See also Pseudogout

Gradenigo Syndrome
(Petrositis)

DESCRIPTION: Skull bone abnormality that causes nerve compression.

CAUSE: Due to infection or tumour of the petrous bone in the skull that damages the 6th cranial nerve.

SYMPTOMS: Headache, double vision, facial pain and a middle ear infection.

INVESTIGATIONS: Skull X-ray or CT scan shows the abnormal bone.

TREATMENT: Potent antibiotics and surgery on the skull to drain any bone abscess or remove a tumour.

COMPLICATIONS: Infection may spread to the brain, ear or other areas.

PROGNOSIS: Good if diagnosed early, but permanent nerve damage may result.

Grand Mal Epilepsy
See Epilepsy

Granuloma Annulare

DESCRIPTION: Harmless, slightly disfiguring lumps on skin.

CAUSE: Unknown. More common in teenagers and young adults.

SYMPTOMS: One or more ring shaped lumps of 1-3cm. diameter on back of hands, elbows or top of feet covered with normal skin but varying in colour from red to white.

INVESTIGATIONS: Diagnosis confirmed by a skin biopsy.

TREATMENT: No ideal treatment exists. Application of potent steroid creams, or injections of steroids into the skin lesion are sometimes successful. Cryotherapy (freezing), ultraviolet light and medications used to treat cancer are other options.

COMPLICATIONS: May be associated with diabetes.

PROGNOSIS: Spontaneous regression possible over years.

Granuloma Inguinale
(Donovanosis; Granuloma Venereum)

DESCRIPTION: Genital skin ulcers caused by a sexually transmitted bacteria.

CAUSE: Caused by the bacteria *Donovania* or *Calymmatobacterium granulomatis* which passes from one person to another during sexual intercourse. Incubation period is one to twelve weeks.

SYMPTOMS: Painless nodules on or around the genitals that break down to shallow ulcers, and may join together into progressively larger ulcers that spread up onto the lower abdomen.

INVESTIGATIONS: Microscopic examination of a biopsy or swab smear from the edge of an ulcer reveals the diagnosis.

TREATMENT: Treatment is difficult, and it may be necessary to take antibiotics such as tetracycline for several months.

COMPLICATIONS: Infection of the ulcers with other bacteria will cause them to fill with pus and become foul smelling.

PROGNOSIS: Relapses common unless full antibiotic course completed.

See also Sexually Transmitted Diseases

Granuloma Venereum
See Granuloma Inguinale

Grave's Disease
See Hyperthyroidism

Grey Baby Syndrome

DESCRIPTION: Rare complication of chloramphenicol use in infants.

CAUSE: Internal use of the potent antibiotic chloramphenicol when the liver has a congenital defect which prevents it from removing the medication from the blood.

SYMPTOMS: Grey coloured skin, heart and liver failure, collapse.

INVESTIGATIONS: Blood tests show the liver damage and high levels of chloramphenicol.

TREATMENT: Stop chloramphenicol, liver transplant if possible.

PROGNOSIS: Very poor.

Grover's Disease
(Transient Acantholytic Dermatosis)

DESCRIPTION: Itchy skin condition of the chest and back that usually affects men over 50, and much less commonly women or younger people.

CAUSE: Frequently follows sweating or some unexpected heat stress.

SYMPTOMS: Sudden onset of very itchy spots on the central back, mid chest and occasionally elsewhere.

INVESTIGATIONS: Skin biopsy can be used to confirm diagnosis.

TREATMENT: Unsatisfactory. Remain cool and avoid sweating. A mild steroid lotion can be applied frequently to give temporary relief.

COMPLICATIONS: None significant.

PROGNOSIS: Most cases settle in six to twelve months, but occasionally it may last longer.

Growing Pains
(Limb Pain Syndrome)

DESCRIPTION: Children who have significant intermittent pain in their legs and (less commonly) their arms for no obvious reason.

CAUSE: May be due to softening of bones at times of rapid growth. There is a tendency for the condition to recur within the one family in successive generations. Affects up to one third of all children of both sexes between the ages of 6 and 14 years.

SYMPTOMS: A deep ache in the limbs that occurs between joints, and not at the joint. Often worse at night, and equal on both sides.

INVESTIGATIONS: No specific tests are necessary, but it is important for other causes of limb pain to be excluded.

TREATMENT: Reassurance, paracetamol and heat packs.

COMPLICATIONS: Nil.

PROGNOSIS: Always settles spontaneously.

Guillain-Barré Syndrome
(Landry-Guillain-Barré Syndrome)

DESCRIPTION: A rare inflammation of nerves (neuropathy).

CAUSE: Usually follows a viral infection, injury, surgery, vaccination or a period of stress.

SYMPTOMS: The nerves in the legs are most commonly involved and the muscles that they supply become paralysed. Sensation to the affected areas may also be lost.

INVESTIGATIONS: None available.

TREATMENT: Steroids are used in treatment, but their use is controversial.

COMPLICATIONS: Up to 20% of patients are left with a permanent disability.

PROGNOSIS: Most patients slowly recover, but in rare cases the muscles of breathing may be paralysed, which can result in death.

Guinea Worm Disease
See Dracunculiasis

Guttae Psoriasis

DESCRIPTION: Very active form of the skin disease psoriasis.

CAUSE: More common in teenagers and young adults and may follow a Streptococcal bacterial infection.

SYMPTOMS: Sudden appearance of multiple small, red, scale covered patches on the arms, leg and trunk. Patches may gradually enlarge and merge.

INVESTIGATIONS: Usually none necessary, but if diagnosis is in doubt it may be confirmed by a skin biopsy.

TREATMENT: One or more of numerous skin preparations including coal tar, dithranol, calcipotriol and steroid creams.

COMPLICATIONS: May progress to normal psoriasis.

PROGNOSIS: May disappear spontaneously after a few weeks, or persist for many years. Controlled, but not cured, by medication.

See also Psoriasis

Guyton's Canal Syndrome

DESCRIPTION: Pinched nerve in the wrist.

CAUSE: Due to the ulnar nerve becoming trapped as it passes the wrist.

SYMPTOMS: Loss of sensation in the 5th finger and half the 4th finger, and wasting and weakness of some muscles in the hand.

INVESTIGATIONS: Electromyograms (EMG) detect the affected muscles.

TREATMENT: Anti-inflammatory medications and an operation to release the ulnar nerve at the wrist.

COMPLICATIONS: Permanent muscle weakness and loss of sensation if not treated adequately.

PROGNOSIS: Good with correct treatment.

See also Carpal Tunnel Syndrome

Gynaecomastia
(Male Breast Enlargement)

DESCRIPTION: Abnormal presence of breast tissue in a male.

CAUSE: The most common reason is the onset of puberty in teenage boys, when there may be a temporary hormone imbalance. Male breasts sometimes enlarge in old age, with an increase in weight, and with oestrogen hormone treatment in men wanting to change sex. May also be a symptom of a significant underlying disease including cirrhosis of the liver, cancer in the adrenal glands, overactivity or cancer of the thyroid gland, an uncommon form of lung cancer, a tumour in the testicles or a genetic condition called Klinefelter syndrome in which there is an extra sex chromosome.

SYMPTOMS: Varying amount of breast tissue, that may be tender, is felt behind the nipple.

222

INVESTIGATIONS: Blood and X-ray tests may be performed to determine the cause.

TREATMENT: Depends on cause. Plastic surgery is sometimes necessary to remove the breast tissue.

COMPLICATIONS: Breast cancer can occur in the male breast.

PROGNOSIS: Depends on cause.

H

Haemangioma
(Angioma)

DESCRIPTION: Localised over growth of arteries and veins.

CAUSE: Blood vessels in the skin, intestine, spinal cord, brain or inside other organs may sometimes dilate and overdevelop dramatically to form a small red lump.

SYMPTOMS: Red lump that blanches on pressure.

INVESTIGATIONS: None necessary in the skin. Internal haemangiomas may be detected by angiography (injecting dye into a blood vessel and taking an X-ray), CT or MRI scans, gastroscopy or colonoscopy.

TREATMENT: Surgical removal if cosmetically unacceptable or causing symptoms.

COMPLICATIONS: May bleed dramatically if injured, and in the gut be responsible for steady blood loss and anaemia. May put pressure on nerves (eg. in spine) to cause pain or loss of nerve function.

PROGNOSIS: Usually harmless, but annoying. Cured by removal.

See also Blue Rubber Bleb Syndrome; Strawberry Naevus

Haemochromatosis

DESCRIPTION: Problem of excessive iron storage in the body.

CAUSE: A congenital disease in which the body stores excessive amounts of iron in the liver, pancreas, kidneys, heart, testes and other tissues. Far more common in males than females.

SYMPTOMS: Very slowly progressive condition that usually causes no problems until the patient is 50 or 60. Common symptoms include liver enlargement and reduced liver function, joint pains, heart enlargement, impaired heart function, diabetes, dark skin discolouration and impotence.

INVESTIGATIONS: Diagnosed by specific blood tests and liver biopsy.

TREATMENT: Blood-letting on a regular basis to remove iron from the body is the main method of dealing with the disease. This may need to be continued weekly for some years to adequately drain iron out of the system. Drugs are also available to increase the rate at which iron is excreted through the kidneys and urine.

COMPLICATIONS: Damage already caused to the body's vital organs by the excess levels of iron (eg. diabetes, liver and heart failure) cannot be reversed.

PROGNOSIS: Good control, but not a permanent cure, possible once diagnosed.

Haemoglobin S Disease
See Sickle Cell Anaemia

Haemolytic Anaemia

DESCRIPTION: Anaemia due to excessive destruction of red blood cells.

CAUSE: Red blood cells may be destroyed at a rapid rate because of an uncommon complication of many diseases including kidney failure, liver failure, transfusion with incompatible blood, cancer, both viral and bacterial infections, and exposure to some drugs and poisons.

SYMPTOMS: Tiredness and weakness are usual, but fever and jaundice (yellow skin) may also be present. In severe cases, the patient may become semiconscious, have severe abdominal pain, and bruise easily.

INVESTIGATIONS: Diagnosed by blood tests and examining the red blood cells under a microscope.

TREATMENT: Emergency treatment involves transfusing the patient with concentrated red blood cells. Prednisone (a steroid) is the usual drug used, but some patients do not respond, and more exotic and toxic drugs are then required. The spleen is responsible for destroying red blood cells, and if this becomes overactive, surgical removal may control the disease.

COMPLICATIONS: Some patients require years of treatment, and in a small number the condition is resistant to treatment and fatal.

PROGNOSIS: Most cases respond well to treatment and recover in a few months.

See also Anaemia

Haemolytic-Uraemic Syndrome
(Uraemic Syndrome)

DESCRIPTION: A serious condition of red blood cell destruction resulting in kidney failure.

CAUSE: Microscopic damage to, and clogging of, the tiny blood vessels in the kidneys due to excessive destruction of red blood cells, can result in poor filtration of the blood and failure to remove waste products that then build up in the body. May be a side effect of severe gut infections, or an inappropriate response to pregnancy or drugs.

SYMPTOMS: Passing bloody urine, tiredness and weakness due to anaemia, and excessive bruising and bleeding due to a drop in the number of platelets (cells in the blood essential for clotting).

INVESTIGATIONS: Diagnosed by blood tests and kidney biopsy.

TREATMENT: Difficult and usually involves blood transfusions, but in about 30% of patients the kidneys fail, and dialysis (artificial kidney machine) is required.

COMPLICATIONS: Extensive internal bleeding.

PROGNOSIS: Although most patients recover, even in the best hospitals, some patients do not survive.

Haemophilia A
(Factor VIII Deficit)

DESCRIPTION: A lack of one of the essential factors responsible for the clotting of blood.

CAUSE: An inherited lack of factor VIII. The gene for the disease is carried by women on the X chromosome, but can only affect men (sex linked inheritance).

SYMPTOMS: Excessive bleeding from a cut, severe bruising from a minor injury, bleeding into joints to cause arthritis, internal bleeding into the gut and other organs.

INVESTIGATIONS: Specific blood tests can confirm the diagnosis.

TREATMENT: Injections of the missing coagulation factor to prevent excessive bleeding when it occurs. Insufficient is available to be given regularly to prevent bleeding at present, but genetic technologies are likely to change this in the near future. The factor is obtained from blood donations at present, but in the future from genetically modified pig milk.

COMPLICATIONS: Arthritis, infertility, damage to other organs from bleeding, chronic weakness, shorter than normal lifespan.

PROGNOSIS: Severity may vary from one patient to another. No permanent cure available. Statistically, half the children of a woman who carries the responsible gene will have the disease. Incidence 1:10,000.

See also Christmas Disease; von Willebrand's Disease

Haemophilia B
See Christmas Disease

Haemophilus Infection
See Chancroid; *Haemophilus influenzae* B Infection

Haemophilus influenzae B Infection
(HiB Infection)

DESCRIPTION: Bacterial infection that in children causes meningitis or epiglottitis, and in adults may affect numerous organs.

CAUSE: *Haemophilus influenzae* type B (HiB) is a bacterium that is spread by close contact and can cause infections in any age group, but is far more serious in children.

SYMPTOMS: CHILDREN

Meningitis — infection of the meninges (covering of the brain) results in a fever, irritability, lethargy, seizures and coma.

Epiglottitis — a life threatening infection of a piece of cartilage at the back of the throat that may swell and block the airways.

ADULTS

May cause serious pneumonia and less serious types of throat infection, sinusitis, middle ear infection, bronchitis, joint infection, skin infection, heart infection and meningitis. Adults with reduced immunity (eg: in AIDS) may have the same serious infections as children.

INVESTIGATIONS: Blood and fluid from the spinal cord can be tested to confirm the diagnosis.

TREATMENT: Infections in adults can be readily treated with appropriate antibiotics (usually as tablets), with minimal long term complications.

In children far more potent antibiotics are needed, and they must be given by injection. The swollen epiglottis (piece of cartilage at the back of the throat) may choke the child before the antibiotics can work, so urgent hospitalisation and intubation (placing a tube into the throat to permit easy breathing) is essential. A vaccine is now available to prevent HiB infections. It is given at two, four and six months of age at the same time as the triple antigen injection.

COMPLICATIONS: The onset of meningitis may be so rapid that the child may be permanently affected (eg: by deafness, learning difficulties and other forms of brain damage) before the antibiotics can work.

PROGNOSIS: Good recovery if diagnosed and treated early. Permanent damage or death possible in children if treatment delayed.

See also Epiglottitis; Meningitis

Haemorrhagic Fever
See Ebola Virus; Lassa Fever; Marburg Virus

Haemorrhoids
See Piles

Hailey-Hailey Disease
(Benign Familial Chronic Pemphigus)

DESCRIPTION: Rare skin condition that starts in middle age and involves the armpits, groin and under the breasts.

CAUSE: Congenital.

SYMPTOMS: Small blisters that break down into red, moist or crusted sore with tiny cracks across it.

INVESTIGATIONS: Diagnosed by skin biopsy.

TREATMENT: Drying agents applied to affected areas. Small areas may be surgically excised.

COMPLICATIONS: Secondary fungal and bacterial infections common.

PROGNOSIS: No cure, but usually settles in old age.

See also Pemphigus

Hair Ball
See Trichobezoar

Hair, Excess
See Hirsutism

Hair Loss
See Alopecia Areata; Baldness; Loose Anagen Syndrome; Telogen Effluvium; Trichotillomania

Hairy Cell Leukaemia
See Leukaemia, Hairy Cell

Hajdu-Cheney Syndrome
DESCRIPTION: Developmental abnormality of joints, teeth and facial structure.
CAUSE: Inherited.
SYMPTOMS: Child with slack joints, premature tooth loss, small unusually shaped face, small jaw, unusual eye and eyebrow shape, slow growth, excess body hair, generalised weakness and pain, and sometimes finger abnormalities.
INVESTIGATIONS: No specific diagnostic tests.
TREATMENT: None available.
PROGNOSIS: No cure.

Hallermann-Streiff Syndrome
DESCRIPTION: A rare birth disorder involving the face.
CAUSE: Congenital condition.
SYMPTOMS: Cataracts in the eyes, facial and teeth abnormalities, lack of hair on head and body, small stature.
INVESTIGATIONS: None specific.
TREATMENT: Surgical correction of deformities and cataract.
PROGNOSIS: No cure, but many effects can be corrected.

Hallux Valgus
See Bunion

Halo Naevus
DESCRIPTION: Area of depigmentation around a benign pigmented spot (naevus) that is common in Caucasian children and young adults.
CAUSE: Autoimmune response to the presence of the naevus.
SYMPTOMS: Dark brown spot surrounded by an area of abnormally white skin.
INVESTIGATIONS: None necessary.
TREATMENT: None necessary.
PROGNOSIS: Often disappear over a few years.

Hamman-Rich Syndrome
(Idiopathic Diffuse Interstitial Fibrosis)

DESCRIPTION: Rare disease causing lung destruction.

CAUSE: Progressive generalised replacement of the lungs with fibrous tissue. May be triggered by acute pneumonia.

SYMPTOMS: Worsening shortness of breath to the point where breathing becomes impossible.

INVESTIGATIONS: Diagnosed by chest X-ray and lung biopsy.

TREATMENT: None available.

PROGNOSIS: Usually fatal.

Hand Foot Mouth Disease

DESCRIPTION: A viral infection that virtually every child will eventually catch.

CAUSE: Infection by a *Coxsackie* virus.

SYMPTOMS: Usually so mild that it causes no symptoms, but in severe cases a child will develop blisters on the soles and palms, and mouth ulcers. It may be accompanied by a mild intermittent fever, headache and irritability.

INVESTIGATIONS: None necessary.

TREATMENT: Paracetamol if necessary.

COMPLICATIONS: None.

PROGNOSIS: Rash persists for three to five days before settling without any problems.

See also Coxsackie Virus Infection

Hand-Schüller-Christian Disease

DESCRIPTION: Condition of children causing serious varied symptoms. One of a group of diseases known as histiocytosis X or Langerhans cell histiocytosis.

CAUSE: Congenital.

SYMPTOMS: Causes diabetes insipidus (see separate entry), patchy bony absorption in the skull, protruding eyes, lung damage and outer ear inflammation. Other symptoms may include skin rashes and gum inflammation.

INVESTIGATIONS: Diagnosis can be made by skull X-rays, biopsy of skin rashes, bone marrow biopsy and chest X-rays.

TREATMENT: Involves irradiation of the bone lesions, very potent medications to prevent further bone and lung damage and conventional management of the diabetes insipidus.

COMPLICATIONS: Numerous organs may fail.

PROGNOSIS: No cure possible.

See also Diabetes Insipidus; Histiocytosis X; Leterer-Siwe Disease

Hansen's Disease
See Leprosy

Happy Puppet Syndrome
See Angelman Syndrome

Hardening of the Arteries
See Arteriosclerosis

Hare Lip
See Cleft Lip and Palate

Harlequin Syndrome
DESCRIPTION: Rare disfiguring disease due to abnormal skin formation.

CAUSE: Congenital.

SYMPTOMS: Severe skin itch, very dry thick skin resulting in formation of hard disfiguring scar tissue and distorted facial features.

INVESTIGATIONS: Diagnosed by skin biopsy.

TREATMENT: Moisturising cream in large quantities.

COMPLICATIONS: Inability to move joints freely due to skin hardening.

PROGNOSIS: Most die before birth. Long-term survival is rare.

Hartnup Disease
DESCRIPTION: A rare disorder of body chemistry that leads to a deficiency of niacin (vitamin B3).

CAUSE: Inherited.

SYMPTOMS: Symptoms similar to those of pellagra (see separate entry) including poor coordination, emotional personality, mental confusion and a sun sensitive red scaling rash.

INVESTIGATIONS: Diagnosed by blood tests.

TREATMENT: Niacin supplements.

PROGNOSIS: Satisfactory control normal, but no cure possible.

See also Pellagra

Hashimoto's Thyroiditis
DESCRIPTION: An inflammation of the thyroid gland in the front of the neck.

CAUSE: Inflammation occurs for no known reasons, but is possibly an autoimmune disease. May occur at any age, tends to run in families and is far more common in women.

SYMPTOMS: Patients have a gradual enlargement of the thyroid gland (goitre) over many months or years. The gland becomes firm, but not tender or painful. Many patients have no other symptoms, and the gland enlargement may be barely noticeable, but in others the gland may gradually cease to function and the patient becomes tired, listless and has other symptoms of hypothyroidism (see separate entry).

INVESTIGATIONS: Diagnosis is made by blood tests.

TREATMENT: Taking thyroid hormone tablets (thyroxine) on a daily basis indefinitely.

COMPLICATIONS: A rapidly progressive form of the disease is known.
PROGNOSIS: Long term outcome is usually very good with normal life expectancy.
See also Goitre; Hypothyroidism; Thyroiditis

Hashish Abuse
See Marijuana Abuse

Hay Fever
(Allergic Rhinitis)
DESCRIPTION: Allergy reaction affecting the lining of the nose.
CAUSE: May be due to any one of several million different pollens, microscopic animals such as the house dust mite, or skin, scale or hair particles from animals. When the sensitive moist membranes that line the nose first come into contact with the sensitising particle (an allergen), there is no reaction, but the body's immune system is primed to react to the next invasion. On the second exposure, the large immunoglobulin proteins that act to defend the body against invasion by any foreign matter react violently. They cluster around mast cells that rupture and release histamine into the nasal tissues. This causes the tissue to become inflamed. After a few hours or days, the body destroys the histamine released, and the tissues return to normal. 10% of the population are affected.
SYMPTOMS: The nose drips constantly and is clogged, the patient sneezes repeatedly, has bad breath, a constant drip of phlegm down the throat and red eyes. Usually occurs for only a few weeks or months of the year.
INVESTIGATIONS: Blood tests may show an increase in certain types of cells and immunoglobulins.
TREATMENT: Antihistamines and pseudoephedrine tablets or nose sprays counteract the histamine released into the tissue and ease the symptoms, but some types of antihistamine may cause drowsiness. Steroid nasal sprays and/or anti-allergy sprays used regularly prevent the nose from reacting to allergens. Patients who suffer repeatedly can have blood or skin tests performed to determine exactly which dusts and pollens cause the hay fever and if a cause can be found, a course of thirty or more weekly injections may be given to permanently desensitise the patient. The last resort is surgery in which part of the lining of the nasal cavity is removed by burning (diathermy), and some of the curly bones within the nose (turbinates) are cut out so that there is less membrane to secrete phlegm.
COMPLICATIONS: A secondary bacterial infection may develop to cause sinusitis.
PROGNOSIS: Good control usually possible.
See also Allergy; Vasomotor Rhinitis

Headache
See Cluster Headache; Headache, Muscle Spasm; Migraine

Headache, Muscle Spasm
(Tension Headache)

DESCRIPTION: Headache from spasm of muscles in the temples, forehead and upper neck.

CAUSE: Stress is the most common trigger, but allergies, infections and injury can also cause muscle spasm. The muscles at the top of the neck, in the forehead and over both temples go into prolonged contraction which tightens the scalp, causing pressure on the skull, and further increases the strain on the muscles.

SYMPTOMS: Constant unrelieved pressure across the head, sharp pains and tenderness around the hairline and neck, poor concentration, tiredness and worsening of the headache by stress, noise and glare.

INVESTIGATIONS: None usually necessary.

TREATMENT: Aspirin or paracetamol, sometimes in combination with muscle relaxants. Commercially available combinations such as Fiorinal, Mersyndol and Panalgesic are useful in the short term, but often cause drowsiness. Mild heat and massaging the tense muscles will give temporary relief. Relief of chronic anxiety by talking through the problems with a doctor or counsellor, accepting help to deal with a stressful situation, and using an anti-anxiety medication may also be useful.

COMPLICATIONS: None significant.

PROGNOSIS: Usually well controlled, but may be recurrent.

Head Injury
See Coma; Concussion; Post Traumatic Cerebral Syndrome; Subarachnoid Haemorrhage; Subdural Haematoma

Head Lice
(Pediculosis)

DESCRIPTION: Infestation of the hairs on the scalp by the 2-3 mm long human head louse.

CAUSE: The human head louse, *Pediculus capitis*, is an insect which lives on human hairs and survives by sucking blood from the skin. They are very common and spread from one person to another very quickly by close contact, by sharing a brush or comb, or by wearing another person's hat. The female louse lays eggs and glues them to the hairs. They hatch after six days, grow into adults capable of further reproduction in about ten days and live for four to six weeks. The nits that can be seen firmly attached to hairs are the egg cases.

SYMPTOMS: Often no symptoms, but in severe cases there may be a mild itching on the scalp. The most common areas for them to congregate are the forehead and behind the ears.

INVESTIGATIONS: It is possible to see the insects or egg cases with a magnifying glass.

TREATMENT: It is advisable to treat all the members of a family with lotions or shampoos that contain malathion or gamma benzene hexachloride. Treatment should be repeated weekly for two or three weeks to kill insects as they hatch. The hair does not need to be cut short unless there are repeated infestations. Eggs that remain after treatment may be removed by a fine comb. Lice cannot survive for long away from humans, so clothing and pillows need only normal washing and no special treatment. If there is any doubt about the diagnosis, or the problem becomes recurrent, medical advice should be sought. Exclusion of children with head lice from school is only necessary until proper treatment has been given.

COMPLICATIONS: None serious.

PROGNOSIS: Cure possible with correct treatment.

See also Crabs

Heart Attack
(MI; Myocardial Infarct)

DESCRIPTION: Blockage of the arterial blood supply to heart muscle for sufficient time to cause the affected muscle to die and be replaced by fibrous scar tissue.

CAUSE: Due to part of the heart not receiving sufficient blood. All the blood to the heart muscle passes through three small arteries. If one of these is blocked, one part of the heart muscle cannot obtain sufficient blood and dies. The arteries may be blocked by fatty deposits because the patient is overweight or has high cholesterol levels, by clots or fat globules breaking off from damaged blood vessels elsewhere in the body, or by damage to the artery from high blood pressure. The severity of a heart attack depends on the amount of heart muscle damaged, and its position in the heart. A small amount of damage in a vital area may cause death, while significant damage in a less important area will not be fatal. In angina (see separate entry) the blood supply to the heart muscle is reduced but not completely cut off, so no permanent damage occurs. Angina may lead to a heart attack in some cases.

SYMPTOMS: A severe crushing pain is felt in the chest and shortness of breath is experienced. The pain builds up rapidly in waves, and then persists for some time before gradually fading. It may be accompanied by sweating, weakness, anxiety, dizziness, cough, nausea and vomiting. Some heart attacks create minimal discomfort, and may be dismissed by the patient as a passing attack of severe indigestion.

INVESTIGATIONS: Diagnosed by an electrocardiogram (ECG) and blood tests. These tests may be negative for a couple of hours after the start of a heart attack, so a doctor's clinical judgment is vital. A chest X-ray and echocardiogram may also be performed. After the initial recovery period, echocardiography, coronary angiography and nuclear scans may be performed to find the cause of the heart attack and to determine further surgical or medical treatment.

TREATMENT: If you feel that someone is having a heart attack, call an ambulance. Once the patient is under the care of a doctor, their chance of survival is good, because medication can be given to stop an abnormal heartbeat, relieve pain and ease the intense anxiety of the patient. Once in hospital, treatment in a coronary care unit will include drugs to break up the blood clot blocking the coronary artery and a complex cocktail of other medications given through a drip into a vein to regulate the functioning of the heart. After a few days, the patient is moved to a normal ward and after 10 to 14 days they can go home for a further six or more weeks rest. The patient will be put on long term medication (eg. beta-blockers and aspirin) to prevent another attack. Gradually increasing levels of exercise are undertaken over many weeks in order to slowly strengthen the heart. If a particular artery can be found to be blocked, coronary artery bypass graft (CABG) surgery may be performed. To prevent a heart attack, keep your weight reasonable, have your blood pressure checked and treated if necessary, avoid excess cholesterol in your diet, exercise regularly, and stop smoking.

COMPLICATIONS: Long-term complications include angina, an irregular heartbeat, heart failure and a heart aneurysm (see separate entries).

PROGNOSIS: 20% of patients will die within the first hour, a further 10% will die in hospital, 5% will die within three months of leaving hospital and another 3% in every year thereafter. The death rate has been significantly lowered by the use of long term medication.

See also Angina; Dressler Syndrome; Stokes-Adams Syndrome

Heartbeat, Rapid
See Tachycardia

Heartburn
See Reflux Oesophagitis

Heart Diseases
See Angina; Atrial Septal Defect; Cardiomyopathy; Congestive Cardiac Failure; Cor Pulmonale; Eisenmenger Syndrome; Ellis-van Creveld Syndrome; Endocarditis; Heart Attack; Hypertension; Hypoplastic Left heart Syndrome; Hypotension; Myocarditis; Myxoma; Patent Ductus Arteriosus; Pericarditis; Sick Sinus Syndrome; Stokes-Adams Syndrome and conditions listed under Arrythmia and Heart Valve Disease

Heart Failure
See Cardiomyopathy; Congestive Cardiac Failure; Cor Pulmonale

Heart Infection
See Endocarditis; Myocarditis; Pericarditis

Heart Tumour
See Myxoma

Heart Valve Disease

See Aortic Valve Incompetence; Aortic Valve Stenosis; Barlow Syndrome; Fallot's Pentalogy; Fallot's Tetralogy; Fallot's Trilogy; Mitral Incompetence; Mitral Stenosis; Pulmonary Valve Incompetence; Pulmonary Valve Stenosis; Tricuspid Incompetence; Tricuspid Stenosis

Heel Spur

DESCRIPTION: Inflammation and bone formation at the point where a tendon or ligament attaches to the heel bone.

CAUSE: Beneath and behind your heel, large ligaments and tendons attach to the calcaneum (heel bone). The attachment can be stressed by prolonged over use or by a sudden injury. After injuring a tendon or ligament attachment, the healing process will involve both the tendon or ligament and the bone to which it attaches. During the healing process, part of the ligament or tendon may be replaced by bone, leading to a spur of bone jutting out from the calcaneum. Spurs are subject to further injury, and may have tiny microscopic stress fractures in them, which involve the equally tiny nerves in the area to cause chronic pain.

SYMPTOMS: Pain and tenderness at the site of the spur formation behind or under the heel that is worsened by exercise.

INVESTIGATIONS: Spurs can be seen on an X-ray.

TREATMENT: Prolonged rest and thick padded insoles in shoes will heal the spur, but further use often results in a recurrence of the pain. Active treatment involves the use of pain killers, heat, anti-inflammatory medications, physiotherapy, steroid injections, or as a last resort, an operation to remove the spur.

COMPLICATIONS: Steroid injections are often very effective, but if used too frequently, can actually damage the surrounding tissue.

PROGNOSIS: Satisfactory treatment sometimes difficult but usually successful.

Heerfordt Syndrome
(Heerfordt-Waldenström Syndrome; Uveoparotid Fever)

DESCRIPTION: Complication of sarcoidosis involving the face, eyes and salivary glands.

CAUSE: Unknown.

SYMPTOMS: Painful inflammation of the salivary glands around the jaw, partial paralysis of one side of the face, inflammation of the eye (iritis) and sarcoidosis (see separate entry).

INVESTIGATIONS: None specific.

TREATMENT: None necessary except for sarcoidosis as it is a self limiting condition.

COMPLICATIONS: Complications of sarcoidosis.

PROGNOSIS: Settles with time and rest, but sarcoidosis may have serious consequences.

See also Iritis; Loeffler Syndrome; Sarcoidosis

Heerfordt-Waldenström Syndrome
See Heerfordt Syndrome

Heiner Syndrome

DESCRIPTION: Form of allergy reaction in lungs.

CAUSE: Cow's milk allergy.

SYMPTOMS: Anaemia, persistent lung inflammation (eg. asthma) and infection (eg. bronchitis).

INVESTIGATIONS: Blood tests show inflammatory reaction and presence of large numbers of inflammatory cells, and a chest X-ray may be abnormal.

TREATMENT: Avoid dairy products and treat lung symptoms.

COMPLICATIONS: Serious lung infections and permanent scarring of lungs.

PROGNOSIS: Reasonable control possible, but no cure.

See also Asthma

HELLP Syndrome

DESCRIPTION: Complication of pregnancy involving destruction of blood cells. Name is an acronym of medical terms for characteristic symptoms.

CAUSE: Unknown.

SYMPTOMS: Haemolysis (breakdown of red blood cells resulting in anaemia), Elevated Liver enzyme activity (due to liver damage from excess waste products from destroyed red blood cells) and Low Platelet count (blood cells essential for blood clotting) in a pregnant woman. Other symptoms that may occur include high blood pressure, pre-eclampsia (see separate entry) and abdominal pain.

INVESTIGATIONS: Blood tests show abnormal blood cells and liver damage.

TREATMENT: Early confinement if possible.

COMPLICATIONS: Eclampsia (see separate entry) and death of foetus are serious possibilities if baby cannot be delivered quickly.

PROGNOSIS: Settles with confinement.

See also Eclampsia; Pre-eclampsia

Helminthiasis
(Worm Infestations)
See Dracunculiasis; Gnathostomiasis; Hookworm; Hydatid Disease; Pinworms; Roundworm Infestation; Strongyloidiasis; Tapeworms; Trichuriasis

Henoch-Schoenlein Syndrome
(Anaphylactoid Purpura)
DESCRIPTION: Generalised inflammation of small blood vessels resulting in the formation of purpura in the skin.

CAUSE: May be a complication of a number of different diseases, but its cause is unknown. More common in children.

SYMPTOMS: Small, slightly raised dilated blood vessels (purpura) appear on the skin

236

as red or purple patches about five to ten millimetres across. There may be bleeding into the intestine, lungs, kidneys and joints to cause belly pain, coughing of blood, blood in the urine and arthritis.

INVESTIGATIONS: Diagnosed by biopsy of one of the purpura in the skin.

TREATMENT: None normally necessary.

COMPLICATIONS: If the kidneys become involved medical treatment is necessary, as long term kidney damage may occur.

PROGNOSIS: Self limiting and usually settles without serious long term problems in one to six weeks.

Hepatic Abscess
See Liver Abscess

Hepatic Carcinoma
See Liver Cancer

Hepatic Metastases
See Metastatic Cancer

Hepatitis A
(Infective Hepatitis)

DESCRIPTION: A viral infection of the liver. The liver is used by the body to process food and eliminate waste products through bile which passes into the gut. If the liver is damaged, it cannot work efficiently, and the main constituent of bile (bilirubin) builds up in the blood stream.

CAUSE: Caught by eating food that has been contaminated by someone who has the disease. The virus lives in the liver, but large numbers pass down the bile duct and into the gut, and contaminate the faeces. If sufferers are not careful with their personal hygiene, the virus may be passed onto someone else. When hepatitis A virus particles are swallowed, they are absorbed with the food into the bloodstream and migrate to the liver, where after an incubation period lasting two to six weeks they start multiplying and cause damage to liver cells. Patients may pass on the virus for a week or two before they develop any symptoms. The vital preventative factor is the standard of hygiene in the community.

SYMPTOMS: Because of the yellow colour of bilirubin, the skin slowly turns a dark yellow (jaundice). The whites of the eyes are affected first, and this may be the only sign of the disease in a dark-skinned person. Other symptoms are nausea, vomiting, marked tiredness, loss of appetite, generalised aches and pains, fever and a large tender liver.

INVESTIGATIONS: Blood tests are available to diagnose the type of hepatitis and monitor its progress.

TREATMENT: The main treatment is bed rest, and a diet that is low in protein and high in carbohydrate. Alcohol is forbidden. Sometimes it is necessary to give medication for nausea and vomiting and to feed severely affected patients by a drip into a vein for a short time. If it continues to worsen, drugs may be used to reduce the liver damage. Hepatitis A can be prevented by a vaccine.

COMPLICATIONS: In rare cases (2 in 1000), the disease may progress despite all efforts of doctors and result in death. This is more common in the elderly.

PROGNOSIS: There is usually an initial worsening of the symptoms, followed by a slow recovery period that may take from one to four months. In children, it may be present, and recovery occur, with no symptoms ever being present. Permanent liver damage is uncommon.

See also Hepatitis B; Hepatitis C; Hepatitis D; Hepatitis E; Hepatitis G

Hepatitis B
(Serum Hepatitis)

DESCRIPTION: A viral infection of the liver.

CAUSE: Can only be caught by intimate contact with the blood or semen of a person who has the disease or is a carrier of the disease. Examples include receiving blood from a carrier, using a contaminated needle, rubbing a graze or cut on an infected person's graze or cut, being bitten by an infected person, or most commonly by having sex (homosexual or heterosexual) with them. 90% of babies born to mothers who are carriers catch the disease. The highest incidences are amongst homosexual men, drug addicts who share needles, Australian Aborigines, and the disease is widespread in southeast Asia. Blood banks screen all donations for hepatitis B. Splashes of blood into an eye or onto a cut or graze can spread the disease, and doctors, dentists, nurses and other health workers are therefore at risk.

SYMPTOMS: There is a long incubation period of six weeks to six months, and the infection cannot be detected during this period. Once active it causes the patient to be very ill with a liver infection, fever, jaundice (yellow skin), nausea and loss of appetite. Some develop only a very mild form of the disease but they are still contagious and may suffer the long term effects.

INVESTIGATIONS: Blood tests are available to diagnose the type of hepatitis and monitor its progress.

TREATMENT: Bed rest, and a diet that is low in protein and high in carbohydrate. Alcohol is forbidden. Sometimes it is necessary to give medication for nausea and vomiting and to feed severely affected patients by a drip into a vein for a short time. If it continues to worsen, drugs may be used to reduce the liver damage. It is possible to vaccinate against hepatitis B.

COMPLICATIONS: Patients must ensure that they are no longer infectious before having sex with anyone and have regular blood tests throughout their life to detect any liver damage. 10% of patients develop cirrhosis, failure of the liver or liver cancer.

PROGNOSIS: Nine out of ten patients recover completely after a few weeks, but one in ten become chronic carriers. About 1% of patients develop a rapidly progressive liver disease that causes death.

See also Hepatitis A; Hepatitis C; Hepatitis D; Hepatitis E; Hepatitis G; Liver Cancer

Hepatitis C

DESCRIPTION: A viral infection of the liver.

CAUSE: Transmitted from one person to another through blood contamination such as the sharing of needles by drug users. All blood donations are screened for this virus. Sexual transmission is uncommon. The incubation period is six to seven weeks.

SYMPTOMS: Usually mild, and the patient may only be vaguely unwell for a few days. A minority progress to develop jaundice, liver enlargement and nausea.

INVESTIGATIONS: Blood tests are available to diagnose the type of hepatitis and monitor its progress.

TREATMENT: Bed rest, and a diet that is low in protein and high in carbohydrate. Alcohol is forbidden. Sometimes it is necessary to give medication for nausea and vomiting and to feed severely affected patients by a drip into a vein for a short time. If it continues to worsen, drugs may be used to reduce the liver damage. It is NOT possible to vaccinate against hepatitis C.

COMPLICATIONS: About a quarter of patients develop permanent liver damage, often after many years.

PROGNOSIS: No cure available. Many patients lead normal long lives, but about half eventually develop cirrhosis (see separate entry) and liver failure.

See also Cirrhosis; Hepatitis A; Hepatitis B; Hepatitis D; Hepatitis E; Hepatitis G

Hepatitis D

DESCRIPTION: A viral infection of the liver.

CAUSE: Can only be caught by patients who already have hepatitis B. The two diseases may be caught at the same time or separately. Hepatitis D is much more common in intravenous drug users with hepatitis B than in patients who have caught hepatitis B in other ways. It is also more prevalent in countries around the Mediterranean.

SYMPTOMS: If hepatitis D is caught at a later time than hepatitis B, there are usually no symptoms.

INVESTIGATIONS: Blood tests are available to diagnose the type of hepatitis and monitor its progress.

TREATMENT: Often no treatment necessary. In severe cases, drugs may be used to reduce the liver damage. There is no specific vaccine against hepatitis D, but vaccination against hepatitis B will effectively prevent both diseases.

COMPLICATIONS: Increases the risk of developing serious liver disease in those who already have hepatitis B.

PROGNOSIS: No cure available. Many patients lead normal lives, but many eventually develop cirrhosis, liver failure and liver cancer.

See also Hepatitis A; Hepatitis B; Hepatitis C; Hepatitis E; Hepatitis G; Liver Cancer

Hepatitis E

DESCRIPTION: A viral infection of the liver.

CAUSE: Caught from contaminated food and water in the same way as hepatitis A. It is rare in western countries with the highest incidence being in central Asia, Algeria and Mexico.

SYMPTOMS: Patients becomes jaundiced, are nauseated and tired, vomit, have no appetite, and develop aches, pains, a fever and a large tender liver.

INVESTIGATIONS: Blood tests are available to diagnose the type of hepatitis and monitor its progress.

TREATMENT: There is no vaccine available, but a gammaglobulin injection will give short term protection. Scrupulous personal hygiene is vital.

COMPLICATIONS: The death rate is far higher in pregnant women.

PROGNOSIS: The immediate death rate from hepatitis E is far higher than in other types of hepatitis, and may occur within a day or two of symptoms appearing. Even so, most patients recover completely, and there are no long term liver problems.

See also Hepatitis A; Hepatitis B; Hepatitis C; Hepatitis D; Hepatitis G

Hepatitis F

There is no such form of hepatitis recognised officially.

Hepatitis G

DESCRIPTION: A viral infection of the liver.

CAUSE: Transmitted from one person to another through blood contamination such as the sharing of needles by drug users, and probably by sex. Very little is yet known about it, as it was only discovered in 1996. It may be widespread, with 1% of normal healthy Americans being infected, and 20% of patients with hepatitis B or C.

SYMPTOMS: Usually minimal.

INVESTIGATIONS: There is no easily available test for the disease, and only research laboratories can distinguish it from other forms of hepatitis.

TREATMENT: No specific treatment or vaccine available.

COMPLICATIONS: Unknown.

PROGNOSIS: Its long term effects are unknown.

See also Hepatitis A; Hepatitis B; Hepatitis C; Hepatitis D; Hepatitis E

Hepatolenticular Degeneration
See Wilson's Disease

Hepatoma
See Liver Cancer

Herald Patch
See Pityriasis Rosea

Hereditary Haemorrhagic Telangiectasia
See Osler-Rendu-Weber Disease

Hernia
See Femoral Hernia; Hiatus Hernia; Incisional Hernia; Inguinal Hernia; Spigelian Hernia; Umbilical Hernia

Heroin Addiction
See Narcotic Addiction

Herpangina
See Coxsackie Virus Infection; Stomatitis

Herpes Simplex Infections
See Cold Sores; Genital Herpes; Whitlow

Herpes Zoster Infections
See Chickenpox; Ramsay-Hunt Syndrome; Shingles

Hers Syndrome
See Glycogen Storage Diseases

Hiatus Hernia

DESCRIPTION: Part of the stomach slips up through the hole in the diaphragm where the oesophagus passes from the chest to the abdomen to form a hiatus hernia.

There are two types of hiatus hernia—

— Paraoesophageal hiatus hernias occur when a pocket of stomach slips up through the hole in the diaphragm beside the oesophagus. Most are small, but sometimes a large proportion of the stomach may push up into the chest.

— Sliding hiatus hernias (90% of hiatus hernias) result from the stomach sliding up into the chest, pushing the oesophagus further up into the chest.

CAUSE: Pressure in the abdominal cavity from heavy lifting, obesity, and tension (muscle spasm occurs), or slack ligaments in the diaphragm in the elderly.

SYMPTOMS: May cause no symptoms, but patients usually describe heartburn (usually worse at night when lying down, or after a meal), excessive burping, a bitter taste on the back of the tongue (waterbrash), difficulty in swallowing and sometimes pain from ulceration inside the hernia or pinching of the hernia. Further symptoms may include a feeling of fullness, and palpitations if a large hernia pushes onto the heart.

INVESTIGATIONS: Barium meal X-ray or gastroscopy.

TREATMENT: Paraoesophageal hiatus hernias should be surgically repaired, unless the patient is elderly or in poor health.

Sliding hiatus hernia can usually be treated with medication (antacids, tablets that reduce the amount of acid secreted by the stomach or increase the emptying rate of the stomach and strengthen the valve at the lower end of the oesophagus), posture and diet. Frequent small meals, rather than three large meals a day, and a diet low in fat and high in protein is beneficial. Obese patients must lose weight.

COMPLICATIONS: Bleeding from ulcers that form in the damaged part of the stomach.

PROGNOSIS: Medications are usually very successful in controlling symptoms. The results of surgery are generally good.

See also Hernias; Reflux Oesophagitis

HiB Infection
See Haemophilus Influenzae B Infection

Hiccoughs
See Hiccups

Hiccups
(Hiccoughs)

DESCRIPTION: Repetitive, annoying brief expulsions of air from the throat.

CAUSE: Due to spasms of the diaphragm, a sheet of muscle that stretches across the body to separate the chest from the abdomen. When it contracts spasmodically, a small amount of air is suddenly forced out of the lungs, causing the characteristic sound. The diaphragm becomes irritated by swallowing large pieces of food, swallowing too quickly, or overfilling the stomach. Sudden laughing, the nervous swallowing of air and a large number of rarer conditions may also be responsible. If the hiccups are long-lasting and constant they may be due to pneumonia, pancreatitis, abscesses in the abdomen, brain disorders (eg. strokes, tumours), chemical imbalances in the bloodstream and heart disease.

SYMPTOMS: Involuntary, repeated spasms of the diaphragm causing the sudden expulsion of air and a brief high pitched noise.

INVESTIGATIONS: None normally necessary unless a specific cause is being sought.

TREATMENT: May be cured by a counter irritation or relieving the stomach pressure. Drinking water, holding a deep breath, a fright, and burping are well-known remedies. Medications can be given to relax the diaphragm muscle in persistent cases.

COMPLICATIONS: Rarely may persist for days, weeks, months or years. The causes need to be investigated and treated in these cases.

PROGNOSIS: Usually lasts no more than a few minutes or an hour or two.

Hidradenitis Suppurativa
DESCRIPTION: Uncommon skin disorder.
CAUSE: Unknown.

SYMPTOMS: Boil-like lumps develop in the groin, armpits and under the breasts.
INVESTIGATIONS: None normally necessary.
TREATMENT: Unsatisfactory. Wash with antiseptics to reduce skin bacteria, use antibiotics (eg. tetracycline, metronidazole) long term, and excise persistent lumps. Some women benefit by taking the oral contraceptive pill. Roaccutane tablets and radical surgery to excise affected area used in very severe cases.
COMPLICATIONS: Abscesses may develop due to secondary bacterial infection.
PROGNOSIS: Often persists long term.

Hidrosadenome
See Fox-Fordyce Disease

High Blood Pressure
See Hypertension

Hip Avascular Necrosis
See Avascular Necrosis of the Femoral Head

Hip Dislocation
DESCRIPTION: Movement of the head of the femur (thigh bone) out of its socket in the pelvis (the hip joint). The hip may be dislocated at birth (congenital dislocation), dislocated in a major injury (traumatic dislocation), or dislocated because of severe arthritis or joint infection (pathological dislocation).
CAUSE: Congenital dislocation — some babies are born with one or both hips dislocated, or able to be easily dislocated. This is five times more common in girls than boys.
Traumatic dislocation — a very serious injury that occurs in severe accidents. The hip joint is forcibly torn from its socket, and the surrounding ligaments and muscles are badly damaged.
Pathological dislocation — because the joint is worn away, weak elderly patients with very severe arthritis of the hip may dislocate it quite easily. In younger patients, a severe infection of the hip may partially destroy the joint and allow it to dislocate.
SYMPTOMS: Congenital dislocation — a delay in walking, uneven skin folds on the buttocks and back of the legs, and limping. A doctor can detect abnormal movement in the hips soon after birth.
Traumatic dislocation — severe pain in the hip and an inability to move the leg.
Pathological dislocation — often minimal pain, but unable to walk or bear weight on the affected leg.
INVESTIGATIONS: All types of dislocation diagnosed by an X-ray.
TREATMENT: Congenital dislocation — if detected early, most patients can be effectively cured by putting the baby's legs in a 'frog position' (widely spread) in a special splint or double nappies for three months. If this is not successful,

or if the condition is not diagnosed until after the child is six months old, an operation to correct the dislocation is required.

Traumatic dislocation — an operation is usually necessary to repair the damage, and many months convalescence are required.

Pathological dislocation — treatment depends on the degree of disability and the patient's general health. An operation to replace the hip joint may be undertaken.

COMPLICATIONS: Congenital dislocation — in severe cases, an artificial hip may need to be inserted once the patient is fully grown.

Traumatic dislocation — permanent arthritis is often a consequence. The dislocation may be associated with a fracture.

PROGNOSIS: Congenital dislocation — good long term results obtained with early treatment.

Traumatic dislocation — reasonable results obtained in many cases but may result in permanent disability.

Pathological dislocation — permanent disability common, depending on patient's general health.

See also Dislocation

Hip Fracture

DESCRIPTION: A fracture of the top of the thigh bone (the femur) that normally does not directly involve the hip joint itself. Usually occurs in elderly people, particularly women.

CAUSE: Falling on the side, particularly when the bone is thinned by osteoporosis (see separate entry).

SYMPTOMS: Pain and loss of function of the hip.

INVESTIGATIONS: Diagnosed by an X-ray.

TREATMENT: Orthopaedic surgeons usually totally replace the hip joint and the ball at the top of the femur, and patients are mobile again in only a few days. In other cases, surgery to fix the fracture in position with steel pins or screws, or many weeks in traction in bed are required to allow healing.

COMPLICATIONS: Failure to heal is common when the fracture is pinned and screwed. Death of a fragment of bone due to an inadequate blood supply may occur. Infection is possible with a hip replacement.

PROGNOSIS: Most hip replacements are very successful, but results are affected by the general health of the patient.

See also Fracture; Osteoporosis

Hirschsprung Disease

DESCRIPTION: A congenital disease of the large intestine which is far more common in boys than girls.

CAUSE: Caused by a failure of the nerves supplying the large intestine (colon) to develop correctly. Without these nerves, the intestine cannot contract to move along the faeces, and it collects to dilate the colon to an enormous size. There is a tendency for the disease to occur in successive generations.

SYMPTOMS: Usually diagnosed soon after birth as the baby is severely constipated, has a distended belly, refuses to feed, is lethargic, small in size, and is very irritable. Foul smelling diarrhoea may develop as a late symptom.

INVESTIGATIONS: Diagnosis confirmed by an X-ray of the gut, and taking a biopsy of the colon.

TREATMENT: Initially, excess faeces is removed by a tube placed up through the anus, but in due course an operation to remove the affected section of gut is necessary.

COMPLICATIONS: Massive overdilation of the large intestine (megacolon).

PROGNOSIS: Without treatment most affected babies will die. After the operation, these children progress very well and have only minor long-term problems.

See also Megacolon

Hirsutism

DESCRIPTION: Excess body hair in women.

CAUSE: May be an inherited characteristic (more commonly in those from the Middle East, southern Europe and India), or due to numerous medical conditions (eg. Stein-Leventhal syndrome, ovarian tumours, Cushing syndrome, adrenal tumours, congenital adrenal hyperplasia etc.) that produce abnormal levels of sex hormones.

SYMPTOMS: Thick hairs appear on the upper lip, chin, belly, nipples, thighs and back.

INVESTIGATIONS: Any underlying cause must be excluded by appropriate investigations.

TREATMENT: Treat the cause if possible. Medications taken long term (eg. spironolactone, cyproterone) control the problem. Individual hair electrolysis permanently removes that particular hair.

PROGNOSIS: Tends to persist once established, even if cause removed. Control reasonable.

Histiocytoma
See Dermatofibroma

Histiocytosis X
(Langerhans Cell Granulomatosis)

DESCRIPTION: A group of diseases that result in replacement of lung, bone and intestinal tissue by fibrous scar tissue. Hand-Schüller-Christian disease and Leterrer-Siwe disease are types of histiocytosis X.

CAUSE: Unknown.

SYMPTOMS: Occurs in young smokers to cause worsening shortness of breath, chronic cough, and gradual destruction of the lungs.

INVESTIGATIONS: Diagnosed by chest X-ray, CAT scan and lung biopsy.

TREATMENT: Stop smoking. Numerous treatments have been tried with varying success including medications normally used for asthma, the drug penicillamine (not the antibiotic penicillin), irradiation and lung transplant.

COMPLICATIONS: Spontaneous pneumothorax.

PROGNOSIS: Usually slowly progressive.

See also Hand-Schüller-Christian Disease; Leterrer-Siwe Disease

Histoplasmosis

DESCRIPTION: An uncommon fungal infection of the lungs.

CAUSE: Caused by the fungus *Histoplasma capsulatum* which is present in soil and can be inhaled to cause a form of pneumonia. Most cases are very mild and may pass unnoticed or cause mild flu-like symptoms. Sometimes a moderately severe lung infection may develop, and in rare cases a severe and fatal pneumonia occurs. Most common in south-east Asia, South America and Africa. It is very rare in developed countries.

SYMPTOMS: Depends on the severity of the infection but in severe cases resemble those of a normal pneumonia with a cough, wheeze, shortness of breath, marked tiredness and a fever.

INVESTIGATIONS: Diagnosed after examining a sample of sputum and culturing it to determine the infecting organism. There is also a specific blood test, and X-rays of the chest show a characteristic pattern.

TREATMENT: Minor cases require no treatment, but more severe ones are treated with specific antifungal medications.

COMPLICATIONS: Permanent lung damage from severe pneumonia may be permanent.

PROGNOSIS: With correct treatment, only the elderly or invalids are likely to die or develop long-term complications.

See also Pneumonia

HIV
See AIDS

Hives
(Angioedema; Urticaria)

DESCRIPTION: An allergic reaction in the skin. Angioedema is a term used more commonly when the lips or eyelid is involved and becomes severely swollen, with only slight itchiness and redness.

CAUSE: Common causes include brushing against plants that may have stinging nettles on their surface, insect bites and chemicals (in creams, cosmetics, soaps) that are applied to the skin. Hives may also occur in a non-allergic form, which may be a response to stress. Some patients with long-term and recurrent forms of urticaria may be reacting to salicylates and tartrazine, chemicals that occur naturally in a wide range of foods.

SYMPTOMS: Red, raised, itchy weals may be limited to a small area, or spread widely over the skin. The rash develops rapidly over a few minutes or a couple of hours, and may persist for up to two weeks, although two or three days is average.

INVESTIGATIONS: Skin and blood tests can be undertaken in an attempt to identify the substance responsible for the reaction.

TREATMENT: Antihistamines or steroids by mouth or injection. Tricyclic antidepressants also seem to benefit some patients with persistent hives. Soothing creams, lotions and baths can give relief to patients during the worst stages of an attack. A diet which is free of salicylates and tartrazine may be of benefit.

COMPLICATIONS: Some rarer forms may become chronic and last for months or years.

PROGNOSIS: Most patients settle with appropriate treatment.

See also Allergy; Familial Angioedema

Hodgkin's Disease
(Lymphoma)

DESCRIPTION: A form of cancer of the lymph nodes. The group of lymphomas that do not fulfil all the criteria to be called Hodgkin's disease are called 'non-Hodgkin's lymphomas'.

CAUSE: Unknown. Tends to occur more in males, young adults and the elderly. There may be a genetic tendency.

SYMPTOMS: Painless swellings of the lymph nodes, often in the neck, armpit and groin. Other symptoms include tiredness, fever, weight loss, night sweats and a generalised itch.

INVESTIGATIONS: Diagnosis confirmed by removing an involved lymph node and examining it under a microscope.

TREATMENT: Most patients can be classified into different stages (1 to 4) depending upon the degree of spread of the disease. The treatment varies depending on the stage of the disease and involves various combinations of radiation, cytotoxic (anti-cancer) drugs, and surgery.

COMPLICATIONS: Spreads to other lymph nodes and organs in other parts of the body.

PROGNOSIS: Survival depends upon the staging. The higher the staging the worse the outcome.

See also Non-Hodgkin's Lymphomas

Hole in the Heart
See Conradi-Hunermann Syndrome; Fallot's Pentalogy; Fallot's Tetralogy; Fallot's Trilogy; Ventricular Septal Defect

Holmes-Adie Syndrome
(Adie's Pupil)

DESCRIPTION: Abnormality of the pupils.

CAUSE: Congenital. More common in women.

SYMPTOMS: The pupils in the eyes are different sizes, respond poorly to light stimulation and tendon reflexes in the arms and legs may be slower than normal.
INVESTIGATIONS: None necessary.
TREATMENT: None available.
COMPLICATIONS: May be adversely affected by bright light, or find it difficult to see in dim light.
PROGNOSIS: Benign condition.

Homosexuality
('Gay'; Lesbian)

DESCRIPTION: A sexual preference for members of the same sex. Homosexuality is not considered to be a medical problem.
CAUSE: There are many theories as to why some people are homosexual, but no absolute reason is known. 6% of adult men and 3% of adult women have partaken in some form of homosexual activity, but only about 1% of men and half that number of women are exclusively homosexual. Homosexual women may be referred to as lesbians.
TREATMENT: Individuals who have trouble accepting their sexual orientation because of peer or society pressures may require psychiatric assistance.
COMPLICATIONS: Higher incidence of sexually transmitted disease than in heterosexuals, mainly because of promiscuity.
PROGNOSIS: Normal lifespan and health.

Hookworm
(Ancylostomiasis)

DESCRIPTION: Infestation of the gut by the nematode worm *Ancylostoma duodenale*. One quarter of the population of the world affected.
CAUSE: The adult hookworm is 1 cm long and lives in the gut. Eggs pass out in the faeces, and if the faeces fall onto moist ground, the larvae will hatch from the eggs. The larvae remain active in the moist soil for up to a week, and during that time, a larva may penetrate the skin of the foot of any person who treads on it. The larva then migrates through the bloodstream to the lung, where it breaks into the air-carrying passageways of the lung. From there it is carried with sputum up into the throat, where it is swallowed, enters the gut, develops into an adult worm and starts the process all over again. May be caught in all the tropical countries of the world.
SYMPTOMS: An itch at the site of skin penetration, a cough, wheeze and fever while the larvae are in the lung, and mild abdominal discomfort and diarrhoea when there are a large number of worms in the gut.
INVESTIGATIONS: Examination of a sample of faeces under a microscope reveals the worm or its eggs.
TREATMENT: Drugs are available to destroy the worms.

COMPLICATIONS: Only in patients who are otherwise ill or malnourished does a hookworm infestation cause significant problems.

PROGNOSIS: Usually cured by appropriate treatment.

Hordeolum, External
See Stye

Horner Syndrome

DESCRIPTION: Bizarre combination of symptoms involving the eye and sweat glands.

CAUSE: Caused by compression of a special network of nerves in the chest due to lung cancer or pneumothorax, or in the brain due to a tumour.

SYMPTOMS: Characterised by a drooping eyelid, contracted pupil and a sunken eye, associated with reduced sweating.

INVESTIGATIONS: Numerous investigations undertaken to find the cause, including X-rays, CT and MRI scans.

TREATMENT: Correct the underlying cause of the nerve compression, usually by surgery.

COMPLICATIONS: May be the first sign of a quite advanced lung cancer.

PROGNOSIS: Depends on cause.

See also Lung Cancer; Pneumothorax

Housemaid's Knee
(Pre-Patellar Bursitis; Water on the Knee)

DESCRIPTION: A swelling and inflammation of the bursa on the front of the knee cap.

CAUSE: Bursae are small sacs that are connected by a fine tube to a joint cavity. Several are present near every joint, and secrete the synovial fluid which acts as an lubricant for the the joint. One of the bursae supplying the knee is in front of the knee-cap, and it may be damaged by prolonged kneeling or a blow.

SYMPTOMS: A painful swelling over the knee cap.

INVESTIGATIONS: None usually necessary.

TREATMENT: Rest, strapping, avoiding kneeling and occasionally draining the excess fluid from the knee.

COMPLICATIONS: Uncommonly, a serious bacterial infection may occur in the knee.

PROGNOSIS: Good, but a recurrence possible.

See also Bursitis

Housewife's Dermatitis
See Contact Dermatitis

HPV Infection
See Genital Warts

Human Papilloma Virus Infection
See Genital Warts

Humerus Fracture

DESCRIPTION: A fracture of the upper arm bone (humerus), usually near the shoulder joint.

CAUSE: Severe injury, but in the elderly may occur after a relatively minor fall or twisting force.

SYMPTOMS: Severe pain and swelling at the site of the fracture, with inability to move the arm.

INVESTIGATIONS: Diagnosed by X-ray.

TREATMENT: It is not practical to immobilise the humerus because it would require a plaster that encased the chest and shoulder, and extended down the arm to the elbow. Most heal very well if the arm is left hanging by the side while the wrist is supported by a sling. Sometimes the elbow is strapped to the body. No attempt should be made to use the arm.

COMPLICATIONS: A false joint may form at the site of the fracture in the elderly with poor healing, or with excessive use of the arm during healing.

PROGNOSIS: Good in most cases, with healing in 6 to 8 weeks, but in the elderly, healing may be slow and painful.

See also Fractures

Hunner's Ulcer
See Interstitial Cystitis

Hunter Syndrome
(Mucopolysaccharoidosis II)

DESCRIPTION: A rare congenital condition in which patients are unable to eliminate certain substances (mucopolysaccharides) from the body.

CAUSE: Inherited abnormality of the metabolic system.

SYMPTOMS: Stiff joints, grotesque facial appearance, enlarged spleen and liver, heart abnormalities and mild mental retardation.

INVESTIGATIONS: Diagnosed by specific blood and bone marrow tests and X-rays.

TREATMENT: Surgery for heart and facial abnormalities.

COMPLICATIONS: Deafness may also be a problem.

PROGNOSIS: No cure possible, but patients have a reasonable life expectancy.

See also Hurler Syndrome

Huntington's Chorea

DESCRIPTION: A distressing, incurable disease that affects muscle function and coordination and is passed from one generation to the next.

CAUSE: Congenital condition that is passed to half the children of a patient, but because the symptoms do not become apparent until between 30 and 50 years of age, it has often already been passed to the next generation before diagnosis. It is likely that all cases in existence can be traced back to previous sufferers.

SYMPTOMS: Irregular, random movements of the arms, legs and face; irritability, mood changes, antisocial behaviour, restlessness, fidgeting, abnormal movements of the body, mental deterioration, premature senility, and rigid muscles. Symptoms develop very slowly over many years.

INVESTIGATIONS: The chromosomal location of the gene that carries the condition from one generation to the next has been identified and the children of a patient can now decide if they wish to know if they are carrying the abnormal gene. This decision will obviously have dramatic effects upon their future lifestyle.

TREATMENT: No effective treatment available, but some psychiatric drugs can control mood changes, and muscle relaxants may ease the abnormal movements.

COMPLICATIONS: Serious psychiatric disturbances.

PROGNOSIS: The inevitable progression cannot be halted. Death within 10 to 20 years of symptoms developing is usual.

Hurler Syndrome
(Mucopolysaccharoidosis I)

DESCRIPTION: A rare congenital condition in which patients are unable to eliminate certain substances (mucopolysaccharides) from the body.

CAUSE: Inherited abnormality of the metabolic system.

SYMPTOMS: Grotesque facial appearance, short stature, stiff joints, spinal deformities, mental retardation, heart abnormalities, blindness and enlarged liver and spleen.

INVESTIGATIONS: Diagnosed by specific blood and bone marrow tests and X-rays.

TREATMENT: Surgery for heart and facial abnormalities.

COMPLICATIONS: Heart failure early in life.

PROGNOSIS: No cure possible. Similar to, but more serious than, Hunter syndrome, and patients usually die in childhood.

See also Hunter Syndrome; Scheie Syndrome; Sly Syndrome

Hutchison's Melanotic Freckle
(Lentigo Maligna)

DESCRIPTION: Skin spot that usually starts on the face of the middle aged or elderly.

CAUSE: Unknown.

SYMPTOMS: Irregular flat black-blue pigmented area on the skin that slowly enlarges.

INVESTIGATIONS: Diagnosed by biopsy.

TREATMENT: Small spots may be frozen (cryotherapy), but larger spots are surgically excised.

COMPLICATIONS: Rarely develops into a malignant melanoma.

PROGNOSIS: Treatment successful. Without treatment, slowly enlarge and thicken.

See also Melanoma

Hutchison's Prurigo
See Photodermatitis

Hyaline Membrane Disease
See Respiratory Distress Syndrome, Infant

Hydatid Disease
(Echinococcosis)

DESCRIPTION: Infestation of human tissue by the larva of the tapeworm *Echinococcus*.

CAUSE: The normal life cycle of *Echinococcus* requires infested meat to be eaten by a dog or other carnivore. The larva enters the gut and grows into a tapeworm which then passes eggs out in the faeces to contaminate grass and soil. The normal hosts are cattle, sheep and other grazing animals which eat the contaminated grass and are eventually killed by the *Echinococcus* infestation in their body. This allows the carcass to be eaten by meat-eating animals, and the life cycle of the parasite starts again. If a human eats food that has been contaminated by the faeces of an infected animal (usually dogs or other meat-eating animals), the larva migrates to the liver, lung, spleen or brain, where it forms a cyst that remains lifelong. The disease is rare in developed countries, but widespread in South America, around the Mediterranean, in east Africa and central Asia.

SYMPTOMS: After the cyst forms in the body, it usually remains dormant for many years, often causing no symptoms. Over a decade or more the cyst slowly enlarges, until the pressure it exerts on its surroundings causes problems. With liver cysts, there may be pain in the upper part of the abdomen, nausea, vomiting and jaundice. In the lung, the cysts may cause part of the lung to collapse, pain and shortness of breath. In the brain symptoms occur earlier, and even a small cyst may cause convulsions or severe headaches. If a cyst ruptures, the reaction in the body to the sudden release of a large number of larvae may cause sudden death or severe illness and the formation of multiple cysts in other parts of the body.

INVESTIGATIONS: Diagnosed by seeing the cyst on a CT or ultrasound scan. Specific blood tests can be performed to determine whether or not a person has a cyst somewhere in their body. Discovering the actual site of the cyst may then prove very difficult.

TREATMENT: If possible, a cyst should be removed surgically. It is vital for the surgeon not to rupture the cyst during its removal, because the spilled larvae can then spread through the body. In other cases, or as an additional form of treatment, potent medications may be prescribed to kill the larvae, but the cyst will remain. Dogs in affected areas can be treated regularly to prevent them carrying the disease.

COMPLICATIONS: If multiple cysts are present, the long-term outlook is grave.

PROGNOSIS: Provided the disease is not widespread, the results of treatment are good.

See also Worm Infestations

Hydatidiform Mole
See Uterine Mole

Hydatid of Morgagni
DESCRIPTION: Gangrene of a residual appendage on the testis.

CAUSE: The hydatid of Morgagni is a small, unnecessary tissue sac that hangs loosely from the top of the testis in the male and the Fallopian tube in the female. In men, it is possible for the sac to become twisted, gangrenous and painful.

SYMPTOMS: Sudden onset of severe testicular pain and tenderness. Torsion of the testis (see separate entry) is a surgical emergency that requires treatment within a few hours and also has the same symptoms.

INVESTIGATIONS: The diagnosis is only made during surgery, after ensuring that the testis itself has not become twisted and gangrenous.

TREATMENT: During a simple operation the offending piece of tissue is removed, with no subsequent adverse effects upon the potency or masculinity of the patient.

COMPLICATIONS: None significant.

PROGNOSIS: Recovery is usually complete within three or four days.

See also Torsion of the Testis

Hydramnios
See Oligohydramnios; Polyhydramnios

Hydrocele
DESCRIPTION: A common problem due to a collection of excess fluid around a testicle.

CAUSE: The testes are surrounded by a fine layer of tissue called the tunica vaginalis. Fluid may accumulate between the testicle and the tunica to cause swelling at almost any age. May follow an injury or infection in the scrotum, or for no apparent reason.

SYMPTOMS: The swelling is painless and there is no discomfort, but the testicle may slowly enlarge to the size of a tennis ball or more.

INVESTIGATIONS: None normally necessary, but an ultrasound scan excludes other conditions.

TREATMENT: In infants the problem sometimes settles without treatment, but in adults a needle is used to drain off the fluid. Unfortunately the fluid often re-accumulates, and a minor surgical procedure may be necessary to give a permanent cure.

COMPLICATIONS: Other cysts and growths that can occur in the scrotum, including cancer, which may not be painful, and the presence of these must be excluded.

PROGNOSIS: No permanent damage to the testicle or its function.

Hydrocephalus

DESCRIPTION: The brain and spinal cord are surrounded by cerebrospinal fluid (CSF). In the brain are a number of cavities, one of which contains a network of veins (the choroid plexus) that secretes the CSF, which passes through small ducts to the outside of the brain. From there it flows down and around the spinal cord in the back, from where it is absorbed into the blood. Hydrocephalus occurs when excess CSF accumulates in or around the brain.

CAUSE: There are two types of hydrocephalus—

— obstructive hydrocephalus occurs if CSF cannot escape from the cavities within the brain due to a blockage in the draining tubes, and the brain is blown up by the fluid it contains.

— communicating hydrocephalus occurs when there is a blockage of the circulation down the spinal cord and the fluid cannot be absorbed back into the bloodstream.

Both types are usually caused by a developmental abnormality of the foetus, or may develop in later life because of brain infections, tumours in the brain or skull, cysts in the brain, blood clots and other rarer conditions.

SYMPTOMS: In babies, the soft skull is grossly dilated by the excess fluid. In older children or adults, a severe headache, personality changes, partial paralysis and loss of consciousness may be symptoms, as the harder skull is unable to expand. Other symptoms will depend upon the effect of the increased fluid pressure on the brain.

INVESTIGATIONS: Diagnosed by a CT or MRI scan.

TREATMENT: Inserting a tube (shunt) into the skull to drain away the excess CSF. The tube has a one way valve allowing the CSF to escape, but preventing other fluids or infection from entering the brain. The far end of the tube is inserted into a vein in the neck or chest, or is run all the way through the chest, and allowed to drain into the abdominal cavity.

COMPLICATIONS: Any brain or intellectual damage that occurs before the condition is treated may be permanent. Shunts can become blocked and require replacement or clearing occasionally.

PROGNOSIS: Treatment is very successful in controlling the condition and allows the patient to lead a normal life with minimal impairment of body function or intelligence.

Hyperadrenocorticism
See Cushing Syndrome

Hyperaldosteronism
See Conn Syndrome

Hypercalcaemia
DESCRIPTION: Excess calcium in the body and blood.

CAUSE: Cancer directly or indirectly (eg. metastatic breast or prostate cancer) affecting bone that releases calcium, hyperparathyroidism, sarcoidosis and excess vitamin D (see separate entries).

SYMPTOMS: Loss of appetite, nausea, vomiting, constipation, passing excess urine, muscle weakness, confusion, tremor, psychiatric disturbances and tiredness.

INVESTIGATIONS: Blood tests demonstrate high calcium levels.

TREATMENT: Treat cause if possible. Fluids given by a drip into a vein to dilute high calcium levels, followed by diuretics (fluid tablets) to wash it out of the body. Other medications can be used to bind calcium (eg. diphosphonates) and reduce inflammation (eg. prednisone).

COMPLICATIONS: Abnormal nerve conduction in the heart may lead to significant abnormalities of rhythm.

PROGNOSIS: Depends on cause.

See also Cancer; Hyperparathyroidism; Sarcoidosis

Hypercholesterolaemia
(Cholesterol, Excess)

DESCRIPTION: A yellow/white fatty substance called cholesterol is essential in the body as it is responsible for cementing cells together, is a major constituent of bile and the basic building block for sex hormones. On the other hand, if excess is present it is harmful.

CAUSE: The level of cholesterol in the body is determined by inherited traits and diet. The people most likely to have high levels of cholesterol are overweight middle-aged men. Women, and people of normal weight, may be affected too, but not as frequently.

SYMPTOMS: If too much cholesterol is present in the blood stream, it may be deposited in gradually increasing amounts inside the arteries. Slowly, the affected artery narrows until the flow of blood is sufficiently obstructed to cause the area supplied by that artery, to suffer. If that area is the heart, a heart attack will result — if it is the brain, a stroke will occur. This deposition of fat is known as arteriosclerosis (hardening of the arteries — see separate entry).

INVESTIGATIONS: Cholesterol levels are determined by a blood test taken after a 12 hour fast from food (usually over night) and no alcohol should be taken for the preceding 72 hours. Cholesterol is divided into high-density and low-density types, and the ratio between these is more important than the total level of cholesterol. High density cholesterol is good for you, while the low density type is bad.

TREATMENT: The cholesterol level that is considered safe varies with risk factors such as family history, obesity, high blood pressure, smoking and any history of heart attacks or strokes. Levels should be lower in young people than old, and males than females. Treatment starts with a diet that is low in cholesterol, not smoking, limiting alcohol intake, exercising more and losing weight if obese. A low-cholesterol diet avoids all dairy products, fatty meats, sausages, offal, and egg yolk. If despite a strict diet, the cholesterol level remains too high, the regular use of medications can be prescribed. There are also surgical techniques available to clean out clogged arteries. As in all diseases, prevention is much better than cure.

COMPLICATIONS: Excess cholesterol is responsible for a large proportion of heart attacks, strokes, circulatory problems and kidney disease.

PROGNOSIS: Patients with normal cholesterol levels have a reduced risk of artery damage, heart attack or stroke. Once cholesterol plaques are deposited inside arteries, they remain there permanently.

See also Arteriosclerosis; Hypertriglyceridaemia

Hyperemesis Gravidarum
See Morning Sickness

Hyper-IgE Syndrome
See Job-Buckley Syndrome

Hyperkeratosis
(Solar Keratosis)

DESCRIPTION: Form of sun damage to exposed areas of skin that may develop into a squamous cell carcinoma (SCC).

CAUSE: Prolonged sun exposure, particularly as a youth.

SYMPTOMS: Patches of raised and scaling skin, but they are not red or itchy.

INVESTIGATIONS: Should be treated when suspected.

TREATMENT: Removed by acid ointments, freezing (cryosurgery), burning (diathermy) or surgical excision.

COMPLICATIONS: In some elderly patients with very large affected areas it may not be practical to remove all the spots, but they should be checked regularly so that any which change can be treated.

PROGNOSIS: Very good, but new spots tend to arise in nearby areas.

See also Squamous Cell Carcinoma of the Skin

Hyperkinetic Syndrome
(Overactivity Syndrome)

DESCRIPTION: A form of minimal brain dysfunction.

CAUSE: Developmental problem starting before birth.

SYMPTOMS: Early onset of personality problems, overactivity, poor coordination of limbs, learning disorders, and antisocial behaviour.

INVESTIGATIONS: An EEG (electroencephalogram) may be abnormal.

TREATMENT: Behaviour modification techniques, drugs such as methylphenidate and dexamphetamine, special education programs, and environmental modification.

COMPLICATIONS: May be associated with epilepsy. Criminal activity common in early adult life.

PROGNOSIS: Although condition persists, satisfactory control usually possible.

See also Attention Deficit Hyperactivity Disorder

Hyperlipidaemia
See Hypercholesterolaemia; Hypertriglyceridaemia

Hypermobility Syndrome
DESCRIPTION: Excessive mobility of joints throughout the body.

CAUSE: Congenital slackness of ligaments.

SYMPTOMS: Dramatically increased ability to move joints beyond their normal limits associated with intermittent joint pain, tenderness and swelling, and ease of joint dislocation. Fingers may bend back at a right angle, the thumb may be able to bend back to touch the forearm, the knees and elbows bend back beyond 10°, and patients can rest palms easily on floor when bending from waist with knees straight.

INVESTIGATIONS: X-rays may show joint damage. Diagnosed by assessing excessive mobility of joints.

TREATMENT: Joint protection, physiotherapy, joint supports and splints, exercise program, counselling, anti-inflammatory drugs, pain killers, local anaesthetic and steroid injections.

COMPLICATIONS: Osteoarthritis may develop.

PROGNOSIS: Disability from recurrent sprains or dislocations.

Hyperopia
See Long Sighted

Hyperparathyroidism
DESCRIPTION: Four small parathyroid glands sit behind the thyroid gland in the neck and secrete the hormone calcitonin which controls the amount of calcium in the bones and blood. If these glands become overactive (hyperparathyroidism), excess calcitonin is secreted, resulting in calcium being taken out of the bones and into the blood.

CAUSE: A rare disease that may be caused by a tumour or cancer in one of the parathyroid glands, but often no cause can be found.

SYMPTOMS: Bones become brittle and painful and break easily. The high levels of calcium in the blood causes kidney stones and damage (which can result in thirst and the passing of large quantities of urine), high blood pressure, constipation and peptic ulcers in the stomach.

INVESTIGATIONS: Diagnosis confirmed by finding high levels of calcium in the blood and urine. CT scans are used to determine the site of the affected gland.

TREATMENT: Intricate surgery to remove the overactive gland. A large fluid intake is necessary to flush out the kidneys. There are no drugs that can be used.

COMPLICATIONS: Damage to the kidneys, which may eventually fail.

PROGNOSIS: Surgery is successful in most cases, but without treatment, the disease will steadily progress until serious complications result.

See also Hypoparathyroidism

Hyperprolactinaemia

DESCRIPTION: Excessive production of the hormone prolactin by the pituitary gland in the centre of the brain. Prolactin is the hormone which is responsible for breast milk production.

CAUSE: May be due to underactive ovaries or testes, or more commonly a tumour in the pituitary gland. Uncommonly, may be due to side effects of some drugs or an underactive thyroid gland.

SYMPTOMS: Abnormal milk production by the breasts in both women (much more commonly) and men. Women usually stop their menstrual periods.

INVESTIGATIONS: The blood level of prolactin is measured, and the pituitary gland is examined by a CT scan.

TREATMENT: Controlled by the drug bromocriptine. Surgery or radiotherapy to the pituitary gland.

COMPLICATIONS: Depends on cause.

PROGNOSIS: Good.

Hyper-Reactive Airways Disease

DESCRIPTION: An inflammatory lung condition similar to asthma.

CAUSE: Often follows a viral infection of the upper airways or lungs, or may be due to inhalation of irritant gases or an allergy.

SYMPTOMS: Persistent wheezing, cough and shortness of breath. More allergy type symptoms and less phlegm production than in asthma.

INVESTIGATIONS: Lung function tests and chest X-ray usually normal.

TREATMENT: Inhaled steroids (eg. beclomethasone, budesonide, flucitasone) or anti-inflammatories (eg. ipratropium).

PROGNOSIS: Settles spontaneously eventually, but responds well to treatment.

See also Asthma

Hypertension
(High Blood Pressure)

DESCRIPTION: Excessive pressure of blood within the arteries that occurs in 20% of adults over 40 years of age.

The heart contracts regularly to pump blood through the arteries under high (systolic) pressure. When the heart relaxes between beats, the blood continues to flow due to the lower (diastolic) pressure exerted by the elasticity of the artery walls. Hypertension occurs when one, or both, of these pressures exceeds a safe level. Blood pressure readings are written as systolic pressure/diastolic pressure (eg. 125/70) and are measured with a sphygmomanometer. Blood pressure varies with exercise, anxiety, age, fitness, smoking and drinking habits, weight and medications. In an elderly person 160/95 may be acceptable, but in a young woman, 110/60 would be more appropriate. Life insurance companies generally require the blood pressure to be under 136/86 for the person to be acceptable at normal rates. The numbers are a measure of pressure in millimetres of mercury.

The arteries of a person with high blood pressure will become hardened, brittle and may eventually rupture, causing a stroke, heart attack or other serious injury to vital organs.

CAUSE: The majority of patients have 'essential' hypertension, for which there is no single identifiable cause. The identifiable causes include smoking, obesity, kidney disease, oestrogen-containing medications (eg. the contraceptive pill), hyperparathyroidism, phaeochromocytoma (see separate entries) and a number of other rare diseases. High blood pressure may also be a complication of pregnancy, when it can lead to quite serious consequences.

SYMPTOMS: The majority of patients have no symptoms for many years. Those who do have symptoms complain of headaches and tiredness, but only when the blood pressure is very high do the further symptoms of nausea, confusion, and disturbances in vision occur.

INVESTIGATIONS: Once diagnosed, blood and urine tests are performed to see if there is any specific cause. X-rays of the kidneys and an electrocardiograph (ECG) may also be performed.

TREATMENT: Prevented by keeping weight within reasonable limits, not eating excessive amounts of salt, not smoking, and by exercising regularly. There is no cure, but hypertension can be successfully controlled by taking tablets regularly lifelong. A wide range of medications are available, and it takes days or weeks for the tablets to work. Regular checks are essential until the correct dosage is determined, then blood pressure checks every 3 to 6 months are necessary.

COMPLICATIONS: Untreated high blood pressure causes strokes and heart attacks at an earlier age than would be expected with normal blood pressure. Other complications may include kidney damage and bleeding into an eye. A rapidly progressive condition known as malignant hypertension can sometimes develop and cause remarkably high levels of blood pressure.

PROGNOSIS: Once controlled, there is no reason why the patient should not lead a full and active working, sporting and sexual life. Untreated, most patients with only moderate hypertension die within 20 years.

See also Heart Attack; Phaeochromocytoma

Hypertension, Pulmonary
See Cor Pulmonale

Hyperthyroidism
(Thyrotoxicosis; Grave's Disease)

DESCRIPTION: Overactivity of the thyroid gland which sits in the front of the neck and is responsible for secreting a hormone called thyroxine. This acts as the accelerator for every cell in the body. If the level of thyroxine is high, the cells function at an increased rate — if the level of thyroxine is low, the cells function at a less than normal rate.

CAUSE: The most common cause is an autoimmune disease, in which antibodies attack the thyroid gland and over stimulate it. There are numerous other rarer causes.

SYMPTOMS: Patients sweat excessively, lose weight, are nervous, tired, cannot tolerate hot weather and have a mild diarrhoea. Other effects include a rapid heart rate, slightly protruding eyes, warm skin, and a slight tremor. Patients tend to fidget, dart quickly in their activity, and speak rapidly. The gland may be grossly enlarged (a goitre) or normal size.

INVESTIGATIONS: The level of thyroxine and gland activity can be measured by blood tests. Abnormalities may also be seen on an electrocardiogram (ECG).

TREATMENT: Overactivity can only temporarily be controlled by medication. A cure can be obtained by surgically removing most of the thyroid gland or destroying it by giving the patient radioactive iodine (Iodine 131) which concentrates in the gland as it is an essential component of thyroxine. Because there is usually insufficient thyroid gland left behind after these procedures to produce adequate amounts of thyroxine, it is necessary for most patients to take thyroxine tablets on a daily basis.

COMPLICATIONS: The complications are serious. The weight loss and muscle wasting may become permanent, liver damage and heart failure may be fatal, psychiatric disturbances may lead to hospitalisation, eye scarring may lead to blindness, and infertility may occur.

PROGNOSIS: If treated early, the prognosis is excellent. If delayed until complications occur the outcome is far less favourable.

See also Goitre; Thyroiditis

Hypertriglyceridaemia
(Triglyceride Excess)

DESCRIPTION: Excess amount of a fat (triglyceride) in blood.

CAUSE: Triglycerides are formed when one of a group of fatty acids (oleic acid, stearic acid and palmitic acid) combines with glycerol. Triglycerides are found in most animal and vegetable fats and form an essential part of the human diet, but when eaten in excess, or excessively concentrated in the blood, they are a problem. Patients with obesity, diabetes, alcoholism, an underactive thyroid gland, and a number of rarer diseases have an increased risk of developing the condition. Some patients have an inherited type of excess triglyceride which cannot be adequately corrected by diet alone but requires medication. Oral contraceptives may also be responsible.

SYMPTOMS: None usually present unless complications occur.

INVESTIGATIONS: Amount of triglyceride in the blood measured. The patient must fast for twelve hours and avoid alcohol for three days before the test.

TREATMENT: Patients can usually be controlled by a diet that excludes most animal and vegetable fat (eg. fried food, dairy products, fatty meats). With hereditary disease or severe cases, medication must be taken long term as well as the diet.

COMPLICATIONS: An increased risk of strokes and heart attacks, as the excess triglyceride is deposited along with cholesterol on the inside wall of arteries to cause hardening of the arteries (Arteriosclerosis).

PROGNOSIS: No cure possible, but control usually satisfactory.

See also Arteriosclerosis; Hypercholesterolaemia

Hypertrophic Cardiomyopathy
See Cardiomyopathy

Hyperuricaemia
See Gout

Hypervitaminosis A
(Carotenaemia)

DESCRIPTION: Vitamin A is found in leafy green vegetables, dairy products, liver and yellow coloured foods such as carrots, pumpkin, mangoes, paw paws, oranges and apricots that contain large quantities of a yellow substance known as carotene. Excess levels of carotene and vitamin A (hypervitaminosis A) therefore occur simultaneously in most cases.

CAUSE: Eating excessive amounts of vitamin A tablets or yellow fruit and vegetables. Huge quantities must be consumed, but patients who develop a craving for one particular type of food can consume sufficient for the symptoms to appear in a few weeks.

SYMPTOMS: Loss of appetite and weight, yellow colouring of the skin (particularly the palms and soles, but unlike liver diseases, not the whites of the eyes), brittle nails, dry and cracked skin, sore gums, headaches and other more bizarre symptoms.

INVESTIGATIONS: All blood tests normal, but yellow palms and soles are diagnostic features.

TREATMENT: Not eating the offending foods and vitamin supplements.

COMPLICATIONS: Can cause deformities to the foetus of a pregnant woman, and therefore large doses of vitamin A should be avoided during pregnancy.

PROGNOSIS: Almost invariably resolves slowly over a few weeks without long-term damage.

Hypoadrenocorticism, Chronic
See Addison's Disease

Hypoaldosteronism

DESCRIPTION: Uncommon kidney disorder in which blood levels of potassium and sodium are abnormal.

CAUSE: Numerous diseases may be responsible (eg. diabetes mellitus), may be inherited, a side effect of drugs (eg. heparin), occur after severe blood loss in an injury, as a result of brain diseases affecting the pituitary gland, after surgery for a tumour of the adrenal glands (which sit on top of each kidney), or may occur spontaneously for no obvious reason.

Hypoaldosteronism

SYMPTOMS: Abnormal urine production and fluid retention.

INVESTIGATIONS: Blood tests show high potassium levels, and other abnormalities of body chemistry.

TREATMENT: Specific types of steroids are given long term, and a low salt diet.

COMPLICATIONS: Kidney and heart failure possible.

PROGNOSIS: No cure, but control reasonable in most patients.

See also Liddle Syndrome

Hypochondriasis

DESCRIPTION: Psychiatric delusion related to hysteria.

CAUSE: Poor experience with physicians on previous occasions, a psychological stress, or excessive reaction to minor bodily aches or changes.

SYMPTOMS: Unvarying belief by a patient that they have a serious illness despite all medical evidence to the contrary.

INVESTIGATIONS: All normal.

TREATMENT: Intensive psychotherapy long term.

COMPLICATIONS: Care must be taken by doctors not to miss a true medical condition that may be present, or arise during treatment.

PROGNOSIS: Generally poor, and delusion persists life long.

See also Briquet Syndrome; Conversion Disorder

Hypoparathyroidism

DESCRIPTION: The four parathyroid glands behind the thyroid gland in the neck regulate the amount of calcium in the blood and bones. In hypoparathyroidism, the glands secrete inadequate amounts of the hormone calcitonin which causes excessive amounts of calcium to be taken from the blood and into the bones.

CAUSE: A rare condition that may occur after thyroid gland surgery, or may be spontaneous for no apparent reason.

SYMPTOMS: Spasms of the small muscles in the hands and feet, tingling lips, tiredness, wheezing, muscle cramps, fungal infections, abdominal pains, anxiety attacks, and behavioural alterations. If present for some time, the nails will become thin and brittle, the teeth will be deformed, cataracts may develop in the eyes, and the skin becomes dry and scaly.

INVESTIGATIONS: Diagnosis confirmed by measuring the amount of calcium in the blood. X-rays show very dense bones and calcium deposits in abnormal areas (eg. brain).

TREATMENT: May be an emergency in serious cases. Calcium injections and tablets, and vitamin D tablets.

COMPLICATIONS: Untreated, may cause irregular heartbeat, reduced growth in children, anaemia and mental retardation.

PROGNOSIS: Once stabilised on treatment, the long-term outlook is good, but damage already done to eyes, teeth and other tissues may be irreversible. Very regular blood tests, follow-up visits, and lifelong medication are essential.

See also Hyperparathyroidism

Hypopituitarism
(Pituitary Failure; Simmonds' Disease)

DESCRIPTION: The pituitary gland sits in the centre of the brain and secretes hormones into the blood stream that control every other hormone producing gland in the body (eg. thyroid gland, adrenal gland, ovary, testes). Hypopituitarism occurs if the pituitary fails to produce appropriate regulating hormones. If the gland fails to produce all the possible hormones it is called **panhypopituitarism.**

CAUSE: A tumour of the pituitary, head injury, stroke, swollen blood vessels, an abscess in the gland, malnutrition or other rare and complex reasons.

SYMPTOMS: When the pituitary gland is underactive, every other gland it controls will also become underactive and the patient will have reduced sexual desire and activity, lose pubic hair, men will stop growing a beard and women will stop having monthly periods. Other problems include weakness, tiredness, poor resistance to infections, low blood pressure, vision defects, and becoming stressed easily. Sometimes only part of the pituitary gland is underactive, so only some glands will malfunction.

INVESTIGATIONS: The diagnosis can be confirmed by blood tests, CT and MRI scans.

TREATMENT: Correcting the cause, if possible, by surgery or irradiation, and giving hormone supplements by tablet or injection.

COMPLICATIONS: Infertility may be a problem in both sexes.

PROGNOSIS: Depends on the cause, but in most cases the condition can be well controlled.

See also Cushing Syndrome

Hypoplastic Left Heart Syndrome

DESCRIPTION: Congenital failure of the heart to develop normally.

CAUSE: Failure of valves in the heart to function properly due to abnormal development, and continuation of the blood flow patterns present before birth.

SYMPTOMS: Newborn infant with rapid onset of heart failure, weak pulses in arms and legs and blue tinged skin (cyanosis).

INVESTIGATIONS: Chest X-ray, ECG, echocardiography and finally passing a fine catheter through arteries into the heart to measure pressures and introduce a dye that can be seen on X-ray.

TREATMENT: None available.

PROGNOSIS: Death within days of birth usual.

Hypospadias

DESCRIPTION: A developmental abnormality in which the tube carrying the urine through the penis (the urethra) fails to close properly in the foetus, and the opening is on the lower side of the penis rather than the end. Very rarely the opening may be on top of the penis (**epispadias**).

CAUSE: Congenital.

Hypospadias

SYMPTOMS: The urethral opening can occur anywhere from the base of the penis to very near the end, depending on the severity of the abnormality.

INVESTIGATIONS: None normally necessary.

TREATMENT: An operation to correct the abnormality and place the urethral opening in the usual position at the end of the penis.

COMPLICATIONS: Patients are more likely to develop urinary infections, must pass urine sitting down, and later in life when having sex, will ejaculate through the abnormal opening in a place that makes it difficult for their partner to fall pregnant.

PROGNOSIS: The operation is completely successful in the vast majority of patients, and the man's future sex life should be completely normal.

Hypostatic Eczema
See Varicose Eczema

Hypotension
(Low Blood Pressure)

DESCRIPTION: Excessively low blood pressure. The heart contracts regularly to pump blood through the arteries under high (systolic) pressure. When the heart relaxes between beats, the blood continues to flow due to the lower (diastolic) pressure exerted by the elasticity of the artery walls. Hypotension occurs when one, or both, of these pressures drops to a low level. Blood pressure readings are written as systolic pressure/diastolic pressure (eg. 125/70) and are measured with a sphygmomanometer. Blood pressure varies with exercise, anxiety, age, fitness, smoking and drinking habits, weight and medications. The numbers are a measure of pressure in millimetres of mercury. Low blood pressure only causes concern when it causes symptoms or is detected in the course of investigation of other diseases (eg. someone with a suspected heart attack). Hypotension is a relative condition — the blood pressure is low compared to what is should be — and not an absolute one. A young woman may have a blood pressure of 90/50 and be perfectly well, but the same pressure in an elderly person may have serious consequences.

CAUSE: May be due to a serious injury resulting in blood loss (shock), heart attack, heart failure, dehydration, alcoholism, serious infections, heat stroke, pregnancy, a large number of less common diseases, and some drugs.

SYMPTOMS: Dizziness, light headedness, fainting and headaches.

INVESTIGATIONS: Measuring the blood pressure, and further investigations to exclude any cause.

TREATMENT: The cause of the low blood pressure needs to be treated, rather than the blood pressure itself. In a very small number of people no specific cause can be found, and a medication may be given to raise the blood pressure slightly.

COMPLICATIONS: Fainting may cause falls and serious injury.

PROGNOSIS: Depends on the cause.

See also Postural Hypotension; Shock

Hypotension, Postural
See Postural Hypotension

Hypothermia
(Exposure)

DESCRIPTION: An abnormally low body temperature below 35 degrees Celsius.

CAUSE: Exposure to cold conditions without adequate protection. Cold air alone can cause hypothermia, but if combined with wind, hypothermia occurs more rapidly. Cold water is the most serious cause, and death may occur in as little as a few minutes in icy water. An inadequately clad person may suffer hypothermia after only half a day in a climate where the temperature does not drop below 20 degrees Celsius. Even in tropical waters shipwreck victims may die from hypothermia. Alcoholics may neglect themselves and even in relatively mild conditions suffer from hypothermia due to inadequate clothing, shelter and nutrition.

SYMPTOMS: The blood vessels to the skin contract so that victims feel far colder to the touch than expected. Other symptoms are weakness, drowsiness, irritability, irrational behaviour and poor coordination. As the temperature drops further, delirium, coma and death from an irregular heartbeat occur.

INVESTIGATIONS: Measuring the temperature using a rectal (through the anus) thermometer. The skin temperature and mouth temperature are often inaccurate.

TREATMENT: Depends on the severity of the hypothermia. Mild cases respond well to good warm clothing, warm bed and rest. Shared body heat may be appropriate. Moderate to severe cases will require hospitalisation for warmed air or oxygen, warm drinks, and warm fluids through a drip into a vein to heat the core of the body. This may be followed by immersion in a lukewarm bath that may have its temperature increased slowly over several hours. Heated blankets may also be used. Patients who appear to have died because of hypothermia must be given mouth-to-mouth resuscitation and external heart massage for several hours while continuing to warm the body. Recovery may not occur until the body temperature rises to 32 degrees Celsius or more. Patients (particularly children) have been known to recover fully after prolonged periods of immersion or apparent death, with appropriate resuscitation, as the low temperature protects the brain and body from damage.

COMPLICATIONS: Rapid warming, and warming the surface of the body only (which may cause premature dilation of the arteries in the skin), can cause heart irregularities and death.

PROGNOSIS: Depends upon the severity, prior health and age. Children recover far better than the elderly.

See also Frostbite

Hypothyroidism
(Myxoedema)

DESCRIPTION: Underactivity of the thyroid gland which sits in the front of the neck and is responsible for secreting a hormone called thyroxine. This acts as the accelerator for every cell in the body. If the level of thyroxine is high, the cells function at an increased rate — if the level of thyroxine is low, the cells function at a less than normal rate. In children, hypothyroidism causes cretinism (see separate entry).

CAUSE: The thyroid gland tends to fail with advancing age, particularly in women. Less commonly, cysts or tumours may destroy the gland tissue.

SYMPTOMS: Tiredness, weakness, muscle cramps, constipation, dry skin, headaches, nervousness, an intolerance to cold weather and a hoarse voice. In more severe cases additional symptoms may include thinning of the hair, brittle nails, weight gain, shortness of breath, a thick tongue and a slow heart rate. The drop in thyroxine levels is usually gradual over many years and the symptoms may be overlooked until the disease is quite advanced. May also be associated with an enlarged thyroid gland (goitre).

INVESTIGATIONS: Diagnosed by blood tests that measures the amount of thyroxine, and other thyroid-related substances.

TREATMENT: Thyroxine tablets are taken long term to replace that not being produced by the gland.

COMPLICATIONS: Untreated, there is an increased risk of developing severe infections and heart failure.

PROGNOSIS: Patients usually notice a remarkable improvement in their quality of life as the thyroxine replacement tablets start to work. With adequate treatment the patient should lead a normal active life. Untreated, premature death will occur.

See also Cretinism; Goitre; Thyroiditis

Hypovitaminosis A
See Vitamin A Deficiency

Hysteria
See Briquet Syndrome; Conversion Disorder; Hypochondriasis

I

Iatrogenic Conditions

DESCRIPTION: Any disease or condition caused by doctors or other medical staff during investigation or treatment.

CAUSE: Side effects of medications, and complications of surgery or investigations, are the most common causes.

SYMPTOMS: Almost any conceivable symptom may be due to iatrogenic conditions.

INVESTIGATIONS: Depends on suspected cause.

TREATMENT: Sometimes stopping treatment is all that is necessary, but in other cases a specific treatment is required.

See also Dermatitis Medicamentosa; Ulysses Syndrome

IBS

See Irritable Bowel Syndrome

ICHABOD Syndrome

DESCRIPTION: Syndrome of imminent death from any chronic cause. The disease name is an acronym for a number of clinical signs used by doctors to predict death in a patient with a long standing incurable disease. As well as being an acronym, the syndrome name may also be derived from the Old Testament daughter-in-law of Eli who, before dying in childbirth, named her son Ichabod, which translates as 'the glory has departed'.

SYMPTOMS: Immobility — fewer than 20% of patients can stand within two days before death

Confusion and coma — 40% become comatose and 30% confused in the two days before death

Homoeostatic (body function regulation) failure — failure of temperature regulation, blood pressure control and circulation to hands and feet common in last two days before death

Anorexia (loss of appetite) — very common in final week before death

Blood — blood test changes indicative of imminent death

Observation — occasional (rather than regular) observation of facial appearance shows marked deterioration in personality features

Dyspnoea (shortness of breath) — 30% of patients become short of breath in last two days. Irregular respiration very common in last few hours.

Ichthyosis

DESCRIPTION: Uncommon congenital (present since birth) skin condition. Numerous sub-types are known (eg. icthyosis vulgaris — most common type; X-linked icthyosis — affects males only; icthyosis linearis circumflexa — affects babies).

CAUSE: Due to lack of oil glands in the skin. Some forms are inherited.
SYMPTOMS: Widespread scaling, dryness and thickening of the skin.
INVESTIGATIONS: Diagnosis confirmed by skin biopsy.
TREATMENT: Massive quantities of moisturising creams and oils applied to the skin.
COMPLICATIONS: More susceptible to other skin diseases, sun damage and poor healing.
PROGNOSIS: No cure possible.

IDDM
See Diabetes Mellitus

Idiopathic Condition
DESCRIPTION: Any disease or condition for which there is no known cause.

Idiopathic Diffuse Interstitial Fibrosis
See Hamman-Rich Syndrome

Idiopathic Lymphadenopathy Syndrome
DESCRIPTION: Probable complication of the earliest stage of the HIV (AIDS) viral infection. More common in the promiscuous, homosexuals and intravenous drug users.
CAUSE: Human immunodeficiency virus (HIV) caught by sex or the exchange of blood with an infected person. Possibly due to other similar viral infections that damage the immune system.
SYMPTOMS: Persistently enlarged lymph nodes in neck, armpit and groin, increased incidence of viral and bacterial infections.
INVESTIGATIONS: Blood tests confirm presence of HIV or other immune deficiency.
TREATMENT: Antiviral medications as used to treat more advanced stages of AIDS.
COMPLICATIONS: Greater chance of rapid progression to more advanced stages of AIDS.
PROGNOSIS: Temporary control of symptoms possible with intensive treatment, but eventual progression inevitable.
See also AIDS

Idiopathic Myelofibrosis
See Myelofibrosis

Idiopathic Pulmonary Fibrosis
(Cryptogenic Fibrosing Alveolitis)
DESCRIPTION: Replacement of normal lung tissue by fibrous tissue.
CAUSE: Unknown. May be a form of autoimmune disease in which the body rejects its own tissue.
SYMPTOMS: Progressively worsening shortness of breath, coughing and attacks of bronchitis.

INVESTIGATIONS: Diagnosed by chest X-ray, nuclear scans, lung function tests, lung biopsy and blood tests.
TREATMENT: None available.
COMPLICATIONS: Pneumonia and heart failure may develop.
PROGNOSIS: Usually slowly progressive until the lungs and/or heart fail.

Idiopathic Renal Acidosis
See Lightwood Syndrome

Idiopathic Thrombocytopenic Purpura
See Thrombocytopenia

Idiot Savant Syndrome
(Savant Syndrome)
DESCRIPTION: Abnormal mental functioning of the brain.
CAUSE: Cause unknown, but may be due to one area of the brain over developing before birth at the expense of other areas.
SYMPTOMS: Patient is usually subnormal in all areas of mental activity except one narrow field (eg. maths, music) in which they are extraordinarily talented.
INVESTIGATIONS: Mental tests differentiate areas of skill from areas of below normal function.
TREATMENT: Intensive education to develop life skills and areas of subnormal ability.
PROGNOSIS: Lifelong problem.
See also Autism

IEC
See Intraepithelial Carcinoma

Ileolumbar Syndrome
DESCRIPTION: Ligamentous strain in the back.
CAUSE: Damage to the ligaments in the lower back from lifting and twisting movements.
SYMPTOMS: Sciatica (pain running down the back of the leg), pain and tenderness of buttocks. Bending sideways away from painful side worsens the pain.
INVESTIGATIONS: No specific tests. X-rays and CT scans of the back are usually normal.
TREATMENT: Anti-inflammatory medications, physiotherapy and injection of local anaesthetic and long lasting steroid into tender area.
COMPLICATIONS: None significant.
PROGNOSIS: Often recurs, although treatment usually successful.

Iliotibial Band Friction Syndrome

DESCRIPTION: Leg injury that usually occurs in long distance runners.

CAUSE: Running on side-sloped surface (eg. beach, road shoulder).

SYMPTOMS: Pain on outside of knee with walking, tenderness when pressure is applied to outside lower end of femur (thigh bone). Grating sensation may be felt in knee joint with walking.

INVESTIGATIONS: None specific.

TREATMENT: Rest, anti-inflammatory medications and physiotherapy.

COMPLICATIONS: None significant.

PROGNOSIS: Settles with appropriate treatment.

Immature Haemangioma

See Strawberry Naevus

Immersion

See Drowning

Immunodeficiency

DESCRIPTION: The immune system is centred on the thymus gland (which sits behind the top of the breast bone), the bone marrow and lymph nodes (mainly in the armpit, groin and neck). These produce white blood cells and antibodies (chemicals that attack specific viruses or bacteria) which circulate in the bloodstream to detect and destroy invading germs. Immunodeficiency (a lack of immunity to infection) is a rare condition that is caused by a lack of or abnormal white blood cells, or a lack of immunoglobulin, which is the building block of antibodies. Most cases occur in children, and usually within a year of birth.

CAUSE: A number of very rare diseases are responsible for immunodeficiency, including di George syndrome (a failure of the thymus to develop), Wiskott-Aldrich syndrome (an inherited failure to produce white cells), and agammaglobulinaemia (a lack of gamma immunoglobulin). Acquired immune deficiency syndrome (AIDS) is also a form of immunodeficiency in which the white cells are destroyed by the virus causing AIDS.

SYMPTOMS: Frequent severe infections, and sometimes patients bleed and bruise easily.

INVESTIGATIONS: Diagnosed by blood tests and biopsy of bone marrow and other organs.

TREATMENT: Medications may slow the progress of the condition and treat resultant infections.

COMPLICATIONS: Increased incidence of cancer.

PROGNOSIS: Patients with most forms of immunodeficiency cannot be cured. Children often die early in life.

See also Agammaglobulinaemia; AIDS; di George Syndrome; Wiskott-Aldrich Syndrome

Impetigo
(School Sores)

DESCRIPTION: A very common skin infection that virtually every child will catch. It may also occur in adults.

CAUSE: Several different bacteria may be responsible, but the most common is *Staphylococcus aureus* ('golden staph'). This is a serious infection inside the body, but relatively mild on the skin. Impetigo spreads from one person to another by close contact. Sometimes an infected animal may act as a source. Once one sore develops on the skin, scratching with fingers can rapidly spread the infection to other parts of the body. More common in warm climates and in summer.

SYMPTOMS: An itchy, red, raised, weeping or crusting sore. If there are many sores, the patient may feel generally unwell, but normally there are no other symptoms.

INVESTIGATIONS: If necessary, swabs can be taken from the sores to confirm the diagnosis, determine the infecting bacteria, and select the correct antibiotic.

TREATMENT: Antibiotic mixtures or tablets, and an antibiotic cream. Antiseptic soaps, not sharing towels and bedding, and careful personal hygiene can be used to prevent the spread of infection. A child must be excluded from school until the sores start to heal.

COMPLICATIONS: In new born babies, impetigo may spread rapidly and become serious. For this reason, infected children should be kept away from infants.

PROGNOSIS: With correct treatment, the sores will heal without scarring in a few days.

Impingement Syndromes

See Anterior Impingement Syndrome; Posterior Impingement Syndrome; Shoulder Impingement Syndrome

Impotence
(Erectile Failure)

DESCRIPTION: Lack of sexual potency.

CAUSE: A penis erection occurs as a reflex which is outside a man's voluntary control. Failure may be due to inadequate levels of testosterone (male hormone), blocked arteries to the penis (eg. from diabetes, arteriosclerosis), abnormal penis anatomy, any form of anxiety, alcohol, anabolic steroids (used illegally to enhance performance and physique), high blood pressure medication and prostate surgery. The main cause is psychological pressure to perform (eg. anxiety about sex with a new partner, conditions that are not ideal). If a man has failed previously, then there is even more anxiety, and every successive failure makes him more anxious to perform and less likely to succeed.

SYMPTOMS: Failure of a man to obtain or sustain an erection when sexually stimulated.

INVESTIGATIONS: All specific causes need to be excluded by appropriate tests.

TREATMENT: Psychological factors may be overcome by not planning sex, but relaxing and waiting until the right circumstances occur spontaneously. Mutual heavy petting and erotic stimulation, but without the expectation of sex, sexual toys, pornography and vacuum pumps to create an erection may be used. Once spontaneous erections develop, sex may start again. Medication is also available:—

— alprostadil (Caverject) injections into the penis

— alprostadil (Muse) pellets may be inserted into the urethra (urine tube in the penis)

— sildenafil (Viagra) tablets.

PROGNOSIS: Most men can be helped by treatment.

See also other diseases listed under **Sex Problems**

Incisional Hernia

DESCRIPTION: In older, obese or debilitated people, the deeper tissue may break down after an operation on the belly, allowing part of the bowel to escape through the deeper layers of the wound to the area just under the skin to cause an incisional hernia.

CAUSE: A wound infection may be responsible, but often the deeper tissue gives way after a fit of coughing or under the strain of supporting the belly after an operation.

SYMPTOMS: A lump under the skin of the belly. Other symptoms are usually minimal, but sometimes intermittent discomfort, and rarely pain at the site of the hernia may occur.

INVESTIGATIONS: None normally necessary.

TREATMENT: A corset is usually all that is required to control the hernia. In other circumstances, further surgery, often with insertion of some surgical mesh to strengthen the area, will be required.

COMPLICATIONS: Rarely, intestine may become caught and twisted in the hernia, causing severe pain, and eventually gangrene of the intestine.

PROGNOSIS: Most cause no serious problem, but may be annoying. There is a significant risk of recurrence after further surgical repair.

See also Hernias

Inclusion Body Myositis

DESCRIPTION: A form of progressive muscle wasting and weakness in the elderly with a very slow insidious onset.

CAUSE: Unknown.

SYMPTOMS: Gradually worsening muscle weakness which starts in the hands and feet and moves towards the trunk.

INVESTIGATIONS: Diagnosed by muscle biopsy and tests on the electrical activity within muscles (electromyography — EMG).

TREATMENT: No specific treatment available, but progress may be slowed in some patients by medication.

PROGNOSIS: No cure.

See also other diseases listed under Muscular Dystrophy and Myositis

Incontinence of Faeces

DESCRIPTION: The inability to control the passing of faeces.

CAUSE: May be due to psychological or psychiatric conditions (particularly in the elderly), a loss of inhibitions associated with a dementia, psychiatric disturbances, behavioural disorders, emotional stress, damage to the brain (eg. a stroke, cerebral palsy), paraplegia, advanced pregnancy, damage to the anus from a difficult birth, and excessive faeces in the rectum.

SYMPTOMS: Inappropriate passing of faeces.

INVESTIGATIONS: Colonoscopy or barium enema X-ray may be necessary.

TREATMENT: Incontinence is not a disease but a symptom, and the responsible disease needs to be diagnosed before treatment can start.

PROGNOSIS: Depends on the cause.

Incontinence of Urine

DESCRIPTION: The inability to control the outflow of urine.

CAUSE: Affects women far more than men. Alcohol and caffeine increase the production of urine, a sudden severe fright or shock, and extreme fear, may cause loss of bladder control. Other causes include infections of the bladder or kidney, childbirth damage to the muscles that control the release of urine, the lack of oestrogen at menopause, obesity, medications (eg. diuretics, tranquillisers), surgery to the pelvis (eg. hysterectomy), stroke, loss of consciousness, epileptic fit, damage to the brain (eg. cerebral palsy, tumour, Parkinson's disease), dementia, Alzheimer disease, tumours or stones in the bladder, damage to the nerve supply to the bladder from pelvic injury, multiple sclerosis, paraplegia, diabetes, and rarely a fistula (abnormal opening) between the bladder and vagina.

SYMPTOMS: Inappropriate passage of urine.

INVESTIGATIONS: X-rays of the bladder and kidneys, and cystoscopy (looking into the bladder through a thin tube).

TREATMENT: Incontinence is not a disease but a symptom, and the responsible disease needs to be diagnosed before treatment can start.

COMPLICATIONS: Repeated urinary infections.

PROGNOSIS: Depends on cause.

See also Bed Wetting

Incontinentia Pigmenti
See Bloch-Sulzberger Syndrome

Indigestion, Functional
See Irritable Bowel Syndrome

Indolent Lymphoma
See Non-Hodgkin's Lymphoma

Infantile Colic
(Baby Colic; Six-Week Colic)
DESCRIPTION: Repeated episodes of belly pain in an infant.
CAUSE: Probably caused by spontaneous spasms of the small intestine, but no reason for these spasms has ever been proved. Some experts blame anxiety in the mother, particularly in a family without extended family support, for causing anxiety in the infant, and subsequent gut spasms.
SYMPTOMS: The baby starts screaming for no apparent reason, draws the legs up and looks pale. After a few minutes, the attack subsides, and the infant appears normal. After a short interval, the screaming starts again. This pattern repeats itself several times a day.
INVESTIGATIONS: No tests can be performed to confirm the diagnosis.
TREATMENT: Changes in diet and formula, different foods for the mother of breastfed infants, alterations to feeding times and positions, increases or decreases in the degree of attention paid to the child, and anti-spasmodic drugs and paracetamol.
COMPLICATIONS: None.
PROGNOSIS: Always goes away in due course, usually at 12 to 16 weeks of age.
See also Intestinal Colic

Infarct, Cerebral
See Stroke

Infarct, Myocardial
See Heart Attack

Infected Glands
See Adenitis

Infection
DESCRIPTION: A microscopic invasion of tissue or body fluids by bacteria, viruses or fungi resulting in cell damage and/or destruction.
CAUSE: About 80 different bacteria, hundreds of different viruses and a score of different fungi.
SYMPTOMS: Vary depending on tissue involved, type and severity of infection, but most cause a fever, pain, swelling and redness of the infected tissue.
INVESTIGATIONS: Swabs, biopsies and blood tests may be performed to determine the infecting organism and the appropriate treatment.

TREATMENT: Most bacteria and fungi are susceptible to antibiotics and antifungal agents. Most viral infections cannot be treated, but many can be prevented by vaccination (eg. measles, hepatitis B, influenza), some may have their reproduction slowed by medication (eg. AIDS), and a very small number may have their reproduction completely blocked by antiviral agents (eg. genital herpes, influenza).

COMPLICATIONS: Untreated infections may spread to other organs, through the bloodstream to the whole body, or form abscesses (see separate entry).

PROGNOSIS: Depends on the infecting organism, its severity, the susceptibility of the patient and the organ(s) involved.

See also specific types of infection (eg. Abscess; Acne; Actinomycosis; Adenitis; AIDS; Appendicitis; Aspergillosis; Bacteremia; Balanitis; Barmah Forest Virus; Bronchitis; Brucellosis; Cellulitis; Chickenpox; Cholera; Chlamydia; Cholecystitis; Cold, Common; Cold Sores; Conjunctivitis; Cystitis; Diphtheria; Diverticulitis; Ebola Virus; Encephalitis; Endocarditis; Epididymo-Orchitis; Erysipelas; Fifth Disease; Folliculitis; Genital Herpes; Glandular fever; Gonorrhoea; Hepatitis A, B, C, D, E and G; Impetigo; Infectious Myositis; Influenza; Laryngitis; Lassa Fever; Leprosy; Marburg Virus; Measles; Meningitis; Molluscum Contagiosum; Mumps; Murray Valley Encephalitis; Mycoplasma Infection; Necrotising Fasciitis; Non-Specific Urethritis; Orf; Osteomyelitis; Otitis Externa; Otitis Media; Paronychia; Pharyngitis; Pilonidal Sinus; Pneumonia; Prostatitis; Psittacosis; Pyelonephritis; Q Fever; Quinsy; Relapsing Fever; Rickettsial Infection; Roseola Infantum; Ross River Fever; Rotavirus Infection; Salpingitis; Scarlet Fever; Septicaemia; Septic Arthritis; Septic Shock; Shigellosis; Sialitis; Sinusitis; Staphylococcal Infections; Syphilis; Tetanus; Thrush; Tinea; Tonsillitis; Tracheitis; Tularaemia; Typhoid; Undulant Fever; Urethritis; Uvulitis; Vaginitis, Bacterial; Vestibulitis; Viraemia; Whooping Cough; Yaws; Yellow Fever etc.)

Infectious Mononucleosis
See Glandular Fever

Infectious Myositis

DESCRIPTION: An uncommon infection of muscle.

CAUSE: Usually starts after a wound penetrates through the skin into the underlying muscle, but sometimes reaches the muscle through the bloodstream. May be due to many different bacteria and viruses.

SYMPTOMS: Muscle pain and tenderness at the area of infection.

INVESTIGATIONS: Blood tests show infection, but not where.

TREATMENT: Antibiotics for bacterial infection. Rest, anti-inflammatories and pain relievers for both viral and bacterial infections.

COMPLICATIONS: Permanent scarring and contraction of muscles involved.

PROGNOSIS: Usually settles with the correct treatment.

See also other diseases listed under Myositis

Infertility, Female

DESCRIPTION: Inability to conceive after 12 months of regular sexual intercourse. Fertility is a joint property, and one third of infertility is due to the male partner.

CAUSE: Failure of the ovaries to develop (eg. Turner syndrome), endometriosis, abnormal development of the uterus, pelvic inflammatory disease, venereal infections of the Fallopian tubes (eg. syphilis, gonorrhoea), hormonal imbalances, and in rare cases a reaction to the partner's sperm.

INVESTIGATIONS: Initially a temperature chart is kept on which the woman's temperature is noted immediately upon waking every morning (there is normally a rise in temperature for the second half of the cycle after the egg has been released from the ovary). Further investigation involves blood tests to measure female hormone levels, special X-rays that outline the uterus (womb) and tubes, and laparoscopy (a small tube is put into the lower abdomen) to directly examine the ovaries and uterus.

TREATMENT: Initially the couple's sexual habits are checked as infrequent sex may miss the few fertile days of the month. Medical treatment depends on the cause but may include fertility drugs to promote ovulation (eg. Clomiphene), other drugs to treat endometriosis and antibiotics for infections. If there is an anatomical abnormality, it may be correctable by surgery. A small number of couples may be considered for IVF (in-vitro fertilisation or 'test-tube babies'), or GIFT (gamete intra-Fallopian transfer). GIFT involves giving ovulation stimulating (egg producing) hormones to an infertile woman, then harvesting an egg directly from her ovary using a laparoscope, and transferring this unfertilised egg along with sperm from her partner, directly into her Fallopian tube. If necessary the sperm or egg may be donated by another man or woman.

COMPLICATIONS: The success rate for any infertility procedure may be as low as 15% for each attempt, although the overall success rate may be over 50%.

PROGNOSIS: 85% of couples conceive normally within 12 months. 15% have below-normal fertility. With medical aid all but 3% of couples can eventually have children.

See also Endometriosis; Infertility, Male and other diseases listed under Sex Problems

Infertility, Male

DESCRIPTION: Inability to impregnate a female partner after 12 months of regular sexual intercourse. Fertility is a joint property, and two thirds of infertility is due to the female partner.

CAUSE: Premature ejaculation, undescended testes (which fail to work because of overheating), injury to the testicles, mumps infection of the testes, venereal infections (eg. syphilis, gonorrhoea), chromosome abnormalities and hormonal disorders.

INVESTIGATIONS: Analysis of sperm (number, shape and activity of sperm) which is collected after masturbation and examined in a laboratory within two hours.

TREATMENT: Depends on cause, but may include hormone supplements, surgery to correct any abnormality of testes or penis, storage and concentration of sperm (artificial insemination by husband — AIH), or fertilisation by donor sperm (artificial insemination by donor — AID).

PROGNOSIS: 85% of couples conceive normally within 12 months. 15% have below-normal fertility. With medical aid all but 3% of couples can eventually have children.

See also Infertility, Female and other diseases listed under Sex Problems

Influenza
(Flu)

DESCRIPTION: Debilitating generalised viral infection. Influenza was once thought to be due to 'influences in the atmosphere', thus giving its name. The various flu virus strains are named after the places where they were first isolated.

CAUSE: Viral infection by one of the more than 80 known strains of the influenza virus. Spreads by microscopic droplets in a cough or sneeze from one person to another.

SYMPTOMS: Muscular aches and pains, overwhelming tiredness, fever, headache, cough, runny nose, stuffed sinuses, painful throat and nausea.

INVESTIGATIONS: None normally necessary, but throat swabs or blood tests can identify the responsible strain of influenza.

TREATMENT: Can now be cured, but only if the inhaled medication (zanamivir) is given within the first 36 hours of symptoms developing. Otherwise rest and time, aspirin, anti-inflammatory drugs and medications to help the phlegm and cough are given. A light nutritious diet that contains minimal fat, and a higher than normal fluid intake are sensible. Flu can be prevented by an annual vaccination which gives more than 80% protection from contracting the infection, but only for one year. Unfortunately the vaccine does not prevent the common cold, and many people who complain that their flu shot has not worked are suffering from a cold caused by yet another group of viruses. Amantadine tablets will prevent some forms of flu while they are being taken.

COMPLICATIONS: Can be a very serious disease, but deaths are now rare except in the elderly and debilitated. Secondary bacterial infections of the throat, sinuses, lungs and ears may occur, which can be treated with antibiotics.

PROGNOSIS: Influenza normally lasts for seven to ten days. The vast majority of patients recover without complications.

See also Cold, Common

Ingrown Toenail

DESCRIPTION: Penetration of the tip of the nail edge into the flesh at the side of the nail, most commonly on the big toe.

CAUSE: The nail has usually been torn, or cut too short, or shoes are too tight. This allows the skin at the end of the toe to override the end of the nail, so that when the nail grows, the corner of the nail cuts into the flesh and causes damage.

SYMPTOMS: Pain and infection in the affected flesh beside the nail.

INVESTIGATIONS: None necessary.

TREATMENT: Infection is treated with antibiotic ointments and tablets. The ingrown corner of the nail must be allowed to break free of the skin by avoiding shoes, and pulling the flesh away from the ingrowing nail corner with tape or regular massage. If this is unsuccessful, one of a number of minor operations may be necessary. The most common operations involve cutting away the excess flesh that is growing over the nail, or cutting away a wedge of the nail, nail bed and tissue beside the nail (a wedge resection) to permanently narrow the nail.

COMPLICATIONS: Serious infections may spread into the foot.

PROGNOSIS: Surgery usually cures an ingrown toe nail.

See also Paronychia

Inguinal Hernia

DESCRIPTION: Occur only in men. The testicles develop inside the abdomen, and before birth they migrate down into the scrotum. Behind them as they move down, they leave a tube called the inguinal canal. Through this canal run the arteries, veins and nerves that supply the testicles, and the vas deferens (a duct that carries the sperm from the testicle to the base of the penis). Shortly before birth, the inguinal canal closes, leaving just enough room for the vital supplies to pass to and from the testes. The inguinal canal remains a source of weakness in the strong muscle wall of the abdomen, and it may tear open again, allowing some of the gut to protrude under the skin of the groin as a hernia.

CAUSE: Excess pressure on the lower part of the belly by heavy lifting, prolonged coughing or some other form of strain. Men who are overweight and have their muscles weakened by fat deposits are more likely to develop this type of hernia, and the slackening of muscle tone with advancing age can also lead to a rupture. There is also an hereditary tendency, so that if your father had a hernia, your chances of developing one are increased.

In some little boys, the tube does not close properly, and this allows a small amount of fat or intestine to move down the tube from the inside of the abdomen, to form a hernia just under the skin beside the penis.

SYMPTOMS: A small lump in the groin that may be only mildly annoying after exercise, or may become intermittently painful.

INVESTIGATIONS: Normally none necessary, but in fat men an ultrasound scan may be needed to confirm the diagnosis.

TREATMENT: Surgical repair of the hernia as an elective procedure.

COMPLICATIONS: Occasionally the gut inside the hernia may become strangled in the inguinal canal, causing severe pain and the trapped section of gut becomes gangrenous. This requires urgent surgery.

PROGNOSIS: Up to 20% of repaired inguinal hernias will recur. A tight sensation in the groin, that may be occasionally painful, may follow the surgery.

See also Hernias

Insecticide Poisoning
(Organophosphate Poisoning)
DESCRIPTION: Poisoning by swallowing, inhaling or touching insecticides containing organophosphates.

CAUSE: Stronger insecticides that contain organophosphate chemicals (eg. parathion, fenthion and malathion).

SYMPTOMS: Wheezing, contracted pupils, excessive sweating, nausea, vomiting, watery eyes, and diarrhoea.

INVESTIGATIONS: Blood tests show serious abnormalities.

TREATMENT: First-aid is vital. If the poison has been swallowed, the patient must be made to vomit, and then given milk. The patient must be thoroughly washed to remove any poison from the skin, and contaminated clothing must be removed. Mouth-to-mouth resuscitation and external cardiac massage may be necessary. Those giving first aid must be careful not to contaminate themselves. In hospital emergency treatment and medication to neutralise the poison can be given.

COMPLICATIONS: In severe cases, can progress to muscle weakness, convulsions, coma and death.

PROGNOSIS: Depends upon the type of poison, its dosage, and the age and fitness of the patient.

Insect Sting
See Sting, Bee or Wasp; Tick Bite

Insulin Dependent Diabetes
See Diabetes Mellitus

Insulinoma
(Beta Cell Tumour)
DESCRIPTION: Uncommon tumour of the insulin producing beta cells in the pancreas gland. Insulin is a hormone that lowers the level of sugar (glucose) in the blood to cause hypoglycaemia. 90% of tumours are benign, while the remaining 10% are cancerous. Usually occur between 50 and 70 years of age, but may occur at any age.

CAUSE: Unknown.

SYMPTOMS: Tiredness, headaches, slurred speech, visual disturbances and confusion relieved by eating which may result in weight gain. If food is not eaten, tremor, palpitations, irregular heart rhythm, coma and death may follow.

INVESTIGATIONS: Blood tests show low glucose, and high insulin levels. Tumour found by CT or MRI scan.

TREATMENT: Surgical removal of the tumour. Chemotherapy for spread of cancer.

COMPLICATIONS: Cancerous tumours can spread to other organs (metastasise).

PROGNOSIS: Good results from surgery, but cancerous tumours eventually kill about half those affected. If left untreated, both forms eventually fatal.

See also Diabetes Mellitus

Insulin Resistance Syndrome
See Syndrome X

Intermediate Coronary Syndrome
(Unstable Angina)

DESCRIPTION: Intermediate stage between angina and myocardial infarct (heart attack).

CAUSE: Damaged arteries supplying the heart muscle from high blood pressure, excess cholesterol in the blood and other causes.

SYMPTOMS: Chest pain (angina) that varies in nature, severity, duration, spread, timing and cause from one attack to another or even during attacks.

INVESTIGATIONS: Abnormal electrocardiograph (ECG).

TREATMENT: Rest, nitrates under tongue or inhaled, and medications to prevent attacks. If possible, coronary artery bypass graft surgery.

COMPLICATIONS: May develop into a heart attack.

PROGNOSIS: Mortality 15% per annum.

See also Angina

Interstitial Cystitis
(Hunner's Ulcer)

DESCRIPTION: Persistent bladder inflammation and ulceration.

CAUSE: Not exactly known but may be an autoimmune disease (inappropriate rejection by the body of its own tissue), allergy, or unidentified bacteria or virus. Middle aged women most commonly affected.

SYMPTOMS: Inflammation, scarring and reduced capacity of the bladder resulting in the frequent painful passing of bloodstained urine.

INVESTIGATIONS: Biopsy of the bladder wall through a cystoscope (instrument passed through the urethra into the bladder) essential for diagnosis.

TREATMENT: Forced dilation of the bladder under anaesthesia, laser or other heat applied to ulcers, drugs to reduce bladder muscle spasm, and surgery to enlarge the bladder or divert urine into an isolated loop of small intestine that opens onto the belly wall.

COMPLICATIONS: May be associated with cancer of the bladder.

PROGNOSIS: Treatment generally unsuccessful, and symptoms persist to some extent long term.

Intertrigo

DESCRIPTION: Inflammatory skin condition.

CAUSE: Heat, sweat and friction in those who are overweight, have poor personal hygiene, live in the tropics, or suffer from diabetes.

SYMPTOMS: Red, damaged, moist, itchy and burning skin in places where the skin folds back upon itself, such as under the breasts, in the groin and armpit, and in skin folds of the abdomen and neck in obese people. In advanced cases, the skin may crack, bleed and become painful.

INVESTIGATIONS: None normally necessary, but blood tests may find diabetes and swabs may be taken to identify a secondary infection.

TREATMENT: Scrupulous hygiene, controlling diabetes, using antibiotics and antifungals to remove infection, losing weight, and applying drying powders to the affected areas. A piece of soft cloth placed under bulky breasts, and a well fitted bra may help. Plastic surgery to reduce large breasts or excessive skin on the belly may be appropriate.

COMPLICATIONS: Fungal and/or bacterial infections may also develop on the damaged skin.

PROGNOSIS: Most patients remain overweight, are not consistent in their hygiene, and the problem persists or recurs.

Intervertebral Disc Prolapse
(Slipped Disc)

DESCRIPTION: Vertebral discs are cushions between the bony vertebrae that form the back bone. They are like a small, thick walled balloon, with walls made of rubbery ligaments and cartilage. The hollow centre is filled with a dense fluid which acts as a shock absorber when walking or running. Discs between the last three or four vertebrae are normally affected, but any disc from the skull down may be involved.

CAUSE: If an excessive amount of pressure is put on a disc from heavy lifting, long term wear and tear or other injury, it may collapse and bulge out between the vertebrae to put pressure on nerves or the spinal cord.

SYMPTOMS: Severe back pain and/or pain in the buttock or leg (sciatica), numbness and other altered sensation, and in extreme cases muscle weakness and paralysis.

INVESTIGATIONS: The space between vertebrae is seen to be narrower than normal on an X-ray, and a CT or MRI scan shows the bulging disc.

TREATMENT: Physiotherapy and exercises, anti-inflammatory medications, pain killers, back supports, steroids, back injections and surgery.

COMPLICATIONS: Permanent damage to nerves possible if treatment delayed.

PROGNOSIS: Usually slowly progressive, but good results from surgery in severe cases.

See also Sciatica

Intracerebral Haemorrhage
See Subarachnoid Haemorrhage

Intracranial Tumour
See Astrocytoma; Glioma; Medulloblastoma; Meningioma

Intestinal Colic

DESCRIPTION: Recurrent abdominal pain.

CAUSE: May be caused by a number of conditions including an obstruction to the gut (eg. by a cancer, tumours, twisting of the gut, adhesions, swallowed foreign body), infections of the intestine, gastroenteritis, food poisoning, over-indulgence in food, parasites in the gut, dehydration and even extreme stress and anxiety.

SYMPTOMS: Intermittent colicky pain in the abdomen due to spasm of the intestine.

INVESTIGATIONS: Serious causes of prolonged colic must be excluded by blood tests, X-rays, colonoscopy and gastroscopy.

TREATMENT: Depends on cause, as colic is a symptom rather than a disease.

PROGNOSIS: Depends on cause.

See also Infantile Colic

Intraepithilial Carcinoma
(IEC)

DESCRIPTION: A common cancer in the outer layers of skin, similar to, but deeper in the skin than, a squamous cell carcinoma.

CAUSE: Usually occur in patients who are over 50 years of age and are caused by prolonged exposure to sunlight. The rims of the ears, the face, scalp, arms and hands are commonly affected.

SYMPTOMS: A red spot covered in fine white scales. They may be itchy or sore and are unsightly.

INVESTIGATIONS: If suspected, excision or biopsy is necessary to make the diagnosis.

TREATMENT: Small IECs are easily removed by burning with a diathermy machine or freezing with liquid nitrogen. If larger, or if the diagnosis is not certain, it is necessary to excise the spot and surrounding tissue. Any IEC that recurs after freezing or burning must be surgically excised.

COMPLICATIONS: Rarely may spread by blood or lymphatics to other parts of the body.

PROGNOSIS: Treatment very effective in early stages of the disease.

See also Bowen's Disease; Hyperkeratosis; Keratoacanthoma; Squamous Cell Carcinoma of the Skin

Intussusception

DESCRIPTION: Uncommon type of obstructions of the small or large gut that usually occurs in children.

CAUSE: A polyp growing in the gut is picked up by the waves of muscular contraction that normally move food along. As the polyp moves down the gut it pulls the piece of gut it is attached to along with it, to cause an infolding of the gut into itself (an intussusception).

SYMPTOMS: Obstruction of the gut, severe intermittent waves of pain, red jelly motions and paralysis of the intestine.

INVESTIGATIONS: May be diagnosed and treated by a barium enema X-ray.

TREATMENT: The intussusception can be relieved by a barium enema (special X-ray)

or colonoscopy (passing a flexible telescope in through the anus) if the large bowel is involved, but in the small intestine surgery is necessary.

COMPLICATIONS: Bowel perforation may rarely occur.

PROGNOSIS: Usually completely cured by appropriate treatment.

Invasive Uterine Mole
See Choriocarcinoma of Uterus

Iritis
(Uveitis)

DESCRIPTION: Inflammation of the iris, the coloured part of the eye. When the surrounding tissues are involved, it is called uveitis.

CAUSE: May be due to an infection such as toxoplasmosis, tuberculosis or syphilis (exogenous iritis), or it may be associated with inflammatory diseases in other parts of the body, including psoriasis, ankylosing spondylitis, and some bowel conditions (endogenous iritis). The latter form is more common.

SYMPTOMS: Usually only one eye is involved which will suddenly become red and painful with blurred vision. Bright lights will aggravate the eye pain and the pupil is small. In the exogenous form, there is less pain and the onset is slower.

INVESTIGATIONS: None specific.

TREATMENT: Any underlying infection or disease must be treated if possible. The eye is made more comfortable with warm compresses. Steroid eye drops are used to reduce inflammation.

COMPLICATIONS: The exogenous form often results in some permanent deterioration in vision.

PROGNOSIS: Usually recovers satisfactorily, but recurrences are common.

Iron Deficiency Anaemia

DESCRIPTION: The most common form of anaemia.

CAUSE: Iron is essential for the manufacture of haemoglobin which transports oxygen in the blood. If iron levels are low, haemoglobin levels drop and the body becomes starved of oxygen. Usually found in women who have very heavy periods or are pregnant, and in those with an iron deficient diet. Serious causes include slow bleeding into the gut from a peptic ulcer, or cancer.

SYMPTOMS: Tiredness, weakness and pallor.

INVESTIGATIONS: Anaemia diagnosed by appropriate blood tests. Cause of the anaemia must be determined by more extensive investigations.

TREATMENT: Iron supplements are given. Iron is found in many foods including meat, poultry, fish, eggs, cereals and vegetables. Vitamin C and folic acid assist in the absorption of iron from the gut into the blood. Because of this, iron tablets often contain folic acid, and sometimes vitamin C as well.

COMPLICATIONS: Some patients with severe degrees of anaemia due to lack of iron, or to intestinal diseases that reduce the absorption of iron, may require iron injections. Usually they can return to tablets, and then a good diet, after only a few shots.

PROGNOSIS: Depends on cause of iron loss, but usually good.

See also Anaemia

Iron Poisoning

DESCRIPTION: Taking excessive amounts of iron into the body, either deliberately or accidentally.

CAUSE: Found in tablets used to treat iron deficiency states and anaemia, many tonics and anti-vomiting drugs. 2000 mg of iron taken at once is sufficient to cause iron poisoning in an adult, but lesser amounts can be very serious in a child.

SYMPTOMS: Vomiting, diarrhoea, black coloured faeces, a rapid and irregular heart rate, low blood pressure, convulsions, and eventually coma and death. Early symptoms may commence within an hour after taking excess iron.

INVESTIGATIONS: Diagnosed by appropriate blood tests.

TREATMENT: Induce vomiting to remove any recently swallowed iron, then urgent hospitalisation. Medications are given to bind the iron and remove it from the body, then a drip into a vein to correct the dehydration caused by vomiting and diarrhoea.

COMPLICATIONS: Even after apparent recovery, liver, pancreas and kidney failure may occur at a later date.

PROGNOSIS: Depends upon the amount of iron taken, and the weight, age and health of the patient.

Irritable Bowel Syndrome
(Functional Indigestion; IBS; Mucus Colitis; Nervous Dyspepsia; Spastic Colon)

DESCRIPTION: Abnormal spasms of the muscles in the wall of the large intestine. The gut is a long tube with bands of muscle running along and around it. The movement of the food from one end to the other is the result of rhythmic contractions of these muscles which send waves and ripples along the gut to push food along. Nutrients are removed from the gut, and only non-absorbable fibre and roughage remains to be passed out through the anus. Up to 20% of adults have symptoms of the irritable bowel syndrome at some time, but only a fraction of these people require medical treatment.

CAUSE: If the diet consists of large amounts of refined foods with little fibre content, the bulk of the faeces is reduced. When the muscles in the large intestine contract, they may have very little to push along, and this may lead to spasms of the gut. People with tense personalities or continuing stress will find that their intestine acts more rapidly than normal due to overstimulation. Over a number of years, the combination of a low-fibre diet, anxiety, stress and hereditary factors may lead to the development of this syndrome. It is more common in women.

SYMPTOMS: Abdominal pain caused by intense spasms of the bowel muscle, alternating constipation and diarrhoea, passage of wind by mouth and anus, nausea, loss of appetite and mucus on the stools. Once established, the pattern may be very difficult to break, as the symptoms cause further anxiety in the victim, which in turn exacerbates the original symptoms.

INVESTIGATIONS: No definite tests can prove the diagnosis, but all other causes must be excluded by exhaustive investigations such as an X-ray of the large intestine (barium enema) or colonoscopy.

TREATMENT: A diet high in fibre and low in dairy products and processed foods, plus high-fibre dietary supplements in some cases. Regular meal and toilet habits should be established, and tobacco and alcohol intake should be restricted. Reassurance is very important, and anti-anxiety drugs, anti-depressants and psychotherapy may all prove useful. In severe cases, drugs are used to reduce the activity of gut muscles. Occasionally pain-killers are also necessary.

COMPLICATIONS: None serious.

PROGNOSIS: Usually occurs intermittently for many years.

Irritant Eczema
See Contact Dermatitis

Irukandji Syndrome

DESCRIPTION: An excessive and abnormal response to the sting of some jellyfish.

CAUSE: Jellyfish sting.

SYMPTOMS: The lungs fill with fluid causing severe shortness of breath, severe widespread pain, rapid heart rate, profuse sweating, generalised shaking and very high blood pressure.

INVESTIGATIONS: None specific.

TREATMENT: Narcotic pain killers and other drugs in high doses through a drip, diuretics (fluid removing drugs) and machine ventilation through a tube into the throat.

COMPLICATIONS: Permanent brain damage and death possible.

PROGNOSIS: Most patients recover, but may have long term nerve damage and pain.

Ischaemic Heart Disease
See Angina; Heart Attack

Itchy Anus
See Pruritus Ani

Itchy Nipple
See Nipple Itch

285

Itchy Upper Arm Syndrome
(Brachioradialis Pruritus)

DESCRIPTION: Abnormal response of the skin to long term sun damage.

CAUSE: Due to constant release of the irritating substance histamine from allergy (mast) cells in the affected skin.

SYMPTOMS: Chronic sun damage to skin, intense itching and burning on outer surface of arm, but no apparent rash. Worse in summer.

INVESTIGATIONS: Skin biopsy shows presence of excessive numbers of mast cells.

TREATMENT: Very strong steroid creams or ointments.

PROGNOSIS: Generally resistant to treatment.

J

Jaccoud Syndrome

DESCRIPTION: Rare condition affecting cartilage in the heart valves and joints.
CAUSE: Unknown.
SYMPTOMS: Repeated attacks of a rheumatic fever like illness causing heart valve damage, and pain free joint inflammation in the hands and feet resulting in joint damage and distortion but no swelling and normal joint movement.
INVESTIGATIONS: No diagnostic tests available. All tests for rheumatic fever are negative. Echocardiograms show heart damage and X-rays show joint damage.
TREATMENT: No specific treatment available. Symptoms are treated.
PROGNOSIS: Slowly progressive.
See also Rheumatic Fever

Jamaican Neuritis
See Strachan Syndrome

Jamestown Canyon Virus
See la Crosse Encephalitis

Japanese Encephalitis

DESCRIPTION: Viral infection of the brain.
CAUSE: Virus spread from other animals (eg. pigs, horses) to man by a mosquito. Found in areas where rice paddies occur throughout east and south Asia and on some Pacific islands. More common in warmer months. Incubation period one to two weeks.
SYMPTOMS: Fever, belly pains, dizziness, sore throat, cough, headache, neck stiffness, nausea, vomiting, tiredness, disturbed mental functions, disorientation, coma and death.
INVESTIGATIONS: Tests on blood and the fluid around the brain are abnormal.
TREATMENT: No specific treatment available. Can be prevented by a vaccine.
COMPLICATIONS: May cause permanent brain damage in up to half of survivors with personality changes, fatigue and inability to concentrate.
PROGNOSIS: Acute attack lasts for one to three weeks, but complete recovery may take months. Mortality rate of up to 50%, but worse in children.
See also Encephalitis

Jaw Joint Inflammation
See Temporomandibular Joint Dysfunction

Jervell-Lange-Nielsen Syndrome

DESCRIPTION: Rare inherited disorder of electrical conduction within the heart.

CAUSE: Congenital, but both parents must carry the gene for an infant to be affected.

SYMPTOMS: Child with deafness and episodes of abnormal heart contraction which cause a sudden collapse.

INVESTIGATIONS: Abnormal ECG (electrocardiograph).

TREATMENT: None available.

PROGNOSIS: Sudden death possible.

Jet Lag
(Rapid Time Change Syndrome)

DESCRIPTION: Varied symptoms caused by longitudinal (east-west) intercontinental flights. Long latitudinal (north-south) flights do not cause jet lag.

CAUSE: Long intercontinental flights, and worse when flying east (against time) than flying west. Children are more upset by time changes and may take several days to adjust.

SYMPTOMS: Tiredness, headaches, nausea, aching muscles, dizziness, irritability, restlessness and disorientation.

INVESTIGATIONS: Mental tests have been used to demonstrate adverse effects.

TREATMENT: Adjust to the local time zone as soon as possible after the start of the flight. Small, frequent carbohydrate rich meals and extra fluids during the flight will aid recovery, but alcohol will slow it. Analgesic preparations (eg. paracetamol and aspirin) and a mild sleeping tablet (eg. temazepam) may be useful. The hormone melatonin, normally produced by the time regulating pineal gland at the front of the brain, is being used to reset the body clocks and prevent jet lag, but the use of this drug is still controversial.

COMPLICATIONS: Poor decisions may be made in the first day or two after a long flight.

PROGNOSIS: Full recovery depends upon the length of the flight, the time of departure and arrival and the direction flown. It may take up to four days to fully recover from a 12 hour time difference.

Job-Buckley Syndrome
(Hyper-IgE Syndrome)

DESCRIPTION: An inborn error of metabolism that results in very high levels of one particular type of immunoglobulin (the protein in the blood responsible for the immune response), IgE.

CAUSE: Congenital, and may pass from one generation to the next in some cases.

SYMPTOMS: Recurrent infections of the skin and lungs, and weakened bones with frequent fractures. Some children may have coarse features and excessive allergies, and a higher proportion than expected have fair skin and red hair.

INVESTIGATIONS: Blood tests show excessively high levels of immunoglobulin E, as well as other abnormalities.

TREATMENT: Long term antibiotics to prevent infections.

COMPLICATIONS: Serious infections may cause permanent scarring and organ damage.

PROGNOSIS: No cure, but control reasonable.

Johanson-Blizzard Syndrome

DESCRIPTION: Inherited abnormality of connective tissue development.

CAUSE: Congenital, but both parents must carry the gene for an infant to be affected.

SYMPTOMS: An infant with abnormal nose structure, failure of the anus to form, underdeveloped and poorly functioning skin, deafness, mild mental retardation, and failure to gain weight and height.

INVESTIGATIONS: Abnormal skin biopsy.

TREATMENT: Plastic surgery to correct some deformities.

PROGNOSIS: No cure available.

Johansson-Sinding-Larsen Syndrome

DESCRIPTION: Damage to the knee cap in athletic adolescents.

CAUSE: Caused by overuse and stress on the knee joint with recurrent knee extension in sports that require running and/or kicking. Results in damage to the lower end of the patella (knee cap) at the point where ligamentous attachment to the tibia (shin bone) occurs. Abnormal bone growth may occur down this ligament from the patella.

SYMPTOMS: Knee pain and tenderness at the lower edge of the patella in a teenager.

INVESTIGATIONS: X-ray of the knee may show abnormal bone deposits in some cases.

TREATMENT: Rest, splint if severe.

PROGNOSIS: Good.

Joint Infection
See Septic Arthritis

Joseph Syndrome
See Machado-Joseph Syndrome

Juvenile Diabetes
See Diabetes Mellitus

Juvenile Rheumatoid Arthritis
See Still's Disease

K

KA
See Keratoacanthoma

Kala-Azar
(Visceral Leischmaniasis)

DESCRIPTION: Widespread internal infection by a protozoan (tiny single celled animal).

CAUSE: The protozoan *Leischmania donovani* is transmitted from one person to another by sand flies. Found throughout the tropics in America, Asia and Africa.

SYMPTOMS: Slow onset with fever, enlarged spleen and liver, anaemia, weight loss, pigmentation of skin on face (mainly forehead) and hands.

INVESTIGATIONS: Diagnosed by blood tests and biopsy of liver or spleen.

TREATMENT: Quite toxic medications must be given regularly by injection for a long time to control the infection.

COMPLICATIONS: Bleeding from the nose and mouth, and warty skin ulcers.

PROGNOSIS: Fatal without treatment. Recurrences common for years after apparent successful treatment. Cure difficult.

See also Cutaneous Leischmaniasis; Mucocutaneous Leischmaniasis

Kallmann Syndrome

DESCRIPTION: Inherited sex hormone abnormality.

CAUSE: Familial (passes from one generation to the next) condition that causes the part of the brain (hypothalamus) that controls hormone production to malfunction.

SYMPTOMS: Poorly developed genitals in a boy, loss of sense of smell, long arms and legs, male but with female body shape.

INVESTIGATIONS: Blood levels of testosterone very low.

TREATMENT: Male hormone replacement therapy.

PROGNOSIS: No cure, but good control usually possible.

Kaposi's Sarcoma

DESCRIPTION: Initially a very rare form of cancer of muscle and fat tissue found only in central Africa, but now far more widespread because of the AIDS virus.

CAUSE: Damage to the immune system by advanced types of AIDS reduces the body's ability to defend itself from this rare type of cancer.

SYMPTOMS: The growth of one or more tender, painful, firm tumours in muscle and other soft tissues.

INVESTIGATIONS: Diagnosed by biopsy of the tumour.

TREATMENT: Surgical excision of the cancer, followed by irradiation and chemotherapy. In advanced cases, only chemotherapy may be practical to slow the progress of the disease.

COMPLICATIONS: Spreads to nearby lymph nodes and other tissues.

PROGNOSIS: No long term cure possible, but progression may be slowed by treatment.

See also AIDS

Kartagener Syndrome

DESCRIPTION: Inherited abnormality of organ position.

CAUSE: Congenital.

SYMPTOMS: The heart is on the right side of the chest instead of the left, and recurrent sinus and lung infections (bronchiectasis) occur. In some patients, the organs in the abdomen (liver, spleen, gut etc.) are also reversed in position.

INVESTIGATIONS: An X-ray of the chest shows the abnormal heart position.

TREATMENT: Surgical correction of defects if required. Antibiotic and symptomatic treatment of lung and sinus problems.

COMPLICATIONS: Recurrent severe lung infections.

PROGNOSIS: No cure, but most problems can be corrected or controlled.

Kawasaki Syndrome
(Mucocutaneous Lymph Node Syndrome)

DESCRIPTION: Uncommon generalised inflammatory condition of infants.

CAUSE: Unknown. Not contagious.

SYMPTOMS: Babies are lethargic, develop high fevers, inflamed mouth, widespread rash, conjunctivitis, enlarged lymph nodes in the neck, artery inflammation and damage, and redness and peeling of the skin on the hands and feet. Patients may also have diarrhoea and heart artery complications.

INVESTIGATIONS: Blood tests show abnormalities but are not diagnostic.

TREATMENT: None effective. Aspirin for inflammation.

COMPLICATIONS: Serious heart complications occur in 30% of survivors.

PROGNOSIS: Fatal in 3% of cases. Others have a prolonged illness.

Kayser-Fleischer Ring
See Wilson's Disease

Kearns-Sayre Syndrome

DESCRIPTION: Rare cause of blindness.

CAUSE: Hereditary. Metabolic abnormality transmitted through women from one generation to the next.

SYMPTOMS: Rapid loss of central vision of both eyes in early adult life, gradual progressive paralysis of eye movement, pigmentation of the retina (light sensitive area at the back of the eye), and abnormal conduction of nerve signals in the heart.

INVESTIGATIONS: Diagnosed by examining the retina with a magnifying light (ophthalmoscope).
TREATMENT: None available.
PROGNOSIS: No cure.
See also Leber Optic Neuropathy

Keloid

DESCRIPTION: Abnormal skin healing that is more common in Negroes, and on the chest, back and neck.
CAUSE: Inherited tendency in which there is excessive healing in a scar.
SYMPTOMS: Red, raised, thick scar at the site of skin injury.
INVESTIGATIONS: None necessary.
TREATMENT: Injection, or application under a plastic dressing, of powerful steroids.
COMPLICATIONS: May become painful or itchy.
PROGNOSIS: Stop enlarging after a few months, and then persist for many years, before very slowly subsiding in some cases.

Keratin Cysts
See Milia

Keratitis
(Snow Blindness)

DESCRIPTION: Inflammation of the cornea, the outer layer of the eye.
CAUSE: Ultraviolet lights, exposure to reflected sun (snow blindness), cement dust, and irritating chemicals (eg. alkalis) that may splash into the eye. May also be due to a bacterial or fungal infection in contact lens wearers.
SYMPTOMS: Severe burning pain in the eye starting some hours after exposure to bright light, but immediately with direct irritants. The eyes water and are very sensitive to bright light. Any contraction or dilation of the pupil causes pain.
INVESTIGATIONS: Examination of the eye under magnification shows damage to cornea.
TREATMENT: Irrigating the eye to remove any irritant chemicals or substances, instilling drops to paralyse any pupil movement, and an eye patch.
COMPLICATIONS: Scarring of the cornea may occur with chemical burns.
PROGNOSIS: Recovery within 24 to 48 hours.
See also Flash Burns to Eye

Keratoacanthoma
(KA)

DESCRIPTION: Rapidly enlarging skin growths that are often confused with skin cancers.
CAUSE: More common in the elderly and on the face, hands and other sun-exposed areas of the body. Rare in dark-skinned races.
SYMPTOMS: Initially appear as small, scale-covered lumps, but over a couple of

months they enlarge rapidly to become red, shiny, firm blisters topped with a plug of hard scaly material that may be 2cm. or more in diameter. Over the next few months, they will slowly disappear, and eventually little or no trace of their presence remains. They take about twice as long to resolve as they take to develop.

INVESTIGATIONS: If there is any doubt at all about the diagnosis a biopsy must be taken.

TREATMENT: No treatment is required unless the KA is very disfiguring. Unsightly ones may be removed surgically.

COMPLICATIONS: None significant.

PROGNOSIS: Except for the temporary disfigurement they cause, they are quite harmless.

See also Squamous Cell Carcinoma of the Skin

Keratoconjunctivitis Sicca

DESCRIPTION: A severe form of dry eye syndrome (xerophthalmia).

CAUSE: Commonly occurs in elderly women whose lacrimal (tear producing) glands fail. Also a complication of autoimmune diseases such as systemic lupus erythematosus, rheumatoid arthritis and Sjögren syndrome (see separate entries).

SYMPTOMS: Continued eye irritation and discomfort from a dry eye surface.

INVESTIGATIONS: A thin strip of blotting paper touched to the lower eye surface for a minute remains abnormally dry.

TREATMENT: Very regular, and long term use of lubricating drops and ointment in the eye. Inserts that are placed under the lower lid and ooze a lubricant constantly for many hours can also be used.

COMPLICATIONS: Rarely a threat to sight.

PROGNOSIS: No cure, difficult to control, and usually continues lifelong.

See also Dry Eye Syndrome

Keratoconus

DESCRIPTION: Protrusion, cone shape and thinning of the cornea (the clear dome over the pupil and iris — coloured part of the eye).

CAUSE: May be inherited or associated with Down syndrome, Turner syndrome, Marfan syndrome (see separate entries) and numerous eye diseases.

SYMPTOMS: Distorted vision (astigmatism) in affected eye that steadily worsens.

INVESTIGATIONS: Diagnosed by examining the eye with a magnifying light (ophthalmoscope).

TREATMENT: In early stages spectacles or contact lenses correct vision. In late stages, surgery to the surface of the cornea or replacement of the cornea with a transplant is necessary.

COMPLICATIONS: Scarring or rupture of the clear corneal membrane.

PROGNOSIS: Good results from treatment. Progressive condition if left untreated.

See also Astigmatism

Keratoderma

DESCRIPTION: Abnormal thickening of skin.

CAUSE: May be inherited, or due to psoriasis, eczema, lichen planus (see separate entries) or other skin diseases.

SYMPTOMS: Very thick, rough, cracked skin on the palms and/or soles.

INVESTIGATIONS: Tests may be performed to determine cause.

TREATMENT: Treat cause if possible. Salicylic acid ointment or urea cream.

PROGNOSIS: Depends on cause, but often persists long term.

Keratosis

See Hyperkeratosis; Keratosis Pilaris

Keratosis Pilaris

DESCRIPTION: Very common skin condition that affects women twice as often as men, and starts in the teenage years. Occurs most commonly on the back of the upper arms, front of thighs and buttocks.

CAUSE: Excess keratin (scale) formation at the opening of hair follicles. Tends to run in families.

SYMPTOMS: Small rough polyps on the skin.

INVESTIGATIONS: None necessary.

TREATMENT: Salicylic acid or urea cream and other scale removing (keratolytic) agents.

PROGNOSIS: Tends to settle in mid-life.

Kerion

DESCRIPTION: Fungal abscess of the scalp.

CAUSE: The fungi *Trichophyton*, *Microsporum* and others that normally cause tinea (ringworm).

SYMPTOMS: A sore, boggy, raised abscess on the scalp.

INVESTIGATIONS: A swab may be taken to identify the responsible fungus.

TREATMENT: Potent antifungal tablets and creams.

COMPLICATIONS: Spread of the fungal infection to other areas.

PROGNOSIS: Very good with appropriate treatment.

See also Tinea Capitis

Ketoacidosis

See Diabetic Ketoacidosis

Kidney Cancer

See Wilms' Tumour

Kidney Failure, Acute
(Acute Renal Failure)

DESCRIPTION: Sudden failure of the kidney to remove waste products from the body and to retain the correct amount of water in the body.

CAUSE: May be triggered by a severe injury (particularly crush injuries), major surgery, poisons (eg. mercury, dry cleaning fluid, mushrooms), heart attacks, severe burns, severe infections, and a number of rarer causes. It may also occur as a complication of pregnancy.

SYMPTOMS: A sudden severe reduction in the output of urine associated with a loss of appetite, tiredness, nausea, vomiting and raised blood pressure.

INVESTIGATIONS: Diagnosis confirmed by blood and urine tests, which show waste products in the blood and very dilute urine.

TREATMENT: Any specific cause must first be treated. In severe cases, an artificial kidney machine may be needed (dialysis). The amount of fluids that the patient drinks must be carefully regulated, and a strict diet that limits the number of waste products in the body is given.

COMPLICATIONS: Bacterial and viral infections are a common complication.

PROGNOSIS: Depends upon the cause. Some patients die within a couple of days, but most can be managed in a good hospital to a successful outcome. After a few days or weeks, the kidney usually starts to work again, and over a month or two the urine and kidney function return to normal. There is usually no long-lasting kidney damage.

See also Kidney Failure, Chronic

Kidney Failure, Chronic
(Chronic Renal Failure; Uraemia)

DESCRIPTION: A slow, gradual failure of the kidneys.

CAUSE: Old age is the most common cause, but may also be due to many other conditions including a damaged blood supply to the kidney from hardened arteries (arteriosclerosis), poisons, infections, the body trying to reject the kidney in auto-immune conditions such as systemic lupus erythematosus, and many rarer diseases.

SYMPTOMS: Because of its slow onset, patients may not present to a doctor until the condition is well advanced, by which time they have weakness, tiredness, lack of appetite, weight loss, nausea, headaches, passing urine frequently and at night, and in advanced cases itchy skin, vomiting, high blood pressure and anaemia.

INVESTIGATIONS: Abnormal blood and urine tests are diagnostic. Further investigations are carried out to discover any specific cause.

TREATMENT: Treat any cause of the condition if possible, followed by a strict diet (low in protein), and control of all fluids that are drunk. Unless the cause can be corrected, long-term treatment with an artificial kidney machine (dialysis), or a kidney transplant operation is necessary.

COMPLICATIONS: Patients must be very careful with medications, as they are likely to be far more effective, last longer in the body than normal, have more side effects and may be toxic.

PROGNOSIS: Kidney transplants have an 80% cure rate. Dialysis can be continued for many years if necessary.

See also Nephrotic Syndrome

Kidney Stone
(Nephrolithiasis; Renal Calculus; Renal Colic; Ureteric Calculus; Ureteric Colic)

DESCRIPTION: Formation of a crystal (stone) in the kidney.

CAUSE: The kidney acts to filter the blood, and removes excess water and wastes. If these wastes become too concentrated or altered in some way, they can precipitate out and form a crystal that slowly grows into a stone. Most stones are flushed down the ureter (the tube that leads to the bladder from the kidney) and are passed out with the urine while still very small. A small number of stones slowly grow in size until they are the size of a grape or larger and completely fill the urine collection chamber of the kidney where they cause repeated kidney infections and pain. Medium sized stones from one to five millimetres in length enter the thin very sensitive ureter, and as the stone is pushed along the tube by the pressure of urine behind, it scrapes the tube wall to cause intense pain (renal colic) that can thus come and go for several days every time the stone moves. Kidney stones are more common in men than women, and in hot climates than cold due to the higher incidence of dehydration.

SYMPTOMS: Excruciating, intermittent pain in the loin (side of the belly) that goes down to the groin. Patients may note blood in their urine because the stone is damaging the ureter to make it bleed.

INVESTIGATIONS: X-rays of the kidney after the injection of a dye (intravenous pyelogram — IVP) show the stone, its size and position. The progress of the stone down the ureter can be seen on repeat X-rays. Blood tests are done to check for the cause of the stone.

TREATMENT: Most patients are given pain relief and lots of fluids to wash the stone down the ureter, and after a few hours or days, the stone enters the bladder and passes out without causing any further pain. Some stones get stuck in the ureter, and must be removed. This can be done in a number of ways—

— lithotripsy uses intense sound shock waves that are passed through the body to shatter the stone, the remnants, which are the size of sand particles, can then be passed normally through the urine.

— passing a tiny umbrella into the bladder and up the ureter to a point above the stone where the umbrella is then opened, and slowly removed, dragging the stone along with it.

— under the control of a radiologist (X-ray specialist), a tube can be placed through the skin into the kidney, and the stone removed.

— rarely an open operation through the abdominal wall may be necessary.

COMPLICATIONS: Severe intractable kidney infections may be due to an undiagnosed stone. A kidney may be so severely damaged by a stone that it fails.

PROGNOSIS: Almost invariably kidney stones can be successfully treated, but up to 50% of patients will have a recurrence within five years if measures are not taken to prevent their formation.

'King's Evil'
See Scrofula

Kissing Disease
See Glandular Fever

Kleine-Levin Syndrome
DESCRIPTION: Sleep and mood disorder.
CAUSE: Unknown.
SYMPTOMS: Recurrent periods of severe excessive sleepiness, increased appetite, mood disturbances, increased sexual activity, disorientation, hallucinations and memory loss. There may be no symptoms for months between attacks. More common in men, with onset from 12 to 20 years of age.
INVESTIGATIONS: None diagnostic.
TREATMENT: Stimulants.
PROGNOSIS: Self-limiting by about 40 years of age.

Klinefelter Syndrome
(XXY Syndrome)
DESCRIPTION: Sexual abnormality that affects one in every 500 males.
CAUSE: Congenital sex chromosome abnormality that occurs at the moment of conception when the sperm fuses with the egg. The chromosomes from the mother and father of these men combine incorrectly with two X chromosomes and one Y being present (XXY) instead of one of each (XY).
SYMPTOMS: Males with very small testes and penis, small breasts develop, they have scanty body hair, and are impotent and sterile.
INVESTIGATIONS: Diagnosed by chromosomal analysis of blood sample.
TREATMENT: Testosterone (male hormone) tablets or injections can be given to improve the body shape and impotence, but infertility cannot be corrected. Plastic surgery to remove the breasts is sometimes necessary.
PROGNOSIS: No cure possible.
See also XYY Syndrome

Klippel-Feil Syndrome
DESCRIPTION: Developmental abnormality of the neck.
CAUSE: Congenital, but not inherited.
SYMPTOMS: Short neck, limited head movement, and sometimes a web of skin at the side of the neck.

INVESTIGATIONS: Neck X-ray shows fusion of 2 or more vertebrae.
TREATMENT: Cosmetic surgery.
PROGNOSIS: No cure.

Klippel-Trenaunay Syndrome

DESCRIPTION: Condition in which there is massive overgrowth of blood vessels within the skin and other tissues.
CAUSE: Unknown.
SYMPTOMS: Artery and vein malformations on the limbs, port-wine stain (large red skin mark), local overgrowth of soft tissue, and sometimes local overgrowth of bone and abnormal connections between arteries and veins elsewhere in the body.
INVESTIGATIONS: None diagnostic.
TREATMENT: Surgery and compression bandages.
COMPLICATIONS: Severe bleeding may occur from an abnormal blood vessel.
PROGNOSIS: No cure.

Klumpke's Palsy

DESCRIPTION: Arm damage to infant during birth.
CAUSE: Due to stretching of the lower nerves in the armpit during a forceps or difficult delivery.
SYMPTOMS: The hand is limp below the wrist in new born infant.
INVESTIGATIONS: Nerve conduction studies sometimes performed.
TREATMENT: Wrist splinted in neutral position.
PROGNOSIS: Most babies fully recover.
See also Erb-Duchenne Palsy

Knee

See Housemaid's Knee; Knee Meniscus Tear; Knock Knees

Knee Meniscus Tear

DESCRIPTION: Damage to one of the two menisci in each knee joint. The menisci are cartilages that run around the top end of the tibia (main lower leg bone) to deepen the socket of the joint and stabilise it.
CAUSE: Abnormal twisting of the knee.
SYMPTOMS: Pain, swelling, clicking and sometimes locking of the knee joint that is worse with movement. Patients often describe a feeling of instability in the joint.
INVESTIGATIONS: Doctors apply various stress tests to the knee in different positions to make the diagnosis.
TREATMENT: Initially, rest of the knee with strapping and using crutches may allow the knee to recover. A locked knee can be released by manipulation. In persistent or severe cases, particularly if there is locking, an operation (meniscectomy) is necessary to remove the torn cartilage. This can usually be

done through an arthroscope (small tube that is passed into the knee joint).

COMPLICATIONS: The knee may become unstable after a meniscectomy, and premature arthritis may develop.

PROGNOSIS: Good results from treatment.

Knock Knees
(Genu Valgum)

DESCRIPTION: A common condition of children, diagnosed when a child who is standing straight tries to bring the bony bumps (medial malleoli) on the inside of the ankles together. If they are unable to do this because the knees come together first, the diagnosis is confirmed.

CAUSE: Usually a developmental and growth problem. In rare cases due to rickets, poorly healed fractures of the leg bones or other very uncommon diseases.

SYMPTOMS: Awkward way of walking and possible knee and ankle discomfort.

INVESTIGATIONS: Sometimes an X-ray of the knees may be taken.

TREATMENT: In the majority of cases the problem corrects itself without any treatment. In severe cases a wedge may be inserted into the inside edge of the shoes to turn the foot slightly outwards. Rarely, if the problem continues into the early teenage years and causes difficulty in walking or abnormal appearance and posture, an operation may be necessary.

COMPLICATIONS: None significant.

PROGNOSIS: Very good.

See also Bow Legs

Koebner Phenomenon
See Psoriasis

Korsakoff's Psychosis
See Wernicke-Korsakoff Psychosis

Kostmann Syndrome

DESCRIPTION: Rare blood white cell disorder.

CAUSE: Inherited lack of neutrophils (a type of white blood cell).

SYMPTOMS: Dramatically increased susceptibility to infection.

INVESTIGATIONS: Blood tests show neutropenia (lack of neutrophils).

TREATMENT: Blood transfusions and aggressive treatment of infections when possible.

PROGNOSIS: Often fatal.

See also Schwachman Syndrome

Kugelberg-Welander Syndrome

DESCRIPTION: Nerve disease that affects muscle function.

CAUSE: Familial (runs in families). Abnormality of the point where a nerve joins to a muscle.

Kugelberg-Welander Syndrome

SYMPTOMS: Muscular weakness of shoulder girdle and pelvis and an abnormal gait. Some patients develop over large calf muscles and tongue weakness.

INVESTIGATIONS: Diagnosed by abnormalities in blood tests, nerve conduction studies and muscle biopsy. Reflexes involving affected muscles are also abnormal.

TREATMENT: Physiotherapy may help, but there is no specific treatment available.

PROGNOSIS: Relatively normal life span, but disease process is slowly progressive.

See also Motor Neurone Disease

Kuru

DESCRIPTION: A now extinct disease that occurred in the cannibalistic Fore tribe in the New Guinea highlands. Closely related to Creutzfeldt-Jakob disease.

CAUSE: A primitive virus like particle known as a prion was probably responsible. Transmitted by eating the infected brains of their victims.

SYMPTOMS: Twitching, incoordination, tremor and mental deterioration.

TREATMENT: None available.

PROGNOSIS: Death inevitable.

See also Creutzfeldt-Jakob Disease

Kwashiorkor

DESCRIPTION: Severe form of malnutrition.

CAUSE: A lack of protein in the diet, although adequate amounts of carbohydrates and fatty foods may be eaten.

SYMPTOMS: Swollen belly, tiredness, thin limbs with swollen ankles, wasted muscles, a dry dermatitis, sparse hair, conjunctivitis and inflamed gums. Protein levels in the blood drop to a very low level which allows water to escape from blood and into tissues to give the characteristic bloated belly appearance.

INVESTIGATIONS: Blood tests show very low protein levels.

TREATMENT: Small amounts of nutritious food frequently over several weeks before returning to a normal diet is essential to prevent an imbalance of chemicals in the blood.

COMPLICATIONS: Permanent organ damage may occur if malnutrition is prolonged.

PROGNOSIS: Good recovery with appropriate diet, but fatal otherwise.

See also Marasmus

Kyphoscoliosis

DESCRIPTION: A combination of both abnormal side to side (scoliosis) and front to back (kyphosis) curvature of the spine.

CAUSE: Minor degrees are seen in many teenagers as they go through periods of rapid growth, particularly if they have poor posture, but in some the deformity becomes severe. Other causes include one leg being shorter than the other, a severe back injury, diseases of the muscles that support the vertebrae, cerebral palsy, osteoporosis, compressed and collapsed vertebrae, ankylosing spondylitis, tuberculous damage to vertebrae, tumours, and a number of less common diseases.

SYMPTOMS: An excessive outward curve of the spine at the back of the chest, and abnormal side to side curvature that may vary from a slightly increased prominence to a severe hunchback deformity.

INVESTIGATIONS: Diagnosis confirmed by X-rays of the spine, which may show the cause at the same time.

TREATMENT: Treat the cause, if possible. Otherwise muscle strengthening exercises, physiotherapy, braces and rarely surgery are used to correct the deformity.

COMPLICATIONS: Nerves pinched as they leave the deformed back may cause severe pain. Permanent deformity is a rare possibility.

PROGNOSIS: Depends upon severity, but most patients cope well with the deformity and have no outward signs of the condition.

See also Kyphosis; Scoliosis

Kyphosis

DESCRIPTION: Abnormal curvature of the back which normally curves gently from front to back in a double S-shape. It curves in at the neck, out over the back of the chest, in at the small of the back, and out again between the buttocks.

CAUSE: Osteoporosis (see separate entry) in older women, compressed and collapsed vertebrae, ankylosing spondylitis (see separate entry) in the elderly, tuberculosis, tumours, constant muscle spasm in spastics, and a number of less common diseases.

SYMPTOMS: An excessive outward curve of the spine at the back of the chest, that may vary from a slightly increased prominence to a severe hunchback deformity.

INVESTIGATIONS: Diagnosis confirmed by X-rays of the spine, which may show the cause at the same time.

TREATMENT: Treat the cause, if possible. Otherwise exercise, physiotherapy, braces and rarely surgery are used to correct the deformity.

COMPLICATIONS: The pinching of nerves as they leave the deformed back may cause severe pain.

PROGNOSIS: Many patients have remarkably pain free backs despite quite horrendous deformities.

See also Kyphoscoliosis; Lordosis; Scoliosis

L

Labyrinthitis

DESCRIPTION: Inflammation or infection of the semicircular canals (labyrinth) in the inner ear that control balance.

CAUSE: Viral, or rarely bacterial, infection of the labyrinth. Sometimes toxins or ear damage may be responsible.

SYMPTOMS: Severe dizziness, abnormal eye movements, and nonexistent noises may be heard.

INVESTIGATIONS: Caloric tests (alternating heat and cold in the outer ear canal) induce worse dizziness.

TREATMENT: Medications to reduce inflammation and dizziness. Antibiotics sometimes necessary.

COMPLICATIONS: Rarely, permanent damage to the balance mechanism may occur.

PROGNOSIS: Most settle in a few days, some persist for weeks.

la Crosse Encephalitis
(Californian Encephalitis; Jamestown Canyon Virus)

DESCRIPTION: Rare viral infection of the brain.

CAUSE: Virus spread from other animals (eg. chipmunks) to man by a mosquito. Found throughout the southern United States. Usually occurs in children and in summer. Incubation period three to seven days.

SYMPTOMS: Fever, belly pains, dizziness, sore throat, cough, headache, neck stiffness, nausea, vomiting, tiredness, disturbed mental functions, disorientation, coma and death.

INVESTIGATIONS: Tests on blood and the fluid around the brain are abnormal.

TREATMENT: No specific treatment or vaccine available.

COMPLICATIONS: May rarely cause permanent brain damage in up to half of survivors with epilepsy and inability to concentrate.

PROGNOSIS: Acute attack lasts for one to three weeks, but complete recovery may take months. Death is uncommon.

See also Encephalitis

Landau-Kleffner Syndrome

DESCRIPTION: Form of epilepsy.

CAUSE: Unknown.

SYMPTOMS: Muscular seizures, followed by a slow failure of the ability to speak or understand language, and behavioural disorders. Usually starts between 4 and 9 years of age.

INVESTIGATIONS: EEG (electroencephalogram) may be abnormal.

TREATMENT: Anticonvulsant medications, speech therapy.

PROGNOSIS: 50% recovery. Poor prognosis with early onset.

See also Epilepsy

Landry-Guillain-Barré Syndrome
See Guillain-Barré Syndrome

Lange Syndrome
See de Lange Syndrome

Langer-Giedion Syndrome
DESCRIPTION: Rare childhood deformity.
CAUSE: Congenital chromosome abnormality.
SYMPTOMS: Sparse hair, bulbous nose, small head, multiple bony overgrowths.
INVESTIGATIONS: Chromosomal analysis abnormal. X-rays show extra bone formation.
TREATMENT: Plastic surgery for deformities.
PROGNOSIS: No cure.

Langerhans Cell Granulomatosis
See Histiocytosis X

Langerhans Cell Histiocytosis
See Hand-Schüller-Christian Disease; Histiocytosis X; Letterer-Siwe Disease

Large Bowel Cancer
See Colo-Rectal Cancer

Large Cell Carcinoma of the Lung
See Lung Cancer

Larva Migrans
See Cutaneous Larva Migrans; Visceral Larva Migrans

Laryngitis
DESCRIPTION: Infection of the larynx (voice box or Adam's apple) at the front of the throat, which contains the vocal cords that are responsible for speech.
CAUSE: Almost invariably it is a viral infection and cannot be cured by antibiotics.
SYMPTOMS: Hoarseness or total loss of voice, pain, difficulty in swallowing, a dry cough and a fever.
INVESTIGATIONS: None necessary.
TREATMENT: Time, voice rest, aspirin and other anti-inflammatory medications to reduce inflammation and swelling of the vocal cords, and to ease the fever.
COMPLICATIONS: Recurrent attacks may cause small nodules to form on the vocal cords, and huskiness in later life.
PROGNOSIS: Complete recovery normal after five to ten days, but recovery will be delayed in smokers and those who persist in using their voice excessively.
See also Pharyngitis

303

Laryngomalacia

DESCRIPTION: A rare condition of the throat in children.

CAUSE: Congenital. The cartilage of the larynx (voice box) is softened, and collapses easily.

SYMPTOMS: When the patient breathes in heavily with exercise, a croupy cough and shortness of breath occur.

INVESTIGATIONS: Diagnosed by laryngoscopy (looking down the throat with an instrument).

TREATMENT: Surgical bracing of the larynx.

COMPLICATIONS: Voice may be permanently distorted.

PROGNOSIS: No cure, but treatment allows a relatively normal life.

Laryngotracheobronchitis

DESCRIPTION: Viral or bacterial infection of the airways from the voice box (larynx) through the trachea to the larger airways (bronchi) of the lungs.

CAUSE: Usually a viral infection, but various bacteria may be responsible.

SYMPTOMS: Hoarseness or total loss of voice, neck and chest pain, difficulty in swallowing, pain with breathing, shortness of breath, a productive cough and a fever.

INVESTIGATIONS: Sputum may be cultured to identify the responsible organism and correct antibiotic to treat it.

TREATMENT: If bacterial, antibiotics can be used. If viral, time, rest, cough mixtures, aspirin and other anti-inflammatory medications to reduce inflammation and ease the fever.

COMPLICATIONS: Untreated bacterial infections may progress to pneumonia.

PROGNOSIS: Bacterial infections settle rapidly with antibiotics. Viral infections recover after five to ten days, but recovery is delayed in smokers.

See also Bronchitis, Acute; Laryngitis; Pharyngitis; Tracheitis

Lassa Fever

DESCRIPTION: An extremely contagious form of viral haemorrhagic fever (viral infection of the blood) that occurs in central and west Africa.

CAUSE: The virus is spread by rats and from person to person in conditions of poor hygiene. Outbreaks have occurred in Sierra Leone, Nigeria and the Congo. More common in women.

SYMPTOMS: Muscle pains, headache, sore throat, joint pains, diarrhoea, vomiting, red eyes and abnormal bleeding.

INVESTIGATIONS: Blood tests show significant abnormalities.

TREATMENT: No cure or vaccine for prevention, but a number of drugs are being used experimentally to modify the disease. Patients must be nursed in strict isolation.

COMPLICATIONS: Internal bleeding causes death.

PROGNOSIS: Fatal in about 90% of patients.

See also Ebola Virus; Marburg Virus

Latent Hepatic Porphyria
See Porphyria Cutanea Tarda

Lateral Epicondylitis
See Tennis Elbow

Laurence-Moon-Biedl Syndrome
DESCRIPTION: Familial condition of the eye, brain and genitals.
CAUSE: Inherited.
SYMPTOMS: Night blindness due to excessive amounts of pigment in the retina at the back of the eye, obesity, mental retardation, extra fingers and toes and underdeveloped genitals.
INVESTIGATIONS: Examination of the back of the eye through an ophthalmoscope (magnifying light) shows excess pigment.
TREATMENT: None available.
PROGNOSIS: No cure.

Lead Poisoning
(Plumbism)
DESCRIPTION: Swallowing or inhaling lead compounds.
CAUSE: Lead has been widely used in industry including batteries, paints (particularly dangerous in flaking old paint), crystal glass, ceramics, old plumbing fixtures, leaded petrol and some old-fashioned medications.
SYMPTOMS: Belly pains, irritability, tiredness, loss of appetite, anaemia, poor coordination, slurred speech, convulsions, coma and death.
INVESTIGATIONS: Detected by specific blood tests.
TREATMENT: If recently swallowed, induce vomiting and give activated charcoal. Medications can slowly remove the lead from the body.
COMPLICATIONS: Permanent damage to nerves (neuropathy) and kidneys possible.
PROGNOSIS: Depends on age, health and weight of patient, and dose of lead.

Leber Congenital Amaurosis
DESCRIPTION: Rare cause of blindness in children.
CAUSE: Familial (runs in families), but both parents must be carriers.
SYMPTOMS: Blindness at birth or developing soon afterwards.
INVESTIGATIONS: No pupil contraction when bright light shone into eye.
TREATMENT: None available.
COMPLICATIONS: May be associated with mental retardation, deafness, epilepsy, kidney and bone abnormalities.
PROGNOSIS: No cure.
See also Leber Optic Neuropathy and other conditions listed under Eye Diseases

Leber Optic Neuropathy

DESCRIPTION: Rare cause of blindness due to inflammation of the optic (eye) nerve.

CAUSE: Hereditary. Metabolic abnormality transmitted through women from one generation to the next.

SYMPTOMS: Rapid loss of central vision of both eyes in early adult life.

INVESTIGATIONS: Diagnosed by examining the light sensitive retina at the back of the eye with a magnifying light (ophthalmoscope).

TREATMENT: None available.

PROGNOSIS: Usually permanent vision loss, but 15% have a spontaneous recovery.

See also Leber Congenital Amaurosis; Kearns-Sayre Syndrome

Ledderhose's Disease

DESCRIPTION: A fibrous sheet (the plantar fascia) stretches under the skin of the sole to give it a smooth appearance, strength and firmness, and to protect and control the movement of the muscle tendons that cross under it to the toes. If damaged, the plantar fascia may become scarred, contract and thicken into hard lumps that can be felt under the skin. As the damage progresses, the contraction of the fibrous sheet pulls on the tendons that run underneath it to prevent their free movement. Men are affected more than women. Similar condition to Dupuytren's contracture of the hand.

CAUSE: Unknown, but may be due to a poor blood supply to the foot (eg. diabetes), and injury to the foot from repeated blows (eg. running).

SYMPTOMS: One or more hard, fixed nodules under the skin of the sole that gradually extend lengthwise along the sole to cause discomfort, pain with walking and loss of toe mobility. Eventually the toes cannot be fully extended, and contract into a claw-like appearance. The middle toes are usually more severely affected than the others.

INVESTIGATIONS: None necessary.

TREATMENT: Soft shoes insoles, injection of steroids around the nodule, and in severe cases only the nodule may be surgically excised.

COMPLICATIONS: Recurrence after surgery common.

PROGNOSIS: Usually persistent.

See also Dupuytren's Contracture of the Hand

Leg Cramps
(Muscle Cramps; Nocturnal Cramps)

DESCRIPTION: Very common painful leg condition.

CAUSE: A combination of minor muscle injury caused by vigorous or unusual exercise, a build up of waste products in the muscle and dehydration. Worsens with age and pregnancy.

SYMPTOMS: Sudden, painful spasm of the muscles in the leg calf, or elsewhere in the body, usually following exercise.

INVESTIGATIONS: In severe intractable cases, blood tests may show a biochemical imbalance.

TREATMENT: Stretching the affected muscles by standing on the balls of the feet can ease the spasm. Prevention is better than cure, and taking adequate amounts of fluid during and after exercise prevents dehydration. If this is insufficient, medications (eg. quinine) can be prescribed to be taken after sport to prevent the cramps. Tonic water or bitter lemon drunk after exercise may also help as these drinks contain quinine.

COMPLICATIONS: Minor muscle tears and persisting muscle aches may occur.

PROGNOSIS: Usually settle quickly, but recurrences common.

Legionnaire's Disease

DESCRIPTION: A serious form of bacterial pneumonia.

CAUSE: Caused by the bacterium *Legionella pneumophila*. Usually spread by contamination of air-conditioning systems in large buildings with water cooling towers. Once an epidemic occurs, it is essential for the responsible building and air-conditioning system to be identified so that it can be thoroughly cleaned and disinfected. Victims inhale the *Legionella* bacteria into their lungs in microscopic droplets of water.

SYMPTOMS: Fever, productive cough and chest pains. Some patients may develop only a mild infection and recover without treatment, but others (particularly smokers) will rapidly deteriorate.

INVESTIGATIONS: Diagnosed by listening to the chest with a stethoscope, chest X-rays and tests on the sputum, to differentiate legionnaire's disease from other types of pneumonia.

TREATMENT: The antibiotic erythromycin will slowly cure most cases. Ancillary treatment, such as physiotherapy and expectorant medications, are also necessary.

COMPLICATIONS: Permanent lung damage such as chronic bronchitis and emphysema may occur.

PROGNOSIS: Even with good hospital care up to 15% of patients will die, particularly if they are elderly, smokers or have other lung disease.

See also Bronchitis, Chronic; Emphysema; Pneumonia

Leigh Disease
(Subacute Necrotising Encephalomyelopathy)

DESCRIPTION: Rare disease of brain metabolism that affects children between 6 months and 6 years of age.

CAUSE: An inherited inability of the body to deal with specific waste products in the brain, that slowly build up until the brain becomes inflamed and symptoms occur.

SYMPTOMS: Child appears normal until s/he suddenly starts vomiting, losing weight, fitting, becomes mentally unstable, blind and then dies. This can occur in a matter of weeks, or may progress slowly over several very distressing months.

INVESTIGATIONS: Blood tests show abnormal levels of waste products.

TREATMENT: No treatment available.

PROGNOSIS: Invariably fatal.

Leiomyoma

DESCRIPTION: Benign, painful skin tumours that usually occur on the arms and legs.

CAUSE: Unknown. Overgrowth of tiny muscles in the skin.

SYMPTOMS: Groups of multiple, small, red-brown, painful lumps (nodules) under the skin.

INVESTIGATIONS: Diagnosed by biopsy.

TREATMENT: Surgical removal.

PROGNOSIS: Cured by surgery, persist life long otherwise.

Leischmaniasis

See Cutaneous Leischmaniasis; Kala-Azar; Mucocutaneous Leischmaniasis

Lennox-Gastaut Syndrome

DESCRIPTION: Very severe form of epilepsy.

CAUSE: Unknown.

SYMPTOMS: Multiple variable types of seizures, mental retardation, sudden drop attacks, and intractable epilepsy.

INVESTIGATIONS: Abnormal EEG (electroencephalogram — measures electrical activity in brain).

TREATMENT: Combinations of potent anti-epilepsy drugs. Brain surgery may be performed in resistant cases

COMPLICATIONS: Self injury or death from persistent fitting possible.

PROGNOSIS: No cure. Control of seizures usually very difficult.

See also Epilepsy

Lentigo

DESCRIPTION: Skin pigmentation condition that starts in childhood and affects mainly Caucasians.

CAUSE: Inherited tendency aggravated by sun exposure.

SYMPTOMS: Small, permanent, pigmented spot on the skin.

INVESTIGATIONS: Rarely it is necessary to biopsy a spot to confirm the diagnosis.

TREATMENT: None necessary. Plastic surgery for disfiguring spots.

PROGNOSIS: Spots are permanent.

Lentigo Maligna

See Hutchison's Melanotic Freckle

Leopard Syndrome

DESCRIPTION: Congenital heart and skin pigmentation disorder.

CAUSE: Inherited and passes through families from one generation to the next.

SYMPTOMS: Multiple brown spots on the skin, excessive skin pigmentation, narrowing of the valve in the artery leading from the heart to the lungs (pulmonary valve), enlarged heart and other organs, and sometimes deafness.

INVESTIGATIONS: Abnormal ECG (cardiograph) and echocardiogram (ultrasound scan of heart).

TREATMENT: Heart valve surgery.

COMPLICATIONS: Heart failure and attacks may occur.

PROGNOSIS: No cure, but controlled reasonably by surgery.

Leprosy
(Hansen's Disease)

DESCRIPTION: Very slowly progressive bacterial infection that damages the skin and nerves (neuropathy).

CAUSE: Caused by the bacterium *Mycobacterium leprae*, which is spread from one person to another by prolonged close contact, most commonly in childhood.

SYMPTOMS: Pale, thick patches of skin on the hands and feet are the first sign, followed by slowly enlarging nodules. The nerves supplying the affected areas of skin become involved and sensation is lost. The cooler parts of the body, furthest from the heart, are affected first. As the disease progresses, a pins and needles sensation may be felt, ulcers form, and bones in the fingers and toes begin to disintegrate. There is rarely any pain.

INVESTIGATIONS: Diagnosis can be confirmed by microscopic examination of a skin biopsy.

TREATMENT: A number of antileprotic drugs are available that will slowly cure leprosy over several years. Any existing deformities must be treated with plastic surgery.

COMPLICATIONS: Damage and deformity is due to unintentional burns and injuries to totally numb tissue. In severe cases, fingers and toes do fall off, but this is very rare.

PROGNOSIS: With good management, cure is possible and patients can live normally in the community. Untreated, the disease progresses to death over 10 to 20 years.

Leptospirosis

DESCRIPTION: A bacterial infection of the liver and other organs.

CAUSE: The bacteria are caught from infected cattle and pigs by abattoir workers, veterinarians and farmers. In third-world countries, dogs and rats may also be carriers. The bacteria enter through minor abrasions or by being swallowed. The incubation period varies from three days to three weeks.

SYMPTOMS: A sudden high fever, headache, stomach pain, muscle aches and inflamed eyes. After a couple of days, these symptoms disappear, and the second stage of the infection commences which lasts for one to four weeks, and the patient complains of swollen lymph nodes, a generalised rash, eye pain, and in severe cases yellowing of the skin (jaundice).

INVESTIGATIONS: Diagnosis confirmed by a specific blood test.

TREATMENT: Antibiotics such as penicillin are prescribed, but sometimes they have remarkably little effect. Careful nursing is important. The disease can usually be prevented by taking a doxycycline antibiotic tablet once a week.

COMPLICATIONS: The second stage may cause permanent liver damage and Weil Syndrome (see separate entry).

PROGNOSIS: Usually cured by correct treatment, but if jaundice develops, the death rate may be as high as 10%.

See also Weil Syndrome

Leriche Syndrome

DESCRIPTION: Reduced blood supply to the legs and genitals.

CAUSE: Patients with high cholesterol levels may develop arteriosclerosis (hardening of the arteries) at the point where the aorta (main artery down back of body) divides at the back of the belly to supply the blood to each leg. This causes narrowing of the aorta and leg arteries, and symptoms due to an inadequate blood supply beyond this point.

SYMPTOMS: Pain in the legs when walking, impotence and cold feet.

INVESTIGATIONS: A characteristic noise can be heard through a stethoscope as blood gurgles through the narrowed section of the aorta. Diagnosis can be confirmed by doppler flow studies (a type of ultrasound) or X-rays of the aorta.

TREATMENT: Surgically cleaning out the artery (thromboendarterectomy), or bypassing the blockage with a synthetic graft (flexible plastic tube).

COMPLICATIONS: Fragments of hard plaque can break off from the artery wall and travel down to small arteries in the feet, blocking them to cause gangrene of toes.

PROGNOSIS: The postoperative outcome is usually very good.

See also Arteriosclerosis

Lesbian
See Homosexuality

Leschke Syndrome

DESCRIPTION: Rare form of diabetes mellitus.

CAUSE: Unknown.

SYMPTOMS: Brown pigment spots on skin, constant tiredness and diabetes mellitus.

INVESTIGATIONS: High blood and urine sugar levels.

TREATMENT: As for diabetes.

PROGNOSIS: Generally more difficult to control than normal diabetes.

See also Diabetes Mellitus

Lesch-Nyhan Syndrome

DESCRIPTION: Rare error of metabolism involving uric acid, which is produced by the breakdown of protein in the diet.

CAUSE: X-linked inherited genetic disorder which passes through the female line but only affects males.

SYMPTOMS: Mental deficiency, severe gout, self-mutilation, and abnormal uncontrolled writhing movements of arms and legs.

INVESTIGATIONS: Blood and urine tests show very high levels of uric acid.
TREATMENT: Medications to remove uric acid and treatment of the other symptoms.
COMPLICATIONS: Severe arthritis.
PROGNOSIS: No cure and control poor.
See also Gout

Letterer-Siwe Disease

DESCRIPTION: One of a number of rare diseases grouped together as Langerhans cell histiocytosis. A lung diseases in which normal tissue is replaced by abnormal fibrous tissue.
CAUSE: Unknown. Occurs in infants under two years of age.
SYMPTOMS: Cause a fever, muscle wasting, a raised itchy rash, enlarged lymph nodes in the neck, armpit and groin, and enlargement of the liver and spleen. There are three stages of the disease, depending on its severity.
INVESTIGATIONS: Diagnosed by X-rays, CT scans and blood tests.
TREATMENT: Treatment involves potent chemotherapy drugs and radiotherapy.
COMPLICATIONS: May spread to bone.
PROGNOSIS: The outcome is very good in stage one of the disease, but worsens in the other two stages, with a 70% mortality rate in stage three.
See also Hand-Schuller-Christian disease; Histiocytosis X

Leucopenia, Malignant
See Agranulocytosis

Leukaemia

DESCRIPTION: Cancer of the white blood cells. Primitive white blood cells are formed in the bone marrow then gradually change into many specialised different types of cell, and so there are many types of leukaemia. At the simplest level, white blood cells are divided into two groups called lymphocytes and myelocytes. Cancer in these can cause lymphatic (or lymphocytic) leukaemia and myeloid leukaemia. There are two other large divisions in leukaemia — the rapidly developing forms (acute leukaemias), and the slowly developing forms (chronic leukaemias). Combining these there are four possible combinations — acute lymphatic, acute myeloid, chronic lymphatic and chronic myeloid leukaemia. These all have separate entries in this book. There are many rarer types of leukaemia known (eg. hairy cell leukaemia, T cell leukaemia).
See also Leukaemia, Acute Lymphatic; Leukaemia, Acute Myeloid; Leukaemia, Chronic Lymphatic; Leukaemia, Chronic Myeloid; Leukaemia, Hairy Cell

Leukaemia, Acute Lymphatic
(Acute Lymphocytic Leukaemia)

DESCRIPTION: Cancer of one type of white blood cell.

CAUSE: Unknown. The most common form of leukaemia in childhood which usually starts between three and seven years, but only 33 in every one million children will develop any form of leukaemia. 20% of this type occurs in adults.

SYMPTOMS: Tiredness, recurrent infections, bruising, nose bleeds and bleeding from the gums. Children develop progressively more severe infections, including skin infections, abscesses and pneumonia. Bleeding into joints may cause arthritic pains. The liver, spleen and lymph nodes in the neck, armpit and groin may be enlarged.

INVESTIGATIONS: Diagnosis confirmed by blood tests and taking a biopsy of bone marrow.

TREATMENT: Treatment will continue intermittently or continuously for some years, and a wide range of drugs are used, including cytotoxics and immuno-supressants, all of which have significant side effects. Constant monitoring and testing of the patient is required. Other treatments include blood transfusions, radiotherapy, spinal injections and bone marrow transplants.

COMPLICATIONS: The child may become very ill with multiple serious infections.

PROGNOSIS: Can be cured in 60% of children, and 95% achieve some remission. Adults have slightly poorer results.

See also Leukaemia

Leukaemia, Acute Myeloid

DESCRIPTION: Cancer of one type of white blood cell.

CAUSE: Unknown. Normally a disease of the elderly but may also occur in children and young adults.

SYMPTOMS: Tiredness, recurrent infections, bruising, nose bleeds, bleeding from the gums and joints, and enlargement of the liver, spleen and lymph nodes.

INVESTIGATIONS: Different types of leukaemia differentiated by blood tests and bone marrow biopsy. The marrow biopsy is usually taken from the breast bone or the pelvic bone under local anaesthetic.

TREATMENT: Cytotoxic and immunosupressant drugs are used initially. Blood transfusions and intensive radiotherapy are commonly required. Bone marrow transplants possible in younger patients.

COMPLICATIONS: Serious bleeding into organs and rapidly progressive infection may occur.

PROGNOSIS: 70% of adults can be given remission but fewer than 30% can be cured. If bone marrow transplantation is possible in younger patients, the cure rate rises to 50%.

See also Leukaemia

Leukaemia, Chronic Lymphatic

DESCRIPTION: A very slowly progressive form of white blood cell cancer.

CAUSE: Unknown. Found almost exclusively in the elderly.

SYMPTOMS: Most patients have only vague symptoms of tiredness or enlarged lymph nodes. The liver and spleen may enlarge, and in severe cases bleeding from nose and gums and into the skin may occur.

INVESTIGATIONS: The diagnosis is frequently made after a routine blood test for another reason.

TREATMENT: Because of its slow progress many patients are given no treatment. If it becomes more active, steroid and cytotoxic drugs are given. Severe anaemia or excessive bleeding may require an operation to remove the spleen.

COMPLICATIONS: About 10% progress at a faster rate.

PROGNOSIS: The disease is slowly but relentlessly progressive, with an average survival time of eight years. Because the patients are elderly, they frequently succumb to other diseases before the leukaemia.

See also Leukaemia

Leukaemia, Chronic Myeloid

DESCRIPTION: A slowly progressive form of white blood cell cancer.

CAUSE: Unknown. A disorder of middle-aged to elderly people.

SYMPTOMS: Patients complain of an intermittent fever, tiredness, excessive sweating and fullness in the abdomen. The spleen may also be enlarged.

INVESTIGATIONS: Often discovered incidentally on a routine blood test. The diagnosis is confirmed by further blood tests and bone marrow biopsy.

TREATMENT: No great urgency in treatment until blood test results reach certain levels, then cytotoxic or immunosuppressive drugs are given. Medication does not cure the disease, but slows its progress and makes the patient feel better. Another form of treatment is bone marrow transplantation but finding a compatible donor is difficult.

PROGNOSIS: Once blood tests deteriorate to the point where treatment is necessary, on drug therapy alone the average survival time is four years. If a donor can be found and marrow can be transplanted, 60% of patients can be cured.

See also Leukaemia

Leukaemia, Hairy Cell

DESCRIPTION: A rare progressive chronic leukaemia.

CAUSE: Unknown. Usually occurs in males over 40 years of age.

SYMPTOMS: Tiredness, enlarged lymph nodes and spleen and bleeding into the skin.

INVESTIGATIONS: Diagnosed by blood tests and bone marrow biopsy.

TREATMENT: The drug cladribine has been remarkably successful in inducing remissions. Splenectomy is the main form of treatment.

COMPLICATIONS: Serious infections due to destruction of white blood cells.

PROGNOSIS: 60% of patients survive for four years. Cure uncommon.

See also Leukaemia

Libido, Reduced

DESCRIPTION: Reduced sexual desire in both men and women.

CAUSE: Menopause (both male and female), diabetes, Parkinson's disease, thyroid disease, pituitary gland disorders, hormone imbalances, stress, anxiety and depression, excess alcohol, illegal drug abuse, prescribed medications (eg. those used to treat high blood pressure), emotional or psychiatric disorders, and old age.

SYMPTOMS: Lack of desire for sex when such desire would reasonably be expected.

INVESTIGATIONS: Any possible cause must be excluded by appropriate investigation.

TREATMENT: Specific cause needs to be treated. Sex hormone therapy may be appropriate, particularly after the menopause.

PROGNOSIS: Depends on cause.

See also Frigidity and other diseases listed under Sex Problems

Lice

See Crabs; Head Lice

Lichen Aureus

See Capillaritis

Lichen Axillaris

See Fox-Fordyce Disease

Lichen Planus

DESCRIPTION: An uncommon skin condition which normally starts in the twenties or thirties.

CAUSE: May start where the skin has been injured, may be a chronic viral infection of the skin, or may be triggered by drugs, but the actual cause is unknown.

SYMPTOMS: Small, shiny, flat topped skin growths that may enlarge and join together to form a plaque. More common in skin creases such as the inside of the wrists and elbows, but can occur anywhere on the body, including the insides of the mouth, nose, ears, vagina and anus.

INVESTIGATIONS: Diagnosed by skin biopsy.

TREATMENT: Mild cases are often not treated, but more serious cases treated with steroid creams and occlusive plastic dressings. Further treatments include steroid tablets or injections under a plaque, ultraviolet light, and potent medications such as retinoic acid and dapsone.

COMPLICATIONS: Some pigmentation of the skin may remain after the rash has cleared.

PROGNOSIS: Long term course is very variable. Some patients recover in a few months, while others may suffer for years, but eventually complete recovery does occur.

See also Lichen Sclerosis; Lichen Simplex

Lichen Sclerosis
(Lichen Sclerosis et Atrophicus)

DESCRIPTION: Scarring of the tissue on one the genitals. Affects women more than men.

CAUSE: Unknown, but infection or injury to the genitals may be a factor.

SYMPTOMS: A thickened area of skin on one side of the penis which causes a sideways curve to the penis that may be painful during an erection. In women, a shiny white itchy area with a red margin appears on the vulva.

INVESTIGATIONS: Biopsy of affected skin sometimes necessary to make diagnosis.

TREATMENT: Minor surgery to stretch the scarred penis tissue. Steroid creams for itch.

COMPLICATIONS: Painful or difficult sexual intercourse. May occur in skin on other parts of the body.

PROGNOSIS: No cure. Treatment unsatisfactory.

See also Lichen Planus; Lichen Simplex

Lichen Simplex
(Circumscribed Neurodermatitis; Lichen Simplex Chronicus)

DESCRIPTION: A type of persistent dermatitis.

CAUSE: Thought to be a form of nerve rash, and patients who are anxious, tense, nervous or aggressive are more likely to develop it. In some cases, mild stimulants such as tea or coffee may aggravate the condition.

SYMPTOMS: Intensely itchy, dry, scaling, thick plaques on the skin. May appear anywhere, but usually occur in areas which are easy to scratch, such as the wrist, neck, thigh and groin.

INVESTIGATIONS: A skin biopsy may help with the diagnosis. Blood tests are normal.

TREATMENT: Stopping tea and coffee may dramatically improve the itch. It is important to avoid any further damage to the skin from scratching by bandages or applying a plaster. Steroid creams and injections into the affected areas of skin may be beneficial. Avoiding stressful situations is helpful, but often not practical.

COMPLICATIONS: Permanent skin scarring from scratching.

PROGNOSIS: If the patient can stop scratching the skin, the disease will cure itself.

See also Eczema; Lichen Planus; Lichen Sclerosis

Lichen Urticatus
See Prurigo

Liddle Syndrome

DESCRIPTION: Rare kidney disease in which sodium is retained in the body and potassium lost.

CAUSE: Inherited.

SYMPTOMS: Hypoaldosteronism (see separate entry) and high blood pressure.

INVESTIGATIONS: Blood tests show significant abnormalities of body chemistry.
TREATMENT: Controlled by the drug triamterene.
PROGNOSIS: No cure, but control reasonable.
See also Hypoaldosteronism

Ligament or Tendon Rupture

DESCRIPTION: Complete or partial rupture of a ligament (eg. at sides of ankle) or tendon (eg. Achilles tendon at back of ankle). A ligament joins one bone to another, while a tendon joins a muscle to a bone.
CAUSE: Excessive force being applied to the tendon or ligament.
SYMPTOMS: Severe pain and loss of function of the joint or muscle, followed by swelling and bruising.
INVESTIGATIONS: X-rays may be taken to exclude fracture. Ultrasound scan can show rupture.
TREATMENT: Depends on site and severity. Joint may be immobilised in a cast for weeks or months, or the rupture may be surgically repaired.
COMPLICATIONS: Ligament may be slack after healing allowing excessive movement in joint, increased risk of further damage, and premature arthritis.
PROGNOSIS: Usually very good results from treatment.
See also Sprain

Lightwood Syndrome
(Idiopathic Renal Acidosis)

DESCRIPTION: Rare syndrome of kidney damage and deterioration in children.
CAUSE: Unknown.
SYMPTOMS: Weight loss, vomiting, constipation.
INVESTIGATIONS: Diagnosed by blood tests and kidney biopsy.
TREATMENT: Kidney transplant may be possible.
PROGNOSIS: Progresses inevitably unless successful transplant possible.

L'Illusion de Sosies
See Capgras Syndrome

Limb Girdle Dystrophy
See Erb's Muscular Dystrophy

Limb Pain Syndrome
See Growing Pains

Lip Cancer
See Mouth Cancer; Squamous Cell Carcinoma of the Skin

Lipoma
(Fat Cyst)
DESCRIPTION: A discrete collection of fat under the skin.
CAUSE: Often appear for no apparent reason, but may be due to injury to the area months before lump noticed.
SYMPTOMS: Soft, movable lump felt under the skin. May be very small or several centimetres in diameter.
INVESTIGATIONS: Usually none necessary, but if there is doubt, diagnosed by excision.
TREATMENT: Surgical excision if cosmetically unacceptable or worrying.
COMPLICATIONS: Pressure on overlying skin rarely causes irritation and an ulcer.
PROGNOSIS: Not serious. Excellent result from treatment.

Lip-Pit Syndrome
DESCRIPTION: Inherited facial deformity.
CAUSE: Dominant inheritance with 50% of siblings and offspring affected.
SYMPTOMS: Small pits on both sides of lower lip, cleft palate and/or cleft lip.
INVESTIGATIONS: None necessary.
TREATMENT: Plastic surgical correction.
PROGNOSIS: Good result from surgery.
See also Cleft Lip and Palate

Lissencephaly Syndrome
DESCRIPTION: Rare brain and developmental disorder.
CAUSE: Inherited, but only if both parents are carriers of a defective gene.
SYMPTOMS: Epileptic seizures, poor muscle tone, jaundice, cataracts in the eye, and wrinkled forehead skin.
INVESTIGATIONS: None diagnostic.
TREATMENT: None available. Seizures difficult to control with normal epilepsy medication.
PROGNOSIS: Early death normal.

Listeriosis
DESCRIPTION: A rare form of meningitis (infection of the membranes surrounding the brain) in newborn babies.
CAUSE: Listeria monocytogenes is the bacteria responsible. It can be caught from contaminated food, particularly soft cheeses (eg. brie) and salads.
SYMPTOMS: In adults and children, the bacteria usually causes no symptoms and is harmless, but if a pregnant woman is infected, the bacteria may spread through her bloodstream to the placenta and foetus, where it can cause widespread infection.
INVESTIGATIONS: Blood cultures are diagnostic.
TREATMENT: Antibiotics can be used in newborn infants, but they are often not successful. Treatment is more successful if started during pregnancy, but the infection is rarely detected before the infant is born.

COMPLICATIONS: Often results in a miscarriage, or death of the foetus and a stillbirth.

PROGNOSIS: Infants that survive birth suffer from a septicaemia (blood infection) that soon contracts to a meningitis that is frequently fatal.

See also Meningitis

Liver Abscess
(Hepatic Abscess)

DESCRIPTION: A collection of pus (abscess) within the liver caused by a bacterial or rarely a fungal infection.

CAUSE: May be due to the spread of bacteria from other organs to the liver through the bloodstream or may spread through the abdomen to the liver from other infections within the belly such as appendicitis, salpingitis (infected fallopian tubes — see separate entry) or an infected gall bladder.

SYMPTOMS: Fever, pain and tenderness in the upper abdomen, loss of appetite, nausea, vomiting and weight loss may all occur.

INVESTIGATIONS: Abscess may be seen by ultrasound or CT scan.

TREATMENT: Surgical drainage of the abscess and appropriate antibiotics.

COMPLICATIONS: Multiple abscesses may develop, and abscesses may burst into the abdominal cavity to cause peritonitis (see separate entry).

PROGNOSIS: Serious, with up to 15% mortality. Those who survive may have long term problems with liver function.

See also Abscess

Liver Cancer
(Hepatic Carcinoma; Hepatoma)

DESCRIPTION: A cancer that starts in the liver and has not spread to the liver from some other organ.

CAUSE: Occur most commonly in patients who have long-standing alcoholic cirrhosis, hepatitis B or C, liver parasites and malnutrition. Far more common in developing countries.

SYMPTOMS: Often no symptoms until the cancer is well advanced, at which point the liver begins to fail and the patient becomes jaundiced (yellow), nauseated, very weak, loses weight and is unable to eat.

INVESTIGATIONS: Diagnosis confirmed by blood tests, liver biopsy, ultrasound and CT scans.

TREATMENT: No surgical or medical treatment available in most cases, as almost invariably the cancer has spread too far by the time it is diagnosed.

COMPLICATIONS: At a late stage of the disease the abdomen may become swollen with fluid.

PROGNOSIS: Unfortunately death within a short time of diagnosis is the usual result.

See also Cirrhosis; Hepatitis B; Hepatitis C

Liver Disease

See Budd-Chiari Syndrome; Cirrhosis; Crigler-Najjar Syndrome; Gallstones; Gilbert Syndrome; Hepatitis A, B, C, D, E and G; Hydatid Cyst; Liver Abscess; Liver Cancer; Wilson's Disease; Yellow Fever

Locked-In Syndrome

DESCRIPTION: Horrendous complication of certain types of brain damage.

CAUSE: Stroke, tumour or injury to particular parts of the brain. May also occur in late stage multiple sclerosis.

SYMPTOMS: Total paralysis of limbs and facial nerves, but normal consciousness. Able to communicate only by eye movements.

INVESTIGATIONS: CT and MRI scans of brain show damage.

TREATMENT: None available.

COMPLICATIONS: Pneumonia from lack of movement and poor function of muscles of breathing.

PROGNOSIS: Poor.

Lockjaw

See Tetanus

Loeffler Syndrome
(PIE Syndrome)

DESCRIPTION: A form of allergy reaction affecting the lungs.

CAUSE: Underlying cause may be a reaction to drugs, an allergy reaction to a huge variety of substances, visceral larva migrans (see separate entry) and other worm infestations. Asthmatics are more prone to this syndrome.

SYMPTOMS: The main characteristic is technically called pulmonary infiltrates with eosinophilia, which gives the syndrome its alternative acronym name of PIE syndrome. In plain English this means that the lungs have too many allergy response cells, which results in a wheeze, cough and fever.

INVESTIGATIONS: Lung biopsy is abnormal, and blood tests show very high levels of eosinophils (allergy response cells).

TREATMENT: Treat underlying cause if possible, otherwise treatment is same as asthma.

COMPLICATIONS: Allergy reactions in other organs and areas of the body.

PROGNOSIS: Depends on cause, but usually good.

See also Asthma

Löfgren Syndrome

DESCRIPTION: Acute form of sarcoidosis (see separate entry).

CAUSE: Complication of acute stage of sarcoidosis that tends to occur in women of Scandinavian or Irish heritage.

SYMPTOMS: Erythema nodosum (skin condition — see separate entry), and enlarged lymph nodes in the chest seen on chest X-ray, in a patient with sarcoidosis.

INVESTIGATIONS: Chest X-ray abnormal and biopsy of affected lymph nodes diagnostic.

TREATMENT: Anti-inflammatory medications control leg and skin symptoms. Sarcoidosis also treated.

COMPLICATIONS: Skin ulcers.

PROGNOSIS: 80% chance of spontaneous recovery.

See also Erythema Nodosum; Heerfordt Syndrome; Sarcoidosis

Long QT Syndrome

DESCRIPTION: Uncommon heart condition.

CAUSE: May occur for no known reason, due to body chemistry abnormalities, follow a heart attack or angina, or may be a side effect of some heart and psychiatric medications.

SYMPTOMS: One or more heart beats are missed.

INVESTIGATIONS: Diagnosed by an electrocardiograph (ECG). Each point on the graph produced by an ECG is labelled with a letter. In this condition there is a long gap between the Q and T points on the graph.

TREATMENT: Depends on cause but may include adding or removing medications, or implanting an artificial pacemaker.

COMPLICATIONS: Very rarely, sudden death may occur.

PROGNOSIS: Depends on cause, but usually a good response to treatment.

See also other conditions listed under Arrhythmia

Long Sighted
(Hyperopia)

DESCRIPTION: Defect in visual acuity.

CAUSE: Usually present from birth. The eyeball is too short, and close objects cannot be focused precisely on the retina (light sensitive cells) at the back of the eye.

SYMPTOMS: Distant objects can be seen clearly, while close objects are blurred.

INVESTIGATIONS: Diagnosed by refractive tests using a number of different lenses until near objects can be seen as clearly as possible.

TREATMENT: Spectacles worn when reading or looking at close objects.

PROGNOSIS: Children may grow out of the problem at puberty, otherwise lifelong problem.

See also Astigmatism; Presbyopia; Short Sighted

Loose Anagen Syndrome

DESCRIPTION: Hair loss in a child.

CAUSE: Unknown.

SYMPTOMS: Child with generalised loss of scalp hair, loose wispy hair and fair colour, but normal hair growth.

INVESTIGATIONS: Hair pulls easily from scalp without pain.

TREATMENT: Improves with age and gentle hair care.

COMPLICATIONS: Bald patches on scalp.
PROGNOSIS: Good.
See also Alopecia Areata; Telogen Effluvium

Lordosis

DESCRIPTION: Abnormal inward curvature of the back, which, when looked at from the side, normally curves in at the neck, out over the back of the chest, in at the small of the back, and out again between the buttocks.

CAUSE: Often associated with poor posture, slack muscles and obesity. It may be present to compensate for kyphosis (outward curvature) of the vertebrae at the back of the chest, or an abnormal hip.

SYMPTOMS: Excessive inward curvature of the lumbar vertebrae in the small of the back. It is the opposite of kyphosis (see separate entry).

INVESTIGATIONS: X-rays of the spine demonstrate the abnormality.

TREATMENT: No treatment is required unless pain and discomfort are present, when weight loss, exercise and physiotherapy are appropriate.

COMPLICATIONS: None significant.

PROGNOSIS: Good.

See also Kyphosis; Scoliosis

Lou Gehrig Disease

See Amyotrophic Lateral Sclerosis

Louis-Bar Syndrome

DESCRIPTION: Rare form of rapidly progressive brain deterioration.

CAUSE: Unknown. Due to degeneration of the cerebellum (lower back portion of brain) and spinal cord.

SYMPTOMS: Dilated capillaries on the whites of the eyes, the face and areas of skin flexion (eg. arm pit, behind knee), mental retardation, recurrent infections of lungs and ears, and poor coordination that steadily worsens. Late symptoms include twitching movements of the eyes and abnormal writhing movements of the arms and legs.

INVESTIGATIONS: Numerous blood tests are abnormal, particularly there are very low immunoglobulin levels.

TREATMENT: None available.

COMPLICATIONS: Above average incidence of cancer.

PROGNOSIS: Death in teenage years usual.

Low Blood Pressure

See Hypotension; Postural Hypotension

Lowe Syndrome

DESCRIPTION: Rare body chemistry disorder.

CAUSE: Inherited condition passed to males only via the female side of the family.

Lowe Syndrome

SYMPTOMS: Boys with mental retardation, eye cataracts, clouding of the cornea (outer surface of eye), abnormal skin folds beside the eyes, and abnormal eye socket shape. Some patients have rickets and Fanconi syndrome (see separate entries).

INVESTIGATIONS: Abnormal levels of amino acids (protein breakdown products) found in urine.

TREATMENT: None available.

PROGNOSIS: No cure, but reasonable life span.

Lown-Ganong-Levine Syndrome

DESCRIPTION: Abnormality of heart rhythm.

CAUSE: The ventricles (main chambers of heart) contract too early in a cycle of heart contraction because of an abnormal nerve pathway from the heart pacemaker to the ventricles.

SYMPTOMS: Irregular heart rate and palpitations.

INVESTIGATIONS: The ECG (electrocardiograph) is diagnostically abnormal.

TREATMENT: Attacks can be stopped by stimulation of nerves supplying the heart (vagus nerve) by swallowing, holding the breath or other manoeuvres. Numerous medications (eg. procainamide, quinidine, verapamil, beta-blockers) can be taken regularly to prevent attacks. In persistent cases, DC cardioversion (electric shock to the heart) can be given.

PROGNOSIS: Usually can be controlled, but recurs if treatment ceased.

See also Paroxysmal Atrial Tachycardia and other conditions listed under Arrhythmia

Lumbago

DESCRIPTION: Form of back and leg pain. Old-fashioned term that describes a collection of symptoms rather than a specific disease.

CAUSE: The pinching of a nerve as it leaves the spinal cord in the lower back due to a ligamentous strain, disc injury, arthritis or a misplaced vertebra. Often triggered by lifting, coughing or straining.

SYMPTOMS: Sudden, severe pain in the lower back triggered by any movement in the back that spreads to the buttocks, leg or groin.

INVESTIGATIONS: X-ray of the spine, and in recurrent cases a CT scan.

TREATMENT: Bed rest, a corset, physiotherapy, pain killers and anti-inflammatory drugs.

PROGNOSIS: Depends on cause, but usually settles with appropriate treatment.

See also Sciatica

Lung Abscess
(Pulmonary Abscess)

DESCRIPTION: Localised collection of pus within the lung.

CAUSE: Complication of pneumonia or a wound that penetrates into the lung.

SYMPTOMS: Chest pain, shortness of breath, fever, a cough and collapse.

INVESTIGATIONS: Chest X-ray or CT scan shows presence and location of abscess.

TREATMENT: Surgery to drain abscess and potent antibiotics.

COMPLICATIONS: Permanent scarring of lungs, uncontrolled spread of infection and rarely death.

PROGNOSIS: Recovery often stormy, but treatment usually successful.

See also Abscess; Pneumonia

Lung Cancer
(Bronchial Carcinoma; Bronchogenic Carcinoma)

DESCRIPTION: Any of several different types of cancer affecting lung tissue. The incidence is steadily increasing in developed countries, particularly in women, and it is the most common form of internal cancer.

CAUSE: Smoking causes 90% of all lung cancers, but this effect of smoking is usually delayed until the patient is 55 or older. Other causes of lung cancer include asbestos dust, irradiation and chrome dust.

Types of lung cancer vary depending on the type of cell affected. The common types are:–

Squamous cell carcinomas — a relatively common form, symptoms usually occur early, it doubles in size every three months on average, and spreads early to lymph nodes.

Oat cell (small cell) carcinomas — far more serious, double in size every month on average, spread rapidly to other parts of the body, and are almost impossible to cure.

Adenocarcinomas and large cell carcinomas — develop at the edge of the lung, have few symptoms, are not easily detected, double in size every three to six months, but spread early to distant parts of the body.

Secondary cancers — spread of cancer from other parts of the body to the lungs is also common, but these cancers are not caused by smoking, and their treatment involves the treatment of the original cancer as well as that in the lung.

Many rarer types of lung cancer are known.

SYMPTOMS: The early warning signs are weight loss, a persistent cough, a change in the normal type of cough, coughing blood and worsening breathlessness. Later symptoms include loss of appetite, chest pain, hoarseness and enlarged tender lymph nodes in the armpit. One quarter of patients have no symptoms when the diagnosis is made, often by a routine chest X-ray. Smokers should consider having a routine chest X-ray every few years.

INVESTIGATIONS: Diagnosed by chest X-rays, CT scans and sputum examination. Occasionally a biopsy of the tumour is necessary.

TREATMENT: Prevention is always better than cure, and that means stop smoking. Even in heavy smokers, after five years of non-smoking, the risk of developing lung cancer will return to normal. Treatment involves major surgery, irradiation, and potent drugs, depending on the type of cancer present. Radiation may be used to shrink the original tumour, but is primarily used to treat cancers that have spread to other organs.

COMPLICATIONS: Spread of the cancer to other organs, most commonly to bone and the brain, and blockage of the veins draining the head and arms (superior vena cava syndrome).

PROGNOSIS: Only 10% of all patients with lung cancer survive more than five years from diagnosis. Those with small cell (oat cell) carcinoma usually die within a year, those with squamous cell carcinoma tend to live a little longer than average.

See also Asbestosis; Mesothelioma; Pancoast Syndrome; Superior Vena Cava Syndrome

Lung Clot
See Pulmonary Embolism

Lung Diseases
See Asbestosis; Asthma; Bronchiolitis; Bronchitis, Acute; Bronchitis, Chronic; Emphysema; Lung Cancer; Melioidosis; Mesothelioma; Mendelson Syndrome; Pleural Effusion; Pleurisy; Pneumonia; Pneumothorax; Pulmonary Embolism; Sarcoidosis; Tuberculosis etc.

'Lupus'
See Systemic Lupus Erythematosus

Lupus Erythematosus
See Discoid Lupus Erythematosus; Systemic Lupus Erythematosus

Luteal Cyst
See Ovarian Cyst

Lyell Syndrome
See Scalded Skin Syndrome

Lyme Disease
DESCRIPTION: Relatively common bacterial blood infection that occurs in the northeast United States.

CAUSE: The bacterium Borrelia burgdorferi which is spread by the bite of the tic Ixodes from infected mice or deer to humans. The tic may lie dormant for up to a year before passing on the infection with a bite.

SYMPTOMS: The disease has three stages:–

— in stage one the patient has a flat or slightly raised red patchy rash, fever, muscle aches and headache.

— stage two comes two to four weeks later with a stiff neck, severe headache, meningitis (inflammation of the membrane around the brain) and possibly Bell's palsy (see separate entry).

— in stage three, which may come three to twelve months later, the patient has muscle pains, and most seriously a long lasting severe form of arthritis that may move from joint to joint.

INVESTIGATIONS: Diagnosis confirmed by specific blood tests.

TREATMENT: Prolonged and repeated courses of antibiotics.

COMPLICATIONS: Persistent crippling arthritis.

PROGNOSIS: Long term, one third of patients may suffer from continuing muscle and joint pains, while a smaller percentage have after effects of the meningitis.

See also Meningitis

Lymphadenitis
See Adenitis

Lymphatic Leukaemia
See Leukaemia, Acute Lymphatic; Leukaemia, Chronic Lymphatic

Lymph Node Inflammation
See Adenitis

Lymphocytic Leukaemia
See Leukaemia, Acute Lymphatic; Leukaemia, Chronic Lymphatic

Lymphoedema

DESCRIPTION: Severe swelling of a limb due to accumulation of lymph.

CAUSE: Lymph is a waste products of all cells that returns to the circulation through a complex network of fine tubes that eventually drain into a major vein near the heart. The lymph ducts pass through the lymph nodes that are concentrated in the arm pit, groin and neck, and act to remove any bacteria or abnormal cells. Lymphoedema is a common complication of surgery when lymph channels are disrupted by the removal of lymph nodes in the arm pit or groin because of breast or other cancers. The lymphatic fluid is unable to return to the circulation normally and accumulates in the limb.

SYMPTOMS: The limb becomes very swollen, tense and sore. In severe cases the arm is rock hard and three times its normal size.

INVESTIGATIONS: None normally necessary.

TREATMENT: Very difficult problem to treat. Elevation, exercises, pressure bandages and a plastic sleeve that envelopes the arm and is rhythmically inflated by a machine, can be tried.

COMPLICATIONS: Ulceration and infection of the skin and deeper tissues in the affected limb. Stewart-Treves syndrome (see separate entry).

PROGNOSIS: Severity varies dramatically from one patient to another, with only a partial relationship to the severity of the surgery. Often persists for many years before gradually subsiding as new lymph channels are formed.

See also Breast Cancer; Milroy's Disease; Stewart-Treves Syndrome

Lymphoepithelial Condition, Benign
See Mikulicz Disease

Lymphogranuloma Venereum

DESCRIPTION: Sexually transmitted disease that is rare in developed countries but common in Africa and Asia.

CAUSE: Caused by the Chlamydia organism which is a bacteria-like germ that lives inside cells and destroys them. The incubation period after sexual contact is one to three weeks.

SYMPTOMS: A sore develops on the penis or vulva, then the lymph nodes in the groin become infected, swollen, soften and suppurate (drain pus) onto the skin. The infection may spread to cause joint, skin, brain and eye infections. If anal intercourse has occurred, sores and pus discharging lymph nodes may form in and around the anus. The initial sore and pus discharging lymph nodes are not painful, and only if the disease spreads does a fever develop.

INVESTIGATIONS: Diagnosed by special skin and blood tests.

TREATMENT: Antibiotic such as tetracyclines. Surgical procedures to drain pus from lymph nodes may be necessary.

COMPLICATIONS: If left untreated disfiguring scarring will occur in the groin at the site of the infected lymph nodes, and the genitals may become permanently swollen. If the infection spreads to other organs, they may be seriously damaged.

PROGNOSIS: The majority of cases are cured by appropriate treatment.

See also other diseases listed under Chlamydial Infections and Venereal Diseases

Lymphoma
See Hodgkin's Disease; Non-Hodgkin's Lymphoma

Lyssavirus Infection
See Rabies

M

Machado-Joseph Syndrome
(Azorean Disease)

DESCRIPTION: Progressive degeneration of the lower part of the brain (cerebellum) and the adjacent spinal cord.

CAUSE: Congenital condition that passes readily from one generation to the next. First discovered in the Azores Islands in the North Atlantic.

SYMPTOMS: Muscle spasticity and rigidity, poor coordination, inability to speak clearly, limb weakness and a fixed facial expression are the common symptoms. Tremor, eye movement paralysis and eye twitching may also occur.

INVESTIGATIONS: Abnormal brain appearance on CT scan.

TREATMENT: Drugs such as levodopa and baclofen help ease rigidity and spasticity.

COMPLICATIONS: Joint damage from muscle spasms.

PROGNOSIS: No cure. Slowly progressive.

Macular Degeneration

DESCRIPTION: A common form of vision deterioration in the elderly.

CAUSE: The macular is the part of the retina at the back of the eye that is most sensitive to light. It degenerates because of a poor blood supply with advancing age, cholesterol build ups in arteries and diabetes.

SYMPTOMS: Gradual loss of central vision while peripheral vision may be normal.

INVESTIGATIONS: Diagnosed by examining the eye through an ophthalmoscope (magnifying light).

TREATMENT: No effective treatment.

PROGNOSIS: Usually very slowly progressive.

See also Drusen

Mad Cow Disease
See Creutzfeldt-Jakob Disease

Madura Foot
See Mycetoma

Majocchis Purpura
See Capillaritis

Malaria

DESCRIPTION: A serious blood parasite infestation that damages liver and red blood cells and is widespread in the tropics.

CAUSE: The single celled parasite *Plasmodium*, of which there are four different types (falciparum, malariae, vivax, ovale) that cause slightly different types of malaria. Spreads from person to person through a bite from the *Anopheles*

Malaria

mosquito. During a bite, the mosquito draws a malaria patient's blood into its belly to be digested, and becomes a carrier to every subsequent person it bites. During a bite a small amount of parasite infested saliva is injected before the blood is drawn up. Found throughout the tropics, but in Indonesia, New Guinea, Thailand, and other south-east Asian and west Pacific nations, a more serious chloroquine resistant form of malaria has developed. The areas of the world affected are shown on the following map—

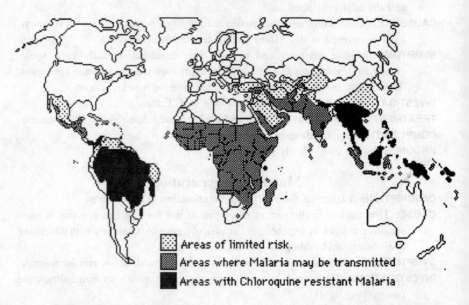

Areas of limited risk.
Areas where Malaria may be transmitted
Areas with Chloroquine resistant Malaria

SYMPTOMS: Attacks of severe fevers, sweats and chills every three to four days, the patient becomes very ill, and red blood cells are destroyed to cause jaundice (yellow skin), headaches and muscle pain. Late symptoms include delirium, convulsions, coma and sometimes death. The pattern of fever attacks and temporary recovery varies from one type of malaria to another. Symptoms develop 8 to 30 days after being bitten by a mosquito, but in some cases may not occur for six months or more.

INVESTIGATIONS: Diagnosis and the type of malaria confirmed by examining the patient's blood under a microscope. Because the parasite goes through cycles of infecting the liver and then the blood, it is sometimes necessary to take several tests before it can be detected.

TREATMENT: Appropriate drugs can slowly cure most cases, but relapses may occur for months or years. No vaccine is yet available, but malaria can be prevented by tablets that are taken either daily (eg. doxycycline) or weekly (eg. chloroquine). Some must be started as much a two weeks before entering a malarial area and continued for up to four weeks after leaving. As an added precaution, use an appropriate insect repellent, and wear long sleeved shirts and slacks or trousers.

COMPLICATIONS: Brain infections, extremely high fevers that may cause brain and other organ damage, and gut infections. **Blackwater fever** is a complication in which large amounts of blood are passed in the urine ('black water') due to the massive breakdown of red blood cells. The patient becomes very anaemic, a deep yellow colour, feverish and desperately ill.

PROGNOSIS: With good treatment, 95% of patients recover, but it kills millions of people in poorer tropical countries every year. With blackwater fever the death rate exceeds 25%.

Male Breast Enlargement
See Gynaecomastia

Male Pattern Baldness
See Baldness

Malignancy
See Cancer

Malignant Astrocytoma
See Astrocytoma; Glioma

Malignant Hypertension
See Hypertension

Malignant Leucopenia
See Agranulocytosis

Mallet Finger

DESCRIPTION: Common injury to a finger resulting in deformity.

CAUSE: Rupture of one of the tendons that straightens (extends) the finger tip from an injury or as a complication of rheumatoid arthritis.

SYMPTOMS: Patient is unable to straighten (extend) the tip of the affected finger, and it droops down.

INVESTIGATIONS: None normally necessary.

TREATMENT: Splinting in the straight position for six weeks or more, or surgery to repair the damaged tendon.

PROGNOSIS: Reasonable results from treatment.

See also Trigger Finger

Mallory-Weis Syndrome

DESCRIPTION: Serious inflammation and damage to the lower end of the oesophagus (gullet).

CAUSE: If a patient vomits forcibly for a prolonged period of time, a tear may occur at the lower end of the oesophagus where it joins the stomach, and massive bleeding occurs from the tear.

SYMPTOMS: Persistent vomiting of fresh blood, sometimes associated with pain behind and below the lower end of the breast bone.

INVESTIGATIONS: Gastroscopy is essential to confirm the diagnosis.

TREATMENT: Medications to stop the vomiting, and gastroscopy, surgery or a balloon device to stop the tear from bleeding.

COMPLICATIONS: Massive blood loss may lead to other organ damage or death.

PROGNOSIS: Most patients recover with good treatment, but there is a significant mortality rate.

See also Reflux Oesophagitis

Malnutrition
See Kwashiorkor; Marasmus

Mammary Carcinoma
See Breast Cancer

Mania

DESCRIPTION: The opposite of depression, but often associated with depression, as patients may swing from one mood extreme to the other (**bipolar personality** or **manic-depressive** disorder). More serious forms of mania include pyromania (the inability to resist the temptation to light fires) and kleptomania (the inability to resist the temptation to steal).

CAUSE: Generally unknown, but attacks may be triggered by stress and anxiety, drug abuse or epilepsy.

SYMPTOMS: Patients change their ideas rapidly, speak quickly on different topics that are not apparently connected, become over-involved in activities, move very quickly to the point where minor accidents are common, require little sleep, are very irritable and lose their temper easily. In severe cases, marked aggression may occur, there may be exceedingly grand ideas about their importance and ability, and rash decisions may be made such as resigning from a job or making inappropriate major purchases. Exhibitionism, excessive sexual desires, pointless travel and attempting to obtain media coverage are other symptoms. The patient may believe that others are persecuting him/her (paranoia), have hallucinations, hear imaginary voices, and feel rejected by society. Episodes usually commence suddenly, and may last from hours to months. They may be preceded or followed by a period of intense depression during which suicide is a risk.

INVESTIGATIONS: None diagnostic.

TREATMENT: One or more antipsychotic medications such as lithium. If the patient is perceived by a doctor to be at risk of suicide or injuring others and refuses to accept treatment, the doctor may, with the cooperation of relatives or another doctor, certify the patient so that the police are empowered to take the patient to a psychiatric hospital for compulsory treatment.

COMPLICATIONS: There is a risk that patients who are manic will injure themselves or others by their actions.

PROGNOSIS: If the patient can be convinced to remain on medication, good control can be obtained. Unfortunately, many patients cannot see why they should take drugs for many months or years, and stop them prematurely which leads to a relapse into the mania or depression.

See also Depression

Manic-Depressive
See Bipolar Affective Disorder; Depression; Mania

Maple Syrup Urine Disease

DESCRIPTION: A metabolic disease that is named after the odour produced by the urine of patients.

CAUSE: Inherited disorder that results in an inability of the body to deal appropriately with certain types of protein in the diet.

SYMPTOMS: Baby with a lack of muscle tone, floppiness and feeding difficulties. If the child survives it will start fitting, have muscle spasms, severe mental retardation and eventually a premature death.

INVESTIGATIONS: Specific blood and urine tests show abnormalities.

TREATMENT: A strict diet that avoids the proteins that cannot be metabolised.

COMPLICATIONS: Often diagnosis is not made until serious organ damage has occurred.

PROGNOSIS: Death within a few weeks of birth is common.

Marasmus

DESCRIPTION: Severe form of malnutrition.

CAUSE: Starvation, with a lack of both protein and carbohydrates in the diet. Some elderly and intellectually handicapped people become malnourished because they are unable to care for themselves adequately.

SYMPTOMS: Wasted muscles, retarded growth, no fat under the skin, dry skin, and patients look older than their years.

INVESTIGATIONS: Blood tests show widespread chemical abnormalities.

TREATMENT: Small amounts of nutritious food frequently over several weeks before returning to a normal diet is essential to prevent an imbalance of chemicals in the blood.

COMPLICATIONS: If weight loss exceeds one third of normal body weight, heart, liver, kidney and other organ damage becomes significant and sudden death may occur. Resistance to infection is reduced, and severe lung and skin infections may also cause death.

PROGNOSIS: Good recovery with appropriate diet, but fatal otherwise.

See also Kwashiorkor

Marburg Virus

DESCRIPTION: An extremely contagious form of viral haemorrhagic fever (viral infection of the blood) that occurs in Africa.

CAUSE: The virus is spread by monkeys and from person to person in conditions of poor hygiene. Outbreaks have occurred throughout central Africa, and in zoo monkey handlers elsewhere in the world. Cases in which the infection has minimal symptoms have occurred, but these patients may pass the infection on to others.

SYMPTOMS: Muscle pains, headache, sore throat, joint pains, diarrhoea, vomiting, red eyes and abnormal bleeding.

INVESTIGATIONS: Blood tests show significant abnormalities.

TREATMENT: No cure or vaccine for prevention, and treatment is restricted to managing the symptoms and nursing care. Patients must be nursed in strict isolation.

COMPLICATIONS: Internal bleeding causes death.

PROGNOSIS: Fatal in about 80% of patients.

See also Ebola Virus; Lassa Fever

March Fracture
(Metatarsal Fracture)

DESCRIPTION: A stress fracture of a forefoot (metatarsal) bone. More significant metatarsal fractures may occur with direct injury.

CAUSE: Prolonged running, jumping or walking, usually on hard surfaces (eg. soldiers on a route march).

SYMPTOMS: Severe pain in the ball of the foot and excruciating pain on attempting to walk.

INVESTIGATIONS: Minimal changes on X-ray and a bone scan may be necessary to detect the fracture.

TREATMENT: Six weeks rest in plaster and on crutches heals these fractures.

PROGNOSIS: Good.

See also Fractures

Marfan Syndrome

DESCRIPTION: Uncommon inherited condition that affects the skeleton, heart and eye, and occurs in all races but only in one out of every 20,000 people.

CAUSE: Congenital.

SYMPTOMS: Characteristics include very long thin bones in the arms, legs, fingers and toes, a tall skull, excessive joint movement and a humped back. Half the patients have an eye lens that is in the wrong position, and may develop a detached retina (the light-sensitive area at the back of the eyes), which results in partial or total blindness. An abnormality in the elastic tissue of the heart valves and major arteries causes these to fail and the pumping of the heart to be inefficient. The main artery of the body, the aorta, becomes overly dilated and distorted and may eventually rupture. Heart infections (endocarditis) are common. Most patients do not have all these symptoms, as there is great variation between them. Some may be totally unaware that they are affected and just appear to be very tall and thin.

INVESTIGATIONS: Diagnosed by the characteristic appearance of the long bones on

X-ray, and by assessing the heart abnormalities with echocardiograms.

TREATMENT: The problems in the heart and aorta are controlled and corrected by both medication and surgery.

COMPLICATIONS: Death in middle age is common unless corrective surgery is successful.

PROGNOSIS: No cure, but treatment reasonably successful.

See also Beal Syndrome

Marijuana Abuse
(Cannabis Abuse; Hashish Abuse; 'Pot')

DESCRIPTION: Addictive drug taken into the body by smoking or eating. The concentrated resin from the plant (hashish) is stronger and more dangerous than marijuana, and produces a more noticeable effect.

CAUSE: Made from the hemp plant, *Cannabis sativa* which has as its active ingredient the chemical tetrahydrocannabinol (THC). THC occurs in all parts of the cannabis plant and is a depressant drug, not a stimulant. Users tend to have a poor self-image and ego. Possibly one in every 100 people is dependent upon illicit drugs in western society, and a far higher percentage have experimented with them at one time or another.

SYMPTOMS: Initially causes excessive happiness, followed by a long period of depression and drowsiness. If used daily for a few weeks it eventually ceases to have its original effect, and the user must increase the dose to reach the same level of intoxication, which is how addiction develops.

INVESTIGATIONS: Blood and urine tests can detect the presence of THC.

TREATMENT: Treatment options available are:

— Gradual withdrawal while receiving counselling and medical support

— Immediate drug withdrawal ('cold turkey') while medically supervised

— Half-way houses that remove the patient from the environment in which drug taking is encouraged

— Individual or group psychotherapy.

COMPLICATIONS: Most drugs dissolve in water, but THC dissolves in the body's fat, and so stores of the drug can be established in the system. This leads to a prolonged withdrawal stage, and the frightening flash-backs that regular users experience when a sudden release of the drug from the body's fat stores occurs. These flash-backs can occur without warning for weeks after the last use of marijuana, and may cause hallucinations while working or driving and can therefore place others at risk. Long-term use may cause an increased risk of bronchitis, lung cancer and other respiratory diseases associated with smoking; decreased concentration, memory and learning abilities; interference with sex hormone production; and cannabis psychosis, which is similar to schizophrenia. Cannabis is often also used with other drugs to intensify its effects, often in unpredictable ways. Using cannabis and alcohol together can be much more dangerous than using either drug by itself.

PROGNOSIS: More addictive and damaging than alcohol. Better long term prognosis than with other illicit drugs, unless patient moves to using stronger and more addictive substances.

See also other problems listed under Addiction

Marinesco-Sjögren Syndrome

DESCRIPTION: Rare progressive degeneration of the cerebellum (lower back part of brain) that starts in early childhood.

CAUSE: Familial (inherited), but both parents must be carriers.

SYMPTOMS: Poor coordination (ataxia), eye cataracts, mental retardation, multiple bony abnormalities and underdeveloped testes or ovaries.

INVESTIGATIONS: No diagnostic test.

TREATMENT: Medication to control ataxia.

PROGNOSIS: No cure. Symptoms steadily worsen to death.

See also Friedrich's Ataxia other conditions listed under Ataxia

Maroteaux-Lamy Syndrome

DESCRIPTION: Metabolic (body chemistry) disorder.

CAUSE: Congenital.

SYMPTOMS: Abnormal bone and heart formation, clouding of the cornea in the eyes, deafness, short body and neck from retarded growth, walk with a waddling gait, knock knees and flat feet.

INVESTIGATIONS: Abnormal specific blood enzyme tests. May be detected before birth by chorionic villus (placenta) sampling.

TREATMENT: None effective.

PROGNOSIS: Survival beyond 40 years unusual.

Mastitis
(Breast Infection)

DESCRIPTION: An infection of the breast tissue, almost invariably in a breastfeeding woman.

CAUSE: Bacterial invasion of the breast in a lactating mother that usually occurs if one of the many lobes in the breast does not adequately empty its milk. May spread from a sore, cracked nipple. Women nursing for the first time are more frequently affected.

SYMPTOMS: The breast becomes painful, very tender, red and sore. The woman may become feverish, and quite unwell.

INVESTIGATIONS: None normally necessary.

TREATMENT: Antibiotic tablets such as penicillin or a cephalosporin. In recurrent cases, bromocriptine may be used to stop or reduce breast milk production. If an abscess forms, an operation to drain away the accumulated pus is necessary.

COMPLICATIONS: An abscess may form in the infected lobe of the breast.

PROGNOSIS: Usually settles rapidly with correct treatment, and the woman can continue breast feeding.

Mastocytosis
See Systemic Mastocytosis; Urticaria Pigmentosa

Mastoiditis
DESCRIPTION: Bacterial infection of the mastoid bone, which is a small bump of bone at the bottom of the skull immediately behind the ear that contains a microscopic honeycomb of air filled spaces.

CAUSE: Almost invariably occurs as a result of infection spreading from the middle ear in patients who have recurrent or severe attacks of middle ear infection (otitis media).

SYMPTOMS: Severe pain and tenderness behind the ear, fever, and redness over the mastoid bone. The ear may discharge pus if the eardrum or a mastoid abscess has ruptured.

INVESTIGATIONS: An X-ray of the mastoid shows the air spaces within it to be destroyed and replaced by pus (an abscess).

TREATMENT: Potent antibiotics which are sometimes given by injection. If these fail, an operation to drain the pus out of the mastoid bone will be necessary (a mastoidectomy).

COMPLICATIONS: In some cases the infection will eat away the bone at the back of the ear canal and allow the pus to escape into the ear. The hole between the ear canal and the mastoid air cells, and the cavity in the mastoid bone that results from the infection, are permanent. If left untreated, the infection may spread into the brain.

PROGNOSIS: Good with appropriate treatment.

See also Abscess; Otitis Media

Mature Capillary Naevus
See Portwine Naevus

Maturity Onset Diabetes
See Diabetes Mellitus

Mauriac Syndrome
DESCRIPTION: Complication of inappropriate insulin usage.

CAUSE: If a short acting insulin is given in a high dose, once daily, blood sugar levels will vary widely from normal to abnormal during the day to adversely affect body chemistry.

SYMPTOMS: A diabetic with reduced stature, obesity and enlarged liver.

INVESTIGATIONS: Blood sugar and insulin levels are abnormal.

TREATMENT: Correct diet, and insulin dose modification.

PROGNOSIS: Good once diagnosed, but existing damage to body cannot be reversed.

See also Diabetes Mellitus

May-Hegglin Anomaly

DESCRIPTION: An abnormality of blood cells.

CAUSE: Unknown.

SYMPTOMS: Inflamed and abnormal white blood cells associated with enlarged platelets (blood clotting cells) which are reduced in number.

INVESTIGATIONS: Abnormal blood cells seen under microscope.

McArdle Syndrome

See Glycogen Storage Diseases

McCune-Albright Syndrome

See Albright Syndrome

ME

See Chronic Fatigue Syndrome

Measles
(Morbilli; Rubeola)

DESCRIPTION: Highly contagious *Morbilli* virus infection.

CAUSE: Viral infection that is contagious from five days before the rash appears until it disappears. The incubation period is 10 to 14 days.

SYMPTOMS: Starts with the cold-like symptoms of a snuffly nose, cough and red eyes. A rash develops about four days later, starting in the mouth where tiny white spots appear on the lining of the cheeks. Dark red blotches then develop on the face and gradually spread across the body, remaining for a week or more before gradually fading. Other symptoms include a high fever and eye discomfort with bright lights. The patient often starts to feel better once the rash has reached its maximum spread.

INVESTIGATIONS: Diagnosis can be confirmed by blood tests if necessary. Previous exposure to the measles virus or vaccine can also be confirmed by blood tests.

TREATMENT: No specific treatment. Rest, paracetamol and medication to relieve the cold symptoms. Vitamin A supplements appear to reduce the severity of an attack. May be prevented by vaccination which is usually given at one and five years of age in combination with the mumps and rubella (German measles) vaccine.

COMPLICATIONS: Include encephalitis (a serious brain infection), pneumonia, ear infections and damage, and possibly the increased risk of developing multiple sclerosis later in life. Immediately after an attack patients are susceptible to other infections, and a significant number will develop tonsillitis, ear and lymph node infections.

PROGNOSIS: Usually very good, but significant complications occur in one in every 200 cases, and death occurs in one in every 5000 cases in developed countries, while in third-world countries one in ten children or adults who catch measles will die.

See also Roseola Infantum; Rubella

Measles, Baby
See Roseola Infantum

Measles, German
See German Measles

Medial Epicondylitis
See Golfer's Elbow

Meckel's Diverticulitis
DESCRIPTION: Infection of a small bowel diverticulum.

CAUSE: Bacterial infection or inflammation of an outpocketing on the last part of the small intestine (ileum) that is left over from the individual's life as a foetus before birth when the diverticulum was attached to the umbilicus. In 2% of people it remains after birth, and may become blocked with food or other debris.

SYMPTOMS: When infected the patient feels pain in the belly and develops a fever. The diagnosis is often confused with appendicitis.

INVESTIGATIONS: Blood tests may show inflammation or infection but not its location. Usually not diagnosed until operation when a normal appendix is found, and further examination of the bowel reveals an infected Meckel's diverticulum.

TREATMENT: Surgical removal.

COMPLICATIONS: Diverticulum may become ulcerated, bleed or cause a gut obstruction.

PROGNOSIS: Easily remedied by surgery, but if left untreated, may burst to cause life threatening peritonitis, or an abscess that results in long term illness.

Meckel Syndrome
DESCRIPTION: Familial defect of numerous body structures.

CAUSE: Inherited, but only if both parents carry the abnormal gene.

SYMPTOMS: Extra fingers and toes, incomplete skull formation with brain protrusion, cleft lip and palate, and small kidneys with multiple cysts. Some patients have eye and liver defects as well.

INVESTIGATIONS: Genetic tests are diagnostic. May be diagnosed before birth by chorionic villus (placenta) sampling.

TREATMENT: None available.

PROGNOSIS: Early death usual.

Mediterranean Fever, Familial
See Familial Mediterranean Fever

Mediterranean Spotted Fever
See Typhus

Medulloblastoma

DESCRIPTION: Cancer of the nerve cells in the brain.

CAUSE: Unknown but more common in children.

SYMPTOMS: Increases the pressure in the brain to cause nausea and headaches.

INVESTIGATIONS: Visualised by CT and MRI scans. Biopsy required for definitive diagnosis.

TREATMENT: Combination of surgery, irradiation and drugs. Usually very sensitive to irradiation.

COMPLICATIONS: May suddenly spread rapidly through the brain.

PROGNOSIS: Unfortunately only one in three can be cured.

See also other tumours listed under Brain Cancer

Meesmann Corneal Dystrophy
See Corneal Dystrophy

Megacolon

DESCRIPTION: Massive distension of the descending and sigmoid colon, the last parts of the large intestine.

CAUSE: Long term constipation and retention of faeces stretches the large bowel. May be a complication of ulcerative colitis, associated with some psychiatric and low intellect disorders, a symptom of an underactive thyroid gland (hypothyroidism), due to excessive use of narcotics, or a birth defect (Hirschsprung disease).

SYMPTOMS: Severe constipation, sometimes associated with lower abdominal pain and a watery diarrhoea as liquid faeces flows around the blockage.

INVESTIGATIONS: Diagnosed by colonoscopy (passing a flexible tube up the bowel through the anus) or X-rays.

TREATMENT: Treat any underlying disease, remove faeces build up, a special high fibre diet, and use laxatives carefully. Surgery in the form of a colostomy (opening bowel onto skin) is a last resort.

COMPLICATIONS: Bowel may rupture causing life threatening peritonitis.

PROGNOSIS: Often a persistent condition that requires constant and repeated treatment.

See also Constipation; Hirshsprung Disease; Ulcerative Colitis

Megaloblastic Anaemia
See Pernicious Anaemia

Meibomian Cyst

DESCRIPTION: Meibomian gland blockage. The upper and lower eyelids each contain about 20 meibomian glands, which secrete an oily substance that lubricates the surface of the eye.

CAUSE: If the tiny tube leading out of a gland becomes blocked, it will swell up into a cyst. More common in those over 40 years of age, and may follow a period of eye irritation or conjunctivitis.

SYMPTOMS: Felt and seen as a lump in the eyelid.

INVESTIGATIONS: None usually necessary.

TREATMENT: A small cut into the cyst will drain out the contents.

COMPLICATIONS: May become infected by bacteria to form a chalazion.

PROGNOSIS: Very good.

See also Chalazion; Stye

Meigs Syndrome
(Demons-Meigs Syndrome)

DESCRIPTION: A type of ovarian tumour.

CAUSE: A fibrous growth in a woman's ovary causes abnormal levels of sex hormone production.

SYMPTOMS: Swelling of the belly from fluid retention.

INVESTIGATIONS: Blood sex hormone levels abnormal.

TREATMENT: Surgical removal of the ovarian tumour.

COMPLICATIONS: Infertility.

PROGNOSIS: Good.

Melancholia
See Depression

Melanoma

DESCRIPTION: The most serious form of skin cancer, which starts in the skin cells that create pigment. In Europeans (Caucasians), these cells are relatively inactive, giving a pale colour to the skin. In Asians (Mongols) they are moderately active, and in Africans (Negroes) they are very active, giving a darker skin colour.

CAUSE: The actual cause is unknown, but exposure to sunlight, particularly in childhood and teen years, dramatically increases the risk. Ultraviolet radiation, most of which is filtered out of sunlight by the ozone layer in the upper atmosphere, is the part of the spectrum that causes the damage. Fair-skinned people have a higher incidence than those with dark complexions. It is rare in children, slightly more common in women than men, and most common between 30 and 50 years of age and on the legs and back. One in every 150 people in Australia will develop a melanoma at some time.

SYMPTOMS: A skin spot that may be black, brown, pink or blue, and the colours may be found individually or mixed. Usually have an irregularly edge, enlarge steadily, have an uneven and bumpy surface, and the pigment can be seen advancing into the surrounding skin. In advanced cases the spot will bleed, scab and ulcerate. Melanomas can occur under the nail (where they may be mistaken for a bruise), in the mouth, under the eyelids, on the retina inside the eye, and in the anus, but the sun-exposed parts of the skin are the most commonly affected.

INVESTIGATIONS: Diagnosed by biopsy or excision of the suspected mole.

TREATMENT: The melanoma and a large area of skin around and under it, must be cut out. The lymph nodes around the melanoma may also need to be removed. If there is evidence that it has spread to other areas, the patient will also be treated with irradiation and injected medications to control its further growth.

COMPLICATIONS: Tendency to grow deep into the body and migrate to other organs, particularly the liver, lungs and lymph nodes in the armpit and groin. The cancer may appear to be cured but can flare up decades later.

PROGNOSIS: In the very early stages there is a 97% cure rate. As the cancer enlarges, the cure rate drops dramatically. One third of all patients who develop a melanoma will eventually die from it.

See also Dysplastic Naevus Syndrome

Melasma
See Chloasma

Melioidosis

DESCRIPTION: Uncommon infection of the lungs.

CAUSE: The bacterium *Pseudomonas pseudomallei* which occurs throughout south and east Asia, and has been reported in Aboriginal communities in northern Australia. Widespread in soil, and is caught by inhaling dust. Person to person spread is rare. Occasionally wounds, the gut and other internal organs can be infected by dirt contamination of a wound or food.

SYMPTOMS: Usually a low grade persistent infection with minimal symptoms. In a minority it develops rapidly with symptoms similar to pneumonia such as a cough, fever, muscle pains, loss of appetite and chest pain.

INVESTIGATIONS: Diagnosed by examination of sputum and specific blood tests.

TREATMENT: Only necessary if the patient has symptoms, and involves long term use of antibiotics. No form of prevention or vaccination available.

COMPLICATIONS: Relapses after treatment has been completed may occur.

PROGNOSIS: Good with appropriate treatment. Without treatment, patients who develop pneumonia usually die.

See also Pneumonia

MEN
See Multiple Endocrine Neoplasia; Werner Syndrome

Mendelson Syndrome

DESCRIPTION: Complication of unconsciousness or anaesthesia.

CAUSE: Due to acid from the stomach coming up the oesophagus, into the throat, and then being inhaled into the lungs.

SYMPTOMS: Severe spasm and inflammation of airways in the lungs similar to, but more serious than, a severe asthma attack.

INVESTIGATIONS: Chest X-rays show lung damage.

TREATMENT: Passing a breathing tube into the lungs to give artificial respiration, oxygen, drugs to open the airways and reduce inflammation (eg. steroids), antibiotics and a drip to control body fluids and chemistry.

COMPLICATIONS: Permanent lung damage may occur.

PROGNOSIS: Most patients recover satisfactorily.

Menétrière's Disease

DESCRIPTION: Excessive infolding of the stomach lining.

CAUSE: Overdevelopment and excessive growth of the stomach lining.

SYMPTOMS: Upper abdominal pain, loss of appetite, nausea, vomiting and weight loss. Patients lose protein through stomach secretions, become malnourished and develop swollen feet and ankles.

INVESTIGATIONS: Diagnosed by barium meal X-ray or gastroscopy.

TREATMENT: High protein diet, anti-ulcer medication and surgery to reduce the size of the stomach.

COMPLICATIONS: Increased risk of stomach bleeding and cancer.

PROGNOSIS: No cure, and control of symptoms difficult.

Ménière's Disease

DESCRIPTION: A syndrome causing dizziness, deafness and a constant noise in the ears.

CAUSE: The inner ear contains both the hearing and balance mechanisms. The latter consists of three tiny semicircular canals full of fluid. The exact cause of the disease is unknown, but there is a build-up of pressure inside the hearing and balance mechanisms, and it may occur after a head injury or ear infection. More common in men and with advancing age. Avoiding prolonged episodes of loud noise (eg. jet engines, rock bands) reduces the incidence.

SYMPTOMS: The most distressing symptom is a constant high-pitched ringing noise (tinnitus) in the ear. Patients also have attacks of dizziness and nausea that come and go for no apparent reason, and a slowly progressive and permanent deafness. Other symptoms may include sweating, nausea and vomiting.

INVESTIGATIONS: No specific tests can diagnose the disease.

TREATMENT: Numerous medications may be tried including betahistine (increases the blood supply to the inner ear), antihistamines, diuretics, prochlorperazine, amitriptyline and chlorpromazine. None have more than a 50-50 chance of success. A tinnitus masker is a hearing-aid device that emits a constant tone that counteracts the noise already heard in the ear. Microsurgical techniques involve draining the high-pressure fluid from the affected parts of the inner ear, or as a last resort destroying the auditory nerve, leaving the patient deaf in that ear but without the distressing buzz saw noise.

COMPLICATIONS: None serious.

PROGNOSIS: No cure and treatment is not very satisfactory, but some cases settle spontaneously.

Meningeal Tuberculosis
See Tuberculosis

Meningioma

DESCRIPTION: Slowly progressive, mildly malignant cancer of the meninges, the membranes that surround and support the brain.

CAUSE: Unknown. More common in women and older people.

SYMPTOMS: Often grow to a large size before symptoms develop. The tumour compresses the brain, causing symptoms that relate to the part of the brain compressed. For example, if the area of the brain controlling the arm is compressed, the arm may become weak or paralysed. Seizures are common.

INVESTIGATIONS: Visualised by CT and MRI scans. Biopsy required for definitive diagnosis.

TREATMENT: Surgical removal of the tumour.

PROGNOSIS: Most cases can be cured.

See also other tumours listed under **Brain Cancer**

Meningitis

DESCRIPTION: Viral (aseptic) or bacterial (septic) infection of the meninges, membranes which wrap all the way around the brain and act to contain the cerebrospinal fluid in which the brain is supported.

CAUSE: Viral (aseptic) meningitis — a relatively benign condition that may be caught by close contact with someone who has a viral infection, or it may be a complication of diseases such as mumps, glandular fever and Herpes.

Bacterial (septic) meningitis — caught from people who are carriers of the bacteria, but the victims are usually weak, ill, under stress or have their ability to resist infection reduced in some way. The most common forms of bacterial meningitis is caused by *Haemophilus influenzae B* (HiB), while the most serious is **Meningococcal meningitis** (caused by *Neisseria meningitidis*).

SYMPTOMS: Viral meningitis — fever, headache, nausea and vomiting, tiredness and sometimes muscle weakness or paralysis. Neck stiffness may be present. Bacterial meningitis — a much more serious condition, with the severity and symptoms varying depending upon which type of bacteria is responsible. Common symptoms include severe headaches, vomiting, confusion, high fevers, patients become delirious, unconscious and may convulse. Neck stiffness is quite obvious, and patients may lie with their neck constantly extended as though they are looking up. Meningococcal meningitis is accompanied by a bruise-like rash on the skin and inside the mouth.

INVESTIGATIONS: The diagnosis of both types of meningitis is confirmed by taking a sample of cerebrospinal fluid from the lower end of the spine (which is an extension of the brain) and examining it under a microscope for the presence of certain cells and it can be cultured to find the responsible bacteria. Blood tests also show abnormalities.

TREATMENT: Viral meningitis — no specific treatment or prevention available. Bed rest, good nursing, paracetamol, and sometimes medication for vomiting are prescribed.

Bacterial meningitis — antibiotics in high doses, usually by injection or a continuous drip into a vein. Patients always require hospitalisation. Both common causes of bacterial meningitis can be prevented by a vaccine. The HiB vaccine is routine in childhood, but the Meningococcal vaccine is only given during epidemics to close contacts of victims. Other forms of bacterial and viral meningitis cannot be prevented.

COMPLICATIONS: Viral meningitis — rare for there to be any after-effects.

Bacterial meningitis — complications include permanent deafness in one or both ears, damage to different parts of the brain, heart or kidney damage, arthritis and the excess production of cerebrospinal fluid which can put pressure on the brain (hydrocephalus). The worst complication is intravascular coagulation, which involves the blood clotting within the arteries and blocking them.

PROGNOSIS: Viral meningitis — patients recover in one or two weeks.

Bacterial meningitis — patients deteriorate very rapidly and most deaths occur within the first 24 hours. The overall mortality rate is about 20%, although it is higher in children and with the Meningococcal form.

See also Arachnoiditis; Haemophilus Influenzae B Infection; Lyme Disease

Meningocele
See Spina Bifida

Meningococcal Infection
See Meningitis; Waterhouse-Friderichsen Syndrome

Meningomyelocele
See Spina Bifida

Meniscus Tear
See Knee Meniscus Tear

Menopause
('Change of Life'; Climacteric)

DESCRIPTION: A natural event that occurs in all women. After the menopause no female hormones are manufactured in the ovaries, the ovaries will no longer produce eggs, the woman is infertile, and the monthly menstrual periods cease.

CAUSE: The sex hormones (oestrogen and progestogen) are released from the ovaries into the blood on regular signals from the pituitary gland, which sits underneath the centre of the brain. These hormones effect every part of the body, but more particularly the uterus, vagina, breasts and pubic areas. For an unknown reason, once a woman reaches an age somewhere between the early forties and mid fifties, the brain breaks rhythm in sending the messages to the ovaries. The signals become irregular, and the ovaries respond by producing sex hormones in varying levels, which causes the symptoms of the menopause.

SYMPTOMS: The first symptom is irregularity in the frequency and nature of the menstrual periods, and their gradual disappearance may be the only symptom in 25% of women. About 50% have other symptoms that cause discomfort, and the remaining 25% go through severe and distressing symptoms. The periods may become very irregular, vary in length and intensity, and become painful. Other symptoms may include bloating and associated headaches and irritability as excess fluid collects in the brain, breasts and pelvis; hot flushes when hormone surges rush through the bloodstream after excess amounts are released by the ovaries; abdominal cramps caused by spasms of the uterine muscles; and depression.

INVESTIGATIONS: Blood tests can determine the sex hormone levels, but they are very difficult to interpret if the woman is taking the contraceptive pill.

TREATMENT: Cannot be cured, because it is a natural occurrence, but most of the symptoms can be relieved. Sex hormone tablets, patches, vaginal preparations, implants or injections are used in varying combinations and dosage patterns to maintain a near normal hormonal balance. Minor symptoms can be controlled individually. Fluid tablets can help bloating and headaches, other agents can help uterine cramps and heavy bleeding, and depression can be treated with antidepressants.

COMPLICATIONS: Osteoporosis, heart disease, skin thinning, Alzheimer's disease and premature aging may occur after the menopause, but can be slowed or prevented by long term use of hormone replacement therapy.

PROGNOSIS: There is no need for any woman to suffer significant symptoms with appropriate management.

See also Atrophic Vaginitis; Vaginal Prolapse

Mercury Poisoning
(Minamata Disease; Pink Disease)

DESCRIPTION: Swallowing mercury or mercury-containing compounds or inhaling mercury vapour.

CAUSE: Used in industry in thermometers, batteries, thermostats, dental fillings and chemical processing. Contamination of the food chain (particularly fish) may lead to poisoning in humans. It used to be present in medications such as teething powders until the 1950s.

SYMPTOMS: If a large amount of mercury is swallowed at one time symptoms include a metallic taste, thirst, burning in the throat, excessive saliva formation, belly pain, vomiting, bloody diarrhoea, collapse and kidney failure.

Inhaling mercury vapour can cause an intractable form of pneumonia.

Chronic mercury poisoning, in which small amounts of mercury are swallowed over a long period of time, causes 'pink disease' with red and swollen hands and feet, irritability, fever, hair loss and damaged nails.

INVESTIGATIONS: Detected by specific blood tests.

TREATMENT: If swallowed, induce vomiting, give egg whites and milk, then go to hospital for stomach wash out. Mercury can slowly be removed from the body by some medications.

COMPLICATIONS: Later problems include tremor, convulsions, brain damage and death. May cause birth defects in the children of mothers with chronic lead poisoning (Minamata disease).

PROGNOSIS: Depends on age, weight and health of patient, and dose of mercury.

Mesenteric Adenitis

DESCRIPTION: The mesentery is a thin membrane which connects the small intestine within the abdomen to the back wall of the abdomen and contains the arteries, veins and nerves that supply the intestine. Scattered through the mesentery are numerous lymph nodes that may become infected or inflamed.

CAUSE: Almost invariably a viral infection that is far more common in children than adults, and is often preceded by another infection such as a bad cold or bronchitis.

SYMPTOMS: Identical to those of appendicitis, and many patients at operation for acute appendicitis are found to have mesenteric adenitis. Both cause severe abdominal pain, nausea, diarrhoea and fever.

INVESTIGATIONS: Blood tests are unable to differentiate between the two diseases, as an infected appendix causes the same changes in the blood as infected lymph nodes.

TREATMENT: No specific treatment available.

COMPLICATIONS: None significant.

PROGNOSIS: Usually settles without treatment after five to ten days.

See also Adenitis

Mesenteric Artery Thrombosis

DESCRIPTION: Reduction of the blood supply to the small intestine, which is loosely attached to the back wall of the belly by a fine membrane (the mesentery) which contains the two mesenteric arteries.

CAUSE: If one of the mesenteric arteries is partially blocked by a plaque of cholesterol, a blood clot (thrombosis) or pressure from another organ or adhesion, the small intestine will not receive sufficient blood to function properly.

SYMPTOMS: After a meal the patient experiences belly pain and aches that vary with the size of the meal, and so they eat very small infrequent meals, and lose weight. When an artery becomes completely blocked, severe belly pain and tenderness occurs, and the patient will collapse.

INVESTIGATIONS: X-rays of the abdomen will show abnormal bowel patterns.

TREATMENT: This is a surgical emergency, as the blocked artery must be cleared and the affected intestine removed as quickly as possible.

COMPLICATIONS: The intestine supplied by the thrombosed artery may become gangrenous.

PROGNOSIS: Depends on severity of bowel damage at time of surgery, but even in good hospitals there is significant mortality.

Mesothelioma

DESCRIPTION: A form of lung cancer that may be a serious complication of asbestosis

CAUSE: Caused by inhalation of asbestos fibres, smoking, or because of the long term inhalation of other irritants (eg. talc dust, coal dust). Up to 7% of patients with asbestosis develop mesothelioma, but half the time it occurs in non-asbestosis sufferers. The average age of onset is 60, and the latent period between exposure to asbestos and development of mesothelioma can be up to 40 years.

SYMPTOMS: Very insidious onset, with symptoms little different to asbestosis itself.

INVESTIGATIONS: X-ray changes may not be apparent until the disease is quite advanced. CT scans are more useful in making the diagnosis in suspicious cases. A biopsy of the cancerous area is the only way to make a definite diagnosis.

TREATMENT: Treatment with surgery, drugs and radiation has been tried, but with virtually no success.

COMPLICATIONS: The cancer is extremely virulent and spreads rapidly.

PROGNOSIS: Three quarters of victims die within a year of the diagnosis, and 98% within two years.

See also Asbestosis; Lung Cancer

Metastatic Cancer
(Secondary Cancer)

DESCRIPTION: Spread of cancer from one organ to another, often to lymph nodes, the liver (hepatic metastases), bone or lungs.

CAUSE: Cancer can eat into a blood vessel or lymph channel and spread to distant parts of the body. Localised spread is also possible.

SYMPTOMS: Depends upon the organ(s) involved. The function of the affected organ is usually affected. Nausea, weight loss, loss of appetite and general tiredness are symptoms of most forms of cancer that occur in addition to the symptoms caused by the failure of the affected organ.

INVESTIGATIONS: Detecting a metastatic deposit of cancer may be difficult. Blood tests, X-rays, ultrasound, CT and MRI scans are used in the search.

TREATMENT: Depends on site of cancer deposits. May involve surgery, anti-cancer drugs and irradiation.

COMPLICATIONS: Depends on site of cancer deposits.

PROGNOSIS: Depends on site of cancer deposits, but metastases indicate a worsening of the cancer and a greater difficulty in treatment.

See also Cancer

Metatarsal Fracture
See March Fracture

Metatarsalgia

DESCRIPTION: Inflammation of one or more of the long bones in the front half of the foot (metatarsals). May be caused by a stress fracture (march fracture — see separate entry), by inflammation of one of the nerves that run beside the metatarsal bone (**Morton's metatarsalgia**), or by flattening and thinning of the forefoot fat pad and transverse arch that protects the foot bones when walking or running.

CAUSE: Running or jogging on hard surfaces and in poor footwear. An unusually long walk or climb, may also trigger an attack. Morton's metatarsalgia is more common in middle-aged women.

SYMPTOMS: Varying degrees of pain in the ball of the foot, or in the front half of the foot beside the ball. Every step may be painful, running excruciating, and patients often adopt an unusual way of walking by taking the weight on their heels or one side of the foot.

INVESTIGATIONS: None diagnostic.

TREATMENT: Morton's metatarsalgia — inserting a shock absorbing insole into the shoes, taking anti-inflammatory medications, steroid injections around the nerve, or in severe cases having an operation to remove the damaged section of nerve. Damage to the forefoot arch and fat pad — physiotherapy to strengthen the small muscles within the foot, sponge rubber insoles and anti-inflammatory medications to give relief from persistent pain.

COMPLICATIONS: Knee, hip and back pain from unusual walking pattern (gait).

PROGNOSIS: Often persistent, but reasonable symptom relief possible.

See also March Fracture

Methicillin-Resistant *Staphylococcus aureus* Infection
See Staphylococcal Infection

MI
See Heart Attack

Middle Ear Effusion
See Glue Ear

Middle Ear Infection
See Otitis Media

Migraine

DESCRIPTION: A form of headache that is usually associated with other significant symptoms. May occur once in a person's life, or three times a week; may cause a relatively mild head pain, or may totally disable the patient.

Migraine

CAUSE: The contraction of an artery in the brain, which may give the patient an unusual sensation and warning of an attack, followed within a few seconds or minutes by an over-dilation of the artery. Excess blood passes to the part of the brain that the artery supplies and it is unable to function properly. The patient feels intense pressure, pain and other symptoms. The artery dilation may occur for no apparent reason, or be triggered by certain foods, anxiety and stress, hormonal changes, allergies, loud noises or flashing lights. The frequency and severity of migraines tends to decrease with age, an initial attack over the age of 40 is unusual, and they may cease in old age.

SYMPTOMS: Effects vary dramatically from one patient to another, depending on the part of the brain involved. As well as intense head pain, most patients suffer nausea and vomiting and loud noises or bright lights aggravate the pain. Other symptoms may include partial blindness, personality changes, loss of hearing, noises in the ears, paralysis, numbness, and violence.

INVESTIGATIONS: No specific diagnostic tests, but doctors can sometimes diagnose a migraine by the visual pattern. If you close your eyes, patterns can be seen on the back of the eyelids which are actually the random activity of the nerves in the light sensitive retina at the back of the eye and in the visual centre of the brain. In normal people, a swirling smooth pattern will be seen, but a patient with a migraine will see flashes of light, bright colours and jagged patterns.

TREATMENT: Migraines may be prevented by regular medication, or treated when they occur.

Prevention — many different drugs can be used including propranolol, methysergide, clonidine, sodium valproate, ketoprofen and pizotifen. It is often a matter of trial and error to find the most effective one.

Treatment — the longer a migraine has been present, the more difficult it is to control. Rapidly cured in most patients by nose sprays, tablets or injections containing naratriptan, sumatriptan or zolmitriptan. The more often these medications are used, the more effective they become. Other treatments include tablets which may be placed under the tongue or swallowed (eg. ergotamine), or normal pain killers (eg. paracetamol, aspirin), antihistamines, mild sedatives and anti-vomiting medications (eg. promethazine). Strong narcotic pain killers should be avoided if possible. Resting in a cool, dark room is also helpful.

COMPLICATIONS: Rarely serious, but patient may be disabled for some hours or days.

PROGNOSIS: Most cases can be prevented or effectively treated, but a small number are resistant to all medications.

Mikulicz Disease
(Benign Lymphoepithelial Condition)

DESCRIPTION: Inflammatory condition of salivary and tear glands.

CAUSE: Unknown. Common in Scandinavia.

SYMPTOMS: Enlargement of the saliva producing glands under and behind the jaw, and enlargement of the lacrimal (tear) glands at the outer corners of the eyes. May also be associated with tuberculosis, sarcoidosis, syphilis, actinomycosis, wasting of the mucous producing glands in the nose, throat and vagina, and dry eyes (keratoconjunctivitis sicca).

INVESTIGATIONS: Specific blood tests and biopsy of the affected glands diagnostic.

TREATMENT: No treatment necessary unless a specific gland becomes painful when it can be surgical removed.

COMPLICATIONS: Recurrent salivary gland infections.

PROGNOSIS: No cure available, but usually a benign condition.

Milia
(Keratin Cysts)

DESCRIPTION: Problem of excess keratin (scale) production by oil glands in the skin.

CAUSE: Unknown, but more common in areas of skin damage.

SYMPTOMS: Tiny, firm, creamy lumps (papules) on the skin, usually of the face.

INVESTIGATIONS: None necessary.

TREATMENT: Removed for cosmetic reasons by piercing with a needle or cryo-surgery (freezing).

PROGNOSIS: Persist long term unless removed.

Milkman Syndrome

DESCRIPTION: Abnormality in bone calcium.

CAUSE: Inability of bones to absorb calcium adequately. Adult version of rickets.

SYMPTOMS: Multiple, bilateral, symmetrical false fractures seen on X-ray, and osteomalacia (see separate entry).

INVESTIGATIONS: X-rays of leg and arm bones are abnormal. The level of calcium in the blood is usually low.

TREATMENT: Vitamin D in high doses.

COMPLICATIONS: Bone deformity.

PROGNOSIS: Usually controlled, but not cured.

See also Osteomalacia; Rickets

Miller-Dieker Syndrome

DESCRIPTION: Birth defect of the head and brain.

CAUSE: Congenital condition localised to chromosome 17.

SYMPTOMS: Abnormal head shape, abnormal facial structure, mentally subnormal, growth retardation and low birth weight.

INVESTIGATIONS: Specific analysis of chromosomes is abnormal, as is a CT scan of the brain. Can be diagnosed before birth by taking a sample from the placenta (chorionic villus sampling).

TREATMENT: None available.

PROGNOSIS: No cure, but reasonable life expectancy.

Miller Syndrome
See Aniridia

Milroy's Disease

DESCRIPTION: A rare condition in which the lymphatic system in one or both legs is faulty, and fails to remove waste products from the leg. The lymphatic system is a fine network of tubes that parallel the veins throughout the body, and take some forms of waste from every cell back into the blood stream, eventually draining into a main vein near the heart.

CAUSE: Hereditary (tends to pass from one generation to the next), and usually starts at puberty (12 to 14 years of age). Far more common in women than men.

SYMPTOMS: Leg becomes very swollen, puffy and uncomfortable.

INVESTIGATIONS: Biopsy of leg tissue shows lack of lymph channels.

TREATMENT: Elevation of the leg as much as possible, and wearing a firm elastic stocking.

COMPLICATIONS: Infections of the swollen tissue, that must be treated with antibiotics.

PROGNOSIS: No cure.

See also Lymphoedema

Minamata Disease
See Mercury Poisoning

Mirrizzi Syndrome

DESCRIPTION: Uncommon complication of gall stones.

CAUSE: Gall stone stuck in the opening of the duct leading from gall bladder.

SYMPTOMS: Inflammation of the common bile duct resulting in obstruction of the flow of bile, severe right upper belly pain and right back pain.

INVESTIGATIONS: Abnormal liver function on blood tests. The stone can be seen on an ultrasound scan of the abdomen.

TREATMENT: Surgical removal of the gall bladder.

COMPLICATIONS: A false opening may occur due to ulceration between the gall bladder and the common bile duct, nearby intestine or into the abdominal cavity causing peritonitis.

PROGNOSIS: Often stormy progress, but surgery usually successful.

See also Gallstones

Miscarriage
(Spontaneous Abortion)

DESCRIPTION: The failure of a pregnancy to progress, due to the death of the foetus, or a developmental abnormality in the foetus or placenta (afterbirth). If the baby is lost before 20 weeks of pregnancy it is a miscarriage, while after 20 weeks it is considered to be a premature birth, although the chances of a baby surviving if born before 28 weeks are very slim, as a normal pregnancy lasts 40 weeks. Most miscarriages occur in the first twelve weeks of pregnancy, and many occur so early that the woman may not even know that she has been pregnant. Up to 15 percent of diagnosed pregnancies, and possibly 50 percent of all pregnancies, end as a miscarriage.

CAUSE: May occur because there is no baby developing (just placental tissue — a **blighted ovum**), the foetus has serious abnormalities, the ovaries do not secrete sufficient hormones to sustain a pregnancy, or malformations of the uterus (womb) or cervix are present. Rarer causes include stress (both mental and physical), other diseases of the mother (eg. diabetes, infections), injuries, and drugs taken in early pregnancy.

SYMPTOMS: Usually starts with a slight vaginal bleed, then menstrual period-type cramps low in the abdomen. The bleeding becomes heavier, and eventually clots and tissue may pass.

INVESTIGATIONS: An ultrasound scan can show if a live foetus is present. Only if a woman has two miscarriages in succession are further investigations undertaken.

TREATMENT: No treatment except rest, sedatives and pain relievers. Once a miscarriage is inevitable, a simple operation may be performed to clean out the uterus and ready it for the next pregnancy. A deformed uterus or cervix may be surgically corrected to prevent future miscarriages.

COMPLICATIONS: Heavy bleeding may lead to anaemia, infections may occur in the uterus, and tissue may be retained in the uterus making it difficult for a further pregnancy to occur.

PROGNOSIS: In most cases, there is no reason why a subsequent pregnancy should not be successful.

See also other diseases listed under Pregnancy

Mitral Valve Incompetence

DESCRIPTION: A leak of the mitral valve between the upper and lower chambers on the left side of the heart. The valve receives its name because its two halves resemble a bishop's mitre.

CAUSE: Rheumatic fever, endocarditis, heart tumours (eg. myxoma) or Marfan syndrome (see separate entries). When the large left ventricle (lower heart chamber) contracts, blood is forced not only into the aorta (where it should go) but back through the damaged valve and up into the smaller left atrium (upper heart chamber) from where it has just come. This puts pressure back into the lungs.

SYMPTOMS: Shortness of breath and abnormal fatigue.

INVESTIGATIONS: Diagnosed by echocardiography (ultrasound scan) or passing a catheter through an artery into the heart.

TREATMENT: Patients with only minimal symptoms require no treatment, but if complications or progressive symptoms develop, surgical repair or replacement of the valve is necessary.

COMPLICATIONS: An irregular heartbeat, lung failure and infections of the damaged valve.

PROGNOSIS: Very good results obtained by surgery.

See also Barlow Syndrome and other diseases listed under Heart Valve Disease

Mitral Valve Stenosis

DESCRIPTION: A narrowing of the mitral valve between the upper and lower chambers on the left side of the heart.

CAUSE: Rheumatic fever is the cause in most patients, but this is becoming a rare disease in developed countries.

SYMPTOMS: Shortness of breath, tiredness, an irregular heartbeat (caused by atrial fibrillation), coughing of blood, and cor pulmonale (see separate entry).

INVESTIGATIONS: Diagnosed by echocardiography (ultrasound scan) or passing a catheter through an artery into the heart.

TREATMENT: Patients with only minimal symptoms require no treatment, but if complications or progressive symptoms develop, medications to control heart rate and surgical repair or replacement of the valve are necessary. Anticoagulants (eg. warfarin) are given to prevent emboli.

COMPLICATIONS: An embolism (blood clot) that may cause a stroke or death if it travels through arteries to the brain.

PROGNOSIS: Very good results obtained by surgery. Irregular heart rate may be difficult to control.

See also other diseases listed under Heart Valve Disease

Mittelschmerz
(Ovulation Pain)

DESCRIPTION: Pain associated with ovulation (release of an egg from the ovary).

CAUSE: Occurs in about 20% of women at the time of ovulation.

SYMPTOMS: A sudden sharp pain occurring on one side or other of the lower belly half way between menstrual periods. Sometimes associated with a small vaginal bleed, which is light and brief.

INVESTIGATIONS: None necessary.

TREATMENT: None normally necessary, but simple pain relievers may be used.

COMPLICATIONS: None.

PROGNOSIS: Pain settles within minutes or an hour or two.

Mixed Parotid Tumour
See Parotid Tumour

Moebius Syndrome

DESCRIPTION: Developmental abnormality of nerves.

CAUSE: The failure of two nerves from the brain (numbers 6 and 7) to develop properly before birth.

SYMPTOMS: Children with drooping eyelids, inability to move their eyes normally, faces that cannot show expressions, difficulty in swallowing and speaking, constant drooling, but normal intelligence.

INVESTIGATIONS: None diagnostic.

TREATMENT: None available.

PROGNOSIS: No cure, but normal lifespan.

Mokola Virus Infection

DESCRIPTION: Infection normally found in wild Nigerian shrews. Only two cases of human infection ever reported.

CAUSE: Virus similar to the rabies virus.

SYMPTOMS: Fever, inflamed throat, convulsions, weakness, vomiting.

INVESTIGATIONS: Virus can be isolated from fluid around the brain (cerebrospinal fluid).

TREATMENT: None available.

PROGNOSIS: One of the two patients died, the other recovered.

Mole, Invasive Uterine
See Choriocarcinoma of Uterus

Molluscum Contagiosum

DESCRIPTION: A mild contagious skin disease.

CAUSE: Viral infection spread from one person to another by close contact. If the blisters occur on the genitals, it has probably been caught by sexual contact.

SYMPTOMS: Multiple small (2-4mm.), dome-shaped, white blisters with a central dimple on scattered parts of their body. The abdomen, chest and face are the most commonly affected areas.

INVESTIGATIONS: None necessary.

TREATMENT: No treatment is normally required, but unsightly or persistent blisters can be removed by a doctor scraping out their contents or heating them with an electrical cautery needle.

COMPLICATIONS: Secondary bacterial infection of a scratched blister can occur.

PROGNOSIS: Rash disappears spontaneously after six weeks to six months.

Mongolism
See Down Syndrome

Moniliasis
See Thrush

Mononucleosis, Infectious
See Glandular Fever

Monteggia Fracture
(Fracture Dislocation of Elbow)

DESCRIPTION: A fracture of the shaft or upper end of the ulnar bone associated with a dislocation of the upper end of the radius bone at the elbow joint. The radius and ulnar are the two bones in the forearm.

CAUSE: A heavy fall onto the arm resulting in severe inwards twisting of the forearm.

SYMPTOMS: Significant pain in the elbow and forearm, inability to use the elbow and distortion of the forearm.

INVESTIGATIONS: Diagnosed on X-ray.

TREATMENT: Accurate reduction of dislocation and fracture into correct position under a general anaesthetic followed by keeping the forearm and elbow in plaster for eight to twelve weeks.

COMPLICATIONS: If the dislocation and fracture cannot be adequately corrected by manipulation, an open operation may be required. Inadequate treatment will result in some permanent loss of movement in the elbow.

PROGNOSIS: Good in most cases.

See also Fractures

Morbilli
See Measles

Morgagni, Hydatid of
See Hydatid of Morgagni

Morning Sickness
(Hyperemesis Gravidarum)

DESCRIPTION: Nausea and vomiting that may affect pregnant women between the sixth and fourteenth weeks of pregnancy. Although more common in the morning, it can occur at any time of the day. About one third of pregnant women have no morning sickness, one half have it badly enough to vomit at least once, and in 5% it is serious enough to result in prolonged bed rest or hospitalisation.

CAUSE: Unusually high levels of oestrogen present in the mother's bloodstream during the first three months of pregnancy. Usually ceases after three months, but may persist for longer, particularly with twins. Usually worse in the first pregnancy.

SYMPTOMS: Nausea and vomiting in early pregnancy aggravated by the smell or sight of food.

INVESTIGATIONS: None normally necessary.

TREATMENT: A self-limiting condition, so treatment is usually given only when necessary. A light diet, with small, frequent meals of dry fat-free foods, is helpful. A concentrated carbohydrate solution (Emetrol) may be taken to help relieve the nausea. Only in severe cases will doctors prescribe more potent medications.

COMPLICATIONS: In rare cases, a woman may become dehydrated because of continued vomiting and fluids must be given by a drip into a vein.

PROGNOSIS: Morning sickness has no effect upon the development of the baby.

Morphoea
(Circumscribed Scleroderma)

DESCRIPTION: Skin condition that occurs more commonly in women and starts in early adulthood. May occur on the forehead (en **Coup de Sabre** — sabre cut), scalp, limbs and chest.

CAUSE: Unknown.

SYMPTOMS: May appear as patches or thick lines on the skin that are initially purplish in colour, then become crusted, thick and shiny. Hairs are lost from affected skin.

INVESTIGATIONS: Diagnosed by skin biopsy.

TREATMENT: Unsatisfactory. Plastic surgery sometimes performed.

COMPLICATIONS: Permanent scarring may occur.

PROGNOSIS: Some cases settle spontaneously over many years. Most persist long term.

Morquio Syndrome

DESCRIPTION: Abnormality of body metabolism that damages numerous organs.

CAUSE: Excess accumulation of keratan sulfate in tissue.

SYMPTOMS: Severe progressive bone damage, heart abnormalities and damage, cataracts in the eyes, deafness, retarded growth leading to a short neck and short trunk, flat fleet and knock knees.

INVESTIGATIONS: Specific blood enzyme tests abnormal.

TREATMENT: None available.

COMPLICATIONS: Bones fracture easily, and heart damage may become significant.

PROGNOSIS: Normal life span expected in most patients.

Morton's Metatarsalgia
See Metatarsalgia

Morton Syndrome

DESCRIPTION: Abnormality of one of the long bones (first metatarsal) in the foot.

CAUSE: May be congenital or due to injury.

SYMPTOMS: Shortening and a bending towards the other foot of the 1st metatarsal (long bone ending in the ball of the foot), and excessive mobility in the joint between the 1st. metatarsal and the mid-foot bones (tarsals).

INVESTIGATIONS: X-ray of foot shows abnormal metatarsal.

TREATMENT: Surgery to correct the deformity if severe.

COMPLICATIONS: May cause nerve entrapment and foot pain.

PROGNOSIS: Good.

Motion Sickness
(Air Sickness; Car Sickness; Sea Sickness; Travel Sickness)

DESCRIPTION: A feeling of nausea or vomiting associated with movement in any form of transport.

CAUSE: A loss of synchronisation between the senses we use to balance — the eyes and the balance mechanism in the inner ears. On a ship, the deck appears to be level, but we sense motion; in an aircraft, the interior of the plane appears to be horizontal, but the aircraft may be climbing steeply. Aggravating factors include being overdressed, too warm, in a stuffy environment, eating too much and drinking alcohol.

TREATMENT: Reconciling the conflicting sensations from the eyes and balance mechanism helps to overcome motion sickness. In a ship, sitting on deck (ideally amidships) and watching the horizon will help. In an aircraft, a window seat from which the person can see the earth below and a seat over the wings where there is least motion are helpful. In a car, sitting in the front seat or in the centre of the rear seat, from where the road can be easily seen, will assist. Patients should be lightly dressed, slightly cold, have plenty of fresh air, eat small amounts of dry easily digestible food before and during the trip (no greasy chips or fatty sausages), and avoid alcohol. Fresh air is available by going on deck in a ship, opening a car window, and opening the air ducts wider on an aircraft. Numerous medications are also available (eg. antihistamines, metoclopramide). Sedatives are used in severely affected people. In chronic cases the problem may be psychological as well as physical, and desensitisation by a psychiatrist or psychologist may be appropriate.

COMPLICATIONS: Fear of travel may become intense.

PROGNOSIS: Not easy to control in all cases, although medications usually successful.

Motor Neurone Disease

DESCRIPTION: Insidious disease that affects the nerves that supply the muscles of the body.

CAUSE: Absolute cause unknown. Nerves are divided into two main groups — sensory nerves that feel heat, cold, touch and pain; and motor nerves that take the signals from the brain to the muscles and instruct the muscles to contract or relax. Motor neurone (neurone means nerve) disease is a steadily progressive degeneration of the motor nerves in the body, or the areas in the brain that control motor nerves. Normally affects adults between 35 and 70 years of age.

SYMPTOMS: Muscles in various parts of the body become steadily weaker until complete paralysis results, but the muscles affected, and therefore the symptoms, vary between patients. Common symptoms include difficulty in swallowing and talking, drooling of saliva, inability to cough effectively, reduced tongue movement, and weakness of the arms and legs. As the disease progresses, weakness of the muscles required for breathing cause severe shortness of breath Some muscles may go into spasms that cause jerking movements and speech.

INVESTIGATIONS: Electrical tests of the motor nerves to determine how well they are functioning, and a nerve biopsy. There are no blood tests to make the diagnosis.

TREATMENT: No cure available, and treatment is aimed at relieving muscle spasm, assisting feeding, preventing infections, aiding breathing and making the patient as comfortable as possible. Physiotherapy on a very regular basis is essential.

COMPLICATIONS: Lung infections such as pneumonia develop, and often lead to death.

PROGNOSIS: Steadily progressive to death within three to five years.

See also Amyotrophic Lateral Sclerosis; Kugelberg-Welander Syndrome; Primary Lateral Sclerosis; Spinal Muscular Atrophy; Werdnig-Hoffman Syndrome

Mountain Sickness
See Altitude Sickness

Mouth Cancer
(Oral Cancer)

DESCRIPTION: Cancer involving the lip, tongue, palate, gums or floor of the mouth. Rare under 45 years of age.

CAUSE: Smoking associated with most cases.

SYMPTOMS: Abnormally coloured or firm patch, tender lump, a persistent ulcer or painful swelling within the mouth.

INVESTIGATIONS: Scrapings taken from the surface of the suspected cancer can be examined under a microscope.

TREATMENT: Surgical removal or irradiation of the cancer.

COMPLICATIONS: Spread to nearby lymph nodes and other organs.

PROGNOSIS: Overall one third of patients survive for five years, but better with early detection.

See also Cancer

Mouth Infection
See Gingivostomatitis; Stomatitis

Mouth Ulcer
(Aphthous Ulcer)

DESCRIPTION: Ulceration of the moist (mucous) membrane that lines the inside of the mouth.

CAUSE: Most common cause is an imbalance between the normal bacteria, viruses and fungi that are present in the mouth. An infection, allergy, being overtired or run-down, or a course of antibiotics may be sufficient to alter this delicate balance and allow one type to overgrow, attack the lining of the mouth, and form an ulcer. Other causes include injuries to the mouth from false teeth, biting on hard food, dental disorders, burns from hot liquids, food allergies, infections of the mouth and numerous less common but sometimes quite serious diseases (eg. leukaemia, coeliac disease, tuberculosis). Some women develop them before their periods every month.

SYMPTOMS: One or more painful ulcers in the mouth that may vary from one or two millimetres in diameter to over a centimetre.

INVESTIGATIONS: If recurrent, tests can be performed to detect any specific cause.

TREATMENT: Antiseptic and pain relieving gels, lotions, pastes or mouthwashes. Vitamin B and folic acid supplements may be beneficial. In resistant cases pastes that contain steroids and antibiotics can be prescribed.

COMPLICATIONS: Cancers in the mouth may first appear as a mouth ulcer, particularly in smokers.

PROGNOSIS: Very good, but recurrences common.

See also Stomatitis

MRSA
See Staphylococcal Infection

MS
See Multiple Sclerosis

Mucinous Cyst of the Cervix
See Nabothian Cyst

Mucocutaneous Leischmaniasis
(Espundia; Naso-Oral Leischmaniasis)

DESCRIPTION: Protozoan (single celled animal) infection of the nose, mouth and surrounding skin.

CAUSE: The protozoan *Leishmania braziliensis* which is transmitted from person to person by direct contact (eg. kissing) or sand flies. Dogs and rats also carry the protozoan. Occurs only in tropical central and south America.

SYMPTOMS: Nodules, warty growths or ulcers on the nose and lips, and ulcers inside the nostrils and mouth.

INVESTIGATIONS: Scrapings from ulcers show characteristic changes under a microscope. Other specific diagnostic tests available.

TREATMENT: Regular injections of medications to destroy the protozoan necessary for several weeks.

COMPLICATIONS: Death may occur from massive ulceration and facial tissue destruction. May spread to affect throat. Disfiguring scars and facial deformities may be left after healing. Secondary bacterial infection of sores common.

PROGNOSIS: Sores heal spontaneously in six to 24 months.

See also Cutaneous Leischmaniasis; Kala-Azar

Mucocutaneous Lymph Node Syndrome
See Kawasaki Syndrome

Mucopolysaccharoidosis
See Hunter Syndrome; Hurler Syndrome; Sanfilippo Syndrome; Scheie Syndrome; Sly Syndrome

Mucormycosis
See Zygomycosis

Mucus Colitis
See Irritable Bowel Syndrome

Multiple Endocrine Neoplasia Type 1
See Werner Syndrome

Multiple Endocrine Neoplasia Type 2
(MEN 2)

DESCRIPTION: Cancers occurring in numerous glands, but particularly the thyroid, that may start in childhood.

CAUSE: Inherited condition that occurs in one in every 25,000 people.

SYMPTOMS: Type 2A — cancer of the thyroid gland in the neck, overactivity of the parathyroid glands (hyperparathyroidism) and a high blood pressure producing tumour of the adrenal glands on top of the kidneys (phaeochromocytoma) (see separate entries).

Type 2B — cancer of the thyroid gland in the neck, a high blood pressure producing tumour of the adrenal glands on top of the kidneys (phaeochromocytoma), Marfan syndrome, and abnormal nerve growth (neuromas) in the mouth, nose, intestine and other areas where a moist membrane lines a body cavity (see separate entries).

INVESTIGATIONS: Specific gene testing.

TREATMENT: Removal of the thyroid gland when first diagnosed, and other tumours and cancers when detected.

COMPLICATIONS: Spread of cancers before detection.

PROGNOSIS: Poor.

See also Werner Syndrome

Multiple Hamartoma Syndrome
See Cowden Disease

Multiple Myeloma
(Myelomatosis)

DESCRIPTION: A cancer of the cells in the bone marrow of the elderly that causes destruction of the marrow and damage to the surrounding bone.

Multiple Myeloma

CAUSE: Unknown.

SYMPTOMS: Bone pain (back, ribs and thighs are the most common sites), tiredness from anaemia, and recurrent infections because of reduced immunity. Further symptoms include fractures of weakened bones, and kidney and heart failure caused by the toxic by-products of the marrow and bone destruction.

INVESTIGATIONS: Because bone is being destroyed by the marrow cancer, calcium is released, and very high levels of calcium are found on blood tests. Diagnosis can be confirmed by specific tests on the blood and a biopsy of bone marrow. X-rays show a 'moth-eaten' appearance of the bone in areas where it has been eaten away, particularly in the skull, ribs and long bones of the arms and legs.

TREATMENT: No cure. Potent cytotoxic drugs and radiotherapy are used to reduce the symptoms and prolong life.

COMPLICATIONS: Blood becomes excessively thick and viscous, which this leads to a wide range of other symptoms including dizziness, vomiting, bleeding gums, mental changes and partial blindness.

PROGNOSIS: Patients survive for one to four years after diagnosis, depending upon their age, the aggressiveness of the cancer, and their general health.

Multiple Personality Disorder

DESCRIPTION: Very rare disorder in which multiple personalities alternate within the one body.

CAUSE: May be started by stress in childhood or adolescence (eg. a sexual assault, emotional cruelty, repressed aggression), but in most cases, no specific cause found.

SYMPTOMS: Two or more (sometimes more than 20) different personalities within the same body that may switch from being dominant and obvious to being totally suppressed in a matter of seconds. One personality is usually present for most of the time, and others for far shorter periods, but in some patients it is difficult to determine which personality is the most common. Each personality is totally independent of the others, with its own likes and dislikes, friends and hobbies; but the different personalities may be aware of each others presence in the one body, and there may be friends and enemies between the personalities. At other times, one personality may not be aware of the activities of the other. The change from one personality to another is often triggered by stress, but sometimes a particular action, activity, place or word may trigger the change. The personalities are often opposites — shy or extrovert, teetotaller or alcoholic, sportsman or studious. A normally faithful husband may suddenly become involved with prostitutes, a rabid anti-smoker may change into a chain-smoker. The possibilities are endless.

INVESTIGATIONS: No specific diagnostic tests, but a CT or MRI brain scan may be performed to exclude structural abnormalities.

TREATMENT: The aim of psychiatrists is to determine which personality is dominant and to promote that personality over the others in a life-long course of psychotherapy.

COMPLICATIONS: The risk of suicide while in one of the alternate personalities is high.

PROGNOSIS: Varies significantly from one patient to another.

See also other diseases listed under Psychiatric Disorders

Multiple Sclerosis
(Disseminated Sclerosis; MS)

DESCRIPTION: An uncommon disease of the brain and spinal cord that interferes with the brain's ability to control the body.

CAUSE: Not known precisely, but there are several theories. It is possibly due to an unidentified virus, or it may be that the body becomes allergic to itself, and starts attacking its own cells in an immune response. May start as a transverse myelitis (see separate entry). Scattered parts of the brain and spinal cord are damaged at random, the affected areas fail to function properly, and nerve messages from the brain to the muscles do not flow smoothly. Sometimes the message cannot get through at all, and paralysis results, while at other times the message may go to the wrong place, causing abnormal movement or a tremor. Often attacks people in the prime of life rather than old age, is more common in people with western European ancestry, and is rare in the tropics between 40°S and 40°N. It is not contagious or preventable.

SYMPTOMS: Vary greatly from one patient to another, but usually include vision problems, unusual forms of paralysis, tremor, loss of balance, poor coordination, general tiredness and numbness. Patients may experience difficulty in controlling an arm or leg, cannot talk, or may have periods of blindness. Symptoms also change in a patient because damaged tissue can repair itself and start functioning again, while other nerves becomes damaged, causing yet another set of symptoms.

INVESTIGATIONS: The diagnosis can be difficult to confirm. Electroencephalograms (EEG), electromyelograms (EMG), blood tests (no specific test is diagnostic) and magnetic resonance imaging (MRI) are all used.

TREATMENT: No effective treatment available, but some medications (eg: beta interferon, steroids) can slow its progress, control acute attacks and bring about remissions. Physiotherapists, speech therapists and occupational therapists are also used.

COMPLICATIONS: Pressure skin areas and bacterial infections of various organs due to lack of movement.

PROGNOSIS: Goes through a series of attacks and remissions, and periods of good health between attacks can last for months or years. Most patients can lead independent, active and satisfying lives and take care of their own needs for many years after the diagnosis is made. The life span of victims is not significantly altered.

See also Transverse Myelitis

Mumps

DESCRIPTION: A viral infection of the salivary glands in the neck that usually occurs in childhood.

CAUSE: The responsible virus spreads in microscopic droplets of fluid that come from the nose and mouth with every breath. Incubation period is two to three weeks, and the patient is infectious from one or two days before the symptoms appear until all the swelling of the glands has disappeared. An attack usually gives lifelong immunity.

SYMPTOMS: Fever, swollen tender salivary glands just under and behind the jaw, headache, and a general feeling of ill-being. Sometimes one side of the neck is involved, and not the other, then the other side may swell up several days after the first side has subsided. Patients often experience additional pain in the gland if spicy or highly flavoured food is eaten, or even smelled.

INVESTIGATIONS: None normally necessary, but diagnosis can be confirmed by blood tests.

TREATMENT: Rest, with aspirin or paracetamol and/or codeine for the pain and fever, but if complications occur, further medical advice should be sought. Exclusion from school is mandatory for the course of the disease. A vaccine available that gives lifelong protection, and is given combined with those against measles and German measles (rubella) at 12 months and 5 years of age.

COMPLICATIONS: May be a significant disease, particularly in adults. Inflammation of the brain, testicles and ovaries may occur. The kidneys, heart and thyroid gland may also be damaged. Very rarely, death may occur.

PROGNOSIS: Recovery is usually uneventful after an eight to twelve day course.

Munchausen Syndrome

DESCRIPTION: A serious psychiatric condition that involves lying and faking the symptoms of a serious illness. A disturbing form occurs when parents induce false illnesses in their children, and demand inappropriate investigations and surgery for them (Polle syndrome or Munchausen's syndrome by proxy).

CAUSE: Unknown, but patients have usually studied medical textbooks, and are able to describe and mimic a wide range of medical symptoms and diseases.

SYMPTOMS: Patients travel from one hospital and doctor to another, and tell extraordinary lies in order to obtain the most elaborate and extensive medical investigations and treatment possible. They may convulse, roll in agony, vomit, pretend to be unconscious and even mutilate themselves so that they bleed in front of examining doctors. By these means, they convince doctors to subject them to numerous operations for imaginary ills, and then they discharge themselves prematurely from hospital so that they can present to another doctor or hospital for further treatment of the 'complications' of the last operation or to complain about the 'incompetence' of the previous doctor.

INVESTIGATIONS: None diagnostic.

TREATMENT: Thorough assessment by a psychiatrist followed by prolonged counselling and psychotherapy.

COMPLICATIONS: Patients may actually succeed in committing suicide or develop serious complications of surgery by the actions of unsuspecting, but caring, doctors.

PROGNOSIS: Treatment is usually difficult, and even after apparent success the relapse rate is high.

See also Polle Syndrome; SHAFT Syndrome

Munchausen Syndrome by Proxy
See Polle Syndrome

Murray Valley Encephalitis

DESCRIPTION: Viral infection of the brain.

CAUSE: Virus spread from water birds to man by a mosquito. Found in the Murray River Valley of Victoria and NSW in Australia. Epidemics occur every few years after flooding. Incubation period three to six days.

SYMPTOMS: Fever and a rash are often the only symptom, but in severe cases may cause eye pain, enlarged tender lymph nodes, dizziness, sore throat, joint pains, headache, neck stiffness, nausea, vomiting, tiredness, disturbed mental functions and disorientation.

INVESTIGATIONS: Tests on blood and the fluid around the brain are abnormal.

TREATMENT: No specific treatment or vaccine available.

COMPLICATIONS: Rarely causes any long term problems.

PROGNOSIS: Acute attack lasts for one to three weeks. Death uncommon.

See also Encephalitis

Muscle Meltdown
See Rhabdomyolysis

Muscular Cramps
See Leg Cramps

Muscular Dystrophy

See Amyotrophic Lateral Sclerosis; Becker's Muscular Dystrophy; Distal Muscular Dystrophy; Duchenne's Muscular Dystrophy; Erb's Muscular Dystrophy; Fascioscapulohumeral Muscular Dystrophy; Inclusion Body Myositis; Kugelberg-Welander Syndrome; Motor Neurone Disease; Myotonic Dystrophy; Oculopharyngeal Muscular Dystrophy; Primary Latewral Sclerosis; Spinal Muscular Atrophy; Werdig-Hoffman Syndrome

Myalgic Encephalomyelitis
See Chronic Fatigue Syndrome

Myasthenia Gravis

DESCRIPTION: A condition characterised by varying weakness of the muscles that control the eyelids, the movement of the eyes and swallowing.

CAUSE: Blocking of signals from the nerves that supply affected muscles, for which there may be an immunological cause when antibodies that normally fight off infection actually attack nerve tissue. May occur at any age, but is most common in young women and may be associated with rheumatoid arthritis, lupus erythematosus (see separate entry), thymus and thyroid disease.

SYMPTOMS: Drooping eyelids (ptosis), double vision and difficulty in swallowing. In severe cases the muscles used in breathing and walking are also affected. Muscle weakness varies in severity during the day and may disappear entirely for days or weeks before recurring. Over a period of months or years, the attacks become more severe.

INVESTIGATIONS: Diagnosis confirmed by the patients reaction to an anticholinergic drug which immediately reverses all the muscle weakness.

TREATMENT: Surgically removing the thymus gland which is the source of most of the antibodies in the blood, and using anticholinergic drugs on a regular basis to control the muscle weakness. Steroids can be used in patients who respond poorly to other treatments.

COMPLICATIONS: Unless adequate treatment is obtained, death eventually results from breathing difficulties.

PROGNOSIS: No cure and patients require treatment for the rest of their lives, but some have lengthy periods when the disease is inactive, during which they may be able to cease their medication.

Myasthenic Syndrome
See Eaton-Lambert Syndrome

Mycetoma
(Madura Foot)

DESCRIPTION: Fungal infection of the foot.

CAUSE: Numerous different fungi that are normally found in the soil enter minor skin wounds on the feet of people in tropical areas who go about barefoot.

SYMPTOMS: Firm, painless lumps under the skin of the foot that eventually break down into persistent discharging sores. The surrounding skin becomes very thickened.

INVESTIGATIONS: Swabs from the sores identify the responsible fungi.

TREATMENT: Antifungal medications for a long time, and sometimes surgery to cut away affected tissue.

COMPLICATIONS: May spread into the bones of the foot causing deformity.

PROGNOSIS: Cured by treatment early in the disease, but long lasting cases may be very resistant to treatment.

Mycoplasma Infection

DESCRIPTION: Bacterial infection that may cause a particularly insidious form of pneumonia (see separate entry).

CAUSE: The bacterium *Mycoplasma pneumoniae*, which tends to attack teenagers and young adults, and often in summer rather than winter.

SYMPTOMS: In the lungs, symptoms are frequently mild at the beginning of the infection and slowly worsen over many weeks. A wheeze, persistent cough, tiredness, intermittent fever and loss of appetite are most common.

INVESTIGATIONS: A chest X-ray shows a typical pneumonia pattern, and a sputum sample can then be cultured to determine the bacteria present. Blood tests show the presence of infection, but not the type.

TREATMENT: Antibiotics such as erythromycin and tetracycline.

COMPLICATIONS: Often confused with asthma or viral infections.

PROGNOSIS: Cured by appropriate antibiotics.

See also Pneumonia

Mycoses

See Fungal Infection

Mycosis Fungoides

DESCRIPTION: A rare form of cancer involving the lymphatic tissue in the skin.

CAUSE: May be caused by spread from other lymphatic cancers (see Hodgkin's disease entry) elsewhere in the body, or may arise in the skin.

SYMPTOMS: Red circular patches appear on the skin, that initially may be confused with a fungal skin infection (thus the disease name), and gradually spread across the body.

INVESTIGATIONS: Diagnosed by taking a biopsy (surgical sample) of the rash.

TREATMENT: Applications of anti-cancer medications directly to the skin, ultraviolet light therapy, irradiation of the affected areas of skin, and in more severe cases, anti-cancer tablets and injections.

COMPLICATIONS: May spread from the skin to other organs.

PROGNOSIS: From when first diagnosed, average life expectancy is seven years.

See also Hodgkin's Disease; Sézary Syndrome

Myelitis

See Multiple Sclerosis; Transverse Myelitis

Myeloid Leukaemia

See Leukaemia, Acute Myeloid; Leukaemia, Chronic Myeloid

Myelodysplastic Syndrome

DESCRIPTION: Abnormality of white blood cell development.

CAUSE: Unknown.

SYMPTOMS: Anaemia that does not respond to normal treatments, abnormal white blood cell and bone marrow cell structure seen when examined under a microscope, general feeling of being unwell, tiredness, frequent infections and abnormal bleeding.

INVESTIGATIONS: Abnormal blood and bone marrow tests.

TREATMENT: Antibiotics, blood transfusions, platelet concentrate transfusions, bone marrow transplantation.

COMPLICATIONS: May be forerunner to acute leukaemia. Severe uncontrollable infections or bleeding may occur.

PROGNOSIS: Poor.

Myelofibrosis
(Idiopathic Myelofibrosis)

DESCRIPTION: Uncommon condition in which white blood cell producing bone marrow is replaced by fibrous scar like tissue.

CAUSE: Unknown in most cases, but may follow a severe infection of the marrow, cancer that spreads to the marrow, or be a complication of a lymphoma (cancer of lymph tissue) or leukaemia.

SYMPTOMS: Often none until disease well advanced when a large spleen and liver, and anaemia are noticed. Later, night sweats, weight loss and fevers occur.

INVESTIGATIONS: Blood cell tests and bone marrow biopsy are abnormal. Bone X-rays may also show marrow damage.

TREATMENT: None specific.

COMPLICATIONS: Fluid accumulation in the belly, bone overgrowth and nerve pinching, severe infections that do not respond to antibiotics, lymphatic cancers, leukaemia and destruction of the body's immune system.

PROGNOSIS: Average survival time of five years from time of diagnosis.

Myeloma, Multiple
See Multiple Myeloma

Myelomatosis
See Multiple Myeloma

Myocardial Infarct
See Heart Attack

Myocarditis
(Heart Infection)

DESCRIPTION: An uncommon but serious infection or inflammation of heart muscle.

CAUSE: Bacterial, viral (most common), parasitic (rarest) or fungal (most serious) infection of the muscle in the heart wall. Inflammation of the heart muscle may be caused by poisons (eg. arsenic), toxins, irradiation and potent drugs (eg. cytotoxics used in cancer treatment). Patients usually remember another infection a week or two prior to the onset.

SYMPTOMS: Chest pain is common, and may be accompanied by a rapid pulse, tiredness, shortness of breath, swollen ankles and a cough.

INVESTIGATIONS: Diagnosis confirmed by an electrocardiogram (ECG), blood tests, and echocardiogram.

TREATMENT: Depends upon the cause. If bacteria are present, antibiotics are prescribed, but if a virus is responsible, no specific treatment is available.

COMPLICATIONS: Heart failure may develop as damaged heart muscle cannot contract normally.

PROGNOSIS: Bacterial infections can be cured, but viral myocarditis tends to persist for many months and then slowly resolve. Permanent heart damage is a common result.

See also Endocarditis

Myoclonus
(Epilepsia Partialis Continua)

DESCRIPTION: Nervous system abnormality.

CAUSE: May be due to uraemia (kidney failure), body chemistry disorders, Creutzfeldt-Jakob disease, epilepsy (see separate entries), brain injury (eg. stroke), side effect of medication (eg. levodopa), alcoholism and sometimes has no apparent cause.

SYMPTOMS: Sudden jerking movements.

INVESTIGATIONS: EEG (electroencephalogram) abnormal.

TREATMENT: Anticonvulsant medications (eg. valproic acid, benzodiazepines).

PROGNOSIS: Reasonable response to treatment, but depends on cause.

Myofascial Pain Syndrome

DESCRIPTION: Painful spasm of muscles.

CAUSE: Overuse (eg. writing, typing) of muscles, poor posture, or injury to a muscle or muscle group, particularly in the back, shoulders, neck and chest. May be associated with osteoarthritis in the neck and back.

SYMPTOMS: Deep, aching, burning pain in affected muscles that is triggered by touch or muscle use. Muscles may twitch uncontrollably.

INVESTIGATIONS: None usually necessary.

TREATMENT: Physiotherapy with ultrasound, maintaining correct posture, anti-inflammatory drugs, muscle relaxants and pain killers.

COMPLICATIONS: Fibrocytis (see separate entry) may occur if condition becomes prolonged.

PROGNOSIS: Good.

Myolysis
See Rhabdomyolysis

Myopia
See Short-Sighted

Myositis

See Dermatomyositis; Focal Nodular Myositis; Gangrene, Gas; Inclusion Body Myositis; Infectious Myositis

Myotonic Dystrophy
(Dystrophia Myotonica; Steinert's Disease)

DESCRIPTION: Progressive condition in which there is delayed relaxation of muscles after contraction. Age of onset varies from mid teens to middle age. Rarely it may start in infancy.

CAUSE: Hereditary disorder affecting muscle cell membranes. Only occurs if both parents are carriers of a defective gene on chromosome 19.

SYMPTOMS: Inability to release grip, muscle weakness and wasting, difficulty in moving arms and legs. Symptoms start in the face, neck, hands and feet, and slowly move towards the trunk.

INVESTIGATIONS: Diagnosed by muscle biopsy.

TREATMENT: Physiotherapy, ankle braces and specific treatments for complications.

COMPLICATIONS: May be associated with cell damage in the heart, eyes (causing cataracts), wasting of the testicles, breathing difficulties, variable bowel habits, worsening mental retardation and confusion, difficulty in swallowing, drowsiness and body chemistry disorders.

PROGNOSIS: No cure available. Slowly progressive. Fatal when heart muscles and muscles of breathing become involved. The older the person at onset of symptoms the more slowly the disease progresses.

See also other diseases listed under Muscular Dystrophy

Myxoedema
See Hypothyroidism

Myxoma
(Cardiac Myxoma)

DESCRIPTION: Most common form of benign tumour occuring inside the heart.

CAUSE: Unknown in most cases, but may be familial (run in families).

SYMPTOMS: Very variable depending upon position within the heart, its size and the effect it has on heart function. Non-specific symptoms may include a fever, weight loss, tiredness and loss of appetite.

INVESTIGATIONS: Diagnosed by echocardiography (ultrasound scan).

TREATMENT: Surgical removal of the tumour.

COMPLICATIONS: Sudden death due to blockage of a heart valve or irregular heart beat (ventricular fibrillation).

PROGNOSIS: Good results from surgery if diagnosed early enough.

N

Nabothian Cyst
(Mucinous Cyst of the Cervix)

DESCRIPTION: Cyst formed from a mucous gland on the cervix, which is the part of the uterus that protrudes into the top of the vagina.

CAUSE: Often unknown, but probably due to injury or infection that damages one of the mucous secreting glands in the cervix.

SYMPTOMS: None. Usually discovered during a routine Pap smear.

INVESTIGATIONS: None necessary.

TREATMENT: None usually needed, but may be cut open and drained if necessary.

COMPLICATIONS: Rarely, may be responsible for abnormal bleeding.

PROGNOSIS: Usually remain for many years, but may burst and disappear spontaneously.

Naevus

DESCRIPTION: Small area of abnormal, but benign, skin pigmentation. May be single or multiple. Many different forms including blue naevus (benign blue coloured and smooth), **Becker naevus** (hairy, male, shoulders), **sebaceous** (yellow, bumpy, on scalp), **epidermal** (very common, may be extensive), halo, portwine, strawberry and spider (see separate entries).

CAUSE: Developmental defect.

SYMPTOMS: Rough raised area of skin of almost any colour, but often brown.

INVESTIGATIONS: If there is any suspicion that the spot may be malignant, it should be biopsied or cut out.

TREATMENT: None necessary. Cosmetic surgery may be performed if desired.

PROGNOSIS: Usually remain life long.

See also Blue Naevus; Halo Naevus; Portwine Naevus; Spider Naevi; Strawberry Naevus

Naffziger Syndrome
(Cervical Rib Syndrome; Scalenus Anticus Syndrome; Thoracic Outlet Obstruction Syndrome)

DESCRIPTION: Additional rib present in lower neck above normal first rib. Nerves and arteries can be compressed between the extra cervical rib and the scalenus anticus muscle in the neck.

CAUSE: Congenital.

SYMPTOMS: Abnormal pressure on ulnar nerve causes pain and pins and needles sensation in arm and hand, muscular weakness of small hand muscles, and altered sensation in forearm and hand. In severe cases patients have cold blue hands, and reduced pulsation and blood flow in the radial and ulnar arteries in the arm.

INVESTIGATIONS: X-ray of the neck shows the extra cervical rib.
TREATMENT: Rest, neck traction, and surgical excision of extra rib.
COMPLICATIONS: Horner syndrome (see separate entry).
PROGNOSIS: Slowly progressive, intermittent course. Good result from surgery.

Nail Bed Infection
See Paronychia

Nail Bruise
See Subungal Haematoma

Nail-Patella Syndrome
See Fong Syndrome

Nappy Eczema
See Seborrhoeic Eczema

Nappy Rash
DESCRIPTION: Baby who develops an angry red area of skin under the nappy. A nappy rash is not a reflection on the mother or a sign of neglect, but a very common problem.
CAUSE: Excess moisture on the skin from wet nappies, pilchers and plastic overpants can cause skin damage, eczema and fungal infections (tinea cruris). Overbathing, soap and detergents left in nappies may also irritate the skin.
SYMPTOMS: Red, pealing, irritated skin on the buttocks. If the skin folds are mainly involved, it is probably eczema. If the skin folds are spared and there are red satellite lesions beyond the edge of the rash, it may be fungal.
INVESTIGATIONS: None normally necessary, but swabs may confirm the presence of a fungus or bacteria.
TREATMENT: Zinc cream, lanolin or petroleum jelly applied to the bottom will protect it against moisture. Fungal infections will settle with antifungal creams, but eczema may require a mild steroid cream.
COMPLICATIONS: Uncommonly bacterial infections may occur.
PROGNOSIS: Good, and even the most resistant cases settle once the child is toilet trained.
See also Seborrhoeic Eczema; Tinea Cruris

Narcolepsy
DESCRIPTION: An unusual disorder of the brain's electrical activity that is characterised by sudden uncontrolled episodes of sleep.
CAUSE: Unknown, but patients go from wakefulness almost immediately into the deepest type of sleep, known as REM (rapid eye movement) sleep, without passing through the normal intermediate stages.
SYMPTOMS: Sudden periods of sleeping for 5 to 30 minutes several times a day,

sudden muscle weakness, hallucinations before and during sleep periods, and paralysis immediately before and during sleep. Patients suddenly fall asleep, sometimes in the middle of a sentence, or when halfway across a pedestrian crossing. Wide range of severity from those who merely appear to sleep excessively, to those who are barely able to function or care for themselves.

INVESTIGATIONS: Diagnosis confirmed by an electroencephalogram (EEG) and by observing the patient in a sleep laboratory.

TREATMENT: Stimulants such as amphetamine used on a regular basis. Patients must not be allowed to drive, swim or operate machinery until they have been well controlled for a long time.

COMPLICATIONS: Obvious danger that the patient may accidentally harm themselves.

PROGNOSIS: In many patients, good control of symptoms is quite difficult to achieve.

Narcotic Addiction
(Heroin Addiction)

DESCRIPTION: Abuse of one of the most addictive substances known. Narcotics including codeine, pethidine, morphine and oxycodone, are all derived from heroin and can be abused if taken regularly or excessively. Used medically as tablets or injections to relieve pain and diarrhoea. Normally used by addicts as an injection directly into the veins, but may also be inhaled or eaten, when they have a much slower effect.

CAUSE: Refined from the milky juice of the opium poppy. Most abusers have personality disorders, antisocial behaviour, or are placed in situations of extreme stress. Possibly one in every 100 people in developed countries is dependent upon illicit drugs, and a far higher percentage have experimented with them at one time or another.

SYMPTOMS: Causes exaggerated happiness, relief of pain, a feeling of unreality, and a sensation of bodily detachment. Contracted pupils that do not respond to light are a sign of use. Tolerance develops quickly, and with time, higher and higher doses must be used to cause the same effect.

INVESTIGATIONS: Blood and urine tests can detect the presence of narcotics.

TREATMENT: The treatment options available are:

— Gradual withdrawal while receiving counselling and medical support.

— Immediate drug withdrawal ('cold turkey') while hospitalised in a specialised unit, sometimes combined with other drugs that are used temporarily to reduce the symptoms associated with the drug withdrawal.

— Substitution of heroin with a prescribed medication (eg. methadone) on a medium to long-term basis before it is slowly withdrawn.

— Naltrexone may be used to flush heroin from the body, and relieve the addiction, within a few days, a process that must be undertaken under strict supervision in a specialised clinic. Naltrexone may also be used long term to reduce the desire for heroin.

— Half-way houses that remove the patient from the environment in which drug taking is encouraged.

— Individual or group psychotherapy.

— Education of intravenous drug users of the dangers associated with their habit (eg. the development of AIDS or hepatitis B).

COMPLICATIONS: Often combined with abuse of alcohol, smoking and synthetic drugs. Physiological problems include vomiting, constipation, brain damage (personality changes, paranoia), nerve damage (persistent pins and needles or numbness), infertility, impotence, stunting of growth in children, difficulty in breathing (to the point of stopping breathing if given in high doses) and low blood pressure. Withdrawal causes vomiting, diarrhoea, coughing, twitching, fever, crying, excessive sweating, generalised muscle pain, rapid breathing and an intense desire for the drug. These symptoms can commence within 8 to 12 hours of the last dose, and peaks at 48 to 72 hours after withdrawal. Mild symptoms may persist for up to six months. As sterile techniques are often not followed when self injecting, the veins and skin at the injection site become infected and scarred.

PROGNOSIS: One quarter of heroin addicts will die within ten years of commencing the habit as a direct result of the heroin use. A rising proportion will die from complications of the intravenous injections such as AIDS, septicaemia and hepatitis B, C and D.

See also other problems listed under Addiction

Naso-Oral Leischmaniasis
See Mucocutaneous Leischmaniasis

Neck Sprain
See Whiplash

Necrotising Encephalomyelopathy, Subacute
See Leigh Disease

Necrotising Enterocolitis

DESCRIPTION: A rare disease of infants in which large segments of the small and large intestines become gangrenous.

CAUSE: Unknown, but may be associated with gut infections, and more common in premature babies.

SYMPTOMS: Bloody diarrhoea, vomiting, and rapid onset of obvious distress as the intestine ruptures and allows its contents to escape into the abdominal cavity.

INVESTIGATIONS: Diagnosis confirmed by X-ray of the abdomen.

TREATMENT: Urgent surgery, massive doses of antibiotics and intensive care are sometimes successful.

PROGNOSIS: Most die within a couple of days.

Necrotising Fasciitis
(Flesh Eating Disease)

DESCRIPTION: A very serious infection and destruction of the fascia, the fibrous material around muscles and other internal organs that binds them together.

CAUSE: Bacteria in the *Streptococci* group. Because the fascia is fibrous tissue, it has a very poor blood supply, and antibiotics have difficulty in reaching the infection.

SYMPTOMS: The bacteria spread extensively through the body and painfully destroy all the flesh surrounded by the infected fascia, converting it into pus or scar tissue.

INVESTIGATIONS: Swabs taken from infected tissue can identify the bacteria responsible.

TREATMENT: Massive doses of potent antibiotics given by a drip into a vein, and extensive and radical surgery to cut away the infected flesh (eg. limb amputation).

COMPLICATIONS: The infecting forms of *Streptococci* are sometimes resistant to many antibiotics.

PROGNOSIS: Difficult to treat and may cause severe tissue damage or death.

Necrotising Ulcerative Gingivostomatitis
(Trench Mouth)

DESCRIPTION: Severe bacterial infection of the mouth and gums.

CAUSE: A mixed infection of two or more different bacteria in the mouth. Common in young adults at times of excessive stress, highly infectious and may spread rapidly through a closely confined group (eg. school children, soldiers living in the trenches during the first world war — thus trench mouth).

SYMPTOMS: Pain, soreness, ulceration and grey membrane formation in the mouth, on the gums and the tonsils associated with very bad breath.

INVESTIGATIONS: None normally necessary, but if required swabs taken from the mouth can identify the responsible bacteria.

TREATMENT: Antibiotic tablets (eg. penicillin) and a hydrogen peroxide gargle.

PROGNOSIS: Responds readily to antibiotics.

See also Gingivostomatitis

Nelson Syndrome

DESCRIPTION: Rare complication of Cushing syndrome.

CAUSE: Usually follows removal of both adrenal glands (which sit on top of the kidneys) for Cushing syndrome.

SYMPTOMS: Skin and tongue pigmentation, and enlargement of the pituitary gland under the brain.

INVESTIGATIONS: Skull X-ray and CT scan show the enlarged pituitary gland and blood tests show low levels of vital hormones (eg. cortisol).

TREATMENT: Replacement of many different hormones by tablets or injection.

COMPLICATIONS: Enlarging pituitary gland may put pressure on the optic nerve from the eye to cause partial visual field loss.
PROGNOSIS: Reasonably good.
See also Cushing Syndrome

Nematode Infestation
(Roundworm Infestation)

See Angiostrongyliasis; Anisakiasis; Ascariasis; Cutaneous Larva Migrans; Gnathostomiasis; Hookworm; Roundworm Infestation; Trichinosis; Visceral Larva Migrans

Neoplasm
See Cancer

Nephritis

See Glomerulonephritis; Nephrotic Syndrome; Pyelonephritis, Acute; Pyelonephritis, Chronic

Nephroblastoma
See Wilms' Tumour

Nephrolithiasis
See Kidney Stone

Nephrotic Syndrome

DESCRIPTION: A form of kidney failure resulting in symptoms that are a result of the kidney's inability to remove fluid and waste products from the body.
CAUSE: Usually caused by glomerulonephritis (see separate entry), but may be a complication of diabetes, multiple myeloma, poisons or other diseases. It is far more common in places where there are poor standards of nutrition and hygiene.
SYMPTOMS: A dramatic swelling (caused by fluid) of the body — the feet, abdomen and hands being the most commonly affected areas. If the chest is affected, the patient becomes very short of breath. Other symptoms include high blood pressure, stretch marks (striae) on the skin of the swollen belly, loss of appetite and a pale complexion. The patient is obviously very ill and may deteriorate rapidly.
INVESTIGATIONS: The diagnosis is confirmed by urine and blood tests. A biopsy of the kidney is often performed to determine the severity of the damage.
TREATMENT: No specific treatment is available, but prolonged bed rest, usually in a hospital, is essential. Steroids are often prescribed to limit further damage. If a specific cause for the disease is present (eg. diabetes), this can be treated.
COMPLICATIONS: Total kidney failure may require kidney transplantation or dialysis.

PROGNOSIS: The outcome in children is far better than in adults, and the majority recover after a few weeks. In adults, long-term kidney problems are more likely.
See also Glomerulonephritis; Kidney Failure, Chronic

Nerve Rash
See Neurodermatitis

Nervous Breakdown
See Depression; Neurosis

Nervous Dyspepsia
See Irritable Bowel Syndrome

Neu-Lexova Syndrome
DESCRIPTION: Rare congenital abnormality.
CAUSE: Familial (runs in families), but only if both parents carry the abnormal gene.
SYMPTOMS: Absent eyelids, underdeveloped nose and jaw, abnormal skin structure and texture, swelling of feet and hands, multiple skin contractures and mental retardation.
INVESTIGATIONS: None specific.
TREATMENT: None available.
PROGNOSIS: Poor.

Neuralgia
DESCRIPTION: Pain in any nerve.
CAUSE: Pinching of a nerve between other tissues (eg. between ribs with prolonged coughing), a reduced blood supply to a nerve (eg. migraine, diabetes), an infection of the nerve (eg. shingles), an injury to the nerve, or joint arthritis (eg. back arthritis causing sciatica).
SYMPTOMS: Sudden, severe, shooting and often brief stabs of pain that may occur anywhere, but the chest, face and arms are more frequently affected.
INVESTIGATIONS: Cause must be investigated by X-rays and sometimes blood tests.
TREATMENT: Depends on the cause. Anti-inflammatory drugs can reduce inflammation associated with muscle strain and arthritis, and steroids can be given as injections into the damaged area. Physiotherapy is often useful.
COMPLICATIONS: Permanent damage to the nerve may cause loss of sensation to the affected area.
PROGNOSIS: Normally good, but depends on cause.
See also Glossopharyngeal Neuralgia; Shingles; Trigeminal Neuralgia

Neurodermatitis
(Nerve Rash)

DESCRIPTION: A rapidly developing form of dermatitis associated with stress.

CAUSE: May be triggered by stress from an exam, job interview, marriage or any other event. It does not mean that you are neurotic or in need of psychiatric care, the rash is merely an outward manifestation of a sometimes minor stress in an otherwise normal person.

SYMPTOMS: Multiple very itchy, small red raised lumps on the skin that may fluctuate quite rapidly in their intensity. The front of the wrist, inside of the elbow and backs of the knees are the most commonly affected areas, but it may occur anywhere.

INVESTIGATIONS: None normally necessary.

TREATMENT: Mild steroid cream to reduce inflammation in the skin.

COMPLICATIONS: None significant.

PROGNOSIS: If the cream is applied as soon as the rash appears, it should settle almost immediately.

See also Dermatitis; Lichen Simplex

Neuroleptic Malignant Syndrome

DESCRIPTION: Very rare (under 200 cases reported) complication of medication used for severe psychiatric disturbances.

CAUSE: May occur early or late in use of major tranquillisers (eg. phenothiazines, butyrophones, thioxanthines, loxapine) at normal dosages.

SYMPTOMS: Very high fever, muscular rigidity, tremor, abnormal sweating, confusion and loss of consciousness.

INVESTIGATIONS: Some blood tests may be abnormal, but none specifically diagnostic.

TREATMENT: Cease medication and support in hospital intensive care unit. Numerous medications have been trialed to help patients, but none proven effective.

COMPLICATIONS: Rhabdomyolysis (muscle meltdown — see separate entry).

PROGNOSIS: Death in 20%. Early treatment improves mortality.

See also Serotonin Syndrome

Neuroma

See Acoustic Neuroma; Multiple Endocrine Neoplasia Type 2; Schwannoma; von Recklinghausen's Disease of Multiple Neurofibromatosis

Neuromyelitis Optica
See Devic Disease

Neuropathy

See Amyloidosis; Autonomic Neuropathy; Bell's Palsy; Diabetes Mellitus; Guillain-Barré Syndrome; Lead Poisoning; Leber Optic Neuropathy; Leprosy; Multiple Sclerosis; Peripheral Neuropathy; Strachan Syndrome; Trigeminal Neuralgia

Neurosis
(Anxiety Neurosis; Nervous Breakdown; Panic Attack)

DESCRIPTION: An illness of the personality in which the patient is aware that a problem is present. In many psychiatric conditions, such as schizophrenia and psychosis (see separate entries), the patient is not aware that there is a problem present. Both severe neuroses and depression may be politely referred to as a 'nervous breakdown'.

CAUSE: Tendency to run in families from one generation to the next, and most are present before the age of 25 years. It is often not possible to define the cause of the anxiety, but patients may try to explain it as a result of some stress in their lives, but in most situations, when questioned closely, the anxiety is found to be 'free floating' and have no real basis. Panic attacks and neurotic episodes tend to be more common in the week immediately before a menstrual period. Caffeine (in coffee and cola drinks) has also been associated with the onset of attacks.

SYMPTOMS: Patients are excessively anxious for no reason, may be unduly scared of something or some place (a phobia), and may become obviously distressed by their anxiety and/or fear. The distress may take the form of shortness of breath, palpitations, nausea, abdominal pain, headaches or a faint. Anxiety and fear can lead to panic attacks, during which the patient becomes breathless, tight in the chest, dizzy, nauseated, bloated, may vomit and collapse in a faint. These usually occur without warning, but once experienced, the patient will be extremely reluctant to place herself in similar circumstances again.

INVESTIGATIONS: No diagnostic tests.

TREATMENT: Many medications available to assist patients through a crisis. Anxiolytics and sedatives are better used in the short term only, while antidepressants may be used for long periods without adverse effects. Additional treatment involves a mixture of behavioural therapy, psychotherapy and social counselling. Behavioural therapy involves gradually taking the patient through more and more stressful and fear-producing circumstances until the anxiety response wears off. Psychotherapy involves analysing the patient's reaction to their past and present situation. Group therapy may be employed to give additional encouragement. Social counselling requires a doctor, psychologist or social worker to advise the family and friends on how they should assist the patient. Activities that accentuate any phobias or anxieties will be discouraged, and the family will be taught how to encourage a more normal interaction with society by the patient.

COMPLICATIONS: Social isolation due to severe phobias, or the inability to perform everyday activities.

PROGNOSIS: The longer the neurosis has been present, the harder it will be to treat. Long-term treatment and encouragement by a sympathetic doctor is essential in all cases.

See also **Obsessive Compulsive Neurosis; Post Traumatic Stress Disorder; Stress** and other diseases listed under **Psychiatric Conditions**

Nezelof Syndrome
(Thymic Dysplasia)

DESCRIPTION: Abnormal development of the thymus gland which sits behind the upper end of the breast bone and is responsible for the body's immune system.

CAUSE: Congenital.

SYMPTOMS: Infant patients have persistent diarrhoea, severe infections, failure to gain weight, fevers, rashes, and fungal infections (thrush) in the mouth.

INVESTIGATIONS: Abnormal blood tests and bone marrow biopsy.

TREATMENT: Bone marrow transplant. Infections are vigorously treated with antibiotics.

COMPLICATIONS: Severe infections may be fatal.

PROGNOSIS: Can be cured with successful bone marrow transplant, but fatal otherwise.

See also **di George Syndrome; Immunodeficiency**

NGU
See Non-Specific Urethritis

NIDDM
See Diabetes Mellitus

Niemann-Pick Disease

DESCRIPTION: Rare congenital metabolic (body chemistry) disorder.

CAUSE: An inability of the body to process some types of fat due to the lack of an enzyme in the liver. Several different forms of the disease, which vary in their severity, depending on the precise enzyme deficiency.

SYMPTOMS: Enlargement of the liver, failure to gain weight after birth, and retarded mental development.

INVESTIGATIONS: Diagnosed by specific blood and bone marrow tests.

TREATMENT: No treatment available.

PROGNOSIS: Poor.

Nipple Cancer
See Paget's Disease of the Nipple

Nipple Itch

DESCRIPTION: Itchy nipples are a relatively common problem.

CAUSE: Women with small breasts may go without a bra and their nipples are irritated by clothing moving across them, or a loose fitting bra may constantly move across the nipple irritating it. Other causes include synthetic materials in a bra, allergies to soaps, perfumes and washing powders, and fungal infections such as thrush (common in breast feeding mothers).

SYMPTOMS: Intense itching of the breast nipple(s).

INVESTIGATIONS: None normally necessary, unless thrush suspected, when a swab may be taken to identify the responsible fungus.

TREATMENT: Lanolin and other skin moisturisers, anti-itch creams, antifungal creams if thrush present, or prescribed mild steroid creams. Padding a bra may help small breasted women. An adhesive dressing over the nipple can give quick relief.

PROGNOSIS: Very good.

Nocardiosis

DESCRIPTION: Infection by bacteria found normally in the soil that seldom infects humans. Usually occurs in patients with reduced immunity.

CAUSE: The bacteria *Nocardia asteroides*, *Nocardia brasiliensis*, *Nocardia farcinica* and several other species of *Nocardia*.

SYMPTOMS: Depends on site of infection. May cause pneumonia, cellulitis (skin infection) and lymph node infections. Abscesses commonly form in association with the infection.

INVESTIGATIONS: Diagnosed by examination of sputum or pus.

TREATMENT: Antibiotics (eg. sulphonamides).

COMPLICATIONS: Abscesses may burst into adjacent organs to open up abnormal connections.

PROGNOSIS: Usually good response to treatment, but risk of death in patients with seriously reduced immune response (eg. AIDS).

Nocturnal Cramps
See Leg Cramps

Non-Gonococcal Urethritis
See Non-Specific Urethritis

Non-Hodgkin's Lymphoma
(Indolent Lymphoma)

DESCRIPTION: A form of cancer of the lymph nodes.

CAUSE: Unknown. Closely related to some forms of leukaemia. Much more common than Hodgkin's disease.

SYMPTOMS: Persistent, painless enlargement of the lymph nodes in the neck, armpit, groin or other areas including the belly. Patients may be tired and develop an itch, but rarely any fever.

INVESTIGATIONS: Diagnosed by biopsy of an affected lymph node. Blood tests may also be abnormal.

TREATMENT: Depends upon the stage at which the cancer is detected. May involve surgery, irradiation and chemotherapy (anti-cancer drugs).

COMPLICATIONS: May spread to distant lymph nodes and other organs.

PROGNOSIS: Remission common, but complete cure rare. Even in advanced stages, ten year survival is now common.

See also Hodgkin's Disease

Non-Specific Urethritis
(Chlamydial Urethritis; NGU; Non-Gonococcal Urethritis; NSU)

DESCRIPTION: Sexually transmitted disease that is carried by women and infects men.

CAUSE: Most (but not all) cases of NSU are caused by a chlamydial infection. Unidentified bacteria are responsible for the other cases. *Chlamydiae* are a group of organisms that are not bacteria, but act as parasites inside human cells and eventually destroy the cell. Spread by passing from the man to female sexual partners where it remains in the vagina to infect the woman's next sex partner. In homosexuals, the infection may occur around the anus.

SYMPTOMS: Men have a white discharge from the penis, painful passing of urine, but rarely other symptoms. In women there are usually no symptoms, but sometimes the infection may spread to cause salpingitis (see separate entry).

INVESTIGATIONS: May be identified by specific blood and swab tests, but they are not always reliable, and a negative test does not mean that the infection is not present.

TREATMENT: Antibiotics such as tetracyclines and erythromycins. All sexual contacts should be treated when the infection is discovered.

COMPLICATIONS: Infection may spread from the penis up into the testes or prostate gland.

PROGNOSIS: Antibiotics cure the infection.

See also Salpingitis and other diseases listed under Chlamydial Infections and Venereal Diseases

Non-Tropical Sprue
See Coeliac Disease

Noonan Syndrome

DESCRIPTION: Uncommon developmental abnormality with widespread effects.

CAUSE: Congenital (present from birth) condition that occurs in both sexes and without any chromosomal defects.

SYMPTOMS: Short stature, wide neck, broad chest, abnormal heart valves, slanted eyes, low set ears, depressed bridge of the nose, broad tip of the nose and some mental retardation.

INVESTIGATIONS: None diagnostic.

TREATMENT: Surgical correction of the heart problems and plastic surgery to cosmetic deformities.

PROGNOSIS: No cure, but relatively normal life expectancy.
See also Turner Syndrome

Norwegian Scabies
See Scabies

Nose Bleed
See Epistaxis

Notalgia Paraesthetica
DESCRIPTION: Condition of nerve and skin damage on the upper back.
CAUSE: The nerves which supply sensation to the upper back emerge from the spinal cord and run a long course through thick muscles in the back before making a right-angled turn and reaching the skin. They are easily damaged by an injury to the area, shingles or even sunburn. The skin is damaged by rubbing and scratching the affected area.
SYMPTOMS: Itch and/or changed sensation in the area of skin just below the shoulder blade on either side of the back. There may be no visible change in the skin or there may be a brown pigmentation, patchy loss of skin colour or thickening due to rubbing.
INVESTIGATIONS: Changed sensation tested for by pinprick, cotton wool or heat and cold.
TREATMENT: Not always successful. Measures that may be tried include cooling lotions (eg. camphor and menthol), capsaicin cream, local anaesthetic creams and amitryptilline tablets at night.
PROGNOSIS: Not serious but often persistent.

NSU
See Non-Specific Urethritis

Nummular Eczema
See Discoid Eczema

O

Oat Cell Carcinoma of the Lung
See Lung Cancer

Obsessive Compulsive Neurosis

DESCRIPTION: A form of neurosis (see separate entry) in which the patient has a totally irrational desire to undertake a repetitive task.

CAUSE: More common in women than in men and occasionally related to previous brain injury or infection (eg. encephalitis).

SYMPTOMS: The desire to perform a task constantly intrudes into the patient's thoughts, and even after completing the task, they feel that they must do it again and again. One of the most common desires is hand washing when patient cannot be convinced that his/her hands are clean, and must scrub them repeatedly, often to the point where serious dermatitis of the hands develops. Other repetitive desires include constantly checking that a tap is turned off, a door is closed, the fly is zipped up, a window is locked, or innumerable other similar routine tasks have been carried out. Compulsive exercise or running to the point of total exhaustion is another form of obsessive compulsive neurosis. The patient may feel that by performing the rituals, s/he will regain control of a personality and emotions that are felt to be out of control. The patient is well aware that the habit is abnormal, but is powerless to stop it. Another form is the **body dismorphic disorder**, in which the patient is obsessed with their appearance, and particularly their facial appearance, and constantly check in mirrors for any abnormality in the way they look.

INVESTIGATIONS: No diagnostic tests.

TREATMENT: Psychotherapy, behavioural therapy and medication (eg. anti-depressants such as paroxetine, sertraline).

COMPLICATIONS: More frightening compulsions may occur such as the constant desire to hit or hurt someone else, to steal, to vandalise or to injure themselves in some way. In extreme cases, these desires may lead to criminal acts or suicide.

PROGNOSIS: Long term treatment usually required. Control of symptoms only reasonable.

See also Neurosis and other diseases listed under Psychiatric Conditions

Occupational Overuse Syndrome
See Repetitive Strain Syndrome

Ocular Larva Migrans
See Visceral Larva Migrans

382

Oculopharyngeal Muscular Dystrophy

DESCRIPTION: A progressive and permanent weakening and wasting of muscles.

CAUSE: Inherited condition that may commence at any age.

SYMPTOMS: Very slowly progressive permanent weakness of muscles that move the eye and enable swallowing.

INVESTIGATIONS: Diagnosed by electrical studies of muscle action, and muscle biopsy.

TREATMENT: No effective treatment. Diet may need to consist of thickened fluids.

COMPLICATIONS: Choking, inhaling food, and lung infections (eg. pneumonia) may occur.

PROGNOSIS: No cure.

See also other diseases listed under Muscular Dystrophy

Oesophageal Achalasia
See Achalasia

Oesophageal Cancer
(Cancer of the Oesophagus; Esophageal Cancer)

DESCRIPTION: Cancer of the gullet (oesophagus).

CAUSE: Excess alcohol (particularly whisky) consumption, smoking, eating very large quantities of pickled vegetables, maize overcooked in iron pots and persistent reflux of stomach acid are known risk factors. Uncommon in western society, but relatively common in central Asia and southern Africa.

SYMPTOMS: Difficulty and pain with swallowing that steadily worsens, and weight loss.

INVESTIGATIONS: Diagnosed by oesophagoscopy (passing a flexible tube into the oesophagus) or a barium swallow X-ray.

TREATMENT: Radical surgery to remove the cancer.

COMPLICATIONS: Food that the patient attempts to swallow may be vomited and inhaled, causing pneumonia.

PROGNOSIS: Very poor with 5% surviving five years.

See also Plummer-Vinson Syndrome; Reflux Oesophagitis

Oesophagitis
See Barrett Syndrome; Plummer-Vinson Syndrome; Reflux Oesophagitis

Oligohydramnios

DESCRIPTION: During pregnancy, the foetus is surrounded by amniotic fluid in the uterus. The fluid protects it from bumps and jarring and removes waste. Oligohydramnios occurs if inadequate fluid is present.

CAUSE: May be due to abnormal development of the foetus, or abnormal placental function, but in most cases there is no obvious cause.

SYMPTOMS: Normally there is about a 1000 mLs. of amniotic fluid present at birth. A volume less than 200 mLs. occurs in oligohydramnios.

INVESTIGATIONS: Diagnosed by an ultrasound scan. Further investigations to determine the cause of the condition must follow.

TREATMENT: Depend upon the cause, but often none is necessary or possible.

COMPLICATIONS: Higher risk of a complicated labour.

PROGNOSIS: Most pregnancies progress normally, but significant risk of foetal abnormality.

See also Polyhydramnios

Onchocerciasis
(River Blindness)

DESCRIPTION: Infestation by the nematode worm *Onchocerciasis volvulus*.

CAUSE: The nematode is carried from one person to another by the bite of a small black fly that only lives along rivers. Larvae are deposited in the skin by the bite, mature after 6 to 36 months into adult worms which are up to 60cm. long and live tightly coiled under the skin. The adult worm releases tiny microfilariae into the blood and these spread throughout the body, particularly to the skin, eyes and lymph nodes. A biting fly can pick up the microfilariae when it sucks up blood, and there they develop into larvae. Adult worms can live up to 18 years. Only occurs in equatorial Africa, southern Arabia and central America.

SYMPTOMS: Extremely itchy skin, generalised rash, lumps under the skin usually over the lower back and thighs, premature ageing and wrinkling of the skin, changes in skin pigmentation and grossly enlarged lymph nodes in the groin.

INVESTIGATIONS: Surgical removal and examination of a skin lump reveals an adult worm.

TREATMENT: Individual skin lumps may be be surgically removed, and medication is given to kill the microfilariae.

COMPLICATIONS: Blindness occurs in 5% of patients when the microfilariae spread to the eye and damage the cornea (clear surface layer of the eye). Rarely, muscles and the intestine may be affected to cause weakness and weight loss.

PROGNOSIS: Medication often must be repeated every six months for some years to give a cure. Death rate in untreated patients about one in one hundred.

Onychogryphosis
(Tinea Unguium)

DESCRIPTION: Fungal infection that occurs under finger and toe nails and distorts the nails.

CAUSE: Fungi such as *Tricophyton rubrum* and *Microsporum* may infect damaged or softened nails and surrounding tissue. If the nail is infected but not damaged the condition is called **onychomycosis**.

SYMPTOMS: Nails appear white or yellow and gradually thicken. More common in the middle-aged and elderly, and toe nails are usually more severely affected than the fingers.

INVESTIGATIONS: Scrapings from under nails are cultured and examined under a microscope to identify the fungus.

TREATMENT: Notoriously difficult to treat but amorolfine paint may be applied to the nail weekly for many months, or terbinafine tablets are taken daily for up to six months. In both cases, as the fungus is destroyed, new normal nail gradually grows out to replace the thick damaged nail.

COMPLICATIONS: Loss of the nail.

PROGNOSIS: Infections may persist for many years, but newer treatments are quite effective.

See also Fungal Infection

Onychomycosis
See Onychogryphosis

Oral Cancer
See Mouth Cancer

Oral Thrush
See Thrush

Orchitis
See Epididymo-Orchitis

Orf

DESCRIPTION: An unusual viral infection of sheep and goats that can infect the skin on the fingers and hands of people (eg. shearers, abattoir workers, veterinarians) who come into close contact with infected animals.

CAUSE: Infection develops if the responsible virus enters a minor injury to the skin.

SYMPTOMS: A sore develops at the site of infection after about ten days. This enlarges to become a large, fluid-filled, ulcerating and scabbing lump that may be one to three centimetres across.

INVESTIGATIONS: None normally necessary, but a biopsy is diagnostic.

TREATMENT: No treatment available or necessary.

COMPLICATIONS: The lymph nodes in the armpit or other areas may become tender and a secondary bacterial infection of the sore may occur.

PROGNOSIS: The lump becomes soft, breaks down, and heals completely after four to eight weeks, leaving no scar.

Organic Brain Syndrome

DESCRIPTION: Deterioration of higher functions in the brain.

CAUSE: Always due to a specific cause such as alcoholism, drugs (prescribed and illegal), cancer or infection anywhere in the body, body chemistry or hormone disorders, autoimmune diseases or epilepsy.

SYMPTOMS: Emotional disturbances (eg. anxiety, depression), poor memory and logic, disorientation, inappropriate sensations, behavioural changes (eg. exhibitionism, aggression).

INVESTIGATIONS: Extensive investigations may be necessary to determine the cause.

TREATMENT: Treat cause when found, give medications to control symptoms, nurse in a supportive environment, and give counselling and behavioural therapy.

PROGNOSIS: May be persistent unless cause treated and reversed early.

See also Alzheimer's Disease; Dementia

Organic Personality Syndrome

DESCRIPTION: Apparently unexplained behaviour changes in an otherwise well person.

CAUSE: Various underlying causes must be sought, but may follow a head injury, stroke or tumour that affects the frontal lobes of the brain.

SYMPTOMS: Personality change, sudden emotional changes, loss of impulse control, inappropriate social behaviour and a lack of concern about consequences of actions.

INVESTIGATIONS: None diagnostic, but any underlying cause must be detected by extensive investigations.

TREATMENT: Treat cause if possible, otherwise managed by medications to control behaviour changes, behavioural therapy and social support.

COMPLICATIONS: May be unable to live normally in society because of grossly abnormal behaviour.

PROGNOSIS: Depends on cause. May be long term or transient.

Organophosphate Poisoning
See Insecticide Poisoning

Orgasm Failure
See Anorgasmia

Oriental Sore
See Cutaneous Leischmaniasis

Ornithosis
See Psittacosis

Orofacial Pain Syndrome

DESCRIPTION: Painful spasm of muscles in the face.

CAUSE: Injury, cold exposure or dental problems may be implicated.

SYMPTOMS: Dull constant ache and tenderness in muscles of jaw, difficulty in opening mouth, and some patients grind their teeth.

INVESTIGATIONS: None usually necessary.

TREATMENT: Physiotherapy, anti-inflammatory drugs, muscle relaxants and pain killers.

COMPLICATIONS: Tooth damage possible if prolonged.

PROGNOSIS: Good.

Osgood-Schlatter's Disease
(Apophysitis of the Tibial Tuberosity)

DESCRIPTION: Relatively common but minor knee condition of children and teenagers.

CAUSE: At the top and front of the tibia (shin bone) in the lower leg, there is a lump just below the knee (the tibial tuberosity). The large patellar tendon runs from the tibial tuberosity up to the knee cap (patella) and through this is connected to the large muscles on the front of the thigh (quadriceps). When the knee is straightened the thigh muscles contract, pull on the patella, which pulls on the patellar tendon, which is attached to the tibial tuberosity, which pulls the tibia into position and straightens the knee. Children who are growing rapidly tend to have slightly softened bones, and in a child who exercises a great deal it is possible for the tibial tuberosity to be pulled slightly away from the softened growing area of the tibia behind it. This separation of the tibial tuberosity from the upper part of the tibia causes considerable pain and is called Osgood-Schlatter's disease.

SYMPTOMS: The patient is usually a boy, a keen sportsman, and between 9 and 15 years of age, who develops pain, tenderness and sometimes an obvious swelling just below the knee. The pain is worse, or may only occur, whenever the knee is straightened, particularly when walking or running. The knee joint itself is pain-free.

INVESTIGATIONS: Diagnosis confirmed by X-rays that show the separation of the tibial tuberosity from the tibia.

TREATMENT: Only treatment is time and rest. In severe cases, strapping or plaster and crutches may be necessary to rest the knee adequately.

COMPLICATIONS: None significant.

PROGNOSIS: Very good, but up to two months rest may be required.

Osler-Rendu-Weber Disease
(Hereditary Haemorrhagic Telangiectasia)

DESCRIPTION: Blood vessel disorder that starts in childhood, but only becomes serious in adult life.

CAUSE: Inherited.

SYMPTOMS: Widespread red dots and lumps caused by dilated small blood vessels (telangiectasia) just under and in the skin of the face, forearms, palms and toes. Moist membranes lining body cavities (eg. nose, mouth, gut, lungs, vagina) may also be affected, resulting in serious internal bleeding and blood noses.

INVESTIGATIONS: Diagnosed by skin biopsy.

TREATMENT: Surgical removal of bleeding internal or large skin telangiectasia.

COMPLICATIONS: Liver involvement causing damage to the organ's blood supply and replacement of normal liver tissue with scar tissue. Blood loss may lead to anaemia.

PROGNOSIS: No cure, but provided bleeding is not serious, life expectancy is normal.

See also Rothmund-Thomson Syndrome

Osteitis Deformans
See Paget's Disease of Bone

Osteoarthritis

DESCRIPTION: A degeneration of one or more joints that affects up to 15% of the population, most of them being elderly.

CAUSE: Degeneration of the cartilage within joints, and inflammation of the bone exposed by the damaged cartilage, which is aggravated by injury and overuse of joint. There is also an hereditary tendency.

SYMPTOMS: Usually mild at first, but slowly worsens with time and joint abuse. The knees, back, hips, feet, and hands are most commonly affected. Stiffness and pain that are relieved by rest are the initial symptoms, but as the disease progresses, swelling, limitation of movement, deformity and partial dislocation (subluxation) of a joint may occur. A crackling noise may come from the joint when it is moved, and nodules may develop adjacent to joints on the fingers in severe cases.

INVESTIGATIONS: X-rays show characteristic changes from a relatively early stage, and repeated X-rays are used to follow the course of the disease. There are no diagnostic blood tests.

TREATMENT: Avoid any movement or action that causes pain in the affected joints, such as climbing stairs and carrying loads (obese patients should lose weight). Paracetamol, aspirin, heat and anti-inflammatory drugs may be used to reduce the pain in a damaged joint. Physiotherapy, acupuncture and massage have also been found to be useful. Surgery to replace affected joints is very successful. The most common joints replaced are the hip, knee and fingers. Surgery to fuse together the joints in the back is sometimes necessary to prevent movement between them, as they cannot be replaced. Steroid injections into an acutely inflamed joint may give rapid relief, but they cannot be repeated frequently because of the risk of damage to the joint.

COMPLICATIONS: Severely damaged joints may dislocate.

PROGNOSIS: Depends on the joints involved and the disease severity. Cures can be achieved by joint replacement surgery, while other patients achieve reasonable control with medications. The inflammation in some severely affected joints can sometimes 'burn out' and disappear with time.

See also other diseases listed under Arthritis

Osteochondritis Dissecans
DESCRIPTION: Injury to the cartilage lining the knee joint.
CAUSE: A fragment of cartilage separates from the joint surface and floats free in the joint (synovial) fluid, usually due to a sudden major injury, or repeated minor injuries, to the knee.
SYMPTOMS: Dull aching pain in the knee joint that is worsened by exercise and may be accompanied by swelling and locking of the knee.
INVESTIGATIONS: X-rays of the knee may be able to confirm the diagnosis, otherwise diagnosed during arthroscopy (looking into the joint through a thin tube).
TREATMENT: Initially rest and strapping may be effective, but persistent or severe cases require surgical treatment, usually by arthroscopy.
COMPLICATIONS: Locking of the knee in one position may become difficult to relieve.
PROGNOSIS: Good results from surgical treatment.
See also Chondromalacia Patellae

Osteoclastoma
See Bone Cancer

Osteogenesis Imperfecta
(Brittle Bone Disease)
DESCRIPTION: A very rare disease in which a child is born with fragile, brittle bones that break easily and heal poorly.
CAUSE: Tends to run in families in an irregular pattern. Varying degrees of severity are possible, and some patients are far more severely affected than others.
SYMPTOMS: Children suffer multiple painful fractures that take months to heal. Other characteristics include deafness, a blue colour to the whites of the eyes, spinal deformities and teeth defects.
INVESTIGATIONS: Diagnosed by X-rays which show a typical appearance in the long bones of the legs and arms.
TREATMENT: No treatment available.
COMPLICATIONS: Healed fractures often leave a permanent deformity.
PROGNOSIS: Many die before puberty, but if they survive to adult life, the disease tends to become less severe, and a relatively normal life expectancy is possible.

Osteogenic Sarcoma
See Osteosarcoma

Osteoma
See Bone Cancer

Osteomalacia

DESCRIPTION: The adult form of the bone disease rickets, which occurs only in growing children, and results in softening of the bones.

CAUSE: A lack of calcium, usually due to overactivity of the parathyroid gland (which controls the calcium balance of the body) in the neck. Other causes include a deficiency in vitamin D or phosphate (both are essential to control calcium activity within the body), kidney failure, alcoholism and other poisons.

SYMPTOMS: May be very mild, or the patient may have muscle weakness, tiredness, and bone pain.

INVESTIGATIONS: Diagnosed by blood tests, X-ray and bone biopsy.

TREATMENT: Improving the diet, prescribing vitamin D, giving calcium supplements and medications that force calcium into the bones.

COMPLICATIONS: Fractures are only slightly more common than would normally be expected.

PROGNOSIS: Further deterioration of bone strength unlikely with correct treatment.
See also Rickets

Osteomyelitis

DESCRIPTION: A serious but uncommon infection of a bone which is more common in children. The femur (thigh bone), tibia (shin bone) and humerus (upper arm bone) are most commonly affected, but any bone in the body may be involved.

CAUSE: Often no obvious cause and the infecting bacteria reaches the bone through the blood. Any cut that penetrates through to the bone leaves it open to infection.

SYMPTOMS: The infected bone becomes painful, tender and warm, the tissue over it is red and swollen, and the patient is feverish and feels ill.

INVESTIGATIONS: X-rays show bone damage, but often not until several days after the infection has started. Blood tests for the presence of bacteria, plus the appearance of the patient, are usually sufficient to allow the commencement of treatment. Once the infecting bacteria have been correctly identified, the antibiotic may be changed.

TREATMENT: Potent antibiotics, which are often given by injection for several weeks. Strict bed rest is also necessary, and if pus is present in the bone, an operation to drain it is essential.

COMPLICATIONS: Septicaemia (see separate entry), permanent damage to the bone and nearby joints, bone death and collapse, persistent infection and damage to the growing area of a bone in a child.

PROGNOSIS: The majority of osteomyelitis cases are controlled and cured by correct treatment.

Osteoporosis

DESCRIPTION: Common bone condition (one quarter of women over the age of 50 affected) in which the basic constituent of bone, calcium, drops to a dangerously low level. The bones soften and may bend, break or collapse.

CAUSE: Calcium is found in all dairy food (particularly cheese), sardines, shellfish, beans, nuts and tripe. Adults require up to 800 mg. of calcium, and children and pregnant women up to 1400 mg. a day. The structure of bones is being constantly renewed, and a lack of calcium over many years leads to a gradual deterioration in bone strength. Once women reach the menopause, the drop in hormone levels accelerates the loss of calcium from bones. May be hereditary and more common in petite, small-boned women.

SYMPTOMS: Most patients do not know they have the disease until they fracture a bone (particularly the hip) with minimal injury, or if on a routine X-ray their bones are seen to be more transparent than normal.

INVESTIGATIONS: A procedure similar to an X-ray, dual photon densitometry, can diagnose osteoporosis at an early stage. There are no diagnostic blood tests.

TREATMENT: Prevention involves adding calcium to the diet before menopause, and by taking calcium supplements and hormone replacement therapy after menopause. Regular exercise is important, as the minor stresses on the bones keep them stronger. In more serious cases, sophisticated, very effective medications (eg. alendronate, calcitriol, disodium etidronate) that force calcium into bones to strengthen them, may be prescribed to be taken daily for several years. Other factors that can help are reducing the intake of coffee and alcohol, and stopping smoking.

COMPLICATIONS: Deformity of the back, severe arthritis, and neuralgia caused by the collapsing bones pinching nerves.

PROGNOSIS: Control good once diagnosed, but reversal of damage difficult.

Osteosarcoma
(Osteogenic Sarcoma)

DESCRIPTION: A form of bone cancer that occurs in teenagers and young adults, and is more common in males than females. The knee and elbow are the most commonly affected areas.

CAUSE: Unknown.

SYMPTOMS: Gradually increasing pain in the arm, leg or other affected bone. The cancer gradually enlarges, causing the covering skin to become warm and tender to touch.

INVESTIGATIONS: Blood tests can give clues to the existence of the cancer, but X-ray and bone biopsy are more important.

TREATMENT: Amputation of the affected arm or leg, or surgical removal of as much cancerous bone as possible if the cancer occurs in other areas. Drugs and irradiation may also be used.

COMPLICATIONS: The cancer may spread to other organs, most commonly to the lungs.

PROGNOSIS: The outcome is better the further out along the limb the cancer develops. The overall cure rate is only 50%, for cancer in the forearm or lower leg it is 70%, but for cancers in the pelvis or breast bone, there are virtually no survivors.

See also Bone Cancer

Otitis Externa
(Swimmer's Ear; Tropical Ear)

DESCRIPTION: Bacterial and/or fungal infection of the ear canal.

CAUSE: Most common cause is retained water in the ear canal, while other causes include irritating the ear canal with a cotton bud or similar object, badly fitting hearing aids, excess ear wax, sweating in dirty and dusty conditions, and dermatitis in the ear canal. Sea water is less likely to be a problem. Bacteria normally live in the outer ear, but if the canal remains constantly wet, the bacteria can invade tissue to cause an infection. If a fungus is the cause it is called tropical ear. More common in children because their narrower ear canals retain water easily. Prevented by drying drops used in the ear after each period of swimming or ear plugs.

SYMPTOMS: The outer ear canal and the outer surface of the eardrum become excruciatingly painful. The onset is often very rapid. As the infection progresses a discharge from the ear usually develops.

INVESTIGATIONS: In most cases, no investigations are necessary, but if the infection is persistent swabs may be taken so that the responsible bacteria and fungi can be identified.

TREATMENT: Involves cleaning the ear of any wax or debris that may be present in the canal, and antibiotic drops or ointment. In difficult cases a wick (piece of light material) soaked in antibiotic ointment or drops may be put in the ear. Tropical ear is more difficult to cure and a prolonged course of antifungal drops or ointment and antifungal tablets is necessary.

COMPLICATIONS: Each infection can injure the ear and repeated attacks may cause permanent damage. Untreated infections can spread through the eardrum and cause a more serious middle ear infection (otitis media).

PROGNOSIS: Very good with correct treatment.

See also Otitis Media

Otitis Media
(Middle Ear Infection)

DESCRIPTION: A bacterial infection of the middle ear.

CAUSE: The middle ear is a cavity which contains three tiny bones that transmit the vibrations of the eardrum to the hearing mechanism in the inner ear. There is a small tube (the eustachian tube) connecting the middle ear to the back of the nose, and infection can enter the middle ear from there. Infection can also spread from the outer ear to the middle ear. Children are more commonly affected than adults.

SYMPTOMS: Sudden onset of severe pain, often at night, and fever. Pressure on the outside of the ear causes additional pain and relative deafness.

INVESTIGATIONS: None normally necessary.

TREATMENT: Antibiotics and medications to dry up phlegm. It is sometimes necessary to perform a small operation on the eardrum to relieve the pressure.

COMPLICATIONS: If left untreated or there is rapid worsening of the infection, the bulging eardrum may burst, and blood and pus will ooze out of the ear canal. The pain may be relieved by a rupture of the eardrum, but treatment with antibiotics is essential to ensure that the eardrum repairs itself. If the hole in the eardrum fails to heal after several months, it may be necessary to have an operation to repair it. Rarer complications include a spread of the infection into the surrounding bone (mastoiditis), or into the bloodstream or brain.

PROGNOSIS: Very good with appropriate treatment. A ruptured eardrum usually heals in one or two weeks.

See also Cholesteatoma; Eustachian Tube Blockage; Glue Ear; Tympanic Rupture

Oto-Palatal-Digital Syndrome

DESCRIPTION: Rare inherited genetic defect of ear, face and hands.

CAUSE: Sex linked trait that can pass through families.

SYMPTOMS: Conductive deafness, abnormal face and nose shape, extra fingers and toes that are joined by webs, and a cleft palate.

INVESTIGATIONS: None diagnostic.

TREATMENT: Surgical correction of deformities.

PROGNOSIS: No cure, but reasonable life expectancy.

Otosclerosis

DESCRIPTION: A relatively common form of arthritis in the tiny bones (malleus, incus and stapes) in the middle ear that vibrate to transmit sounds from the ear drum to the hearing mechanism in the inner ear. Eventually affects approximately one person in every 200 in old age.

CAUSE: The middle ear bones become soft and enlarged which reduces their ability to transmit vibration, and thus sounds. More common in women, usually starts in the late teens or twenties, and its onset may be triggered by pregnancy. Significant tendency for it to pass from one generation to the next.

SYMPTOMS: Steadily worsening deafness and a constant ringing noise in the ears (tinnitus).

INVESTIGATIONS: Special tests on ear function used to make the diagnosis.

TREATMENT: A hearing aid can be very effective, but a permanent operative cure in which the affected bones in the middle ear are replaced with Teflon substitutes is the treatment of choice.

COMPLICATIONS: Dizziness occurs in some patients.

PROGNOSIS: Progresses very slowly, but never results in total deafness. The earlier in life the condition starts, the greater the final hearing loss and the worse the noises become.

Ovarian Cancer
(Cancer of the Ovary)

DESCRIPTION: Any of several different types of cancer of the ovary.

CAUSE: Absolute cause is unknown, but there is a family tendency. A relatively uncommon cancer, affecting about one in every 20,000 women in developed countries every year, and the majority of them will be over 60 years of age.

SYMPTOMS: Most women present with a large, painless lump in the lower abdomen, or with pelvic discomfort.

INVESTIGATIONS: Diagnosed by a CT or ultrasound scan of the pelvis.

TREATMENT: Surgery to remove the affected ovary and surrounding tissue, followed by drug treatment (chemotherapy) with cytotoxics.

COMPLICATIONS: Spread of the cancer to other parts of the body.

PROGNOSIS: The overall five-year survival rate for all ovarian cancer patients is only 35%.

See also Teratoma

Ovarian Cyst

DESCRIPTION: A cyst (fluid-filled sac) that occurs in the ovary. Usually less than 5cm across, but rarely they may form giant cysts the size of a football. Several types are known including follicular cysts, luteal cysts, cysts caused by infections of the ovary and tubes, cysts associated with endometriosis (see separate entry), and in rare cases cysts associated with some types of ovarian cancers.

CAUSE: Every time a woman releases an egg from her ovary it is surrounded by a tiny sac of fluid, and some women experience a slight stab of pain (mittelschmerz — see separate entry) as the fluid around the egg is released with ovulation in the middle of each month. If these normal tiny cysts re-form and enlarge after releasing the egg, a cyst of the ovary results.

SYMPTOMS: Follicular cysts — the woman is often not aware that the cyst is present unless it is discovered at surgery, or bursts. They cause some irregularity of the periods, but if a cyst bursts, the woman experiences sudden, severe pain on one side, low down in her abdomen. The pain eases slowly over several hours or days, as the irritating fluid contained in the cyst disperses. They are quite common in teenage girls and young women.

Luteal cysts — cause delayed or irregular periods and rarely any other trouble.

INVESTIGATIONS: Diagnosed by an ultrasound scan of the lower abdomen.

TREATMENT: Follicular cysts — women who develop them frequently can be given the oral contraceptive pill, which will prevent ovulation, and therefore the formation of further cysts. The pill will also shrink existing cysts, but large cysts need to be removed surgically.

Luteal cysts — no treatment necessary unless the cyst is very large, when it must be surgically removed.

COMPLICATIONS: Infertility may occur until a large cyst is removed. The fluid from a ruptured cyst may cause inflammation of the bowel and other abdominal organs which results in adhesion formation.

PROGNOSIS: Generally very good.

See also Polycystic Ovarian Syndrome

Ovarian Torsion

DESCRIPTION: Uncommon cause of severe ovary pain.

CAUSE: The twisting of an ovary on the stalk of tissue that supplies it with blood and nerves, cutting off the blood supply and inflaming the nerves.

SYMPTOMS: Sudden severe pain and tenderness low down in the abdomen on one side.

INVESTIGATIONS: An ultrasound scan may show some abnormalities, but often diagnosed at surgery.

TREATMENT: Urgent surgery is required to untwist, or more commonly remove, the affected ovary.

COMPLICATIONS: The loss of the affected ovary, and inflammation in the abdomen that may cause adhesions (see separate entry).

PROGNOSIS: Although one ovary may be lost, fertility and normal production of female hormones can be maintained by the remaining ovary.

See also Torsion of the Testis

Overactivity Syndrome
See Hyperkinetic Syndrome

Ovulation Pain
See Mittelschmerz

P

Paedophilia
(Pederasty)

DESCRIPTION: A psychiatric disturbance that results in the sexual abuse of a child by adult men (most commonly) or women.

CAUSE: May develop from childhood abuse of the paedophile by his or her parents, or other psychological traumas as a child. Paedophilia is NOT more common in homosexuals, but pederasty is by definition a homosexual act between a man and a boy.

SYMPTOMS: Mentally disturbed adults who use children to become sexually aroused to the point of orgasm. Sexual contact varies from feeling, to oral sex, or sexual penetration that may progress to serious injury or rarely murder. Paedophiles have difficulty in establishing normal intimate relationships with adults of the opposite sex, have inadequate personalities, low self esteem, and male paedophiles are often impotent.

INVESTIGATIONS: No diagnostic tests, but any cause of mental disturbance needs to be excluded.

TREATMENT: Prolonged counselling by a psychiatrist and sometimes medications to reduce sexual desire and increase control.

COMPLICATIONS: If discovered, paedophiles are invariably charged in the courts.

PROGNOSIS: Long term success is poor.

See also other diseases listed under **Psychiatric Disturbances**

Paget's Disease of Bone
(Osteitis Deformans)

DESCRIPTION: Bone in scattered parts of the body becomes thickened and soft, causing compression of nerves and collapse of those bones that support weight.

CAUSE: No known cause, but unusual under 60 years of age.

SYMPTOMS: Very insidious onset, may be quite advanced before diagnosis, and can vary from very mild to rapidly progressive. The skull, thighbone (femur) and shinbone (tibia) are often involved, giving a characteristic head appearance and bowing of the legs as they bend under the body's weight. Skull enlargement causes pressure on nerves and a constant headache. Fractures may occur with only slight injury, and the back becomes bent and deformed.

INVESTIGATIONS: Diagnosis made on the characteristic X-ray appearance. Blood tests show specific chemical imbalances, including excess calcium.

TREATMENT: Medications such as disodium etidronate are taken regularly for the rest of the patient's life to control the disease.

COMPLICATIONS: Excess calcium may cause kidney damage, extra blood flow to the bones can cause circulatory and heart problems, and a small number of patients develop a form of bone cancer.

PROGNOSIS: Drugs slow disease progress, but there is no cure. The earlier it occurs in life, the more likely it is to be severe.

Paget's Disease of the Nipple
(Nipple Cancer)

DESCRIPTION: An uncommon type of cancer that starts in the milk ducts of the nipple, and may spread rapidly along these ducts, deep into the breast.

CAUSE: Unknown. Only one in every 100 breast cancers.

SYMPTOMS: Often very few symptoms until well advanced, and no lump is felt. Symptoms include itching and irritation of the nipple, a thickening of the nipple and in advanced cases an ulcer may form.

INVESTIGATIONS: Diagnosed by biopsy of the nipple.

TREATMENT: Surgery to remove the nipple and the affected part of the breast. Radiotherapy and chemotherapy may also be necessary.

COMPLICATIONS: Spread of the cancer to breast tissue and nearby lymph nodes.

PROGNOSIS: The more advanced when first treated, the poorer the survival rate.

See also Breast Cancer

Painful Arc Syndrome

DESCRIPTION: Pain in part the range of movement of the shoulder.

CAUSE: An injury or fracture to the very top of the humerus (upper arm bone), stretching damage (tendinitis) to the tendon that pulls the arm through the painful arc, inflammation of the bursae (fluid producing sacs for the shoulder joint) that surround the shoulder joint, or microscopic bone formation (calcification) in tendons that move the shoulder joint.

SYMPTOMS: If the arm is held by the side, and then moved away from the body while being kept straight until it is above the head, it describes an arc of 180°. In this syndrome there is pain with movement through the mid part of the arc between about 45° and 135°. There is no pain in the lower or upper parts of the arc of movement.

INVESTIGATIONS: X-rays may show microscopic calcification of a tendon, but in most cases are normal.

TREATMENT: Combinations of physiotherapy, anti-inflammatory drugs and rarely surgery.

PROGNOSIS: Slow recovery common, but long term good recovery normal.

See also Rotator Cuff Syndrome.

Painful Bruising Syndrome

DESCRIPTION: Abnormal development of bruising in women.

CAUSE: Unknown, but may follow emotional or physical stress.

SYMPTOMS: Pins and needles sensation of limbs and trunk followed by crops of bruises without injury in young women.

INVESTIGATIONS: All blood and other tests normal.

TREATMENT: None necessary.

PROGNOSIS: Self-limiting condition.

Painless Thyroiditis Syndrome

DESCRIPTION: Complication of childbirth involving the thyroid gland in the front of the neck.

CAUSE: Unknown, but more common in North America and Japan.

SYMPTOMS: Intermittent episodes of thyroid gland over activity (hyperthyroidism) or under activity (hypothyroidism) with enlargement of the thyroid gland (goitre) in a woman shortly after childbirth.

INVESTIGATIONS: Blood tests of thyroid function abnormal.

TREATMENT: Medication (propranolol) for hyperthyroidism or thyroxine replacement therapy for hypothyroidism as necessary.

COMPLICATIONS: Some women progress to develop permanent hypothyroidism.

PROGNOSIS: Most settle with appropriate treatment.

See also Goitre; Hyperthyroidism; Hypothyroidism

PAN

See Polyarteritis Nodosa

Pancoast Syndrome

DESCRIPTION: Complication of lung cancer, and a sign that the cancer is progressing very rapidly.

CAUSE: Occurs in patients with cancer in the top part of the lung.

SYMPTOMS: Shoulder, arm and chest pain with an associated Horner syndrome (a drooping eyelid, lack of sweating on one side of the face and a contracted pupil in the eye — see separate entry).

INVESTIGATIONS: None necessary.

TREATMENT: None available other than powerful narcotic pain killers.

PROGNOSIS: Death usually follows soon after the condition is diagnosed.

See also Horner Syndrome; Lung Cancer

Pancreatic Cancer

DESCRIPTION: Cancer of the pancreas, which is an organ that sits in the centre of the belly behind the umbilicus and secretes digestive enzymes that are discharged via a duct, that it shares with the gall bladder, into the small intestine.

CAUSE: Unknown. Cancer usually occurs in the end nearest the discharging duct (the head of the pancreas).

SYMPTOMS: The enlarging cancer puts pressure on the adjacent duct from the gall bladder, preventing bile from escaping. The build up in bile results in liver damage and jaundice (yellow skin), which is often the first symptom. Other symptoms include vague belly and back pain, weight loss, poor food digestion, diarrhoea and blood clots in veins.

INVESTIGATIONS: Diagnosis confirmed by blood tests and a CT or MRI scan.

TREATMENT: Involves major surgery to remove the cancer and reroute the duct from the gall bladder to the gut. Follow up radiotherapy and chemotherapy may be undertaken.

COMPLICATIONS: Liver failure and spread of the cancer to adjacent lymph nodes and organs.

PROGNOSIS: Depends upon the type of cancer and how far it has spread, but is generally poor.

See also Bard-Pic Syndrome

Pancreatitis

DESCRIPTION: A well recognised but uncommon complication of alcoholism causing inflammation or infection of the pancreas gland, which sits in the centre of the abdomen directly behind the navel. Its main task is to produce the digestive enzymes that attack your food. A tiny duct leads from the pancreas to the bile duct and then to the small intestine to transport these enzymes to the food.

CAUSE: The pancreas may become infected, damaged by excess alcohol intake, injured in an accident, or the duct leading from it may be blocked by a gallstone. The digestive enzymes leak out of the pancreas ducts and start dissolving the gland itself, the intestines and other abdominal organs.

SYMPTOMS: Excruciating pain in the centre of the abdomen that may also be felt in the back and sides, nausea, vomiting, weakness, fever and sweats.

INVESTIGATIONS: Diagnosis confirmed by specific blood tests.

TREATMENT: Difficult, and often involves long hospital stays for resuscitation, prolonged bed rest and pain relief. The cause of the pancreatitis must also be treated, with antibiotics and occasionally surgery.

COMPLICATIONS: Recurrences of attacks, particularly in alcoholics, are common.

PROGNOSIS: Significant death rate, which rises with subsequent attacks.

See also Alcoholism

Panhypopituitarism
See Hypopituitarism

Panic Attack
See Neurosis

Panniculitis

DESCRIPTION: Inflammation of the fat layer under the skin that usually affects young women. Numerous subtypes known.

CAUSE: Unknown, but due to inflammation of the small arteries (vasculitis) supplying the fat, and reduced blood supply.

SYMPTOMS: Tender lumps (nodules) under the skin, which is red.

INVESTIGATIONS: Diagnosed by biopsy of fatty lump.

TREATMENT: None necessary except for severe forms, when steroids are given to settle inflammation.

COMPLICATIONS: Weber-Christian panniculitis is most severe form and may rarely lead to death from reduced blood supply to internal organs.

PROGNOSIS: Usually settle without treatment over many months to leave a dent in the skin due to lack of fat.

Papillon-Le Fevre Syndrome

DESCRIPTION: Abnormality of tooth development.
CAUSE: Congenital.
SYMPTOMS: A child with loose front teeth, receding gums and widely spaced teeth.
INVESTIGATIONS: Diagnosed by physical examination only. No diagnostic tests.
TREATMENT: Impeccable dental hygiene.
COMPLICATIONS: May result in premature loss of teeth.
PROGNOSIS: No cure, and may require dental plate.

Paralysis Agitans
See Parkinson's Disease

Paranoia
See Paranoid Disorder

Paranoid Disorder
(Paranoia)

DESCRIPTION: A delusion that makes a patient believe that they are being persecuted by individuals or organisations.
CAUSE: Unknown.
SYMPTOMS: The preoccupation with imagined persecutions may have a marked effect upon the patient's home life, and may cause disruption to a marriage or family. Examples include the belief that the secret service has bugged the home and is listening to all the conversations of the family, or that the next-door neighbour is deliberately undertaking activities that are constantly irritating. May occur alone, or as a part of schizophrenia (see separate entry).
INVESTIGATIONS: None diagnostic.
TREATMENT: Antipsychotic medications and psychotherapy.
COMPLICATIONS: Seriously antisocial behaviour.
PROGNOSIS: Patients can usually live relatively normally in society, but may express their unreasoned fears of persecution at inappropriate times.
See also Schizophrenia and other diseases listed under Psychiatric Conditions

Parapertussis
See Whooping Cough

Paraphimosis

DESCRIPTION: Entrapment of the head of the penis in a tight band of foreskin.
CAUSE: Penile erection in a man suffering from phimosis (narrow opening in foreskin).
SYMPTOMS: Tight foreskin becomes painfully trapped behind head of penis after an erection has subsided.
INVESTIGATIONS: None necessary.
TREATMENT: Manipulation of the foreskin back over the head of the penis by firm pressure, or surgically cutting the tight band of foreskin around the head. Circumcision may be necessary to prevent recurrences.

COMPLICATIONS: If unrelieved, permanent damage to the head of the penis may occur.

PROGNOSIS: Good results from treatment.

See also Phimosis

Paraplegia

DESCRIPTION: Complication of a back injury that severs the spinal cord.

CAUSE: All parts of the human body are capable of healing and repairing damage, except the central nervous system, which comprises the brain and spinal cord. The spinal cord runs from the base of the brain, down through the vertebrae that form the backbone, and ends just below the waist. Nerves run out from it to the muscles, skin and other tissues, with one bundle of nerves emerging from between each of the 24 vertebrae. If the spinal cord is cut by a broken back or other injury, it is impossible for nerve signals to pass backwards and forwards from the brain to the body. Involuntary muscles which control the internal organs such as the gut and heart movements, are supplied by a different set of nerves, and are not affected by spinal injury.

SYMPTOMS: Paralysis below the waist. Patients cannot feel heat or cold, hard or soft, sharp or dull, or any sensation below the level of the injury. There is no control of muscles, so patients cannot walk or control their bladder.

INVESTIGATIONS: Diagnosed by X-rays, CT and MRI scans, and electrical tests on nerves and muscles.

TREATMENT: The only help that can be offered is rehabilitation so patients can cope with their disability.

COMPLICATIONS: Pressure sores on the skin and urinary infections from immobility.

PROGNOSIS: No cure, but normal life span.

See also Brown-Séquard Syndrome; Quadriplegia

Paraumbilical Hernia
See Umbilical Hernia

Parinaud Syndrome
(Pretectal Syndrome)

DESCRIPTION: Complication of disease or injury to the front (pretectal region) of the brain.

CAUSE: Due to pinealoma, glioma, head injury, tumour or stroke (see separate entries).

SYMPTOMS: Loss of ability to look upwards, the eye retracts into the head when attempting to look up, the eye pupils do not contract in bright light and do not dilate when looking at something that is very close to the eyes. Some patients have drooping eyelids and inability to look downwards as well.

INVESTIGATIONS: Cause must be found by CT and MRI scans of the brain.

TREATMENT: Underlying cause treated if possible.

PROGNOSIS: Depends entirely on cause.

See also Glioma; Pinealoma; Stroke

Parkinsonism

See Parkinson's Disease

Parkinson's Disease

(Paralysis Agitans; Parkinsonism; Shaking Palsy)

DESCRIPTION: One of the more common causes of a tremor in elderly people.

CAUSE: No known cause, but what happens in the brain to cause the symptoms is understood. When a muscle contracts, the opposite muscle must relax. For example, when you bend your finger, the muscles on the palm side of the finger contract, while those on the back of the finger must relax. This coordination occurs in the brain. In parkinsonism, the brain cells that control this coordination have degenerated so that smooth control of movement is lost.

SYMPTOMS: Early signs are failure to swing the arm when walking, a deterioration in handwriting, and poor balance. Later symptoms are a constant tremor, general body stiffness, loss of facial expression, a stiff way of walking and lack of coordination. The intelligence and mental powers of victims are not affected in the early stages of the disease, and this causes great frustration, particularly when speech may be impaired.

INVESTIGATIONS: No blood or other test is diagnostic. CT scans (special X-rays) may reveal changes in certain parts of the brain, as may electroencephalograms (EEG) which measure the electrical brain waves. Magnetic resonance imaging (MRI) is now being used in some centres.

TREATMENT: A number of drugs are available to control the symptoms and slow the progress of the disease, but it is a matter of trial and error to determine which medications will help any particular patient. Physiotherapy is also very important. In rare cases, brain surgery, in which part of the brain is destroyed in an attempt to block nerve pathways that cause the constant tremor, is performed.

COMPLICATIONS: Patients may become depressed, anxious and emotionally disturbed.

PROGNOSIS: No cure, but medications allow some patients to lead normal lives. The disease process progresses steadily over many years, rarely causing death, but causing otherwise normal people to become invalids, totally dependent on others for everyday tasks.

See also Essential Tremor; Steele-Richardson-Olszewski Syndrome

Paronychia

(Nail Bed Infection)

DESCRIPTION: Infection of the nail bed (pink tissue under a nail) and surrounding tissues.

CAUSE: An ingrown nail, damage to the side and base of the nail from habitually picking at the area, working in water, working with chemicals (eg. detergents and soaps), dermatitis, and gardening when particles of dirt may be pushed between nail and skin.

SYMPTOMS: Red, tender, painful swelling at the side and base of the nail.

INVESTIGATIONS: None necessary.

TREATMENT: Applying antibiotic ointment to the infected skin around the nail, taking antibiotic tablets, and if an abscess is present, having it lanced to drain pus.

COMPLICATIONS: If not treated, infected tissue can break down to form an abscess, which may damage the nail bed and cause the nail to come off.

PROGNOSIS: Most settle quickly with treatment.

See also Ingrown Toenail

Parotid Tumour

DESCRIPTION: The parotid glands sit under the angle of the jaw on each side to secrete saliva into the back of the mouth. Several different types of tumour can develop in this gland, and the other salivary glands (submandibular and submental glands) that sit under the chin. The most common form is called a **mixed parotid tumour**, which is not malignant (cancerous).

CAUSE: Unknown.

SYMPTOMS: A slowly enlarging painless lump at the angle of the jaw, but as it enlarges the tumour puts pressure on surrounding tissue and nerves to eventually cause discomfort and pain.

INVESTIGATIONS: Diagnosis is often difficult, but can be made by a CT or MRI scan and needle biopsy (sticking a needle into the gland to take a tissue sample).

TREATMENT: Extremely intricate surgery to remove the enlarged gland and the tumour it contains. If the tumour is cancerous, irradiation of the area to prevent a recurrence is necessary.

COMPLICATIONS: The nerve supplying the face runs through the gland, and it is very easy to damage this during surgery, leaving the face numb and paralysed.

PROGNOSIS: Generally very good, but if the tumour is cancerous it is far more serious.

Parotitis
See Sialitis

Paroxysmal Atrial Tachycardia
(PAT)

DESCRIPTION: Sudden onset of irregular rapid heart rate.

CAUSE: Relatively common in women, and may be triggered by hormonal, emotional or other factors.

SYMPTOMS: A sudden rapid beating of the heart. Most attacks last only a few minutes and cause minimal discomfort, but often significant anxiety.

INVESTIGATIONS: Diagnosis confirmed by an electrocardiogram (ECG) while an attack is present, but this is normal at other times.

TREATMENT: If the attacks last for long periods or occur frequently, medication (eg. propranolol, lanoxin, sotalol) can be given to prevent them. Firm massage of the eyeballs, holding the breath and dunking the face in icy water may also stop an attack.

COMPLICATIONS: None significant.

PROGNOSIS: Not harmful, and most attacks settle spontaneously within a couple of hours. Preventive medication very successful.

See also Lown-Ganong-Levine Syndrome

Paroxysmal Ventricular Tachycardia

DESCRIPTION: Sudden very rapid heart rate.

CAUSE: Often due to a heart attack.

SYMPTOMS: Chest tightness, palpitations, shortness of breath and collapse.

INVESTIGATIONS: ECG (electrocardiograph) shows abnormal rhythm.

TREATMENT: Medications (eg. lignocaine) injected into a vein followed by cardioversion (electric shock), stabilisation in hospital, and then tablets to prevent a recurrence.

COMPLICATIONS: May progress to ventricular fibrillation (see separate entry), which is frequently fatal.

PROGNOSIS: Depends on cause and severity.

Parvovirus Infection
See Fifth Disease

PAT
See Paroxysmal Atrial Tachycardia

Patau Syndrome
(Trisomy 13-15)

DESCRIPTION: Rare developmental defect affecting numerous parts of the body.

CAUSE: Congenital defect in which three copies of chromosomes 13 and 15 are present instead of two.

SYMPTOMS: Infant with extra fingers and toes, abnormal heart structure, cleft lip and palate, small eyes and brain malformations.

INVESTIGATIONS: Tests on heart and brain function (eg. CT scan, echocardiogram) performed to confirm diagnosis.

TREATMENT: None available.

PROGNOSIS: Poor.

Patello-Femoral Pain Syndrome

DESCRIPTION: Common knee injury.

CAUSE: Overuse or strain to knee.

SYMPTOMS: Pain in the front of part of the knee behind or around patella (knee cap) that is a dull ache with sharp exacerbations aggravated by climbing or descending stairs or slopes.

INVESTIGATIONS: No specific diagnostic tests, but on examination there is pain when pressing on the patella which is eased by pushing the patella towards the other knee during knee movement. Pushing the patella away from the other knee worsens pain during knee movement.

TREATMENT: Physiotherapy, strapping, rest and anti-inflammatory medications.

PROGNOSIS: Good.

See also Chondromalacia Patellae

Patent Ductus Arteriosus
(PDA)

DESCRIPTION: Failure of an artery near the heart that bypasses the lungs, to close immediately after birth.

CAUSE: A foetus inside the mother's womb (uterus) does not breathe, but obtains its oxygen directly from the mother's blood. The foetal blood is diverted away from the lungs through an artery (ductus arteriosus) which connects the pulmonary artery to the aorta. Immediately after birth, this special artery contracts and closes, diverting the full supply of blood into the lungs, which assists in their expansion, and enables the newborn baby to obtain its oxygen requirements by breathing. If the ductus arteriosus remains open after birth ('patent') it will divert unoxygenated blood away from the lungs and into the general circulation. This prevents sufficient oxygen from reaching the body, and eventually the baby may become blue.

SYMPTOMS: No early symptoms, but as the heart has to work harder it will gradually enlarge, and over a period of several months or years, the heart will gradually fail because of the extra work it is required to undertake.

INVESTIGATIONS: A characteristic heart murmur can be heard. Diagnosis confirmed by sophisticated X-rays of the heart, electrocardiographs and other specialised tests.

TREATMENT: The drug indomethacin, commonly used for treating arthritis, causes a patent ductus arteriosus to close. In some cases surgery is necessary.

COMPLICATIONS: There may be other serious malformations of the heart present.

PROGNOSIS: In some patients, the ductus arteriosus may be partially closed, and the problem is not significant enough to warrant treatment. In others, the dilated patent ductus arteriosus may be life-threatening. Normal life expectancy once ductus arteriosus has been closed.

See also Eisenmenger Syndrome; Fallot's Tetralogy

Paterson-Brown-Kelly syndrome
See Plummer-Vinson Syndrome

PDA
See Patent Ductus Arteriosus

Pederasty
See Paedophilia

Pediculosis
See Crabs; Head Lice

Pellagra
(Vitamin B₃ Deficiency)

DESCRIPTION: Dietary vitamin deficiency.

CAUSE: Lack of niacin (vitamin B_3) in the diet. Niacin is essential for the normal functioning of the body, and is found in many foods including rice, meats, vegetables and dairy products. Occurs in countries where the diet is primarily corn, which has minimal amounts of niacin.

SYMPTOMS: In the early stages patients have a poor appetite, general weakness, irritability, sore mouth and weight loss. More advanced cases develop dermatitis, diarrhoea, and become demented.

INVESTIGATIONS: Diagnosis can be confirmed by blood tests.

TREATMENT: Vitamin B supplements by mouth.

COMPLICATIONS: Severe psychiatric disturbances in advanced cases.

PROGNOSIS: Easily cured by vitamin supplements. If left untreated, death will eventually occur.

See also Hartnup Disease

Pellegrini-Stieda Lesion

DESCRIPTION: Inflammation of the ligament on the inside of the knee that attaches the lower end of the femur (thigh bone) to the top end of the tibia (main lower leg bone) at the point where it attaches to the femur. Bone may form in the ligament.

CAUSE: Injury to the knee, usually in the form of a blow to the side of the knee.

SYMPTOMS: Pain, swelling and tenderness at the point where the ligament attaches to the femur above the inside of the knee.

INVESTIGATIONS: X-ray shows bone formation in ligament.

TREATMENT: Physiotherapy, ultrasound to affected area, strengthening and mobilising exercises, and injections of a steroid around the ligament at monthly intervals.

COMPLICATIONS: None significant.

PROGNOSIS: Responds well, but slowly, to treatment.

Pelvic Congestion Syndrome

DESCRIPTION: Pelvic discomfort in women.

CAUSE: Associated with fluid retention in the pelvis before a menstrual period.

SYMPTOMS: A dull ache and heaviness is felt in the pelvis.

INVESTIGATIONS: None necessary.

TREATMENT: Relieved by fluid tablets or sexual orgasm.
PROGNOSIS: Self-limiting condition.
See also Premenstrual Tension Syndrome

Pelvic Inflammatory Disease
(PID)

DESCRIPTION: An infection of the uterus (womb), Fallopian tubes, ovaries and the tissues immediately around these organs.

CAUSE: Usually associated with the sexual transmission of bacteria from one person to another, although less commonly it may occur as a result of non-sexually transmitted infections. Most common in young, sexually promiscuous women. The use of intrauterine devices (IUD) doubles the risk of developing PID, while condoms provide significant protection. A wide range of different bacteria may be responsible, and frequently two, three or more different types are present.

SYMPTOMS: Pain low in the abdomen, fevers, a vaginal discharge, abnormal menstrual periods, pain with intercourse, and infertility. The pain may become very severe, and the patient appear extremely ill. There may be no symptoms in the male partner of the patient, although a discharge from the penis is sometimes present.

INVESTIGATIONS: Swabs are usually taken from the vagina and cervix (opening into the womb) to determine the responsible bacteria and appropriate antibiotic.

TREATMENT: Antibiotics by mouth or injected in severe cases. Sex should be avoided until complete recovery, which may take several weeks or months. If an abscess develops in the pelvis, an operation will be necessary to drain it.

COMPLICATIONS: One quarter of all women who develop PID will have long-term problems including repeat infections, infertility (10% after one attack of PID, 55% after three attacks of PID), persistent pain in the pelvis or with sex, and ectopic pregnancy (pregnancy that develops in the wrong position).

PROGNOSIS: Many women are cured by early treatment.

See also Salpingitis; Vaginitis, Bacterial

Pemphigoid
(Bullous Pemphigoid)

DESCRIPTION: An uncommon but serious skin disease that usually affects elderly women.

CAUSE: Auto-immune disease in which there is an inappropriate immune reaction within the body that causes the skin to be rejected in the same way as a transplanted kidney is rejected by the body. The actual cause of the auto-immune reaction is unknown.

SYMPTOMS: Red, scaling, itchy patches, which after a few days break down into large, fluid-filled blisters on widespread areas of the body. These huge, soft bubbles develop on the arms and legs initially, but soon spread to the trunk. The face and head are rarely affected.

INVESTIGATIONS: Diagnosis confirmed by a skin biopsy (taking a sample of the affected skin, and examining it under a microscope).

TREATMENT: High doses of prednisone, a steroid that reduces the immune response and allows the skin to repair itself. Once the disease is under control, the dosage is slowly reduced over a period of many months, but some patients need to remain on a low dose for years. Cytotoxic drugs may also be used.

COMPLICATIONS: Severe fluid loss from the body through the blisters may cause dehydration and heart rhythm irregularities.

PROGNOSIS: Without treatment, pemphigoid is fatal in one third of patients. With treatment, deaths are very rare, and one third of patients will require no treatment after two years.

See also Pemphigus

Pemphigus

DESCRIPTION: A rare but severe skin disease that occurs in all age groups and both sexes, but is very uncommon in children.

CAUSE: Auto-immune disease in which there is an inappropriate immune reaction within the body that causes the skin to be rejected in the same way as a transplanted kidney is rejected by the body. The actual cause of the auto-immune reaction is unknown.

SYMPTOMS: Rash varies dramatically in its form from shallow ulcers, to multiple blisters, red scaling patches or massive peeling of skin. Any part of the body, including the face and the inside of the mouth, may be affected.

INVESTIGATIONS: A biopsy (sample) of the affected skin is examined to confirm the diagnosis.

TREATMENT: Large doses of prednisone or other steroids, immunosuppressive and cytotoxic drugs, all of which may have significant side effects, must be used long-term.

PROGNOSIS: Without treatment, pemphigus is invariably fatal. With adequate treatment, the mortality rate is below 25%.

See also Hailey-Hailey Disease; Scalded Skin Syndrome

Pemphigus Neonatorum
See Scalded Skin Syndrome

Pendred Syndrome

DESCRIPTION: Rare abnormality of the ear and thyroid gland.

CAUSE: Inherited, but only if both parents carry the gene.

SYMPTOMS: Deaf from birth, and a goitre (enlarged thyroid gland) from puberty.

INVESTIGATIONS: None diagnostic.

TREATMENT: Thyroxine tablets are taken to control the goitre.

PROGNOSIS: No cure, but normal life expectancy.

Penis Cancer
See Erythroplasia of Queyrat; Squamous Cell Carcinoma

Penis Infection
See Balanitis

Penis, Short
DESCRIPTION: The size of the penis varies from one person to another. Measured along the top, the average male erect penis is 12.9cm. in length, and 90% of men have an erect penis that is between 9cm. and 17cm. in length. The other 10% are evenly divided between longer and shorter. There is no direct correlation between height, or any other obvious physical attribute, and penis size.

CAUSE: Congenital.

SYMPTOMS: A penis that the man considers to be less than normal size.

INVESTIGATIONS: None necessary.

TREATMENT: Usually none necessary as a small penis has no effect upon a man's fertility, and does not determine whether a man is a good lover. During intercourse, the most sensitive part of a woman's sexual organs are the clitoris, which is at the outside entrance to the vagina, and the 'G spot' which is just inside, and on the front wall of the vagina, at a point where even the shortest penis can give stimulation. If desired, there are plastic surgery procedures available that will both lengthen and thicken the penis, but these may have significant complications.

PROGNOSIS: No man with a relatively small penis should underestimate his sexual prowess, as he will be able to satisfy the sexual appetite of any woman if he approaches her in the right way.

See also other diseases listed under Sex Problems

Peptic Ulcer
See Ulcer, Peptic

Periarteritis Nodosa
See Polyarteritis Nodosa

Pericardial Effusion
See Pericarditis

Pericarditis
DESCRIPTION: Uncommon inflammation or infection of the pericardium, the fibrous sack that surrounds the heart.

CAUSE: May be caused by a viral (common — often secondary to mumps, hepatitis or influenza) or bacterial (rare) infection. May also occur if the pericardium is affected by the spread of cancer cells from the lung, lymph nodes or other organs. Other causes include heart attacks, tuberculosis, kidney failure and irradiation.

Pericarditis

SYMPTOMS: All forms cause chest pain, shortness of breath and a fever.

INVESTIGATIONS: Diagnosed by a combination of X-ray, CT scan, electrocardiogram (ECG), blood tests and biopsy examinations.

TREATMENT: No specific cure for a viral infection, and treatment involves aspirin, anti-inflammatory drugs and prednisone. Bacterial pericarditis can be treated with antibiotics. A pericardial effusion (collection of fluid within the pericardial sac) can be treated by inserting a long needle through the chest wall and draining the fluid. Patients with constrictive pericarditis (fibrous sack becomes scarred and contracts tightly around the heart) may require surgery on the heart to cut away the scarred part of the pericardium.

COMPLICATIONS: The secretion of fluid by the damaged pericardium into the tiny space between the pericardium and heart (**pericardial effusion**) which puts pressure on the heart, and scarring of the pericardium from infection which contracts and constricts the heart. In both these cases, the heart may not be able to expand fully between each beat, and becomes steadily more constricted (**constrictive pericarditis**), causing the heart to fail as a pump (see Heart Failure entry).

PROGNOSIS: Depends upon the cause and severity of the infection, and the age and health of the patient. Death occurs in a significant number of cases, particularly if the patient is elderly or debilitated.

See also Dressler Syndrome; Endocarditis; Heart Failure; Myocarditis

Perineal Descent Syndrome

DESCRIPTION: Weakness of the muscles in the pelvic floor (perineum).

CAUSE: Old age, difficult labour or chronic constipation results in excessive slackness of the muscles that form the floor of the pelvis, and bulging of the tissue in front of the anus when attempting to pass faeces.

SYMPTOMS: Slack pelvic floor muscles cause constipation, straining at stool, and incontinence of urine.

INVESTIGATIONS: Diagnosed by an X-ray of the lower bowel while passing a barium stool.

TREATMENT: Surgical tightening of the slack muscles.

COMPLICATIONS: Persistent straining and constipation may result in overdilation of the colon (megacolon — see separate entry).

PROGNOSIS: Reasonable results from surgery, but depends on age.

Peripheral Neuropathy

DESCRIPTION: Abnormal nerve function in the arms and legs.

CAUSE: Many causes including toxins, poisons, alcoholism, poor blood supply, poorly controlled diabetes mellitus, kidney failure, vitamin deficiencies, liver failure (eg. cirrhosis), underactive thyroid gland.

SYMPTOMS: Tingling and burning sensations in the hands and feet, abnormal sensations, abnormal reflexes.

INVESTIGATIONS: Electromyography (EMG) measures the electrical activity and function of muscles. Numerous clinical tests can be performed to check sensation. Blood and other tests are undertaken to find the cause.

TREATMENT: Appropriately treating the cause may slow the progress of the disease, or reverse its affects.

COMPLICATIONS: Clumsiness and difficulty in walking, muscle wasting and weakness.

PROGNOSIS: Depends on the cause, its severity and response to treatment.

See also Alcoholism; Cirrhosis; Wernicke-Korsakoff Psychosis

Peritonitis

DESCRIPTION: Within the belly (abdomen) is a large membranous sack called the peritoneum which contains the intestine and other organs. Peritonitis occurs if this sack becomes inflamed or infected.

CAUSE: A wide range of diseases of any organ within the abdomen may cause peritonitis. Examples include gut infections such as appendicitis or diverticulitis, a hole in the gut from an ulcer that allows the gut contents to escape into the abdominal cavity, liver infections such as hepatitis and cirrhosis, pancreatitis, pelvic inflammatory disease, bleeding within the abdomen from injury, a ruptured ovarian cyst, cancer of any organ in the abdomen, mesenteric adenitis, or it may be a rare side effect of some drugs and poisons.

SYMPTOMS: Patients have severe abdominal pain, nausea, fever and sometimes diarrhoea. They may become shocked and collapse.

INVESTIGATIONS: It is essential that the cause of the peritonitis be determined by further investigations before treatment is started. Investigations may include blood tests, X-rays, placing a needle into the abdomen to sample any fluid that may be present, vaginal and rectal examinations, or an operation to explore the abdomen.

TREATMENT: Appropriate antibiotics by injection.

COMPLICATIONS: May cause temporary paralysis of the gut, abscess formation in the abdomen, liver damage and adhesions.

PROGNOSIS: With good treatment, recovery is normal, but without adequate medical care, death can occur.

Peritonsillar Abscess
See Quinsy

Pernicious Anaemia
(Megaloblastic Anaemia; Vitamin B$_{12}$ Deficiency)

DESCRIPTION: Common cause of anaemia due to a lack of vitamin B$_{12}$.

CAUSE: Vitamin B$_{12}$ (cyanocobalamin) is essential for the formation of haemoglobin, the oxygen-carrying substance in red blood cells. For vitamin B$_{12}$ to be absorbed from the stomach and into the blood a substance called intrinsic factor is required. Patients with pernicious anaemia lack intrinsic factor and therefore develop a lack of vitamin B$_{12}$, which in turn leads to an inability to produce haemoglobin. It is common in middle aged women and is given its name because of its very gradual and 'pernicious' onset over many years.

SYMPTOMS: In addition to tiredness and pallor, patients have a smooth and sore tongue, indigestion, lack of appetite, and occasionally jaundice (yellow skin).

INVESTIGATIONS: Diagnosed by blood tests which show abnormal blood cells (megaloblasts).

TREATMENT: Regular injections of vitamin B_{12} for the rest of the patient's life. The injections may be weekly at first, then reduced to one every two or three months.

COMPLICATIONS: None significant if effectively treated.

PROGNOSIS: Pernicious anaemia cannot be cured, but it can be effectively controlled. Untreated, the disease is fatal.

See also Anaemia

Perthes' Disease

DESCRIPTION: A disease of the hip that occurs in children.

CAUSE: Softening of the growing area of the thigh bone (femur) in children between 5 and 11 years of age, immediately below the hip joint, due to an abnormal blood supply to the bone. The softened bone becomes distorted and damaged as the child continues to walk on it.

SYMPTOMS: The first sign is a limp, as the affected leg does not grow as well as the other, and becomes slightly shorter. Pain is the next symptom, and eventually walking may become impossible.

INVESTIGATIONS: Diagnosis confirmed by an X-ray of the hip.

TREATMENT: Resting the affected leg by keeping the child in bed, on crutches or in a calliper. If there is significant deformity, or the bone at the top of the femur dies, an operation is necessary.

COMPLICATIONS: Permanent deformity of the hip, and the development of early arthritis.

PROGNOSIS: Treatment has varying success. In most cases, the condition settles after two years.

Pertussis
See Whooping Cough

Pes Cavus

DESCRIPTION: Increased height of foot arch causing shortening of the foot.

CAUSE: May be a developmental abnormality, due to injury, or secondary to muscle spasm diseases such as cerebral palsy and polio.

SYMPTOMS: The foot is painful, abnormally shaped and the toes are often clawed.

INVESTIGATIONS: X-rays show bone deformity.

TREATMENT: Depends on severity and varies from supportive arches in shoes to strengthening exercises under the supervision of a physiotherapist and surgery to reduce the height of the arch.

COMPLICATIONS: Premature osteoarthritis in the foot and a limp.
PROGNOSIS: Good results from treatment.
See also Flat Feet

Pes Planus
See Flat Feet

Petit mal
See Epilepsy

Petrositis
See Gradenigo Syndrome

Peutz-Jegher Syndrome
DESCRIPTION: Abnormal polyp development in the gut.
CAUSE: Congenital (present from birth).
SYMPTOMS: Brown or black pigment in the mouth and on the lips and fingers, and multiple polyps throughout the intestine that can bleed and sometimes obstruct the gut.
INVESTIGATIONS: Diagnosed by gastroscopy and/or colonoscopy (passing a flexible tube into the gut through the mouth or anus).
TREATMENT: Removal of the bleeding and largest polyps by gastroscopy, colonoscopy or open surgery.
COMPLICATIONS: Anaemia from loss of blood.
PROGNOSIS: No cure, and repeated operations to remove polyps required.

Peyronie Disease
DESCRIPTION: An uncommon problem that causes deformity of the erect penis.
CAUSE: Injury to the penis, narrowing of the artery to one side of the penis (common with poorly controlled diabetes or high cholesterol), abnormal nerve supply to the penis or most frequently, for no known cause. Incidence increases with age.
SYMPTOMS: Significant side to side (not vertical) curvature of the erect penis and a less firm than normal erection as the normal tissue of the penis is replaced by fibrous tissue on one side only. A small degree of side to side curvature (up to 15°) is quite normal. A hard piece of tissue can often be felt at the base of the penis on the affected side.
INVESTIGATIONS: Ultrasound scans can show abnormal fibrous tissue in the penis.
TREATMENT: Surgery, steroid injections and radiotherapy may be tried. The most radical, and most successful treatment, is surgical replacement of the contents of the penis with an inflatable bladder that can be pumped up when an erection is desired.
PROGNOSIS: Most forms of treatment are not very successful. Replacement surgery is up to 80% effective.

Phaeochromocytoma

DESCRIPTION: A rare black-celled tumour in the adrenal glands (which sit on top of each kidney) which releases a substance into the blood stream that causes very high blood pressure (hypertension).

CAUSE: Sometimes an hereditary tendency, but most arise for no apparent reason.

SYMPTOMS: Extremely high blood pressure, severe headaches, palpitations of the heart, abnormal sweating, nausea and vomiting, abdominal pains, blurred vision, and brain damage that may result in loss of speech, blindness or unconsciousness. Other symptoms may include increased appetite, nervousness and irritability, shortness of breath, weight loss, light-headedness and chest pain (angina).

INVESTIGATIONS: Diagnosis confirmed by special blood tests that measure excessive levels of catecholamines (the chemical released by the tumour). A CT scan or a magnetic resonance imaging scan (MRI) is performed to locate the tumour.

TREATMENT: Controlling the high blood pressure with medication, and then surgically removing the tumour. Long-term management with medication, but without surgery, is not practical.

COMPLICATIONS: Some patients have multiple tumours in other parts of the body. Unexplained sudden deaths may be due to a heart attack caused by an undiagnosed tumour. Some forms are associated with cancer, but a phaeochromocytoma is not a cancer itself.

PROGNOSIS: Depends on damage caused by the hypertension before diagnosis, and how many tumours are present. If tumour is removed early, a complete recovery is expected. Without treatment, the disease is invariably fatal, and even in the best medical centres, a small percentage of patients will die from complications of the disease or the surgery.

See also Hypertension

Pharyngitis
(Throat Infection)

DESCRIPTION: Very common bacterial or viral infection of the throat (pharynx).

CAUSE: The vast majority are caused by viruses, while a minority are due to bacteria. The most serious bacterial pharyngitis is caused by *Staphylococcus aureus* (golden staph), but by the most common is caused by *Streptococci*. The infection is passed from one person to another in tiny water droplets in the breath. Most cases occur in winter.

SYMPTOMS: May vary from one day of mild discomfort to a severe infection that may cause dramatic swelling of the throat for more than a week. Symptoms include fever, throat pain and soreness, pain on swallowing, dry cough, headache and sometimes enlarged lymph nodes in the neck.

INVESTIGATIONS: Most require no investigation, but if the infection is serious, a throat swab may be taken to identify the responsible bacteria and appropriate antibiotic. Blood tests may be performed if diseases such as glandular fever (see separate entry) which also cause throat pain are suspected.

TREATMENT: Viral pharyngitis — aspirin, paracetamol or ibuprofen; anaesthetic gargles, and soothing lozenges.

Bacterial pharyngitis — antibiotics such as penicillin can be prescribed as well as the medications for a viral infection.

COMPLICATIONS: Severe bacterial infections may rarely cause a throat abscess.

PROGNOSIS: Viral infections last for a week or ten days. Antibiotics will cure a bacterial infection in a day or two.

See also Cold, Common; Laryngitis; Tonsillitis; Uvulitis

Phenylketonuria
(PKU)

DESCRIPTION: Uncommon metabolic (body chemistry) disorder that may have serious consequences.

CAUSE: Congenital (present from birth) disease that runs in families from one generation to the next, and more common in people of Scottish or Irish descent (1 in 5000 children), but extremely rare in Negroes (1 in 300,000).

SYMPTOMS: A baby with PKU cannot tolerate foodstuffs which contain the amino acid, phenylalanine, and a build-up of this in the blood causes brain damage, mental retardation, epilepsy, behaviour problems and eczema.

INVESTIGATIONS: Every baby in developed countries is routinely tested a couple of days after birth using a single drop of blood taken from a heel prick. Further blood tests are performed regularly to ensure that the amount of phenylalanine does not rise above normal.

TREATMENT: A protein free diet from before two months of age until child is at least eight years old. Phenylalanine is found in most proteins, but other amino acids (the building blocks of protein) are provided in a special formula.

PROGNOSIS: A correct diet started early will prevent the disease from damaging the brain, and the child will grow up to be a normal adult with normal intelligence.

Phimosis

DESCRIPTION: Narrow opening in foreskin of penis.

CAUSE: Normal up to six years of age in boys. The foreskin should never be forcibly retracted before this age. In men it may be due to infection in or under the foreskin, injury or a minor birth defect.

SYMPTOMS: Inability to retract the foreskin over the head of the penis, and sometimes ballooning of foreskin when passing urine.

INVESTIGATIONS: None normally necessary.

TREATMENT: Circumcision.

COMPLICATIONS: Balanitis (an infection of the head of the penis) due to an inability to clean under the foreskin.

PROGNOSIS: Very good result from surgery.

See also Balanitis; Paraphimosis

Phlebitis

DESCRIPTION: Inflammation of a vein.

CAUSE: Usually due to a blood clot (thrombosis) in a vein, but may occur for no apparent reason.

SYMPTOMS: Pain, tenderness and redness along the course of a vein.

INVESTIGATIONS: Blood tests in an attempt to determine cause.

TREATMENT: Anti-inflammatory medication.

COMPLICATIONS: Swelling of tissue drained by affected vein due to reduced blood flow.

PROGNOSIS: Good.

See also Thrombophlebitis; Thrombosis

Phobia

DESCRIPTION: An unnecessary fearful reaction that provokes severe anxiety. May be due to a fear of enclosed spaces (**claustrophobia**), spiders (**arachnophobia**), open spaces (**agoraphobia**), heights (**acrophobia**), sharp implements, specific animals, eating in public or almost any thing or activity imaginable.

CAUSE: Most commonly develop in anxious people in the late teens and early adult years, and more common in women than men. Some patients have a fear of a particular circumstance because of an unpleasant experience in the past (eg. claustrophobia after being trapped in a lift), but this is not a true phobia as it is a rational fear triggered by a previous unpleasant experience.

SYMPTOMS: An unreasonable fear of something, place or activity that should not provoke fear. An anxious patient may rationalise their anxiety and the palpitations, sweating, nausea and headaches it causes by considering it to be a fear of something. It may become an obsession that dominates the patients life, particularly if the fear is of contamination, dirt or disease, which leads to repetitive actions such as constant, excessive hand-washing. In other situations, patients may go to extreme lengths to avoid the object of their fear (eg. stay in rooms on the ground floor of hotels), or undertake rituals that make a fearful activity safe (eg. always wear a certain piece of clothing when flying). The patient with one serious phobia usually develops more and more phobias of less and less fearful objects and situations, as the neurotic disease or anxiety worsens.

INVESTIGATIONS: No diagnostic tests.

TREATMENT: Psychiatrists can help patients deal with the underlying anxieties, give behavioural treatment that gradually exposes the patient to the fear, and prescribe medication that controls the problem.

COMPLICATIONS: Patient may become housebound or unable to function in society.

PROGNOSIS: Most can cope with appropriate treatment, but phobia often lasts lifelong.

See also Neurosis; Obsessive Compulsive Neurosis and other diseases listed under Psychiatric Conditions

Photodermatitis

DESCRIPTION: Abnormal reaction of skin to sunlight. Several different forms (eg. Hutchison's prurigo, polymorphic light eruption, solar urticaria).
CAUSE: Congenital (present since birth) allergy type reaction.
SYMPTOMS: Red, raised itchy rash on sun exposed skin.
INVESTIGATIONS: No specific diagnostic tests.
TREATMENT: Using clothing that covers all skin and broad brimmed hats.
COMPLICATIONS: Permanent skin damage and scarring.
PROGNOSIS: No cure.
See also Dermatitis

Photosensitive Eczema

DESCRIPTION: Uncommon type of eczema that affects areas of skin that are exposed to light.
CAUSE: A reaction in the skin to ultraviolet wavelengths in sunlight. Fluorescent lights also give off ultraviolet radiation and can cause this reaction. Usually occurs in middle-aged and elderly men.
SYMPTOMS: Red rash covered with scales that is intensely itchy. The face, forearms and hands are the most common areas affected.
INVESTIGATIONS: A biopsy may assist in the diagnosis.
TREATMENT: Wearing long-sleeved shirts and hats, and applying UV sun screen creams and very strong steroid creams. Occasionally steroid tablets are also required.
COMPLICATIONS: In rare cases, may be so severe that the patient cannot go outside during the day, and they must reverse their lifestyle — sleeping during the day and being active at night — in order to avoid the sun.
PROGNOSIS: Once established, the condition persists for life.
See also Eczema

Phthisis
See Tuberculosis

Pick's Disease

DESCRIPTION: Similar to Alzheimer's disease, except that only one lobe of the brain (usually the frontal or temporal lobe) wastes away (atrophies) rather than the brain as a whole.
CAUSE: Unknown, but may be familial (passed from one generation to the next) in some cases.
SYMPTOMS: Slowly progressive dementia, excessive use of the mouth in a baby-like manner, deliberate vomiting after meals, disturbances in speech and use of words, loss of normal social inhibitions, irritability and persistent aimless wandering.
INVESTIGATIONS: CT scan shows degeneration of part of the brain.

TREATMENT: None available.
PROGNOSIS: Slow inevitable progression.
See also Alzheimer's Disease; Dementia

Pickwickian Syndrome

DESCRIPTION: Complication of being seriously overweight that usually occurs in women.
CAUSE: Gross obesity.
SYMPTOMS: Significant shortness of breath, obesity, tiredness, blue skin (cyanosis), shallow breathing, cor pulmonale (see separate entry), high blood pressure (hypertension) and heart failure.
INVESTIGATIONS: Abnormal levels of acid, oxygen, carbon dioxide and red blood cells in blood, abnormal respiratory function tests and chest X-ray.
TREATMENT: Significant weight loss and medications to control heart failure and hypertension.
COMPLICATIONS: Pneumonia and other serious infections.
PROGNOSIS: Poor unless patient succeeds in losing large amount of weight.
See also Cor Pulmonale; Hypertension

PID
See Pelvic Inflammatory Disease

PIE Syndrome
See Loeffler Syndrome

Pierre-Robin Syndrome

DESCRIPTION: Rare abnormality of upper and lower jaw development.
CAUSE: Congenital.
SYMPTOMS: Cleft palate and lip, abnormally small lower jaw.
INVESTIGATIONS: X-rays of face show extent of abnormality.
TREATMENT: Extensive facial surgery.
COMPLICATIONS: Maintenance of airway and feeding prior to surgery often difficult.
PROGNOSIS: Good results from surgery.

Pigmented Purpura
See Capillaritis

Pigmented Purpuric Lichenoid Dermatosis
See Capillaritis

Pigmented Villonodular Synovitis

DESCRIPTION: A specific type of synovitis of the knee, in which the smooth synovial membrane that lines the inside of the joint becomes covered with dark-coloured (ie. pigmented) microscopic protuberances and lumps.

CAUSE: Inflammation of the synovial membrane due to injury to the knee, or may be associated with rheumatoid arthritis.

SYMPTOMS: Painful, swollen, red knee that has limited movement.

INVESTIGATIONS: Diagnosed at arthroscopy (looking into the knee joint through a small tube) by a biopsy of the synovial membrane.

TREATMENT: Pain controlled by anti-inflammatory drugs and the swelling eased by removing excess fluid from the joint through a needle. These measures are only temporary, and most patients will needle to have the knee joint replaced.

COMPLICATIONS: Knee joint may fuse solid and immovably if left untreated.

PROGNOSIS: Good results from knee replacement surgery.

See also Rheumatoid Arthritis; Synovitis

Piles
(Haemorrhoids)

DESCRIPTION: Dilation, damage to, bleeding from and blood clot formation in veins around the anus. Internal and external versions, depending on whether veins inside or outside the anus are damaged.

CAUSE: Constipation, passing hard motions, squatting and heavy lifting.

SYMPTOMS: Intermittent, painless swelling beside the anus, or they may become excruciatingly tender, painful, and bleed profusely.

INVESTIGATIONS: Proctoscopy (passing an examination tube through the anus into the rectum).

TREATMENT: Keeping the bowels regular and soft prevents piles. Initially, ice packs and simple soothing creams can be used, but if relief is not obtained, steroid and antiseptic creams or soothing suppositories are prescribed. If there is a clot of blood in the haemorrhoid, it is cut open to allow the clot to escape. If it persists, further treatment may involve clipping a rubber band around the base of the pile, injected or electrically coagulating the pile, or an operation to cut away part of the anal canal.

COMPLICATIONS: Excessive bleeding from the pile may cause anaemia.

PROGNOSIS: The operation is normally successful in permanently removing the problem.

See also Anal Fissure

Pilonidal Sinus

DESCRIPTION: Infection of a hair follicle on or between the buttocks.

CAUSE: Hair is found all over the body, except on the palms and soles. Every hair follicle is supplied with a gland that secrete a thick, viscous oil. If the hair follicle becomes clogged with oil, it may become infected. More common in hairy men who sit all day at work (eg. truck drivers). Waxing the hairs will aggravate the situation by damaging the hair follicles.

SYMPTOMS: A painful infection that rapidly develops into an abscess.

INVESTIGATIONS: None necessary.

TREATMENT: Antibiotic tablets and surgical drainage of the abscess. Long term

antibiotics, may be necessary in some patients to prevent recurrences.
COMPLICATIONS: Severe abscesses may require significant surgery to remove a large area of surrounding tissue.
PROGNOSIS: Generally good, although recurrences common.

Pimples
See Acne

Pinealoma
(Pineal Tumour)
DESCRIPTION: Rare benign or cancerous growth of the pineal gland, which acts as the body's clock and sits underneath and between the frontal lobes of the brain.
CAUSE: Unknown.
SYMPTOMS: Headache, difficulty in looking upwards, personality changes, nausea and tiredness.
INVESTIGATIONS: Diagnosed by CT and MRI scans.
TREATMENT: Surgical removal or irradiation of the tumour.
COMPLICATIONS: Increase in pressure of cerebrospinal fluid that surrounds the brain may cause epileptic fits.
PROGNOSIS: Good if tumour is benign, poor if cancerous.
See also Parinaud Syndrome

Pineal Tumour
See Pinealoma

Pingueculum
DESCRIPTION: A growth on the eye surface that develops very slowly over many years.
CAUSE: Recurrent mild sunburn to the cornea (eye surface) which irritates tissue that overgrows.
SYMPTOMS: A pale yellow fleshy overgrowth of the white part of the eye (cornea) that occurs on the side of the eye closest to the nose. May become irritated, red and itchy.
INVESTIGATIONS: None necessary.
TREATMENT: Simple drops ease any redness and irritation. Cure requires simple surgery. Prevented by wearing good quality (polarised) sun glasses.
COMPLICATIONS: A pterygium develops with further irritation and growth.
PROGNOSIS: Good.
See also Pterygium

Pink Disease
See Mercury Poisoning

Pinta

DESCRIPTION: Bacterial skin infection that occurs in children and young adults who are malnourished and living in conditions of poor hygiene. More common on the forearms and lower legs.

CAUSE: The bacterium *Treponema carateum*. Incubation period one to three months.

SYMPTOMS: Starts with a small, pink scaly lump (papule), which gradually enlarges to form a scale covered plaque with raised edges. Further spots appear around the original one, and then elsewhere on the body.

INVESTIGATIONS: Diagnosed by a biopsy of affected skin. Blood tests for syphilis, which is caused by a similar bacteria, are positive.

TREATMENT: Antibiotics (penicillin or tetracycline).

COMPLICATIONS: In a second stage of the disease, the plaques become extensive, thicken, enlarge, and merge together, and pigment is lost or gained to change the skin colour.

PROGNOSIS: Very good response to treatment, but pigment changes in second stage disease are permanent.

See also Syphilis; Yaws

Pinworms
(Enterobiasis; Threadworms)

DESCRIPTION: Infestation of the gut by the pinworm (*Enterobius vermicularis*).

CAUSE: 1cm long, the pinworm lives in the large intestine, but migrates to around the anus to lay eggs, from where they may be transferred to the fingers during wiping or scratching, and then re-enter the original patient's mouth or pass to another person, where the cycle starts again. The worm dies after depositing the eggs and passes out with the faeces, where they may sometimes be seen. The eggs can survive for up to three weeks outside the body. Children are the most commonly affected group, and they spread the infestation to others by poor personal hygiene. It is very easy for all the members of one family to be affected.

SYMPTOMS: Most patients have no symptoms but some will experience anal itching at night, mild diarrhoea and minor abdominal pains.

INVESTIGATIONS: Diagnosed by microscopically examining the faeces for the presence of worms or eggs.

TREATMENT: Treatment should involve all members of the patient's immediate family. A number of anthelmintic medications can be used to kill the worms. Good hygiene involves careful hand-washing after going to the toilet and not scratching the anus. If the patient does not reinfected themselves the worms will die out in six to seven weeks.

COMPLICATIONS: In rare cases the worms may migrate to the vagina and urethra of women and girls.

PROGNOSIS: Virtually all patients will recover with time and good personal hygiene.

See also Worm Infestations

Piriformis Syndrome

DESCRIPTION: Uncommon cause of sciatica.

CAUSE: Injury, strain or sprain to the piriformis muscle of the pelvis. Aggravated by osteoarthritis of the hip joint. More common in women.

SYMPTOMS: Sciatica (pain running across the buttock and down the leg) caused by compression of the sciatic nerve at the back of the pelvis by spasm of the piriformis muscle. For comfort when lying down, the hip is held turned out so that the foot points outwards.

INVESTIGATIONS: Pain and muscle weakness occur when the legs are moved apart or rolled outwards by a doctor while the patient attempts to prevent this by muscle use.

TREATMENT: Injection of local anaesthetic and steroid combination into the piriformis muscle, or in resistant cases, the muscle is surgically cut.

PROGNOSIS: Often persistent.

See also Sciatica

Pituitary Failure
See Hypopituitarism

Pityriasis Rosea

DESCRIPTION: Skin disease of older children and adults up to middle age.

CAUSE: Unknown.

SYMPTOMS: Dark red, scaling, slightly raised, oval-shaped patches on the chest, upper arms, thighs, neck, abdomen and back. Usually a large patch ('**herald patch**') precedes other smaller patches by a week or two. Only very slight itching or irritation, and minimal discomfort. The forearms, lower legs and face are not usually affected.

INVESTIGATIONS: None normally required. Sometimes a blood test may be performed to exclude more serious diagnoses.

TREATMENT: Antihistamine tablets taken at night, and steroid creams applied.

COMPLICATIONS: None.

PROGNOSIS: Settles without treatment in six to eight weeks.

Pityriasis Versicolor
(Tinea Versicolor)

DESCRIPTION: A relatively common fungal skin disease of the tropics.

CAUSE: A fungal infection that affects young adults more than the elderly and children. The chest, upper arms, neck, upper back and armpits are the most commonly affected areas.

SYMPTOMS: Pink/brown patches on the skin, which may have a very faint scale upon them. After a few weeks, the skin underlying the rash has less pigment, so the rash appears as white patches which are due to sunlight being unable to tan the skin underlying the fungus. Areas not exposed to sunlight (eg. armpits, breasts) may retain the pink/brown patch appearance. This effect does

422

not occur on Aborigines, Chinese and other dark-skinned races. No other symptoms other than an occasional very mild itch.

INVESTIGATIONS: None normally necessary, but diagnosis can be proved by examining skin scrapings under a microscope.

TREATMENT: Regular use of antifungal lotions, rinses or creams. An antifungal tablet (ketaconazole) is used in persistent and widespread cases.

COMPLICATIONS: White patches will remain for some time after the fungus has been destroyed, until the sun tans the area again.

PROGNOSIS: Episodes of infection are quite easy to clear, but often recurs in the next summer.

See also Fungal Infections

PKU
See Phenylketonuria

Placental Cancer
See Choriocarcinoma of the Uterus

Plague, Bubonic
(Black Death)

DESCRIPTION: A severe generalised bacterial infection that is very rare in developed nations, but still present in many poorer Asian and African countries.

CAUSE: The bacterium *Yersinia pestis* which normally infects rats, and passes from one rat to another, or from rat to humans, by the bite of a flea.

SYMPTOMS: Large, pus-filled glands (buboes) in the neck, groin and armpit; accompanied by a high fever, severe muscle pain, headache, rapid heart rate, profound tiredness and eventually coma. The infection may spread to the blood and cause black spots (bruises — thus the 'black death') under the skin.

INVESTIGATIONS: Diagnosis confirmed by special blood tests and cultures from the discharging glands.

TREATMENT: Isolation in hospital, antibiotics and intravenous drip feeding. Prevented by a plague vaccine or taking tetracycline tablets every day.

COMPLICATIONS: Plague pneumonia or meningitis may develop.

PROGNOSIS: In good hospitals virtually all patients will recover, but untreated the death rate exceeds 50%, and death may occur within a few hours in patients who are malnourished or in poor health. Complications are fatal without excellent medical care.

Plantar Fasciitis

DESCRIPTION: Inflammation of the fibrous band of tissue that forms the support for the sole of the foot.

CAUSE: May start after excessive exercise (eg. an unusually long run or walk), after a sudden sharp injury (eg. landing heavily after jumping), or for no apparent reason.

SYMPTOMS: A constantly aching foot sole, that becomes sharply painful with every step when walking.

INVESTIGATIONS: None normally necessary.

TREATMENT: Complete rest, sometimes requiring several weeks on crutches. Other treatments include anti-inflammatory drugs, pain killers, physiotherapy and occasionally steroid injections into the foot. As a last resort, the foot may be put in plaster for a few weeks to ensure total rest.

PROGNOSIS: Good with correct treatment.

Plantar Wart
(Verruca)

DESCRIPTION: Warts on the soles of the feet, which tend to grow inwards rather than out.

CAUSE: A very slow developing virus that attacks softened skin.

SYMPTOMS: A hard, slightly raised, scar like growth on the sole of the foot that becomes painful with walking. Verrucae are like icebergs, with only a small part showing on the surface and a much larger area affected deeper in the sole.

INVESTIGATIONS: None necessary.

TREATMENT: Diathermy (burning), acid ointments, freezing, cutting out, or injecting under the wart. After surgery, a far larger hole than expected is usually left in the sole that may take some weeks to heal.

COMPLICATIONS: May become so large, widespread and painful that walking is very difficult.

PROGNOSIS: Recurrences common despite the best treatment.

See also Warts

Pleural Effusion

DESCRIPTION: Accumulation of a large amount of fluid between the pleura (a smooth, slippery, shiny membrane that lines the inside of the chest cavity) and the lung.

CAUSE: Heart failure, cirrhosis, nephrotic syndrome, lung embolus, cancer, tuberculosis (see separate entries) and bacterial or viral infections of the lung.

SYMPTOMS: Fluid restricts lung movement and may cause significant shortness of breath and a dry cough.

INVESTIGATIONS: Excess fluid can be seen on a chest X-ray.

TREATMENT: Fluid removed by passing a needle through the chest wall and into the fluid collection, then drawing it off into a syringe. The fluid is examined to determine which disease is responsible for the effusion. Further treatment will depend upon the cause of the effusion.

COMPLICATIONS: Pleurisy (see separate entry).

PROGNOSIS: Depends on cause, but effusion itself usually controllable.

See also Pleurisy

Pleurisy
(Pleuritis)

DESCRIPTION: Infection (pleurisy) or inflammation (pleuritis) of the pleura (a smooth, slippery, shiny membrane that lines the inside of the chest cavity) which allows the lung to move freely within the chest as it contracts and expands with every breath. The pleura is covered with a very thin layer of fluid that acts as a lubricant.

CAUSE: Occurs with viral infections of the chest, a fractured rib that damages the pleura, and bacterial infections associated with acute bronchitis, pneumonia and tuberculosis.

SYMPTOMS: Severe pain that can often be localised to one point on the chest or back and is worse with breathing, sneezing, coughing, laughing or any movement of the chest.

INVESTIGATIONS: Chest X-ray may show area of fluid accumulation or inflammation.

TREATMENT: Viral and inflammatory pleurisy will settle with rest and minor pain killers or anti-inflammatory drugs (eg. indomethacin). Bacterial pleurisy associated with pneumonia requires antibiotics and stronger pain-killers.

COMPLICATIONS: Pleural effusion (see separate entry).

PROGNOSIS: Good, but depends on underlying cause.

See also Bronchitis, Acute; Pleural Effusion; Pneumonia

Pleurodynia
See Bornholm Disease

Plica Syndrome
See Synovial Plica Syndrome

Plumbism
See Lead Poisoning

Plummer-Vinson Syndrome
(Paterson-Brown-Kelly syndrome)

DESCRIPTION: Inflammatory condition of gullet (oesophagus).

CAUSE: Unknown, but tends to occur in middle aged women.

SYMPTOMS: Difficulty and pain on swallowing, fibrous web formation across the oesophagus, enlarged spleen, iron deficiency anaemia, inflamed mouth, finger nails curve upwards, and in some patients the lips are thin and the mouth is beak shaped.

INVESTIGATIONS: X-ray barium swallow and oesophagoscopy (passing a flexible tube down the oesophagus) both abnormal. Blood tests show anaemia.

TREATMENT: Swallowing oesophageal dilators under sedation, iron supplements, and a good diet.

COMPLICATIONS: Often leads to cancer of the oesophagus.

PROGNOSIS: Often recurs after treatment.

See also Oesophageal Cancer

PMR
See Polymyalgia Rheumatica

PMT
See Premenstrual Tension Syndrome

PND
See Post-Nasal Drip

Pneumoconiosis

DESCRIPTION: Replacement of normal lung tissue by fibrous scar tissue. A form of chronic obstructive airways disease.

CAUSE: Long-term inhalation of fine coal dust particles in underground coal miners. Aggravated by cigarette smoking.

SYMPTOMS: No symptoms until the condition is quite advanced, when patients become short of breath.

INVESTIGATIONS: Chest X-ray shows numerous small pellets of coal dust concentrated in the lungs. The upper part of the lung is more affected than the lower.

TREATMENT: None available.

COMPLICATIONS: Lung infections such as pneumonia.

PROGNOSIS: No cure, but the disease does not necessarily lead to lung cancer in the same way as asbestosis.

See also **Asbestosis; Silicosis; Talcosis**

Pneumonia
(Bronchopneumonia)

DESCRIPTION: A bacterial, or rarely fungal, infection of the lung alveoli (tiny air bubbles that form the major part of the lung and enable the oxygen to cross into the bloodstream), which fill with pus. Usually only one part of the lungs, often at the bottom of the chest, is affected, but it may spread to other parts of the lung. Once one type of bacteria are present, a second type may also infect the lungs as well to cause **double pneumonia**. Almost invariably the bronchi (main air tubes) are also infected, so the disease should correctly be called bronchopneumonia.

CAUSE: Bacteria are inhaled into the lungs, and overcome the body's defence mechanisms, particularly if the patient is tired, run-down, overworked, elderly, bedridden or suffering from other illnesses.

SYMPTOMS: The symptoms of pneumonia may be obvious with fever, productive cough and chest pains, but some infections are more insidious and cause minimal symptoms for some months while the patient feels tired, short of breath and has intermittent sweats.

INVESTIGATIONS: Chest X-rays are diagnostic, and are repeated at regular intervals to ensure that the infection is resolving. A sample of sputum is taken before treatment is started, and is sent to a laboratory to identify the infecting bacteria.

TREATMENT: One or more antibiotics are given by tablet, injection or drip into a vein. Expectorants to open up the airways and loosen the phlegm are also prescribed, along with cough mixtures and pain-killers. Regular physiotherapy is very important to drain phlegm and pus out of the chest. Rest and the cessation of smoking are vital. Occasionally oxygen is required for seriously ill patients, and in rare cases, surgery to drain out collections of pus or remove areas of chronically infected lung is required. Some forms of pneumonia can be prevented by a vaccine (Pneumovax).

COMPLICATIONS: Inadequately treated pneumonia can cause chronic ill health, an abscess may form in the lung and lead to permanent lung damage. Once the lung is damaged, the chances of developing a subsequent attack of pneumonia is increased, and smoking will accelerate this process. Pneumonia puts a great strain on the heart, and it may fail in older or debilitated patients.

PROGNOSIS: With correct treatment the majority of patients recover in a couple of weeks, but some may take months, and there is a small mortality rate amongst the elderly and debilitated, even in the best hospitals. Up to half of all patients affected died before the advent of modern antibiotics in the 1940s.

See also Bronchitis, Acute; Emphysema; Lung Abscess; Psittacosis

Pneumothorax

DESCRIPTION: The presence of air between the lung and its surrounding pleura. The lung lies in a smooth, slippery sack (the pleura). If the lung develops a puncture, air will leak into the pleural sack around the lung and is unable to escape. More and more air accumulates in the sack, causing pressure on the lung, which eventually collapses.

CAUSE: Often occurs for no apparent reason (**spontaneous pneumothorax**), or may be due to a chest injury, and lung diseases such as asthma, tuberculosis, cancer or cystic fibrosis.

SYMPTOMS: Worsening shortness of breath and chest pain.

INVESTIGATIONS: A chest X-ray will show the partly collapsed lung.

TREATMENT: A small pneumothorax may be observed and its progress checked by regular X-rays. If the pneumothorax is large or growing larger, a tube is placed through the chest wall to remove the escaped air, which allows the lung to expand. The outside end of the tube is placed under water to stop air reentering the lungs. Patients who have repeated attacks of spontaneous pneumothorax, may require surgery to repair the damaged area of lung. All patients must stop smoking.

COMPLICATIONS: A **tension pneumothorax**, may be fatal in a few minutes, as every breath pumps large amounts of air out of the lungs and into the pleural cavity. The pressure in the pleural cavity builds up rapidly and causes the lungs to collapse. A large needle or tube must be immediately pushed through the chest wall into the pleural cavity to save the patient's life.

PROGNOSIS: Complete recovery in a few hours or a day or two is normal with correct treatment.

Poikiloderma, Congenital
See Rothmund-Thomson Syndrome

Poikiloderma of Civatte
DESCRIPTION: Common weathering effect on the skin at the sides and front of the neck, that spares the shaded area under the chin.

CAUSE: Exact cause unknown, but contributing factors include fair skin, long term sun exposure, cosmetics, perfumes and hormonal changes.

SYMPTOMS: Affected skin is thin, red-brown with prominent hair follicles and dilated small blood vessels (telangiectasia).

INVESTIGATIONS: None normally necessary.

TREATMENT: Difficult. Sun protection with hats and sunscreen, avoid perfumes and soaps on affected area, preparations to help fade the pigmentation, lotions containing tretinoin and laser treatment to reduce the telangiectasia.

PROGNOSIS: Persistent. Treatment often unsatisfactory.

Poisoning
See Arsenic Poisoning; Ciguatera Poisoning; Cyanide Poisoning; Insecticide Poisoning; Iron Poisoning; Lead Poisoning; Mercury Poisoning; Strychnine Poisoning

Polio
(Poliomyelitis)
DESCRIPTION: A generalised infection that involves muscles. Very rare in developed countries, but widespread in many poorer countries.

CAUSE: A virus which passes from one person to another through droplets in the breath or by touch.

SYMPTOMS: Severe muscle spasm followed by paralysis and muscle contractures.

INVESTIGATIONS: Diagnosed by specific blood tests.

TREATMENT: None available other than general physical support and muscle relaxants. An oral (Sabin) vaccine is available that is extremely effective, safe, and has no side effects.

COMPLICATIONS: If the muscles of breathing or the heart are affected, the patient may die or remain on a respirator for life.

PROGNOSIS: Poor. Many patients recover, but most of them have significant disabilities.

See also Post-Polio Syndrome

Polle Syndrome
(Munchausen Syndrome by Proxy)
DESCRIPTION: Obscure forms of child abuse.

CAUSE: Psychiatric disturbance.

SYMPTOMS: Apparently caring parents who consult excessively with doctors and hospitals about their child, demand extensive investigation of the child who is emotionally stressed. Parents deliberately falsify symptoms or tests.

INVESTIGATIONS: None diagnostic. Usually over investigated by innumerable tests before diagnosis made.

TREATMENT: Psychotherapy, family counselling.

COMPLICATIONS: Child may be injured by unnecessary procedures.

PROGNOSIS: Poor result for family as child may need to be taken into protective custody.

See also Munchausen Syndrome

Polyarteritis Nodosa
(PAN; Periarteritis Nodosa)

DESCRIPTION: Inflammation of small to medium-sized arteries. The damaged artery may become weakened and balloon out to several times its normal diameter, it may scar and shrink down, or the blood passing through the inflamed section of artery may clot and completely block the artery (a thrombosis). The arteries affected may be anywhere in the body, but the gut, liver, heart, testes, kidney, and muscles are most commonly involved.

CAUSE: Unknown, but more common in drug abusers and in patients with hepatitis B. Rarely it may be a side effect of medication. Men are three times more likely to develop the disease than women, and it is most common in young adults.

SYMPTOMS: Very varied, depending on which arteries and organs are involved. The patient is usually feverish, and has pain in the area involved. Specific complaints may include muscle pain, palpitations, arthritis, skin ulcers, spots in the vision, abdominal pain, nausea, vomiting, diarrhoea and high blood pressure.

INVESTIGATIONS: No diagnostic blood tests. A biopsy (sample) taken from an involved artery confirms the diagnosis.

TREATMENT: Taking steroids (eg. prednisone) in high doses for a long period of time. Immunosuppressive drugs may also be used.

PROGNOSIS: Varies markedly from one patient to another, depending upon the areas and arteries involved. Some patients do recover, but the majority slowly deteriorate to die within a few months or years.

Polychondritis, Relapsing
See Relapsing Polychondritis

Polycystic Kidney

DESCRIPTION: Multiple fluid-filled cysts in the kidneys that are formed when tiny urine-collecting tubes within the kidney become blocked or do not connect up to the main urine-collecting system of the kidney.

CAUSE: Familial (inherited).

SYMPTOMS: Usually no symptoms, and found during investigations of a family that is known to have the disease, during an operation or other routine investigation. In other cases may be a cause of high blood pressure, blood in the urine, or constant pain in one loin.

INVESTIGATIONS: Diagnosed by ultrasound scan, CT scan or special X-rays of the kidney.

TREATMENT: Most patients require no treatment. In serious cases where the kidneys do fail, dialysis (artificial kidney machine) or a kidney transplant are possible.

COMPLICATIONS: Liver and pancreas may be involved in a small number of patients.

PROGNOSIS: Good. Although damaged, the kidney tissue remaining between the cysts is able to function adequately.

Polycystic Ovarian Syndrome
(Stein-Leventhal Syndrome)

DESCRIPTION: Multiple small cysts form in one or both ovaries.

CAUSE: Unknown. Cysts interfere with the production of hormones by the ovaries.

SYMPTOMS: The patient develops facial hairs, gains weight, stops her menstrual periods, is infertile and losses breast firmness.

INVESTIGATIONS: Abnormal levels of hormones can be measured in the bloodstream. Often discovered on an ultrasound scan during investigations for infertility.

TREATMENT: Surgically cutting away part of the affected ovarian tissue, and using hormones to stimulate the ovary to restart its correct function. Specific medications (eg. spironolactone or progestagens) used for excessive hair growth. Some women find the discomfort of the condition and the side effects of medication unacceptable and decide to have a total hysterectomy.

COMPLICATIONS: No serious long-term effects.

PROGNOSIS: Good results from treatment.

See also Ovarian Cyst

Polycythaemia Rubra Vera
See Polycythaemia Vera

Polycythaemia Vera
(Polycythaemia Rubra Vera)

DESCRIPTION: Excess production of red blood cells that is most common in middle-aged to elderly, overweight men, but may occur in both sexes. Rare under 40 years of age.

CAUSE: Red blood cells are made in the bone marrow, primarily of the breastbone (sternum), pelvis and thighbone (femur). If the marrow becomes overactive, excessive numbers of cells may be produced.

SYMPTOMS: Headache, dizziness, tiredness, blurred vision, generalised itching, noises in the ears, high blood pressure and an enlarged spleen.

INVESTIGATIONS: Diagnosis confirmed by finding excess red blood cells in a blood test. Further tests on bone marrow determine the severity of the disease.

TREATMENT: Controlled, but not cured, by draining large quantities of blood out of a vein initially, and smaller amounts on a regular basis long term. Medications to reduce the activity of the bone marrow may also be used.

COMPLICATIONS: Blood clots in vital organs (eg. brain to cause a stroke), and some patients develop a form of chronic leukaemia (see separate entry).

PROGNOSIS: Average survival time after diagnosis is twelve years.

Polyglandular Autoimmune Syndromes

DESCRIPTION: Autoimmune (inappropriate rejection of normal body tissue) damage to multiple hormone secreting glands in the body. Three different types have been identified.

CAUSE: All types are inherited, but with type 1 both parents must carry the abnormal gene, while with types 2 and 3 only one parent needs to be a carrier.

SYMPTOMS: Type 1 — Child with thrush (fungal infection) in the mouth, under active parathyroid glands in the neck and under active adrenal glands (sit on top of each kidney). Some patients may have loss of body hair, under-developed genitals and an underactive thyroid gland.

Type 2 — Adult with under active adrenal glands, autoimmune thyroid gland disease and insulin dependent diabetes. Some patients may have under-developed genitals, myasthenia gravis and vitiligo (see separate entries).

Type 3 — Adult with autoimmune thyroid disease and insulin dependent diabetes mellitus, OR under active adrenal glands and Hashimoto's thyroiditis (see separate entry).

INVESTIGATIONS: Depending on form abnormal results may occur with numerous blood tests.

TREATMENT: Missing hormones are replaced and inflamed glands individually treated.

COMPLICATIONS: Significant organ damage and body function failures.

PROGNOSIS: Potentially fatal.

Polyhydramnios

DESCRIPTION: In a pregnant woman, the baby floats in a uterus filled with amniotic fluid which acts to protect it from bumps and jarring and removes waste. Polyhydramnios occurs if excess fluid is present.

CAUSE: Occurs in one in every 100 pregnancies, and may be a sign that the foetus has a significant abnormality that prevents it from drinking or causes the excess production of urine. Other causes include a twin pregnancy, and diabetes or heart disease in the mother. In over half the cases no specific cause for the excess fluid can ever be found.

SYMPTOMS: A uterus that is larger than expected for the length of pregnancy. Normally there is about 1000 mLs. of amniotic fluid at birth. A volume greater than 1500 mLs. is considered to be diagnostic of polyhydramnios, but it may not become apparent until 2500 mLs. or more is present.

INVESTIGATIONS: Diagnosed by an ultrasound scan. Further investigations to determine the cause of the condition must follow (eg. amniocentesis — taking a sample of the fluid for analysis).

TREATMENT: Depends upon the cause, but often none is necessary.

COMPLICATIONS: Increased risk to mother of amniotic fluid embolism, a potentially fatal complication that occurs when some of the fluid enters the mother's blood stream.

PROGNOSIS: Most pregnancies proceed relatively normally, but increased risk of foetal abnormality.

See also Oligohydramnios

Polymorphic Light Eruption
See Photodermatitis

Polymyalgia Rheumatica
(PMR)

DESCRIPTION: Random inflammation of the muscles anywhere in the body. Women are affected five times more often than men.

CAUSE: PMR is one of a number of post-viral syndromes. In some people, for no known reason, a viral infection such as influenza is followed by a chronic inflammation of many muscles.

SYMPTOMS: Severe aches and pains in a group of muscles for a few days before the pain subsides, then another muscle group is attacked. The muscles are also weak and the patient is irritable, tired, unable to concentrate, and depressed. Other symptoms may include nausea, headache, arthritis and loss of appetite.

INVESTIGATIONS: No investigations can confirm the diagnosis but blood tests indicate a generalised inflammation of the body.

TREATMENT: Heat, pain-killers and anti-inflammatory medications. If these are not successful, steroids can be used.

COMPLICATIONS: Many patients will also suffer from temporal arteritis (see separate entry).

PROGNOSIS: May last for weeks or months, then recur after a long absence. Eventually recovery occurs in most patients.

Polymyositis
See Dermatomyositis

Polyposis Coli
(Familial Polyposis)

DESCRIPTION: Multiple polyps in the colon (large intestine).

CAUSE: Often familial (runs in families), but may arise for no apparent reason.

SYMPTOMS: Vague abdominal pain, irregular bowel habits, bleeding from the bowel and anaemia.

INVESTIGATIONS: Diagnosed by colonoscopy or barium enema X-ray.

TREATMENT: Removal of as many polyps as possible through a colonoscope. In severe cases, sections of, or the whole large intestine may need to be surgically removed.
COMPLICATIONS: Significant risk of bowel cancer.
PROGNOSIS: Guarded.
See also Blue Rubber Bleb Syndrome; Cowden Disease; Cronkhite-Canada Syndrome; Gardener Syndrome; Peutz-Jegher Syndrome; Turcot Syndrome

Pompe Syndrome
See Glycogen Storage Diseases

Pompholyx
(Dyshidrosis)
DESCRIPTION: A skin condition that affects the sides of the palms of the hands and soles of the feet, and is more common in young adults.
CAUSE: May be triggered by excess sweating, emotional stress, fungal infections of the skin, and touching irritating substances or plants.
SYMPTOMS: Small blisters that are deep in the skin and moderately itchy form at the edges of the palms and soles. With irritation, the blisters burst, the skin peels and leaves small brown scale-covered ulcers.
INVESTIGATIONS: None normally necessary.
TREATMENT: Avoiding all soaps, irritants, detergents and chemicals only treatment necessary for mild cases. Steroid or coal tar creams used for moderate attacks, while severe attacks may require steroid tablets.
COMPLICATIONS: None significant.
PROGNOSIS: Settles slowly and frequently recurs.

Porokeratosis
See Disseminated Superficial Actinic Porokeratosis

Porphyria
See Acute Hepatic Porphyria; Porphyria Cutanea Tarda

Porphyria Cutanea Tarda
(Latent Hepatic Porphyria)
DESCRIPTION: The most common form of porphyria, which are a group of liver diseases.
CAUSE: Usually inherited, but may be triggered by some poisons. Occurs in all races but is more common amongst the Bantu tribes of Africa.
SYMPTOMS: Skin that is very sensitive to sunlight, with skin thickening and pigmentation occurring in sun exposed areas such as the face and forearms. The urine turns a dark purple colour, then brown, if left standing. Occurs in varying degrees of severity from so mild that it is undetected to a rapidly fatal form.

INVESTIGATIONS: Diagnosed by special blood tests.

TREATMENT: Treatment involves careful genetic counselling of families and the use of a complex drug regime.

COMPLICATIONS: Liver damage, which may progress to liver failure or liver cancer (hepatoma).

PROGNOSIS: May be controlled, but not cured. Rarely fatal.

See also See also Acute Hepatic Porphyria

Portal Hypertension

DESCRIPTION: An increase in the blood pressure in the portal veins of the abdomen that take nutrition from the intestine to the liver.

CAUSE: Many different liver diseases (eg. cirrhosis), a blood clot (thrombosis) in the portal vein or spleen, and schistosomiasis (see separate entry) may be responsible.

SYMPTOMS: No symptoms other than piles until severe bleeding occurs from massively dilated veins around the lower oesophagus (gullet) and in the stomach.

INVESTIGATIONS: Angiography (X-rays of arteries) of portal veins in the abdomen diagnostic. Liver biopsy and blood tests may be abnormal if liver disease is responsible for the problem. Gastroscopy shows enlarged veins in oesophagus and stomach.

TREATMENT: Surgery to bypass any blockage in the veins or liver. The spleen may be removed if veins in this organ are thrombosed.

COMPLICATIONS: Torrential internal bleeding into the stomach may be fatal.

PROGNOSIS: Depends on cause, but often poor.

See also Cirrhosis

Portwine Naevus
(Mature Capillary Naevus)

DESCRIPTION: Often disfiguring skin condition due to overdilated blood vessels.

CAUSE: Congenital.

SYMPTOMS: Flat or slightly raised, pale pink to red or dark purple stain on the skin, usually on the face or upper chest, and on only one side of the body.

INVESTIGATIONS: None necessary.

TREATMENT: Plastic surgery sometimes possible, depending on site of naevus.

COMPLICATIONS: None significant.

PROGNOSIS: Persists life long.

See also Naevus

Positional Hypotension
See Postural Hypotension

Posner-Schlossman Syndrome
(Glaucomatocyclitic Crisis)

DESCRIPTION: Rare condition characterised by recurrent attacks of glaucoma in one eye associated with uveitis. Young adults affected.

CAUSE: Inflammation of the drainage system for the fluid in the eye.

SYMPTOMS: Halos around lights, blurred vision and sometimes pain.

INVESTIGATIONS: Diagnosed by measuring the pressure in the eye using a tonometer (device that rests on the anaesthetised eye, or a brief puff of air onto the eye).

TREATMENT: Steroid eye drops, glaucoma drops, and indomethacin tablets.

COMPLICATIONS: Repeated attacks may cause permanent eye damage.

PROGNOSIS: Good response to treatment for each attack, but future attacks cannot be prevented.

See also Glaucoma; Uveitis

Posterior Facet Syndrome

DESCRIPTION: Form of persistent lower back pain.

CAUSE: Long standing inflammation of the synovial membrane which lines the small joints between the back outer edges on the arch of the vertebrae (posterior facet joints), and degeneration (osteoarthritis) and instability of these joints in the lower back (lumbar vertebrae).

SYMPTOMS: Pain in lower back that runs down one or both legs. Greatest pain occurs with bending back sideways and backwards.

INVESTIGATIONS: X-rays or CT scans of the lower back may show joint degeneration.

TREATMENT: Physiotherapy, manipulation, injection of local anaesthetic and steroid into facet joints, and as a last resort surgical fusion of the adjacent joint surfaces.

COMPLICATIONS: Degenerative disc disease and spinal stenosis (narrowing of the spinal canal — see separate entry).

PROGNOSIS: Often persistent. Cure difficult but control reasonable.

Posterior Impingement Syndrome

DESCRIPTION: Impingement (abnormal coming together) of bone at back of foot under the ankle (talus) and the lower end of the tibia (shin bone).

CAUSE: Common in footballers, ballet dancers, gymnasts and others who forcibly bend their feet down.

SYMPTOMS: Pain and tenderness at back of ankle when walking.

INVESTIGATIONS: Ankle X-ray shows abnormal bone development at back of ankle.

TREATMENT: Rest, physiotherapy, anti-inflammatory medications and surgery to remove bony overgrowths.

COMPLICATIONS: Pain will steadily worsen until walking becomes impossible if not treated.

PROGNOSIS: Good if treatment program followed.

See also Impingement Syndromes

Postgastrectomy Syndrome
See Dumping Syndrome

Post-Herpetic Neuralgia
See Shingles

Post-Menopausal Vaginitis
See Atrophic Vaginitis

Post-Nasal Drip
(Cattarh; PND)

DESCRIPTION: The inside of the nose and sinuses is lined with a moist (mucus) membrane. If inflamed, the glands in the mucus membrane swell up and secrete extra amounts of mucus that overflows the sinus cavities, and runs down the back of the throat.

CAUSE: Infections with bacteria (eg. sinusitis) or a virus (eg. the common cold or flu), allergies (eg. hay fever, cigarette smoke), temperature changes (vasomotor rhinitis), hormone changes (more mucus may be produced at certain times in a woman's monthly cycle), anxiety and stress (eg. an exam or interview), eating, drinking alcohol and changes in position (eg. getting out of bed may start a sneezing fit).

SYMPTOMS: Episodes of sneezing, irritated throat, recurrent cough, bad breath, blocked nose and nausea (from swallowed mucus).

INVESTIGATIONS: Examination of the nose with a special instrument, and X-rays or CT scans of the sinuses may be useful.

TREATMENT: Bacterial infections cured by antibiotics. Antihistamines shrink down the swollen mucus membranes and reduce the production of mucus, mucolytics liquefy the phlegm, decongestants in tablets and nasal sprays clear the airways, and steroid or anti-allergy nasal sprays prevent the nose from reacting excessively. The minority who continue to have long term symptoms may be helped by surgery to reduce the amount of mucus membrane in the nose, and removing some curled up bones inside the nose (turbinates) that are covered with mucus membrane.

COMPLICATIONS: Secondary bacterial infections may cause sinusitis or pharyngitis. Flying or changing altitude can force phlegm up the eustachian tubes into the middle ears to cause pain and infection.

PROGNOSIS: Usually settles spontaneously, but sometimes persistent. Control reasonable.

See also Hay Fever; Pharyngitis; Sinusitis; Vasomotor Rhinitis

Postnatal Depression
(Postpartum Depression)

DESCRIPTION: Spontaneous form of depression that occurs in some women after childbirth.

436

CAUSE: A response to the effect on the brain of sudden changes in hormone levels.

SYMPTOMS: Constant unhappiness for which there is no reason. Patients are unable to sleep, lose appetite and weight, and feel there is no purpose in living. They may feel unnecessarily guilty, have a very poor opinion of themselves, feel life is hopeless, find it difficult to think or concentrate, worry excessively about their infant or neglect the child.

INVESTIGATIONS: Diagnosed after careful psychiatric assessment.

TREATMENT: Medications to control the production of depressing chemicals in the brain (eg. fluvoxamine, moclobemide, nefazadone, paroxetine, venlafaxine) while hospitalised or given intensive home support. Shock therapy (electroconvulsive therapy — ECT) may be used as a last resort.

COMPLICATIONS: Rarely may lead to attempted or actual suicide.

PROGNOSIS: Virtually all cases settle with support and medication in a few weeks.

See also Depression

Postpartum Depression
See Shingles

Postphlebitic Syndrome

DESCRIPTION: Complication of blood clot in veins deep in the muscles of the leg (deep vein thrombosis — see separate entry).

CAUSE: Due to destruction of valves in leg veins by blood clot, and subsequent increase in superficial vein pressure.

SYMPTOMS: Dermatitis due to pooling of blood under skin, leg ulcers near the ankle, swelling (oedema) of legs and formation of varicose veins.

INVESTIGATIONS: Ultrasound scans or special X-rays of leg veins (venography) shows damaged valves and blood clots.

TREATMENT: Bed rest, elevation of legs, support stockings, specific medications for dermatitis and ulcers, and surgical removal of varicose veins.

COMPLICATIONS: Ulcers may spread, become infected, and rarely gangrene of leg possible.

PROGNOSIS: Persistent and difficult to treat.

See also Deep Vein Thrombosis

Post-Polio Syndrome

DESCRIPTION: Occurs in some survivors of polio, 30 to 40 years after recovery from the infection.

CAUSE: May be due to the overuse of muscles previously damaged by polio.

SYMPTOMS: Unaccustomed tiredness, joint and muscle pain and muscle weakness.

INVESTIGATIONS: None diagnostic.

TREATMENT: Anti-inflammatory medications and steroids may help.

COMPLICATIONS: Because of muscle weakness, more stress is put on joints, and arthritis of major joints and in the back may also occur. In a small number of severely affected patients, difficulty in breathing may lead to sleep apnoea and the necessity for breathing aids.

PROGNOSIS: No cure, and condition persists.

See also Polio

Post-Traumatic Cerebral Syndrome

DESCRIPTION: Side effect of head injury.

CAUSE: Occurs after head injury, sometimes of a minor nature. Aggravated by changes in temperature or posture, alcohol or exercise.

SYMPTOMS: Dizziness, headache, persistent tiredness, poor memory, poor concentration, and sometimes a personality change.

INVESTIGATIONS: No diagnostic tests. Brain CT scan usually normal.

TREATMENT: No specific treatment, but individual symptoms may be controlled.

PROGNOSIS: Slow recovery normal.

See also Concussion

Post-Traumatic Stress Disorder
(PTSD; Shell Shock)

DESCRIPTION: Occurs after experiencing a situation that causes extreme stress and a feeling of helplessness (eg. armed holdup, serious accident, war violence, being assaulted or raped, observing atrocities etc.). Most symptoms start between two weeks and three months of the triggering catastrophe, but may start as late as six months.

CAUSE: Experience of a threatening or traumatic event, or a period of provoked fear, helplessness or horror.

SYMPTOMS: Patients must have at least one symptom from each of the following categories:–

General

Symptom duration more than one month, with significant distress or inability to function normally in society.

Re-experiencing phenomena

Experience intrusive recollections, nightmares, flashbacks as if the event was recurring, psychological distress on exposure to cues that may trigger memories, or physiological effects (eg. rapid pulse, rapid breathing) on exposure to cues.

Avoidance behaviour

Avoiding thoughts, feelings or conversations about the incident; avoiding places, people or activities connected with the incident; selective amnesia about the traumatic event; reduced interest in everyday activities or detachment from others; unable to look forward to future events with pleasure; or abnormal personality compared to before the incident.

Excessively aroused

Insomnia, irritability, anger, poor concentration, increased vigilance or increased startle response to frights.

INVESTIGATIONS: No specific diagnostic tests.

TREATMENT: Psychological counselling and debriefing immediately after the event, and a trained counsellor should follow up the victim for at least six months. Normal work and activities should be resumed as soon as possible. Referral to a psychiatrist is necessary if the patient does not appear to recover within six months, or deteriorates sooner, when medication may be necessary.

COMPLICATIONS: May lead to recurrent minor illnesses, poor physical health, and in extreme cases, suicide.

PROGNOSIS: Usually settles within 3 to 6 months, but may become chronic.

See also Neurosis; Stress

Postural Hypotension
(Positional Hypotension)

DESCRIPTION: Low blood pressure and lack of blood to the brain caused by a change in position.

CAUSE: A brief drop in blood pressure caused by the altered relative positions of the brain and the heart when the patient moves from lying to sitting or standing. The heart must pump harder, and the arteries must contract more to maintain blood flow by means of the blood pressure to a brain that is 30 cm above the heart, rather than one that is at the same level as the heart. It takes a few seconds for this adjustment to be made, particularly in patients who have hardening of the arteries (arteriosclerosis). Sometimes, medications to lower blood pressure and remove fluid may aggravate the condition.

SYMPTOMS: Light-headedness and dizziness, and sometimes blackouts or faints, when rising quickly from lying or sitting to a standing position.

INVESTIGATIONS: Diagnosed by measuring the blood pressure when the patient is lying, and again immediately after standing.

TREATMENT: Advise elderly patients to be slow in changing position. Review medications that may be responsible.

COMPLICATIONS: Fainting and falling may cause serious injuries.

PROGNOSIS: Depends on cause, but may be difficult to control.

See also Arteriosclerosis; Hypotension

Post-Viral Syndrome
See Chronic Fatigue Syndrome

'Pot'
See Marijuana Abuse

Potassium Wastage Syndrome

DESCRIPTION: Serious abnormality of blood chemistry.

CAUSE: May be due to Fanconi syndrome, Conn syndrome, Cushing syndrome, chronic kidney (renal) failure (see separate entries), and rarely side effects of medication. Sometimes no specific cause can be found.

SYMPTOMS: Passing large amount of very dilute urine and muscle weakness.

INVESTIGATIONS: Urine levels of potassium very high, and blood levels very low. Blood is abnormally alkaline.

TREATMENT: Treat underlying cause and give potassium supplements.

COMPLICATIONS: Heart rhythm abnormalities and heart attack may occur.

PROGNOSIS: May be fatal if left untreated. Good prognosis if cause can be adequately treated.

Potter Syndrome

DESCRIPTION: Developmental failure of kidneys.

CAUSE: Congenital. Risk of recurrence in subsequent pregnancy 1 in 40.

SYMPTOMS: No urine passed as kidneys are absent, lungs underdeveloped, small jaw, low set ears, loose upper lip, exaggerated eye folds, wide set eyes, and limbs are contracted.

INVESTIGATIONS: Ultrasound, CT scans and X-rays of abdomen reveal abnormalities.

TREATMENT: None available.

PROGNOSIS: Death within days of birth.

See also Prune Belly Syndrome

Pott's Fracture

DESCRIPTION: Fracture above the ankle, when the bottom ends of the two bones in the lower leg (the tibia and fibula) are broken off.

CAUSE: A twisting force to the lower leg often after catching the foot in a hole while running.

SYMPTOMS: Pain, swelling, tenderness and loss of function of the lower leg and ankle.

INVESTIGATIONS: Diagnosed by an X-ray.

TREATMENT: Manipulation of bone ends under anaesthetic to achieve good alignment, then the ankle is encased in plaster. Sometimes open operation and fixation of the bones by plates and screws is required.

COMPLICATIONS: Failure to heal, poorly aligned bone ends and infection after open operation.

PROGNOSIS: Require up to three months to heal adequately.

See also Fracture

Prader-Willi Syndrome

DESCRIPTION: Rare congenital brain condition (present since birth) that affects only boys.

CAUSE: Chromosomal defect.

SYMPTOMS: Small infant who develops into an obese child due to compulsive overeating from an abnormality in the part of the brain that controls hunger. Child is usually short, has underdeveloped genitals, is mentally retarded, muscles are weak and have very poor tone, and the belly is very flabby.

INVESTIGATIONS: Chromosome analysis abnormal.
TREATMENT: No effective treatment.
COMPLICATIONS: Tendency to develop diabetes later in life.
PROGNOSIS: Poor long term.

Pre-Eclampsia

DESCRIPTION: A potentially serious disease that occurs only in pregnancy. In developed countries it is detected early because most women undertake regular antenatal visits which find it in about 10% of all pregnant women.
CAUSE: Exact cause unknown, but it may be due to the production of an abnormal amount of hormones by the placenta. More common in first pregnancies, twins and diabetes, and normally develops in the last three months of pregnancy, but may not develop until labour commences, when it may progress rapidly to eclampsia if not detected.
SYMPTOMS: Not until the condition is well established does the patient develop a headache, nausea, vomiting, abdominal pain and disturbances of vision.
INVESTIGATIONS: The early detection of pre-eclampsia is essential for the good health of both mother and baby. Diagnosed by noting high blood pressure, swollen ankles, abnormalities (excess protein) in the urine and excessive weight gain (fluid retention).
TREATMENT: Strict bed rest, drugs to lower blood pressure and remove excess fluid, sedatives, and in severe cases, early delivery of the baby.
COMPLICATIONS: If no treatment is given, the mother may develop eclampsia which causes convulsions, coma, strokes, heart attacks, death of the baby and possibly death of the mother. The correct treatment of pre-eclampsia prevents eclampsia.
PROGNOSIS: Very good if detected early and treated correctly.
See also Eclampsia

Pregnancy

Pregnancy is not a disease, but a variation of the normal human condition.
Only the complications of pregnancy are dealt with in this book.
See Asherman Syndrome; Chiari-Frommel Syndrome; Choriocarcinoma of the Uterus; Eclampsia; Ectopic Pregnancy; Miscarriage; Morning Sickness; Oligohydramnios; Painless Thyroiditis Syndrome; Polyhydramnios; Postnatal Depression; Pre-Eclampsia; Scheehan Syndrome; Stretch Marks; Uterine Mole

Pregnancy, Ectopic
See Ectopic Pregnancy

Premature Ejaculation

DESCRIPTION: Early ejaculation of semen when not desired. Ejaculation cannot be brought about by conscious effort, but is a subconscious reflex.
CAUSE: Often no apparent cause, but may be due to sexual anxiety or performance stress.

Premature Ejaculation

SYMPTOMS: Ejaculation of semen at a very early stage before or during sexual intercourse.

INVESTIGATIONS: None normally necessary.

TREATMENT: Requires the cooperation of the sex partner to use either the 'stop-start' or 'squeeze' techniques. The 'stop-start' technique involves repeatedly stopping all sexual activity at a point just short of ejaculation when the man indicates by a signal or word that ejaculation is imminent, until the couple are ready to orgasm. In the 'squeeze' technique, the man again indicates when ejaculation is imminent, but instead of stopping all activity, the woman grasps the man's penis firmly just behind the head (glans) of the penis, and squeezes firmly until the man loses part of his erection, at which point she lets go and continues sexual activity. With practice, the man can learn to control his ejaculation until these techniques are no longer required.

PROGNOSIS: Reasonable results with a well motivated couple.

See also other diseases listed under Sex Problems

Premenstrual Tension Syndrome
(PMT)

DESCRIPTION: May vary from a slight discomfort for a couple of hours before the onset of a woman's menstrual period to a severely distressing condition.

CAUSE: During the two weeks leading up to a menstrual period, the body retains fluid. If the balance between the sex hormones oestrogen and progestogen is not quite right, an excessive amount of fluid may be retained in the pelvis, brain, breasts, hands and feet.

SYMPTOMS: Gradually increasing discomfort in the pelvis and breasts, with swelling of the hands and feet, pounding headaches and depression. The worst sufferers will experience abdominal pain, swollen tender breasts, anxiety, irritability and clumsiness, and may be unable to concentrate, work or exercise effectively.

INVESTIGATIONS: None normally necessary.

TREATMENT: The oral contraceptive pill or similar hormones regulate the hormonal balance and prevent excess fluid retention. Diuretics (tablets that remove fluid from the body) may be used alone or in combination with the contraceptive pill. Other medications that may be beneficial include vitamin B_6, mefenamic acid, naproxen, indomethacin and evening primrose oil. Other approaches include a sensible balanced diet, and avoiding coffee, chocolate and rich foods in the two weeks before the period.

COMPLICATIONS: Depression, very rarely severe enough to lead to suicide, and a psychosis that has been used in court as a defence for murder.

PROGNOSIS: Disappears within a few hours when the period starts. The majority of women can be helped adequately by good treatment.

See also Pelvic Congestion Syndrome

Pre-Patellar Bursitis
See Housemaid's Knee

Presbyopia
DESCRIPTION: A deterioration of close vision which starts in middle age.
CAUSE: Stiffening of the lens with age which prevents it focussing light rays from close objects accurately on the retina (light sensitive layer of cells at the back of the eye).
SYMPTOMS: Steadily worsening difficulty in reading small print or seeing close objects in detail.
INVESTIGATIONS: Specific tests on vision.
TREATMENT: Correct spectacles to assist with focusing.
PROGNOSIS: Very good.
See also Long-Sighted

Pressure Ulcer
See Bed Sore

Pretectal Syndrome
See Parinaud Syndrome

Priapism
DESCRIPTION: Abnormally prolonged penis erection.
CAUSE: Spinal cord injury, bladder stones, blood diseases (eg. leukaemia in children), stroke, uncontrolled diabetes, some forms of widespread cancer, injury to the penis, excess dose of alprostadil (Caverject, Muse), illegal drugs (eg. cocaine, marijuana) and prescription drugs (eg. prazosin, heparin). Rarely a result of excessive sexual stimulation.
SYMPTOMS: Penis remains persistently, inappropriately and painfully erect for a long period of time.
INVESTIGATIONS: Any underlying cause needs to be excluded by appropriate tests.
TREATMENT: Warm packs, pseudoephedrine (Sudafed) tablets, and syringes to draw excess blood from the penis.
COMPLICATIONS: Permanent damage to the penis may occur due to the constant pressure on the tissue.
PROGNOSIS: Settles well with treatment.
See also other diseases listed under Sexual Problems

Primary Lateral Sclerosis
DESCRIPTION: Very rare form of motor neurone disease (see separate entry) that affects the nerves that supply the muscles of the limbs.
CAUSE: Unknown, but results in a progressive degeneration of the motor cortex (muscle controlling part) of the brain.
SYMPTOMS: Muscles in the limbs and throat go into spasms and become

progressively weaker. Movement, speech and swallowing become difficult.

INVESTIGATIONS: Biopsy of the affected part of the brain is the only diagnostic test.

TREATMENT: No cure available, and treatment is aimed at relieving muscle spasm, assisting feeding, preventing infections, aiding breathing and making the patient as comfortable as possible. Physiotherapy on a very regular basis is essential.

COMPLICATIONS: Lung infections such as pneumonia develop, and often lead to death.

PROGNOSIS: Slowly progressive, but may not cause death for many years.

See also Motor Neurone Disease; Spinal Muscular Atrophy

Proctalgia Fugax

DESCRIPTION: Pain in and around the anus.

CAUSE: Spasm of the muscle that controls the opening and closing of the anus (the sphincter). Normally this is in constant contraction to prevent the passage of faeces and gas, but if it contracts excessively into a cramp, pain is felt.

SYMPTOMS: Severe, brief, very sharp pain that is felt in the anus for a few seconds or minutes several times a day. Patients describe the sensation as having a thin knife pushed into the anal canal and twisted.

INVESTIGATIONS: None diagnostic.

TREATMENT: Difficult, and involves using ice packs, ice suppositories (large tablets inserted into the anus) and anal injections. Strangely, inhaling salbutamol (Ventolin — normally used for asthma) will sometimes ease the pain.

COMPLICATIONS: None serious.

PROGNOSIS: May persist for months or years, but eventually settles.

See also Proctitis; Pruritus Ani

Proctitis
(Anal Inflammation)

DESCRIPTION: Inflammation or infection of the anal canal.

CAUSE: Bacterial, viral (eg. Herpes) or fungal infection, or injury to the anus (eg. homosexual penetration).

SYMPTOMS: Pain and irritation in the anus that is worse with passing faeces, constant feeling that there is a motion to be passed when there is none, and sometimes a discharge.

INVESTIGATIONS: Swab taken from the anus to identify responsible infecting organism.

TREATMENT: Appropriate antibiotic or antifungal creams and antibiotic or antiviral tablets by mouth. Soothing steroid creams and suppositories (anal tablets) may also be used.

COMPLICATIONS: Persistent infection may cause scar tissue formation and a narrowing of the anal canal.

PROGNOSIS: Depends on cause, but usually good with treatment.

See also Anal Fissure; Proctalgia Fugax

Progressive Pigmented Purpura
See Capillaritis

Progressive Supranuclear Palsy
See Steele-Richardson-Olszewski Syndrome

Progressive Systemic Sclerosis
See Scleroderma

Prolapse
See Rectal Prolapse; Vaginal Prolapse

Pronator Syndrome
DESCRIPTION: Nerve injury resulting in arm pain, function and sensation abnormalities.

CAUSE: Due to entrapment of median nerve between muscles or ligaments and bone in forearm near elbow.

SYMPTOMS: Pain and tenderness in forearm; pins and needles sensation in thumb, 2nd and 3rd fingers and half 4th finger; and weakness of muscles that bend the thumb down onto the palm.

INVESTIGATIONS: Electromyography (EMG) measures muscle and nerve activity.

TREATMENT: Surgical release of median nerve entrapment.

PROGNOSIS: Good results from surgery.

Prostate Cancer
(Prostatic Cancer)

DESCRIPTION: Any one of several different types of cancer of the prostate gland, depending on which cells in the gland become cancerous.

CAUSE: Unknown, but those who have sex infrequently may be more susceptible. Rare before 50 years of age, but up to 20% of all men over 60 may have an enlargement of the prostate. The percentage of these men whose enlargement is due to cancer steadily increases with age, with virtually every male over 90 years of age having some degree of prostate cancer.

SYMPTOMS: A very slow-growing cancer that may give no symptoms until many years after it has developed. Symptoms usually start with difficulty in passing urine and difficulty in starting the urinary stream.

INVESTIGATIONS: Specific blood tests can detect most cases, but it is often diagnosed by feeling the gland using a gloved finger in the back passage. Ultrasound scans and biopsy of the gland may also be performed.

TREATMENT: Treated with a combination of surgery, drugs and irradiation. Early stages may not be treated in the very elderly, because it is unlikely to cause trouble in their life time. Brachytherapy is a process in which tiny radioactive particles are injected into the prostate to create radiation which destroys the cancer. Orchidectomy (removal of the testes) is sometimes performed to

445

remove all testosterone from the man's body, as this stimulates growth of the cancer.

COMPLICATIONS: Spread of cancer to the bones of the pelvis and back.

PROGNOSIS: If cancer is localised to the gland itself, the five-year survival rate is over 90%. With local spread, the survival rate drops to about 70%, but with spread to the bone, only 30% of patients survive five years.

Prostate Enlargement
See Prostatomegaly

Prostate Infection
See Prostatitis

Prostatic Cancer
See Prostate Cancer

Prostatitis
(Prostate Infection)

DESCRIPTION: Infection of the prostate gland which sits behind the base of the penis.

CAUSE: Infection by bacteria that may enter the prostate by moving up the urethra (urine tube) from the outside, from a sexually transmitted infection (eg. gonorrhoea), or uncommonly from an infection spreading from other parts of the body.

SYMPTOMS: Pain behind the base of the penis, a discharge from the penis, pain on passing urine, fever and passing urine frequently.

INVESTIGATIONS: Diagnosis confirmed by taking a swab from the urethra, and identifying the bacteria present.

TREATMENT: Long course of antibiotics.

COMPLICATIONS: Infection may spread to the man's sexual partner, in whom it can cause pelvic inflammatory disease (see separate entry).

PROGNOSIS: Acute case usually settles with treatment, but recurrences are common and a low-grade persistent infection may develop, which is difficult to treat.

Prostatomegaly
(Prostate Enlargement)

DESCRIPTION: Up to 20% of all men over 60 have benign enlargement of the prostate gland, which is usually associated with a drop in sexual activity.

CAUSE: Absolute cause unknown, but as the gland enlarges, it squeezes the urethra (urine-carrying tube) which passes through it, making it steadily harder to urinate.

SYMPTOMS: Difficulty in passing urine, and eventually the urethra becomes completely blocked, causing extreme distress as the pressure of urine in the bladder increases.

INVESTIGATIONS: Diagnosed by feeling the prostate gland through the anus, ultrasound scans and blood tests.

TREATMENT: In the acute situation, a flexible tube is passed up the urethra through the penis into the bladder to release urine, but if this is unsuccessful a large needle must be pushed through the lower wall of the abdomen into the bladder. In some cases drugs (eg. finasteride, prazosin, terazosin) can be used to shrink the enlarged prostate slightly. Most cases require surgery once symptoms develop. The operation can vary from simply dilating the urethra, to scraping away the part of the prostate constricting the urethra by passing a specially shaped knife up it (transurethral resection of prostate — TURP), or completely removing the gland.

COMPLICATIONS: If back pressure of urine in the bladder becomes persistent, kidney damage can occur.

PROGNOSIS: Treatment almost invariably successful, with no subsequent effect on the sexual or general health of the patient.

See also Prostate Cancer

Proteus Syndrome
(Elephant Man Deformity)

DESCRIPTION: Rare bone and tissue growth abnormality.

CAUSE: Congenital. Excessive and unequal bone growth in face, arms, legs and hands.

SYMPTOMS: Severe facial and body disfigurement, bony growths on skull causing a great increase in skull circumference, wrinkled bumps on feet, face and hands.

INVESTIGATIONS: X-rays show abnormal bone growth.

TREATMENT: Plastic surgery helps some deformities.

PROGNOSIS: Near normal life expectancy, but deformities persist.

Prune Belly Syndrome

DESCRIPTION: Rare developmental abnormality.

CAUSE: Congenital. Occurs in 20% of infants with Potter syndrome. Risk of recurrence in subsequent pregnancies less than 1 in 100.

SYMPTOMS: Potter syndrome, very distended and wrinkled abdomen from poor muscle development, hugely dilated ureters (tubes from kidneys to bladder) and bladder, and undescended testes.

INVESTIGATIONS: Ultrasound, CT scans and X-rays of abdomen reveal abnormalities.

TREATMENT: None available.

PROGNOSIS: Inevitably fatal within days of birth.

See also Potter Syndrome

Prurigo
(Lichen Urticatus)

DESCRIPTION: Very itchy skin reaction that is more common in middle aged women and poorly cared for children. Usually occurs on the back of the arms, front of the legs, buttocks, face and neck.

CAUSE: Allergic reaction, possibly to food, insect bites or medications.

SYMPTOMS: Multiple, pink, dome shaped, intensely itchy lumps (papules) topped with a tiny blister (vescicle). The vescicle is soon scratched off and replaced by a brown crust.

INVESTIGATIONS: None diagnostic.

TREATMENT: Antihistamine tablets and creams containing a steroid.

PROGNOSIS: Attacks eventually settle spontaneously, sometimes taking only a few days, or may persist for months.

See also Allergy

Pruritus Ani
(Anal Itch)

DESCRIPTION: Itchy skin around the anus.

CAUSE: Possibly due to fungal infections, diabetes, worm infestations, antibiotics, cancer and a number of skin diseases, but usually no obvious cause.

SYMPTOMS: Excruciatingly itchy anus, and except for the scratch marks left by the patient's finger nails, there is often no rash. Usually worse at night, and some patients find it is aggravated by red wine and spicy food.

INVESTIGATIONS: Underlying causes excluded by examination of the faeces, skin scrapings for fungi, and blood tests for diabetes.

TREATMENT: Scratching must be stopped, as this will prolong and exacerbate the problem. Anal area kept cool and dry by avoiding nylon underwear, tight clothing and sweating. The anus should be rinsed with warm water for washing, but no soap should be used, and should be patted dry, not rubbed. A mild steroid cream and sitz baths in potassium permanganate or silver nitrate may be beneficial.

COMPLICATIONS: Skin around the anus damaged by scratching may become infected by a fungus or bacteria.

PROGNOSIS: Not serious, but often recurrent, long-lasting and very annoying.

See also Proctalgia Fugax

Pseudocushing Syndrome

DESCRIPTION: Excessive levels of steroids in the blood.

CAUSE: Secondary to alcoholism and liver damage which prevents steroids that are normally produced in the body from being destroyed, allowing their blood levels to increase. Unlike Cushing syndrome, there is no excess steroid production.

SYMPTOMS: Combination of symptoms due to Cushing syndrome and alcoholism (see separate entries).

INVESTIGATIONS: Blood tests confirm the diagnosis.

TREATMENT: Once alcoholism has been controlled, symptoms may settle, provided organ damage not severe.

COMPLICATIONS: Liver damage may be so severe that the organ is unable to recover, and a liver transplant is required.

PROGNOSIS: Reasonable if alcohol ceased, fatal if alcohol consumption continued.

See also Alcoholism; Cushing Syndrome

Pseudoexfoliation Syndrome

DESCRIPTION: Degenerative disease of the eye(s).

CAUSE: Unknown, but more common in females and elderly.

SYMPTOMS: White granular deposits on edge of iris (coloured part of the eye) and lens, glaucoma (increased pressure in the eye), defects in the iris that allow light to pass through into the eye, poor dilatation of pupil, and pigmentation of the cornea (white part of eye).

INVESTIGATIONS: Examination of eye with a magnifying light and measuring the pressure in the eye.

TREATMENT: Specific eye drops to treat glaucoma, argon laser to remove deposits, and surgery to the eye.

COMPLICATIONS: One third of patients have the disease in both eyes. Loss of vision more rapid than in glaucoma alone.

PROGNOSIS: Reasonable, but usually there is a slow deterioration in vision.

See also Glaucoma

Pseudofolliculitis Barbae
See Razor Rash

Pseudogout
(Calcium Pyrophosphate Deposition Disease)

DESCRIPTION: Sudden, repeated attacks of severe arthritis in a major joint.

CAUSE: The deposition of calcium pyrophosphate crystals in joints due to a metabolic disorder.

SYMPTOMS: Pseudogout has exactly the same symptoms as gout with acute pain in, and redness over a joint, but affects the knees and other large joints. Patients are usually elderly, and complain of recurrent, severe attacks of pain.

INVESTIGATIONS: Diagnosed by identifying the responsible crystals in the fluid that may be drawn out of the affected joint through a needle. X-rays show arthritis and calcification around the joint.

TREATMENT: Involves use of anti-inflammatory drugs (eg. indomethacin, naproxen), and injections of steroids into the joint. Unlike gout, there are no medications that can be used in the long term to prevent further attacks.

COMPLICATIONS: Permanent arthritis in repeatedly affected joints.

PROGNOSIS: Control of each attack is usually good, but repeated attacks may occur.

See also Chondrocalcinosis; Gout

Pseudomembranous Colitis

DESCRIPTION: Form of severe inflammation of the large intestine associated with a fine membrane over the gut wall.

CAUSE: Overgrowth in the bowel of the bacteria *Clostridium difficile* as an adverse reaction to antibiotics (eg. clindamycin, ampicillin, cephalosporins).

SYMPTOMS: Severe intractable watery diarrhoea, cramping belly pain and fever. Sometimes the motions become bloody.

INVESTIGATIONS: Colonoscopy reveals the inflamed gut and false membrane.

TREATMENT: The antibiotic vancomycin and a drip into a vein to replace fluid loss.

COMPLICATIONS: Dehydration, body chemistry abnormalities, perforation of the inflamed bowel, and rarely death.

PROGNOSIS: Most patients recover with appropriate treatment.

Pseudomonas Infection

DESCRIPTION: A serious bacterial infection, usually of the lungs, that causes bronchitis or pneumonia.

CAUSE: The bacterium *Pseudomonas aeruginosa*.

SYMPTOMS: Persistent cough that produces yellow to green phlegm, chest pain, fever and tiredness.

INVESTIGATIONS: Sputum samples cultured to identify bacteria and appropriate antibiotic.

TREATMENT: Antibiotics (eg. gentamicin).

COMPLICATIONS: If left untreated, may cause permanent lung damage and chronic poor health.

PROGNOSIS: Slow but successful response to treatment.

See also Bronchitis, Acute; Pneumonia

Psittacosis
(Bird Fancier's Lung; Ornithosis)

DESCRIPTION: A rare form of pneumonia caught from birds.

CAUSE: The bacteria-like organism *Chlamydia*, which is normally an infection of parrots, pigeons, chickens and ducks, may very occasionally be transmitted to humans, but rarely passes from one person to another.

SYMPTOMS: Gradual onset of fever, headache, muscle pains, tiredness, dry cough and nose bleeds. Some patients develop skin spots, shortness of breath, and abdominal pains. Incubation period one to two weeks after exposure to an infected bird. The diagnosis may be suspected in bird fanciers, chicken farmers and veterinarians.

INVESTIGATIONS: Diagnosis confirmed by sputum culture or a specific blood test. A chest X-ray can show the presence of pneumonia, but not that the pneumonia is caused by psittacosis.

TREATMENT: Appropriate antibiotics, sometimes by injection.

COMPLICATIONS: Spread of the infection to the heart or brain, and sometimes a second bacterium may cause double pneumonia.

450

PROGNOSIS: Although the infection is sometimes prolonged, the vast majority of patients can be completely cured.

See also Pneumonia and other diseases listed under Chlamydial Infections

Psoriasis

DESCRIPTION: An annoying, distressing, persistent and difficult to treat skin disease that affects 2% of the population.

CAUSE: An autoimmune disease in which the body's immune system is inappropriately triggered to reject tissue as though it was a foreign material. In psoriasis, varying parts of the skin are rejected. It is unusual in children but becomes more common as age increases.

SYMPTOMS: Appears as a small patch of red skin covered with fine scales that gradually enlarges, roughens and thickens the skin. Other spots may start over a period of months. The elbows, knees and scalp are the most common sites. On the scalp, it may appear to be a bad case of dandruff. The nails may also be affected, and become rough and pitted. The **Koebner phenomenon** occurs when psoriasis develops on areas of skin that have been injured, and may appear as a line of inflamed skin along a healed cut or surgical incision, or a patch at the site of a previous graze.

INVESTIGATIONS: Psoriasis has many subtypes, and it is often necessary to perform a biopsy to confirm the diagnosis.

TREATMENT: Involves one or more of a number of creams or ointments that are used regularly on the skin. Coal tar is the mainstay of treatment, but calcipotriol and steroid creams are also very effective. Other skin preparations include dithranol, salicylic acid and psoralen. Ultraviolet light may be used in conjunction with psoralen to promote healing. In very severe cases, steroid tablets or injections, or acitretin tablets, may be given.

COMPLICATIONS: In severe cases the joints may be attacked to cause a type of arthritis.

PROGNOSIS: May come and go without any treatment. There is no cure for psoriasis, but it can usually be successfully controlled.

See also Dermatitis; Guttae Psoriasis

Psoriatic Arthritis

DESCRIPTION: A form of inflammatory joint disease.

CAUSE: Complication of the skin disease psoriasis when the lining of a joint is affected in the same way as the skin. Arthritis usually worse when the skin disease flares.

SYMPTOMS: Painful, red, swollen joint.

INVESTIGATIONS: Fluid removed by a needle from the joint is examined to confirm the diagnosis.

TREATMENT: Treated in the same way as osteoarthritis (eg. paracetamol, aspirin, heat, anti-inflammatory drugs, physiotherapy) with the addition of medication to control the psoriasis (eg. acitretin).

COMPLICATIONS: Permanent joint damage and osteoarthritis.

PROGNOSIS: Easier to control than osteoarthritis. Most patients have reasonable symptom relief, but no cure.
See also Osteoarthritis; Psoriasis

Psychiatric Disturbances

See Anorexia Nervosa; Apotemnophilia; Bipolar Affective Disorder; Briquet Syndrome; Bulimia Nervosa; Catatonic Syndrome; Charles Bonnet Syndrome; Clérambault Syndrome; Conversion Disorder; da Costa Syndrome; Depression; Diogenes Syndrome; Episodic Dyscontrol Syndrome; Hypochondriasis; Hysteria; Mania; Multiple Personality Disorder; Munchausen Syndrome; Neurosis; Obsessive Compulsive Neurosis; Paedophilia; Paranoid Disorder; Phobia; Polle Syndrome; Postnatal Depression; Post Traumatic Stress Disorder; Psychosis; Schizophrenia; Seasonal Affective Disorder; SHAFT Syndrome; Stress etc.

Psychosis
(Psychotic)

DESCRIPTION: A mental disorder in which the patient has no understanding that they are mentally ill. A classification that covers a large group of more serious mental diseases such as schizophrenia, paranoid disorders and manic depressive states (see separate entries).
CAUSE: Generally unknown, but varies from one form to another.
SYMPTOMS: Various forms of loss of contact with reality.
INVESTIGATIONS: None diagnostic.
TREATMENT: Medications and psychotherapy.
PROGNOSIS: Usually no cure, but long term control reasonable.
See also Diogenes Syndrome; Paranoid Disorders; Schizophrenia; other diseases listed under Psychiatric Conditions

Psychotic
See Psychosis

Pterygium

DESCRIPTION: Damage to the eye surface resulting in overgrowth of tissue.
CAUSE: Glare and sun exposure cause recurrent mild sunburn to the cornea. The irritated tissue overgrows to form a pingueculum, then spreads across the eye. More common in tropical climates.
SYMPTOMS: A pale yellow fleshy overgrowth of the white part of the eye (cornea) that spreads across the coloured part of the eye (iris). May become irritated, red and itchy at times.
INVESTIGATIONS: None necessary.
TREATMENT: Once present it will remain until removed by a simple surgical procedure. Prevented by wearing good quality (polarised) sun glasses.
COMPLICATIONS: Growth spreads across the pupil and causes blindness.
PROGNOSIS: Very good results from surgery.
See also Pingueculum

PTSD
See Post Traumatic Stress Disorder

Pubic Pediculosis
See Crabs

Pulmonary Abscess
See Lung Abscess

Pulmonary Embolism
(Lung Clot; Pulmonary Thromboembolism)

DESCRIPTION: Occurs when a blood clot or other substance (embolus — eg. fatty plaque from high cholesterol) travels through the blood to a small artery in the lung (pulmonary artery) which it then blocks.

CAUSE: Blood clots may occur in the veins of leg muscles (see Deep Venous Thrombosis), but may also arise in other parts of the body. They travel through veins to the right side of the heart, and then into the lungs where they cut off the blood supply to a segment of lung which will collapse and die. More common after major surgery, in patients who are bedridden for long periods, and in the elderly.

SYMPTOMS: Chest pain, shortness of breath, coughing of blood, fainting, heart rate increases, and a fever.

INVESTIGATIONS: Diagnosed by chest X-ray or CT scans. Blood tests can show signs of clotting within the body, and an electrocardiogram (ECG) shows strain on the heart. Specialised tests of lung function are sometimes necessary. An X-ray in which dye is injected into the veins and can be seen moving through the arteries in the lung may be performed in cases of doubt.

TREATMENT: Must start as soon as possible to prevent extension of the clot and further damage to the lung. Anticoagulants drugs that prevent blood clotting (eg. heparin) are initially given as an injection, and later as tablets (eg. warfarin, aspirin). Regular blood tests are performed throughout treatment with anticoagulants to check the dosage required. Anticoagulant therapy is continued for some months after the attack, but in high risk patients it may be continued for life. In severe cases thrombolytics (clot dissolving drugs) are injected directly into the involved veins. In rare circumstances, surgery to remove the clot from the lungs or leg is undertaken, or a filter is inserted surgically into the main vein of the body leading from the legs to the heart, to filter out any blood clots that may form in the future. Blood clots in the legs can be prevented by using pressure stockings during long operations, early mobilisation after surgery, physiotherapy to keep leg muscles active, and elevation of the legs in bed-bound patients.

COMPLICATIONS: Increased back pressure of blood on the heart may lead to right heart failure (cor pulmonale — see separate entry). An extending clot can cut off more pulmonary arteries, and destroy a larger area of lung.

PROGNOSIS: Rapid death occurs in 10% of patients who have a large area of lung involved, but the majority of patients recover provided appropriate treatment is given quickly.
See also Deep Venous Thrombosis; Thrombosis

Pulmonary Fibrosis, Idiopathic
See Idiopathic Pulmonary Fibrosis

Pulmonary Hypertension
See Cor Pulmonale

Pulmonary Thromboembolism
See Pulmonary Embolism

Pulmonary Tuberculosis
See Tuberculosis

Pulmonary Valve Incompetence
(Pulmonic Regurgitation)

DESCRIPTION: Leakage of the pulmonary heart valve which controls the flow of blood from the right ventricle (right lower chamber) of the heart to the pulmonary artery, which goes to the lungs.
CAUSE: Uncommon form of heart valve disease that is often a result of endocarditis or cor pulmonale (see separate entry).
SYMPTOMS: No significant symptoms present, and usually found by accident when listening to the heart for other reasons.
INVESTIGATIONS: Diagnosed by hearing a characteristic heart murmur or echocardiography (ultrasound scan).
TREATMENT: None normally necessary, but cause must be treated.
PROGNOSIS: Good.
See also other diseases listed under Heart Valve Disease

Pulmonary Valve Stenosis

DESCRIPTION: Narrowing of the pulmonary heart valve which controls the flow of blood from the right ventricle (right lower chamber) of the heart to the pulmonary artery, which goes to the lungs.
CAUSE: Usually a birth defect.
SYMPTOMS: Mild stenosis causes no symptoms. Severe stenosis causes chest pain, fainting on exertion, and shortness of breath.
INVESTIGATIONS: Diagnosed by echocardiography (ultrasound scan).
TREATMENT: If the stenosis is causing symptoms it must be corrected surgically.
PROGNOSIS: Good results from surgery. If left untreated, sudden death or heart failure may occur.
See also other diseases listed under Heart Valve Disease

Pulmonic Regurgitation
See Pulmonary Valve Incompetence

Pulse, Rapid
See Tachycardia

Punch Drunk Syndrome
DESCRIPTION: Form of brain injury.

CAUSE: Recurrent blows to the head over a period of months or years may result in repeated episodes of brain damaging concussion. Damaged brain tissue is replaced by scar tissue, and the patient's brain is unable to function normally. Boxers are almost the only people who suffer from this condition, although others who suffer repeated accidental head injuries may also be affected.

SYMPTOMS: Unsteady walk, tremors, personality changes, poor coordination and deterioration in mental ability.

INVESTIGATIONS: Diagnosis confirmed by CT scans and electroencephalograms (EEG).

TREATMENT: Some of the worst symptoms can sometimes be controlled by medication.

COMPLICATIONS: Dementia.

PROGNOSIS: No cure.

Purpura Annularis Telangiectodes
See Capillaritis

Pyelonephritis, Acute
DESCRIPTION: An infection of the kidneys.

CAUSE: A bacterial infection may reach the kidney through the blood stream, or up the ureter from the bladder. More common in women, after operations to the urinary tract, during pregnancy, and in those who are very sexually active.

SYMPTOMS: Starts suddenly with pain in the loin, fever, nausea, headaches and sometimes nausea and vomiting. May be associated with cystitis (see separate entry) which causes pain on passing urine, and urinary frequency.

INVESTIGATIONS: Diagnosis confirmed by examining a sample of urine to identify the responsible bacteria and the correct antibiotic. Further tests may be indicated if infections are repeated, including X-rays and/or ultrasound scans of the kidney, and cystoscopy (a fine flexible tube is passed into the bladder).

TREATMENT: Antibiotics, usually as a tablet or capsule by mouth for five to ten days, but occasionally by injection. Patients should take as much fluid as possible to flush out the infection. Passing urine after sex will reduce the incidence of recurrences.

COMPLICATIONS: Some patients will require long courses of antibiotics to prevent further attacks.

PROGNOSIS: With correct treatment, settles quickly.

See also Cystitis; Pyelonephritis, Chronic

455

Pyelonephritis, Chronic

DESCRIPTION: A persistent infection of the kidneys.

CAUSE: Recurrent bacterial infection of the kidney that may occur in both sexes and at any age, but those most commonly affected are elderly, incontinent (unable to control their bladder), and may have a catheter into the bladder.

SYMPTOMS: Often no symptoms, but detected on a routine urine test. Some patients have vague loin pain, feel tired and pass urine frequently.

INVESTIGATIONS: X-rays, CT and ultrasound scans of the kidneys, blood tests, urine culture tests, and cystoscopy (passing a flexible tube into the bladder).

TREATMENT: A very long course of the appropriate antibiotic, urinary antiseptics and alkalysing agents (eg. Ural, Citravescent). Patients are encouraged to drink large quantities of fluids. If a kidney abnormality is found, this may be surgically corrected.

COMPLICATIONS: Scarring of the kidney, high blood pressure, anaemia and functional failure of the kidney.

PROGNOSIS: One third of patients cured by a six-week course of antibiotics, another third cured after six months of antibiotics and antiseptics, 10% progress to severe kidney damage and failure, and the remainder continue to have a chronic infection without symptoms or kidney damage.

See also Pyelonephritis, Acute

Pyloric Ulcer
See Ulcer, Peptic

Pyridoxine Deficiency
See Vitamin B$_6$ Deficiency

Q

Q Fever

DESCRIPTION: Lung infection by primitive bacteria of the genus Rickettsia, which was unidentified for many years. The disease may derive its name from the fact that doctors were constantly questioning (Q) the cause of the fever, or Q may stand for Queensland, where the disease was very common and first researched.

CAUSE: *Coxiella burnetti* is the responsible Rickettsia. It is a parasite of sheep, cattle and goats, and passes from these animals in the milk and faeces, then droplets and dust containing the bacteria may be inhaled by humans. Farmers, shearers and abattoir workers are at a high risk. It does not spread from one human to another. Incubation period is one to three weeks.

SYMPTOMS: Often causes very mild, barely noticeable symptoms, but in more severe cases the patient will develop a fever, weakness, headache, muscle pains and a dry cough. In advanced cases, jaundice (yellow skin) and stomach pains occur.

INVESTIGATIONS: A specific blood test can diagnose the disease, and a chest X-ray may show lung abnormalities in severe cases.

TREATMENT: Tetracyclines (antibiotic) used to suppress the infection, but it does not always eliminate the disease completely. Prevented by a vaccination given to those who are at high risk.

COMPLICATIONS: Heart and brain involvement possible.

PROGNOSIS: Treatment not completely satisfactory, and relapses are common. Death rare unless heart becomes involved.

See also Brucellosis

Quadriplegia
(Tetraplegia)

DESCRIPTION: Complication of a neck injury that severs the spinal cord.

CAUSE: All parts of the human body are capable of healing and repairing damage, except the central nervous system, which comprises the brain and spinal cord. The spinal cord runs from the base of the brain, down through the vertebrae that form the backbone, and ends just below the waist. Nerves run out from it to the muscles, skin and other tissues, with one bundle of nerves emerging from between each of the 24 vertebrae. If the spinal cord is cut by a broken neck or other injury, it is impossible for nerve signals to pass backwards and forwards from the brain to the body. Involuntary muscles which control the internal organs such as the gut and heart movements, are supplied by a different set of nerves, and are not affected by spinal injury.

SYMPTOMS: Paralysis from the neck down. Patients cannot feel heat or cold, hard or soft, sharp or dull, or any sensation below the level of the injury. There is

457

no control of muscles, so patients cannot walk, move their arms or control their bowels or bladder.

INVESTIGATIONS: Diagnosed by X-rays, CT and MRI scans, and electrical tests on nerves and muscles.

TREATMENT: The only help that can be offered is rehabilitation so patients can cope with their disability.

COMPLICATIONS: Pressure sores on the skin, and lung and urinary infections from immobility.

PROGNOSIS: No cure. Life span often slightly shortened by lung complications.

See also Paraplegia

Quinsy
(Peritonsillar Abscess)

DESCRIPTION: An abscess (see separate entry) involving the tonsil at the side and back of the throat. More common in adults and males.

CAUSE: If tonsillitis is severe enough to cause destruction of the tonsil tissue, pus will form and collect between the tonsil and the wall of the throat to form an abscess.

SYMPTOMS: An attack of tonsillitis may initially appear to settle, but then the patient develops a high fever, severe pain on one side of the throat, a swollen throat, and difficulty in swallowing and opening the mouth.

INVESTIGATIONS: Swabs are taken from the tonsil to identify the bacteria responsible and the appropriate antibiotic to treat it.

TREATMENT: Large doses of antibiotics (often penicillin) by injection or tablet, and an operation to either drain the abscess or remove the tonsil and abscess together.

COMPLICATIONS: If the pus alone is drained at operation, the tonsils are often removed a few weeks later to prevent a recurrence. Rarely, the infection can spread to the bloodstream to cause septicaemia (see separate entry).

PROGNOSIS: Most patients settle well with appropriate treatment.

See also Septicaemia; Tonsillitis

R

Rabies

DESCRIPTION: Invariably fatal viral infection spread by animal bites (eg. dog, cat, bat, monkey, rats). Found throughout Asia, Europe (except Spain, Italy, Scandinavia and Britain), Africa and the Americas, but not present in Australia and the Pacific. Other forms of the rabies virus have been implicated in rare infections, including a fatal encephalitis that can be caught from infected bats in northeastern Australia.

CAUSE: The *Lyssavirus*, which infects the salivary glands of animals, so that any bite causes the injection of the virus into the victim's wound. Incubation period after a bite is three to seven weeks. If possible, the animal causing the bite should be isolated and observed to see if it is affected.

SYMPTOMS: The classic symptom is fear of water (hydrophobia) which is due to the severe pain that swallowing any food or liquid causes as a result of muscle spasm in the throat. Further symptoms include skin pain and tingling, generalised muscle spasms, convulsions, the production of copious amounts of thick saliva and eventually muscle paralysis.

INVESTIGATIONS: Diagnosis confirmed by a specific blood test.

TREATMENT: First aid after a bite is thorough washing of the wound with soap and water, then drenching the bite in antiseptic (eg. Betadine). If rabies is suspected it is essential for the patient to receive a rabies vaccine. No treatment available once symptoms appear.

PROGNOSIS: Death within two or three days of symptoms appearing.

Radiation Sickness

DESCRIPTION: A high dose of irradiation will damage all body tissues, but bone marrow, which is responsible for producing cells that maintain the immune system, is particularly susceptible and will cease to function and allow the body to be overwhelmed by what would otherwise be minor infections. Other vulnerable organs include the liver, lungs, thyroid, testes, ovaries and breasts.

CAUSE: A nuclear reactor accident, the mishandling of radioactive material used in medicine or industry, or an atomic bomb.

SYMPTOMS: Nausea, vomiting, weakness, delirium, blindness (the cornea of the eye being damaged to cause a cataract), mouth ulcers, bleeding gums, bleeding into the skin (bruises), and convulsions.

INVESTIGATIONS: Tests are performed to assess the function of specific organs and the types of cells present in the blood.

TREATMENT: First aid involves removing the patient from the contaminated area, thorough washing, providing fresh uncontaminated clothing, and purging the gut. If evacuation is not immediately practical, place as many walls and objects (eg. upturned table) as possible between the source of radiation and any people. Further treatment involves blood transfusions, marrow transplants and drugs that will remove any inhaled or swallowed radioactive dust from the body. The thyroid gland can be protected by taking high doses of normal iodine in pill form, to prevent the thyroid from absorbing any radioactive iodine from the environment.

COMPLICATIONS: The testes and ovaries may be affected to cause deformities or infertility. Unborn babies are at particular risk of irradiation, and miscarriages are common. Some body damage may be permanent (eg. skin scarring, thyroid destruction), and there are long-term risks of increased cancer rates.

PROGNOSIS: With time, natural repair of radiation damage is possible, but the risk of death will depend upon the dosage of radiation received.

Ramsay-Hunt Syndrome

DESCRIPTION: Infection of a facial nerve with the virus *Herpes zoster*.

CAUSE: Shingles (see separate entry) may affect any nerve leading out from the brain or spinal cord. If the nerve affected (the geniculate ganglion) is the one supplying the ear and face, the patient will develop this syndrome.

SYMPTOMS: Severe earache, dizziness, and a painful blistering rash across the upper face and ear.

INVESTIGATIONS: None normally necessary, but if required the diagnosis can be confirmed by taking special swabs from a sore.

TREATMENT: Antiviral medication (eg. aciclovir, valaciclovir) must be taken as soon as the shingles starts to prevent its spread. Steroids may also be used to reduce complications.

COMPLICATIONS: Permanent deafness and dizziness can result if treatment starts too late.

PROGNOSIS: Usually settles rapidly with treatment.

See also Shingles

Rapid Time Change Syndrome
See Jet lag

Raynaud's Disease

DESCRIPTION: Widespread constriction of small arteries.

CAUSE: Unknown, but aggravated by cold conditions.

SYMPTOMS: Raynaud's phenomenon (see below) plus constriction of blood vessels to the feet, face, chest, abdomen and sometimes internal organs. Patients have intense feelings of cold in these areas.

INVESTIGATIONS: None diagnostic.

TREATMENT: A wide range of medications may be used regularly to dilate the constricted arteries.

COMPLICATIONS: Poor blood supply to the fingers and toes may lead to ulceration and eventually gangrene.

PROGNOSIS: No cure, but medical control reasonable.

See also Raynaud's Phenomenon

Raynaud's Phenomenon

DESCRIPTION: Distressing spasm of small arteries, almost invariably affecting women.

CAUSE: Spasm of small arteries which restricts blood flow. Attacks usually triggered by cold conditions, such as entering an air-conditioned building or a cold climate. Other triggers may be hormonal changes, stress and anxiety, exercise and some foods. Raynaud's disease (see separate entry) is the most common cause, but in most cases no specific cause can be found.

SYMPTOMS: Hands go white then blue, swell and become very painful episodically. Usually starts in the teenage years or early twenties, may remain lifelong, and affects one in every five women. Often eases after the menopause.

INVESTIGATIONS: None diagnostic.

TREATMENT: Keep hands warm. Alcohol in low doses may be useful. A wide range of tablets and ointments can be used to dilate the tiny arteries in the fingers. As a last resort, operations to cut the nerves that cause the artery spasm can be performed.

COMPLICATIONS: Often associated with rheumatoid arthritis, and CREST syndrome and scleroderma are rare diseases that may be a cause.

PROGNOSIS: Persistent, but control reasonable with appropriate treatment. Surgery may be curative.

See also CREST Syndrome; Raynaud's Disease; Scleroderma

Razor Rash
(Pseudofolliculitis Barbae)

DESCRIPTION: Skin irritation of face and neck.

CAUSE: Minor damage to facial hair follicles by the scraping of a razor and ingrowing of hairs. Occurs more commonly in people who have curly hair.

SYMPTOMS: Ugly, raised, red, itchy rash on the neck and face.

INVESTIGATIONS: None necessary.

TREATMENT: Initially, let the beard grow for a month to eliminate ingrown hairs. Use a polyester skin-cleansing pad twice a day or a moisturising shaving foam, a single blade razor or shave frequently and as lightly as possible with an electric razor. Do not stretch the skin. Astringents and alcohol rubs may harden the skin to prevent the problem, and a mild steroid cream will settle the rash when it flares. As a last resort, grow a beard!

PROGNOSIS: Control good with treatment, but often flares repeatedly.

Reactive Arthritis
See Reiter Syndrome

Reactive Depression
See Depression

461

Reaven Syndrome
See Syndrome X

Rectal Cancer
See Colo-Rectal Cancer

Rectal Prolapse

DESCRIPTION: Slippage of part of the lining of the lower gut out through the anus.

CAUSE: Babies and frail elderly who strain at stool with constipation, and severe diarrhoea.

SYMPTOMS: Anal pain, discomfort and constant moistness, and a lump protrudes through the anus.

INVESTIGATIONS: Proctoscopy (passing a viewing tube into the anus) may be performed to inspect the rectum (last part of the large intestine).

TREATMENT: Surgery to correct prolapse.

COMPLICATIONS: Ulceration and bleeding from the prolapsed bowel. In severe cases the prolapsed bowel may become gangrenous.

PROGNOSIS: Good results from surgery.

Rectocoele
See Vaginal Prolapse

Rectovaginal Fistula
See Fistula

Rectovescical Fistula
See Fistula

Red-Back Spider Bite

DESCRIPTION: The Australian red-back spider is found in dark and protected areas, often hiding under cast-off tins and other rubbish. Only the female bites, and her body is the size of a pea, dark brown to black in colour, with the distinctive red or orange stripe running down the back.

SYMPTOMS: Intense pain at site of bite, tingling around the mouth, generalised pain, nausea and vomiting, profuse sweating, weakness and faintness, swelling around the bite and a rapid pulse.

INVESTIGATIONS: None normally necessary.

TREATMENT: Reassure the victim, relieve the pain by applying an ice cube wrapped in damp material to the bite (but do not freeze or damage the skin) and get medical help. Do NOT apply pressure immobilisation. An antivenine injection is available.

COMPLICATIONS: Ulcer formation at the site of the bite.

PROGNOSIS: The venom is relatively slow-acting, and provided there is no undue delay in obtaining treatment the victim should recover. Deaths have occurred in infants, but not older children.

Red Man Syndrome

DESCRIPTION: Side effect of a potent antibiotic used for very serious bacterial infections.

CAUSE: Occurs in up to 80% of patients receiving vancomycin through a drip into a vein (intravenous infusion).

SYMPTOMS: Very red itchy swollen skin on face, neck and torso, and a fever.

INVESTIGATIONS: None normally necessary.

TREATMENT: Reduce rate of vancomycin infusion. Antihistamines if required.

COMPLICATIONS: Low blood pressure and heart attack may occur if not treated.

PROGNOSIS: Usually mild and transient.

Reflex Sympathetic Dystrophy Syndrome
(Complex Regional Pain Syndrome Type One; Sudeck's Atrophy)

DESCRIPTION: Overstimulation of the sympathetic nervous system, which controls subconscious bodily functions (eg. sweating).

CAUSE: Self-perpetuating closed cycle of sensory nerves stimulating sympathetic nerves and vice versa. Often triggered initially by major injury or surgery to a limb.

SYMPTOMS: Prolonged exaggerated burning pain associated with very minor injury to affected area, hot dry limb initially, cold clammy blue limb later. The limb may also be swollen. When the foot is involved, it is known as Sudeck's atrophy.

INVESTIGATIONS: None diagnostic.

TREATMENT: Strong pain killers, physiotherapy, injections into sympathetic nerves, and medications to reduce the perception of pain (psychotropics).

PROGNOSIS: Treatment often unsatisfactory. Often settles spontaneously after a prolonged period.

See also Causalgia

Reflux Oesophagitis
(Gastro-Oesophageal Reflux)

DESCRIPTION: The back flow of acid from the stomach up through a normally closed muscle ring into the lower end of the oesophagus (gullet). Most commonly occurs in babies and overweight elderly men.

CAUSE: Some infants have a defect or temporary weakness in the muscle ring at the bottom of the oesophagus.

In adults, factors such as obesity, smoking, overeating, a hiatus hernia (see separate entry), rapid eating, alcohol, stress, anxiety, and poor posture may cause the excessive production of acid in the stomach and/or slackness in the muscle ring.

SYMPTOMS: Infants — pain, crying and irritability.

Adults — burning sensation behind the breast bone (heartburn), a bitter taste on the back of the tongue and burping as gas escapes easily from the stomach. Often worse at night after a large meal when the patient is lying down. If attacks are regular, ulcers may develop.

INVESTIGATIONS: Proved by gastroscopy or a barium meal X-ray.

TREATMENT: Children — most will grow out of the problem. Position child with head elevated while feeding, give small frequent thickened feeds, burp the baby regularly, and loosen nappy before feeds. If not adequately helped, preventive medication is given as a mixture. Do not allow child to lie flat after a feed.

Adults — weight loss, raising the head of the bed, having the main meal in the middle of the day, avoiding bending and heavy lifting, stopping smoking and reducing alcohol. Antacids to reduce the acid concentration in the stomach, and medication to empty the stomach faster (eg. cisapride) and reduce acid production (eg. nizatadine). In resistant cases is it necessary to resort to quite major surgery.

COMPLICATIONS: Scarring and narrowing of the lower end of the oesophagus to the point where it may be difficult to swallow food (Barrett syndrome — see separate entry), severe bleeding from ulcers in the oesophagus, and cancer of the oesophagus.

PROGNOSIS: Majority of patients can be controlled with appropriate treatment.

See also Barrett Syndrome; Hiatus Hernia; Mallory-Weis Syndrome; Sandifer Syndrome

Refsum Syndrome

DESCRIPTION: Rare disorder of nerve metabolism (chemistry) that results in the accumulation of damaging phytanic acid in nerve tissue.

CAUSE: Congenital, but onset usually between 5 and 10 years of age.

SYMPTOMS: Child with poor sensation and muscle control of the hands, forearms, feet and lower legs that affects the legs more than the arms. Other symptoms include nerve deafness, thickened skin and pigmentation of the light sensitive retina at the back of the eye.

INVESTIGATIONS: Nerve biopsy shows characteristic deformity.

TREATMENT: None available.

COMPLICATIONS: Heart failure and nerve defects in the heart.

PROGNOSIS: Poor.

Regional Enteritis
See Crohn's Disease

Reis-Bücklers Corneal Dystrophy
See Corneal Dystrophy

Reiter Syndrome
(Reactive Arthritis)

DESCRIPTION: An inflammatory condition involving the eyes, urethra and joints.

CAUSE: Unknown, but more commonly in young men, and often follows a bacterial infection.

SYMPTOMS: Unusual and apparently unconnected symptoms of conjunctivitis (eye inflammation), urethritis (inflammation of the urine tube — the urethra) and arthritis (joint inflammation). Other symptoms that may occur include mouth ulcers, skin sores, inflammation of the foreskin of the penis and a fever.

INVESTIGATIONS: Blood tests are not diagnostic, but indicate presence of inflammation. X-rays show arthritis in the joints of the back only after several attacks.

TREATMENT: Disease shortened by anti-inflammatory drugs such as indomethacin.

COMPLICATIONS: Rarely, the heart becomes inflamed.

PROGNOSIS: Heals without treatment after a few days or weeks, but the arthritis tends to last longer and recurrences are common.

Relapsing Fever

DESCRIPTION: Generalised infection of the body found worldwide in areas of poor hygiene. Particularly common in the western United States, but rare in western Europe and Australasia.

CAUSE: Infection by several bacteria of the species *Borrelia* that is spread from rats to man by the bite of a tick, or may spread from man to man by the bite of human body lice.

SYMPTOMS: Some days after being bitten by an infected insect, patient suddenly develops a fever, chills, nausea, vomiting, rapid heart rate, joint pains, rash and headache. Sometimes they become delirious and hallucinate. The attack stops as suddenly as it started after three to ten days, but relapses occur after one or two weeks.

INVESTIGATIONS: Diagnosed by specific blood tests.

TREATMENT: Antibiotics.

COMPLICATIONS: Uncommonly, in the elderly and debilitated, it may be fatal.

PROGNOSIS: Up to a dozen relapses may occur before final recovery, but five is the average, and each subsequent attack is milder than the preceding one. Treatment with appropriate antibiotics cures the infection and stops the relapses.

Relapsing Polychondritis

DESCRIPTION: Uncommon, intermittent, recurrent inflammation of cartilage.

CAUSE: Probably an autoimmune disorder (body inappropriately rejects its own tissue).

SYMPTOMS: Inflammation, swelling, redness, ulceration and pain in the cartilages that form the ear, nose, larynx (voice box), trachea (upper airway to lungs) and rib ends. Patients may also have a fever, anaemia, heart valve damage, arthritis and uveitis (eye inflammation — see separate entry).

INVESTIGATIONS: No specific diagnostic test, but general blood tests of inflammation are abnormal.

TREATMENT: Prednisone (a steroid).

COMPLICATIONS: Deafness, permanent deformity of nose and ear, and swelling of the larynx may choke patient.

PROGNOSIS: No cure, but reasonable control of each attack possible.

Renal Calculus
See Kidney Stone

Renal Colic
See Kidney Stone

Renal Failure, Acute
See Kidney Failure, Acute

Renal Failure, Chronic
See Kidney Failure, Chronic

Rendu-Osler-Weber Syndrome

DESCRIPTION: Abnormal overgrowth of small blood vessels throughout the body.

CAUSE: Inherited, and passes from one generation to the next in families.

SYMPTOMS: Polyp like outgrowths of dilated small blood vessels on the skin, tongue and throughout gastrointestinal tract, that bleed easily to cause severe anaemia.

INVESTIGATIONS: Biopsy of skin or intestinal polyp diagnostic. Blood found in faeces.

TREATMENT: Surgical removal of as many bleeding points as possible, iron supplements and blood transfusion.

COMPLICATIONS: Large connections between arteries and veins may short circuit blood supply to an organ or tissue and place strain on heart.

PROGNOSIS: No cure.

Repetitive Strain Injury
(Occupational Overuse Syndrome; RSI)

DESCRIPTION: A controversial diagnosis as the symptoms are almost invariably due to a condition such as tenosynovitis, tendonitis, carpal tunnel syndrome, osteoarthritis, rheumatoid arthritis, synovitis (see separate entries), or a combination of these.

CAUSE: Tends to occur in those undertaking repetitive tasks such as typing, playing the piano, or working on a production line.

SYMPTOMS: Pain, swelling and stiffness of the wrist, elbow or the small joints in the hand. The pain may actually be worse while the patient is at rest and immediately upon returning to work after a break.

INVESTIGATIONS: No specific tests, but diagnosis only made after all other possible conditions have been excluded by X-ray and other investigations.

TREATMENT: Resting the affected joint in a splint for a short time, altering the type of work undertaken, physiotherapy, alternating heat and cold to the area, and anti-inflammatory medications. A prolonged rest such as a holiday often settles the disorder.

COMPLICATIONS: May result in long-term stiffness, pain, and limited joint movement.

PROGNOSIS: Some cases become chronic while others resolve completely after treatment.

Respiratory Distress Syndrome, Adult

DESCRIPTION: Difficulty in breathing due to blood loss.

CAUSE: Only occurs in association with severe shock, very low blood pressure or serious injury.

SYMPTOMS: Anxiety, shortness of breath, rapid breathing, excess fluid in the lungs and a blue tinge may develop in the skin (cyanosis).

INVESTIGATIONS: Chest X-ray and specific blood tests to measure oxygen in the blood.

TREATMENT: Managed in a hospital intensive care unit. Control any bleeding and replace lost blood, give oxygen, ventilate mechanically if necessary, manage body fluids by a drip into a vein and fluid removing medications (diuretics), and antibiotics to prevent infection.

COMPLICATIONS: Permanent organ damage may occur.

PROGNOSIS: Depends on cause, but recovery normally expected.

Respiratory Distress Syndrome, Infant
(Hyaline Membrane Disease)

DESCRIPTION: A lung disease that occurs only in very premature babies. The more premature the infant, the greater the risk of developing the condition. Of babies born 8 weeks premature, 75% will be affected.

CAUSE: Surfactant is a fluid essential within the lungs to enable them to open and fill with air after birth. It is not produced in adequate quantity in some premature babies, so their lungs do not open and they cannot obtain sufficient air and oxygen. The hyaline membrane that lines the tiny airways within the lungs, is responsible for producing surfactant. Hyaline membranes are not anatomical structures but restrictive membranes, formed by proteins exuded from the tiny blood vessels in the immature lungs of premature babies, which decrease the elasticity of the lungs and make breathing more difficult.

SYMPTOMS: Develops some hours after birth, when the baby starts to breath rapidly, grunt with each breath, and has very marked movements of the chest and abdomen as it tries to breath. The baby will become blue in colour, and lapse into a coma.

INVESTIGATIONS: The diagnosis is confirmed by a chest X-ray. A special test performed on a sample of the amniotic fluid in which the baby floats in the womb can assess the risk of developing the disease.

TREATMENT: Can be prevented if the mother is given an injection of a steroid at least 48 hours before the birth. Every effort is made to delay a birth until the 48 hours has elapsed. Once the disease is present, oxygen is given in a humidicrib.

COMPLICATIONS: A small number of children have permanent lung damage.

PROGNOSIS: Death common without treatment. If the baby survives for 48 hours, it is almost certain to recover.

Respiratory Syncitial Virus Infection
See Bronchiolitis

Restless Legs Syndrome
(Wittmaack-Ekbom Syndrome)

DESCRIPTION: Patient's legs feel as though they want to exercise when body is trying to rest.

CAUSE: Unknown, but more common in women, made worse by pregnancy and heat, and sometimes aggravated by antihistamine medications. Not related to previous exercise.

SYMPTOMS: When patient goes to bed, they can't get to sleep because they feel that they have to keep moving their legs.

INVESTIGATIONS: None diagnostic.

TREATMENT: Keeping the legs cooler than the body, and the use of paracetamol or a small dose of a mild muscle relaxant such as diazepam (Valium). Getting out of bed and going for a run doesn't help.

COMPLICATIONS: None.

PROGNOSIS: Distressing but not serious problem that often occurs episodically for years, but is usually well controlled by treatment.

Retarded Ejaculation
See Ejaculatory Failure

Retinal Detachment

DESCRIPTION: The light-sensitive retina at the back of the eye is loosely attached to the eyeball, but if it detaches from the back of the eye, full or partial blindness results. May occur very slowly over a period of years, or be complete in a few minutes.

CAUSE: Retina may detach if a blood vessel ruptures and bleeds behind the retina, or if the fluid in the eye leaks behind the retina. May follow an injury to the eye, or be caused by high blood pressure or a tumour in the eye. Frequently, there is no obvious cause.

SYMPTOMS: Patient describes a black curtain slowly moving across the field of vision, as the retina progressively lifts away from the eyeball and causes at first partial, and later complete blindness.

INVESTIGATIONS: Detachment seen by examining the eye with an ophthalmoscope (small magnifying glass attached to a light).

TREATMENT: Rapid treatment is essential to save the sight. Surgical procedures, or a laser that is shone in short, sharp, accurately aimed bursts into the eye, are used to seal the retina back onto the eyeball.

PROGNOSIS: 95% of retinal detachments can now be cured or controlled if treated immediately they occur.

See also other conditions listed under Eye Diseases

Retinitis Pigmentosa

DESCRIPTION: A disease of the light-sensitive cells in the retina at the back of the eye that starts with night blindness in childhood, and slowly progresses to cause near total blindness in old age. The retinal cells steadily deteriorate, and pigmented cells replace them. The degeneration starts at the edge of the retina and progressively moves towards the centre.

CAUSE: Inherited and passes from one generation to the next.

SYMPTOMS: The field of vision slowly decreases until the patient can only see straight ahead as though through a tunnel, and has no peripheral vision.

INVESTIGATIONS: The retina has a characteristic pigmented appearance when viewed by a magnifying light (ophthalmoscope).

TREATMENT: No treatment available.

PROGNOSIS: Slowly progressive over many years.

See also Usher Syndrome other conditions listed under Eye Diseases

Retinoblastoma

DESCRIPTION: Cancer of the retina (light sensitive cells at the back of the eye) that usually occurs in children under three years of age.

CAUSE: May be a familial (inherited tendency) in 40% of cases, but cause in others is unknown.

SYMPTOMS: The pupil becomes white, a squint is noticed, the affected eye bulges forward, becomes reddened and the vision is affected.

INVESTIGATIONS: Diagnosed by examining the eye with a magnifying light (ophthalmoscope) and a CT scan.

TREATMENT: Small tumours may be treated by laser or chemotherapy (medication), but most are not diagnosed until large, and the eye must be removed.

COMPLICATIONS: May spread (metastasise) from the eye along the optic (vision) nerve to the brain.

PROGNOSIS: Depends on size of tumour at time of diagnosis. Survival rate with no spread is 85%, but this drops dramatically if cancer cells are found in the optic nerve. Overall five year survival about 70%.

See also Cancer

Retrograde Ejaculation

DESCRIPTION: Semen is ejaculated from the sac at the base of the penis (seminal vescicle), but instead of passing along the urethra in the penis to the outside, it travels in the other direction and enters the bladder.

CAUSE: Complication of surgery in the area (eg. to the prostate), due to advanced diabetes or a side effect of some uncommon drugs.

SYMPTOMS: Sensation of orgasm during sex, but no ejaculation occurs.

INVESTIGATIONS: Examination of urine passed after sex reveals sperm.

TREATMENT: None available.

COMPLICATIONS: Infertility which may be overcome by microsurgical techniques to remove sperm from the man and artificially inseminate a woman.

PROGNOSIS: No cure.

See also other diseases listed under Sex Problems

Retrovirus Infection
See AIDS

Rett Syndrome

DESCRIPTION: Rare brain condition of girls that affects about one in 20,000 women.

CAUSE: Congenital (present from birth) condition that only affects females.

SYMPTOMS: Episodes of rapid over breathing (hyperventilation), seizures, subnormal mentality, autism (see separate entry), constipation and repetitive movement disorders of the hands. Symptoms become apparent at 12 to 18 months of age.

INVESTIGATIONS: None diagnostic.

TREATMENT: Medication to control the seizures.

PROGNOSIS: No cure.

Reye Syndrome

DESCRIPTION: Rare brain and liver inflammation that is more common in children under six years of age.

CAUSE: Unknown, but may be associated with the use of aspirin. Invariably follows two to three weeks after a viral infection such as influenza, chickenpox or a cold.

SYMPTOMS: Liver failure and brain inflammation (encephalitis) that cause vomiting, mental confusion and convulsions.

INVESTIGATIONS: None diagnostic, but blood tests of liver function are abnormal.

TREATMENT: No specific treatment is available, but attempts are made to control the brain swelling and assist breathing.

COMPLICATIONS: Permanent liver or brain damage in survivors.

PROGNOSIS: Death rate in excess of 30% and often rapidly fatal.

Rhabdomyolysis
(Muscle Meltdown)

DESCRIPTION: Muscle destruction caused by massive overuse.

CAUSE: In conditions of extreme exertion, when a muscle is forced to work despite an inadequate blood supply of oxygen and energy, the muscle will briefly use its own material as an energy source and destroy itself.

SYMPTOMS: Sudden collapse during extreme exertion and inability to use affected muscles, which become excruciatingly painful.

INVESTIGATIONS: Muscle biopsy diagnostic.

TREATMENT: None available.

PROGNOSIS: Muscle is permanently damaged and is replaced by scar tissue or fat.

Rheumatic Fever

DESCRIPTION: A damaging inflammation of the heart valves that was common before antibiotics were readily available, but is now rare in developed countries.

CAUSE: Follows some types of bacterial infections.

SYMPTOMS: Patients have two or more of a number of widely different symptoms, so every case is completely different. Symptoms include inflammation of the heart and its valves, a rapid pulse, irregular heart beat, irregular shaped red patches and rings on the skin, chorea (uncontrolled twitching of the arms, legs and face), fever, and arthritis that moves from one large joint to another.

INVESTIGATIONS: Diagnosis confirmed by blood tests, and an electrocardiogram (ECG).

TREATMENT: Antibiotics (commonly penicillin) to remove any remaining bacterial infection, aspirin to reduce fever and joint pains, and strict bed rest for several weeks or months.

COMPLICATIONS: In 70% of patients causes permanent damage to heart valves which leak and fail in later life, and are susceptible to infection (endocarditis). All patients who have had rheumatic fever must take antibiotics whenever they have any dental treatment or operation.

PROGNOSIS: Usually lasts a few weeks to months, with children taking far longer to recover than adults. A significant number of patients have recurrences for years afterwards. 98% of patients recover from the first attack, but multiple repeat attacks may lead to death from heart damage.

See also Endocarditis; Sydenham's Chorea

Rheumatoid Arthritis

DESCRIPTION: An inflammatory disease that affects the entire body, and is not limited to the joints. The main effect is inflammation (swelling and redness) of the smooth moist synovial membrane that lines the inside of joints. Those most affected are the hands and feet.

CAUSE: An autoimmune disease in which the immune system is triggered off inappropriately, and the body starts to reject its own tissue. Tends to run in families from one generation to the next, and the onset may be triggered by a viral infection or stress. Occurs in one in every 100 people, and females are three times more frequently affected than males. Usually starts between 20 and 40 years of age.

SYMPTOMS: Initial symptoms are very mild, with early morning stiffness in the small joints of the hands and feet, loss of weight, a feeling of tiredness and being unwell, pins and needles sensations, sometimes a slight intermittent fever, and gradual deterioration over many years. Occasionally the disease has a sudden onset with severe symptoms flaring in a few days, often after emotional stress or a serious illness. As the disease worsens, it causes increasing pain and stiffness in the small joints, progressing steadily to larger joints, the back being only rarely affected. The pain becomes more severe and constant, and the joints become swollen, tender and deformed. Other organs may also be affected.

INVESTIGATIONS: Diagnosed by specific blood tests, X-rays, examination of joint fluid and the clinical findings. The level of indicators in the blood stream can give doctors a gauge to measure the severity of the disease and the response to treatment.

TREATMENT: Requires constant care by doctors, physiotherapists and occupational therapists. The severity of cases varies greatly, so not all treatments are used in all patients, and the majority will only require minimal care.

In acute stages, general physical and emotional rest, and splinting the affected joints are important. Physiotherapists undertake regular passive movement of the joints to prevent permanent stiffness developing, and apply heat or cold as appropriate to reduce the inflammation.

In chronic stages, carefully graded exercise under the care of a physiotherapist, is used. Medications for the inflammation include aspirin and other anti-inflammatory drugs. Steroids such as prednisone give dramatic, rapid relief from all the symptoms, but they may have long-term side effects (eg. bone and skin thinning, fluid retention, weight gain, peptic ulcers, lowered resistance to infection, etc.), and their use must balance the benefits against the risks. In some cases, steroids may be injected into a particularly troublesome joint. A number of unusual drugs are also used, including gold by injection or tablet, antimalarial drugs (eg. chloroquine) penicillamine (not the antibiotic), and cell-destroying drugs (cytotoxics).

Surgery to isolated, painful joints can be useful in a limited number of patients.

COMPLICATIONS: Additional effects can include wasting of muscle, lumps under the skin, inflamed blood vessels, heart and lung inflammation, an enlarged spleen and lymph nodes, dry eyes and mouth, and changes to cells in the blood.

PROGNOSIS: There is no cure, but effective controls are available for most patients, and the disease tends to burn out and become less debilitating in old age. Some patients have irregular acute attacks throughout their lives, others may have only one or two acute episodes at times of physical or emotional stress, while others steadily progress until they become totally crippled by the disease.

See also other diseases listed under Arthritis

Rhinitis
See Hay Fever; Vasomotor Rhinitis

Rhinophyma

DESCRIPTION: Abnormal growth of the nose.

CAUSE: A severe form of rosacea (see separate entry) that usually occurs in men.

SYMPTOMS: Increase in size of the nose due to a dramatic enlargement of the skin oil glands and excessive deposition of fat and other tissue under the skin. In advanced cases it becomes very disfiguring and gives the appearance of a large growth on the nose.

INVESTIGATIONS: Skin biopsy sometimes necessary to confirm diagnosis.

TREATMENT: Plastic surgery to remove the excess tissue.

PROGNOSIS: Reasonable results from surgery.

See also Rosacea

Richner-Hanhart Syndrome
(Tyrosinaemia Type II)

DESCRIPTION: Protein body chemistry abnormality affecting the eyes, skin and brain.

CAUSE: Familial (runs in families from one generation to the next). Due to deficiency of specific liver enzymes used to break down the protein tyrosine.

SYMPTOMS: Eyes unable to cope with bright lights, ulceration of the eye surface (cornea), spasms of the eyelids, dry scaly skin, mental retardation and seizures.

INVESTIGATIONS: Blood levels of tyrosine very high.

TREATMENT: Protein restricted diet with exclusion of the proteins phenylalanine and tyrosine.

COMPLICATIONS: Permanent brain and eye damage if not treated early.

PROGNOSIS: Symptoms resolve with treatment.

Rickets

DESCRIPTION: A rare disease in developed countries, growing children in poorer countries may develop rickets if they have an inadequate intake of vitamin D. Vitamin D is essential for the body to absorb calcium, which is the main constituent of bone. In adults the same condition is known as osteomalacia (see separate entry).

CAUSE: Vitamin D is obtained from dairy products (milk, cheese, yoghurt, etc.), eggs and fish. Vitamin D can also be formed in the body by the action of sunlight on certain substances in the skin.

SYMPTOMS: Children with rickets have soft bones and grow slowly. The legs tend to bow outwards because of walking on the soft long bones of the legs. Abnormalities in the growth of the ribs, and excessive enlargement of the forehead may occur. Patients may also be 'double-jointed', with slack ligaments around the joints, and may have weak muscles.

INVESTIGATIONS: Measurement of calcium and vitamin D levels in the blood, X-rays of long bones.

TREATMENT: Supplying adequate amounts of vitamin D in the diet.

COMPLICATIONS: Any bone deformity present may become permanent, resulting in premature arthritis.
PROGNOSIS: No further damage likely once good diet started.
See also Osteomalacia

Rickettsial Infection

See Q Fever; Rickettsialpox; Rocky Mountain Spotted Fever; Typhus

Rickettsialpox

DESCRIPTION: Uncommon mild infection that has widespread effects.
CAUSE: The primitive bacteria *Rickettsia akari*, which passes from mice to humans through a mite bite in over crowded unhygienic conditions. Incubation period seven to twelve days.
SYMPTOMS: Sudden onset of fever, chills, a single red lump on the skin at site of mite bite, headache and widespread muscular and joint pains. Two to four days later swelling of skin occurs with chickenpox-like blisters on the affected skin.
INVESTIGATIONS: Diagnosed by specific blood tests.
TREATMENT: Tetracycline antibiotic tablets.
COMPLICATIONS: None significant.
PROGNOSIS: Complete recovery normal.
See also other diseases listed under Rickettsial Infection

Riedel's Thyroiditis

DESCRIPTION: A rare form of inflammation involving the thyroid gland at the front of the neck.
CAUSE: The normal structure of the thyroid is replaced by hard fibrous scar tissue for no known reason.
SYMPTOMS: The gland becomes irregularly enlarged, inadequate thyroid hormone is produced and the patient develops a slow heart beat, dry skin, cold intolerance and other symptoms of hypothyroidism (see separate entry). Other effects are caused by the enlargement of the gland and include difficulty in swallowing, shortness of breath and hoarseness.
INVESTIGATIONS: Diagnosed by blood tests and thyroid gland biopsy.
TREATMENT: Partial removal of the gland by surgery and taking thyroid hormone tablets long term.
COMPLICATIONS: Often associated with other widespread organ damage.
PROGNOSIS: Satisfactory.
See also Hypothyroidism; Thyroiditis

Rieger Syndrome

DESCRIPTION: Developmental abnormality of the teeth and eyes.
CAUSE: Familial (runs in families from one generation to the next).
SYMPTOMS: Abnormal formation of the iris (coloured part) of the eye, and the teeth are reduced in number and smaller than normal.

INVESTIGATIONS: None diagnostic.
TREATMENT: None available.
PROGNOSIS: No cure, but normal life expectancy.

Right Heart Failure
See Cor Pulmonale

Riley-Day Syndrome
DESCRIPTION: Uncommon inherited syndrome that occurs in Jews of Middle Eastern extraction.
CAUSE: Familial (runs in families from one generation to the next).
SYMPTOMS: Lack of tears in the eyes, excessive sweating, intermittent fevers and episodes of low body temperature, blood pressure swings between being too high and too low, the surface of the eye may feel no pain, and generally patients feel only the most severe pains. As a result they may have fractures and other injuries of which they have no knowledge. Less commonly, they may have poor coordination, difficulty in swallowing, difficulty in talking, and extreme mood swings.
INVESTIGATIONS: None diagnostic.
TREATMENT: None available.
COMPLICATIONS: Serious personal injury, particularly to the eye resulting in blindness.
PROGNOSIS: Poor.

Ringworm
See Tinea Corporis

Ritter's Disease
See Scalded Skin Syndrome

River Blindness
See Onchocerciasis

Rocky Mountain Spotted Fever
DESCRIPTION: Serious widespread infection that occurs throughout the Americas, but most commonly in the western United States.
CAUSE: The primitive bacteria *Rickettsia rickettsii*, which is transmitted from numerous small wild mammals and dogs to man by a tick bite. Incubation period 3 to 12 days.
SYMPTOMS: Sudden onset of severe headache, shaking, very high fever, muscle pains, nausea, restlessness, delirium and collapse. Belly muscles may become very sore and pain occurs in numerous joints. A faint pink large spotted rash appears on the arms and legs about four days after other symptoms. The rash steadily darkens to a deep red, tends to be more severe over bony prominences

(eg. sides of ankles), and bleeding may occur into the spots which may then degenerate into ulcers. Rapid pulse and low blood pressure develop when the heart becomes affected.

INVESTIGATIONS: Diagnosed by specific blood tests.

TREATMENT: Potent antibiotics (eg. chloramphenicol, tetracycline) by drip into a vein.

COMPLICATIONS: Pneumonia, ear and salivary gland infections, dehydration, enlarged spleen, and blood clots (thrombosis) in limbs which may lead to gangrene. Permanent effects rarely occur after recovery, but may include permanent paralysis and epilepsy.

PROGNOSIS: Up to 20% of patients die, even with good medical care, but the mortality rate is higher in the elderly.

See also other diseases listed under Rickettsial Infection

Rodent Ulcer
See Basal Cell Carcinoma

Rosacea
(Acne Rosacea)

DESCRIPTION: A skin disease of the face, found most commonly in middle-aged women.

CAUSE: Unknown.

SYMPTOMS: Intermittent flushing of the face that becomes a permanent redness of the facial skin. After a few days or weeks, sores similar to a severe case of acne develop. In advanced cases, the surface of the eyes may be involved in a form of conjunctivitis.

INVESTIGATIONS: No diagnostic tests available.

TREATMENT: Antibiotic tablets (eg. tetracycline, erythromycin) and/or metronidazole gel applied to the affected skin that are continued for two or three months.

COMPLICATIONS: Relapses are common for years afterwards, but if medication is used immediately, it suppresses each attack effectively.

PROGNOSIS: Eventual cure expected with good treatment.

See also Rhinophyma

Roseola Infantum
(Baby Measles)

DESCRIPTION: Viral infection that is caught by virtually every child in the first two or three years of life.

CAUSE: Contagious virus with an incubation period from 7 to 17 days.

SYMPTOMS: Most children will have such a mild attack that it will be passed off as a slight cold. Those with a severe attack will develop a fever and a measles-like rash on the trunk and neck, which usually appears after the fever has gone.

INVESTIGATIONS: None necessary.

TREATMENT: No treatment other than paracetamol for the fever.

COMPLICATIONS: None.

PROGNOSIS: The child recovers completely within two or three days.

See also German Measles; Measles

Ross River Fever
(Epidemic Polyarthritis)

DESCRIPTION: Generalised viral infection found throughout northern Australia, in the NSW Riverina irrigation area, New Guinea, Solomon Is., Samoa and Fiji.

CAUSE: Virus transmitted by mosquitoes between animals (possibly bats) and humans.

SYMPTOMS: Fevers, muscle aches, arthritis (particularly of the hands and feet), swollen joints, headaches, swollen tender lymph nodes, poor appetite, nausea, flu-like symptoms and tiredness. A rash occurs in some patients. Symptoms worsen with age and children may be infected without having symptoms, but still act as reservoirs for further spread of the disease.

INVESTIGATIONS: Diagnosed by a specific blood test.

TREATMENT: Aspirin and anti-inflammatory medications to ease pain and remove the fever. Prevented by control of mosquitoes, insect repellents, window screens and protective clothing.

COMPLICATIONS: No serious consequences.

PROGNOSIS: No cure. May be debilitating for months and recur repeatedly when the patient becomes run-down.

See also Barmah Forest Virus

Rotator Cuff Syndrome

DESCRIPTION: The shoulder can move through a greater range than any other joint in the body because the socket of this ball and socket joint is very shallow, but as a result, the joint is very unstable and dislocates easily. To stabilise the joint, a number of muscles and tendons crowd around the joint as a 'cuff' of firm tissue, inside which the shoulder can still freely rotate. Damage to this rotator cuff causes the rotator cuff syndrome.

CAUSE: Any tear, stretching or rupture of the muscles, ligaments or tendons forming the rotator cuff around the shoulder joint, caused by an obvious injury, overuse or aging.

SYMPTOMS: Pain and tenderness around the shoulder joint. Depending upon the muscles injured, some movements of the joint may be very painful, while others cause no discomfort.

INVESTIGATIONS: None diagnostic.

TREATMENT: Combination of rest, physiotherapy, anti-inflammatory medications, and in severe cases injections of steroids and anaesthetics into the affected muscles.

COMPLICATIONS: If a muscle or tendon is torn badly or completely ruptured, surgery to repair the damage will be necessary.

PROGNOSIS: Slow, but complete, recovery normal.

See also Painful Arc Syndrome

Rotavirus Infection
See Gastroenteritis

Rothmund-Thomson Syndrome
(Congenital Poikiloderma)

DESCRIPTION: Abnormality of skin development.

CAUSE: Congenital birth defect.

SYMPTOMS: Skin is thin, red and pigmented, with red dots caused by dilated small blood vessels (telangiectasia) just under the skin. Patients are short, have under developed genitals, and the skin is very sensitive to sunburn.

INVESTIGATIONS: Diagnosed by skin biopsy.

TREATMENT: None available.

COMPLICATIONS: Scarring of skin from sunburn and serious bleeding from telangiectasia.

PROGNOSIS: No cure.

See also Osler-Rendu-Weber Disease

Rotor Syndrome

DESCRIPTION: Cause of yellow skin (jaundice) in a newborn infant.

CAUSE: Hereditary.

SYMPTOMS: Jaundice with no other symptoms.

INVESTIGATIONS: All liver function tests and liver biopsy normal except for high levels of bilirubin.

TREATMENT: None necessary.

COMPLICATIONS: None.

PROGNOSIS: Complete recovery normal within a week or so.

See also Dubin-Johnson Syndrome

Roundworm Infestation
(Nematode Infestation)

See Ascariasis; Cutaneous Larva Migrans; Gnathostomiasis; Hookworm; Roundworm Infestation; Trichinosis; Visceral Larva Migrans

Roussy-Levy Syndrome

DESCRIPTION: Developmental defect of nerves in arms and legs.

CAUSE: Familial (inherited).

SYMPTOMS: Poor coordination, curvature of the spine and hump back, thin arms and legs with very weak muscles.

INVESTIGATIONS: Tendon reflexes in arms and legs absent.
TREATMENT: None available.
PROGNOSIS: Slowly progressive.

Royal Free Disease
See Chronic Fatigue Syndrome

RSI
See Repetitive Strain Injury

RSV
See Bronchiolitis

Rubella
See German Measles

Rubenstein-Taybi Syndrome
DESCRIPTION: Developmental abnormality of numerous structures.
CAUSE: May be hereditary or occur spontaneously as a congenital malformation.
SYMPTOMS: Under developed cheek bones, broad thumbs and toes, slanted eyes, patent ductus arteriosus (see separate entry), heart malformations, and mild to moderate subnormal mentality.
INVESTIGATIONS: None diagnostic.
TREATMENT: Surgery for heart and cosmetic deformities.
PROGNOSIS: No cure, but reasonable life span provided heart abnormalities not severe.

Rubeola
See Measles

Russell-Silver Syndrome
DESCRIPTION: Form of dwarfism.
CAUSE: Due to retarded development of growth plates at bone ends in the arms and legs. Sporadic inheritance within families.
SYMPTOMS: Small stature and small at birth, significant variation in size between left and right sides of body which tends to correct itself with growth, early onset of puberty and brown spots on skin. Some patients may have an incurved and short little finger, down turning at the corner of the mouth, triangular shaped face, webbed toes, mental retardation, and kidney and penis abnormalities.
INVESTIGATIONS: X-rays show bone growth plate abnormalities.
TREATMENT: None available.
COMPLICATIONS: 10% develop Wilms' tumour (see separate entry).
PROGNOSIS: No cure, but growth and appearance improve in adolescence.

479

S

Saccular Aneurysm
See Aneurysm

St.Louis Encephalitis

DESCRIPTION: Viral infection of the brain.

CAUSE: Virus spread from birds to man by a mosquito. Found in central and western United States. More common in warmer months and the elderly. Incubation period one to three weeks.

SYMPTOMS: Fever, belly pains, dizziness, sore throat, cough, headache, neck stiffness, nausea, vomiting, tiredness, disturbed mental functions, disorientation, coma and death. In children the symptoms may be minimal.

INVESTIGATIONS: Tests on blood and the fluid around the brain are abnormal.

TREATMENT: No specific treatment or vaccine available.

COMPLICATIONS: Commonly causes permanent brain damage in elderly survivors with paralysis, epilepsy, tremor and personality changes.

PROGNOSIS: Acute attack lasts for one to three weeks, but complete recovery may take months. Mortality rate of about 5%, but worse in elderly.

See also Encephalitis

St. Vitus Dance
See Sydenham's Chorea

Salivary Stone

DESCRIPTION: Uncommon formation of a stone in a saliva producing gland in the mouth. Under the tongue and in the side of the jaw there are six salivary glands, three on each side (the parotid glands at the angle of the jaw, submandibular glands under the side of the jaw, and submental glands under the chin). A small tube leads from each gland to open into the mouth under the tongue or at the back corner of the mouth. They produce saliva to keep the mouth moist and to start the digestion of food.

CAUSE: If a salivary gland becomes infected or injured, or the saliva becomes too concentrated, a stone may form in the gland.

SYMPTOMS: Salivation at the sight, smell or taste of food causes excruciating pain as the pressure of saliva behind the stone moves it in the delicate duct.

INVESTIGATIONS: Special X-ray of the salivary gland after a passing a fine tube into its duct through the opening into the mouth.

TREATMENT: Medication to temporarily dry up the saliva and ease the pain, followed by surgery to remove the stone.

COMPLICATIONS: Sialitis (see separate entry) and abscess formation in the gland.

PROGNOSIS: Responds well to treatment.

See also Parotid Tumour; Sialitis

Salmonellosis, Intestinal
See Typhoid Fever

Salpingitis

DESCRIPTION: An infection of the Fallopian tubes that lead from the ovaries to the uterus.

CAUSE: Numerous sexually transmitted bacteria including *Chlamydia trachomatis* and *Neisseria gonorrhoea*.

SYMPTOMS: Pain low in the abdomen, fevers, a vaginal discharge, abnormal menstrual periods and pain with intercourse.

INVESTIGATIONS: Blood tests, vaginal examination and vaginal swabs to determine which bacteria are present and the appropriate antibiotic.

TREATMENT: Antibiotics by tablet or injection to clear the infection, and avoidance of sex until cured.

COMPLICATIONS: The Fallopian tubes may be damaged so eggs have difficulty in passing down to the uterus resulting in infertility, or fertilised eggs may implant in the tube as an ectopic pregnancy (pregnancy develops outside the uterus — see separate entry).

PROGNOSIS: Up to one quarter of women will have continuing problems including repeat infections, infertility, ectopic pregnancies, persistent pelvic pain and painful sex.

See also Fitz-Hugh-Curtis Syndrome; Gonorrhoea; Pelvic Inflammatory Disease and other diseases listed under Venereal Diseases.

Sandifer Syndrome

DESCRIPTION: Restless infant with irritated oesophagus.

CAUSE: Reflux oesophagitis caused by concentrated hydrochloric acid flowing back up from the stomach into the gullet to cause sudden severe pain.

SYMPTOMS: Sudden spasms of neck extension and muscle stiffening in an infant.

INVESTIGATIONS: Trial of treatment usually successful, but in cases of doubt a barium swallow X-ray may be performed.

TREATMENT: Antacids, anti-reflux (eg. cisapride) and anti-ulcer (eg. ranitidine) treatments.

COMPLICATIONS: May be confused with epileptic seizure.

PROGNOSIS: Good response to treatment.

See also Reflux Oesophagitis

Sanfilippo Syndrome
(Mucopolysaccharidosis III)

DESCRIPTION: A rare congenital condition in which patients are unable to eliminate certain substances (mucopolysaccharides) from the body.

CAUSE: Inherited abnormality of the metabolic system.

SYMPTOMS: Severe mental retardation starting at age 5 years or later, excess body hair, abnormal face structure, and enlarged liver and spleen.

481

INVESTIGATIONS: Urine tests show excess levels of heparitin sulfate.
TREATMENT: None available.
PROGNOSIS: No cure.
See also Hunter Syndrome; Hurler Syndrome

Sarcoidosis

DESCRIPTION: An uncommon disease which causes damage and inflammation to a wide range of organs within the body, but most commonly to the lungs.
CAUSE: Unknown. Women are more commonly affected than men, and the usual age of onset is 40 to 60 years.
SYMPTOMS: The symptoms can be very varied and sometimes bizarre because almost any part of the body may be involved as affected tissues fail to function correctly. Patients may have a fever, tiredness, shortness of breath, rashes, enlarged glands, liver or spleen enlargement, pain, arthritis, pins and needles sensation and heart failure.
INVESTIGATIONS: Blood tests and lung X-rays show abnormalities, but cannot specifically diagnose sarcoidosis. Definitive diagnosis requires the microscopic examination of a biopsy.
TREATMENT: Steroids to reduce the inflammation.
COMPLICATIONS: Gradual destruction of the lungs and other organs.
PROGNOSIS: Slowly progressive and cannot be cured, but control is usually sufficient to give the victim a relatively long life.
See also Heerfordt Syndrome; Loeffler Syndrome

Sarcoma

See Angiosarcoma; Cancer; Kaposi's Sarcoma; Osteosarcoma; Stewart-Treves Syndrome

Savant Syndrome

See Idiot Savant Syndrome

Scabies

DESCRIPTION: An infestation (not an infection) by a tiny insect that burrows for 1cm. or more through the outer layers of the skin. Most common areas affected are the fingers, palms, heels, groin and wrists, but it can spread across the entire body, although it is unusual for the head and neck to be involved. The scabies mite is just visible to the naked eye, appearing like a spot of dust on a piece of black paper, but it cannot be seen on the skin. In many third-world countries, the disease is in epidemic proportions, but relatively uncommon in developed countries.
CAUSE: The tiny insect mite *Sarcoptes scabiei* which spreads by close contact (eg. shaking hands) with someone who already has the disease. Can occur despite scrupulous personal cleanliness.
SYMPTOMS: Incessant itching caused by the burrowing mite, and the tissue around

them becomes red, itchy and inflamed. Scratching often damages the skin, making diagnose difficult, and allowing a secondary bacterial infection to enter the skin.

INVESTIGATIONS: A skin scraping is examined under a microscope, when the mites and their eggs can be seen.

TREATMENT: Painting the entire body with a lotion or cream (eg. benzyl benzoate, permethrin, crotamiton) that kills the mites. All other members of the family, and anyone else closely connected with the patient, should be treated at the same time. Advisable to change all the bed linen, and to repeat the treatment after a week, so that any mites that hatch from the remaining eggs after the initial treatment will be killed.

COMPLICATIONS: Itch may continue for 10-20 days after treatment due to an allergy to the scabies bodies or their products (eggs, droppings, etc.). Norwegian scabies is a very severe form that causes thickening and scaling of the skin (particularly the palms and soles) from huge numbers of mites.

PROGNOSIS: Good response to treatment, but recurrences common.

Scald
See Burn

Scalded Skin Syndrome
(Lyell Syndrome; Ritter's Disease; Toxic Epidermal Necrolysis)

DESCRIPTION: Severe bacterial skin infection known as Ritter's disease in newborn infants, and toxic epidermal necrolysis in older children. Milder forms are known as **pemphigus neonatorum** or **bullous impetigo**. Scalded skin syndrome and Lyell syndrome are terms that cover all forms.

CAUSE: Superficial skin infection caused by the bacterium *Staphylococcus aureus* (golden Staph) that spreads from nose, eyes, mouth or umbilicus to areas of skin damaged by eczema or injury. May be a complication of Stevens-Johnson syndrome.

SYMPTOMS: An infant or child with severe peeling of skin that commences on the face and genitals and spreads across body. The skin appears similar to a very severe sunburn.

INVESTIGATIONS: Culture swabs from nose, eyes, throat and umbilicus to confirm responsible bacteria and appropriate antibiotic.

TREATMENT: Antibiotics such as penicillin or erythromycin.

COMPLICATIONS: Death from fluid loss through damaged skin or internal spread of infection possible.

PROGNOSIS: Responds slowly to antibiotics, but most children recover.

See also Stevens-Johnson Syndrome

Scalenus Anticus Syndrome
See Naffziger Syndrome

Scaphoid Fracture
(Wrist Fracture)

DESCRIPTION: Fracture of one of the eight small wrist bones (scaphoid) on the thumb side of the wrist.

CAUSE: Falling on the outstretched hand.

SYMPTOMS: Pain and tenderness on the thumb side of the wrist.

INVESTIGATIONS: These fractures are often hard to detect, and X-rays ten days apart may be necessary.

TREATMENT: Immobilisation of the wrist in plaster.

COMPLICATIONS: In a small number of cases, part of this small bone may die after a fracture and result in a constantly painful wrist joint. An artificial scaphoid bone can now be inserted if complications occur.

PROGNOSIS: Most heal after four to six weeks.

See also Colles' Fracture; Fracture; Smith's Fracture

Scapulo-Costal Syndrome

DESCRIPTION: Cause of shoulder, head, arm and neck pain. One of the thoracic outlet group of syndromes.

CAUSE: May be due to muscle fatigue associated with long term faulty posture.

SYMPTOMS: Pain in back of the neck spreading to back of the head, the inside edge of the shoulder blade (scapula) and down the inside of the arm to the little finger. May be associated with tenderness along the inside edge of the scapula, shoulder stiffness, and tender muscles down the back.

INVESTIGATIONS: None diagnostic.

TREATMENT: Posture correction, exercise, anti-inflammatory medications, and local anaesthetic and steroid injections.

PROGNOSIS: Usually settles with time, rest and treatment.

See also Naffziger Syndrome; Subclavian Steal Syndrome

Scarlet Fever

DESCRIPTION: Infection of children that is now very uncommon because of the widespread use of antibiotics for minor infections.

CAUSE: Bacteria from the Streptococcal family.

SYMPTOMS: Patient is unwell with a fever and sore throat for a few hours to two days before the typical 'scarlet red' rash develops, which consists of bright red, pin-head size dots on the face, neck, armpits, groin and other areas. The skin immediately around the mouth often remains a normal colour. The tonsils are usually enlarged, red and painful, and the tongue may be red and swollen. The skin of the palms and soles may flake away in severe cases.

INVESTIGATIONS: Diagnosis confirmed by taking a swab from the throat, and by specific blood tests.

TREATMENT: Can be both treated and prevented by antibiotics such as penicillin and erythromycin.

PROGNOSIS: Very good with antibiotic treatment.

SCC
See Squamous Cell Carcinoma of the Skin

Schamberg's Disease
See Capillaritis

Scheie Syndrome
DESCRIPTION: Rare mucopolysaccharidosis closely related to Hurler syndrome which starts at one to two years of age. Patients are unable to eliminate complex carbohydrates (mucopolysaccharides) from the body.

CAUSE: Inherited abnormality of the metabolic system.

SYMPTOMS: Recurrent respiratory infections, enlarged liver and spleen, excessive forward curvature of the spine, heart murmurs, eye cataracts and slow growth.

INVESTIGATIONS: Specific blood enzyme tests abnormal.

TREATMENT: None available.

PROGNOSIS: Progresses to death by 10 years of age.

See also Hurler Syndrome

Scheuermann's Disease
DESCRIPTION: A relatively uncommon bone condition that affects the shape of the vertebrae in rapidly growing teenagers. May not be diagnosed until later in life when back pain occurs.

CAUSE: Vertebrae in the middle part of the back, behind the chest, do not grow properly, and instead of being roughly square in cross section, become slightly wedge-shaped.

SYMPTOMS: Back curves forward excessively giving a slightly humped appearance. Back movement is reduced and pain may occur due to compression of nerves.

INVESTIGATIONS: Diagnosis made by seeing abnormal vertebrae on a back X-ray.

TREATMENT: Physiotherapy to correct posture, anti-inflammatory medications and exercise. In rare cases surgery is required.

COMPLICATIONS: Osteoarthritis develops prematurely.

PROGNOSIS: No cure, but reasonable control of symptoms.

See also Osteoarthritis

Schistosomiasis
(Bilharzia)
DESCRIPTION: Fluke infestation transmitted by a species of snail that is found in fresh water streams, rivers and lakes in Egypt, tropical Africa as far south as Zimbabwe, the Caribbean and eastern South America. Often caught by bathing or washing in fresh water.

CAUSE: A microscopic animal (trematode fluke) that enters the body by burrowing through the skin, often of the foot. Once in the blood it travels to the veins around the large intestine, where eggs are laid. These pass out with the faeces or urine to infect water supplies. Once in fresh water, the eggs hatch, and the

485

larvae seek out and burrow into the flesh of specific species of fresh water snail. They mature in the snail, and emerge from it ready to enter and infect another human. Patients do not pass out all the eggs that are laid by the fluke, and they may spread to the liver, lungs or spinal cord to cause further symptoms.

SYMPTOMS: The first symptom is an itchy patch at the site of skin penetration. Varying symptoms then follow, depending on the areas affected by the fluke as it moves through the body, and the individual's reaction to those changes. Long-term symptoms include diarrhoea, abdominal pain and bloody urine.

INVESTIGATIONS: Diagnosis involves blood, urine and skin tests, and liver and gut biopsies.

TREATMENT: Difficult, particularly late in the disease. A number of drugs can be used to kill the fluke inside the body.

COMPLICATIONS: Damage caused to organs by the fluke may be permanent.

PROGNOSIS: Untreated may cause a low-grade chronic illness, or may progress to death in a matter of months. Result of treatment is good if commenced early in the course of the disease. Advanced disease may be incurable.

Schizophrenia

DESCRIPTION: A mental illness which causes abnormal behaviour and perceptions. When treatment starts or an attack passes, the patient returns to normal giving the impression of two different personalities, but this is not the case.

CAUSE: Exact cause unknown, but there is a family tendency and the environment in which the patient is raised, and emotional stress, may trigger a person to escape into schizophrenia.

SYMPTOMS: A distorted view of the world because of delusions and hallucinations. Patients often change the topic of conversation for no apparent reason, may not look after themselves, become dishevelled in appearance, withdrawn, and fail to communicate properly with others. Their mood and behaviour changes seem bizarre and they often believe that others are persecuting them. They may hear unfriendly voices, or have frightening hallucinations.

INVESTIGATIONS: No diagnostic blood or other tests.

TREATMENT: A wide range of effective medications (antipsychotics) such as clozapine, fluphenazine, olanzapine, promazine, risperidone, thioridazine, thiothixene and trifluoperazine can be given as tablets or injections to control the disease. Just as important are a supportive environment and psychological counselling for the patient and their family.

COMPLICATIONS: Suicide and harmful behaviour towards themselves and others are possible. Many patients refuse medication because they lack insight into their condition.

PROGNOSIS: Permanent cure is not usually possible, but well controlled if the patient remains on long term medication.

See also Diogenes Syndrome and other diseases listed under Psychiatric Conditions

Schmidt Syndrome

DESCRIPTION: Very rare condition in which there is inadequate production of hormones by both the thyroid and adrenal glands.

CAUSE: Autoimmune disorder in which the body inappropriately rejects its own tissue.

SYMPTOMS: Combined symptoms of hypothyroidism and Addison's disease (see separate entries).

INVESTIGATIONS: Diagnosed by specific blood tests that show low levels of thyroxine and cortisol.

TREATMENT: Treat both hypothyroidism and Addison's disease.

PROGNOSIS: No cure and management difficult.

See also Addison's Disease; Hypothyroidism

Schnyder Corneal Dystrophy
See Corneal Dystrophy

School Sores
See Impetigo

Schwachman Syndrome

DESCRIPTION: Rare disorder of white blood cells (neutrophils) and the pancreas.

CAUSE: Unknown, but may be inherited.

SYMPTOMS: Digestive disorders, diabetes, increased incidence of infections.

INVESTIGATIONS: Very low levels of neutrophils (neutropenia) and other abnormalities on blood tests.

TREATMENT: Infections and diabetes can be treated.

COMPLICATIONS: Very severe infections and poor food absorption.

PROGNOSIS: Usually fatal in childhood.

See also Kostmann Syndrome

Schwannoma

DESCRIPTION: Slow growing tumour that usually occurs in the acoustic (hearing) nerve (acoustic neuroma — see separate entry), and is formed from cells that normally act as the insulating sheath around the nerve (Schwann cells). Often occurs near the point where the nerve leaves the brain. These growths may also occur on other nerves leading from the brain and in the spinal cord.

CAUSE: May be inherited or arise spontaneously. Sometimes associated with von Recklinghausen's disease of multiple neurofibromatosis (see separate entry).

SYMPTOMS: Impaired function of the involved nerve. If the auditory nerve is involved, progressive deafness in one ear occurs.

INVESTIGATIONS: CT and MRI scans, and measuring brain waves when involved nerve stimulated (eg. when different sounds heard).

TREATMENT: Microsurgical removal of the Schwann cells from around the remaining nerve cells at an early stage of tumour development may result in preservation of nerve function and hearing. Radiation may be used for more advanced growths.

COMPLICATIONS: Damage to skull bone and other tissues around tumour.

PROGNOSIS: Not malignant. If left untreated will cause total loss of nerve function (eg. deafness in one ear) and eventually bone pain. Good results from treatment, but depends on stage of progression when diagnosed.

See also Acoustic Neuroma; von Recklinghausen's Disease of Multiple Neurofibromatosis

Sciatica

DESCRIPTION: Pain in the back and leg.

CAUSE: The pinching of a nerve as it emerges from the spinal cord and passes between two vertebrae in the lower back due to arthritis, ligament strains or disc damage. More sinister diseases (eg. bone cancer) may also be responsible. The sciatic nerve is made from several spinal nerves that join together in the middle of the buttock, at a point where the pain of sciatica is often first felt, then it runs down the back of the thigh and calf to the foot.

SYMPTOMS: Severe pain that spreads from the lower back to the buttock and then down one or both legs. The pain is felt where the nerve runs, not usually at the point in the back where the nerve is pinched. Shooting pains may be experienced all the way from the back to the foot.

INVESTIGATIONS: X-rays and CT scans of the lower back can usually determine where the nerve is damaged. In difficult cases, an MRI scan or myelogram (X-ray of dye injected into the back) may be performed.

TREATMENT: Pain killers, anti-inflammatory medications, physiotherapy, rest, heat, back braces, steroid or other injections into the back and occasionally surgery.

COMPLICATIONS: Severe nerve damage can cause temporary or eventually permanent paralysis of muscles or a leg.

PROGNOSIS: Most patients can be helped by adequate treatment.

See also Intervertebral Disc Prolapse and other diseases listed under Back Diseases

Scleritis

DESCRIPTION: Uncommon inflammation of the whites (sclera) of an eye. Numerous types recognised (eg. anterior scleritis, posterior scleritis, diffuse scleritis, nodular scleritis).

CAUSE: Often unknown, but may be associated with rheumatoid arthritis, polyarteritis nodosa, systemic lupus erythematosus and other autoimmune diseases.

SYMPTOMS: Redness, discomfort, and sometimes painful ulceration, of the sclera.

INVESTIGATIONS: No specific diagnostic tests.

TREATMENT: Anti-inflammatory or steroid eye drops and tablets.

COMPLICATIONS: Sclera may become thickened and affect vision. Cataracts and glaucoma (see separate entries) may occur in severe forms.

PROGNOSIS: Good response to treatment.
See also Episcleritis

Scleroderma
(Progressive Systemic Sclerosis)

DESCRIPTION: An inflammatory condition most commonly affecting the skin and gut, then the oesophagus (gullet), lungs, heart and other internal organs.

CAUSE: Auto-immune disease, in which the body inappropriately rejects its own tissue. Usually starts between 30 and 50 years of age, and women are more commonly affected.

SYMPTOMS: Vary widely but include thickening of the skin, arthritis that moves between joints, patchy changes in skin colouration, poor circulation to the hands, difficulty in swallowing, lung infections, fevers and diarrhoea.

INVESTIGATIONS: Blood tests show abnormalities but are not diagnostic. A biopsy (sample) of skin or other affected tissue confirms the diagnosis.

TREATMENT: Medications to relieve the symptoms.

COMPLICATIONS: Damage to vital organs such as the heart.

PROGNOSIS: No cure. Slowly progressive over many years. Men and the elderly deteriorate more rapidly.

See also CREST Syndrome; Morphoea

Scoliosis

DESCRIPTION: Abnormal curvature of the spine.

CAUSE: Minor degrees are seen in many teenagers as they go through periods of rapid growth, particularly if they have poor posture, but in some the deformity becomes severe. If one leg is shorter than the other due to injury or other causes, the pelvis will be tilted, and the spine will curve to compensate. Other causes include abnormal vertebrae in the back that may have been present since birth or damaged by a severe injury, diseases of the muscles that support the vertebral bones (eg. polio or quadriplegia), or spasm of muscles in cerebral palsy that can pull the backbone out of shape.

SYMPTOMS: Abnormal lateral (side to side) curvature of the spine. Only significant curvature warrants medical attention.

INVESTIGATIONS: When the patient touches their toes, looking from behind along the back, one side will be seen to rise higher than the other, even though the spine may appear relatively straight when erect. X-rays of the back are also abnormal.

TREATMENT: Initially, careful measurements are taken, and the patient is then checked at regular intervals to assess the progress of the scoliosis. If there is deterioration or the curvature exceeds 15-20 degrees, treatment is necessary, by means of physiotherapy, structured exercises, braces, or in severe cases surgery. Surgical techniques include the insertion of steel rods into the back to keep it straight, or fusing several vertebrae together in a straight line to prevent them from moving.

COMPLICATIONS: Permanent deformity is possible.

PROGNOSIS: The younger the onset of the problem, the greater the need for concern, but babies nearly always recover spontaneously. With proper medical care severe deformity is almost unknown.

See also Kyphoscoliosis; Kyphosis; Lordosis

Scrapie
See Creutzfeldt-Jakob Disease

Scrofula
('King's Evil')

DESCRIPTION: Tuberculosis occurring in the lymph nodes of the neck.

CAUSE: The bacterium *Mycobacterium tuberculosis.*

SYMPTOMS: Large, hard masses in the lymph nodes of the neck that may drain pus out onto the skin.

INVESTIGATIONS: Swabs taken from discharging lymph nodes are examined to confirm the diagnosis.

TREATMENT: Cutting out the affected lymph nodes and giving antituberculotic medications.

COMPLICATIONS: May spread from the lymph nodes to other organs including the lungs, brain and heart.

PROGNOSIS: Good with appropriate treatment, but permanent scarring usually occurs.

See also Tuberculosis

Scurvy
(Vitamin C Deficiency)

DESCRIPTION: The scourge of sailors on long voyages over two centuries ago, particularly voyages of exploration to places where fresh food supplies could not be relied upon, but a very uncommon condition today. Captain James Cook made a name for himself early in his career by insisting that all his crew had rations of lime juice (which contains high levels of vitamin C) every day.

CAUSE: Lack of ascorbic acid (vitamin C) in the diet. May occur in people on unusual fad diets or in malnourished alcoholics.

SYMPTOMS: In early stages vague tiredness and weakness occur. As the vitamin deficiency becomes more severe, bleeding into the skin, rashes, bleeding gums, joint pain and bleeding into joints, slow wound healing and tender bones are experienced. The patient becomes severely anaemic, and bleeds readily.

INVESTIGATIONS: Diagnosis confirmed by measuring ascorbic acid level in blood, and noting the marked anaemia.

TREATMENT: Between 100 and 300 mg. of vitamin C a day is required for treatment, while 50 mg. a day is sufficient for prevention.

COMPLICATIONS: In advanced cases the kidneys fail, the body swells, bleeding occurs in the brain, and death follows. Large doses of vitamin C may cause toxicity, particularly in children.

PROGNOSIS: Good response to treatment. Easily prevented.

Sea Sickness
See Motion Sickness

Seasonal Affective Disorder

DESCRIPTION: Common condition in far northern climates where there may be daylight for only two or three hours a day during winter.

CAUSE: Inappropriate time regulation by the body's internal clock, which is controlled by the hormone melatonin produced in the pineal gland at the front of the brain.

SYMPTOMS: Irritability and depression.

INVESTIGATIONS: No diagnostic tests.

TREATMENT: Living in very bright light for part of the day, antidepressant medications, or taking melatonin.

COMPLICATIONS: Suicide may occur in severe cases.

PROGNOSIS: Difficult to manage.

See also Depression

Sebaceous Cyst

DESCRIPTION: Cyst full of sebum (the oil that keeps our skin moist and supple) which is produced in sebaceous glands beneath the skin all over the body, and is discharged through small ducts.

CAUSE: In areas that become sweaty, dirty or injured it is possible to block the duct draining the sebaceous gland. Sebum continues to be produced, and a cyst slowly forms under the skin.

SYMPTOMS: Cysts usually appear on the back, chest and neck, are slightly soft and often have a tiny dimple at the point where the original duct opened onto the skin. Sometimes pressure in the cyst is sufficient for its contents to be discharged through the previously blocked duct, but the cyst usually reforms.

INVESTIGATIONS: Diagnosis confirmed by cutting out the cyst.

TREATMENT: Any cyst that is unsightly may be cut out. Infected cysts are treated with antibiotic tablets.

COMPLICATIONS: Cysts may become infected, and if antibiotics are not given soon enough, an abscess may form.

PROGNOSIS: Good result from surgery.

Sebaceous Naevus
See Naevus

Seborrhoeic Eczema
(Cradle Cap; Nappy Eczema)

DESCRIPTION: A widespread, common form of eczema that can occur at any age.

CAUSE: Due to inflammation of the oil producing sebaceous glands in the skin, but the cause of the inflammation is unknown.

SYMPTOMS: In infants, seborrhoeic eczema frequently affects the scalp to cause 'cradle cap' or the buttocks to cause 'nappy eczema'. Other frequently affected areas are the cheeks, neck, armpits, groin and folds behind the knees and elbows and under the breasts. In adults, it is responsible for some forms of dandruff. On the scalp, it appears as a red, scaly, greasy rash. In skin folds, the skin is red, moist and breaks down into tiny ulcers. On exposed areas such as the face, the rash is red, scaling and may contain tiny blisters.

INVESTIGATIONS: None normally necessary.

TREATMENT: The scalp is treated with a lotion or cream to remove the oil and scale, and regular shampooing. Tar solutions are applied in resistant cases. In other areas, mild steroid lotions or creams are used. Soap should be avoided and substitutes used.

COMPLICATIONS: There may be a secondary fungal infection present.

PROGNOSIS: Tends to be chronic and recurrent. Children often grow out of it in the early teens, but in adults it may persist intermittently for years.

See also Dandruff; Eczema

Seckel Syndrome

DESCRIPTION: Rare genetic abnormality.

CAUSE: Inherited, but both parents must be carriers for it to affect their children.

SYMPTOMS: Reduced growth as a foetus before birth, low set ears, hip and elbow dislocation, mental retardation and a beaked nose.

INVESTIGATIONS: None diagnostic.

TREATMENT: None available.

PROGNOSIS: Poor.

Secondary Cancer
See Metastatic Cancer

Second Childhood
See Alzheimer's Disease; Dementia

Seizure
See Epilepsy

Seminoma
See Testicular Cancer

Senile Dementia
See Alzheimer's Disease

Senile Vaginitis
See Atrophic Vaginitis

Septicaemia
(Blood Poisoning)

DESCRIPTION: A bacterial infection of the blood.

CAUSE: Infection usually starts in another part of the body, such as the lungs, tonsils (quinsy — see separate entry) or after childbirth (now very rare), but in some cases the origin of the infection may never be found. Many different bacterial infections have septicaemia as a complication.

SYMPTOMS: Patients are usually very ill, with a high fever, prostration and generalised aches and pains.

INVESTIGATIONS: Many different bacteria may be responsible for the infection, and it is important to identify them by blood tests before antibiotic treatment commences.

TREATMENT: Potent antibiotics by mouth, injection or drip infusion in hospital. The original site of infection must also be treated.

COMPLICATIONS: A small number of patients will have an overwhelming infection with resistant bacteria, which leads to death.

PROGNOSIS: Provided an appropriate antibiotic can be found, most patients can be cured.

See also Bacteremia; Infection; Quinsy; Septic Shock

Septic Arthritis
(Joint Infection)

DESCRIPTION: Uncommon but serious bacterial infection of a joint that requires urgent and effective treatment.

CAUSE: Responsible bacteria usually enter the joint through the bloodstream, but sometimes injury to the joint or adjacent bone can allow a bacteria to enter. May also follow an injection into, or the draining of fluid from a joint. Premature babies are at a particularly high risk.

SYMPTOMS: Starts with a fever and the sudden onset of severe pain in a joint that is tender to touch, swollen, hot, red, and painful to move. The knees, hips and wrists are most commonly involved.

INVESTIGATIONS: Blood tests show infection is present in the body, but not the location or type. Fluid drawn from the joint through a needle is cultured to identify the responsible bacteria. X-rays only show changes late in the disease.

TREATMENT: Culture of joint fluid should be started before treatment is commenced, so that the bacteria can be correctly identified. While awaiting results, antibiotics are started and are initially given by intramuscular injection. Regular removal of the infected fluid from the joint by needle aspiration or open operation, is also necessary. Further treatment involves hot compresses, elevation and immobilisation of the joint, and pain relieving medication. Gentle movement of the joint should commence under the supervision of a physiotherapist as recovery occurs.

COMPLICATIONS: Joint destruction, severe chronic arthritis, or complete fusion and stiffness of a joint can occur if the disease is not treated correctly.

PROGNOSIS: Recovery within a week to ten days is normal with good treatment.

See also other diseases listed under Arthritis

Septic Meningitis
See Meningitis

Septic Shock

DESCRIPTION: Widespread reaction to infection.

CAUSE: Severe bacterial infection of the blood (septicaemia).

SYMPTOMS: High fever, very low blood pressure, rapid breathing and heart rate, confusion, poor output of urine and eventually coma.

INVESTIGATIONS: Responsible bacteria identified by blood culture.

TREATMENT: Fluids by drip into a vein to increase blood pressure, and potent antibiotics into the drip. Management in intensive care unit and if necessary kidney dialysis and artificial respiration.

COMPLICATIONS: Permanent damage to organs from poor blood supply or blood clots (thrombosis).

PROGNOSIS: Mortality rate of 50% within a month in good hospitals, and further deaths later from organ damage. Survival rates better in the young, but worse in the elderly or debilitated.

See also Septicaemia; Shock

Serotonin Syndrome

DESCRIPTION: Rare complication of antidepressant medication use.

CAUSE: Caused by interaction between different antidepressants after inadequate rest period between stopping one medication and starting another, or interaction between antidepressants and other drugs (eg. pethidine, pseudoephedrine, dextromethorphan — last two found in cold remedies).

SYMPTOMS: Agitation, vomiting, tremor, muscle spasm, dizziness, incoordination, rapid heart rate, overactive reflexes and abnormal eye movements (nystagmus).

INVESTIGATIONS: None diagnostic.

TREATMENT: Stop all antidepressant medication, and medications given to reverse adverse effects (eg. cyproheptadine, diazepam).

COMPLICATIONS: Some patients develop a very high fever, flushing and diarrhoea.

PROGNOSIS: Good.

See also Neuroleptic Malignant Syndrome

Serum Hepatitis
See Hepatitis B

Serum Sickness

DESCRIPTION: An uncommon blood allergy reaction that may be immediate, or delayed for up to two weeks.

CAUSE: Reaction to a blood or serum (liquid part of blood without the cells) transfusion, or use of a blood product (eg. globulin or proteins). Uncommonly it may be caused by the use of a drug.

SYMPTOMS: Patient feels unwell, tired, nauseated and feverish. The lymph nodes in the neck, armpit and groin become enlarged, an itchy rash develops, cramps occur in the belly, and joints may become painful.

INVESTIGATIONS: None diagnostic, but blood tests show generalised abnormalities characteristic of an allergy.

TREATMENT: Antihistamines to counteract the allergy reaction, and steroids or adrenaline to treat the results of the reaction.

PROGNOSIS: May be mild and pass almost unnoticed, or a very severe condition that can lead to death in a few hours, depending on the severity of the reaction.

See also Allergy

Sex Problems
See Anorgasmia; Failure of Ejaculation; Frigidity; Impotence; Infertility, Female; Infertility, Male; Libido, Reduced; Penis, Short; Premature Ejaculation; Priapism; Retrograde Ejaculation; Vaginismus

Sexually Transmitted Diseases
(Venereal Diseases)
See AIDS (HIV); Amoebiasis; Chancroid; Crabs; Cytomegolovirus (CMV); Donavanosis; Gay Bowel Syndrome; Genital Herpes; Genital Warts; Giardiasis; Gonorrhoea; Granuloma Inguinale; Hepatitis B; Hepatitis C; Hepatitis D; Lice; Lymphogranuloma Venereum; Non-Specific Urethritis; Pelvic Inflammatory Disease; Syphilis; Thrush; Trichomoniasis, Venereal; Vaginitis, Bacterial

Sézary Syndrome

DESCRIPTION: Form of cancer that is a variant of mycosis fungoides (see separate entry) and starts in middle age.

CAUSE: Unknown.

SYMPTOMS: Persistently itchy patches of thick red skin, overlying hair loss on affected skin, and enlarged lymph nodes in neck, groin, armpits and elsewhere.

INVESTIGATIONS: Skin and lymph node biopsy abnormal, and a blood test reveals abnormal blood white cells.

TREATMENT: Low grade irradiation of skin, and cytotoxic drugs (chemotherapy).
COMPLICATIONS: May spread to other areas of the body. Nails may be damaged. Eventually progresses to leukaemia or a type of sarcoma.
PROGNOSIS: Very slowly progressive despite treatment.
See also Mycosis Fungoides; Sarcoma

SHAFT Syndrome

DESCRIPTION: Personality disorder. Disease name is an acronym for major symptom characteristics.
CAUSE: Form of neurosis that is a variation of Munchausen syndrome.
SYMPTOMS: Sad, hostile, anxious, frustrated, tenacious patient who praises a doctor excessively to obtain unnecessary surgery, then has worsening of imagined symptoms after surgery, for which the doctor is blamed.
INVESTIGATIONS: Extensive investigations invariably carried out, but all are normal.
TREATMENT: Psychotherapy.
PROGNOSIS: Poor, and patients often persist with symptoms long term.
See also Munchausen Syndrome

Shaking Palsy
See Parkinson's Disease

Sheehan Syndrome

DESCRIPTION: Varied progressive symptoms of pituitary gland failure that follows pregnancy. The pituitary gland lies under the brain and controls all the other hormone producing glands in the body.
CAUSE: Due to blood clot (thrombosis) in the blood vessels supplying the pituitary gland during labour.
SYMPTOMS: Heavy uterine bleeding after delivery of a baby in labour, failure of breast milk production, and failure of periods to return after delivery. Some patients have very low blood pressure (hypotension).
INVESTIGATIONS: Widespread abnormalities of hormone function in blood and urine tests.
TREATMENT: Replacement of missing hormones (eg. thyroxine, cortisone, oestrogens) by tablet or injection.
PROGNOSIS: No cure, but well controlled by treatment.
See also Hypopituitarism

Shell Shock
See Post-Traumatic Stress Disorder

Shigellosis
(Bacillary Dysentery; Bacterial Dysentery)

DESCRIPTION: A common intestinal disease in third-world countries and the poorer areas of some developed countries.

CAUSE: A number of different bacteria from the *Shigella* family can infect the gut under poor sanitary conditions. Spreads when bacteria in the faeces of a patient contaminates the food of another person.

SYMPTOMS: Severe intermittent abdominal pain, copious diarrhoea, blood and mucus mixed in with the faeces, and a high fever.

INVESTIGATIONS: Diagnosed by examining a sample of faeces for the presence of the infecting bacteria.

TREATMENT: Appropriate antibiotics, adequate fluid intake by an intravenous drip in severe cases, medications to relieve abdominal cramps, and a strict diet to avoid foods that may irritate the gut (eg. milk products, eggs and fatty foods). Carers should be very careful in the disposal of the faeces and soiled linen to prevent spread of the infection.

COMPLICATIONS: Severe dehydration may lead to blood clots (thrombosis) that damages the organ supplied by the affected artery.

PROGNOSIS: In children under three years of age and the elderly may be life-threatening. In older children and adults it can be readily treated, or may persist for several weeks without adequate treatment.

See also Campylobacter Enteritis; Cryptosporidiosis; Gastroenteritis; Giardiasis, Intestinal; Typhoid Fever

Shingles
(Herpes Zoster; Varicella)

DESCRIPTION: An infection of nerves and skin by the *Herpes zoster* virus.

CAUSE: Shingles is caused by the *Herpes zoster* virus, which is the same virus that causes chickenpox (see separate entry), and is usually caught as a child. The virus never leaves the body, but migrates to the roots of nerves along the spinal cord, where it remains inactive lifelong. At times of stress, the virus may reactivate and move along the nerve to cause the skin and other tissues to become very painful. Far more common in older people, and uncommon in children. You cannot catch shingles from another person, but a child who has not had chickenpox may catch this from a person who has active shingles.

SYMPTOMS: An acutely tender blistering rash occurs, often in a belt-like line on one side of the body. Even the slightest touch causes severe shooting pain. Any nerve may be affected, and it can occur on the abdomen or chest (most common sites), or on the face or legs.

INVESTIGATIONS: None normally necessary, but if required the diagnosis can be confirmed by taking special swabs from a sore.

TREATMENT: Shingles can be cured by specific antiviral tablets, but only if treatment is started within 72 hours of the rash first appearing. If treatment is neglected until after three days from the onset of the rash, the only treatment is pain-killers, drying antiseptic lotions and mild sedatives. Steroids may be used in severe cases.

COMPLICATIONS: Occasionally leaves permanent scars, particularly on the face. A small number of elderly people can develop chronic inflammation in the nerve, and pain that persists for years (**post-herpetic neuralgia**). The worst complication occurs if nerves around the eye and ear are involved, when dizziness, ear noises and rarely blindness may occur (see Ramsay-Hunt syndrome entry).

PROGNOSIS: The rash dries out slowly and disappears over several weeks, usually healing completely. The pain is slower to disappear, and may last a month longer than the rash. The vast majority of patients make an excellent recovery.

See also Chickenpox; Ramsay-Hunt Syndrome

Shin Splints
(Tibial Stress Syndrome)

DESCRIPTION: Inflammation of the periosteum (thin membrane) that covers the tibia (larger of the lower leg bones).

CAUSE: Excessive stress on the periosteum at the point where major muscles attach to the back and outside surfaces of the tibia, particularly in novice athletes who exercise excessively. Running on a hard surface is notorious for triggering the condition because of the jarring at every step.

SYMPTOMS: Pain and tenderness of the tibia that is worsened by running, jumping or sometimes just walking.

INVESTIGATIONS: None necessary.

TREATMENT: Prolonged rest and anti-inflammatory medications.

PROGNOSIS: Recovers slowly with correct treatment.

Shock
(Shock Syndrome)

DESCRIPTION: Any condition in which there is inadequate circulation of blood around the body.

CAUSE: Many serious causes including loss of blood from a major injury, severe burns, several fractures, extensive bleeding into the gut from an ulcer or other disease, massive diarrhoea, various forms of heart damage and failure, lung disease (eg. thrombosis or embolism), heart valve disease or septicaemia (see separate entry).

SYMPTOMS: The patient collapses, is obviously very ill, pale, sweaty, has a weak thready pulse, the blood pressure is very low, and may become unconscious. Further symptoms depend on the cause, and may vary from pain to shortness of breath and fever.

INVESTIGATIONS: Extensive blood, urine, X-ray and other tests performed in order to determine cause.

TREATMENT: First aid involves lying the patient flat with legs raised if conscious to improve blood flow to the brain, or lying down flat and on the side if unconscious, controlling any bleeding, maintaining body temperature by the use of warm blankets, splinting fractures, protecting burnt areas, and if the patient deteriorates, mouth-to-mouth resuscitation and external cardiac massage may be necessary. In a hospital intensive care unit fluids or blood are given through a drip into a vein, and oxygen and pain-killing injections are given when appropriate. Further treatment depends on the cause and may include a wide range of drugs and possibly surgery.

COMPLICATIONS: Permanent damage to almost any organ (including the brain and heart) may occur due to poor blood supply or blood clots (thrombosis).

PROGNOSIS: Depends upon a multitude of factors including the cause of the shock, the patient's age and general health, and the speed with which medical assistance can be obtained.

See also Anaphylaxis; Defibrination Syndrome; Hypotension; Septic Shock

Short Bowel Syndrome

DESCRIPTION: Complication of extensive bowel surgery.

CAUSE: Usually due to removal of a large part of the bowel for Crohn's disease or cancer.

SYMPTOMS: Fatty foul smelling diarrhoea, pernicious anaemia and osteomalacia (see separate entries).

INVESTIGATIONS: Fat levels in faeces very high.

TREATMENT: Antidiarrhoeal medications, low fat diet, folic acid supplements and vitamin B12 injections.

PROGNOSIS: No cure, but reasonable control.

Short Penis
See Penis, Short

Short-Sighted
(Myopia)

DESCRIPTION: Developmental vision defect.

CAUSE: The eye ball is too long, and light rays from distant objects are focussed in front of the retina (layer of light sensitive cells at back of the eye).

SYMPTOMS: Distant objects appear blurred while close objects are clearly seen. Reading is easy but moving around difficult.

INVESTIGATIONS: Specific tests on vision using lenses of varying strength.

TREATMENT: Spectacles with accurately prescribed corrective lenses. In some people, laser keratotomy, in which the shape of the cornea (outer layer of the eye) is permanently reshaped, may cure the problem. This procedure is not carried out before the late teen years as vision can change with growth.

PROGNOSIS: Very good.

See also Long-Sighted; Presbyopia

Shoulder Dislocation

DESCRIPTION: Disruption of the joint between the scapula (shoulder blade) and humerus (upper arm bone). The shoulder is a ball and socket joint, but the socket is very shallow to allow maximum movement. A cuff of muscles and ligaments surrounds the joint to keep it in position. This joint can move through a greater range than any other, but as a result is relatively unstable, and it is the most commonly dislocated major joint.

CAUSE: If excessive force is applied to the shoulder joint, it may dislocate forwards, or less commonly, backwards.

SYMPTOMS: Patients experience severe pain, do not like the shoulder joint to be moved, and often hold the elbow of the affected arm at right angles and against their side with the other hand.

INVESTIGATIONS: Diagnosed by X-rays.

TREATMENT: The dislocated shoulder can be put back into place by one of a number of different techniques, often with little or no anaesthetic if treated immediately, or after giving pain-killing injections or a brief general anaesthetic if there is any delay. After treatment the arm is kept in a sling for a month.

COMPLICATIONS: Any shoulder dislocation is associated with tearing and damage to the surrounding muscles and ligaments of the rotator cuff and joint capsule. A dislocation may be associated with a fracture. Recurrent shoulder dislocations may occur by merely picking up a heavy object or raising the arm and these patients require an operation (the Putti-Platt procedure) to repair the damaged tissues and prevent further dislocations.

PROGNOSIS: Good after one dislocation, but after further dislocations surgery is advisable, and is usually very successful.

See also Dislocation

Shoulder-Hand Syndrome

DESCRIPTION: Disorder of shoulder and hand that is more common in middle aged diabetics.

CAUSE: Unknown, but over use may play a part.

SYMPTOMS: Variable painful disorders of hand and shoulder of one arm, shoulder arthritis and Sudeck's atrophy of hand and wrist (see separate entry).

INVESTIGATIONS: None diagnostic.

TREATMENT: Pain killers, passive exercise, steroid injections, and manipulation while under a general anaesthetic for shoulder. Physiotherapy, medication (eg. trifluoperazine), pain killers, prednisone tablets and surgery to cut sympathetic nerves for hand.

PROGNOSIS: Poor if treatment delayed.

Shoulder Impingement Syndrome

DESCRIPTION: Painful tissue inflammation and pinching between bones in shoulder.

CAUSE: Overuse or inappropriate use of shoulder joint.

SYMPTOMS: Pain at top of shoulder in arc of movement between 60 and 120° when moving arm away from body.

INVESTIGATIONS: Diagnosis confirmed if local anaesthetic injected into top of shoulder joint temporarily relieves pain.

TREATMENT: Rest, anti-inflammatory drugs, corticosteroid injections into shoulder, physiotherapy, and surgery to release trapped tissue.
PROGNOSIS: Good with appropriate treatment.

Shy-Drager Syndrome
DESCRIPTION: Severe form of multiple system failure.
CAUSE: Unknown.
SYMPTOMS: Low blood pressure, reduced sweating, slight tremor, difficulty in speaking, rigidity, poor coordination, impotence, dizziness, varying muscle paralysis and incontinence.
INVESTIGATIONS: MRI scan of the brain abnormal.
TREATMENT: Unsatisfactory. Care in postural changes, elastic stockings, support girdle and medication (eg. fludrocortisone, ephedrine sulfate).
COMPLICATIONS: Fainting with changes in position.
PROGNOSIS: Progressive to death in 5-7 years.

Sialadenitis
See Sialitis

Sialitis
(Sialadenitis)
DESCRIPTION: Infection or inflammation of one or more of the three salivary glands on each side of the mouth (the parotid, submandibular and submental glands) that supply the saliva to the mouth. If the parotid gland (which is situated at the angle of the jaw and is the largest of the glands) alone is infected the condition is called **parotitis**.
CAUSE: May be caused by a stone in the duct of the salivary gland (see salivary stone entry), may be associated with Sjögren syndrome (see separate entry), a tumour, or may start for no apparent reason.
SYMPTOMS: Acutely painful swelling of the gland which may exude pus into the mouth.
INVESTIGATIONS: None diagnostic.
TREATMENT: Potent antibiotics that are often given by an intravenous drip, and massage of the gland to expel any pus.
COMPLICATIONS: If the infection is not adequately treated an abscess may form.
PROGNOSIS: Good with appropriate treatment.

Sicard Syndrome
(Collet-Sicard Syndrome)
DESCRIPTION: Damage to nerves from brain that control muscles in the head and neck.
CAUSE: Due to a tumour (eg. of parotid salivary gland) or injury involving cranial nerves 9, 10, 11 and 12.
SYMPTOMS: Paralysis of muscles in the larynx, tongue, pharynx, palate and neck on one side.

501

INVESTIGATIONS: CT or MRI scan used to detect tumour.
TREATMENT: Treat cause if possible.
PROGNOSIS: Usually no cure.

Sicca Syndrome

DESCRIPTION: Failure of salivary and tear (lacrimal) glands.
CAUSE: May be complication of Sjögren syndrome, a drug reaction or autoimmune disease.
SYMPTOMS: Swelling of salivary and lacrimal glands, dry mouth, dry eyes, dry vagina and dry throat.
INVESTIGATIONS: Salivary gland biopsy diagnostic.
TREATMENT: Artificial tears, saliva and lubricants.
PROGNOSIS: Self-limiting benign condition.
See also Mikulicz Disease

Sick Building Syndrome

DESCRIPTION: Condition affecting workers in air conditioned buildings.
CAUSE: In order to conserve energy, some large air conditioned buildings allow minimal amounts of fresh air into circulation with each cycle. This allows organic solvents (eg. from photocopiers, glues, paints), fungal spores, pollens, dusts and other contaminants to recirculate in increasing concentrations, particularly if the air conditioning filters are poorly maintained.
SYMPTOMS: Residents and workers in the building develop snuffly noses, eye irritation, dry skin, headaches and tiredness. The longer they spend in the building, the worse the symptoms become.
INVESTIGATIONS: Examination and culture of dust in air conditioning filters.
TREATMENT: Increase the amount of fresh air entering building and carefully maintain filters.
PROGNOSIS: Good.

Sickle Cell Anaemia
(Haemoglobin S Disease)

DESCRIPTION: A form of abnormal red cell development in Negroes.
CAUSE: Inherited condition that causes red blood cells to become sickle shaped (like a crescent moon) rather than round because of an abnormal form of haemoglobin called haemoglobin S. The abnormal gene is found only in Negroes.
SYMPTOMS: Victims are tired and weak, have large spleens, may become jaundiced (yellow), heal poorly, develop gallstones easily and cope poorly with infections.
INVESTIGATIONS: Adults carrying the abnormal gene can be identified by blood tests, and if two carriers marry, one in four of their children will suffer from sickle cell anaemia. Can be diagnosed before birth by amniocentesis or other tests on the unborn child. After birth, examining blood under a microscope reveals the abnormal cells.

TREATMENT: Treatment with folic acid supplements and occasional transfusions control most cases. Maintaining adequate water intake and treating infections early are important.

COMPLICATIONS: Clumping of the abnormal red cells may block small arteries, cause severe pain in wide areas of the body and permanently damage the heart, liver and other organs.

PROGNOSIS: There is no cure but its effects can usually be controlled. Interestingly, the disease gives protection against malaria.

See also Anaemia

Sick Sinus Syndrome
(Sinus Bradycardia)

DESCRIPTION: Abnormality of heart rhythm.

CAUSE: Due to failure of heart pacemaker (sinus node) or nerve conduction in heart.

SYMPTOMS: Variable heart rate from brief standstill or very slow to markedly rapid beat or atrial fibrillation (see separate entry) and resultant fainting or collapse.

INVESTIGATIONS: Continuous ECG reading (Holter monitor) for 24 hours abnormal.

TREATMENT: Artificial pacemaker and drugs to stabilise heart rhythm.

COMPLICATIONS: Heart attack and death may rarely occur.

PROGNOSIS: Good control from treatment once diagnosed.

SIDS
See Cot Death

Sight Problems
See Amblyopia; Astigmatism; Cataract; Glaucoma; Long Sighted; Presbyopia; Short Sighted; Squint

Silicosis

DESCRIPTION: Permanent lung damage caused by the long-term inhalation of dust particles.

CAUSE: The inhalation of tiny particles of silica in workers involved in rock quarrying, stone cutting, tunnelling, pottery and those who use diatomaceous earth, resulting in the formation of multiple small hard round nodules in the lung.

SYMPTOMS: No symptoms in early stages of the disease. In advanced cases there is shortness of breath, and a poor tolerance to exercise.

INVESTIGATIONS: Chest X-ray shows characteristic abnormalities.

TREATMENT: None available.

COMPLICATIONS: Lung infections such as pneumonia.

PROGNOSIS: No cure, and slowly progressive over many years.

See also Asbestosis; Pneumoconiosis; Talcosis

503

Simmonds' Disease
See Hypopituitarism

Sinus Bradycardia
See Sick Sinus Syndrome

Sinusitis

DESCRIPTION: A bacterial or viral infection of the moist membrane that lines the air filled sinuses in the face. They lie in the skull bone below, above, between and behind the eyes and are connected together and to the nose by small holes and drainage tubes.

CAUSE: Some people secrete excess amounts of fluid in the sinuses because of hay fever, smoking or irritating fumes, while others may have drainage holes and tubes that are too small to cope with the secretions produced. If bacteria or viruses infect the sinus lining or secretions, sinusitis results.

SYMPTOMS: Thick and pus-like phlegm drains from the nose and down the throat, the face is very painful and tender, and there is a fever, headache and tiredness.

INVESTIGATIONS: X-rays of the sinuses shows the abnormal presence of fluid. Swabs may be taken from the back of the nose so that the type of bacteria causing the infection can be determined and the correct treatment selected.

TREATMENT: Appropriate antibiotics when the cause is bacterial, and other medications to dry phlegm and clear the sinuses. Inhalations of steam and nasal decongestant drops are beneficial. In patients who suffer from repeated attacks, surgical procedures to more effectively drain the sinuses can be performed.

COMPLICATIONS: Infection may spread to the middle ear, and in severe cases, it may be necessary to insert needles through the nose into the sinuses to wash out the pus. Untreated the infection can spread to the teeth, eyes or brain, and abscesses may form.

PROGNOSIS: Most settle quickly with appropriate treatment, but recurrences common.

See also Cold, Common

Six-Week Colic
See Infantile Colic

Sjögren-Larsson Syndrome

DESCRIPTION: Rare disease of skin and brain.

CAUSE: Inherited trait, but both parents must be carriers.

SYMPTOMS: Widespread thick dry scaly skin, and muscle spasms.

INVESTIGATIONS: None diagnostic.

PROGNOSIS: No cure.

Sjögren Syndrome

DESCRIPTION: A chronic widespread inflammatory condition.

CAUSE: Auto-immune disease in which the body inappropriately rejects tissue. Closely related to rheumatoid arthritis, but affects more organs.

SYMPTOMS: Common symptoms include widespread arthritis, dry eyes, dry mouth, dry skin and dry throat. Other symptoms may include difficulty in swallowing, decaying teeth, loss of taste and smell, and a hoarse voice. Nearly all patients are women, and it usually commences in the fifth decade.

INVESTIGATIONS: Diagnosed by specific blood tests.

TREATMENT: Anti-inflammatory drugs, steroids (eg. prednisone), and a number of unusual drugs such as gold by injection or tablet, antimalarial drugs (eg. chloroquine) penicillamine (not the antibiotic), and cell-destroying drugs (cytotoxics). Artificial tears and skin moisturisers, and good dental hygiene are also necessary.

COMPLICATIONS: Complications may involve inflammation of the pancreas, thyroid and other organs.

PROGNOSIS: No cure, but reasonable long-term control is usually possible.

See also Rheumatoid Arthritis

Skin Cancer

DESCRIPTION: Various forms of skin cancer vary from the relatively innocuous to those which can spread rapidly enough to eventually kill.

CAUSE: Usually caused by sun exposure, primarily in childhood, but some chemicals may also be responsible and there is sometimes a familial tendency. Tropical nations with a predominantly white-skinned population have a far higher incidence.

SYMPTOMS: Fall into several different categories — squamous cell carcinomas (SCC), intraepithelial carcinoma (IEC), basal cell carcinomas (BCC), Bowen's disease and melanomas are the most common and are dealt with separately. Signs to watch for in a spot or sore that may indicate that it is a skin cancer are any irregularity in colour, shape or outline; soreness or itchiness; bleeding or weeping.

INVESTIGATIONS: Biopsy can give a definitive diagnosis, but may be more practical to excise whole growth.

TREATMENT: Prevention involves protecting the skin from the sun. May be treated by freezing with liquid nitrogen, diathermy (burning), cutting out the growth, injecting anti-cancer drugs in and under it, or applying acid or anticancer ointments.

PROGNOSIS: Depends on type and stage.

See also Basal Cell Carcinoma; Bowen's Disease; Intraepithelail Carcinoma; Melanoma; Squamous Cell Carcinoma of the Skin

Skin Diseases

See Acne; Albinism; Allergic Eczema; Alopecia Areata; Anthrax; Athlete's Foot; Atopic Eczema; Baldness; Basal Cell Carcinoma; Bed Sore; Blastomycosis; Bloch-Sulzberger Syndrome; Blue Naevus; Boil; Bowen's Disease; Bunion; Capillaritis; Cellulitis; Cold Sore; Contact Dermatitis; Cutaneous Larva Migrans; Cutaneous Leischmaniasis; Dandruff; Dermatitis; Dermatitis Artefacta; Dermatitis Herpetiformis; Dermatofibroma; Dermatomyositis; Discoid Eczema; Discoid Lupus Erythematosus; Disseminated Superficial Actinic Porokeratosis; Dysplastic Naevus Syndrome; Eczema; Ehlers-Danlos Syndrome; Epidermolysis Bullosa; Erysipelas; Erythema Nodosum; Exfoliative Dermatitis; Frostbite; Fungal Infection; Genital Warts; Gianotti Crosti Syndrome; Goltz Syndrome; Gorlin-Goltz Syndrome; Granuloma Annulare; Granuloma Inguinale; Grover's Disease; Haemangioma; Harlequin Syndrome; Henoch-Schoenlein Syndrome; Hidradenitis Suppurativa; Hives; Hyperkeratosis; Hypervitaminosis A; Ichthyosis; Impetigo; Intertrigo; Intraepithelial Carcinoma; Itchy Upper Arm Syndrome; Keratoacanthoma; Kerion; Klippel-Trenaunay Syndrome; Leprosy; Lichen Simplex; Lipoma; Loose Anagen Syndrome; Melanoma; Molluscum Contagiosum; Mycosis Fungoides; Nappy Rash; Necrotising Fasciitis; Neurodermatitis; Notalgia Paraesthetica; Osler-Rendu-Weber Disease; Pemphigoid; Pemphigus; Photodermatitis; Photosensitive Eczema; Pityriasis Rosea; Pityriasis Versicolor; Plantar Wart; Poikiloderma of Civatte; Pompholyx; Porphyria Cutanea Tarda; Psoriasis; Razor Rash; Rhinophyma; Rosacea; Rothmund-Thomson Syndrome; Scabies; Scalded Skin Syndrome; Scleroderma; Sebaceous Cyst; Sebborhoeic Eczema; Sézary Syndrome; Shingles; Sjögren-Larsson Syndrome; Skin Cancer; Spider Naevi; Squamous Cell Carcinoma of the Skin; Stretch Marks; Subcutaneous Emphysema; Sweet Syndrome; Systemic Mastocytosis; Telangiectasia Eruptiva Macularis Perstans; Telogen Effluvium; Tinea; Ulcer, Skin; Ulcer, Venous; Urticaria Pigmentosa; Varicose Eczema; Vitiligo; von Recklinghausen's Disease of Multiple Neurofibromatosis; Warts; Whitlow etc.

Skin Ulcer
See Ulcer, Skin

Slapped Cheek Disease
See Fifth Disease

SLE
See Systemic Lupus Erythematosus

Sleep Apnoea
DESCRIPTION: A cessation of breathing (apnoea) during sleep.

CAUSE: Most common cause in overweight middle-aged men is a complete relaxation of the small muscles at the back of the throat, which allows the tissue to become very soft, flabby and collapse as the patient breathes in, closing off the throat and preventing breathing. Snoring is caused in the same way. The other cause tends to occur in elderly men with high blood pressure and is due to suppression of the urge to breathe by the brain during very deep sleep.

SYMPTOMS: Breathing stops for periods from 10 to 60 seconds on many occasions while asleep, resulting in tiredness during the day, morning headaches, personality changes, poor concentration, bed-wetting and impotence. The sleeping partner complains about the patient's loud snoring and thrashing restless sleep.

INVESTIGATIONS: Diagnosis is best made in a sleep laboratory, where the patient's sleep and breathing pattern can be monitored through an entire night.

TREATMENT: Weight loss, and avoiding alcohol, sedatives and smoking. In persistent cases a small mask is fitted to the patient's nose, and air is blown up the nose at a slight pressure with a small electrically driven blower (continuous positive airway pressure — CPAP). In severe cases surgery to the back of the throat and nose to remove the uvula and part of the soft palate opens the airway.

COMPLICATIONS: Minor brain damage may occur with every episode of apnoea, that eventually leads to a noticeable deficit in brain function.

PROGNOSIS: A significant deterioration in the quality of life may occur unless successfully treated.

See also Snoring

Sleeping Sickness
(African Trypanosomiasis)

DESCRIPTION: Parasitic disease of lymph nodes and the brain that only occurs in tropical Africa.

CAUSE: The tiny parasite *Trypanosoma brucei* (of which there are three further subtypes), which is transmitted from game animals, cattle and sheep to humans by the bite of the tsetse fly.

SYMPTOMS: A sore develops at the site of the tsetse fly bite, followed a few days later by tender and enlarged lymph nodes in the groin armpit and neck, fever, headache, rashes and joint pain. Often there are week long periods of perfect health, followed by a recurrence of the symptoms. As the disease progresses, the patient loses weight, becomes very tired and, as the brain becomes involved, wants to sleep constantly.

INVESTIGATIONS: Diagnosed by specific blood tests.

TREATMENT: Travellers to tropical Africa should avoid tsetse bites by wearing trousers and long-sleeved shirts, using insect nets at night and an insect repellent by day. Drugs are available to treat the disease, but early treatment is essential.

COMPLICATIONS: Permanent brain damage after recovery.

PROGNOSIS: May take many months to run its course but without treatment, it is almost invariably fatal.

See also Chaga's Disease

Slipped Disc
See Intervertebral Disc Prolapse

Slipping Rib Syndrome

DESCRIPTION: Abnormality of the lower ribs.

CAUSE: Injury to chest or developmental abnormality.

SYMPTOMS: The cartilage that normally attaches the end of the tenth rib to the lower end of the breast bone (sternum), becomes unattached and overrides the rib above causing pain.

INVESTIGATIONS: Chest X-ray abnormal.

TREATMENT: Usually none required, but if particularly annoying can be injected with a mixture of a steroid and local anaesthetic, or cartilage can be removed by surgery.

PROGNOSIS: Usually a nuisance rather than serious.

See also Twelfth Rib Syndrome

Sly Syndrome

DESCRIPTION: A rare congenital condition in which children are unable to eliminate certain substances (mucopolysaccharides) from the body that starts at one to two years of age.

CAUSE: Inherited abnormality of the metabolic system (mucopolysaccharidosis) that is closely related to Hurler syndrome.

SYMPTOMS: Recurrent respiratory infections, enlarged liver and spleen, excessive forward curvature of the spine, heart murmurs, eye cataracts and slow growth.

INVESTIGATIONS: Specific blood enzyme tests abnormal.

TREATMENT: None effective.

PROGNOSIS: Progresses to death by 10 years of age.

See also Hurler Syndrome

Small Cell Carcinoma of the Lung
See Lung Cancer

Small Penis
See Penis, Short

Smallpox
(Variola Major)

DESCRIPTION: The first disease in history to be totally eradicated by vaccination, the last case occurring in Somalia in 1978. Vaccination is no longer necessary anywhere in the world.

CAUSE: Highly contagious virus infection.

SYMPTOMS: Blistering sores on the skin, severe headache and high fever.

INVESTIGATIONS: None normally necessary, but diagnosis could be confirmed by specific blood tests.

TREATMENT: None available, but prevented by a vaccination.
COMPLICATIONS: Permanent skin scarring.
PROGNOSIS: More than half the patients died.
See also Vaccinia

Smith-Lemli-Opitz Syndrome

DESCRIPTION: Genetic abnormality causing varied deformities.
CAUSE: Inherited, but both parents must be carriers.
SYMPTOMS: Droopy eyelids, narrow forehead, mental retardation, abnormal penis, malformed nostrils and webbed toes.
INVESTIGATIONS: None diagnostic.
TREATMENT: Surgical correction of deformities.
PROGNOSIS: No cure.

Smith-Magenis Syndrome

DESCRIPTION: Rare genetic abnormality causing head and face deformities.
CAUSE: Congenital condition localised to chromosome 17.
SYMPTOMS: Small abnormally shaped head, underdeveloped face, protruding lower jaw and hoarse voice.
INVESTIGATIONS: Specific chromosomal analysis abnormal.
TREATMENT: None available.
PROGNOSIS: No cure.

Smith's Fracture

DESCRIPTION: The wrist is bent forward excessively to cause a fracture of the forearm bones (ulna and radius) just above the wrist.
CAUSE: Falling onto the back of the outstretched hand.
SYMPTOMS: Pain, tenderness, swelling, deformity and loss of function of the forearm and wrist.
INVESTIGATIONS: Diagnosed by an X-ray.
TREATMENT: The bones must be put back into place under an anaesthetic and held in position by plaster.
COMPLICATIONS: Persistent deformity if incorrectly aligned.
PROGNOSIS: Normally heal well after six weeks in plaster in an adult, three to four weeks in a child.
See also Colles' Fracture; Fracture

Smokers Foot
See Buerger's Disease

Smoking
Diseases that may be caused or aggravated by smoking include—
Asbestosis; Amblyopia; Aneurysm; Angina; Asthma; Bronchiectasis; Bronchitis;
Buerger's Disease; Cattarh; Cervical Cancer; Common Cold; Cor Pulmonale;

Emphysema; Histiocytosis X; Hypercholesterolaemia; Hypertension; Laryngitis; Laryngotracheobronchitis; Legionnaire's Disease; Lung Cancer; Mesothelioma; Mouth Cancer; Oesophageal Cancer; Osteoporosis; Pneumoconniosis; Pneumonia; Reflux Oesophagitis; Sleep Apnoea; Snoring; Tachycardia; Talcosis; Thrombosis; Ulcer, Peptic and many others.

Snake Bite

DESCRIPTION: Bite from a snake. More serious in a child than an adult because the proportion of venom relative to body size is greater.

CAUSE: Snakes usually retreat from humans intruding into their habitat unless surprised or cornered. Most non-venomous snakes do not bite (the carpet python is an exception).

SYMPTOMS: Nausea, vomiting, headache, giddiness, double vision, drowsiness, tightening in the chest, diarrhoea, sweating, and difficulty in breathing may occur from 15 minutes to two hours after the bite. May be reddening, swelling, bruising or persistent bleeding at the site of the bite.

INVESTIGATIONS: The responsible snake can be identified by taking swabs from around the bite site. Specific blood and other tests will be used to monitor a patient's progress in hospital.

TREATMENT: First aid:—

— keep the victim calm and move them as little as possible to prevent spread of poison.

— apply pressure directly to the bite.

— if the bite is on a limb, apply pressure immobilisation by bandaging the limb firmly starting at the bitten area and working to the fingers or toes, then back up the limb to the armpit or groin.

— immobilise the limb with a splint (eg. a small branch) or by bandaging it to the other limb.

— check the victim's breathing and pulse regularly, and give mouth-to-mouth resuscitation if breathing stops, and cardiopulmonary resuscitation if the pulse stops.

— get medical assistance as soon as possible.

Antivenenes are available for all poisonous snake bites.

COMPLICATIONS: Ulceration and permanent damage to tissue around site of bite.

PROGNOSIS: In developed countries with good health care, only 2% of bites from potentially deadly snakes are now fatal.

Snapping Scapula Syndrome

DESCRIPTION: Abnormality of the shoulder blade (scapula).

CAUSE: Falling heavily on the shoulder or upper back damages the scapula and causes a bony spur to develop.

SYMPTOMS: Dull ache along the inside edge of the scapula and a loud snapping sound when the shoulder is used to move the arm away from the body.

INVESTIGATIONS: X-ray may show bony spur.

TREATMENT: Avoid movements that cause the snap, inject tender area with a steroid, or surgery to remove bony spur.

COMPLICATIONS: May cause persistent pain despite treatment.

PROGNOSIS: Most cases settle spontaneously, and most of the remainder with appropriate treatment.

Snoring

CAUSE: May occur intermittently during colds, flu or throat infections because of the excess production of phlegm and the swelling of tissues, but in persistent cases it is due to the vibration of the soft part at the back of the palate on the roof of the mouth with the movement of air.

SYMPTOMS: Harsh rough noise produced by the movement of air in and out of the throat and nose with breathing during sleep.

INVESTIGATIONS: If severe, may need to be investigated in a sleep laboratory, where the patient can be monitored through an entire night.

TREATMENT: Changing the position during sleep from the back to the side, using pillows or straps if necessary. Patients should lose weight if obese, and stop sedatives, alcohol and smoking. Nose clips and dilating springs may prove successful. Sometimes medications (eg. antidepressants, respiratory stimulants, anti-inflammatory drugs, steroids) may be beneficial. In very severe cases surgery to remove part of the soft palate can allow a clear airway and stop the problem.

COMPLICATIONS: Sleep apnoea when the breathing stops completely for up to a minute.

PROGNOSIS: Control eventually possible if patient is prepared to follow a full treatment program.

See also Sleep Apnoea

Snow Blindness
See Keratitis

Solar Keratosis
See Hyperkeratosis

Solar Urticaria
See Photodermatitis

Somatisation Disorder
See Briquet Syndrome

Soto Syndrome

DESCRIPTION: Developmental abnormality.

CAUSE: Inherited trait.

SYMPTOMS: Developmental delay during childhood, prominent forehead, reverse eye slant, and accelerated late childhood growth resulting in normal adult stature.

INVESTIGATIONS: EEG (electroencephalogram) abnormal, and CT brain scan shows dilated chambers (ventricles).
TREATMENT: None necessary.
PROGNOSIS: Good.

Spastic
See Cerebral Palsy

Spastic Colon
See Irritable Bowel Syndrome

'Speed'
See Amphetamine Abuse

Spherocytic Anaemia
See Spherocytosis

Spherocytosis
(Spherocytic Anaemia)
DESCRIPTION: Uncommon form of anaemia caused by abnormal red blood cells.
CAUSE: Inherited condition that causes red blood cells to swell and become more rounded (spherical) than they should be. These large cells cannot fit through the smallest capillaries, block them, and damage organs such as the spleen.
SYMPTOMS: Severity can vary markedly from one patient to another. Most patients are ill from soon after birth with weakness, jaundice (yellow skin) from excess red cell destruction and an enlarged spleen.
INVESTIGATIONS: Diagnosed by the abnormal appearance of red blood cells seen through a microscope on a blood film.
TREATMENT: Folic acid supplements and surgery to remove the spleen, which is responsible for the anaemia by destroying too many red cells.
COMPLICATIONS: The incidence of gall stone formation is far higher than average.
PROGNOSIS: No cure, but reasonable control usually possible.
See also Anaemia

Spider Bite
See Funnel Web Spider Bite; Red-Back Spider Bite

Spider Naevi
(Telangiectasia)
DESCRIPTION: Over dilation of a capillary that becomes visible on the skin.
CAUSE: Commonly caused by sun damage to the skin, but pregnancy and a number of diseases may also be responsible including liver failure, an overactive thyroid gland, alcoholism and rheumatoid arthritis.
SYMPTOMS: Dilated blood vessels on the nose and cheeks that look like tiny red spiders can be seen diverging from a central point.

INVESTIGATIONS: None necessary.

TREATMENT: Each individual naevus can be treated by cryotherapy (freezing), laser or diathermy (electrical heat) to the central blood vessel which destroys it. A small white spot will remain at the site.

COMPLICATIONS: May bleed excessively if damaged.

PROGNOSIS: Good results from treatment.

Spigelian Hernia

DESCRIPTION: A rare hernia occurring between muscle bundles in the lower belly wall.

CAUSE: Weakness in the muscle wall of the lower belly from obesity, or wasting of muscles in chronic disease.

SYMPTOMS: A soft lump appears just above the pubic bone to the left or right of centre in the lower belly. If the hernia becomes trapped, it may be painful and tender.

INVESTIGATIONS: Usually the lump can be pushed back into the belly when the patient lies down. No specific tests are diagnostic.

TREATMENT: Surgery to repair the defect in the muscle wall.

COMPLICATIONS: The hernia may become trapped or twisted, which cuts off the blood supply to the intestine in the hernia, which then becomes gangrenous.

PROGNOSIS: Surgery is usually very successful, but obesity may make it complicated.

See also other conditions listed under Hernia

Spina Bifida

DESCRIPTION: The spinal cord runs from the base of the brain, through the vertebrae of the back, and carries nerve messages from the brain to the body. Spina bifida is a failure of the vertebra to close over the spinal cord during development as a foetus. There are several degrees of severity—

— **spina bifida occulta** is the mildest form in which only the vertebral arch is affected, and the spinal cord works normally.

— **meningocele** is more serious as there is a protuberant sac at the level of the failed fusion, which contains cerebrospinal fluid only, but the spinal cord has some damage.

— **meningomyelocele** is the most serious form in which a raw, uncovered sac containing nerve tissue and cerebrospinal fluid protrudes onto the surface of the back.

CAUSE: Unknown, but its incidence is higher in subsequent pregnancies after one child has been born with the condition, and in those of Irish and Welsh ancestry. The foetus develops its spinal cord and vertebrae in the first three months of pregnancy from a flat strip of nerve tissue that folds in upon itself lengthwise and fuses into a rod. It is then surrounded by the bony arch of the vertebrae. Spina bifida is the failure of the vertebral arch to form, usually in the lower back, allowing the spinal cord to be easily damaged. The unfused vertebral arch has a double pointed (bifid) appearance on X-ray examination.

SYMPTOMS: Spina bifida occulta — no symptoms.

Meningocele — only some of the necessary nerve messages are transmitted to the legs and bladder causing some muscle weakness, abnormal sensations and poor bladder control.

Meningomyelocele — paralysis and loss of all sensation below the level of damage and no control of the bladder or legs (paraplegia).

INVESTIGATIONS: Mothers who are at high risk can have a test performed on the amniotic fluid that surrounds the baby in the womb between the 14th and 16th week of pregnancy to detect the defect. May also be detected by ultrasound scan during pregnancy. After birth, X-rays, and MRI and CT scans of the back show every detail of the defect.

TREATMENT: Some evidence that folic acid supplements during pregnancy prevent the condition.

Spina bifida occulta — none normally necessary.

Meningocele — operation to close the defect in the back is performed in childhood.

Meningomyelocele — major operation to close the defect in the back is performed early, but this does not cure the paraplegia.

COMPLICATIONS: Spina bifida occulta — none significant.

Meningocele — back is weakened and more easily damaged.

Meningomyelocele — significant risk of infection in the spine and brain and may be associated with other birth deformities such as hydrocephalus (see separate entry) and anencephaly (failure of the brain to develop).

PROGNOSIS: No cure, but control of the condition enables the sufferers to have a normal life span.

See also Paraplegia

Spinal Muscular Atrophy

DESCRIPTION: Rare form of motor neurone disease (see separate entry) that destroys the nerves that supply the muscles of the trunk and adjacent limb muscles.

CAUSE: Congenital due to inherited chromosome damage. Occurs in infants and children.

SYMPTOMS: Floppy babies, with weakness of the muscles in the chest, shoulders, abdomen, back and thighs.

INVESTIGATIONS: Muscle biopsy shows death of motor nerve fibres. Electrical tests on muscles (electromyography) are also abnormal.

TREATMENT: None available.

COMPLICATIONS: Pneumonia often leads to death.

PROGNOSIS: Death within months or a few years of birth.

See also Motor Neurone Disease; Primary Lateral Sclerosis

Spinal Stenosis

DESCRIPTION: Narrowing (stenosis) of the canal in the vertebrae through which the spinal cord runs, resulting in pressure on the cord that affects its function.

CAUSE: Injury to the back, collapse of vertebrae with osteoporosis (bone thinning), Paget's disease of bone, a tumour of bone or the membranes (meninges) that surround the spinal cord, or may be a birth defect.

SYMPTOMS: Back and leg pain that are worsened by walking or prolonged standing, and relieved by sitting or lying. As the stenosis worsens, there may be abnormal sensations (eg. pins and needles), then loss of sensation and muscle weakness. Finally paralysis (paraplegia — see separate entry) occurs below the level in the back where the narrowing occurs.

INVESTIGATIONS: Narrowing demonstrated by CT or MRI scans, or special X-rays in which a dye is injected into the spinal canal (myelogram).

TREATMENT: Anti-inflammatory medications, exercise and physiotherapy, and pain relievers may be used initially, but as the condition progresses surgery is essential to relieve the pressure on the spinal cord.

COMPLICATIONS: Loss of control of bladder and bowels.

PROGNOSIS: Depends on cause, but overall one quarter have progressive disease that eventually results in paraplegia.

See also Osteoporosis; Paget's Disease of Bone

Spinocerebellar Degeneration
See Friedrich's Ataxia

Spleen, Ruptured

DESCRIPTION: The spleen weighs about 100g, is roughly the same size as your fist, is shaped rather like an inverted pudding bowl, and is tucked under the last couple of ribs on your left side. Its functions are to remove damaged cells from the blood, store vital elements such as iron, store antibodies that the body develops after an infection, produce new white blood cells that fight off infection, and produce red blood cells to transport oxygen.

CAUSE: In a car or other accident, the chest may be squashed, and the spleen may be pierced by a rib or ruptured by the pressure.

SYMPTOMS: Pain in the lower left chest and upper left abdomen, weakness, shortness of breath and collapse.

INVESTIGATIONS: Ultrasound scan of the spleen may show damage. Free blood may be found in the abdominal cavity when a needle is pushed through the muscle wall.

TREATMENT: Repairing the spleen surgically is difficult as it is too friable, and as a result it is often necessary to remove it it in order to stop bleeding.

COMPLICATIONS: Blood loss into the abdomen can be life-threatening.

PROGNOSIS: Removal of the spleen is lifesaving and has remarkably little effect on an adult, as bone marrow can take over most of its functions. In babies the spleen is essential for the early formation of blood cells, and it is removed from children only in extreme circumstances.

Spondylitis

DESCRIPTION: Inflammation of the spine. There are several different types, the most common being rheumatoid spondylitis, ankylosing spondylitis (see separate entry) and arthritic spondylitis.

CAUSE: Rheumatoid form is caused by a rejection reaction of the body to the tissue lining the small joints of the back (autoimmune condition). Arthritic form is usually a wear and tear injury to a part of the spine in heavy manual workers or those who have participated in rugged sports.

SYMPTOMS: Significant pain in localised areas of the back bone.

INVESTIGATIONS: Damage may be seen on an X-ray or CT scan. Blood tests show inflammatory changes.

TREATMENT: Anti-inflammatory medications, pain killers, physiotherapy (most important), surgery and some exotic drugs for the rheumatic form (eg. chloroquine, gold).

COMPLICATIONS: Rheumatoid form usually affects the small joints of the hands and feet as well.

PROGNOSIS: No permanent cure for most forms, and continuing care is normally required.

See also Ankylosing Spondylitis; Spondylosis

Spondylolisthesis

DESCRIPTION: An abnormality of the vertebrae in the lower back in which one vertebra moves forward in the back in relation to the adjacent vertebrae causing nerves to be pinched.

CAUSE: May be present from birth, or caused by injury or degeneration (arthritis).

SYMPTOMS: Significant back pain that spreads to the buttocks and down the legs (sciatica).

INVESTIGATIONS: Diagnosed by X-ray and CT scan.

TREATMENT: Physiotherapy, anti-inflammatory drugs, and in intractable cases, surgery.

COMPLICATIONS: Severe nerve pinching may cause muscle spasm or weakness.

PROGNOSIS: Management often difficult, but in most cases surgery eventually successful.

See also Osteoarthritis

Spondylosis

DESCRIPTION: Abnormality of the mechanical structure of the spine.

CAUSE: Incorrect alignment of the joints between the vertebral arches (the arch of bone protecting the spinal cord) in the back. Usually occurs in the elderly, obese or after a back injury. If the joints become inflamed, the condition is spondylitis (see separate entry).

SYMPTOMS: Dull aching pain in the neck or back that is relieved by a change in position. May be associated with a protective spasm of the back muscles.

INVESTIGATIONS: X-rays and CT scans of the back may show arthritic changes in the involved joints.

TREATMENT: Exercises and spine movements under the supervision of a physiotherapist, anti-inflammatory medications, support corset or neck brace, pain killers, and in severe cases surgery.

COMPLICATIONS: May progress to spondylitis.

PROGNOSIS: Often persistent and recurrent, with good temporary response to treatment. Surgery may be curative.

See also Spondylitis

Spongieform Encephalitis
See Creutzfeldt-Jakob Disease

Spontaneous Pneumothorax
See Pneumothorax

Sprain

DESCRIPTION: Tearing of ligaments that support a joint.

CAUSE: Excessive force being applied to the joint.

SYMPTOMS: Pain, swelling and bruising in and around the joint.

INVESTIGATIONS: X-ray may be performed to exclude any possible fracture.

TREATMENT: Rest, ice, compression and elevation initially, followed by immobilisation of the joint to allow ligaments to heal by use of bandages or plaster, and a sling or crutches.

COMPLICATIONS: If healing is poor, there may be permanent slackness in the ligaments, allowing excessive movement in the joint and increased risk of further injury and premature arthritis.

PROGNOSIS: Usually heal very well.

See also Ligament or Tendon Rupture; Strain; Whiplash

Sprue
See Coeliac Disease; Tropical Sprue

Spur, Heel
See Heel Spur

Squamous Cell Carcinoma of the Lung
See Lung Cancer

Squamous Cell Carcinoma of the Skin
(SCC)

DESCRIPTION: A cancer of the outermost layer of skin.

CAUSE: Occur on sun-exposed parts of the body, usually in patients who are over 50 years of age and are caused by prolonged exposure to sunlight or irritant chemicals. The rims of the ears, the face, scalp, arms and hands are commonly affected, but may also occur on the penis.

SYMPTOMS: Look like a red spot covered in fine white scales. They may be itchy or sore but often attract attention because they are unsightly.

INVESTIGATIONS: If suspected, excision or biopsy is necessary to make the diagnosis.

TREATMENT: Small SCCs are easily removed by burning with a diathermy machine or freezing with liquid nitrogen. If it is larger, or if the diagnosis is not certain, it is necessary to excise the spot and surrounding tissue. Any SCC that recurs after freezing or burning must be surgically excised.

COMPLICATIONS: Can spread by blood or lymphatics to distant parts of the body.

PROGNOSIS: Treatment very effective in early stages of the disease.

See also Bowen's Disease; Hyperkeratosis; Intraepithelial Carcinoma; Keratoacanthoma

Squint
(Strabismus)

DESCRIPTION: Abnormal alignment of eyes. When the eyes are both turned inwards the condition is called esotropia.

CAUSE: Weakness or abnormal development of the tiny muscles within the eye socket which move and align the eyes, or abnormal vision in one eye.

SYMPTOMS: The two eyes do not align equally when looking at a distant object and appear to be looking in different directions. This is normal when looking at a very close object, as both eyes turn in to look at it. May not be constant and occur only when a child is very tired.

INVESTIGATIONS: The diagnosis is not easy as a number of normal conditions may mimic it. Specific tests must be carried out on eye movement and vision.

TREATMENT: Special spectacles may be used long term to correct the problem by reducing the angle of the squint. In more severe cases an eye patch may cover the good eye to strengthen the poorer one and eye exercises may be added. In marked degrees of squint, it is necessary to operate to change the tightness of the tiny muscles that control eye movement, which is a technically a difficult operation for the surgeon, but relatively minor surgery for the patient.

COMPLICATIONS: If untreated, the brain will gradually suppress the sight in one eye to avoid double vision resulting in blindness in that eye. Successful management is a slow process that takes several years, and there can be a temptation for the patient to stop treatment and to miss follow-up appointments, but for the long-term future vision of the child, good care is essential.

PROGNOSIS: Provided medical advice is followed, the long-term cosmetic and vision results are excellent. The success rate of surgery is very high.

See also other diseases listed under Visual Problems

Stagardt Syndrome

DESCRIPTION: Form of vision loss in adolescents.

CAUSE: Deterioration and eventual death of the cells in the centre of the light sensitive retina at the back of the eye where central vision is focused. Inherited, but both parents must be carriers.

SYMPTOMS: Deteriorating central vision while peripheral vision remains.

INVESTIGATIONS: Eye examination with a magnifying light (ophthalmoscope) abnormal. Special dye (fluorescein) injected into an artery shows damaged blood supply to retina.

TREATMENT: None available.

PROGNOSIS: No cure. Slowly progressive.

Stammer
See Stutter

Staphylococcal Infections

DESCRIPTION: Staphylococcal bacterial infections in the lungs (pneumonia), eye, skin, brain (meningitis), gut and other parts of the body. Methicillin is one of the most potent forms of penicillin, and methicillin-resistant *Staphylococcus aureus* (MRSA) is becoming a serious problem, because it is difficult to treat and tends to occur in hospitals where large quantities of antibiotics are used. A fortunately rare development is that of vancomycin and methicillin-resistant *Staphylococcus aureus* (VMRSA) infections, which usually cause pneumonia in debilitated patients admitted to large hospitals.

CAUSE: The bacterium *Staphylococcus aureus* (golden staph).

SYMPTOMS: Depends on area involved, but will include a fever, tiredness, loss of appetite and pain in the infected tissue.

INVESTIGATIONS: Blood tests will show presence of infection, and pus, tissue swab or sample from infected area can be cultured to identify the responsible bacteria.

TREATMENT: Most forms susceptible to antibiotics such as penicillin and cephalosporins.

MRSA — patients will need to be given high doses of special antibiotics (eg. vancomycin) by injection or drip, and isolated and nursed in such a way that the hospital staff cannot transmit the infection to other patients (barrier nursing).

VMRSA — at present there are no antibiotics available to treat this infection.

COMPLICATIONS: Permanent damage to infected organs.

PROGNOSIS: Very good with normal infections. Most patients with MRSA can be successfully treated, but it may take several weeks of intensive treatment. VMRSA is often fatal.

See also Toxic Shock Syndrome and other diseases listed under Infections

Starvation
See Kwashiorkor; Marasmus; Strachan Syndrome

Status Epilepticus
See Epilepsy

Steele-Richardson-Olszewski Syndrome
(Progressive Supranuclear Palsy)
DESCRIPTION: Deterioration of the part of the brain responsible for muscle control that is often confused with Parkinson's disease. Occurs twice as often in males as females.

CAUSE: Unknown.

SYMPTOMS: Elderly person whose back is rigidly extended, falls backwards easily, is demented, eyes are unable to look down, reflexes are increased and has difficulty swallowing.

INVESTIGATIONS: None specifically diagnostic.

TREATMENT: Physiotherapy, occupational and speech therapy, and medications to ease muscle rigidity and spasm.

PROGNOSIS: Slowly progressive.

See also Parkinson's Disease

Steinert's Disease
See Myotonic Dystrophy

Stein-Leventhal Syndrome
See Polycystic Ovarian Syndrome

Sternocleidomastoid Torticollis
See Torticollis

Stevens-Johnson Syndrome
DESCRIPTION: Severe complication of erythema multiforme (see separate entry).

CAUSE: May be triggered by drugs or infection.

SYMPTOMS: Erythema multiforme; severe purulent ulcerating conjunctivitis; high fever; inflamed mouth (stomatitis); blisters or ulcers in nose, vagina, urethra, and anal canal; ulceration, pain and swelling extending down the throat and into the lungs to give a form of bronchitis.

INVESTIGATIONS: No specific diagnostic test.

TREATMENT: Intensive steroid therapy, and remove cause of erythema multiforme if possible.

COMPLICATIONS: Heart and lungs may become involved. Scalded skin syndrome (see separate entry) may develop.

PROGNOSIS: Most patients recover slowly, but death possible in the elderly and debilitated.

See also Erythema Multiforme; Scalded Skin Syndrome

Stewart-Morgagni-Morel Syndrome

DESCRIPTION: Disorder of the pituitary gland and adjacent part of the brain (hypothalamus) that controls the gland, resulting in excess production of androgenic (male sex) hormones.

CAUSE: Unknown.

SYMPTOMS: Acromegaly (enlarged head and major bones) and a very prominent forehead.

INVESTIGATIONS: X-rays and CT scans used to investigate condition and cause.

TREATMENT: Surgery or irradiation to the pituitary gland to reduce androgen production, but this causes hypopituitarism (see separate entry) as a side effect.

PROGNOSIS: Reasonable, but depends on success of treatment.

Stewart-Treves Syndrome

DESCRIPTION: Sarcoma (form of cancer) of an arm affected by lymphoedema (hard swelling) in the elderly.

CAUSE: Lymphoedema often follows mastectomy (breast removal) for cancer.

SYMPTOMS: Purplish red growth (angiosarcoma) on a lymphoedematous limb.

INVESTIGATIONS: Diagnosed after surgical removal of the tumour and examination under a microscope.

TREATMENT: Wide surgical excision of the tumour.

PROGNOSIS: Relentlessly aggressive tumour with a poor prognosis.

See also Angiosarcoma; Breast Cancer; Lymphoedema

Sticky Platelet Syndrome

DESCRIPTION: Uncommon cause of abnormal blood clots (thromboses) in young patients. Platelets are the cells in blood that stick together to form a clot.

CAUSE: Unknown.

SYMPTOMS: Excess stickiness of platelets causes migraines and thromboses. Symptoms vary depending on organs affected.

INVESTIGATIONS: Platelet agglutination rate on blood test very high.

TREATMENT: Medications that reduce platelet stickiness such as aspirin and dipyridamole are taken long term.

COMPLICATIONS: Stroke may occur in the brain.

PROGNOSIS: Good control possible, but serious permanent organ damage may occur before diagnosed.

See also Thrombosis

Stiff-Man Syndrome

DESCRIPTION: Rare cause of muscle stiffness and spasm.

CAUSE: Unknown.

SYMPTOMS: Rigid limbs with severely painful muscle cramps.

INVESTIGATIONS: Abnormal electromyogram (EMG) which measures electrical activity in muscles.

TREATMENT: Medications to relax muscles (eg. diazepam, suxamethonium) and injections or surgery to block or destroy nerves to muscles.

COMPLICATIONS: Bones may develop stress fractures and joints may partially dislocate (subluxate) due to constant muscle spasm.

PROGNOSIS: No cure and management difficult.

Still's Disease
(Juvenile Rheumatoid Arthritis)

DESCRIPTION: A rare rheumatoid arthritis-type disease that occurs in children and teenagers. There are several forms of the disease that vary in their symptoms, severity and outcome.

CAUSE: Unknown.

SYMPTOMS: Widespread measles-type rash; a fever that rises and falls rapidly; enlarged lymph nodes, spleen and liver; and one or more hot, red, painful, swollen joints. Nodules may develop under the skin near affected joints, and the heart, lungs and muscles may also become inflamed. The knees, hips, elbows and ankles are the joints most commonly affected. Rare under one year of age and over fourteen, and girls are twice as likely as boys to develop the condition.

INVESTIGATIONS: Blood tests show signs of inflammation, but the tests that diagnose adult rheumatoid arthritis are usually normal.

TREATMENT: Prolonged rest, with passive movement of affected joints by physiotherapists on a regular basis. Heat often relieves the pain and swelling. Drug treatment includes aspirin, anti-inflammatory drugs, and steroids.

COMPLICATIONS: Some have long term joint damage and deformity.

PROGNOSIS: Although the course is often prolonged, most children eventually recover.

See also Rheumatoid Arthritis

Sting, Bee or Wasp

DESCRIPTION: Bee stings are barbed and are usually left behind in the skin with the venom sac attached and the bee dies. Some wasps can sting repeatedly.

CAUSE: Sting from a bee or wasp. Same principles apply to stings from other insects.

SYMPTOMS: Painful red swollen mark on skin.

TREATMENT:

- remove bee sting by scraping it sideways with fingernail or side of a knife. Do not pull or squeeze the sac of venom attached to the sting.
- wipe affected area clean and apply a block of ice wrapped in damp material.
- in moderately severe cases antihistamine tablets or injections are given, and steroid creams applied.
- if the victim has an allergic reaction, apply pressure immobilisation (firmly wrapped bandage) and obtain urgent medical attention. If breathing or pulse stops, give mouth-to-mouth resuscitation or cardiopulmonary resuscitation.
- adrenaline and steroid injections for very severe reactions (anaphylaxis).

COMPLICATIONS: A few people are allergic to stings, and their reaction may be worse with severe pain, swelling and irritation, puffy eyelids and wheezy breathing. If the reaction is extreme (anaphylaxis), it can affect breathing and the heart. It is not unknown for bees and wasps to crawl into an open can of drink, and then sting the victim in the mouth and throat which can be very serious as the airway may swell up and block.

PROGNOSIS: Recovery is usually swift and uneventful. Severe allergy reactions respond well once appropriate treatment given. Massive stings from multiple insects may rarely be fatal.

See also Anaphylaxis; Funnel-Web Spider Bite; Red Back Spider Bite

Stokes-Adams Attack
(Adams-Stokes Syndrome)

DESCRIPTION: Complication of irregular heart beat.

CAUSE: Sudden slowing of the heart beat from an electrical problem within the heart resulting in inadequate blood supply to the brain. Often occurs after a heart attack, may have no apparent cause, or may be due to a side-effect of medication.

SYMPTOMS: Sudden faint, convulsive movements, and slow heart rate or multiple missed heart beats. Facial flushing occurs for a minute or so on recovery.

INVESTIGATIONS: Monitoring of heart electrical activity for a prolonged period (Holter monitor) while maintaining normal lifestyle until an attack occurs and heart electrical problem can be identified.

TREATMENT: Appropriate medications to regulate heart rate or surgical implantation of an electrical pacemaker.

COMPLICATIONS: Injuries from fall during attack. Rarely may cause permanent damage to heart leading to further heart complications.

PROGNOSIS: Recovery from sudden attack usually rapid, but recurrences frequent. Usually well controlled by appropriate treatment once cause identified. Good result from pacemaker.

See also Faint; Heart Attack

Stomach Cancer
(Gastric Carcinoma)

DESCRIPTION: Cancer of the stomach.

CAUSE: One of the less common cancers in Europeans (4% of all cancers), but very common amongst Japanese. More than twice as common in men than women, and usually occurs over the age of 60 years. The consumption of green and yellow vegetables decreases the risk, but it rises in lower socioeconomic groups and in those who have pernicious anaemia.

SYMPTOMS: Often has mild symptoms such as indigestion and heartburn, so patients frequently do not attend a doctor until it is quite advanced. Other symptoms include burping, feeling very full in the upper belly, nausea, weight loss and a loss in appetite. Vomiting blood and passing black faeces are late complications.

INVESTIGATIONS: Confirmed by gastroscopy and biopsy of any suspicious areas. Stomach cancer often looks like, and may be confused with, an ulcer.

TREATMENT: Surgical removal of the stomach, and surrounding lymph nodes to which the cancer may have spread. Irradiation may be used as additional treatment.

COMPLICATIONS: The liver is a common site for the spread of the cancer, but once this is involved, a cure is most unlikely.

PROGNOSIS: The five-year survival rate is about 20%.

Stomach Ulcer
See Ulcer, Peptic

Stomatitis
(Mouth Infection)

DESCRIPTION: An infection of the mouth.

CAUSE: May be the result of one or more mouth ulcers, or a fungal, viral or bacterial infection.

Fungal infection (thrush) — common in babies and in those who are on antibiotics or taking anti-cancer drugs (cytotoxics).

Viral infection — include chickenpox, hand foot and mouth disease, and most seriously, Herpes simplex — cold sores (see separate entries). Herpangina is a special type of stomatitis that occurs in children under 6 years of age and is caused by the coxsackievirus.

Bacterial infection — may arise from poor dental hygiene.

SYMPTOMS: Fungal infection — inside of the mouth and tongue have patches of off-white slough sticking to them, and if this is scratched away, a red sore area is exposed. The infection is often painful and aggravated by sweet or spicy foods.

Viral infection — painful ulcers that are worse with eating or drinking.

Herpangina — sudden pain in the mouth, fever, difficulty in swallowing, mouth ulcers and grey coloured blisters.

Bacterial infection — generalised soreness of the mouth and bad breath.

INVESTIGATIONS: Mouth swabs may be taken to identify the responsible organism.

TREATMENT: Fungal infection — anti-fungal drops, ointments or lozenges.

Viral infection — anaesthetic gels.

Bacterial infection — hydrogen peroxide mouth washes and antibiotics.

COMPLICATIONS: Mouth pain may prevent eating and drinking and lead to dehydration and malnutrition.

PROGNOSIS: Fungal infection — treatment is rapidly effective.

Viral infection — heals after seven to ten days.

Bacterial infection — respond rapidly to treatment.

See also Cold Sores; Gingivostomatitis; Mouth Ulcer; Thrush

Stone
See Gallstones; Kidney Stone; Salivary Stone

Strabismus
See Squint

Strachan Syndrome
(Jamaican Neuritis)
DESCRIPTION: Widespread nerve and skin damage from poor diet.

CAUSE: Poor nutrition, particularly a lack of vitamin B. Often occurs in alcoholics and with starvation. Worse in smokers.

SYMPTOMS: Amblyopia (dim vision — see separate entry), dermatitis around mouth and genitals, and painful and excessively sensitive areas of skin. Some patients have muscle weakness or spasms.

INVESTIGATIONS: Abnormalities of the retina (light sensitive area at back of eye) when examined through an ophthalmoscope (magnifying light), blood test abnormalities, and over active reflexes.

TREATMENT: Vitamin supplements and good diet.

COMPLICATIONS: Permanent vision damage if left untreated for a prolonged period.

PROGNOSIS: Cured by correct treatment.

See also Amblyopia

Strain
DESCRIPTION: Overstretching of a muscle or tendon. Tendons attach muscles to bones.

CAUSE: Excessive stress being placed on muscle or tendon, often during sport.

SYMPTOMS: Pain, swelling and inability to use the muscle without discomfort.

INVESTIGATIONS: X-rays and ultrasound scans sometimes necessary to exclude a sprain or fracture.

TREATMENT: Rest, ice, compression and elevation initially. Strapping, pain killers and anti-inflammatory medications may be necessary.

COMPLICATIONS: Weakness in affected muscle may make future injury easier.

PROGNOSIS: Full recovery in a few days usual.

See also Sprain

Strawberry Naevus
(Immature Haemangioma)
DESCRIPTION: Temporarily disfiguring skin blemish of children.

CAUSE: Unknown. Overgrowth of small blood vessels.

SYMPTOMS: Bright red, raised, irregular, rapidly enlarging spot that appears shortly after birth. Growth ceases by nine months of age.

INVESTIGATIONS: None normally necessary.

TREATMENT: None, until at least the age of six years, when surgery may be considered.

COMPLICATIONS: Surgery to remove naevus leaves a permanent scar.

PROGNOSIS: Virtually all disappear spontaneously, completely and without a scar by the age of five years.

See also Haemangioma; Naevus

Streptococcal Infection

DESCRIPTION: Common bacterial infection.

CAUSE: Beta-haemolytic streptococci bacteria, which are divided into two major groups — A and B.

SYMPTOMS: Group A is responsible for infections in the throat and on the skin. Group B causes some types of genital infections, meningitis and pneumonia (see separate entries).

INVESTIGATIONS: A specific blood test is available to detect the A group anywhere in the body. B group detected by a culture of the blood, sputum or other infected tissue.

TREATMENT: Antibiotics such as penicillin, erythromycin and cephalosporins.

COMPLICATIONS: Group A may cause rheumatic fever or glomerulonephritis (see separate entries).

PROGNOSIS: Rapid recovery in most cases with appropriate treatment.

Stress

DESCRIPTION: Excessive anxiety about problems of daily living.

CAUSE: Mortgage repayments, marriage strife, young children, job security, family finances, separation and divorce, leaving home, poor health, work responsibilities, or a death in the family. All of these, and hundreds of other situations, are causes of stress.

SYMPTOMS: May cause a very wide range of symptoms including a persistent headache, peptic ulcers, heart disease, migraines, diarrhoea, shortness of breath, sweating, passing excess urine, rashes and vomiting.

INVESTIGATIONS: Cause of stress needs to be determined.

TREATMENT: Three possible treatment strategies:—

— remove the cause of the stress, which is much easier said than done in most cases.

— rationalise stress by talking over the problem with a spouse, relatives, friends, doctor or priest. Writing down details of the problem makes it appear more manageable, particularly when all possible options are diagrammatically attached to it to give a rational view of the situation. Professional assistance may be given by a general practitioner, psychiatrist, psychologist, marriage guidance counsellor, child guidance officer or social worker.

— Medications that alter mood, sedate or relieve anxiety are used in a crisis, intermittently or for short periods of time. Some antidepressant drugs and treatments for psychiatric conditions are designed for long-term use, but most of the anxiety-relieving drugs can cause dependency if used regularly.

COMPLICATIONS: May worsen or trigger other physical illnesses, or progress to a neurosis, depression, or in severe cases, suicide is possible.

PROGNOSIS: Depends on cause, but most people eventually cope with their problems.

See also Conversion Disorder; Neurosis; Post Traumatic Stress Disorder; Suicide

Stress Fracture
(Fatigue Fracture)

DESCRIPTION: Abnormal break of a bone, often in the foot (see March Fracture entry), or lower leg (fibula or tibia).

CAUSE: Repeated abnormal stress on a bone causes it to break.

SYMPTOMS: Pain and tenderness in the affected bone that is worsened by use.

INVESTIGATIONS: Diagnosed by X-ray, CT or radionucleotide scan.

TREATMENT: Rest in a plaster cast.

PROGNOSIS: Settles well with treatment.

See also March Fracture

Stress Incontinence
See Incontinence of Urine

Stretch Marks
(Striae)

DESCRIPTION: Disfiguring skin condition.

CAUSE: A break down and stretching of the elastic fibres in the skin due to changes in the body's hormone levels and stretching of the skin. Pregnancy, obesity, Cushing syndrome, or taking large doses of cortisone are the most common causes. The tendency to develop striae may be inherited.

SYMPTOMS: Disfiguring bands of thinned and scar like skin develop on the belly and breasts.

INVESTIGATIONS: None necessary.

TREATMENT: Unsatisfactory. Selected streaks may be removed by plastic surgery or reduced by creams containing retinoic acid.

COMPLICATIONS: None.

PROGNOSIS: Usually remain permanently.

Striae
See Stretch Marks

Stroke
(Cerebral Infarct; Cerebrovascular Accident; CVA)

DESCRIPTION: An accident involving the blood vessels in the brain. If a clot, or piece of material from elsewhere in the body blocks an artery in the brain (cerebral thrombosis), or if an artery bursts in the brain, a stroke may occur.

Stroke

CAUSE: The risk of stroke is higher in those who smoke, have high blood pressure, high cholesterol levels, are diabetic, and drink alcohol to excess.

SYMPTOMS: Any blood vessel in the brain may be involved, so any part of the brain may be damaged, and the area damaged determines the effects on that person's body. The symptoms can therefore be varied. If a motor area of the brain which controls movement is affected, the patient becomes paralysed down the opposite side of the body because the nerves supplying the body cross over to the opposite side at the base of the brain (the right side of the brain controls the left arm and leg). Other patients may lose their memory, power of speech, become uncoordinated, unbalanced, start fitting, have strange smells, hear abnormal noises or any of dozens of other possibilities.

INVESTIGATIONS: The cause of the stroke can be determined by using special X-rays, CT scans, MRI (magnetic resonance imaging), blood tests, tests on the fluid around the brain, and measuring the brain waves electrically (EEG).

TREATMENT: A wait-and-watch attitude is adopted in most cases, with medication given to prevent the stroke from worsening and to protect other organs. Surgery to a bleeding or blocked artery in the brain may be appropriate in some cases. Physiotherapists, speech pathologists and occupational therapists will assist in recovery. Further strokes can often be prevented by the long term use of low dose aspirin or warfarin, which prevent blood clots. Patients who are at a high risk can also use these medications.

COMPLICATIONS: The area of the brain affected may increase as a blood clot extends along an artery, or bleeding into the brain continues.

PROGNOSIS: It will be several days or even weeks before doctors can give an accurate prognosis. The brain does not repair itself, but it can often find different ways of doing a task and bypassing damaged areas. Most improvement occurs in the first week, but full recovery may take months. Patients who become unconscious during a stroke generally have a poorer outcome than those who do not. Strokes are the third major cause of death in developed countries after heart disease and cancer.

See also Transient Ischaemic Attack

Strongyloidiasis

DESCRIPTION: Infestation of the human by the tiny 2 mm. long worm **Strongyloides stercoralis**.

CAUSE: Strongyloides can live freely in moist soil or its larvae may penetrate the skin of a human, enter the bloodstream, pass through the heart into the lungs, and pass from the blood into the air passages of the lung. From there it moves up into the throat, is swallowed and develops into an adult worm, which then produces eggs which pass out with the faeces and contaminate the soil. The eggs may also hatch into larvae in the intestine and these larvae can penetrate the bowel wall to enter the blood and reinfect the host human. There are no male and female worms, only a single asexual form. Found throughout the tropics.

SYMPTOMS: Many patients have no or minimal symptoms. In long standing or severe cases symptoms may include itchy buttocks and wrists, raised rashes, belly pains, nausea, diarrhoea and weight loss.

INVESTIGATIONS: Diagnosed by finding the eggs or worms in the faeces or by a specific blood test.

TREATMENT: Appropriate medication can eradicate the infestation.

COMPLICATIONS: Rarely in long standing cases the larvae may invade the liver, kidney and brain.

PROGNOSIS: A cure can be expected in most cases.

See also Worm Infestations.

Strychnine Poisoning

DESCRIPTION: Swallowing strychnine overstimulates the nervous system.

CAUSE: Poison used in some animal baits.

SYMPTOMS: Muscle spasms, convulsions and vomiting. Symptoms start within 15 to 30 minutes of swallowing poison.

INVESTIGATIONS: Diagnosed by specific blood tests.

TREATMENT: In hospital intensive care unit, medications are given to paralyse patient and prevent convulsions. Life is sustained by artificial ventilation.

COMPLICATIONS: Permanent heart, nerve or muscle damage possible.

PROGNOSIS: Depends on dose. If patient survives for twelve hours, recovery likely.

See also Poisoning

Sturge-Weber Syndrome

DESCRIPTION: Developmental disorder of the brain and skin.

CAUSE: Congenital (present from birth).

SYMPTOMS: Mental retardation, a red stain across part of the face, convulsions, paralysis down one side of the body and eye abnormalities.

INVESTIGATIONS: No diagnostic tests.

TREATMENT: Medication can control the convulsions, surgery can correct the cosmetic deformities, and a combination of drugs and surgery are used for the eye abnormalities.

PROGNOSIS: No cure, but reasonable control of symptoms.

Stutter
(Stammer)

DESCRIPTION: The involuntary repetition of a sound during speech. Tends to start with the commencement of speech between two and four years of age.

CAUSE: Unknown, but more common in boys than girls, and more likely if one parent is or was a stutterer. Causation theories include emotional insecurity, anxiety and family disturbances in childhood. There is an association between left-right confusion and stuttering. Rarely may be due to brain damage.

SYMPTOMS: The speaker is unable to proceed past a certain point in speech for some seconds but eventually overcomes the barrier, and the remaining part of the sentence or phrase comes out in a rush. Worsens if the person is tense, hurried or confused. Consonants are the usual blocks for stammerers, and the letters 'p' and 'b' are the most commonly involved. Patients can usually sing without stammering, and some use a sing-song cadence to their speech pattern to overcome the problem.

INVESTIGATIONS: None usually necessary.

TREATMENT: Long-term treatment by a speech pathologist. Psychologists and/or psychiatrists may also be involved. Other than brief use of minor anti-anxiety drugs, no medication can help.

PROGNOSIS: With persistence over many months or years, most patients can learn to cope with their disorder.

Stye
(External Hordeolum)

DESCRIPTION: A miniature abscess in an eyelid.

CAUSE: A bacterial infection of one of the tiny sweat or oil glands (glands of Zeiss) on the margin of the eyelid that keep the eyelashes moist and lubricated. Often no apparent reason, but may follow excessively rubbing the eye or an injury to the eyelid.

SYMPTOMS: Infected gland becomes painful, red, swollen, and fills with pus.

INVESTIGATIONS: None necessary.

TREATMENT: Frequent warm compresses to the eye, and antibiotic ointment under the upper eyelid. A persistent sty can be incised to drain away pus.

COMPLICATIONS: None significant.

PROGNOSIS: Very good.

See also Meibomian Cyst

Subacute Bacterial Endocarditis
See Endocarditis

Subacute Necrotising Encephalomyelopathy
See Leigh Disease

Subacute Thyroiditis
See de Quervain's Thyroiditis

Subarachnoid Haemorrhage
(Intracerebral Haemorrhage)

DESCRIPTION: Bleeding into the substance of the brain. The arachnoid mater is the middle of the three meninges (membranes) that surround and support the brain, so by definition a subarachnoid haemorrhage is a bleed within the arachnoid membrane. The innermost membrane is the pia mater.

CAUSE: Rupture of a blood vessel in the brain due to high blood pressure (stroke), the rupture of an aneurysm (ballooning on the side of an artery), bleeding disorders (eg. thrombocytopenia, leukaemia), brain tumours, head injury or as a side effect of medication (eg. warfarin).

SYMPTOMS: Sudden loss of consciousness or confusion, vomiting, dizziness, headache and abnormal brain function (eg. partial paralysis, strange sensations) depending on the position of the bleed within the brain.

INVESTIGATIONS: CT scan or angiography (X-ray of arteries after injecting a dye) used to find site of bleed.

TREATMENT: Depends on cause, and can vary from time and rest to surgery to stop continued bleeding.

COMPLICATIONS: Permanent brain damage and epilepsy.

PROGNOSIS: Very variable depending on position and severity. Some patients recover rapidly, while other may lapse into a long term coma or die.

See also Stroke; Subdural Haematoma

Subclavian Steal Syndrome

DESCRIPTION: Restricted blood supply to left arm and head.

CAUSE: Due to pressure from one of the thoracic outlet syndromes (see separate entry) on the left subclavian artery or innominate artery, which supply blood to the left side of the head and the left arm. Results in restricted blood supply to arm and brain.

SYMPTOMS: Arm pain, particularly with exercise, and varying brain symptoms similar to a transient ischaemic attack (see separate entry).

INVESTIGATIONS: Angiography (X-ray of arteries after injection of a dye) abnormal.

TREATMENT: None unless severe, when surgical bypass of the affected artery is necessary.

COMPLICATIONS: Significant brain damage may occur if correct diagnosis not made.

PROGNOSIS: Good results from surgical treatment.

See also Naffziger Syndrome; Scapulocostal Syndrome

Subcutaneous Emphysema

DESCRIPTION: Gas (air) in tissues under the skin.

CAUSE: Lung injury, major surgery, fractured rib, gas gangrene, serious gas producing skin infections (cellulitis), severe tissue injuries, or damage to the throat (larynx).

SYMPTOMS: Spongy crackling sensation and/or sound when skin is indented.

INVESTIGATIONS: May show on ultrasound scan. Cause must be investigated by X-rays or blood tests.

TREATMENT: Depends on cause. Usually settles without treatment if cause not serious.

PROGNOSIS: Depends on cause, but not serious in itself.

Subdural Haematoma

DESCRIPTION: A collection of blood between the brain and the skull that puts pressure on the brain and affects its function. The dura mater is the outermost of the three meninges (membranes) that surround and support the brain, so by definition this is a bleed between the dura mater and the arachnoid mater which is the middle membrane. The innermost membrane is the pia mater.

CAUSE: Usually due to a significant head injury, but sometimes due to the rupture of a blood vessel affected by arteriosclerosis (see separate entry), high blood pressure or for no obvious reason. Onset may be sudden, or may be delayed for some weeks after a head injury if the bleed and build up of pressure is very gradual.

SYMPTOMS: Confusion, vomiting, dizziness, headache and abnormal brain function (eg. partial paralysis, strange sensations) depending on the position of the blood collection and the pressure it applies to the brain.

INVESTIGATIONS: CT or MRI scan used to find blood collection.

TREATMENT: Urgent surgical removal of blood collection.

COMPLICATIONS: Permanent brain damage possible but uncommon.

PROGNOSIS: May be fatal or cause permanent disability if left untreated. Good results from surgical treatment.

See also Concussion; Subarachnoid Haemorrhage

Subluxation
See Dislocation

Subungal Haematoma
(Nail Bruise)

DESCRIPTION: Collection of blood under a finger or toe nail.

CAUSE: Injury to the nail.

SYMPTOMS: Very painful nail that is black in colour and loose on its bed.

INVESTIGATIONS: None necessary.

TREATMENT: Hot tip of paper clip used to burn hole in nail and release blood.

COMPLICATIONS: Uncommonly, infection of the nail bed occurs.

PROGNOSIS: Nail usually lost as new nail grows out underneath old one.

Sudden Infant Death Syndrome
See Cot Death

Sudeck's Atrophy
See Reflex Sympathetic Dystrophy Syndrome

Sugar Diabetes
See Diabetes Mellitus

Suicide

DESCRIPTION: Eighth in importance as a cause of all deaths in western countries, but in young adults it is far higher in the rankings. Twice as many women as men attempt suicide, but men are three times more successful and are more likely to use violent means (eg. gun, jumping). Those who live alone and who have poor general health are also at a higher risk.

CAUSE: May be triggered by an emotional crisis such as divorce, death of a close family member, loss of a job, financial crisis or as a result of some other form of rejection, but often there is no apparent reason. Alcoholism makes suicide attempts more likely, and the sudden excessive use of alcohol in an already stressed or depressed person is cause for considerable concern.

SYMPTOMS: Those who contemplate suicide often provide clues of their intentions, but unfortunately these clues are sometimes not obvious or are ignored. A person who jokes about 'ending it all', or that the family is 'better off without me', may well be trying to judge the reaction of others to this idea. Other similar conversational clues may be introduced in the third person by expressing ideas such as 'my friend often talks of suicide' or 'did you read about that suicide in the paper'. Further clues may include changes in behaviour such as giving away prized possessions, enquiring about cremations, or sudden changes in religious attitudes and investigating alternate religions. A decision to attempt suicide may be a long slow process over many weeks or months, in which cases clues may be identified and a doctor alerted, or a sudden bout of deep depression may result in the decision being made in a matter of minutes.

TREATMENT: Once there is reasonable suspicion that an individual may attempt suicide, a medical practitioner (usually the person's general practitioner) should be made aware of the clues that have been noticed. The doctor will then take all possible measures to ensure that the person is treated and counselled appropriately. No-one can be forced to undergo medical treatment, but if the doctor's efforts to persuade the patient to accept treatment are unsuccessful, and if the doctor is convinced that a suicide attempt is imminent, documents may be signed to allow the person to be taken into a hospital for further assessment and treatment. This measure is only taken as a last resort. If the patient accepts treatment, it will involve counselling and medication to correct the biochemical imbalance in the brain that may be causing depression (see separate entry).

PROGNOSIS: Suicide attempts are at least ten times more common than successful suicides. Many can be prevented, and the patient can be successfully treated so that they can lead a happy and productive life, but the early involvement of doctors is essential.

See also Depression; Post Traumatic Stress Disorder; Stress

Sunburn
See Burn

SUNCT Syndrome

DESCRIPTION: Form of headache whose name is an acronym of major symptoms.

CAUSE: Variant of cluster headaches. May be triggered by alcohol, stress, exercise, certain foods and glare.

SYMPTOMS: Severe headaches that are shortlasting (seconds to minutes), one sided (unilateral) and piercing (neuralgiform) with associated red eyes (conjunctival injection) and excess tear production. May occur regularly or spasmodically.

INVESTIGATIONS: None diagnostic.

TREATMENT: Medication (eg. sumatriptan, ergotamine), nasal capsaicin spray, and inhaling pure oxygen.

COMPLICATIONS: None serious.

PROGNOSIS: Often recurrent. Very annoying but not serious.

See also Cluster Headache

Superficial Venous Thrombosis
(SVT)

DESCRIPTION: Blood clot (thrombosis) in the superficial veins just under the skin in the legs or arms.

CAUSE: May follow injury to the area, an intravenous drip insertion, or other localised disease.

SYMPTOMS: Affected vein becomes red, hard and tender.

INVESTIGATIONS: None normally necessary.

TREATMENT: Heat, rest of the limb, and aspirin or other anti-inflammatory medication.

COMPLICATIONS: Rarely there may be secondary infection or skin ulceration over the thrombosis.

PROGNOSIS: Recovery without complications in a week or two is normal.

See also Deep Venous Thrombosis; Thrombosis; Varicose Veins

Superior Vena Cava Syndrome

DESCRIPTION: Complication of cancer in the chest.

CAUSE: Invariably secondary to lung cancer or other chest cancers that cause blocking of the superior vena cava (the main vein draining into the heart from the head and arms).

SYMPTOMS: Firm swelling (brawny oedema) and flushing of head and neck, and dilated neck and arm veins.

INVESTIGATIONS: Venography (X-ray of veins) shows blocked superior vena cava.

TREATMENT: Potent anticancer drugs and chest irradiation.

COMPLICATIONS: Treatment urgent or heart failure occurs.

PROGNOSIS: Very poor. Cancer usually inoperable by time this syndrome occurs.

See also Lung Cancer

Suppurative Thyroiditis
See Thyroiditis

Supraspinatus Tendonitis
See Tendonitis

SVT
See Superficial Venous Thrombosis

Sweet Syndrome
(Acute Febrile Neutrophilic Dermatosis)
DESCRIPTION: Skin disease with generalised effects that is more common in women.

CAUSE: Unknown.

SYMPTOMS: Multiple tender red or purple skin plaques on neck and limbs, muscle pains, fever, and joint pains and swelling.

INVESTIGATIONS: Blood tests show excess white cells (neurtophils). Skin plaque biopsy is diagnostic.

TREATMENT: Prednisone.

COMPLICATIONS: Acute myeloid leukaemia develops in 20% of patients, and rarely ulcerative colitis occurs.

PROGNOSIS: Heals spontaneously over 2 or more months, but recurrences common.

Swimmer's Ear
See Otitis Externa

Sydenham's Chorea
(St.Vitus Dance)
DESCRIPTION: Complication of rheumatic fever. Now a rare condition, but more common before the development of antibiotics.

CAUSE: Follows some types of bacterial infections.

SYMPTOMS: Irregular jerky movements of a limb or the body, with a complete loss of muscle tone between each movement.

INVESTIGATIONS: No specific diagnostic tests.

TREATMENT: Treat rheumatic fever with antibiotics (eg. penicillin).

PROGNOSIS: As for rheumatic fever.

See also Rheumatic Fever

Syncope
See Faint

Syndrome
A syndrome is a collection of several symptoms that occur consistently in patients with a particular medical condition. Several hundred syndromes are recognised.
See under individual syndrome names.

Syndrome of Inappropriate Antidiuretic Hormone Secretion
(Syndrome of Inappropriate Vasopressin Secretion)

DESCRIPTION: A complex condition in which excess ADH (anti-diuretic hormone or vasopressin) is released by the pituitary gland in the centre of the head. ADH controls the rate at which the kidneys produce urine and excrete salt and if excess is produced, the kidneys do not release sufficient water in the urine, and it builds up in the body.

CAUSE: May occur as a result of a pituitary gland tumour, strokes in the part of the brain (hypothalamus) which controls the pituitary gland, or bleeding into the brain from a head injury. Some types of cancer, particularly of the lungs and pancreas, can start producing ADH independent from the pituitary gland. A number of other diseases (eg. tuberculosis, thyroid gland underactivity) may rarely also inappropriately produce ADH. Uncommon side effects from drugs and prolonged resuscitation may also trigger the syndrome.

SYMPTOMS: Weight gain, reduced urine output, generalised weakness, mental confusion, and eventually convulsions due to retention of excessive amounts of water and very low levels of salt in the blood.

INVESTIGATIONS: Blood and urine tests abnormal.

TREATMENT: Controlled by medications (diuretics) to make the kidneys produce more urine, taking salt and restricting fluid intake.

COMPLICATIONS: Heart, brain and other organ damage occur if not controlled.

PROGNOSIS: Good control with treatment, but a cure may be difficult as the exact cause must be found and corrected. Fatal if not controlled.

Syndrome of Inappropriate Vasopressin Secretion
Syndrome of Inappropriate Antidiuretic Hormone Secretion

Syndrome X
(Insulin Resistance Syndrome; Reaven Syndrome)

DESCRIPTION: Newly recognised cause of high blood pressure.

CAUSE: Autoimmune condition, in which the body inappropriately rejects its own tissue, in this case the cells that respond to insulin.

SYMPTOMS: High blood pressure, a tendency to develop diabetes, obesity and cholesterol imbalances.

INVESTIGATIONS: Diagnosed by sophisticated blood tests.

TREATMENT: Medication to control blood pressure, diabetes and cholesterol levels.

COMPLICATIONS: Significantly increased risk of stroke and heart attack.

PROGNOSIS: No cure possible, but good control normally achieved.

Synovial Plica Syndrome
(Plica Syndrome)

DESCRIPTION: Form of significant knee pain and disability.

CAUSE: Vigorous knee exercise.

SYMPTOMS: Pain in the front of the knee caused by a fold of synovial membrane (the smooth membrane lining the joint) on the inside of the knee being caught between the patella (knee cap) and femur (thigh bone).

INVESTIGATIONS: Arthroscopy (looking into the joint) can be used for both diagnosis and treatment.

TREATMENT: Rest, splinting, arthroscopic removal of excess synovial membrane, anti-inflammatory drugs and physiotherapy.

PROGNOSIS: Good result from treatment.

Synovitis

DESCRIPTION: Inflammation or infection of the synovial membrane which lines all joint cavities, covering all surfaces within the joint except those where weight-bearing cartilage is present. The membrane secretes synovial fluid which acts as a lubricant within joints, and allows them to move smoothly and freely.

CAUSE: A bacterial infection, injury to the joint, rheumatoid arthritis, tuberculosis (now rare), gonorrhoea (see separate entry) or other infecting organisms. Usually associated with the excessive secretion of synovial fluid into the joint.

SYMPTOMS: Swelling, restricted movement, pain and sometimes redness and heat in the joint. Any joint may be involved, but the hip, knee and ankle are the most commonly affected ones.

INVESTIGATIONS: Sometimes necessary to drain some fluid from the joint through a needle and examine it to diagnose the cause.

TREATMENT: The cause must be treated (eg. antibiotics for a bacterial infection) and the joint must be rested until pain and swelling subside.

COMPLICATIONS: If left untreated, permanent damage to the joint may occur, or arthritis may develop prematurely.

PROGNOSIS: Depends on cause, but usually good result from treatment.

See also Pigmented Villonodular Synovitis; Repetitive Strain Injury; Rheumatoid Arthritis

Syphilis

DESCRIPTION: Infection that is usually sexually transmitted, and which passes through three main stages over many months or years. Relatively uncommon in developed countries, but still widespread in poorer societies.

CAUSE: The spirochete bacterium *Treponema pallidum* which is transmitted by heterosexual or homosexual contact, sharing injecting needles, blood transfusions, or from a mother to her child during pregnancy (congenital syphilis). The same bacteria also causes yaws (see separate entry) which is transmitted by close body contact, but not necessarily sexual contact.

SYMPTOMS: First stage — a painless sore (chancre) on the penis, the female genitals, or around the anus of homosexuals which heals after three to six weeks. There may be painless enlarged lymph nodes in the armpit and groin that also disappear.

Second stage — starts a few weeks or months later with a widespread rash, mouth and vaginal ulcers, and a slight fever. The patient is highly infectious but will usually recover and enter a latent period that may last many years.

Third (tertiary) stage — years later tumours (gumma) develop in the liver, major arteries, bones, brain, spinal cord (tabes dosalis), skin and other organs. Symptoms vary depending on organs involved but may include arthritis, bone weakness, severe bone pain, paralysis, strokes, heart attacks, internal bleeding from aneurysms (see separate entry), blindness, headaches, jaundice (liver failure), muscle spasms, skin ulcers, scars, nodules in the larynx and lungs, vomiting, confusion, insanity and death.

Congenital syphilis — newborn infant with teeth abnormalities, deafness, misshapen bones, deformed nose, pneumonia, and mental retardation.

INVESTIGATIONS: Diagnosed at all stages by specific blood tests, or by finding the responsible bacteria on a swab taken from a genital sore in the first stage of the disease. All pregnant women are routinely tested.

TREATMENT: First and second stages — antibiotics such as penicillin (often as an injection), tetracycline or erythromycin.

Third (tertiary) stage — antibiotics used, but can merely prevent further deterioration as organ damage is irreversible.

Congenital syphilis — child is infectious when born and is treated with antibiotics.

COMPLICATIONS: First stage — usually none.

Second stage — spread of the infection to involve the joints, brain, liver and kidney which may be severely damaged.

Third (tertiary) stage — almost any organ can be seriously damaged.

Congenital syphilis — may develop more serious problems if the condition is not treated aggressively.

PROGNOSIS: A course of antibiotics for a few weeks almost invariably cures the disease in its first two stages. No cure for tertiary or congenital syphilis. Plastic surgery may correct the more obvious congenital deformities.

See also Tabes Dorsalis; Yaws and other diseases listed under Venereal Diseases

Syringomyelia

DESCRIPTION: Expansion of a cavity within the spinal cord that places pressure on the nerves passing this point, and affects nerve function and circulation of the surrounding cerebrospinal fluid below it. Usually occurs in the neck.

CAUSE: May be a developmental disorder (congenital), or due to tumours, injury or inflammation. Sometimes associated with the Arnold-Chiari malformation, in which the lowest part of the brain (cerebellum) slips down into the spinal canal.

SYMPTOMS: Gradually worsening reduction in sensation and muscle weakness below the affected point of the spine.

INVESTIGATIONS: Diagnosed by CT and MRI scans.

TREATMENT: Surgical drainage of the cavity in the spinal cord, and removal of any tumour.

COMPLICATIONS: Untreated, quadriplegia or paraplegia may occur.
PROGNOSIS: Good results from treatment.

Systemic Lupus Erythematosus
(Disseminated Lupus Erythematosus; 'Lupus'; SLE)

DESCRIPTION: Relatively common inflammatory condition affecting joints, skin, liver, and kidney most commonly, but almost any tissue in the body may be involved. 85% of cases occur in women (usually young), and more common in Negroes than Caucasians.

CAUSE: Auto-immune disorder in which the body inappropriately rejects normal tissue for no known reason. Attacks may be precipitated by stress, some medications or chemicals. There is also a familial tendency.

SYMPTOMS: Common symptoms are arthritis of several joints, a red rash across both cheeks and the bridge of the nose ('butterfly rash'), rashes on other areas that are exposed to sunlight, mouth ulcers, poorly functioning kidneys and anaemia. Additional symptoms may include a fever, loss of appetite, tiredness, weight loss, damaged nails, loss of hair and painfully cold fingers. Less common complaints include conjunctivitis, blurred vision, chest pain, pneumonia, heart failure, belly pain, constipation, depression and convulsions. The symptoms vary significantly from one patient to another, and none will have them all. Many patients are free of symptoms for months before a recurrence.

INVESTIGATIONS: Specific blood tests can diagnose the condition.

TREATMENT: Depends upon the severity of the disease. With mild symptoms, no treatment is required. Sun exposure should be avoided, and all non-essential medications ceased. In severe cases, a wide range of drugs, including steroids, cytotoxics, immunosuppressives and antimalarials may all be used. Regular blood tests follow the course of the condition.

COMPLICATIONS: After each attack, there is slightly more permanent liver, kidney or heart damage, and eventually these problems accumulate to the point where the disease becomes life-threatening. In rare cases it proceeds relentlessly to death within a relatively short time.

PROGNOSIS: Very variable course, from a mild arthritic complaint to a rapidly progressive disease. No cure, but with careful management, compliance with treatment, and regular checkups, 90% of patients are alive more than ten years after the diagnosis is made.

See also Discoid Lupus Erythematosus

Systemic Mastocytosis

DESCRIPTION: Form of urticaria pigmentosa that arises in an adult and affects internal organs as well as the skin.

CAUSE: Skin and internal collections (patches) of mast cells that contain histamine. When the patch is disturbed, histamine is released into the tissue, and makes blood vessels leak, resulting in localised itching, swelling, redness and damage specific to the affected organ.

SYMPTOMS: Brown patches on the skin that steadily increase in number over several months or years. They blister and become itchy when rubbed. Internal patches may cause fever, weight loss, diarrhoea and abdominal pain.

INVESTIGATIONS: A skin biopsy can confirm the diagnosis of skin disease. The internal disease can be diagnosed by X-rays of the skull and long bones that may show areas of bone thinning. Liver function blood tests are only sometimes abnormal, and urinary histamine levels may be high.

TREATMENT: Unsatisfactory, but antihistamines, steroids and interferon may be tried.

COMPLICATIONS: Rarely associated with cancer of the bone, liver, spleen, lymph nodes or gut, and causes a type of leukaemia.

PROGNOSIS: Tends to persist long term.

See also Urticaria Pigmentosa

Systemic Sclerosis
See Scleroderma

T

Tabes Dorsalis

DESCRIPTION: Rare complication of third stage syphilis (see separate entry).

CAUSE: Development of a syphilitic deposit in the spinal cord.

SYMPTOMS: Repetitive, brief, severe pain in the legs, back, chest, and sometimes arms and face. Some patients develop poor coordination of the legs and difficulty in walking.

INVESTIGATIONS: Tests for syphilis positive. Abnormal reflexes detected.

TREATMENT: Antibiotics treat the syphilis and prevent progression of the disease.

COMPLICATIONS: Loss of bladder control, vomiting, abdominal pain, and abnormal sensations.

PROGNOSIS: No cure for existing symptoms.

See also Syphilis

Tachycardia
(Ventricular Tachycardia)

DESCRIPTION: Normally the heart beats without any conscious awareness. If a patient becomes aware of the heartbeat, it is usually because it is beating faster than normal (tachycardia).

CAUSE: Exertion, fear or emotion, eating or drinking too much caffeine (eg. colas, coffee), smoking, diseases (eg. anaemia, overactive thyroid gland, cancer, chronic kidney or liver disease), numerous heart disease (eg. paroxysmal atrial or ventricular tachycardia), and drugs (eg. thyroxine, appetite suppressants).

SYMPTOMS: Rapid heart beat and pulse, tiredness, and patients feel the cold more than normal.

INVESTIGATIONS: ECG (electrocardiograph) shows tachycardia and sometimes its cause. Blood and other tests necessary to find cause.

TREATMENT: Depends on cause.

COMPLICATIONS: Heart failure a possibility with some causes.

PROGNOSIS: Depends on cause.

See also Paroxysmal Atrial Tachycardia; Paroxysmal Ventricular Tachycardia

Taeniasis
See Tapeworms

Takayasu's Arteritis
(Aortic Arch Syndrome)

DESCRIPTION: Uncommon inflammation of the aortic arch (very large artery running up from the heart and arching over to run down the back of the chest) and the arteries leading off from this to the neck, head and arms. Tends to occur more in young women, and oriental Asians.

541

Takayasu's Arteritis

CAUSE: Unknown, but probably an autoimmune disease.

SYMPTOMS: Generalised symptoms of tiredness, fever, night sweats, joint pains, loss of appetite. Specific symptoms include chest pain, high blood pressure, heart enlargement, fainting and vision deterioration.

INVESTIGATIONS: Poor or loss of pulses in the neck and arms. Diagnosis confirmed by arteriography (X-ray of arteries after injection of a dye).

TREATMENT: Prednisone (a steroid) eases the symptoms, but does not change the prognosis.

COMPLICATIONS: A stroke occurs in 15% of patients.

PROGNOSIS: Very variable. May settle spontaneously without treatment, or progress rapidly to death in 10%.

See also Temporal Arteritis

Talcosis

DESCRIPTION: Replacement of normal lung tissue by fibrous scar tissue.

CAUSE: Long-term inhalation of fine talcum powder in the milling and rubber industries. Aggravated by cigarette smoking.

SYMPTOMS: No symptoms until the condition is quite advanced, when patients become short of breath.

INVESTIGATIONS: Chest X-ray shows scar tissue in lungs.

TREATMENT: None available.

COMPLICATIONS: Lung infections such as pneumonia.

PROGNOSIS: No cure, but only slowly progressive, and the disease does not necessarily lead to lung cancer in the same way as asbestosis.

See also Asbestosis; Pneumoconiosis; Silicosis

Talipes Equinovarus
See Club Foot

Tapanui Flu
See Chronic Fatigue Syndrome

Tapeworms
(Cestode Infestation; Taeniasis)

DESCRIPTION: Six different types of tapeworm (*Taeniasis*) can infect man. They vary in length from half a centimetre (dwarf tapeworm) to more than 25 metres (beef tapeworm) and are members of a class of worms known as Cestodes. Tapeworms were named because they are divided into segments in much the same way as a tape measure. At one end there is a head (scolex) that has a large sucker on it, and this is used to attach the worm to the inside of the gut.

CAUSE: Mature tapeworms that live in the gut of humans or other animals. Segments that are full of eggs constantly drop off from the end of the worm and pass out with the faeces and remain in the soil until eaten by another animal. When the egg is swallowed, it hatches an embryo that burrows into

542

the muscle of the animal and remains there for the rest of that animal's life. If the animal's flesh is eaten, the embryo enters the gut of the new host, attaches to it and grows into a mature tapeworm. Tiny tapeworm embryos may be found in the flesh of cattle, pigs, and fish but are destroyed by cooking. Less common tapeworms can be transmitted by fleas and other insects from rats and dogs to man, and another uncommon form passes directly from the gut of one human to another through faeces and contaminated food. Tapeworms may be caught in many parts of the world but are rare in developed countries.

SYMPTOMS: There may be no symptoms until the number of worms present is quite high when nausea, diarrhoea, abdominal discomfort, hunger, weight loss and tiredness may occur. Sometimes patients find segments of the worm in their underclothes or bedding.

INVESTIGATIONS: Confirmed by examining the faeces under a microscope for the presence of segments or eggs.

TREATMENT: Cured by appropriate medication.

COMPLICATIONS: Except for the rare cases where the embryo stage spreads to the brain, there are no long-term complications after treatment.

PROGNOSIS: Good with correct treatment.

See also Worm Infestations

Tarsal Tunnel Syndrome

DESCRIPTION: Damage to one of the main nerves supplying the foot.

CAUSE: Due to compression on the posterior tibial nerve as it passes the ankle joint after an injury to the area from repetitive use or a sudden strain.

SYMPTOMS: Pins and needles sensation in toes and sole of the foot, and weakness of muscles in the foot.

INVESTIGATIONS: Electromyography (EMG) shows abnormal nerve and muscle function.

TREATMENT: Corticosteroid injection around the nerve at the point where it is being pinched, or surgery to release trapped nerve.

COMPLICATIONS: Permanent damage to the nerve may result in loss of sensation and function in the foot.

PROGNOSIS: Good results from treatment.

See also Carpal Tunnel Syndrome

TB

See Tuberculosis

T Cell Leukaemia

See Leukaemia

Tear Duct, Blocked

See Conjunctivitis

Teeth Grinding
See Bruxism

Teething
(Cutting Teeth)

DESCRIPTION: Teeth normally start to appear around five or six months, although some children cut a tooth as early as three months and some have even been born with teeth, while in others they do not appear until seven or eight months. By the time they are nine or ten months, most babies have both the top and bottom four front teeth. The molars appear around the age of one year and are likely to cause more discomfort since their larger, broader shape makes it difficult to push through the gum.

CAUSE: A child cries when teething because its gums really are hurting.

SYMPTOMS: An infant with gum discomfort while teeth are pushing through, excess drooling, irritability, food refusal and sometimes bowel movements become slightly loose.

TREATMENT: Chewing on a teething ring, rubbing the gums with gels that contain a mild pain reliever, and paracetamol drops or elixir.

COMPLICATIONS: Infants are more susceptible to infections while stressed by teething.

PROGNOSIS: Discomfort settles after a few days or weeks.

Telangiectasia
See Ataxia Telangiectasia; Osler-Rendu-Weber Disease; Rothmund-Thomson Syndrome; Spider Naevi; Telangiectasia Eruptiva Macularis Perstans

Telangiectasia Eruptiva Macularis Perstans

DESCRIPTION: A rare form of the skin disease urticaria pigmentosa (see separate entry).

CAUSE: Skin patches that are made of abnormal collections of mast cells. These contain histamine and when the cell is disturbed, this is released into the skin. Histamine makes blood vessels leak, resulting in localised itching, swelling and redness.

SYMPTOMS: Diffuse red skin patches occur associated with overlying dilated capillaries (telangiectasia).

INVESTIGATIONS: Skin biopsy confirms the diagnosis.

TREATMENT: Potent steroid creams, antihistamines and PUVA (ultraviolet radiation) two or three times a week for several months.

PROGNOSIS: Usually persistent.

See also Urticaria Pigmentosa

Telogen Effluvium

DESCRIPTION: Diffuse hair loss.

CAUSE: Both men and women have fewer hairs as they grow older, but it may be a symptom of disease such as sex hormone disturbances (eg. pregnancy, menopause), an over- or underactive thyroid gland, pituitary gland diseases, many other serious illness, drugs used to treat cancer, radiation therapy, too much vitamin A, and sudden and excessive loss of weight (eg. anorexia nervosa). Extreme mental or physical stress may also be responsible.

SYMPTOMS: Excessive generalised hair loss from the scalp, and sometimes other hairy areas of the body (eg. eyebrows, pubic area, chest).

INVESTIGATIONS: Blood and other tests may be done to exclude specific causes.

TREATMENT: If a cause can be found this should be treated. When the cause is medication, the hair usually grows back when it is ceased.

PROGNOSIS: Depends on cause.

See also Alopecia Areata; Baldness

Temporal Arteritis
(Giant Cell Arteritis)

DESCRIPTION: Inflammation of medium to large arteries throughout the body, but most commonly the arteries in the temples at the side of the head.

CAUSE: The cause is unknown but may an autoimmune disease. Often follows a significant viral infection.

SYMPTOMS: Involved arteries become extremely tender and swollen. Symptoms depend on which arteries are inflamed, but may include headache, scalp tenderness, pain in the jaw with chewing, throat pain and vision disturbances. Less commonly a cough, shoulder pain, weakness and a fever occur.

INVESTIGATIONS: Blood tests to detect the inflammation, and biopsy of an artery which reveals the presence of giant cells.

TREATMENT: Steroid tablets (eg: prednisone) taken for months.

COMPLICATIONS: Blindness due to involvement of the arteries in the eye, and aneurysms (dilations) of arteries. About half the patients have polymyalgia rheumatica (see separate entry).

PROGNOSIS: Usually well controlled and eventually cured. Recurrences when medication is ceased are common.

Temporal Lobe Epilepsy
See Epilepsy

Temporomandibular Joint Dysfunction
(Jaw Joint Inflammation)

DESCRIPTION: Common cause of face pain due to inflammation of the jaw joint that lies just in front of the ear. More common in women.

CAUSE: May be due to poor alignment of teeth, muscle imbalances in the face associated with emotional stress, grinding of the teeth (bruxism) or an injury to the joint.

SYMPTOMS: Tight aching pain which spreads to the ear and across the face, is worse with chewing and may be associated with a click in the joint.

545

INVESTIGATIONS: X-rays and other tests are usually normal.

TREATMENT: Muscle relaxants (eg. diazepam), mobilisation of the joint under the supervision of a physiotherapist, anti-inflammatory medications and pain relievers, and as a last resort surgery may be performed.

COMPLICATIONS: Arthritis may develop in the joint.

PROGNOSIS: Good response to treatment.

Tendonitis

DESCRIPTION: Inflammation of a tendon due to overuse or injury. Tendons connect a muscle to a bone so that when a muscle contracts, the bone is pulled by the tendon.

CAUSE: If a tendon becomes strained, stretched, overused or damaged it will become inflamed. **Supraspinatus tendonitis** is one of the most common types of tendonitis, and is caused by inflammation of the tendon that runs across the top of the shoulder to move the arm away from the body.

SYMPTOMS: The tendon swells, becomes acutely painful and does not work effectively.

INVESTIGATIONS: Sometimes tiny flecks of bone form in the tendon if it has been inflamed for a long time, and these can be seen on X-ray.

TREATMENT: Rest of the affected part, which may be strapped, bandaged, splinted or plastered to ensure there is no movement. Anti-inflammatory medicines and steroid injections may also be used along with physiotherapy, which is particularly valuable on return to work to prevent a recurrence of the problem.

COMPLICATIONS: None significant.

PROGNOSIS: Good.

See also Repetitive Strain Injury; Tenosynovitis

Tendon Rupture
See Ligament or Tendon Rupture

Tennis Elbow
(Lateral Epicondylitis)

DESCRIPTION: Inflammation of the tendon on the outside of the bony lump at the back of the elbow (olecranon).

CAUSE: Overstraining of the extensor tendon at the outer back of the elbow due to excessive bending and twisting movements of the arm. In tennis, the injury is more likely if the backhand action is faulty, with excessive wrist action and insufficient follow-through. Being unfit, having a tautly strung racquet, a heavy racquet and wet balls all add to the elbow strain. This leads to tears of the minute fibres in the tendon, scar tissue forms which is then broken down again by further strains. May also occur in tradesmen who undertake repetitive tasks, housewives, musicians and many others who may put excessive strain on their elbows.

SYMPTOMS: Painful inflammation occurs, which can be constant or may only occur when the elbow is moved or stressed. The whole forearm can ache in some patients, especially when trying to grip or twist with the hand.

INVESTIGATIONS: None usually necessary.

TREATMENT: Prolonged rest is most important. Exercises to strengthen the elbow and anti-inflammatory drugs may also be used. Cortisone injections may be given in resistant cases. The strengthening exercises are done under the supervision of a physiotherapist and involve using the wrist to raise and lower a weight with the palm facing down. Some patients find pressure pads over the tendon, or elbow guards (elastic tubes around the elbow) help relieve the symptoms and prevent recurrences by adding extra support.

COMPLICATIONS: Not easy to treat and can easily become chronic.

PROGNOSIS: No matter what form of treatment is used, most cases seem to last for about 18 months and then settle spontaneously.

See also Golfer's Elbow

Tenosynovitis

DESCRIPTION: Inflammation of the fibrous sheath that surrounds a tendon, particularly in the hands and feet.

CAUSE: Overuse or repetitive use may reduce the volume of the very thin film of lubricating synovial fluid that allows a tendon to slide smoothly through its sheath, triggering inflammation.

SYMPTOMS: Pain with any movement involving use of the inflamed tendon sheath, and tenderness if pressure is applied to the tendon.

INVESTIGATIONS: None diagnostic.

TREATMENT: Resting the affected part by strapping, bandages, splints or even plaster to prevent any movement of the tendon. Anti-inflammatory medicines may also be used along with physiotherapy. In severe cases injections of steroids may be given around the tendon sheath, but these cannot be repeated too frequently. The last resort is an operation to remove the tendon sheath.

COMPLICATIONS: Rarely permanent contractures of the tendon and limited movement of the joint may occur.

PROGNOSIS: Generally good.

See also Repetitive Strain Injury; Tendonitis

Tension Headache
See Headache, Muscle Spasm

Tension Pneumothorax
See Pneumothorax

Teratoma

DESCRIPTION: An uncommon and unusual form of cancer that occurs in the ovaries or testes.

CAUSE: As the ovaries are the source of eggs, and the testes of sperm, that are used for fertilisation and growth into new humans, the cells in the ovary and testes, when cancerous may develop into many different types of tissue. All types of strange tissue may develop in the tumour, including gland tissue, muscle tissue, skin and even teeth.

SYMPTOMS: In women, symptoms are often minimal until the cancer is quite large, or bleeding occurs into it to cause an abdominal lump or pain. Men feel a hard, tender lump in a testicle.

INVESTIGATIONS: Diagnosed by X-ray, CT scan and biopsy of the tumour.

TREATMENT: Surgical removal of the cancer and surrounding tissue is usually all that is necessary.

COMPLICATIONS: Rarely, an aggressive cancer may be present, that spreads to other parts of the body.

PROGNOSIS: The overall cure rate is close to 90%.

See also Ovarian Cancer; Testicular Cancer

Testicle, Undescended
(Cryptorchidism)

DESCRIPTION: The testes remain inside the abdomen and do not descend into the scrotum. The migration of the testes from where they develop inside the abdomen to the scrotum occurs in 97% of boys by the time they are born, but may be delayed in premature babies.

CAUSE: Developmental abnormality.

SYMPTOMS: The scrotum is empty and no testicles can be felt, but in some boys the testes can be found in the groin and manipulated into the scrotum by gentle finger movements.

INVESTIGATIONS: An ultrasound scan is sometimes performed to find the missing testes.

TREATMENT: If the testes can be manipulated out of the groin into the scrotum no treatment is usually required, but they must be checked regularly to ensure that they do eventually enter and stay in the scrotum. If the testes do not descend in the first year of life, an operation to place them in the correct position is necessary.

COMPLICATIONS: A testicle that remains undescended will eventually fail due to overheating, and if both testes are involved, sterility will result. Long-term problems include an increased risk of inguinal hernias, torsion of the testicle and cancer.

PROGNOSIS: Very good results from surgery.

Testicular Cancer

DESCRIPTION: Any of several different types of cancer that may develop in the testicles. The types include embryomas, seminomas (most common and least serious), choriocarcinoma, teratomas (see separate entry), and a number of rarer ones.

CAUSE: Unknown. Rare form of cancer that develops in one in every 50,000 adult men every year. Most common in early adult and middle-age.

SYMPTOMS: A firm lump, hardening, unusual tenderness or gradual enlargement of the testicle. There is often no pain, but unusually some patient's develop small breasts due to excess production of female oestrogen by the tumour.

INVESTIGATIONS: Some types of cancer can be detected by blood tests, but any hard lump in the scrotum must be investigated by ultrasound, and if necessary surgically biopsied, to determine the exact cause.

TREATMENT: Involves removing the affected testicle and nearby lymph nodes, followed by irradiation or cytotoxic drugs depending upon the type of cancer present.

COMPLICATIONS: May spread to the lymph nodes in the groin, the lungs and liver.

PROGNOSIS: Overall cure rate is 90%.

See also Teratoma

Testicular Infection
See Epididymo-Orchitis

Testicular Torsion
See Torsion of the Testis

Tetanus
(Lockjaw)

DESCRIPTION: A very serious worldwide disease that attacks muscles.

CAUSE: The bacterium Clostridium tetani which lives harmlessly in the gut of many animals, particularly horses. When it passes out in faeces it forms a hard microscopic cyst which contaminates soil. It can remain inactive for many years until it enters a cut or wound where it starts multiplying and produces a chemical (toxin) which spreads throughout the body in the blood. Deep wounds, such as treading on a nail, are particularly susceptible to a tetanus infection.

SYMPTOMS: The toxin attacks the small muscles used for chewing making it difficult to open the mouth (thus the common name of lockjaw). Larger and larger muscles are then attacked, irritating them and causing severe spasm. Excruciating pain from widespread muscle spasms may be triggered by the slightest noise. The patient remains conscious, but eventually the muscles which control breathing and the heart are affected.

INVESTIGATIONS: Diagnosed by a specific blood test.

TREATMENT: No effective treatment other than muscle relaxants and mechanical ventilation. Although the bacteria may be killed by antibiotics, the toxin remains in the body. A vaccine is available, but it does not give lifelong protection, and revaccination is necessary every ten years, or after five years if you have a deep wound.

PROGNOSIS: Death occurs in about 50% of patients, even in good hospitals.

Tetany

DESCRIPTION: Form of muscle spasm that is totally different to a tetanus infection.

CAUSE: Rapid shallow breathing (hyperventilation) may start after a shock, surprise, injury or vigorous exercise, and can cause the amount of carbon dioxide in the lungs to increase. This dissolves in the blood to make it more alkaline (high ph) than normal, and small muscles in the hand and elsewhere are sensitive to this change in blood chemistry. Hormonal and calcium imbalances in the blood may also be responsible.

SYMPTOMS: Small muscles in the hand go into spasm with the wrist bent and fingers and thumb bunched together and pointed towards the wrist. Sometimes muscles in the forearms and feet also go into a firm spasm.

INVESTIGATIONS: None normally necessary, but in repeated cases blood tests may detect abnormal calcium or hormone levels.

TREATMENT: Breathing into a paper bag for a few minutes increases the level of carbon dioxide in the lungs, slows the breathing and eases the spasm. Assisted by giving repeated reassurance.

COMPLICATIONS: None significant.

PROGNOSIS: Not serious. Settles spontaneously eventually, but sometimes not until after the patient has collapsed. Quick recovery with treatment.

See also Tetanus

Tetralogy of Fallot
See Fallot's Tetralogy

Tetraplegia
See Quadriplegia

Thalassaemia beta Major

DESCRIPTION: A blood disease that may cause severe anaemia, and occurs in two main forms, minor and major. There are a number of further subdivisions.

CAUSE: Familial disease (passes from one generation to the next) found in people who live in an area that stretches across Europe and Asia from southern Italy to Malaya, and in some Negro tribes. Major form only occurs if both parents have minor form (see following entry).

SYMPTOMS: Severe anaemia, generalised weakness, increased susceptibility to other diseases, children grow slowly, develop large livers and spleens, and may become jaundiced (yellow).

INVESTIGATIONS: Diagnosed by specific blood tests.

TREATMENT: Regular blood transfusions for severe anaemia.

COMPLICATIONS: The heart is put under great strain trying to cope with severe anaemia, and becomes very enlarged.

PROGNOSIS: Death from heart failure, infection or other complications is common in early adult life. The outcome will depend on the severity of the disease.

See also Thalassaemia beta Minor

Thalassaemia beta Minor

DESCRIPTION: A blood disease that may cause mild anaemia, and occurs in two main forms, minor and major. The minor form is far more common than the major.

CAUSE: Familial. If someone with thalassaemia beta minor marries a normal person, half their children have the chance of having the minor form of the disease. If two people with thalassaemia beta minor marry, statistically one quarter of their children will have the far more serious and disabling major form of the disease, one half will have the minor form, and the other quarter will have neither.

SYMPTOMS: Only slight anaemia, and usually no symptoms.

INVESTIGATIONS: Diagnosed by specific blood tests. Those with a family history should have tests to see if they have the minor form. If a person is positive any marriage partner should also have the test.

TREATMENT: None normally necessary.

COMPLICATIONS: None significant.

PROGNOSIS: Very good, and only an inconvenience.

See also Thalassaemia beta Major

Thiamine Deficiency
See Beriberi

Thoracic Outlet Syndromes
See Naffziger Syndrome; Scapulocostal Syndrome; Subclavian Steal Syndrome

Threadworm
See Pinworm

Throat Infection
See Laryngitis; Pharyngitis; Post-Nasal Drip; Tonsillitis

Thromboangiitis Obliterans
See Buerger's Disease

Thrombocytopenia
(Idiopathic Thrombocytopenic Purpura)

DESCRIPTION: Complex uncommon condition due to a lack of platelets (also known as thrombocytes), the blood cells that are responsible for controlling the rate at which blood clots.

CAUSE: In children the condition often follows a viral illness and settles quickly, but in adults it is usually an autoimmune condition (body rejects its own cells) in which platelets are inappropriately destroyed by the spleen for no apparent reason. Can also occur as a result of adverse drug reactions, infections and other rare disorders.

Thrombocytopenia

SYMPTOMS: Patients are unable to clot their blood as quickly as normal, and they bleed excessively. They develop purpura (red dots under the skin caused by microscopic bleeding) across a wide area, bleed internally to cause black motions, have nosebleeds that are difficult to stop, may vomit and cough blood, bruise very easily, bleed around their teeth after eating and may bleed very heavily during a menstrual period.

INVESTIGATIONS: Diagnosis confirmed by a simple blood test.

TREATMENT: In some children, rest and time only necessary. In all adults and most children high doses of prednisone (a steroid) are given to settle the condition and allow more platelets to be made in the bone marrow. Immunoglobulin injections may also be used. As the spleen is the organ destroying the platelets, surgical removal of this can cure the disease in resistant cases. Other exotic medications may be used in severe cases.

COMPLICATIONS: Bleeding into the brain may cause a stroke, or very rarely, death.

PROGNOSIS: May last for a long time in adults, but the vast majority of patients respond well to treatment, although there are significant dangers before the patient presents to a doctor and in the first few days of treatment. May occasionally recur in adults, but rarely in children.

Thromboembolism, Pulmonary
See Pulmonary Embolism

Thrombophlebitis

DESCRIPTION: A combination of thrombosis and phlebitis (see separate entries) in a vein.

CAUSE: Thrombosis is a clot in a vein and phlebitis is inflammation of the involved blood vessel. Often occurs in a vein which has had a drip inserted into it.

SYMPTOMS: A long rope like, painful, hard, red lump can be felt under the skin along the course of an artery or vein.

INVESTIGATIONS: None normally necessary.

TREATMENT: Anti-inflammatory medication for phlebitis and appropriate treatment for thrombosis (see separate entry).

COMPLICATIONS: Clot may spread and damage blood supply to or from major organs.

PROGNOSIS: Settles with treatment, but rope like lump may remain long term.

See also Phlebitis; Thrombosis

Thrombosis

DESCRIPTION: A thrombus occurs when blood clots inside a vein or artery, partially or completely blocking it. Blood vessels in any part of the body may be involved.

CAUSE: An injury, prolonged immobility, hardening of the arteries from cholesterol deposits (atherosclerosis), smoking, cancer, major surgery and a number of rarer conditions.

SYMPTOMS: Pain at the site of the thrombus, and other symptoms depending on blood vessel affected.

INVESTIGATIONS: Blood tests can demonstrate the presence of a thrombus somewhere in the body, but not its location. Sophisticated X-rays, ultrasound and CT scans are used to find the blood clot.

TREATMENT: Depends on site and severity, but generally anticoagulant medication (eg. warfarin, heparin) is given to prevent both the spread of the thrombus and the formation of new clots.

COMPLICATIONS: If a thrombus occurs in an artery supplying the heart muscle a heart attack occurs, in the brain a stroke, and in the lung a pulmonary embolism (see separate entries).

PROGNOSIS: Depends on site and size of thrombus.

See also Deep Venous Thrombosis; Mesenteric Artery Thrombosis; Pulmonary Embolism; Sticky-Platelet Syndrome; Stroke; Superficial Venous Thrombosis; Thrombophlebitis

Thrombosis, Cerebral
See Stroke

Thrush
(Candidiasis; Moniliasis)

DESCRIPTION: A fungal infection that occurs most commonly in the mouth and the vagina.

CAUSE: The fungus Candida albicans is responsible for the infection in all sites.

Oral — quite common in infancy, particularly in bottle-fed babies, and may be triggered by a course of antibiotics that destroy the bacteria in the mouth that normally control the growth of excess fungi.

Vaginal — Candida albicans lives in the gut where it causes little or no trouble. When it comes out on to the skin around the anus, it dies off; but if that skin is warm, moist and irritated, it can grow and spread forward to the lips of the vagina (the vulva). A warm climate and the aggravating factors of tight jeans, pantyhose, the contraceptive pill, nylon bathers, antibiotics and sex give the area between a woman's legs the right degree of warmth, moisture and irritation to make the spread of the fungus relatively easy. Antibiotics aggravate the problem as they can kill off the bacteria that normally keep fungi under control. Entry of the fungus into the vagina is aided by the mechanical action of sex and the alteration in the acidity of the vagina caused by the contraceptive pill.

SYMPTOMS: Oral — grey/white patches on the tongue, gums and inside of the cheeks that cannot be rubbed away with a finger tip or cotton bud. May spread through the intestine and emerge to infect the skin around the anus, where it causes a bright red rash that is slightly paler towards the centre.

Vaginal — an unpleasant white vaginal discharge, intense itching of the vulva and surrounding skin, and often inflammation of the urine opening so that passing urine causes discomfort.

INVESTIGATIONS: Swabs may be taken from mouth, buttocks or vagina to confirm the identity of the responsible fungus.

TREATMENT: Oral — antifungal drops or gels in the mouth, and antifungal creams around the anus.

Vaginal — antifungal vaginal pessaries (tablets), vaginal creams or antifungal tablets taken by mouth. The sex partner must also be treated as he can give the infection back to the woman after she has been successfully treated. Prevented by wearing loose cotton panties, drying the genital area carefully after swimming or showering, avoiding tight clothing, wiping from front to back after going to the toilet and not using tampons when an infection is likely.

COMPLICATIONS: Oral — rarely causes serious complications.

Vaginal — many women have repeated attacks, which may be due to inadequate treatment, contamination from the gut, or reinfection from their sex partner.

PROGNOSIS: Oral — most babies respond rapidly to the correct treatment.

Vaginal — usually settles with treatment, but reinfection common.

See also Fungal Infections; Stomatitis

Thymic Dysplasia
See Nezelof Syndrome

Thymic Hypoplasia
See di George Syndrome

Thymoma

DESCRIPTION: Rare cancerous or benign tumour of the thymus gland, which is a small irregular strip of glandular tissue that lies behind the upper part of the breast bone and extends up into the front of the neck. The thymus is proportionally much larger and more important in children, and reaches its maximum size at puberty. It plays a major role in the development and maintenance of the immune system, produces specific types of white blood cells that are vital in allowing the body to become immune to infection, and secretes a hormone that maintains the cells it produces.

CAUSE: Unknown.

SYMPTOMS: Vague discomfort in neck, cough, shortness of breath, tiredness.

INVESTIGATIONS: CT or MRI scan of neck and chest shows the tumour.

TREATMENT: Surgical removal.

COMPLICATIONS: Cancerous types may spread to nearby tissues.

PROGNOSIS: Very variable depending on type of tumour present and stage at which surgery is performed.

Thyroid Cancer

DESCRIPTION: Any of several different types of cancer of the thyroid gland, which sits in the front of the neck between the Adam's apple and the top of the breast bone, and produces hormones that control the metabolic rate of the body.

CAUSE: Unknown, but more common in elderly women. Cancers may also spread from other organs to the thyroid.

SYMPTOMS: Usually felt as a painless lump in the gland that steadily enlarges. It does not normally interfere with the workings of the gland until it is very advanced, and there are no other symptoms in the early stages. Any hard lump in the thyroid gland is considered to be a cancer until proved otherwise.

INVESTIGATIONS: The proof usually involves scanning the thyroid gland with radioactive iodine, an ultrasound scan, taking a biopsy of the lump, or removing the lump surgically. It cannot be detected by a blood test.

TREATMENT: Surgery to remove the gland. Irradiation and cytotoxic drugs may be added in some cases.

COMPLICATIONS: May spread to surrounding lymph nodes, bone, liver and other organs.

PROGNOSIS: Several different types of cancer occur in the thyroid, and outcome will depend upon the type present. Anaplastic carcinoma of the thyroid has the worst prognosis and usually proceeds rapidly to death, while papillary tumours are rarely fatal.

Thyroid Gland Enlargement
See Goitre; Painful Thyroiditis Syndrome

Thyroid Gland Underactivity
See Cretinism; Goitre; Hypothyroidism

Thyroiditis

DESCRIPTION: An inflammation or infection of the thyroid gland, which lies in the front of the neck. The most common type is Hashimoto's disease (see separate entry). Other forms include de Quervain's thyroiditis, Riedel's thyroiditis (see separate entries) and suppurative thyroiditis.

CAUSE: See separate entries for information on inflammatory types.

Suppurative thyroiditis is a rare disorder caused by a bacterial infection of the gland.

SYMPTOMS: Patients with suppurative thyroiditis have severe pain in the front of the neck, tenderness, redness and swelling of the gland.

INVESTIGATIONS: Diagnosed by blood tests.

TREATMENT: Suppurative thyroiditis — high doses of antibiotics and drainage of any abscess that may form.

Other forms — depends on cause. Thyroid hormone supplements usually required.

Thyroiditis

COMPLICATIONS: An abscess may develop in the gland.
PROGNOSIS: Most forms can be easily controlled, but only the suppurative form can be cured.
See also de Quervain's Thyroiditis; Hashimoto's Thyroiditis; Painful Thyroiditis Syndrome; Riedel's Thyroiditis

Thyrotoxicosis
See Hyperthyroidism

TIA
See Transient Ischaemic Attack

Tibial Stress Syndrome
See Shin Splints

Tic Doloureux
See Trigeminal Neuralgia

Tick Bite

DESCRIPTION: Ticks are distantly related to spiders. They have a round black body from which mouth parts protrude and grasp the skin, but do not have a head as such. The tube-like mouth part pierces the skin to suck up blood, and when full it drops off to digest its meal, then waits sometimes for more than a year, for its next victim. They feed from almost any warm-blooded animal, although some species preferentially attack certain animals. They are more active in spring and summer and are usually found on the head, burrowing in amongst the hair, or in body crevices.
CAUSE: Bite from any one of a number of different species of tick.
SYMPTOMS: Usually only painful irritation and a raised lump on the skin at the bite site. In children or severe cases there may be a pins and needles sensation around the bite, nausea, double vision, unsteadiness, and eventually weakness and difficulty in moving the limb.
INVESTIGATIONS: None normally necessary.
TREATMENT: To remove a tick, wash it and the surrounding skin with an alcohol solution (eg. methylated spirits). Place a pair of tweezers flat on the skin so that the jaws are on either side of the tick. Grasp the tick firmly, as close to the skin as possible, twist through 90 degrees, and then lift off. The tick will come away easily with minimal pain. Some tiny black marks, the mouth parts, may be left behind, but rarely cause any trouble. Antiseptic cream or lotion may be put on the bite.
COMPLICATIONS: If the bite area becomes red and angry, it may have become infected by a bacteria. Rarely in children a tick bite may lead to paralysis of the face and breathing apparatus. Very rarely death occurs in infants.
PROGNOSIS: Bite heals without scarring over a couple of days.

Tick Typhus
See Typhus

Tietze Syndrome
(Anterior Chest Wall Syndrome; Costochondral Syndrome)
DESCRIPTION: A harmless, relatively common chest wall condition which tends to mimic the pain of a heart attack. Patients are usually middle aged, and there is normally only one attack. The ribs sweep around the chest from the back towards the breast bone (sternum) but stop a few centimetres short. The ribs are joined to the breast bone by a strip of cartilage (costal cartilage). Inflammation occurs at the point where the cartilage joins onto the rib (costochondral junction). The second rib is most commonly involved, but any rib, and any number of ribs may be affected.

CAUSE: Unknown.

SYMPTOMS: Painful, tender swellings of one or more costal cartilages just under the skin on the front of the chest to either side of the sternum.

INVESTIGATIONS: None necessary.

TREATMENT: Anti-inflammatory drugs, steroid injections and pain-killers.

COMPLICATIONS: None significant.

PROGNOSIS: Settles spontaneously in two weeks to six months.

See also Xiphoidalgia

Tinea
See Athlete's Foot; Fungal Infections; Onychogryphosis; Pityriasis Versicolor; Tinea Capitis; Tinea Corporis; Tinea Cruris; Tinea Manum

Tinea Capitis
DESCRIPTION: A fungal infection of the skin on the scalp that usually occurs in children.

CAUSE: The fungi usually come from the Trichophyton, Microsporum and Epidermophyton families. Caught by close contact with another infected human or animal (eg. cat, dog).

SYMPTOMS: An irregular, relatively bald patch on the scalp covered in a fine scale and broken hair stubble (the fungi invades the hairs and causes them to become fragile and break).

INVESTIGATIONS: Diagnosis proved by taking a skin scraping or hair sample, and examining it under a microscope for fungal spores. Ultraviolet light (Wood's light) in an otherwise dark room, will cause a bright green fluorescence of hair and skin affected by a fungus.

TREATMENT: Antifungal ointments, lotions, tinctures and shampoos.

COMPLICATIONS: A severely affected patch may develop a thick build-up of scale and form a fungal abscess (kerion — see separate entry).

PROGNOSIS: Very good.

See also other diseases listed under Fungal Infections

Tinea Corporis
(Ringworm)

DESCRIPTION: A fungal infection of the skin that is NOT caused by a worm.

CAUSE: The fungi usually come from the Trichophyton, Microsporum and Epidermophyton families. Caught by close contact with another infected human or animal (eg. cat, dog). Prefer areas of the body where there is heat (under clothing, in shoes), friction (from tight clothes or skin folds rubbing together) and moisture (from sweat), and more common in the tropics. Affects both sexes and all ages equally.

SYMPTOMS: The fungus settles in one spot on the skin, and a red dot may be seen. This slowly enlarges as the fungus spreads, and after a few days the centre of the red patch becomes pale again and similar to normal skin, because the infection is no longer active at this point. The infection continues to spread and forms an enlarging red ring on the skin. Multiple ring-shaped spots with a pale centre are seen on the chest, abdomen and back. Usually does not cause an itch or discomfort.

INVESTIGATIONS: Diagnosis proved by taking a skin scraping and examining it under a microscope for fungal spores.

TREATMENT: Antifungal creams, ointments, lotions and tinctures. Antifungal tablets are available for more serious infections, but sometimes they are very slow to work, and may need to be taken for up to six months.

COMPLICATIONS: Without treatment, the ringworm may persist for many months.

PROGNOSIS: Good with proper treatment, but recurs if treatment ceased prematurely.

See also other diseases listed under **Fungal Infections**

Tinea Cruris
('Crotch Rot')

DESCRIPTION: A fungal infection of the skin in the groin.

CAUSE: The fungi usually come from the Trichophyton, Microsporum and Epidermophyton families. Caught by close contact (eg. sexual) with an infected person, or in babies may be due to wet nappies or sweaty skin. More common in men than women, has a peak incidence in the 20s and 30s, and tends to occur more in summer and with exercise.

SYMPTOMS: A red, scaly rash spreads out from the skin folds in the groin to cover the inside of the thighs, the lower abdomen and the buttocks. Often itchy and feels constantly uncomfortable.

INVESTIGATIONS: Diagnosis proved by taking a skin scraping and examining it under a microscope for fungal spores.

TREATMENT: Antifungal creams, ointments, lotions and tinctures. Antifungal tablets are available for more serious infections, but sometimes they are very slow to work, and may need to be taken for up to six months.

COMPLICATIONS: Secondary bacterial infection of damaged skin possible.

PROGNOSIS: Good with proper treatment, but recurrences common.

See also other diseases listed under **Fungal Infections**

Tinea Manum

DESCRIPTION: A fungal infection of the hand.

CAUSE: The fungi usually come from the Trichophyton, Microsporum and Epidermophyton families. Caught by close contact with another infected human or animal (eg. cat, dog). Uncommon in children.

SYMPTOMS: A fine scale with a faint red edge that affects the palms and palm side of the fingers.

INVESTIGATIONS: Diagnosis proved by taking a skin scraping and examining it under a microscope for fungal spores.

TREATMENT: Antifungal tablets for a month or more, rather than cream, because the thick skin of the palm makes it difficult for creams to penetrate.

COMPLICATIONS: None significant.

PROGNOSIS: Good with proper treatment.

See also other diseases listed under **Fungal Infections**

Tinea Pedis
See Athlete's Foot

Tinea Unguium
See Onychogryphosis

Tinea Versicolor
See Pityriasis Versicolor

Tocopherols
See Vitamin E Deficiency; Vitamin E Excess

Toenail, Ingrown
See Ingrown Toenail

Togavirus Infection
See German Measles

Tolosa-Hunt Syndrome

DESCRIPTION: Rare injury to nerve supplying eye muscles and sensation.

CAUSE: Aneurysm (ballooning) on the side of the internal carotid artery at the base of the skull puts pressure on nerves.

SYMPTOMS: Painful paralysis of one eye.

INVESTIGATIONS: Angiography (X-ray of an artery after injection of a dye), CT or MRI scan.

TREATMENT: Surgical removal of the aneurysm.

PROGNOSIS: Surgery usually cures the problem.

See also Aneurysm

Tonsillitis

DESCRIPTION: Infection of the tonsils, which are modified lymph nodes that sit on either side of the throat at the back of the mouth. They intercept and destroy bacteria and viruses that enter the body, but if a tonsil is overwhelmed by these organisms tonsillitis occurs. May occur at any age, but far more common amongst children.

CAUSE: Bacteria (eg. Streptococci, Staphylococci, Haemophilus) or viruses (eg. glandular fever) that enter through the mouth or nose.

SYMPTOMS: Tonsil becomes enlarged, red and covered in pus. Patient develops a sudden high fever, headache, throat pain, has offensive breath and finds it difficult to swallow or speak. Can easily spread to the other tonsil and to lymph nodes below the jaw and around the ear.

INVESTIGATIONS: Bacterial infection — types of bacteria differentiated by a throat swab.

Viral infection — blood tests can detect glandular fever and likelihood of other viral infections.

TREATMENT: Bacterial infection — bed rest, fluid diet, aspirin or paracetamol, antiseptic mouth washes and antibiotics (eg. penicillin, erythromycin, tetracycline).

Viral infection — no cure available, and pain-killing tablets and gargles used to give relief, while prolonged rest allows recovery.

Recurrent attacks — surgical removal of the tonsils (tonsillectomy).

COMPLICATIONS: The eustachian tube that drains fluid from, and allows air to enter into the middle ear, opens into the back of the throat between the tonsils and adenoids. As a result infection may spread from the tonsils to the ear. Uncontrolled bacterial infection may cause an abscess (quinsy) or septicaemia (see separate entries). Infectious, and may be passed to another person who is in close contact with the patient.

PROGNOSIS: Very good with appropriate treatment.

See also Quinsy

Torsion Dystonia

DESCRIPTION: Nervous system abnormality.

CAUSE: May be inherited or occur for no apparent reason.

SYMPTOMS: Child or young adult with progressively worsening abnormal movements and posture of the head, face (grimaces, opening and closing mouth), neck and limbs.

INVESTIGATIONS: No specific diagnostic tests.

TREATMENT: Unsatisfactory. Numerous medications may be tried, including those used for Parkinson's disease.

PROGNOSIS: No cure. One third of patients are severely disabled, one third moderately and one third only mildly.

Torsion of the Testis
(Testicular Torsion)

DESCRIPTION: Cutting off the blood supply to the testicle due to twisting of the organ.

CAUSE: Torsion occurs if a testicle, hanging in the scrotum from its network of veins, arteries and nerves, twists horizontally, and its blood supply is cut off.

SYMPTOMS: Severe testicular pain, tenderness, redness and swelling. Usually occurs in teenage boys, and is almost unknown over 30 years of age.

INVESTIGATIONS: None necessary.

TREATMENT: Torsion of the testes is a medical emergency, and the testis will die unless it is surgically untwisted within about 12 hours.

COMPLICATIONS: Gangrene and death of the testicle necessitating its removal. Infection of the testes can also occur (see epididymo-orchitis), and may be confused with torsion, but the pain is usually less severe, the patient is febrile and both testes may be involved.

PROGNOSIS: Depends on how quickly surgery is undertaken. A man is still able to function normally sexually, and is still fertile, with only one testicle.

See also Epididymo-Orchitis; Hydatid of Morgagni; Ovarian Torsion

Torticollis

DESCRIPTION: Severe spasm of a muscle in the neck. The sternocleidomastoid muscle that runs diagonally from the mastoid process at the base of the skull behind the ear across the neck to the top of the breast bone (sternum) is most commonly involved.

CAUSE: Usually caused by repeated turning of the head (eg. watching a tennis match) or sleeping heavily and awkwardly (eg. after excess alcohol), but rarely may be due to a tumour of the brain affecting the nerves to the involved muscles.

SYMPTOMS: Very painful spasm of muscles, usually on only one side of the neck, that limits neck movement and causes the head to be held at an abnormal angle.

INVESTIGATIONS: None normally necessary unless a brain cause is suspected in intractable cases, when a CT scan is performed.

TREATMENT: Muscle relaxants (eg. diazepam) and powerful pain killers (eg. pethidine), often by injection, with pain relieving tablets to follow. Heat and physiotherapy are also useful.

COMPLICATIONS: None significant.

PROGNOSIS: Usually settles in a day or so with treatment.

Tourette Syndrome
(Gilles de la Tourette Syndrome)

DESCRIPTION: Severe behaviour disorder of children.

CAUSE: Unknown.

SYMPTOMS: Patients suffer seizures, other forms of uncontrollable body movements, and often swear and shout excessively.

INVESTIGATIONS: None will specifically diagnose the condition.

TREATMENT: Medications are available to control the more serious symptoms.

COMPLICATIONS: Possibly associated with the Crigler-Najjar syndrome (see separate entry).

PROGNOSIS: Persists long term, but often fades in adult life.

Toxic Epidermal Necrolysis
See Scalded Skin Syndrome

Toxic Erythema
See Dermatitis Medicamentosa

Toxic Shock Syndrome

DESCRIPTION: Rare syndrome that usually affects women in which a toxin (poison) damages tissue.

CAUSE: Toxin released by the bacterium Staphylococcus aureus (golden staph). May occur after confinement, using contraceptive diaphragms, gynaecological surgery, with an abscess, or as a complication of influenza. More than 90% of cases are associated with the use of menstrual tampons. The blood-soaked material in a tampon may become invaded by the bacteria, which release the toxin into the bloodstream through the vaginal wall. The woman herself is not infected by the bacteria.

SYMPTOMS: Fever, widespread red rash, headache, muscle aches, vomiting, diarrhoea and dangerously low blood pressure.

INVESTIGATIONS: Numerous blood tests performed in an attempt to identify the cause and monitor progress. No specific diagnostic test available.

TREATMENT: Injected steroids, kidney dialysis (artificial kidney machine), blood transfusions and antibiotics in a hospital intensive care unit.

COMPLICATIONS: Low blood pressure may threaten the blood supply to the brain, liver, kidney and other vital organs, and eventually causes them to fail.

PROGNOSIS: Overall mortality rate is 15%.

Toxocariasis
See Visceral Larva Migrans

Toxoplasmosis

DESCRIPTION: Parasitic infestation of the intestine.

CAUSE: The single-celled animal Toxoplasma gondii which is found world-wide as a parasite of cats, other animals and birds, from whom it may spread to humans. The eggs pass out in the faeces of the animal and may then enter a human mouth (eg. after careless handling of cat litter, or soil contamination of fingers or food). Once in the gut, the microscopic egg hatches and multiplies into millions of single-celled animals.

SYMPTOMS: Often so mild that they are ignored, but in severe cases a low-grade fever, tiredness, muscle aches, joint pains, headache, sore throat, a mild rash and enlarged lymph nodes may occur. In rare severe cases, the liver, spleen, lungs, eye, heart and brain may be involved.

INVESTIGATIONS: Detected by a specific blood test.

TREATMENT: Normally none necessary. If symptoms are significant or complications develop, medications are available (eg. pyrimethamine) to destroy the parasite. No vaccination or other form of prevention available. Pregnant women should not associate closely with cats.

COMPLICATIONS: In pregnant women the infestation may cause miscarriages, still birth, and deformities in the baby (eg. small head, hydrocephalus, mental retardation, fits, blindness).

PROGNOSIS: Patients usually recover without treatment in four to eight weeks.

Tracheitis

DESCRIPTION: Infection of the trachea (windpipe), usually by viruses, but sometimes by bacteria.

CAUSE: The infecting viruses or bacteria are inhaled from the breath of someone who has some form of respiratory tract infection (eg. common cold, bronchitis, sinusitis).

SYMPTOMS: Painful breathing, persistent dry cough, pain in the chest behind the upper end of the breast bone, fever and tiredness.

INVESTIGATIONS: None normally necessary.

TREATMENT: Antibiotics can cure the condition if caused by bacteria, but viral infections can only be treated with aspirin and other anti-inflammatory medications, cough suppressants, and paracetamol for pain. In severe cases inhaled steroids may be used to settle the inflammation.

COMPLICATIONS: The infection may spread up to the throat to cause laryngitis, or down into the lungs to cause bronchitis.

PROGNOSIS: Bacterial infections settle rapidly with antibiotics, while viral infections may persist for two or more weeks before settling.

See also Bronchitis, Acute; Laryngitis; Laryngotracheobronchitis; Pharyngitis

Trachoma

DESCRIPTION: A type of conjunctivitis (superficial eye infection).

CAUSE: The bacteria-like Chlamydia organism, which is very common in areas of low hygiene where flies can transmit the infection from one person to another. It is particularly common among Australian Aborigines.

SYMPTOMS: Mild infections may not be very noticeable, and in children may cause no symptoms. In more severe cases, eye pain, intolerance to bright lights, and a weeping swollen eye develop. Small bubbles on the underside of the eyelids are the earliest sign of the disease.

INVESTIGATIONS: Diagnosed by culture and examination of swabs from the eye.

TREATMENT: A one to three month course of antibiotics and antibiotic eye ointment. Once blindness has occurred from corneal scarring, the only treatment is surgical replacement of the damaged cornea by one donated by a deceased person.

COMPLICATIONS: Chronic trachoma causes scarring of the cornea (the outer surface of the eye) and subsequent blindness. Blood vessels grow into the scar tissue, and the coloured part of the eye and the pupil may be covered with a thick scar and obvious small arteries and veins. The gland that produces tears (the lacrimal gland) can also be damaged so that tears no longer form, the eye dries out, and is further damaged and scarred.

PROGNOSIS: Usually cured if treated within the first year, and the outcome is excellent, but if left longer some scarring of the eye surface may occur.

See also Conjunctivitis

Transfusion Reaction

DESCRIPTION: Abnormal reaction to a blood transfusion. Most patients have no reaction at all.

CAUSE: It is necessary to cross-match blood before it is given to a patient, so that the blood of the patient and the donor are compatible. There are four main blood groups (A, B, O, AB) that are further subdivided into those that are Rhesus negative and Rhesus positive. A person can therefore be one of eight different combinations (ie. A+ or A-, O+ or 0-, B+ or B-, AB+ or AB-). There are several dozen subgroups beyond this classification and usually these make no significant difference to the patient receiving the blood, but in some cases a transfusion reaction can occur if there is a very slight mismatch of the blood between one of these minor subgroups.

SYMPTOMS: Most commonly only a raised temperature occurs. Other possible symptoms include muscle pains, headaches, and shortness of breath. Very rarely do symptoms become worse than this.

INVESTIGATIONS: None normally necessary.

TREATMENT: Often none required, but in more severe cases aspirin, antihistamines or steroids may be necessary.

COMPLICATIONS: Very rarely a severe reaction may permanently damage organs or be life threatening.

PROGNOSIS: Recovery within a few hours or days usual.

Transient Acantholytic Dermatosis
See Grover's Disease

Transient Ischaemic Attack
(TIA)

DESCRIPTION: Type of funny turn in elderly people due to a temporary miniature stroke.

CAUSE: Most caused by hardening and narrowing of arteries (arteriosclerosis) in the neck and brain by excessive deposition of cholesterol that causes small blood clots to form. A clot may break off from the artery wall and travel through the arteries into the brain, where it may briefly obstruct an artery, causing temporary damage to the brain tissue beyond the blockage. Spasms of arteries caused by stress, toxins or allergies may also be responsible.

SYMPTOMS: The patient feels strange and acts peculiarly. There may be weakness in one arm or leg, abnormal sensations (eg. pins and needles, numbness), disturbances in vision, abnormally slurred speech, dizziness, confusion, tremor and blackouts. The symptoms may last for a few seconds or several hours.

INVESTIGATIONS: Blood tests, ultrasound examination of arteries in the neck, special X-rays of arteries in the brain, and CT scans of the brain may be performed to determine the cause.

TREATMENT: There is no specific treatment. Aspirin or warfarin taken long term in low doses prevent most TIAs, and often prevent strokes too, by preventing blood clots.

COMPLICATIONS: May be an early warning of narrowed arteries in the brain, and can forewarn of strokes. All patients experiencing a TIA need to be fully investigated.

PROGNOSIS: Temporary condition, and the patient returns to normal within 24 hours.

See also Stroke

Transverse Myelitis

DESCRIPTION: Inflammatory disorder of the spinal cord.

CAUSE: Autoimmune condition often associated with a recent viral (eg. influenza, measles, mumps) or bacterial (eg. Mycoplasma) infection, or very rarely a vaccination.

SYMPTOMS: Neck or back pain, followed by altered sensations (eg. pins and needles, loss of sense of touch) and muscle weakness in the body below the area of pain.

INVESTIGATIONS: Reflexes are abnormal. Diagnosed by an MRI scan.

TREATMENT: Steroid injections into the spinal cord may be tried, but are often ineffective.

COMPLICATIONS: May progress to complete paraplegia or quadriplegia.

PROGNOSIS: May be some recovery, but effects usually permanent.

See also Devic's Disease; Multiple Sclerosis; Paraplegia; Quadriplegia

Traumatic Cervical Syndrome
See Whiplash

Travel Sickness
See Motion Sickness

Treacher-Collins Syndrome

DESCRIPTION: Rare developmental disorder of the face.

CAUSE: Transmitted within a family by an irregularly dominant gene.

SYMPTOMS: Under developed lower jaw, large mouth, absent angle between nose and forehead, abnormal eye slant, notched lower eye lids, sparse eyelashes, hairy cheeks, low set ears, deafness and middle ear abnormalities.

INVESTIGATIONS: No diagnostic tests.

TREATMENT: Plastic surgery may correct some deformities.

PROGNOSIS: No cure.

Tremor, Essential
See Essential Tremor

Trench Mouth
See Necrotising Ulcerative Gingivostomatitis

Trichinosis

DESCRIPTION: Roundworm infestation not found in Australia, but otherwise a world wide disease with maximum incidence in North America and Europe.

CAUSE: Infestation of the intestine and muscle tissue of humans, pigs and a wide range of other animals caused by a tiny nematode (round worm). Wild pigs are the most common source, but it has been caught from eating walrus in Alaska and bear in Canada. The nematode forms a cyst in the animal meat, and if not adequately cooked, may survive and enter the human intestine where larvae are released from the cyst, mature and reproduce. The larvae pass through the lining of the gut into veins and are distributed by the blood throughout the body to form cysts in the tissue, where they may remain for up to ten years waiting to be eaten by another mammal.

SYMPTOMS: Diarrhoea, muscle pain, fevers, tiredness and sometimes facial swelling.

INVESTIGATIONS: Detected by specific blood and skin tests.

TREATMENT: Larvae can be killed by appropriate medication.

COMPLICATIONS: In more serious cases the heart, lungs and brain may be invaded.

PROGNOSIS: Cysts remain in the tissue after the larvae they contain have been destroyed, and symptoms may continue long term.

Trichobezoar
(Bezoar; Hair Ball)

DESCRIPTION: A bezoar is a solid mass in the stomach formed from swallowed foreign bodies. A trichobezoar is the most common form and is composed of hair that may completely fill the stomach.

CAUSE: May occur as a side effect of stomach surgery (eg. vagotomy, partial gastrectomy) if the emptying ability of the stomach is affected and fibrous vegetable matter accumulates, but more commonly occurs in psychiatric patients who eat inappropriate objects that can vary from asphalt and cloth to leaves and plastic bags. Women with very long hair who chew their hair as a habit, and psychiatric patients who pull out their hair and eat it, may form a trichobezoar.

SYMPTOMS: Stomach pain, nausea, vomiting, loss of appetite and weight loss.

INVESTIGATIONS: Diagnosed by a barium meal X-ray or gastroscopy.

TREATMENT: Difficult. Removal through a gastroscope is usually attempted, but if it cannot be broken and allowed to pass on naturally, or withdrawn with or through the gastroscope, open surgery may be necessary.

COMPLICATIONS: Stomach ulcers or rarely bowel obstruction.

PROGNOSIS: Good results from treatment once diagnosed.

Trichomoniasis, Venereal

DESCRIPTION: Infection of a woman's vagina, and the urethra (urine tube) of both men and women.

CAUSE: The single-celled animal, Trichomonas vaginalis . Transmitted from one victim to another by heterosexual or homosexual intercourse.

SYMPTOMS: In women, vaginal infection causes a foul-smelling, yellow/green, frothy discharge, and there may be mild itching or soreness around the outside of the vagina. In men, there are often minimal symptoms, or discomfort on passing urine, often first thing in the morning.

INVESTIGATIONS: Diagnosis can be confirmed by examining a swab taken from the vagina or urethra.

TREATMENT: Antibiotic tablets (eg. azithromycin) and/or vaginal cream. All sexual contacts need to be treated at the same time.

COMPLICATIONS: None serious.

PROGNOSIS: Very good result from treatment.

See also other conditions listed under Sexually Transmitted Diseases.

Trichotillomania

DESCRIPTION: Self induced cause of hair loss that often starts in childhood or the teen years. Females far more commonly affected than males, and any body hair, including pubic and eyebrows, may be involved.

CAUSE: Pulling and twisting the hair until it breaks, usually as a subconscious habit, but sometimes in association with a psychiatric disturbance.

SYMPTOMS: Patchy hair loss, with hair of varying lengths in the affected area.

INVESTIGATIONS: None necessary.

TREATMENT: Strangely, shaving the head or pubic area (but not the eyebrows) may break the habit. Sometimes psychiatric medications required.

PROGNOSIS: Most patients grow out of the habit.

Trichuriasis
(Whipworm Infestation)

DESCRIPTION: Infestation of the large intestine with the 3 to 5 cm. long worm Trichuris.

CAUSE: Adult whipworms live in the colon and produce eggs which pass out with the faeces to contaminate the soil. If contaminated food or water is consumed the eggs will hatch in the small intestine to form larvae that then migrate to the large intestine and mature into adult worms. The cycle takes a minimum of three months and adult worms may live for three years. They are found throughout the tropics.

SYMPTOMS: Most patients have no symptoms, but with severe infestations abdominal pain, loss of appetite and diarrhoea may occur.

INVESTIGATIONS: Diagnosed by finding the eggs on microscopic examination of the faeces.

TREATMENT: Effectively treated by the drug mebendazole.

COMPLICATIONS: Badly infested children may have bloody diarrhoea and become malnourished.

PROGNOSIS: Treatment is very effective.

See also Worm Infestations.

Tricuspid Incompetence
(Tricuspid Regurgitation)

DESCRIPTION: Leaking of the three leafed tricuspid valve which controls the flow of blood between the upper chamber (the atrium) and lower chamber (the ventricle) on the right side of the heart.

CAUSE: Cor pulmonale, heart attack, heart tumours (eg. myxoma), or endocarditis (see separate entries).

SYMPTOMS: Distended neck veins, enlarged liver, fluid accumulates in belly and around the lungs, and the ankles and feet become swollen.

INVESTIGATIONS: Diagnosed by hearing a characteristic heart murmur, abnormal electrocardiograph (ECG), echocardiography (ultrasound scan) or passing a catheter through a vein and into the heart.

TREATMENT: Often controlled by medication rather than surgery, which is performed only in severe cases.

COMPLICATIONS: Reduced outflow of blood from the heart to the lungs may lead to heart failure or attack.

PROGNOSIS: Good.

See also other diseases listed under Heart Valve Disease

Tricuspid Regurgitation
See Tricuspid Incompetence

Tricuspid Stenosis

DESCRIPTION: Narrowing of the three leafed tricuspid valve which controls the flow of blood between the upper chamber (the atrium) and lower chamber (the ventricle) on the right side of the heart.

CAUSE: Uncommon in developed countries and usually occurs as a result of rheumatic fever.

SYMPTOMS: Fluid accumulation in the belly, large liver, shortness of breath, fatigue, dilation of the veins in the neck and a redness in the neck and face as blood finds it difficult to progress from the body and into the heart.

INVESTIGATIONS: Diagnosed by hearing a characteristic heart murmur, abnormal electrocardiograph (ECG) and echocardiography (ultrasound scan).

TREATMENT: Surgical correction of narrowed heart valve.

COMPLICATIONS: Heart failure.

PROGNOSIS: Good results from surgery.

See also other diseases listed under **Heart Valve Disease**

Trigeminal Neuralgia
(Tic Doloureux)

DESCRIPTION: Inflammation of the trigeminal nerve which leaves the brain and passes through a hole in the skull just beside the ear. It fans out across the face, to receive sensations from the skin of the face, and to give movement instructions to the muscles in the face.

CAUSE: Occasionally may be caused by a brain or nerve disease such as multiple sclerosis, or a tumour that presses on the nerve, but usually no specific cause.

SYMPTOMS: Sudden severe pain in the face which often arises beside the mouth and spreads almost instantly up to the eye, down to the jaw, and across to the ear. May last a few seconds or several minutes and only one side of the face is affected. Attacks may be started by cold winds, eating, yawning, or touching the face. They tend to come in episodes, with attacks coming every few minutes for a few days or weeks, and then disappearing for a time. Unfortunately, each successive attack tends to last longer than the preceding one, and the pain-free periods become shorter.

INVESTIGATIONS: No tests available to prove the diagnosis.

TREATMENT: Pain-killers are not particularly effective, but anti-epileptic drugs such as carbamazepine and phenytoin are quite successful. If these medications prove unsuccessful, surgical exploration of the nerve may find an area of compression or abnormality as a cause of the pain. As a last resort, the nerve may be destroyed to give relief from intractable pain, but this leaves the face numb and paralysed.

PROGNOSIS: Control usually reasonable, but cure difficult. Spontaneous, permanent cures do occur.

See also Multiple Sclerosis; Neuralgia

Trigger Finger

DESCRIPTION: Consequence of an injury or inflammation of the tendon to the affected finger.

CAUSE: Formation of a nodule (lump) in the tendon that bends (flexes) the finger or thumb, restricting its movement.

SYMPTOMS: Finger is difficult to straighten (extend) and may do so with a sudden painful jerk, or may need to be moved back by pushing on an object.

INVESTIGATIONS: None normally necessary.

TREATMENT: Injecting steroids around the swollen nodule on the tendon, or surgical removal of the nodule.

COMPLICATIONS: Finger may become fixed in the bent position.

PROGNOSIS: Good results from treatment.

See also Mallet Finger

Triglyceride Excess
See Hypertriglycleridaemia

Trigonitis

DESCRIPTION: Inflammation of the lower part (trigone) of the bladder around the opening of the urethra (tube leading out of the bladder). Usually occurs in women.

CAUSE: Lack of oestrogen after the menopause or after a total hysterectomy causes the tissue of the vagina and adjacent bladder base to become thin, less supple, easily damaged and the sensory nerves in the bladder base become exposed to urine.

SYMPTOMS: Painful frequent passage of urine and aching pain in the lower belly. The involuntary passage of urine with a cough or exercise is also common.

INVESTIGATIONS: Diagnosed by cystoscopy (passing a tube into the bladder through which it can be inspected).

TREATMENT: Long term oestrogen supplementation by local application of cream in the vagina, tablets, patches, implants or injection. Progestogens may need to be given as additional treatment with the oestrogen.

COMPLICATIONS: Bladder and urinary tract bacterial infections can easily occur.

PROGNOSIS: Good while oestrogen hormone replacement therapy is continued.

Trisomy 13-15
See Patau Syndrome

Trisomy 18
See Edwards Syndrome

Trisomy 21
See Down Syndrome

Tropical Ear
See Otitis Externa

Tropical Sprue
DESCRIPTION: A failure to absorb fat from the gut.
CAUSE: Inflammation of the small intestine that develops in people used to a European diet who live for prolonged periods in tropical countries.
SYMPTOMS: Explosive diarrhoea with watery stools, rapid weight loss, indigestion, burping, abdominal cramps, muscle cramps, and as a result of the failed fat absorption, a failure to absorb vitamins A, D, E and K, which are all soluble in fat.
INVESTIGATIONS: Diagnosis is made by examination of the faeces, which is found to contain high levels of fat, and by X-rays of the small intestine. Blood tests show a particular type of anaemia.
TREATMENT: Tetracycline (an antibiotic) for a week, and folic acid for several months. Further treatment may be required if severe anaemia has developed.
PROGNOSIS: Recovery within a few weeks is usual.
See also Coeliac Disease; Vitamin A Deficiency

Trousseau Syndrome
DESCRIPTION: Uncommon complication of cancer.
CAUSE: Cancer of organs in the abdomen, including the intestine.
SYMPTOMS: Thrombophlebitis (blood clots and vein inflammation — see separate entry) that occurs in multiple areas.
INVESTIGATIONS: Blood tests show presence of blood clots (thrombosis). Other tests must be performed to find cancer.
TREATMENT: Treat underlying cancer.
COMPLICATIONS: Thrombosis may affect blood supply to or from vital organs.
PROGNOSIS: Depends on specific cause, but generally poor.

Trypanosomiasis
See Chagas' Disease; Sleeping Sickness

Tubal Pregnancy
See Ectopic Pregnancy

Tuberculosis
(Phthisis; TB)
DESCRIPTION: A bacterial infection that affects one third of the people on the planet. Usually occurs in the lungs (pulmonary tuberculosis), but may attack bone, skin, joints, lymph nodes, kidney, gut, heart and membranes around the brain (meningeal tuberculosis). Uncommon in developed countries, but widespread in poorer parts of Asia, Africa and South America. Cattle and other animals may carry TB, making its total eradication difficult.

Tuberculosis

CAUSE: The bacterium Mycobacterium tuberculosis passes from one person to another in moist droplets with every breath. When inhaled the bacteria may infect the lung and the surrounding lymph nodes, or may lie dormant for years, and then start multiplying to cause an initial or subsequent attack of the disease at a time when the patient's resistance is down.

SYMPTOMS: Productive cough, night sweats, loss of appetite, fever, weight loss and generalised tiredness.

INVESTIGATIONS: Chest X-rays show a characteristic pattern, and the infection may be confirmed by collecting sputum samples and identifying the bacteria through a microscope. Skin tests can determine whether the person has ever been exposed to tuberculosis.

TREATMENT: Combination of different antibiotic and antituberculotic medications for a year or more. Patients must be hospitalised and isolated until they are no longer infectious. All the other members of the patient's family must be investigated for early signs of the disease, and may be given treatment as a routine preventative measure. The BCG vaccine gives lifelong protection, and is given routinely at birth to babies in many poorer countries.

COMPLICATIONS: May gradually spread to almost every other organ in untreated patients. Symptoms depend upon which areas are affected.

PROGNOSIS: With effective treatment regimes, a complete cure can be expected, and most recurrences are due to patients failing to complete the full course of treatment. Without treatment, death occurs in a significant proportion of victims.

See also Scrofula

Tuberous Sclerosis
(Epiloia)

DESCRIPTION: Uncommon nodule formation in organs of young children.

CAUSE: Congenital condition (present since birth) that may occur in successive generations in the one family or develop randomly.

SYMPTOMS: Repeated convulsions in infancy from brain nodules. Later in childhood, mental retardation is noted and a rash consisting of red nodules (small lumps) appears on the face and neck. Other unusual rashes may develop elsewhere on the body, and lumps may form under the nails.

INVESTIGATIONS: No specific diagnostic test.

TREATMENT: No curative treatment available. Medication given to control convulsions, and surgery for some of the more serious nodules.

COMPLICATIONS: Eye damage, cysts in the heart, bone and lungs, and nodules in the bowel.

PROGNOSIS: No cure. Mental retardation steadily worsens with age.

Tularaemia

DESCRIPTION: Bacterial infection of rats and rabbits that can spread to humans.

CAUSE: Spread through a tick bite or direct contact with an infected animal.

SYMPTOMS: Fever, headache, enlarged lymph nodes, tender spleen and vomiting. A sore can usually be found at the site where the bacteria entered the body. In severe cases, pneumonia and diarrhoea may develop.

INVESTIGATIONS: Diagnosis can be confirmed by a blood culture.

TREATMENT: Antibiotic in high doses by injection or intravenous drip.

COMPLICATIONS: Meningitis, bone and heart infection.

PROGNOSIS: Most patients recover.

Tumour Lysis Syndrome

DESCRIPTION: Complication of cancer treatment.

CAUSE: Body chemistry (metabolic) disturbance due to rapid release of toxins from inside a large number of cancer cells destroyed by chemotherapy (medication).

SYMPTOMS: Weakness, tiredness, paralysis of bowels, constipation, irregular heart beat and acute kidney failure.

INVESTIGATIONS: Blood tests show significant abnormalities in electrolytes (essential elements).

TREATMENT: Prevented by giving lots of fluids during chemotherapy, and medication to make urine alkaline and remove toxins (eg. allopurinol). Treated in hospital by giving fluids through an intravenous drip and monitoring electrolytes carefully.

COMPLICATIONS: Death from heart or kidney failure.

PROGNOSIS: Depends on type of cancer being treated. Syndrome can usually be controlled.

Turcot Syndrome

DESCRIPTION: Very rare cancer.

CAUSE: Unknown.

SYMPTOMS: Malignant brain tumours and multiple bowel polyps (polyposis coli — see separate entries).

INVESTIGATIONS: Tumours and polyps detected by CT and MRI scans and colonoscopy.

TREATMENT: Surgery.

PROGNOSIS: Very poor.

Turner Syndrome
(XO Syndrome)

DESCRIPTION: Rare defect in sex chromosomes.

CAUSE: The person is born with only one X chromosome (XO), and no matching X or Y sex chromosome. The sex chromosomes are named X and Y. Normally two X chromosomes (XX) occur in a female, and one of each (XY) in a male.

SYMPTOMS: Patients look female, but are really asexual, as they do not develop testes or ovaries and are infertile. At puberty, the breasts and pubic hair fail to develop, the genitals remain child-like in appearance, and menstrual periods do not start. Other signs are short stature and a web of skin that runs from the base of the skull down the neck and onto the top of the shoulder.

INVESTIGATIONS: Diagnosis confirmed by blood and cell tests that show the chromosome structure.

TREATMENT: Giving female hormones (oestrogens) in a cyclical manner from the time of expected puberty to encourage the development of female characteristics. Growth hormone can be used to improve height, and surgery can correct the heart defects and neck webbing.

COMPLICATIONS: Eye disorders, heart valve defects, narrowing of the aorta (main body artery), a stocky chest, the early development of diabetes and thin frail bones (osteoporosis).

PROGNOSIS: Patients can function as females in every way except fertility, and can lead a normal life.

See also Noonan Syndrome

Twelfth Rib Syndrome

DESCRIPTION: Pain due to damage to the lowest (twelfth) rib.

CAUSE: The lateral arcuate ligament in the side of the chest and abdomen becomes trapped under the 12th rib, usually after an injury or strain to the chest.

SYMPTOMS: Loin (side) pain aggravated by movement and pressure on 12th rib.

INVESTIGATIONS: X-rays and all other scans are normal.

TREATMENT: Anti-inflammatory medications, steroid injection into the damaged ligament, and sometimes surgery.

COMPLICATIONS: None serious.

PROGNOSIS: Good.

See also Slipping Rib Syndrome

Tympanic Rupture
(Burst Ear Drum)

DESCRIPTION: Rupture of the ear drum to leave it with a slit or round hole.

CAUSE: Increased pressure in the middle ear (eg. eustachian tube blockage), infection (eg. otitis media), glue ear or direct injury to the ear (eg. extremely loud sudden noise, poking stick into ear).

SYMPTOMS: Pain and deafness. If infection is present there may be a discharge.

INVESTIGATIONS: Diagnosed by examining the ear with an otoscope (magnifying light).

TREATMENT: Antibiotics to prevent or treat infection and in persistent cases, surgery in which a tiny skin graft is put over the defect.

COMPLICATIONS: Infection in the ear may lead to permanent deafness.

PROGNOSIS: Most heal in a few days to weeks, depending on size of hole and cause.

See also Eustachian Tube Blockage; Glue Ear; Otitis Media

Typhoid Fever
(Enteric Fever; Salmonellosis, Intestinal)

DESCRIPTION: A widespread bacterial infection of the gut and surrounding lymph nodes, including the spleen. Incubation period is 5-14 days. Occurs throughout Asia, Africa and South America.

AREAS OF THE WORLD AFFECTED BY TYPHOID FEVER

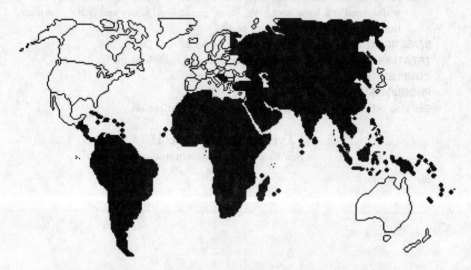

CAUSE: Caught by eating food contaminated with Salmonella typhi bacteria, which pass out in the faeces and urine of those who have the infection or are symptom-free carriers of the bacteria.

SYMPTOMS: Fever, headache, tiredness, cough, sore throat, abdominal pain and constipation. After a day or two, the constipation suddenly gives way to a massive diarrhoea.

INVESTIGATIONS: Diagnosis confirmed by specific blood, urine and faeces tests

TREATMENT: Antibiotics to destroy invading bacteria, steroids to reduce inflammation, a low-residue diet and intravenous fluids. Prevention available as three tablets that give at least six months protection, or injections that give three years protection.

COMPLICATIONS: Massive bleeding into the gut and perforation of the gut, which usually cause the death of the patient. In severe cases, it is possible for the infection to spread to the lungs, brain, kidneys and gall bladder. Bacteria may be almost impossible to eradicate from people who become symptom-free carriers of the disease.

PROGNOSIS: Death occurs in up to 30% of untreated cases, but only in 2% of those who are treated in good facilities. With no treatment, survivors slowly improve after about ten days, but relapses may occur for the next two or three weeks.

See also Shigellosis

Typhus
(Mediterranean Spotted Fever; Tick Typhus)

DESCRIPTION: Worldwide infection that causes significant generalised illness. More common around the Mediterranean, in the Middle East and in East Africa.

CAUSE: Various types of the primitive bacteria Rickettsia, which pass to humans through a tick bite.

SYMPTOMS: Black spot on the skin at the site of the tick bite, swelling of skin, widespread red large spot rash, fever, generalised aches and pains, tiredness, headache and enlarged lymph nodes.

INVESTIGATIONS: Diagnosed by specific blood tests.

TREATMENT: Antibiotics such as tetracycline and ciprofloxacin.

COMPLICATIONS: Liver damage and skin ulceration.

PROGNOSIS: Good.

See also other diseases listed under Rickettsial Infection

Tyrosinaemia Type II
See Richner-Hanhart Syndrome

U

Ulcer

See Bed Sore; Eye Ulcer; Mouth Ulcer; Ulcerative Colitis; Ulcer, Peptic; Ulcer, Skin; Ulcer, Venous

Ulcerative Colitis

DESCRIPTION: A severe and potentially life-threatening inflammation and subsequent ulceration of the large intestine (colon). Repeated attacks cause thickening and scarring of the colon to the point where it cannot adequately undertake its task of absorbing excess fluid from the faeces.

CAUSE: Unknown, but more common in whites than in blacks and orientals, and six times more common in Jews than other Caucasians. The overall incidence in developed countries is about one in every thousand people.

SYMPTOMS: Often quite mild at first, but subsequent attacks steadily worsen to cause bloody diarrhoea with severe abdominal cramps and pain. Large amounts of mucus may be present in the diarrhoea, and in severe cases the diarrhoea may occur 20 times a day, consist entirely of blood and mucus, and be severe enough to cause the patient to collapse. Occasionally, periods of apparent constipation can occur between attacks of diarrhoea. Further symptoms include fever, loss of appetite, weight loss and overwhelming tiredness.

INVESTIGATIONS: Diagnosis confirmed by a barium meal X-ray or colonoscopy (a tube is passed through the anus into the colon to allow it to be examined).

TREATMENT: Passes through phases of active disease and remission, and treatment is aimed at treating the active disease when it occurs and preventing an attack from developing. Severe attacks require admission to hospital for drips into a vein, antibiotics, and steroids. Milder attacks may be treated by steroid tablets or suppositories (given through the anus). Prevention and the treatment of mild attacks require a specific diet that is high in protein but excludes dairy products, and the regular use of sulphasalazine, which reduces gut inflammation. Uncontrolled disease may require the surgical removal of the entire colon and an ileostomy (the small intestine is opened out onto the skin of the abdomen and wastes are collected in a bag).

COMPLICATIONS: Numerous serious complications including abscesses around the anus, a rupture of the colon (urgent surgery may be necessary), colon cancer, massive overdilation of the large intestine (megacolon), or false connections (fistula) from the gut to the bladder or vagina caused by ulcers breaking through to these adjacent organs. Inflammation in the colon may be associated with inflammation in other parts of the body, including the skin, joints, eye, mouth and liver.

PROGNOSIS: No permanent cure, but most cases can be adequately controlled by medication. Because of the long-term complications and related conditions in other organs, the average life expectancy of these patients is slightly less than normal.

See also Colo-Rectal Cancer; Megacolon

Ulcer, Mouth
See Mouth Ulcer

Ulcer, Peptic
(Duodenal Ulcer; Gastric Ulcer; Pyloric Ulcer; Stomach Ulcer)

DESCRIPTION: Ulceration of the stomach or duodenum (first part of the small intestine) caused by hydrochloric acid.

CAUSE: Hydrochloric acid is a potent acid naturally produced in the stomach to aid food digestion. The stomach protects itself with a layer of thick mucus. If there is excess acid or insufficient mucus present, the acid may eat into the stomach wall. The most common causes for excess acid or reduced mucus are smoking, stress, anxiety, alcohol, aspirin and the nonsteroidal anti-inflammatory drugs used to treat arthritis. The bacterium *Helicobacter pylori* may damage the mucus lining of the stomach. The acid can cause a **gastric ulcer** in the stomach, or the first part of the small intestine may be ulcerated to form a **duodenal ulcer**. **Pyloric ulcers** develop at the point where a muscle ring acts as a valve between the stomach and duodenum. The term peptic ulcer refers to all three types of ulcer.

SYMPTOMS: The ulcer may penetrate into a blood vessel to cause bleeding, anaemia and weakness before any pain is felt. Most ulcers cause pain high up in the belly which is often worst just before a meal and relieved by eating. Other symptoms include a feeling of fullness, excess burping and indigestion.

INVESTIGATIONS: Proved by a barium meal X-ray or gastroscopy. During gastroscopy a biopsy can be taken of an ulcer to exclude cancer, and a test can be performed to identify the presence of *Helicobacter pylori*. The bacteria can also be detected by a test on a sample of breath that is collected in an air-tight container. A blood test is also available, but less accurate.

TREATMENT: A sensible diet, stopping smoking and relaxation. If *Helicobater pylori* is detected, a specific course of antibiotics and anti-ulcer medication (triple therapy) can be given to eradicate it, heal the ulcer, and prevent a recurrence. Numerous tablets are available to control and often cure peptic ulcers. Because of the effectiveness of these medications, surgery for peptic ulcers is now rarely required.

COMPLICATIONS: Excessive bleeding from an ulcer can cause serious anaemia. A very small percentage of ulcers can be cancerous.

PROGNOSIS: Most patients respond very well to medical treatment.

Ulcer, Pressure
See Bed Sore

Ulcer, Skin

DESCRIPTION: Occurs when the outer layers of the skin are destroyed and the underlying tissue is exposed.

CAUSE: Constant pressure (bed sore), injury, poor blood supply (venous ulcer), a cut or sore that is constantly irritated by scratching or rubbing from clothing and certain types of skin cancer that are left untreated. Sometimes mentally disturbed patients, prisoners and people trying to draw attention to themselves deliberately irritate an ulcer to prevent it from healing.

SYMPTOMS: A persistent open sore on the skin.

INVESTIGATIONS: Sometimes a biopsy of the edge of an ulcer is necessary to exclude skin cancer as a cause.

TREATMENT: Covering the ulcer with a dressing that prevents irritation, removing excessive pressure on the area by regularly changing position or special mattresses or cushions, and special healing gels, plasters and dressings. Surgically excising a persistent ulcer and closing the defect by suturing or with a skin graft can be used in some cases.

COMPLICATIONS: A secondary bacterial infection may develop in the ulcer.

PROGNOSIS: Depends on cause, but usually reasonable results with good treatment.

See also Bed Sore; Ulcer, Venous

Ulcer, Venous
(Varicose Ulcer)

DESCRIPTION: Occur on the shin and ankle in middle-aged and elderly due to a poor return of blood from the ankles and feet to the heart. The ankles may be swollen, and the skin may be thin and discoloured by eczema. Women are affected far more often than men.

CAUSE: A slight injury to a leg affected by varicose veins may cause an ulcer, and because of the high pressure from the swollen veins in the area, the poor quality of the skin, and the poor blood supply, healing may be very slow. Aggravated by diabetes.

SYMPTOMS: Persistent ulcer on the lower leg and ankle associated with varicose veins.

INVESTIGATIONS: Diabetes and other significant generalised diseases need to be excluded.

TREATMENT: Prolonged elevation of the leg to reduce the pressure in the veins, wearing compression bandages or stockings when walking, avoiding standing still for prolonged periods, and careful dressing of the ulcer with antiseptics and specialised pads or powders. In persistent cases, surgery to the swollen veins to relieve the pressure may be necessary before healing can occur.

COMPLICATIONS: Secondary bacterial infection of the ulcer.

PROGNOSIS: Often very slow recovery, but most heal with persistence.

See also Ulcer, Skin

Ulysses Syndrome

DESCRIPTION: The more tests that are performed, the greater the chance that one abnormality will be found. That abnormality should not be pursued unless clinically significant or this syndrome may develop.

CAUSE: Over investigation of a patient by doctors.

SYMPTOMS: A patient with no symptoms is taken through a long, costly and potentially hazardous series of investigations and procedures in order to explain one randomly abnormal pathology test result.

INVESTIGATIONS: Stop all investigations.

TREATMENT: Reassure patient that abnormality is not significant. Observe for any symptoms.

PROGNOSIS: Good for patient, bad for doctor!

Umbilical Hernia

DESCRIPTION: Protrusion of the gut under the skin of the navel. There are two forms—

— In children, there is a hole between the muscle layers of the abdomen where the arteries and veins that passed down the umbilical cord from the mother entered the baby. This hole normally closes quickly after birth, but in some children the hole is very large, or is slow to close. In these cases, bulging of the intestine into the area just below the skin of the umbilicus can occur.

— In adults, the hernia is not strictly speaking an umbilical hernia, but a **paraumbilical hernia**, as the rupture occurs not immediately underneath the umbilicus but in the slightly weakened fibrous tissue just above (more common) or below the navel. They steadily increase in size with time.

CAUSE: Children — more common in premature babies, as the processes involved in closing the hole behind the umbilicus are slower.

Adults — common in women who have had multiple pregnancies, in the very obese and those who have other causes of excess pressure in the abdomen.

SYMPTOMS: Children — hernia bulges out while the infant is crying or active, but usually disappears when the child is lying quietly. The hernia almost never gives pain or discomfort to the child.

Adults — large hernias can contain a significant amount of intestine and may cause discomfort and constipation.

INVESTIGATIONS: None necessary.

TREATMENT: Children — vast majority close spontaneously within twelve months but may take until three years of age. If the hernia persists, surgery may be necessary.

Adults — Small paraumbilical hernias are repaired surgically when discovered, as delay may lead to a larger hernia and more difficult repair later. In older patients with particularly large hernias, surgical repair may not be practical.

COMPLICATIONS: Rarely the intestine may become trapped in the hernia, very painful and gangrenous. If this occurs, emergency surgery is essential.

PROGNOSIS: The recurrence rate after surgery depends upon the original size of the hernia, but is generally low.

See also Hernias

Unconscious
See Coma

Undescended Testicle
See Testicle, Undescended

Undulant Fever
See Brucellosis

Unstable Angina
See Intermediate Coronary Syndrome

Upper Respiratory Tract Infection (URTI)
See Cold, Common; Influenza; Laryngitis; Pharyngitis; Sinusitis; Tonsillitis

Uraemia
See Kidney Failure, Chronic

Uraemic Syndrome
See Haemolytic-Uraemic Syndrome

Ureteric Calculus
See Kidney Stone

Ureteric Colic
See Kidney Stone

Urethral Syndrome
DESCRIPTION: Inflammation of the urethra (tube draining urine from bladder to outside) in women.

CAUSE: May be due to unidentified bacterial infection (eg. *Ureaplasma urealyticum*), interstitial cystitis, trigonitis (see separate entries), bladder tumours or bladder prolapse into vagina (see Vaginal Prolapse entry).

SYMPTOMS: Pain when passing urine and passing urine very frequently. No bacterial infection can usually be found.

INVESTIGATIONS: Urine tests completely normal, but cystoscopy (passing a thin examining tube through the urethra into the bladder) may show inflammation.

TREATMENT: Often unsatisfactory. Antibiotics, mixtures to make urine alkaline and bladder irrigation with antiseptic solution can be tried. Prevented by passing urine after sex.

COMPLICATIONS: None significant.
PROGNOSIS: Often persistent, but settles eventually.
See also Interstitial Cystitis; Trigonitis; Vagina Prolapse

Urethritis
See Non-Specific Urethritis

Urge Syndrome
DESCRIPTION: Bladder problem affecting 10% of adult population at some time, but nearly always women.
CAUSE: Unknown.
SYMPTOMS: Passing urine very frequently and several times a night, urgency to pass urine when desire felt, incontinence of urine and sometimes bed wetting.
INVESTIGATIONS: No diagnostic tests, but tests to exclude diabetes, infection, bladder tumours and stones, and kidney disease must be performed.
TREATMENT: Avoid bladder stimulants (eg. coffee, cola, tea, alcohol), restrict fluids, bladder training exercises (eg. practise retaining urine for longer periods), fluid intake/output recording, medications (eg. oxybutynin, propantheline, amitriptyline, imipramine, temazepam), psychiatric assessment and rarely surgery.
PROGNOSIS: Often persistent, but usually settles eventually.
See also Incontinence of Urine

Urine Incontinence
See Incontinence of Urine

Urine Infection
See Cystitis; Non-specific Urethritis; Pyelonephritis, Acute; Pyelonephritis, Chronic; Trigonitis

URTI
(Upper Respiratory Tract Infection)
See Cold, Common; Influenza; Laryngitis; Pharyngitis; Sinusitis; Tonsillitis

Urticaria
See Hives; Photodermatitis

Urticaria Pigmentosa
(Mastocytosis)
DESCRIPTION: Allergy-like patch reaction in skin that most often affects infants.
CAUSE: Patches are made of abnormal collections of mast cells. These contain histamine and when the cell is disturbed, this is released into the skin. Histamine makes blood vessels leak, resulting in localised itching, swelling and redness.
SYMPTOMS: Brown patches on the skin of young children that steadily increase in

number over several months or years and blister when rubbed. If many patches are activated at the same time the skin becomes itchy and the infant may become irritable, but it is uncommon for severe symptoms to arise.

INVESTIGATIONS: Rubbing a patch causes redness, swelling and itching within a few minutes (Darier's sign). Occasionally a skin biopsy is needed to confirm the diagnosis.

TREATMENT: None normally necessary. Exercise, heat, alcohol and some medications (eg. aspirin, narcotics — codeine and morphine) can aggravate the condition. If symptoms are significant antihistamine mixture or tablets, and steroid creams can be used.

COMPLICATIONS: A severe attack can result in flushing and faintness. Rarely occurs in adults, when the condition is usually worse, spots are itchier, and may spread to involve internal organs (systemic mastocytosis).

PROGNOSIS: Over the next few years becomes less irritable and eventually the patches fade away. By the teenage years, most patches will have gone.

See also Systemic Mastocytosis; Telangiectasia Eruptiva Macularis Perstans

Usher Syndrome

DESCRIPTION: Rare cause of deafness.

CAUSE: Inherited, but both parents must carry the defective gene.

SYMPTOMS: Child that is deaf and has retinitis pigmentosa (see separate entry).

INVESTIGATIONS: No diagnostic test.

TREATMENT: None available.

PROGNOSIS: No cure.

Uta
See Cutaneous Leischmaniasis

Uterine Fibroids
See Fibroids of the Uterus

Uterine Mole
(Hydatidiform Mole)

DESCRIPTION: Abnormal development of the placenta during pregnancy.

CAUSE: One in every 750 pregnancies develops into a uterine (or hydatidiform) mole, which is a dramatic overdevelopment of the placenta. Any foetus that is present dies at a very early stage.

SYMPTOMS: Multiple cysts develop in the placenta so that it appears like a large bunch of grapes. The woman may not be aware of the problem until it is well advanced, at 14 to 20 weeks of pregnancy, when an abnormal vaginal bleed or discharge may occur, and the womb feels much larger than expected. Occasionally, some of the grape-like cysts may be passed.

INVESTIGATIONS: An ultrasound scan and blood tests will confirm the diagnosis.

TREATMENT: Immediate surgical removal of the abnormal placenta from the uterus through the cervix is essential.

COMPLICATIONS: One complication is an invasive mole, in which the abnormal placenta penetrates through the wall of the uterus and damages it to the point where a hysterectomy is necessary. More seriously, 4% of women develop cancer in the abnormal tissue (choriocarcinoma).

PROGNOSIS: Usually very good. Careful follow-up with blood tests and gynaecological examinations is essential.

See also Choriocarcinoma of the Uterus

Uterine Prolapse
See Vaginal Prolapse

Uveitis
See Fuchs Uveitis Syndrome; Iritis

Uveoparotid Fever or Syndrome
See Heerfordt Syndrome

Uvulitis

DESCRIPTION: Infection of the uvula, which is the soft tag of flesh that hangs down the back of the throat from the soft palate.

CAUSE: Bacterial, viral or fungal infection.

SYMPTOMS: Painful throat, pain with swallowing, excess saliva production, enlarged lymph nodes in neck and a fever.

INVESTIGATIONS: None normally necessary, but sometimes a swab is taken to identify the responsible organism.

TREATMENT: Antibiotics for bacterial infections, and antifungal lozenges or gels for fungal infections. All types of infection, including viral, eased by anaesthetic and antiseptic gargles or lozenges, and paracetamol or aspirin.

COMPLICATIONS: Uvula may ulcerate, and infection may spread to tonsils or other nearby tissues.

PROGNOSIS: Bacterial and fungal infections settle rapidly with treatment. Viral infections settle after a few days.

See also Pharyngitis; Tonsillitis

V

Vaccinia

DESCRIPTION: Complication of smallpox vaccination. This vaccination is now unavailable and unnecessary as smallpox has been eliminated world wide.

CAUSE: Smallpox vaccination was given by scratching the vaccine into the skin. If the patient had eczema, dermatitis, significant burns or other skin damage this complication could occur. Patients with vaccinia can spread the reaction to close contacts.

SYMPTOMS: Spread of vaccination reaction across skin to cause varying rashes, ulceration and rarely internal spread to vital organs such as the brain (encephalitis).

INVESTIGATIONS: None usually necessary.

TREATMENT: None available.

PROGNOSIS: Variable.

See also Smallpox

Vaginal Infection
See Vaginitis

Vaginal Prolapse
(Cystocoele; Prolapse of Vagina; Rectocoele; Uterine Prolapse; Womb Prolapse)

DESCRIPTION: A protrusion of an organ into the vagina, caused primarily by gravity. A uterine prolapse occurs when the uterus moves down the vagina and completely fills it. Occasionally the cervix, which is the lowest part of the uterus, may protrude through the vulva to the outside. Part of the bladder which is in front of the vagina, may push back into the vagina causing a bladder prolapse (cystocoele). The rectum (last part of the large intestine) may push forward into the vagina as a rectal prolapse (rectocoele). Occasionally there is a combination of all three types of prolapse.

CAUSE: During childbirth, the vagina becomes very stretched, and does not always return to its original size. The muscles around the vagina become weakened and the ligaments supporting the uterus may become stretched and sag.

SYMPTOMS: Cystocoele causes difficulty in passing urine, urinary infections and incontinence. A rectocoele causes difficulty in passing faeces and other bowel problems. A uterine prolapse causes discomfort, pain, and ulceration of the cervix may result in infections and bleeding.

INVESTIGATIONS: None normally necessary.

TREATMENT: Operation that uses strong natural material in the pelvis and artificial slings to support the prolapsing organ. In elderly women, a ring inserted into the vagina may be used to hold prolapse in the correct place. Younger women can prevent the problem by pelvic floor exercises under the guidance of a physiotherapist both before and after the delivery of their babies.

PROGNOSIS: Reasonable results from surgery, but recurrences possible.

See also Rectal Prolapse

Vaginal Thrush
See Thrush

Vaginismus

DESCRIPTION: Strong spasm of the muscles around the vagina.

CAUSE: Unconscious reaction, normally triggered by anxiety related to sex. The initial trigger may be fear (of pregnancy, pain, etc.), guilt, lack of privacy, anxiety about expectations, lack of self confidence, previous rape or sexual assault, and other psychological factors.

SYMPTOMS: Sexual intercourse impossible as the man is unable to penetrate the woman.

INVESTIGATIONS: None normally necessary other than a doctor examining the woman internally.

TREATMENT: Psychological counselling, medication to reduce anxiety and vaginal dilators (dildo — artificial penises) of gradually increasing width. Confidence must be gained in using one size of dildo before the next size is attempted.

PROGNOSIS: Reasonable results if woman is well motivated.

See also other diseases listed under Sex Problems

Vaginitis, Bacterial
(Vaginal Infection)

DESCRIPTION: Vaginal infection by any of a number of different bacteria.

CAUSE: Bacteria such as *Gardnerella vaginalis*, which is slightly unusual in that it requires an oxygen-free and alkaline environment. The upper end of the vagina can be oxygen-free, but is normally slightly acid. It may become alkaline with semen after sex, changing sexual partners, hormonal changes at different times of the month, and using antibiotics.

SYMPTOMS: A greyish fish-smelling vaginal discharge, soreness and redness.

INVESTIGATIONS: Diagnosis and type of bacteria present determined by taking a swab from the vagina and having it examined and cultured.

TREATMENT: Appropriate antibiotic tablets by mouth, antiseptic douches (eg. iodine solution), and acidic gels or creams in the vagina. In recurrent cases the male sexual partner may need to be treated.

COMPLICATIONS: Infection may spread into the uterus and cause pelvic inflammatory disease, or to adjacent glands to cause a Bartholin's cyst infection (see separate entries).

PROGNOSIS: Good results from treatment.

See also Atrophic Vaginitis; Bartholin's Cyst; Pelvic Inflammatory Disease; Sexually Transmitted Diseases

Vancomycin and Methicillin-Resistant *Staphylococcus aureus* Infection
See Staphylococcal Infection

Varicella
See Chickenpox; Congenital Varicella Syndrome; Shingles

Varicocoele
DESCRIPTION: A knot of varicose veins surrounding the testes in the scrotum.

CAUSE: Unknown, but probably an inherited tendency.

SYMPTOMS: A soft, slightly tender blue swelling in the scrotum.

INVESTIGATIONS: None necessary.

TREATMENT: Surgical removal if uncomfortable or if infertility a problem.

COMPLICATIONS: The extra heat produced by these veins can sometimes affect sperm production and fertility.

PROGNOSIS: Good results from surgery.

Varicose Eczema
(Hypostatic Eczema)
DESCRIPTION: Chronic skin deterioration that affects women more than men, and is far more common in the elderly.

CAUSE: A poor return of blood through the veins from the feet to the heart. Blood pools in the feet, causing pressure on the skin. More common if varicose veins are present.

SYMPTOMS: The skin is itchy, red, shiny, swollen, dry and covered with scales. It is easily injured and very slow to heal. The inside of the shin, just above the ankle, is the area usually affected.

INVESTIGATIONS: None necessary, although blood tests may be performed to exclude other conditions such as diabetes.

TREATMENT: Elevating the leg as much as possible, using support stockings or pressure bandages, and raising the foot of the bed slightly. If varicose veins are present, it may be appropriate to remove them surgically. Mild steroid creams and coal tar solutions are used on the eczema.

COMPLICATIONS: Ulcers are a common complication, as are bacterial skin infections, and allergy reactions. These must be treated separately from the varicose eczema.

PROGNOSIS: Usually persistent, and the results of treatment are often poor.
See also Eczema

Varicose Ulcer
See Ulcer, Venous

Varicose Veins

DESCRIPTION: Over dilation of the superficial veins in the legs. Two networks of veins in the legs move the blood from the feet back to the heart. One is deep inside the muscles of the calf and thigh, the other is outside the muscles and just under the skin (superficial).

CAUSE: Contraction of muscles in the leg squeezes the veins, and with the aid of one-way valves scattered through the venous network, the blood is steadily pushed back towards the heart. Pregnancy (because the growing baby puts pressure on veins in the pelvis) and prolonged standing (eg. hairdressing, shop assistant) make it difficult for the blood to move up from the legs into the body and stretch the veins, which damages the one-way valves. The damaged valves allow more blood to remain in the veins, stretching them further. Reducing the amount of standing, wearing elastic support stockings and regularly exercising the muscles in the legs while standing may prevent varicose veins.

SYMPTOMS: Tired, aching, swollen legs, with large, ugly, blue, knotted veins under blotchy, red and sometimes ulcerated skin.

INVESTIGATIONS: None normally necessary.

TREATMENT: Tablets (eg. hydroxyethyl rutosides) can reduce the leg ache, but only surgical procedures can permanently remove the veins. Injections of a type of glue, diathermy (hot electric needle) or lasers may be used to destroy small, fine, spider-like networks of veins. Larger isolated veins can be removed one at a time by a 'nick and pick' procedure, with a small cut being made over each vein to allow its removal. Vein stripping involves removing most of the superficial veins on one side of the leg from the groin to the ankle.

COMPLICATIONS: Rupture of a vein may cause severe bruising, or a cut will bleed profusely (treated by elevating the leg and applying compression).

PROGNOSIS: No cure, but symptoms can usually be reduced. Surgery is successful in most patients, but does not prevent the development of new veins, and skin staining caused by the varicosities is usually permanent.

See also Superficial Venous Thrombosis

Variola Major
See Smallpox

Vascular Haemophilia
See von Willebrand's Disease

Vasculitis
Inflammation of an artery or vein.
See Buerger's Disease; Pannicultis; Phlebitis; Takayasu's Arteritis; Temporal Arteritis

Vasomotor Rhinitis

DESCRIPTION: The inside of the nose and sinuses is lined with a moist (mucus) membrane. If inflamed, the glands in the mucus membrane swell up and secrete extra amounts of mucus that overflows the sinus cavities.

CAUSE: Temperature changes (eg. walking into an air-conditioned building), hormonal changes (more mucus may be produced at certain times in a woman's monthly cycle), anxiety and stress (eg. an exam or interview), eating, drinking alcohol and changes in position (eg. getting out of bed may start a sneezing fit).

SYMPTOMS: Episodes of constant sneezing, and a constant drip of clear watery mucus from the nose.

INVESTIGATIONS: None normally necessary.

TREATMENT: Antihistamines shrink down the swollen mucus membranes and reduce the production of mucus, and steroid or ipratropium nasal sprays prevent the nose from reacting excessively. The minority who continue to have long term symptoms may be helped by surgery to reduce the amount of mucus membrane in the nose, and removing some curled up bones inside the nose (turbinates) that are covered with mucus membrane.

COMPLICATIONS: Secondary bacterial infections may cause sinusitis or pharyngitis. Flying or changing altitude can force phlegm up the eustachian tubes into the middle ears to cause pain and infection.

PROGNOSIS: Usually settles spontaneously, but sometimes persistent. Control reasonable.

See also Hay Fever; Pharyngitis; Sinusitis

Vasovagal Syndrome

DESCRIPTION: Cause of repeated fainting attacks.

CAUSE: Stress, anxiety or significant emotional or physical upset in past. Attacks triggered by memory or association with past incident at times when there is another minor stress or possibility of fainting.

SYMPTOMS: Recurrent episodes of fainting, low blood pressure, pale complexion and slow heart rate.

INVESTIGATIONS: Low blood pressure, slow pulse and abnormal ECG (electro-cardiograph) during attack.

TREATMENT: Avoid precipitating causes (eg. prolonged standing), lie down or bend forward with start of symptoms, and aromatic inhalations.

COMPLICATIONS: Injury from falling.

PROGNOSIS: Settles eventually, but slowly.

See also Faint; Post-Traumatic Stress Disorder

VD
See Venereal Diseases

Venereal Diseases
(Sexually Transmitted Diseases; VD)
See AIDS (HIV); Amoebiasis; Chancroid; Crabs; Cytomegolovirus (CMV);
Donavanosis; Gay Bowel Syndrome; Genital Herpes; Genital Warts; Giardiasis;
Gonorrhoea; Granuloma Inguinale; Hepatitis B; Hepatitis C; Hepatitis D; Lice;
Lymphogranuloma Venereum; Non-Specific Urethritis; Pelvic Inflammatory
Disease; Syphilis; Thrush; Trichomoniasis, Venereal; Vaginitis, Bacterial

Venereal Warts
See Genital Warts

Venezuelan Equine Encephalitis
See Equine Encephalitis

Venomous Bite
See Funnel Web Spider Bite; Red-Back Spider Bite; Snake Bite; Tick Bite

Venous Thrombosis
See Deep Venous Thrombosis; Superficial Venous Thrombosis; Thrombosis

Venous Ulcer
See Ulcer, Venous

Ventricular Extrasystoles
DESCRIPTION: Abnormal heart beat.
CAUSE: An abnormal nerve impulse from part of the left ventricle (larger chamber on the left side of the heart) fires off before the normal heart pacemaker to cause a premature or extra heart beat.
SYMPTOMS: Momentary irregularity in the heart beat that may occur very infrequently, or every three or four beats.
INVESTIGATIONS: Diagnosed by electrocardiograph (ECG).
TREATMENT: Often none necessary, but if frequent, medications can be given to regulate heart rhythm.
COMPLICATIONS: May progress to ventricular flutter (see Ventricular Fibrillation entry).
PROGNOSIS: Good response to treatment.
See also other conditions listed under Arrhythmia

Ventricular Failure
See Congestive Cardiac Failure

Ventricular Fibrillation
(VF)

DESCRIPTION: Extremely rapid vibration of heart muscle in the ventricles (larger heart chambers) that prevents any blood from being pumped out of the heart. A slower, but still very rapid, heart contraction rate that allows a small amount of blood flow, is **ventricular flutter**.

CAUSE: Heart attack and electrocution most common causes.

SYMPTOMS: Sudden collapse, coma and death within minutes if not adequately treated.

INVESTIGATIONS: Diagnosed by ECG (electrocardiograph).

TREATMENT: Cardio-pulmonary resuscitation (CPR — heart massage and mouth to mouth breathing) may save some patients long enough for specific treatment to be given. Electrical shock to heart (cardioversion) applied immediately after patient collapses and repeated until normal rhythm occurs, followed by injections into a vein of medications to prevent further heart beat irregularities.

PROGNOSIS: If VF occurs in a hospital intensive care ward, a significant percentage of patients can be saved. In the community, death usually occurs before effective treatment can be given.

See also Heart Attack

Ventricular Flutter
See Ventricular Fibrillation

Ventricular Septal Defect
(Blue Baby; Hole in the Heart)

DESCRIPTION: Abnormal opening between the two main chambers (ventricles) in the heart.

CAUSE: Congenital.

SYMPTOMS: Depends on size of abnormal opening. May have no symptoms or in severe cases may cause congestive cardiac failure, cor pulmonale (see separate entries), shortness of breath, blue tinged skin (cyanosis), chest pain, fainting attacks, coughing up blood and numerous other symptoms related to the heart and lungs.

INVESTIGATIONS: Diagnosed by ultrasound examination of heart (echocardiography).

TREATMENT: Small holes may close spontaneously. Open heart surgery used to close larger holes.

COMPLICATIONS: Often combined with other heart and other organ developmental defects.

PROGNOSIS: Usually good results from treatment, but if very severe, death in infancy before surgery can be performed is possible.

See also Conradi-Hunermann Syndrome; Fallot's Pentalogy; Fallot's Tetralogy; Fallot's Trilogy

Ventricular Tachycardia
See Paroxysmal Ventricular Tachycardia; Tachycardia

Verruca
See Plantar Wart

Vestibular Neuronitis
See Vestibulitis

Vestibulitis
(Vestibular Neuronitis)
DESCRIPTION: Disturbance to the three semicircular canals of the balance mechanism in the inner ear.

CAUSE: Inflammation or viral infection of the nerve endings supplying the balance mechanism (vestibular apparatus) in the inner ear, that may be associated with almost any viral infection, including influenza. Excess fluid accumulates in the balance mechanism to make it malfunction.

SYMPTOMS: Constant dizziness and unsteadiness, often at rest, but certainly with any movement. May be associated with nausea, vomiting and a ringing noise in the ears. Abnormal side to side eye movements (nystagmus) may be present.

INVESTIGATIONS: Usually none necessary, but sometimes special balance tests carried out on the ear.

TREATMENT: Medications (eg. prochlorperazine, diuretics) ease the symptoms.

COMPLICATIONS: None serious.

PROGNOSIS: No cure but settles slowly with time.

VF
See Ventricular Fibrillation

Vincent's Angina
See Gingivostomatitis; Necrotising Ulcerative Gingivostomatitis

Viraemia
DESCRIPTION: A generalised viral infection of the blood.

CAUSE: Almost any virus that enters the body (often through the nose or mouth) and circulates in the blood, rather than attacking any specific area.

SYMPTOMS: General feeling of being unwell, variable fever, tiredness and generalised aches and pains.

INVESTIGATIONS: None normally necessary. Blood tests will show the presence of a virus, and sometimes which one.

TREATMENT: Aspirin or other anti-inflammatory medications, and pain killers such as paracetamol. Time and rest are the only cures.

COMPLICATIONS: Infection may attack a specific organ to cause localised symptoms.

PROGNOSIS: Good. Eventually settles spontaneously.

592

Viral Conjunctivitis
See Conjunctivitis

Viral Encephalitis
See Equine Encephalitis; Japanese Encephalitis; la Crosse Encephalitis; Murray Valley Encephalitis; St.Louis Encephalitis; West Nile Encephalitis

Viral Enteritis
See Gastroenteritis

Viral Haemorrhagic Fever
See Ebola Virus; Lassa Fever; Marburg Virus

Viral Infection
See Adenitis; AIDS; Barmah Forest Virus; Bronchiolitis; Bronchitis, Acute; Chickenpox; Cold, Common; Cold Sores; Conjunctivitis; Coxsackie Virus Infection; Croup; Cytomegalovirus Infection; Ebola Virus; Encephalitis; Fifth Disease; Gastroenteritis; Genital Herpes; German Measles; Glandular fever; Hand Foot Mouth Disease; Hepatitis A, B, C, D, E and G; Influenza; Labyrinthitis; Laryngitis; Laryngotracheobronchitis; Lassa Fever; Marburg Virus; Measles; Meningitis; Mokola Virus Infection; Molluscum Contagiosum; Mumps; Murray Valley Encephalitis; Orf; Pericarditis; Pharyngitis; Pleurisy; Polio; Rabies; Rocky Mountain Spotted Fever; Roseola Infantum; Ross River Fever; Rotavirus Infection; Smallpox; Vestibulitis; Viraemia; Warts; Whitlow; Yellow Fever etc.

Viral Meningitis
See Meningitis

Visceral Larva Migrans
(Ocular Larva Migrans)
DESCRIPTION: Internal infestation by the larvae of a roundworm (nematode).

CAUSE: Dogs infected by the roundworm (*Toxocara canis*) pass worm eggs out with their faeces to contaminate the soil. Eggs swallowed by humans (often children) hatch into larvae which penetrate through the gut wall into the bloodstream by which they are carried to a variety of organs, particularly the lungs, liver, brain and eye (ocular larva migrans).

SYMPTOMS: Very variable, depending on which organ the larvae are carried to, and the number of larvae present. Usually include fever, tiredness, loss of appetite and weight loss. Organ specific symptoms include cough, wheeze, rash, large liver and spleen, visual disturbances, seizures and behavioural disorders.

INVESTIGATIONS: There is a specific blood test to detect the presence of the larvae, and other blood tests show significant reactive changes. Chest X-rays may show lung inflammation. Masses of larvae in the eye can be seen by looking through the pupil with an ophthalmoscope (magnifying light).

TREATMENT: Medication is available to destroy the larvae, and steroids are used to reduce inflammation.

COMPLICATIONS: Heart infestation and pneumonia may lead to death.

PROGNOSIS: Larvae cannot develop into worms in humans, and die off naturally after several months, but permanent organ damage may occur. Treatment of eye disease is unsatisfactory.

See also Cutaneous Larva Migrans

Visceral Leischmaniasis
See Kala-Azar

Vision Problems
See Amblyopia; Astigmatism; Cataract; Colour Blind; Corneal Dystrophy; Drusen; Episcleritis; Floaters in Eye; Glaucoma; Keratoconus; Leber Congenital Amaurosis; Long Sighted; Macular Degeneration; Presbyopia; Retinal Detachment; Scleritis; Short Sighted; Squint; Strachan Syndrome

Vitamin A Deficiency
(Hypovitaminosis A)

DESCRIPTION: Vitamin A is found in all green leafy vegetables and a lack is uncommon except in places where food supplies are inadequate.

CAUSE: Starvation, tropical sprue, poor or fad diet that lacks vitamin A, and alcoholism or narcotic addiction which may lead to the other causes.

SYMPTOMS: Reduced night vision, dry eye surface, eye ulceration and dry skin.

INVESTIGATIONS: Blood test measurements of low vitamin A levels are inaccurate. Diagnosis made by history and clinical signs.

TREATMENT: Vitamin A supplements.

COMPLICATIONS: Permanent damage to the retina (light sensitive area at the back of the eye).

PROGNOSIS: Good response to treatment.

See also Eye Ulcer; Tropical Sprue

Vitamin A Excess
See Hypervitaminosis A

Vitamin B$_1$ Deficiency
See Beriberi

Vitamin B$_3$ Deficiency
See Hartnup Disease; Pellagra

Vitamin B$_6$ Deficiency

DESCRIPTION: Rare. A lack of vitamin B$_6$ (pyridoxine), which is widely distributed in all foods including meats, vegetables and cereals.

CAUSE: May be an uncommon side effect of some medications (eg. isoniazid, penicillamine), genetic disorders and in poor nutrition.

SYMPTOMS: Epileptic like seizures, dermatitis, mouth sores and dryness, vomiting, weakness and dizziness.

INVESTIGATIONS: Blood levels of pyridoxine can be measured.

TREATMENT: Correct cause or give vitamin B_6 supplements.

PROGNOSIS: Good response to treatment.

Vitamin B_{12} Deficiency
See Pernicious Anaemia

Vitamin B Excess

DESCRIPTION: Excess of any of the B group vitamins.

CAUSE: Taking too many vitamin B supplements.

SYMPTOMS: Usually no serious effects as excess passes out in the urine. Very high doses of pyridoxine (vitamin B_6) may cause nerve damage and poor coordination, numbness around the mouth, clumsiness, muscle weakness and loss of position sense. Very high doses of niacin (vitamin B_3) may cause severe flushing, itchy skin, diarrhoea and liver damage.

INVESTIGATIONS: Level of different B group vitamins can be measured in blood.

TREATMENT: Stop vitamin B supplements.

PROGNOSIS: Long term complications uncommon.

Vitamin C Deficiency
See Scurvy

Vitamin C Excess

DESCRIPTION: Excess vitamin C.

CAUSE: Taking too many vitamin C (ascorbic acid) supplements.

SYMPTOMS: Increase blood levels of oestrogens which cause breast tenderness and menstrual period irregularities, increased risk of kidney stones, reduced absorption of vitamin B_{12} and the development of pernicious anaemia, and rebound scurvy in babies born to mothers who take too much vitamin C during pregnancy.

INVESTIGATIONS: Level of vitamin C can be measured in the blood.

TREATMENT: Stop vitamin C supplements.

PROGNOSIS: Long term complications uncommon.

See also Scurvy

Vitamin D Deficiency
See Osteomalacia; Rickets

Vitamin D Excess
See Hypercalcaemia

Vitamin E Deficiency

DESCRIPTION: Lack of vitamin E (tocopherols), which results in nerve damage. Widely distributed in nearly all types of food, and acts as an anti-oxidant.

CAUSE: Starvation, poor diet, malabsorption of fats (eg. abetalipoproteinaemia — see separate entry).

SYMPTOMS: Reduced reflexes, abnormal gait (way of walking), decreased senses of position and vibration, and eye movement abnormalities.

INVESTIGATIONS: Diagnosed by measuring vitamin E levels in blood.

TREATMENT: Vitamin E supplements.

COMPLICATIONS: Degeneration of the spinal cord.

PROGNOSIS: Good response to treatment provided there has not been permanent nerve damage.

See also Abetalipoproteinaemia

Vitamin E Excess

DESCRIPTION: Excess vitamin E (tocopherols).

CAUSE: Taking too many vitamin E supplements.

SYMPTOMS: Usually none, but in some patients may cause tiredness, diarrhoea, headaches and high blood pressure. May be harmful to the foetus in pregnancy, and prevent blood clotting in those who are taking warfarin.

INVESTIGATIONS: Diagnosed by measuring vitamin E level in blood.

TREATMENT: Stop taking vitamin E supplements.

PROGNOSIS: Good, but foetal abnormalities may be permanent.

Vitamin K Deficiency

DESCRIPTION: A lack of vitamin K (phylloquinone) which is present in most vegetables, particularly those with green leaves.

CAUSE: Relatively common in newborn infants. Diseases which prevent fat absorption from the gut (eg. abetalipoproteinaemia), and long term potent antibiotic use may be responsible.

SYMPTOMS: Excessive bleeding and bruising.

INVESTIGATIONS: Diagnosed by measuring blood level of vitamin K.

TREATMENT: Vitamin K injections, which rarely, may be given to infants.

COMPLICATIONS: Excessive bleeding may lead to anaemia.

PROGNOSIS: Good response to treatment.

See also Abetalipoproteinaemia

Vitamin K Excess

DESCRIPTION: Excess vitamin K (phylloquinone).

CAUSE: Taking too many vitamin K supplements.

SYMPTOMS: Stop anticoagulants (eg. warfarin) from working and may lead to strokes or heart attacks. In pregnancy, the baby may be born jaundiced (yellow skin due to liver damage).

INVESTIGATIONS: Diagnosed by measuring vitamin K level in blood.

TREATMENT: Stop taking vitamin K supplements.
PROGNOSIS: Good.

Vitiligo

DESCRIPTION: Skin pigmentation disorder that can occur in all races, in both sexes, and at all ages, but onset is uncommon over 50 years of age.
CAUSE: Unknown, but probably an autoimmune disease, in which the body's defence mechanisms inappropriately attack normal cells and tissue, in this case destroying pigment producing melanin cells (melanocytes) in the skin.
SYMPTOMS: Loss of skin pigmentation in multiple patches that are sharply defined, may appear anywhere on the body, in any size and number, and overlying hair is usually white or grey. Affected skin is very sensitive to sunlight, and burns easily. In pale-skinned northern Europeans the patches may be barely noticed, but in southern Europeans, Arabs, Negroes and Chinese the resultant large white patches are quite disfiguring.
INVESTIGATIONS: Skin biopsy shows destruction of melanocytes.
TREATMENT: Cosmetic stains or dyes to disguise the affected areas of skin are most effective. A number of other treatments are available, but require long-term use of tablets and/or ultraviolet light exposure, and have only moderate success.
COMPLICATIONS: No side effects or complications.
PROGNOSIS: Affected area of skin usually slowly extends to involve larger areas but eventually stabilises after several years. Spontaneous recovery is uncommon.

VMRSA
See Staphylococcal Infection

Vogt-Koyanagi-Harada Syndrome

DESCRIPTION: Inflammation of brain, eyes and ears.
CAUSE: Unknown.
SYMPTOMS: Recurrent encephalitis and meningitis (see separate entries) with iritis (eye inflammation), detachment of the light sensitive retina from the back of the eye to cause patches of blindness, fever, headache and dizziness. May be associated with white patch of hair and skin, hair loss (alopecia), cataracts and glaucoma in the eyes, and deafness and ringing in the ears (tinnitus). May occur in one or both eyes.
INVESTIGATIONS: No specific diagnostic test.
TREATMENT: None available.
PROGNOSIS: Most cases settle spontaneously with time, but permanent eye damage often occurs.

Volkmann's Contracture

DESCRIPTION: Deformity of the forearm.
CAUSE: Damage to the artery (brachial artery) supplying the muscles in the forearm

from an elbow injury results in them being replaced by scar tissue.

SYMPTOMS: Pain in the forearm and an inability to straighten the wrist and fingers, which become fixed in a claw position.

INVESTIGATIONS: Radial pulse is missing in the wrist.

TREATMENT: Surgical repair of artery in early stages sometimes possible.

PROGNOSIS: Poor once contractures are present.

von Gierke Syndrome
See Glycogen Storage Diseases

von Hippel-Lindau Syndrome

DESCRIPTION: Developmental abnormality of blood vessels in the eye and brain that affects young adults.

CAUSE: Inherited.

SYMPTOMS: Visual disturbances from growth of tumours made of overgrown capillaries on the light sensitive retina at the back of the eye.

INVESTIGATIONS: Ophthalmoscopy (examining the eye with a magnifying light) shows abnormal growths. CT scan of brain may show tumours.

TREATMENT: Laser photocoagulation or surgical resection of retinal tumours, and brain surgery to remove any tumours that develop.

COMPLICATIONS: Tumours may develop in cerebellum (lower back part of brain) and cause varied disturbances.

PROGNOSIS: No permanent cure, and outcome depends on number, severity and location of tumours.

von Recklinghausen's Disease of Multiple Neurofibromatosis

DESCRIPTION: Disfiguring condition of skin and nerves that affects one in every 3000 Europeans. Fatty lumps grow from cells that form the soft sheath around nerves.

CAUSE: Familial (passes from one generation to next in families). Both partners must carry the gene for a child to be affected.

SYMPTOMS: Multiple light brown marks on the skin and soft fatty lumps under the skin, most commonly found on the trunk, pelvis and in the armpits. Spots and lumps increase in size and number with age, and in some patients, nerves may be damaged. One third of patients merely have a couple of brown spots that never concern them, while 10% are severely disfigured and disabled by large soft lumps under the skin, nerve weakness and multiple brown patches.

INVESTIGATIONS: Diagnosis confirmed by examining a biopsy of the patches or lumps.

TREATMENT: Plastic surgery for particularly bad lumps and patches.

COMPLICATIONS: Nerve damage due to soft lumps developing in the spinal canal, and in other areas where they can put pressure on nerves to the point where the nerve is no longer able to function. Deafness, blindness and paralysis may be the long-term result in a small number of cases. Scoliosis (curvature of the spine), bone cysts, uneven growth of the limbs (one arm or leg larger than the other), arthritis and sometimes mild mental retardation may occur. There is an increased risk of cancer (sarcoma) developing in affected tissues.

PROGNOSIS: No cure, but reasonable life expectancy.

von Willebrand's Disease
(Vascular Haemophilia)

DESCRIPTION: Rare cause of prolonged bleeding.

CAUSE: Inherited. Patients lack one of the essential factors involved in the complex process of blood clotting.

SYMPTOMS: Most cases are mild, and patients experience nose bleeds, heavy periods, bleeding gums and bleeding into the gut. Excessive bleeding also occurs with any cut or surgery and is dramatically worsened by aspirin.

INVESTIGATIONS: Diagnosis confirmed by appropriate blood tests.

TREATMENT: None required in the majority of patients, but aspirin must be avoided. An injection of a blood extract that contains the missing factors is given before surgery and to those who experience excessive bleeding from a severe case of the disease.

COMPLICATIONS: Bleeding into joints may cause premature arthritis.

PROGNOSIS: Disease is normally mild, and has an excellent long term prognosis.

See also Christmas Disease; Haemophilia A

Vulvodynia
See Burning Vulva Syndrome

W

Waardenburg-Klein Syndrome

DESCRIPTION: Genetic developmental abnormality.

CAUSE: Familial (passes through families).

SYMPTOMS: Deafness in one or both ears, broad root of nose with sideways displacement of corner of eye, eyebrows join together, white forelock and eye irises different colours.

INVESTIGATIONS: No specific diagnostic test.

TREATMENT: Plastic surgery for facial abnormalities.

PROGNOSIS: No cure.

WAGR Syndrome

DESCRIPTION: Genetic developmental abnormality. Name is an acronym for the principal features.

CAUSE: Congenital condition localised to chromosome 11.

SYMPTOMS: Wilms' tumour of kidney (see separate entry), no iris in eyes (Aniridia), ovarian or testicular tumours (Gonadoblastoma) and mental Retardation.

INVESTIGATIONS: Chromosome analysis abnormal.

TREATMENT: Treatment of Wilms' and gonad tumours.

PROGNOSIS: Very poor.

See also Wilms' Tumour

Warts

DESCRIPTION: Unsightly growth on the skin.

CAUSE: A very slow-growing virus, which takes months or years to cause a wart. Only a quarter of the population is susceptible to the wart virus, the rest have natural immunity. Most common in children from 8 to 16 years of age. People with warts should not be isolated for fear of spreading the disease as the virus is widespread in the community.

SYMPTOMS: Hard, rough, raised growth on the skin. The most common sites are the knees, elbows, hands and feet.

INVESTIGATIONS: None necessary.

TREATMENT: Acid paints applied regularly eat away wart tissue, freezing (cryotherapy) with liquid nitrogen causes the wart to fall off after a few days, burning the wart tissue away with a high voltage electric current (diathermy), injecting a cell destroying substance (bleomycin) under the wart, or cutting the wart out surgically.

COMPLICATIONS: Warts may recur after all forms of treatment. Only warts that are causing disfigurement or discomfort should be treated, as a scar may remain after any form of surgery, diathermy or cryotherapy.

PROGNOSIS: Usually go away by themselves without any treatment, but this may take many months or years. The average life span of a wart is about 18 months.
See also Genital Warts; Plantar Warts

Warts, Genital
See Genital Warts

Wasp Sting
See Sting, Bee or Wasp

Water on the Knee
See Housemaid's Knee

Waterhouse-Friderichsen Syndrome
(Fulminant Meningococcaemia)
DESCRIPTION: Catastrophic infection of the adrenal glands which sit on top of each kidney and secrete steroids to sustain the body.
CAUSE: Severe Meningococcal bacterial infection causes bleeding into both adrenal glands, destroying them and causing an acute Addisonian crisis (see separate entry).
SYMPTOMS: Collapse, bleeding into and under the skin, blue tinge to skin around the mouth, pale complexion. Followed by coma, heart failure and death.
INVESTIGATIONS: Blood culture identifies the bacteria and blood tests show numerous body chemistry abnormalities.
TREATMENT: Immediate treatment critically urgent. Large doses of antibiotics by drip into a vein, hydrocortisone injections and fluids into the drip.
COMPLICATIONS: Permanent Addison's disease, brain or heart damage.
PROGNOSIS: Poor. Death may occur within a few hours.
See also Addison's Disease; Meningitis

Weber-Christian Panniculitis
See Panniculitis

Wegener's Granulomatosis
DESCRIPTION: Rare condition causing inflammation of blood vessels and kidneys, and ulcerating sores in the lungs, larynx, nose and sinuses. Diagnosis is often difficult.
CAUSE: Unknown.
SYMPTOMS: Fever, weakness, sinusitis, shortness of breath, cough, chest pain, coughing up blood and joint pain.
INVESTIGATIONS: May be detected on a chest X-ray, or by taking a biopsy (sample) of one of the sores.
TREATMENT: Cyclophosphamide.
COMPLICATIONS: Permanent damage to involved organs.
PROGNOSIS: The condition is invariably fatal without treatment, but good results have been obtained with treatment.

Weil Syndrome

DESCRIPTION: A severe form of leptospirosis (see separate entry).

CAUSE: The spirochete bacteria *Leptospira interrogans* or *Leptospira biflexa*, which passes from rats and other rodents to man in conditions of poor hygiene.

SYMPTOMS: Pharyngitis (inflamed throat), muscle pains, diarrhoea with blood in faeces, excessive bleeding internally and externally (eg. blood nose, unusual bruising), kidney and liver failure, a large spleen and severe jaundice (yellow skin).

INVESTIGATIONS: Specific blood tests for Leptospira are positive.

TREATMENT: Antibiotics (eg. penicillin, tetracycline), kidney dialysis (artificial kidney machine).

COMPLICATIONS: Lung involvement causes cough, blood stained sputum, shortness of breath and adult respiratory distress syndrome (see separate entry). Heart involvement (myocarditis) possible.

PROGNOSIS: Significant morbidity (permanent organ damage), occasionally fatal.

See also Leptospirosis

Werdig-Hoffman Syndrome

DESCRIPTION: A progressive and permanent weakening and wasting of muscles.

CAUSE: Inherited condition that runs in families.

SYMPTOMS: Muscle weakness which attacks muscles of the trunk more than the limbs and makes breathing more and more difficult.

INVESTIGATIONS: Diagnosed by electrical studies of muscle action, and muscle biopsy.

TREATMENT: No effective treatment available, but physiotherapy may be beneficial.

COMPLICATIONS: Pneumonia from the failure of muscles of breathing.

PROGNOSIS: No cure. Most patients die before the age of five years.

See also Motor Neurone Disease and other diseases listed under Muscular Dystrophy

Werner Syndrome
(MEN 1; Multiple Endocrine Neoplasia Type 1)

DESCRIPTION: Multiple cancers developing in the hormone producing glands of children.

CAUSE: Inherited.

SYMPTOMS: Cancer involving the pituitary gland under the brain, parathyroid glands in the neck and pancreatic islet cells in the pancreas that produce insulin. Other symptoms may include carcinoid tumours of the intestine, high blood pressure producing tumours in the adrenal glands on top of each kidney (phaeochromocytoma), thin wasted skin and eye cataracts (see separate entries for details of these diseases).

INVESTIGATIONS: Diagnosed by genetic tests, and can be detected before birth. Regular screening of gland function by blood tests.

TREATMENT: Surgery to remove cancers, and management of affected glands by hormone replacement.

COMPLICATIONS: Spread of cancer to other organs.

PROGNOSIS: Poor.

See also Multiple Endocrine Neoplasia Type 2

Wernicke's Encephalopathy
See Wernicke-Korsakoff Psychosis

Wernicke-Korsakoff Psychosis
(Korsakoff's Psychosis; Wernicke's Encephalopathy)

DESCRIPTION: Damage to the brain caused by a vitamin deficiency.

CAUSE: A deficiency in vitamin B, particularly thiamine (vitamin B_1), that occurs most commonly in alcoholics who neglect their diet. Elderly people who are malnourished may also develop the condition.

SYMPTOMS: Tremor, poor coordination, confusion, sudden eye movements, double vision, and pins and needles in the hands and feet.

INVESTIGATIONS: Blood tests can confirm the low levels of thiamine in the blood.

TREATMENT: Thiamine by injection initially, and later by tablet, to replace that which is missing. A good well-balanced diet and strictly no alcohol.

COMPLICATIONS: If alcoholics are not treated early, permanent brain damage may result.

PROGNOSIS: Good treatment and patient cooperation brings most back to a reasonable lifestyle.

See also Alcoholism; Peripheral Neuropathy

West Nile Encephalitis

DESCRIPTION: Viral infection of the brain.

CAUSE: Virus spread from birds to man by a mosquito. Found throughout north Africa, the Middle East and southeast Europe. More common in children and the elderly. Incubation period three to six days.

SYMPTOMS: Fever and a rash are often the only symptoms, but in severe cases may cause eye pain, enlarged tender lymph nodes, dizziness, sore throat, joint pains, headache, neck stiffness, nausea, vomiting, tiredness, disturbed mental functions and disorientation.

INVESTIGATIONS: Tests on blood and the fluid around the brain are abnormal.

TREATMENT: No specific treatment or vaccine available.

COMPLICATIONS: Rarely causes any long term problems.

PROGNOSIS: Acute attack lasts for one to two weeks. Death uncommon.

See also Encephalitis

Western Equine Encephalitis
See Equine Encephalitis

Wheezy Bronchitis
See Asthma

Whiplash
(Neck Sprain; Traumatic Cervical Syndrome)
DESCRIPTION: Injury that damages the ligaments and muscles that support the neck and head.

CAUSE: If a person is suddenly accelerated forwards (eg. in a rear-end automobile accident), the head has a tendency to remain behind and the neck is bent backwards suddenly and excessively. The ligaments and muscles on the front of the vertebral column and neck are stretched and torn (sprained). In severe cases, nerve fibres may also be overstretched and damaged.

SYMPTOMS: Vary dramatically from one patient to another. Pain, limited neck movement and stiffness may commence shortly after the injury or be delayed by 24 hours or more. Pain may spread to the shoulders, chest and back. Other possible symptoms include numbness in the fingers and forearm, difficulty in swallowing, blurred vision, dizziness, noises in the ears (tinnitus) and nausea.

INVESTIGATIONS: Neck X-rays are often performed, but are usually normal.

TREATMENT: Rest, immobilisation (neck brace), anti-inflammatory medications, pain relievers, heat and physiotherapy.

COMPLICATIONS: Damage to the bony vertebrae in the neck, or very rarely the spinal cord.

PROGNOSIS: Most patients recover within a couple of weeks, but a very small number continue with long-term discomfort, pain and movement limitation.

Whipple's Disease
DESCRIPTION: Rare disorder of the lymphatic system, which drains waste products back from cells to the heart.

CAUSE: Obstruction of the lymphatic ducts draining the small intestine and persistent bacterial infection of the gut.

SYMPTOMS: Joint and belly pain, diarrhoea, weight loss and a slight fever. Patients may also have increased pigmentation of the skin and enlarged lymph nodes.

INVESTIGATIONS: Faeces examination shows the presence of excess fat, and small bowel X-rays are abnormal. Diagnosed by a biopsy of the small intestine.

TREATMENT: Long term antibiotics (eg. sulfas).

COMPLICATIONS: Heart failure, uveitis (eye inflammation), confusion, memory loss and abnormal eye movements.

PROGNOSIS: No cure, but most cases controlled by treatment.

Whipworm Infestation
See Trichuriasis

Whistling Face Syndrome
See Freeman-Sheldon Syndrome

Whitlow
(Herpes Simplex Type 1 Infection)

DESCRIPTION: A skin infection beside a finger nail, with the virus Herpes simplex type 1.

CAUSE: Initially, the infection is caught as a child, when it is a simple mouth infection. The virus then migrates to the nerve endings around the finger or toe nail, and remains inactive there for many years. It may later reactivate at times of stress or illness. Recurrences tend to develop at the same spot.

SYMPTOMS: Redness and soreness of the skin, usually beside a nail, followed a day or two later by an eruption of small blisters, which rapidly burst to leave a shallow, weeping, painful ulcer.

INVESTIGATIONS: None normally necessary, but if required the diagnosis can be confirmed by taking special swabs from the sore.

TREATMENT: If treated by appropriate creams and lotions immediately the redness and discomfort is felt and before the blisters form, it may be possible to stop further progress. Once established, a cure is not normally possible, but drying, antiseptic and anaesthetic creams or lotions may be used.

COMPLICATIONS: In rare cases, the infection can spread into the throat and lungs, and these patients become extremely ill.

PROGNOSIS: The sore heals and the pain eases in about ten days.

See also Cold Sores

Whooping Cough
(Pertussis)

DESCRIPTION: A preventable bacterial infection of the respiratory tract that is very serious in children. A much milder form of the disease (parapertussis) is also known, against which the pertussis vaccine gives no protection.

CAUSE: The bacterium *Bordetella pertussis*, which is widespread in the community. In adults an infection merely has the symptoms of a cold, but in young children the disease is more severe. Spreads from person to person in the microscopic droplets exhaled or coughed out in the breath of a patient, so an adult with minimal symptoms may carry the disease from one infant to another. The incubation period is one to two weeks.

SYMPTOMS: Starts in a child as a cold that lasts a week or two, but then the cough becomes steadily more severe and occurs in increasingly distressing spasms, characterised by a sudden intake of breath before each cough. Coughing spasms may last up to 30 minutes, and leave the child exhausted, then another spasm starts after only a few minutes. As the infection worsens, the child may become blue, lose consciousness, and thick stringy mucus is coughed up and vomited. The patient has no appetite and rapidly loses weight. Severe coughing may cause bleeding in the lungs, throat and nose, that may be severe enough to cause suffocation. If the child survives, the spasms start to ease off after a few weeks, but mild recurrences may occur for months.

INVESTIGATIONS: Diagnosed by analysis of a sputum sample.

TREATMENT: No cure available, but may be completely prevented by a vaccination that is combined with those for tetanus and diphtheria (see separate entries). Usually given at two, four, six and 18 months, and again at five years of age. Treatment involves oxygen, sedatives and careful nursing, isolated within a hospital for several weeks. Antibiotics can prevent the spread of the disease to others.

COMPLICATIONS: Permanent lung damage possible.

PROGNOSIS: In good hospitals about 2% die, and up to 10% have long term complications. In poorer countries, the mortality rate is much higher.

Williams Syndrome

DESCRIPTION: Genetic developmental abnormality.

CAUSE: Sporadic inheritance.

SYMPTOMS: Blue and lacy irises (coloured part of eyes), abnormally long distance between nose and upper lip, prominent eye folds and lips, pendular cheeks, slight mental deterioration and an outgoing personality. Some patients also have excess calcium in their blood and narrowing of the aorta (aortic stenosis).

INVESTIGATIONS: None diagnostic.

TREATMENT: None available.

PROGNOSIS: No cure, but reasonable life expectancy.

Wilms' Tumour
(Nephroblastoma)

DESCRIPTION: A form of cancer that arises in the supportive tissue immediately surrounding the kidneys of children.

CAUSE: Unknown. More than 80% of patients are under four years of age when diagnosed, and it accounts for nearly 10% of all childhood cancers.

SYMPTOMS: The children develop a swollen abdomen, but only one in five has pain, and even fewer develop the other possible symptoms of fever, bloody urine, weight loss and loss of appetite. Usually detected by a parent feeling the large hard mass in the abdomen.

INVESTIGATIONS: Diagnosis confirmed by X-ray or CT scan of the kidney, followed by a biopsy.

TREATMENT: The affected kidney is removed surgically, followed by irradiation of the abdomen to destroy any remaining cancer cells. Chemotherapy with cytotoxic drugs may also be given.

COMPLICATIONS: Spread of the cancer to other tissues and organs, particularly the liver and lungs, and in rare cases to the bone and brain.

PROGNOSIS: With localised disease 90% of patients now survive more than five years, and even if the cancer has spread to other organs, more than 50% survive for five years.

Wilson's Disease
(Hepatolenticular Degeneration)

DESCRIPTION: A rare disorder of copper metabolism with symptoms relating to the brain, the liver or both.

CAUSE: Inherited disorder that results in the excessive deposition of copper in the liver and brain. Occurs in both sexes and is usually diagnosed between 10 and 30 years of age.

SYMPTOMS: Excess copper in the brain may cause psychiatric disorders, rigid muscles and a tremor. Liver disease symptoms include jaundice (yellow skin), an enlarged liver and/or spleen, anaemia and hepatitis. A brown/green ring (Kayser-Fleischer ring) around the iris (coloured part) in the eye is easily visible.

INVESTIGATIONS: Diagnosis confirmed by blood tests that detect the excessive copper.

TREATMENT: Copper can be removed by a number of drugs (eg. penicillamine), and a diet low in copper (eg. avoiding shellfish, beans and offal). Lifelong treatment is necessary to keep copper levels low.

COMPLICATIONS: Any damage to the brain or liver caused before the treatment is started cannot usually be reversed.

PROGNOSIS: The long-term outlook is normally good.

See also other diseases listed under Liver Diseases

Wiskott-Aldrich Syndrome

DESCRIPTION: Abnormal destruction of the cells (platelets) which are responsible for blood clotting, and a lack of the cells necessary to protect the body from infection.

CAUSE: Inherited condition, which passes from one generation to the next through the mother (X linked), but only affects boys.

SYMPTOMS: Widespread eczema, recurrent severe infections, and excessive bleeding and bruising because of a lack of platelets in the blood.

INVESTIGATIONS: Diagnosed by blood tests and bone marrow biopsy.

TREATMENT: Vigorous treatment of infections, blood transfusions, bone marrow transplants and sometimes removal of the spleen (which is responsible for destroying the platelets).

COMPLICATIONS: Severe life threatening infections.

PROGNOSIS: Few of these children survive into their teen years.

See also Immunodeficiency

Witkop
See Favus

Wittmaack-Ekbom Syndrome
See Restless legs Syndrome

Wolff-Parkinson-White Syndrome
(Accelerated Conduction Syndrome)

DESCRIPTION: Abnormal nerve pathway in heart allows short circuit between the upper (atria) and lower (ventricles) chambers of the heart.

CAUSE: May be congenital or develop later in life.

SYMPTOMS: Very abnormal heart rhythm and distressing palpitations.

INVESTIGATIONS: Electrocardiograph (ECG) shows typical abnormal pattern.

TREATMENT: Acute attacks treated by medications (eg. verapamil, propranolol, procainamide) injected into a vein and cardioversion (electric shock to heart). Long term prevention of further attacks involves the regular use of medication and sometimes surgery on the heart to cut abnormal nerve pathways.

COMPLICATIONS: Rarely, sudden death may occur.

PROGNOSIS: Adequate control normal.

See also Ebstein Anomaly and other conditions listed under Arrhythmia

Wolf-Hirschhorn Syndrome

DESCRIPTION: Developmental abnormality of the face.

CAUSE: Congenital condition localised to chromosome 4.

SYMPTOMS: Mental retardation, slow growth, abnormal nasal bridge ('Greek helmet' appearance), cleft lip and abnormally short distance between nose and upper lip.

INVESTIGATIONS: Chromosomal analysis abnormal.

TREATMENT: Plastic surgery.

PROGNOSIS: No cure.

Womb Prolapse
See Vaginal Prolapse

Worm Infestation
(Helminthiasis)

See Angiostrongyliasis; Anisakiasis; Ascariasis; Cutaneous Larva Migrans; Dracunculiasis; Gnathostomiasis; Hookworm; Hydatid Disease; Pinworms; Strongyloidiasis; Tapeworms; Trichuriasis; Trichinosis; Visceral Larva Migrans

Wrist Fracture
See Colles' Fracture; Scaphoid Fracture; Smith's Fracture

X

Xanthomatosis

DESCRIPTION: Skin complication of high cholesterol levels.

CAUSE: Excess cholesterol in the blood that settles in the skin.

SYMPTOMS: Small, fatty, yellow lumps that appear to be almost on top of the skin. Most commonly occur around the eyes, on the knees, elbows and buttocks.

INVESTIGATIONS: Blood cholesterol levels raised.

TREATMENT: Diet and medication to lower cholesterol. Skin lumps can be destroyed by cautery (burning) or surgically cut out.

PROGNOSIS: Skin lumps persist after cholesterol controlled.

Xeroderma Pigmentosa

DESCRIPTION: Rare disorder of skin and nerves resulting in an inability to repair damage to the skin, brain and other tissues.

CAUSE: Familial (inherited). Sun exposure causes skin damage.

SYMPTOMS: Skin sores, inflammation and abnormal pigmentation. Children have small heads, mental deterioration, poor coordination (ataxia), muscle spasms (spasticity), abnormal movements of the limbs (athetosis) and underdeveloped testes or ovaries. Other abnormalities may include deafness, seizures, abnormal sensations and abnormal heart nerves.

INVESTIGATIONS: No specific diagnostic test.

TREATMENT: Avoid sun. Otherwise none available.

COMPLICATIONS: High incidence of cancer.

PROGNOSIS: Poor.

See also other diseases listed under Ataxia

Xerophthalmia

See Dry Eye Syndrome; Keratoconjunctivitis Sicca

Xiphoidalgia

DESCRIPTION: The xiphoid is a piece of cartilage at the bottom end of the breast bone (sternum) that sticks down into the gap between the ribs on either side.

CAUSE: Inflammation of the xiphoid for no known reason.

SYMPTOMS: Significant pain and tenderness of the xiphoid cartilage that is worse with chest movement (eg. deep breath, cough).

INVESTIGATIONS: None necessary.

TREATMENT: Anti-inflammatory medications, anti-inflammatory and anaesthetic injections, or steroids.

COMPLICATIONS: Irritation of underlying stomach may cause nausea and vomiting.

PROGNOSIS: Settles with time and treatment.

See also Tietze Syndrome

X-Linked Agammaglobulinaemia
See Agammaglobulinaemia

XO Syndrome
See Turner Syndrome

XXX Syndrome

DESCRIPTION: Chromosomal abnormality affecting one in 800 women.

CAUSE: Congenital. Three X chromosomes present instead of the normal two in a woman.

SYMPTOMS: Woman appears totally normal but may suffer minor mental retardation.

INVESTIGATIONS: Chromosome analysis abnormal.

TREATMENT: None available.

COMPLICATIONS: Increased incidence of psychoses.

PROGNOSIS: No cure. Normal fertility, children genetically normal, and normal life span.

XXY Syndrome
See Klinefelter Syndrome

XYY Syndrome

DESCRIPTION: Sex chromosome abnormality of males.

CAUSE: Congenital. Usually males have an X and Y chromosome (XY) and females two X chromosomes (XX). In one in 500 males, an extra Y chromosome is found to cause the XYY syndrome. Rarely even more Y chromosomes may be added to create XYYY and XYYYY.

SYMPTOMS: Males who are tall, heavily built, aggressive and violent.

INVESTIGATIONS: Diagnosed by examining the chromosomes in almost any bodily cell, and may be made before birth by amniocentesis or chorionic villus sampling.

TREATMENT: Behavioural therapy.

COMPLICATIONS: The population in jails has a far higher proportion of men with this syndrome than is found in the general population.

PROGNOSIS: No cure.

See also Klinefelter Syndrome

Y

Yaws

DESCRIPTION: Bacterial infection that occurs in some third-world countries with very poor hygiene.

CAUSE: The *Treponema pallidum* bacterium is responsible, which is the same bacteria that causes syphilis (see separate entry). Transmitted from one person to another by close contact and poor personal cleanliness.

SYMPTOMS: Sores on the skin and in the nose and mouth, and inflamed lymph nodes in the armpits and groin.

INVESTIGATIONS: Diagnosed by taking swabs from sores.

TREATMENT: Antibiotics (eg. penicillin) and improved personal hygiene.

COMPLICATIONS: Sores may become large, ulcerate, penetrate to the bone and cause permanent disfigurement.

PROGNOSIS: Cured by antibiotics.

See also Pinta; Syphilis

Yellow Fever

DESCRIPTION: A serious tropical liver infection.

CAUSE: Viral infection transmitted from one person to another by the Aedes mosquito. Occurs only in central Africa, and tropical Central and South America. The incubation period is three to six days.

SYMPTOMS: Vary from vomiting, headache, tiredness, and eye pain in mild cases, to severe generalised body pains, high fevers, bleeding from the gums and intestine, bruising, copious vomiting, delirium, kidney failure and liver failure (which causes yellow skin — jaundice).

INVESTIGATIONS: Specific blood tests to confirm the diagnosis may not turn positive until a week or two after the symptoms develop, which makes early diagnosis difficult.

TREATMENT: No effective treatment or cure. The patient must be carefully nursed, given fluids through a drip into a vein, and sedated. A single vaccination gives protection for at least ten years.

COMPLICATIONS: Severe constipation.

PROGNOSIS: Death through massive internal bleeding and liver failure is common, even in good hospitals.

See also other diseases listed under Liver Diseases

Yellow Nail Syndrome

DESCRIPTION: Uncommon form of damage to finger and toe nails.

CAUSE: Poor blood and oxygen supply to nails. Chronic bronchitis and bronchiectasis (see separate entries) often responsible.

SYMPTOMS: Long term lung disease and/or lymphoedema (hard swelling of a limb

Yellow Nail Syndrome

— see separate entry) causes nails to stop growing and become thick and yellow, with excessive side to side curvature of nail, no cuticle (white half moon at base), and swelling and redness of skin fold at base of nail.

INVESTIGATIONS: Investigate cause.

TREATMENT: Treat underlying lung problem or lymphoedema. Apply azelaic acid to nail. Take vitamin E and zinc supplements.

COMPLICATIONS: Nails drop off and do not regrow.

PROGNOSIS: Very little chance of nails recovering.

See also Bronchiectasis; Bronchitis, Chronic; Lymphoedema

Z

Zellweger Syndrome
(Cerebro-Hepato-Renal Syndrome)

DESCRIPTION: Genetic abnormality of brain, liver and kidneys.

CAUSE: Familial (runs through families), but both parents must be carriers.

SYMPTOMS: Flat long face, large fontanelle (soft spot) in skull, poor muscle tone, difficulty in breathing from birth, large liver that fails to function, and seizures. The eyes may be affected by glaucoma and cataracts, joints may be contracted, bony abnormalities occur and the testes do not descend in boys.

INVESTIGATIONS: Numerous blood, urine and skeletal X-ray abnormalities detected.

TREATMENT: None available.

PROGNOSIS: Death within two months of birth.

Zollinger-Ellison Syndrome
(Gastrinoma)

DESCRIPTION: Rare form of severe peptic ulceration in the stomach or small intestine.

CAUSE: A tumour of the pancreas that produces high levels of a hormone which promotes excessive acid production in the stomach.

SYMPTOMS: Exaggerated symptoms of a peptic ulcer with severe pain in the upper abdomen, bloating, nausea and diarrhoea. Usually starts at a younger age than normal for a peptic ulcer.

INVESTIGATIONS: A specific blood test can measure the hormone 'gastrin' which is responsible for stimulating the stomach to produce hydrochloric acid. Other tests include gastroscopy and measuring the amount of acid in the stomach.

TREATMENT: Medications as for normal peptic ulcers, but in higher doses. Surgery is often required to control recurrent ulceration.

COMPLICATIONS: Severe bleeding from ulcers leading to anaemia.

PROGNOSIS: Treatment must be continued lifelong, but is usually successful in controlling the disease.

See also Ulcer, Peptic

Zygomycosis
(Mucormycosis)

DESCRIPTION: Fungal infection of the nose and sinuses that usually occurs in patients who are having chemotherapy for cancer or are debilitated.

CAUSE: The fungi Rhizopus and Mucor.

SYMPTOMS: Low grade fever, dull pain in the face and forehead, nasal congestion and discharge.

Zygomycosis

INVESTIGATIONS: Diagnosed from examining a biopsy of the lining of the nose and sinuses under a microscope.

TREATMENT: Surgical clearance of the nose and sinuses combined with potent antifungal drugs for several months.

COMPLICATIONS: Worsening fever, bloody nasal discharge, reduced eye movement, lung involvement and collapse.

PROGNOSIS: About half the patients with sinus infection are cured. It is not usually possible to cure any spread of the fungal infection to the lungs.

See also Fungal Infections.

TOPIC LISTING

Abetalipoproteinaemia

Abortion, Spontaneous

Abscess

Acanthosis Nigicans

Accelerated Conduction Syndrome

Achalasia

Achilles Tendon Rupture

Acne

Acne Conglobata

Acne Rosacea

Acne Vulgaris

Acoustic Neuroma

Acquired Immune Deficiency Syndrome

Acrocephalopolysyndactyly

Acrocephalosyndactyly of Apert

Acromegaly

Acrophobia

Actinomycosis

Acute Brain Syndrome

Acute Bronchitis

Acute Confusional Syndrome

Acute Febrile Neutrophilic Dermatosis

Acute Hepatic Porphyria

Acute Leukaemia

Acute Kidney Failure

Acute Pyelonephritis

Acute Renal Failure

Adams-Stokes Syndrome

ADD

Addiction

Addisonian Crisis

Addison's Disease

Adenitis

Adenocarcinoma of the Lung

ADHD

Adhesions

Adhesive Capsulitis

Adie's Pupil

Adrenal Gland Insufficiency

Adrenal Hyperplasia, Congenital

Adrenocortical Hyperfunction

Adrenocortical Insufficiency

Adrenogenital Syndrome

Adult Respiratory Distress Syndrome

Affective Disorder

Afferent Loop Syndrome

African Trypanosomiasis

Agammaglobulinaemia

Agoraphobia

Agranulocytosis

AIDS

Air Sickness

Alagille Syndrome

Albinism

Albino

Albright Syndrome

Alcoholism

Aldosteronism

Allergic Conjunctivitis

Allergic Eczema

Allergic Rhinitis

Allergy

Alopecia Areata

Alopecia Totalis

Alport Syndrome

Altitude Sickness

Alveolitis

Alzheimer's Disease

Amaurosis

Amblyopia

American Trypanosomiasis

Amnestic Syndrome

Amoebiasis

Amoebic Dysentery

Amphetamine Abuse

Amsterdam Dwarf

Amyloidosis

Amyotrophic Lateral Sclerosis

Anaemia

Anaerobic Infections

Anal Atresia

Anal Fissure

Topics

Anal Fistula
Anal Inflammation
Anal Itch
Anaphylactic Shock
Anaphylactoid Purpura
Anaphylaxis
Anaplastic Carcinoma of the Thyroid Gland
Ancylostomiasis
Andersen Syndrome
Anencephaly
Aneurysm
Angelman Syndrome
Angina
Angina, Vincent's
Angioedema
Angioma
Angioneurotic Oedema
Angiosarcoma
Angiostrongyliasis
Aniridia
Anisakiasis
Ankle Sprain
Ankylosing Spondylitis
Anorexia Nervosa
Anorgasmia
Anterior Chest Wall Syndrome
Anterior Compartment Syndrome
Anterior Impingement Syndrome
Anthrax
Antiphospholipid Syndrome
Anxiety Neurosis
Aortic Aneurysm
Aortic Arch Syndrome
Aortic Regurgitation
Aortic Stenosis
Aortic Unfolding
Aortic Valve Incompetence
Aortic Valve Stenosis
Apert Syndrome
Aphthous Ulcers
Aplastic Anaemia
Apophysitis of the Tibial Tuberosity
Apotemnophilia
Appendicitis

Arachnoiditis
Arachnophobia
Arcus Senilis
Arnold-Chiari Malformation
Arrhythmia
Arsenic Poisoning
Arterial Gas Embolism
Arteriosclerosis
Arteriovenous Fistula
Arteritis
Artery, Hardened
Arthritis
Asbestosis
Ascariasis
Ascites
Asorbic Acid Deficiency and Excess
Aseptic Meningitis
Asherman Syndrome
Asperger Syndrome
Aspergillosis
Asthma
Astigmatism
Astrocytoma
Ataxia
Ataxia Telangiectasia
Atherosclerosis
Athlete's Foot
Atopic Conjunctivitis
Atopic Dermatitis
Atopic Eczema
Atrial Extrasystoles
Atrial Fibrillation
Atrial Flutter
Atrial Septal Defect
Atrophic Vaginitis
Attention Deficit Disorder
Attention Deficit Hyperactivity Disorder
Auriculotemporal Syndrome
Autism
Autoimmune Diseases
Autonomic Neuropathy
Avascular Necrosis of the Femoral Head
Azorean Disease

Baby Colic

Baby Measles

Bacillary Dysentery

Back Diseases

Bacteraemia

Bacterial Conjunctivitis

Bacterial Endocarditis

Bacterial Meningitis

Bacterial Vaginitis

Baker's Cyst

Balanitis

Baldness

Bard-Pic Syndrome

Barlow Syndrome

Barmah Forest Virus

Barrett Syndrome

Bartholin's Cyst

Bartter Syndrome

Basal Cell Carcinoma

Basal Cell Carcinoma Naevus Syndrome

Bassen-Kornzweig Syndrome

Bat Ears

Bazin's Disease

BCC

Beal Syndrome

Becker's Muscular Dystrophy

Becker's Naevus

Beckwith-Wiedemann Syndrome

Bed Sore

Bed Wetting

Bee Sting

Behçet Syndrome

Bell's Palsy

Bends

Benign Familial Chronic Pemphigus

Benign Lymphoepithelial Condition

Bernard-Soulier Syndrome

Beriberi

Berry Aneurysm

Beta Cell Tumour

Bezoar

Bilharzia

Biliary Colic

Binge-Purge Syndrome

Bipolar Affective Disorder

Bipolar Personality

Bird Fancier's Lung

Bite

Black Death

Blackfan-Diamond Syndrome

Blackwater Fever

Bladder Infection

Blastocystis

Blastomycosis

Blepharitis

Blighted Ovum

Bloch-Sulzberger Syndrome

Blocked Tear Duct

Blood Poisoning

Blood Pressure, High

Blood Pressure, Low

Blood Transfusion Reaction

Bloom Syndrome

Blount's Disease

Blue Baby

Blue Diaper Syndrome

Blue Naevus

Blue Rubber Bleb Naevus Syndrome

Body Dismorphic Disorder

Boerhaave Syndrome

Boil

Bone, Broken

Bone Cancer

Bone Infection

Bonnet Syndrome

Bornholm Disease

Botulism

Bowel Cancer

Bowen's Disease

Bow Legs

Brachioradialis Pruritus

Brachmann-de Lange Syndrome

Brain Aneurysm

Brain Cancer or Tumour

Brain Haemorrhage

Brain Syndrome, Organic

Breakbone Fever

Breast Cancer

Topics

Breast Enlargement, Male
Breast Infection
Briquet Syndrome
Brittle Bone Disease
Broken Bone
Bronchial Carcinoma
Bronchiectasis
Bronchiolitis
Bronchitis, Acute
Bronchitis, Chronic
Bronchitis, Wheezy
Bronchogenic Carcinoma
Bronchopneumonia
Brown-Séquard Syndrome
Brucellosis
Bruise
Bruton Syndrome
Bruxism
Bubonic Plague
Buerger's Disease
Budd-Chiari Syndrome
Bulimia Nervosa
Bullous Impetigo
Bullous Pemphigoid
Bunion
Burn
Burning Vulva Syndrome
Bursitis
Burst Ear Drum

Caisson Disease
Calcium, Excess
Calcium Pyrophosphate Deposition Disease
Calculus, Renal
Californian Encephalitis
Callosity
Callus
Campylobacter Enteritis
Cancer
Cancer of the Cervix
Cancer of the Oesophagus
Cancer of the Ovary
Candidiasis
Cannabis Abuse

Capgras Syndrome
Capillaritis
Capsulitis
Carbuncle
Carcinoid Syndrome
Carcinoma
Carcinoma of the Cervix
Cardiac Failure
Cardiac Myxoma
Cardiomyopathy
Carney's Complex
Carotenaemia
Carotodynia Syndrome
Carpal Tunnel Syndrome
Carpenter Syndrome
Car Sickness
Cataract
Cat Scratch Disease
Catatonic Syndrome
Cattarh
Causalgia
CCF
Celiac Disease
Cellulitis
Cerebral Aneurysm
Cerebral Infarct
Cerebral Palsy
Cerebral Thrombosis
Cerebral Tumour
Cerebro-Hepato-Renal Syndrome
Cerebrovascular Accident
Cerumen
Cervical Cancer
Cervical Rib Syndrome
Cervix Cyst
Cestode Infestation
CFS
Chagas' Disease
Chalazion
Chancroid
'Change of Life'
Charcot-Marie-Tooth Disease
CHARGE Syndrome
Charles Bonnet Syndrome

Chédiak-Higashi Syndrome

Cheyne-Stokes Respiration

Chiari-Frommel Syndrome

Chickenpox

Chiclero's Ulcers

Chilblains

Chinese Restaurant Syndrome

Chlamydial Infections

Chlamydial Urethritis

Chloasma

Choledocoduodenal Fistula

Cholecystitis

Cholelithiasis

Cholera

Cholesteatoma

Cholesterol, Excess

Chondrocalcinosis

Chondrodermatitis Nodularis Chronica
  Helicis

Chondromalacia Patellae

Chondrosarcoma

Chorda Tympani Syndrome

Chorea

Choriocarcinoma of the Testicle

Choriocarcinoma of the Uterus

Christmas Disease

Chronic Bronchitis

Chronic Fatigue Syndrome

Chronic Hypoadrenocorticism

Chronic Kidney Failure

Chronic Leukaemia

Chronic Obstructive Airways (Pulmonary)
  Disease

Chronic Pyelonephritis

Chronic Renal Failure

Churg-Strauss Syndrome

Ciguatera Poisoning

Circumscribed Neurodermatitis

Circumscribed Scleroderma

Cirrhosis

CJD

Claudication

Claustrophobia

Cleft Lip and Palate

Clérambault Syndrome

Climacteric

Clostridial Myositis

Club Foot

Cluster Headache

CMV

Coagulation, Disseminated Intravascular

COA(P)D

Coarctation of the Aorta

Cocaine Addiction

Coeliac Disease

Coeliac Sprue

Coffin-Lowry Syndrome

Coffin-Siris Syndrome

Cogan Microcystic Corneal Dystrophy

Cogan Syndrome

Cold, Common

Cold Sore

Colic

Colitis

Colles' Fracture

Collet-Sicard Syndrome

Colo-Rectal Cancer

Colour Blind

Coma

Common Cold

Complex Regional Pain Syndrome
  Type One

Complex Regional Pain Syndrome
  Type Two

Concussion

Condylomata Acuminata

Congenital Adrenal Hyperplasia

Congenital Dislocation of Hip

Congenital Poikiloderma

Congenital Syphilis

Congenital Varicella Syndrome

Congestive Cardiac Failure

Conjunctivitis

Conn Syndrome

Conradi-Hunermann Syndrome

Conrad Syndrome

Constipation

Constrictive Pericarditis

Topics

Contact Dermatitis
Contractural Arachnodactyly
Conversion Disorder
Cori Syndrome
Corneal Dystrophy
Corneal Ulcer
Cor Pulmonale
Coryza
Costen Syndrome
Costochondral Syndrome
Cot Death
Cowden Disease
Coxsackie Virus Infection
Crabs
Crack
Cradle Cap
Cramps, Leg and Muscular
Craniopharyngioma
Craniostenosis
Creeping Eruption
CREST Syndrome
Cretinism
Creutzfeldt-Jakob Disease
Cri du Chat Syndrome
Crigler-Najjar Syndrome
Crocodile Tears Syndrome
Crohn's Disease
Cronkhite-Canada Syndrome
Cronkhite Syndrome
'Crotch Rot'
Croup
Crouzon Syndrome
CRST Syndrome
Cryptococcosis
Cryptogenic Fibrosing Alveolitis
Cryptorchidism
Cryptosporidiosis
Cubital Tunnel Syndrome
Cushing Syndrome
Cutaneous Larva Migrans
Cutaneous Leischmaniasis
Cutis Hyperelastica
Cutting Teeth
CVA

Cyanide Poisoning
Cyclothymic Disorder
Cyst
Cystic Duct Syndrome
Cystic Fibrosis
Cystinosis
Cystitis
Cystitis, Interstitial
Cystocoele
Cytomegalovirus Infection

da Costa Syndrome
Dandruff
Dandy Syndrome
Dandy-Walker Syndrome
Darier's Disease
Deaf
de Clérambault Syndrome
Deep Vein Thrombosis
Defibrination Syndrome
Dehydration
Deja Vu
de Lange Syndrome
Delirium Tremens
Dementia
Demons-Meigs Syndrome
Denervation Syndrome
Dengue Fever
Depression
de Quervain's Tenosynovitis
de Quervain's Tenovaginitis
de Quervain's Thyroiditis
Dermatitis
Dermatitis Artefacta
Dermatitis, Atopic
Dermatitis Herpetiformis
Dermatitis Medicamentosa
Dermatofibroma
Dermatomyositis
de Toni-Fanconi-Debré syndrome
Devic's Disease
Diabetes Insipidus
Diabetes Mellitus
Diabetes Type One and Two

Diabetic Ketoacidosis

Diabetic Neuropathy

Diarrhoea

DIC

Diencephalic Syndrome

di George Syndrome

Diogenes Syndrome

Diphtheria

Discoid Eczema

Discoid Lupus Erythematosus

Disc, Slipped

Dislocation

Dissecting Aneurysm

Disseminated Intravascular Coagulation

Disseminated Lupus Erythematosus

Disseminated Sclerosis

Disseminated Superficial Actinic
   Porokeratosis

Distal Muscular Dystrophy

Diverticular Disease

Diverticulitis

Donovanosis

Double Pneumonia

Down Syndrome

Dracunculiasis

Dressler Syndrome

Drowning

Drug Addiction

Drug Eruption

Drusen

Dry Eye Syndrome

DSAP

DTs

Duane Syndrome

Dubin-Johnson Syndrome

Dubowitz Syndrome

Duchenne Muscular Dystrophy

Ductus Arteriosus

Dumping Syndrome

Duodenal Ulcer

Dupuytren's Contracture of the Hand

DVT

Dyscontrol Syndrome, Episodic

Dysentery

Dyshidrosis

Dyspepsia, Nervous

Dysplastic Naevus Syndrome

Dystrophia Adiposgenitalis

Dystrophia Myotonica

Ear Drum Rupture

Ear Infection

Ears, Protruding

Ear Wax

Eastern Equine Encephalitis

Eaton-Lambert Syndrome

Ebola Virus

Ebstein Anomaly

EBV Infection

Echinococcosis

Eclampsia

E. coli Infection

Ectopic Pregnancy

Ectropion

Eczema

Edwards Syndrome

Effort Syndrome

Ehlers-Danlos Syndrome

Eisenmenger Syndrome

Ejaculation Problems

Ejaculatory Failure

Ekbom Syndrome

Elastic Skin Syndrome

Elbow Fracture/Dislocation

Elephantiasis

Elephant Man Deformity

Ellis-van Creveld Syndrome

Embolism, Pulmonary

Embryoma

Emphysema

Emphysema, Subcutaneous

Empyema

Encephalitis

Encephalomyelopathy, Subacute Necrotising

Enchondroma

en Coup de Sabre

Endocarditis

Endogenous Depression

Topics

Endometriosis
Enteric Fever
Enteritis
Enterobiasis
Enterocolitis, Necrotising
Entropion
Enuresis
Eosinophilia-Myalgia Syndrome
Eosinophilic Meningoencephalitis
Epicondylitis
Epidemic Polyarthritis
Epidermal Naevus
Epidermolysis Bullosa
Epididymo-Orchitis
Epiglottitis
Epilepsia Partialis Continua
Epilepsy
Epiloia
Episcleritis
Episodic Dyscontrol Syndrome
Epispadias
Epistaxis
Epstein-Barr Virus Infection
Equine Encephalitis
Erb-Duchenne Palsy
Erb's Muscular Dystrophy
Erb's Palsy
Erectile Failure
Erotomania
Erysipelas
Erythema Induratum
Erythema Infectiosum
Erythema Multiforme
Erythema Nodosum
Erythrasma
Erythroderma, Generalised
Erythrogenesis Imperfecta
Erythroplasia of Queyrat
Escherichia coli Infection
Esophageal Cancer
Esophagitis
Esotropia
Espundia
Essential Hypertension

Essential Tremor
Eustachian Tube Blockage
Ewing's Tumour
Exfoliative Dermatitis
Exposure
External Hordeolum
Extrasystoles
Eye Cancer
Eye Diseases
Eye Floaters
Eye Ulcer

Factor VIII Deficit
Factor IX Deficit
Failure of Ejaculation
Faint
Fallot's Pentalogy
Fallot's Tetralogy
Fallot's Trilogy
Familial Angioedema
Familial Mediterranean Fever
Familial Polyposis
Familial Tremor
Fanconi Syndrome
Fascioscapulohumeral Muscular Dystrophy
Fat Cyst
Fatigue Fracture
Favus
Felty Syndrome
Femoral Hernia
Fetal Alcohol Syndrome
Fibrillation
Fibrocystic Disease
Fibroids of the Uterus
Fibromyalgia Syndrome
Fibromyositis
Fibrosarcoma
Fibrosing Alveolitis, Cryptogenic
Fibrositis
Fibrous Dysplasia
Fifth Disease
Filariasis
Fissure in Ano
Fistula

Fistula in Ano
Fit
Fitz-Hugh-Curtis Syndrome
Fixed Drug Eruption
Flash Burns to Eye
Flat Feet
Flesh Eating Disease
Floaters in Eye
Floppy Baby Syndrome
Floppy Eyelid Syndrome
Flu
Focal Dermal Hypoplasia
Focal Nodular Myositis
Foetal Alcohol Syndrome
Follicular Ovarian Cyst
Folliculitis
Fong Syndrome
Food Poisoning
Footballer's Ankle
Foot Ganglion
Fox-Fordyce Disease
Fracture
Fragile X Syndrome
France's Triad
Freeman-Sheldon Syndrome
Freiberg's Disease
Frey Syndrome
Friedrich's Ataxia
Frigidity
Fröhlich Syndrome
Frostbite
Frozen Shoulder
Fuchs Heterochromic Cyclitis
Fuchs Uveitis Syndrome
Fulminant Meningococcaemia
Functional Indigestion
Fungal Infection
Fungal Nail Infection
Fungal Skin Infection
Funnel Web Spider Bite
Furuncle
Furunculosis, Ear

Galactokinase Deficiency

Galactosaemia
Gallstones
Gambling, Pathological
Ganglion of a Tendon
Gangrene, Gas
Gardner Syndrome
Gas Bloat Syndrome
Gas Embolism
Gas Gangrene
Gastric Carcinoma
Gastric Ulcer
Gastrinoma
Gastritis
Gastro-Oesophageal Reflux
Gastroenteritis
Gaucher Disease
'Gay'
Gay Bowel Syndrome
Generalised Erythroderma
Genital Herpes
Genital Warts
Genu Valgum
Genu Varum
Geographic Tongue
German Measles
Gerstmann Syndrome
Gerstmann-Straussler-Scheinker Syndrome
Gianotti Crosti Syndrome
Giant Cell Arteritis
Giant Cell Tumour
Giardiasis, Intestinal
Gilbert Syndrome
Giles de la Tourette syndrome
Gillespie Syndrome
Gingivitis
Gingivostomatitis
Gland Infection
Glandular Fever
Glanzmann Syndrome
Glaucoma
Glaucomatocyclitic Crisis
Glioblastoma
Glioma
Globus

Topics

Glomerulonephritis
Glomus Tumour
Glossopharyngeal Neuralgia
Glue Ear
Glycogen Storage Diseases
Gnathostomiasis
Goitre
Golfer's Elbow
Goltz Syndrome
Gonorrhoea
Goodpasture Syndrome
Gorlin-Goltz Syndrome
Gourgerot-Blum Disease
Gout
Gradenigo Syndrome
Grand Mal Epilepsy
Granuloma Annulare
Granuloma Inguinale
Granuloma Venereum
Grave's Disease
Grey Baby Syndrome
Grover's Disease
Growing pains
Guillain-Barré Syndrome
Guinea Worm Disease
Guttae Psoriasis
Guyton's Canal Syndrome
Gynaecomastia

Haemangioma
Haemochromatosis
Haemoglobin S Disease
Haemolytic Anaemia
Haemolytic-Uraemic Syndrome
Haemophilia A
Haemophilia B
Haemophilus Infection
Haemophilus Influenzae B Infection
Haemorrhagic Fever
Haemorrhoids
Hailey-Hailey Disease
Hair Ball
Hair, Excess
Hair Loss

Hairy Cell Leukaemia
Hajdu-Cheney Syndrome
Hallermann-Streiff syndrome
Hallux Valgus
Halo Naevus
Hamman-Rich Syndrome
Hand Foot Mouth Disease
Hand-Schüller-Christian Disease
Hansen's Disease
Happy Puppet Syndrome
Hardening of the Arteries
Hare Lip
Harlequin Syndrome
Hartnup Disease
Hashimoto's Thyroiditis
Hashish Abuse
Hay Fever
Headache
Headache, Muscle Spasm
Head Injury
Head Lice
Heart Attack
Heartbeat, Rapid
Heartburn
Heart Diseases
Heart Failure
Heart Infection
Heart Tumour
Heart Valve Disease
Heel Spur
Heerfordt Syndrome
Heerfordt-Waldenström Syndrome
Heiner Syndrome
HELLP Syndrome
Helminthiasis
Henoch-Schoenlein Syndrome
Hepatic Abscess
Hepatic Carcinoma
Hepatic Metastases
Hepatitis A
Hepatitis B
Hepatitis C
Hepatitis D
Hepatitis E

Hepatitis G
Hepatolenticular Degeneration
Hepatoma
Herald Patch
Hereditary Haemorrhagic Telangiectasia
Hernia
Heroin Addiction
Herpangina
Herpes Simplex Infections
Herpes Zoster Infections
Hers Syndrome
Hiatus Hernia
HiB Infection
Hiccoughs
Hiccups
Hidradenitis Suppurativa
Hidrosadenome
High Blood Pressure
Hip Avascular Necrosis
Hip Dislocation
Hip Fracture
Hirschsprung Disease
Hirsutism
Histiocytoma
Histiocytosis X
Histoplasmosis
HIV
Hives
Hodgkin's Disease
Hole in the Heart
Holmes-Adie Syndrome
Homosexuality
Hookworm
Hordeolum, External
Horner Syndrome
Housemaid's Knee
Housewife's Dermatitis
HPV Infection
Human Papilloma Virus Infection
Humerus Fracture
Hunner's Ulcer
Hunter Syndrome
Huntington's Chorea
Hurler Syndrome

Hutchison's Melanotic Freckle
Hutchison's Prurigo
Hyaline membrane Disease
Hydatid Disease
Hydatidiform Mole
Hydatid of Morgagni
Hydramnios
Hydrocele
Hydrocephalus
Hyperadrenocorticism
Hyperaldosteronism
Hypercalcaemia
Hypercholesterolaemia
Hyperemesis Gravidarum
Hyper-IgE Syndrome
Hyperkeratosis
Hyperkinetic Syndrome
Hyperlipidaemia
Hypermobility Syndrome
Hyperopia
Hyperparathyroidism
Hyperprolactinaemia
Hyper-Reactive Airways Disease
Hypertension
Hypertension, Pulmonary
Hyperthyroidism
Hypertriglyceridaemia
Hypertrophic Cardiomyopathy
Hyperuricaemia
Hypervitaminosis A
Hypoadrenocorticism, Chronic
Hypoaldosteronism
Hypochondriasis
Hypoparathyroidism
Hypopituitarism
Hypoplastic Left Heart Syndrome
Hypospadias
Hypostatic Eczema
Hypotension
Hypotension, Postural
Hypothermia
Hypothyroidism
Hypovitaminosis A
Hysteria

Topics

Iatrogenic Conditions
IBS
ICHABOD Syndrome
Ichthyosis
IDDM
Idiopathic Condition
Idiopathic Diffuse Interstitial Fibrosis
Idiopathic Lymphadenopathy Syndrome
Idiopathic Myelofibrosis
Idiopathic Pulmonary Fibrosis
Idiopathic Renal Acidosis
Idiopathic Thrombocytopenic Purpura
Idiot Savant Syndrome
IEC
Ileolumbar Syndrome
Iliotibial Band Friction Syndrome
Immature Haemangioma
Immersion
Immunodeficiency
Impetigo
Impingement Syndromes
Impotence
Incisional Hernia
Inclusion Body Myositis
Incontinence of Faeces
Incontinence of Urine
Incontinentia Pigmenti
Indigestion, Functional
Indolent Lymphoma
Infantile Colic
Infarct, Cerebral
Infarct, Myocardial
Infected Glands
Infection
Infectious Mononucleosis
Infectious Myositis
Infertility, Female
Infertility, Male
Influenza
Ingrown Toenail
Inguinal Hernia
Insecticide Poisoning
Insect Sting
Insulin Dependent Diabetes

Insulinoma
Insulin Resistance Syndrome
Intermediate Coronary Syndrome
Interstitial Cystitis
Intertrigo
Intervertebral Disc Prolapse
Intracerebral Haemorrhage
Intracranial Tumour
Intestinal Colic
Intraepithelial Carcinoma
Intussusception
Invasive Uterine Mole
Iritis
Iron Deficiency Anaemia
Iron Poisoning
Irritable Bowel Syndrome
Irritant Eczema
Irukandji Syndrome
Ischaemic Heart Disease
Itchy Anus
Itchy Nipple
Itchy Upper Arm Syndrome

Jaccoud Syndrome
Jamaican Neuritis
Jamestown Canyon Virus
Japanese Encephalitis
Jaw Joint Inflammation
Jervell-Lange-Nielsen Syndrome
Jet Lag
Job-Buckley Syndrome
Johanson-Blizzard Syndrome
Johansson-Sinding-Larsen Syndrome
Joint Infection
Joseph Syndrome
Juvenile Diabetes
Juvenile Rheumatoid Arthritis

KA
Kala-Azar
Kallmann Syndrome
Kaposi's Sarcoma
Kartagener Syndrome
Kawasaki Syndrome

Kayser-Fleischer Ring
Kearns-Sayre Syndrome
Keloid
Keratin Cysts
Keratitis
Keratoacanthoma
Keratoconjunctivitis Sicca
Keratoconus
Keratoderma
Keratosis
Keratosis Pilaris
Kerion
Ketoacidosis
Kidney Cancer
Kidney Failure, Acute
Kidney Failure, Chronic
Kidney Stone
'King's Evil'
Kissing Disease
Kleine-Levin Syndrome
Klinefelter Syndrome
Klippel-Feil Syndrome
Klippel-Trenaunay Syndrome
Klumpke's Palsy
Knee
Knee Meniscus Tear
Knock Knees
Koebner Phenomenon
Korsakoff's Psychosis
Kostmann Syndrome
Kugelberg-Welander Syndrome
Kuru
Kwashiorkor
Kyphoscoliosis
Kyphosis

Labyrinthitis
la Crosse Encephalitis
Landau-Kleffner Syndrome
Landry-Guillain-Barré Syndrome
Lange Syndrome
Langer-Giedion Syndrome
Langerhans Cell Granulomatosis
Langerhans Cell Histiocytosis

Large Bowel Cancer
Large Cell Carcinoma of the Lung
Larva Migrans
Laryngitis
Laryngomalacia
Laryngotracheobronchitis
Lassa Fever
Latent Hepatic Porphyria
Lateral Epicondylitis
Laurence-Moon-Biedl Syndrome
Lead Poisoning
Leber Congenital Amaurosis
Leber Optic Neuropathy
Ledderhose's Disease
Leg Cramps
Legionnaire's Disease
Leigh Disease
Leiomyoma
Leischmaniasis
Lennox-Gastaut Syndrome
Lentigo
Lentigo Maligna
Leopard Syndrome
Leprosy
Leptospirosis
Leriche Syndrome
Lesbian
Leschke Syndrome
Lesch-Nyhan Syndrome
Letterer-Siwe Disease
Leucopenia, Malignant
Leukaemia
Leukaemia, Acute Lymphatic
Leukaemia, Acute Myeloid
Leukaemia, Chronic Lymphatic
Leukaemia, Chronic Myeloid
Leukaemia, Hairy Cell
Libido, Reduced
Lice
Lichen Aureus
Lichen Axillaris
Lichen Planus
Lichen Sclerosis
Lichen Simplex

Topics

Lichen Urticatus
Liddle Syndrome
Ligament or Tendon Rupture
Lightwood Syndrome
L'Illusion de Sosies
Limb Girdle Dystrophy
Limb Pain Syndrome
Lip Cancer
Lipoma
Lip-Pit Syndrome
Lissencephaly Syndrome
Listeriosis
Liver Abscess
Liver Cancer
Liver Disease
Locked-In Syndrome
Lockjaw
Loeffler Syndrome
Löfgren Syndrome
Long QT Syndrome
Long Sighted
Loose Anagen Syndrome
Lordosis
Lou Gehrig Disease
Louis-Bar Syndrome
Low Blood Pressure
Lowe Syndrome
Lown-Ganong-Levine Syndrome
Lumbago
Lung Abscess
Lung Cancer
Lung Clot
Lung Diseases
'Lupus'
Lupus Erythematosus
Luteal Cyst
Lyell Syndrome
Lyme Disease
Lymphadenitis
Lymphatic Leukaemia
Lymph Node Inflammation
Lymphocytic Leukaemia
Lymphoedema
Lymphoepithelial Condition, Benign

Lymphogranuloma Venereum
Lymphoma
Lyssavirus Infection

Machado-Joseph Syndrome
Macular Degeneration
Mad Cow Disease
Madura Foot
Majocchis Purpura
Malaria
Male Breast Enlargement
Male Pattern Baldness
Malignancy
Malignant Astrocytoma
Malignant Hypertension
Malignant Leucopenia
Mallet Finger
Mallory-Weis Syndrome
Malnutrition
Mammary Carcinoma
Mania
Manic-Depressive
Maple Syrup Urine Disease
Marasmus
Marburg Virus
March Fracture
Marfan Syndrome
Marijuana Abuse
Marinesco-Sjögren Syndrome
Maroteaux-Lamy Syndrome
Mastitis
Mastocytosis
Mastoiditis
Mature Capillary Naevus
Maturity Onset Diabetes
Mauriac Syndrome
May-Hegglin Anomaly
McArdle Syndrome
McCune-Albright Syndrome
ME
Measles
Measles, Baby
Measles, German
Medial Epicondylitis

628

Meckel's Diverticulitis

Meckel Syndrome

Mediterranean Fever, Familial

Mediterranean Spotted Fever

Medulloblastoma

Meesmann Corneal Dystrophy

Megacolon

Megaloblastic Anaemia

Meibomian Cyst

Meigs Syndrome

Melancholia

Melanoma

Melasma

Melioidosis

MEN

Mendelson Syndrome

Menétrière's Disease

Ménière's Disease

Meningeal Tuberculosis

Meningioma

Meningitis

Meningocele

Meningococcal Infection

Meningomyelocele

Meniscus Tear

Menopause

Mercury Poisoning

Mesenteric Adenitis

Mesenteric Artery Thrombosis

Mesothelioma

Metastatic Cancer

Metatarsal Fracture

Metatarsalgia

Methicillin-Resistant *Staphylococcus aureus*
Infection

MI

Middle Ear Effusion

Middle Ear Infection

Migraine

Mikulicz Disease

Milia

Milkman Syndrome

Miller-Dieker Syndrome

Miller Syndrome

Milroy's Disease

Minamata Disease

Mirrizzi Syndrome

Miscarriage

Mitral Valve Incompetence

Mitral Valve Stenosis

Mittelschmerz

Mixed Parotid Tumour

Moebius Syndrome

Mokola Virus Infection

Mole, Invasive Uterine

Molluscum Contagiosum

Mongolism

Moniliasis

Mononucleosis, Infectious

Monteggia Fracture

Morbilli

Morgagni, Hydatid of

Morning Sickness

Morphoea

Morquio Syndrome

Morton's Metatarsalgia

Morton Syndrome

Motion Sickness

Motor Neurone Disease

Mountain Sickness

Mouth Cancer

Mouth Infection

Mouth Ulcer

MRSA

MS

Mucinous Cyst of the Cervix

Mucocutaneous Leischmaniasis

Mucocutaneous Lymph Node Syndrome

Mucopolysaccharoidosis

Mucormycosis

Mucus Colitis

Multiple Endocrine Neoplasia Type 1

Multiple Endocrine Neoplasia Type 2

Multiple Hamartoma Syndrome

Multiple Myeloma

Multiple Personality Disorder

Multiple Sclerosis

Mumps

Topics

Munchausen Syndrome
Munchausen Syndrome by Proxy
Murray Valley Encephalitis
Muscle Meltdown
Muscular Cramps
Muscular Dystrophy
Myalgic Encephalomyelitis
Myasthenia Gravis
Myasthenic Syndrome
Mycetoma
Mycoplasma Infection
Mycoses
Mycosis Fungoides
Myelitis
Myeloid Leukaemia
Myelodysplastic Syndrome
Myelofibrosis
Myeloma, Multiple
Myelomatosis
Myocardial Infarct
Myocarditis
Myoclonus
Myofascial Pain Syndrome
Myolysis
Myopia
Myositis
Myotonic Dystrophy
Myxoedema
Myxoma

Nabothian Cyst
Naevus
Naffziger Syndrome
Nail Bed Infection
Nail Bruise
Nail-Patella Syndrome
Nappy Eczema
Nappy Rash
Narcolepsy
Narcotic Addiction
Naso-Oral Leischmaniasis
Neck Sprain
Necrotising Encephalomyelopathy, Subacute
Necrotising Enterocolitis

Necrotising Fasciitis
Necrotising Ulcerative Gingivostomatitis
Nelson Syndrome
Nematode Infestation
Neoplasm
Nephritis
Nephroblastoma
Nephrolithiasis
Nephrotic Syndrome
Nerve rash
Nervous Breakdown
Nervous Dyspepsia
Neu-Lexova Syndrome
Neuralgia
Neurodermatitis
Neuroleptic Malignant Syndrome
Neuroma
Neuromyelitis Optica
Neuropathy
Neurosis
Nezelof Syndrome
NGU
NIDDM
Niemann-Pick Disease
Nipple Cancer
Nipple Itch
Nocardiosis
Nocturnal Cramps
Non-Gonococcal Urethritis
Non-Hodgkin's Lymphoma
Non-Specific Urethritis
Non-Tropical Sprue
Noonan Syndrome
Norwegian Scabies
Nose Bleed
Notalgia Paraesthetica
NSU
Nummular Eczema

Oat Cell Carcinoma of the Lung
Obsessive Compulsive Neurosis
Occupational Overuse Syndrome
Ocular Larva Migrans
Oculopharyngeal Muscular Dystrophy

Oesophagael Achalasia
Oesophageal Cancer
Oesophagitis
Oligohydramnios
Onchocerciasis
Onychogryphosis
Onychomycosis
Oral Cancer
Oral Thrush
Orchitis
Orf
Organic Brain Syndrome
Organic Personality Syndrome
Organophosphate Poisoning
Orgasm Failure
Oriental Sore
Ornithosis
Orofacial Pain Syndrome
Osgood-Schlatter's Disease
Osler-Rendu-Weber Disease
Osteitis Deformans
Osteoarthritis
Osteochondritis Dissecans
Osteoclastoma
Osteogenesis Imperfecta
Osteogenic Sarcoma
Osteoma
Osteomalacia
Osteomyelitis
Osteoporosis
Osteosarcoma
Otitis Externa
Otitis Media
Oto-Palatal-Digital Syndrome
Otosclerosis
Ovarian Cancer
Ovarian Cyst
Ovarian Torsion
Overactivity Syndrome
Ovulation Pain

Paedophilia
Paget's Disease of Bone
Paget's Disease of the Nipple

Painful Arc Syndrome
Painful Bruising Syndrome
Painless Thyroiditis Syndrome
PAN
Pancoast Syndrome
Pancreatic Cancer
Pancreatitis
Panhypopituitarism
Panic Attack
Panniculitis
Papillon-Le Fevre Syndrome
Paralysis Agitans
Paranoia
Paranoid Disorder
Parapertussis
Paraphimosis
Paraplegia
Paraumbilical Hernia
Parinaud Syndrome
Parkinsonism
Parkinson's Disease
Paronychia
Parotid Tumour
Parotitis
Paroxysmal Atrial Tachycardia
Paroxysmal Ventricular Tachycardia
Parvovirus Infection
PAT
Patau Syndrome
Patello-Femoral Pain Syndrome
Patent Ductus Arteriosus
Paterson-Brown-Kelly syndrome
PDA
Pederasty
Pediculosis
Pellagra
Pellegrini-Stieda Lesion
Pelvic Congestion Syndrome
Pelvic Inflammatory Disease
Pemphigoid
Pemphigus
Pemphigus Neonatorum
Pendred Syndrome
Penis Cancer

Topics

Penis Infection
Penis, Short
Peptic Ulcer
Periarteritis Nodosa
Pericardial Effusion
Pericarditis
Perineal Descent Syndrome
Peripheral Neuropathy
Peritonitis
Peritonsillar Abscess
Pernicious Anaemia
Perthes' Disease
Pertussis
Pes Cavus
Pes Planus
Petit mal
Petrositis
Peutz-Jegher Syndrome
Peyronie Disease
Phaeochromocytoma
Pharyngitis
Phenylketonuria
Phimosis
Phlebitis
Phobia
Photodermatitis
Photosensitive Eczema
Phthisis
Pick's Disease
Pickwickian Syndrome
PID
PIE Syndrome
Pierre-Robin Syndrome
Pigmented Purpura
Pigmented Purpuric Lichenoid Dermatosis
Pigmented Villonodular Synovitis
Piles
Pilonidal Sinus
Pimples
Pinealoma
Pineal Tumour
Pingueculum
Pink Disease
Pinta

Pinworms
Piriformis Syndrome
Pituitary Failure
Pityriasis Rosea
Pityriasis Versicolor
PKU
Placental Cancer
Plague, Bubonic
Plantar Fasciitis
Plantar Wart
Pleural Effusion
Pleurisy
Pleurodynia
Plica Syndrome
Plumbism
Plummer-Vinson Syndrome
PMR
PMT
PND
Pneumoconiosis
Pneumonia
Pneumothorax
Poikiloderma, Congenital
Poikiloderma of Civatte
Poisoning
Polio
Polle Syndrome
Polyarteritis Nodosa
Polychondritis, Relapsing
Polycystic Kidney
Polycystic Ovarian Syndrome
Polycythaemia Rubra Vera
Polycythaemia Vera
Polyglandular Autoimmune Syndromes
Polyhydramnios
Polymorphic Light Eruption
Polymyalgia Rheumatica
Polymyositis
Polyposis Coli
Pompe Syndrome
Pompholyx
Porokeratosis
Porphyria
Porphyria Cutanea Tarda

632

Portal Hypertension

Portwine Naevus

Positional Hypotension

Posner-Schlossman Syndrome

Posterior Facet Syndrome

Posterior Impingement Syndrome

Postgastrectomy Syndrome

Post-Herpetic Neuralgia

Post-Menopausal Vaginitis

Post-Nasal Drip

Postnatal Depression

Postpartum Depression

Postphlebitic Syndrome

Post-Polio Syndrome

Post Traumatic Cerebral Syndrome

Post Traumatic Stress Disorder

Postural Hypotension

Post-Viral Syndrome

'Pot'

Potassium Wastage Syndrome

Potter Syndrome

Pott's Fracture

Prader-Willi Syndrome

Pre-Eclampsia

Pregnancy

Pregnancy, Ectopic

Premature Ejaculation

Premenstrual Tension Syndrome

Pre-Patellar Bursitis

Presbyopia

Pressure Ulcer

Pretectal Syndrome

Priapism

Primary Lateral Sclerosis

Proctalgia Fugax

Proctitis

Progressive Pigmented Purpura

Progressive Supranuclear Palsy

Progressive Systemic Sclerosis

Prolapse

Pronator Syndrome

Prostate Cancer

Prostate Enlargement

Prostate Infection

Prostatic Cancer

Prostatitis

Prostatomegaly

Proteus Syndrome

Prune Belly Syndrome

Prurigo

Pruritus Ani

Pseudocushing Syndrome

Pseudoexfoliation Syndrome

Pseudofolliculitis Barbae

Pseudogout

Pseudomembranous Colitis

Pseudomonas Infection

Psittacosis

Psoriasis

Psoriatic Arthritis

Psychiatric Disturbances

Psychosis

Psychotic

Pterygium

PTSD

Pubic Pediculosis

Pulmonary Abscess

Pulmonary Embolism

Pulmonary Fibrosis, Idiopathic

Pulmonary Hypertension

Pulmonary Thromboembolism

Pulmonary Tuberculosis

Pulmonary Valve Incompetence

Pulmonary Valve Stenosis

Pulmonic Regurgitation

Pulse, Rapid

Punch Drunk Syndrome

Purpura Annularis Telangiectodes

Pyelonephritis, Acute

Pyelonephritis, Chronic

Pyloric Ulcer

Pyridoxine Deficiency

Q Fever

Quadriplegia

Quinsy

Rabies

Topics

Radiation Sickness
Ramsay-Hunt Syndrome
Rapid Time Change Syndrome
Raynaud's Disease
Raynaud's Phenomenon
Razor Rash
Reactive Arthritis
Reactive Depression
Reaven Syndrome
Rectal Cancer
Rectal Prolapse
Rectocoele
Rectovaginal Fistula
Rectovescical Fistula
Red-Back Spider Bite
Red Man Syndrome
Reflex Sympathetic Dystrophy Syndrome
Reflux Oesophagitis
Refsum Syndrome
Regional Enteritis
Reis-Bücklers Corneal Dystrophy
Reiter Syndrome
Relapsing Fever
Relapsing Polychondritis
Renal Calculus
Renal Colic
Renal Failure, Acute
Renal Failure, Chronic
Rendu-Osler-Weber Syndrome
Repetitive Strain Injury
Respiratory Distress Syndrome, Adult
Respiratory Distress Syndrome, Infant
Respiratory Syncitial Virus Infection
Restless Legs Syndrome
Retarded Ejaculation
Retinal Detachment
Retinitis Pigmentosa
Retinoblastoma
Retrograde Ejaculation
Retrovirus Infection
Rett Syndrome
Reye Syndrome
Rhabdomyolysis
Rheumatic Fever

Rheumatoid Arthritis
Rhinitis
Rhinophyma
Richner-Hanhart Syndrome
Rickets
Rickettsial Infection
Rickettsialpox
Riedel's Thyroiditis
Rieger Syndrome
Right Heart Failure
Riley-Day Syndrome
Ringworm
Ritter's Disease
River Blindness
Rocky Mountain Spotted Fever
Rodent Ulcer
Rosacea
Roseola Infantum
Ross River Fever
Rotator Cuff Syndrome
Rotavirus Infection
Rothmund-Thomson Syndrome
Rotor Syndrome
Roundworm Infestation
Roussy-Levy Syndrome
Royal Free Disease
RSI
RSV
Rubella
Rubenstein-Taybi Syndrome
Rubeola
Russell-Silver Syndrome

Saccular Aneurysm
St. Louis Encephalitis
St. Vitus Dance
Salivary Stone
Salmonellosis, Intestinal
Salpingitis
Sandifer Syndrome
Sanfilippo Syndrome
Sarcoidosis
Sarcoma
Savant Syndrome

Scabies

Scald

Scalded Skin Syndrome

Scalenus Anticus Syndrome

Scaphoid Fracture

Scapulo-Costal Syndrome

Scarlet Fever

SCC

Schamberg's Disease

Scheie Syndrome

Scheuermann's Disease

Schistosomiasis

Schizophrenia

Schmidt Syndrome

Schnyder Corneal Dystrophy

School Sores

Schwachman Syndrome

Schwannoma

Sciatica

Scleritis

Scleroderma

Scoliosis

Scrapie

Scrofula

Scurvy

Sea Sickness

Seasonal Affective Disorder

Sebaceous Cyst

Sebaceous Naevus

Seborrhoeic Eczema

Seckel Syndrome

Secondary Cancer

Second Childhood

Seizure

Seminoma

Senile Dementia

Senile Vaginitis

Septicaemia

Septic Arthritis

Septic Meningitis

Septic Shock

Serotonin Syndrome

Serum Hepatitis

Serum Sickness

Sex Problems

Sexually Transmitted Diseases

Sézary Syndrome

SHAFT Syndrome

Shaking Palsy

Sheehan Syndrome

Shell Shock

Shigellosis

Shingles

Shin Splints

Shock

Short Bowel Syndrome

Short Penis

Short-Sighted

Shoulder Dislocation

Shoulder-Hand Syndrome

Shoulder Impingement Syndrome

Shy-Drager Syndrome

Sialadenitis

Sialitis

Sicard Syndrome

Sicca Syndrome

Sick Building Syndrome

Sickle Cell Anaemia

Sick Sinus Syndrome

SIDS

Sight Problems

Silicosis

Simmonds' Disease

Sinus Bradycardia

Sinusitis

Six-Week Colic

Sjögren-Larsson Syndrome

Sjögren Syndrome

Skin Cancer

Skin Diseases

Skin Ulcer

Slapped Cheek Disease

SLE

Sleep Apnoea

Sleeping Sickness

Slipped Disc

Slipping Rib Syndrome

Sly Syndrome

Topics

Small Cell Carcinoma of the Lung

Small Penis

Smallpox

Smith-Lemli-Opitz Syndrome

Smith-Magenis Syndrome

Smith's Fracture

Smokers Foot

Smoking

Snake Bite

Snapping Scapula Syndrome

Snoring

Snow Blindness

Solar Keratosis

Solar Urticaria

Somatisation Disorder

Soto Syndrome

Spastic

Spastic Colon

'Speed'

Spherocytic Anaemia

Spherocytosis

Spider Bite

Spider Naevi

Spigelian Hernia

Spina Bifida

Spinal Muscular Atrophy

Spinal Stenosis

Spinocerebellar Degeneration

Spleen, Ruptured

Spondylitis

Spondylolisthesis

Spondylosis

Spongieform Encephalitis

Spontaneous Pneumothorax

Sprain

Sprue

Spur, Heel

Squamous Cell Carcinoma of the Lung

Squamous Cell Carcinoma of the Skin

Squint

Stagardt Syndrome

Stammer

Staphylococcal Infections

Starvation

Status Epilepticus

Steele-Richardson-Olszewski Syndrome

Steinert's Disease

Stein-Leventhal Syndrome

Sternocleidomastoid Torticollis

Stevens-Johnson syndrome

Stewart-Morgagni-Morel Syndrome

Stewart-Treves Syndrome

Sticky Platelet Syndrome

Stiff-Man Syndrome

Still's Disease

Sting, Bee or Wasp

Stokes-Adams Attack

Stomach Cancer

Stomach Ulcer

Stomatitis

Stone

Strabismus

Strachan Syndrome

Strain

Strawberry Naevus

Streptococcal Infection

Stress

Stress Fracture

Stress Incontinence

Stretch Marks

Striae

Stroke

Strongyloidiasis

Strychnine Poisoning

Sturge-Weber Syndrome

Stutter

Stye

Subacute Bacterial Endocarditis

Subacute Necrotising Encephalomyelopathy

Subacute Thyroiditis

Subarachnoid Haemorrhage

Subclavian Steal Syndrome

Subcutaneous Emphysema

Subdural Haematoma

Subluxation

Subungal Haematoma

Sudden Infant Death Syndrome

Sudeck's Atrophy

Sugar Diabetes
Suicide
Sunburn
SUNCT Syndrome
Superficial Venous Thrombosis
Superior Vena Cava Syndrome
Suppurative Thyroiditis
Supraspinatus Tendonitis
SVT
Sweet Syndrome
Swimmer's Ear
Sydenham's Chorea
Syncope
Syndrome
Syndrome of Inappropriate Antidiuretic
   Hormone Secretion
Syndrome of Inappropriate Vasopressin
   Secretion
Syndrome X
Synovial Plica Syndrome
Synovitis
Syphilis
Syringomyelia
Systemic Lupus Erythematosus
Systemic Mastocytosis
Systemic Sclerosis

Tabes Dorsalis
Tachycardia
Taeniasis
Takayasu's Arteritis
Talcosis
Talipes Equinovarus
Tapanui Flu
Tapeworms
Tarsal Tunnel Syndrome
TB
T Cell Leukaemia
Tear Duct, Blocked
Teeth Grinding
Teething
Telangiectasia
Telangiectasia Eruptiva Macularis Perstans
Telogen Effluvium

Temporal Arteritis
Temporal Lobe Epilepsy
Temporomandibular Joint Dysfunction
Tendonitis
Tendon Rupture
Tennis Elbow
Tenosynovitis
Tension Headache
Tension Pneumothorax
Teratoma
Testicle, Undescended
Testicular Cancer
Testicular Infection
Testicular Torsion
Tetanus
Tetany
Tetralogy of Fallot
Tetraplegia
Thalassaemia beta Major
Thalassaemia beta Minor
Thiamine Deficiency
Thoracic Outlet Syndromes
Threadworm
Throat Infection
Thromboangiitis Obliterans
Thrombocytopenia
Thromboembolism, Pulmonary
Thrombophlebitis
Thrombosis
Thrombosis, Cerebral
Thrush
Thymic Dysplasia
Thymic Hypoplasia
Thymoma
Thyroid Cancer
Thyroid Gland Enlargement
Thyroid Gland Underactivity
Thyroiditis
Thyrotoxicosis
TIA
Tibial Stress Syndrome
Tic Douloureux
Tick Bite
Tick Typhus

Topics

Tietze Syndrome

Tinea

Tinea Capitis

Tinea Corporis

Tinea Cruris

Tinea Manum

Tinea Pedis

Tinea Unguium

Tinea Versicolor

Tocopherols

Toenail, Ingrown

Togavirus Infection

Tolosa-Hunt Syndrome

Tonsillitis

Torsion Dystonia

Torsion of the Testis

Torticollis

Tourette Syndrome

Toxic Epidermal Necrolysis

Toxic Erythema

Toxic Shock Syndrome

Toxocariasis

Toxoplasmosis

Tracheitis

Trachoma

Transfusion Reaction

Transient Acantholytic Dermatosis

Transient Ischaemic Attack

Transverse Myelitis

Traumatic Cervical Syndrome

Travel Sickness

Treacher-Collins Syndrome

Tremor, Essential

Trench Mouth

Trichinosis

Trichobezoar

Trichomoniasis, Venereal

Trichotillomania

Trichuriasis

Tricuspid Incompetence

Tricuspid Regurgitation

Tricuspid Stenosis

Trigeminal Neuralgia

Trigger Finger

Triglyceride Excess

Trigonitis

Trisomy 13-15

Trisomy 18

Trisomy 21

Tropical Ear

Tropical Sprue

Trousseau Syndrome

Trypanosomiasis

Tubal Pregnancy

Tuberculosis

Tuberous Sclerosis

Tularaemia

Tumour Lysis Syndrome

Turcot Syndrome

Turner Syndrome

Twelfth Rib Syndrome

Tympanic Rupture

Typhoid Fever

Typhus

Tyrosinaemia Type II

Ulcer

Ulcerative Colitis

Ulcer, Mouth

Ulcer, Peptic

Ulcer, Pressure

Ulcer, Skin

Ulcer, Venous

Ulysses Syndrome

Umbilical Hernia

Unconscious

Undescended Testicle

Undulant Fever

Unstable Angina

Upper Respiratory Tract Infection

Uraemia

Uraemic Syndrome

Ureteric Calculus

Ureteric Colic

Urethral Syndrome

Urethritis

Urge Syndrome

Urine Incontinence

Urine Infection
URTI
Urticaria
Urticaria Pigmentosa
Usher Syndrome
Uta
Uterine Fibroids
Uterine Mole
Uterine Prolapse
Uveitis
Uveoparotid Fever or Syndrome
Uvulitis

Vaccinia
Vaginal Infection
Vaginal Prolapse
Vaginal Thrush
Vaginismus
Vaginitis, Bacterial
Vancomycin and Methicillin-Resistant
    Staphylococcus aureus Infection
Varicella
Varicocoele
Varicose Eczema
Varicose Ulcer
Varicose Veins
Variola Major
Vascular Haemophilia
Vasculitis
Vasomotor Rhinitis
Vasovagal Syndrome
VD
Venereal Diseases
Venereal Warts
Venezuelan Equine Encephalitis
Venomous Bite
Venous Thrombosis
Venous Ulcer
Ventricular Extrasystoles
Ventricular Failure
Ventricular Fibrillation
Ventricular Flutter
Ventricular Septal Defect
Ventricular Tachycardia

Verruca
Vestibular Neuronitis
Vestibulitis
VF
Vincent's Angina
Viraemia
Viral Conjunctivitis
Viral Encephalitis
Viral Enteritis
Viral Haemorrhagic Fever
Viral Infection
Viral Meningitis
Visceral Larva Migrans
Visceral Leischmaniasis
Vision Problems
Vitamin A Deficiency
Vitamin A Excess
Vitamin B_1 Deficiency
Vitamin B_3 Deficiency
Vitamin B_6 Deficiency
Vitamin B_{12} Deficiency
Vitamin B Excess
Vitamin C Deficiency
Vitamin C Excess
Vitamin D Deficiency
Vitamin D Excess
Vitamin E Deficiency
Vitamin E Excess
Vitamin K Deficiency
Vitamin K Excess
Vitiligo
VMRSA
Vogt-Koyanagi-Harada Syndrome
Volkmann's Contracture
von Gierke Syndrome
von Hippel-Lindau Syndrome
von Recklinghausen's Disease of Multiple
    Neurofibromatosis
von Willebrand's Disease
Vulvodynia

Waardenburg-Klein syndrome
WAGR Syndrome
Warts

Topics

Warts, Genital
Wasp Sting
Water on the Knee
Waterhouse-Friderichsen Syndrome
Weber-Christian Panniculitis
Wegener's Granulomatosis
Weil Syndrome
Werdig-Hoffman Syndrome
Werner Syndrome
Wernicke's Encephalopathy
Wernicke-Korsakoff Psychosis
West Nile Encephalitis
Western Equine Encephalitis
Wheezy Bronchitis
Whiplash
Whipple's Disease
Whipworm Infestation
Whistling Face Syndrome
Whitlow
Whooping Cough
Williams Syndrome
Wilms' Tumour
Wilson's Disease
Wiskott-Aldrich Syndrome
Witkop

Wittmaack-Ekbom Syndrome
Wolff-Parkinson-White Syndrome
Wolf-Hirschhorn Syndrome
Womb Prolapse
Worm Infestations
Wrist Fracture

Xanthomatosis
Xeroderma Pigmentosa
Xerophthalmia
Xiphoidalgia
X-Linked Agammaglobulinaemia
XO Syndrome
XXX Syndrome
XXY Syndrome
XYY Syndrome

Yaws
Yellow Fever
Yellow Nail Syndrome

Zellweger Syndrome
Zollinger-Ellison Syndrome
Zygomycosis